A Professional Approach

Access

Core & Expert

Kathleen Stewart

 **Glencoe McGraw-Hill**

New York, New York   Columbus, Ohio   Chicago, Illinois   Peoria, Illinois   Woodland Hills, California

This program has been prepared with the assistance of Gleason Group, Inc., Norwalk, CT.

Editorial Director: Pamela Ross

Developmental Editors: John Carter, Jon Juarez

Copy Editor: Malinda McCain, Sharon Wilkey

Composition: The Format Group LLC; Creative Ink, Inc., PDS Associates

Design: Leggitt Associates; Creative Ink, Inc.

Screens were captured using FullShot V6 For Windows from Inbit Incorporated, Mountain View, CA.

Glencoe/McGraw-Hill

A Division of The McGraw-Hill Companies

Access 2002: A Professional Approach, Core & Expert
Student Edition
ISBN 0-07-827401-X

2   3   4   5   6   7   8   9   10   071/071   07   06   05   04   03   02

Microsoft, Microsoft Access, Microsoft Excel, Microsoft Word, Windows, and the Microsoft Office User Specialist logo are either registered trademarks or trademarks of Microsoft Corporation in the United States and/or other countries.

PostScript is a registered trademark of Adobe Systems, Inc.

Glencoe/McGraw-Hill is independent from Microsoft Corporation, and not affiliated with Microsoft in any manner. This publication may be used in assisting students to prepare for a Microsoft Office User Specialist Exam. Neither Microsoft, its designated review company, nor Glencoe/McGraw-Hill warrants that use of this publication will ensure passing the relevant exam.

Between the time that Web site information is gathered and published, it is not unusual for some sites to have closed. URLs will be updated in reprints when possible.

Visit the Professional Approach Series Web site www.pas.glencoe.com

Contents

Unit 1

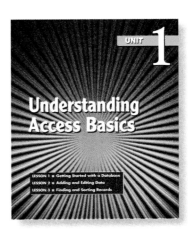

UNDERSTANDING ACCESS BASICS   5

UNIT 2

BUILDING A DATABASE   141

Building a
Database

LESSON 4 ■ Creating Databases and Tables
LESSON 5 ■ Managing Data Integrity
LESSON 6 ■ Adding Forms to a Database
LESSON 7 ■ Adding Reports to a Database

UNIT 3

GETTING INFORMATION FROM A DATABASE   305

UNIT 4

ADDING OBJECTS AND DATA TO A DATABASE   419

UNIT 5

USING ADVANCED FEATURES   561

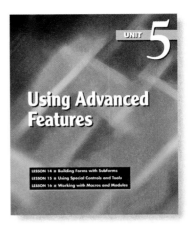

LESSON 16: WORKING WITH MACROS AND MODULES

What Is a Microsoft Office User Specialist?

A Microsoft Office User Specialist (MOUS) is an individual who has certified his or her skills in one or more Microsoft Office desktop applications, including Microsoft Word, Microsoft Excel, Microsoft PowerPoint, Microsoft Outlook, and Microsoft Access, as well as Microsoft Project.

What Is the Microsoft Office User Specialist Program?

The Microsoft Office User Specialist Program typically offers certification exams at the "Core" and "Expert" skill levels.* This program is the only Microsoft-approved program in the world for certifying proficiency in Microsoft Office desktop applications and Microsoft Project. This certification can be a valuable asset in any job search or career advancement.

What Does Mean?

It means this courseware has been approved by the Microsoft Office User Specialist Program to be among the finest available for learning Microsoft Office desktop applications. It also means that upon completion of this courseware, you may be prepared to become a Microsoft Office User Specialist.

For More Information

- www.microsoft.com/mous is the official Web site of the MOUS program and contains the latest information on available tests, testing centers, costs, and resources.
- Certiport oversees and administers the MOUS certification program for Microsoft. The Certiport Web site provides more information about the program, test centers, and more.
- Your Glencoe regional sales office can tell you more about other MOUS-approved courseware from Glencoe/McGraw-Hill.

---

* The availability of Microsoft Office User Specialist certification exams varies by application, application version, and language. Visit www.microsoft.com/mous for exam availability.

Microsoft, the Microsoft Office User Specialist Logo, PowerPoint, and Outlook are either registered trademarks or trademarks of Microsoft Corporation in the United States and/or other countries.

Preface

Access 2002 is written to help you master Microsoft Access for Windows. The text takes you step-by-step through the Access features that you're likely to use in both your personal and business life.

Case Study

Learning about the features of Access is one thing, but applying what you learn is another. That's why a *Case Study* runs through the text. The Case Study offers the opportunity to learn Access in a realistic business context. Take the time to read the Case Study about Carolina Critters, a fictional business located in Charlotte, North Carolina. All the documents for this course involve Carolina Critters.

Organization of the Text

The text includes five *units*. Each unit is divided into smaller *lessons*. There are 16 lessons, each building on previously learned procedures. This building block approach, together with the Case Study and the features listed below, enable you to maximize the learning process.

Features of the Text

- ☑ *Objectives* are listed for each lesson.
- ☑ Required skills for the *Microsoft Office User Specialist (MOUS) Certification Program* are listed for each lesson.
- ☑ The *estimated time* required to complete each lesson (up to the "Using Help") is stated.
- ☑ Within a lesson, each *heading* corresponds to an objective.
- ☑ Easy-to-follow *exercises* emphasize "learning by doing."
- ☑ *Key terms* are italicized and defined as they are encountered.
- ☑ Extensive *graphics* display screen contents.
- ☑ *Toolbar buttons* and *keyboard keys* are shown in the text when used.
- ☑ *Large toolbar buttons in the margins* provide easy-to-see references.
- ☑ Lessons contain important *Notes*, useful *Tips*, and helpful *Reviews*.
- ☑ *Using Help* introduces you to a Help topic related to lesson content.
- ☑ A *Lesson Summary* reviews the important concepts taught in the lesson.
- ☑ A *Command Summary* lists the commands taught in the lesson.
- ☑ *Concepts Review* includes true/false, short answer, and critical thinking questions that focus on lesson content.
- ☑ *Skills Review* provides skill reinforcement for each lesson.

☑ *Lesson Applications* ask you to apply your skills in a more challenging way.

☑ *On Your Own exercises* lets you apply your skills creatively.

☑ *Unit Applications* give you the opportunity to use the skills you learn in a unit.

☑ Includes *Appendices*, *Glossary*, and *Index*.

MOUS Certification Program

For a complete listing of the MOUS skills for the Access 2002 "Core" and "Expert" certification exams (and correlations to the lessons in the text), see Appendix E: "MOUS Certification."

Professional Approach Web Site

Check out the Professional Approach Web site at www.pas.glencoe.com. A helpful *Task Reference List*—handy for remembering how to perform over 200 Access tasks—is available for downloading.

Conventions Used in the Text

This text uses a number of conventions to help you learn the program and save your work.

• Text to key appears either in **boldface** or as a separate figure.

• Filenames appear in **boldface**.

• Options that you choose from menus and dialog boxes appear in a font that is similar to the on-screen font; for example, "Choose P̲rint from the F̲ile menu." (The underline means you can press Alt and key the letter to choose the option.) Some options that you choose from a task pane or Help window appear in blue text, as they appear on-screen; for example, "Click F̲ont in the Reveal Formatting task pane."

If You Are Unfamiliar with Windows

If you're unfamiliar with Windows, review *Appendix A: "Windows Tutorial"* before beginning Lesson 1. This tutorial provides a basic overview of the program and shows you how to use the mouse. You might also want to review *Appendix B: "File Management"* to get more comfortable with files and folders.

Screen Differences

As you practice each concept, illustrations of the screens help you follow the instructions. Don't worry if your screen is different from the illustration. These differences are due to variations in system and computer configurations.

Acknowledgments

We thank the Developmental Editors of this text for their valuable assistance: John Carter and Jon Juarez, both of Doña Ana Community College, Las Cruces, NM. We also thank the reviewers for their thoroughness: Eric Ecklund, Cambria Rowe Business College, Johnstown, PA; Melissa Wertz, Pittsburgh Technical Institute, Oakdale, PA; Ken Andrews, Computer Tech, Pittsburgh, PA.

Installation Requirements

You'll need Microsoft Access 2002 to work through this textbook. Access needs to be installed on the computer's hard drive (or on a network). Use the following checklist to evaluate installation requirements.

Hardware

- ☑ Pentium computer with between 32 MB and 72 MB of RAM depending on the version of Windows installed
- ☑ 3.5-inch high-density disk drive and CD-ROM drive
- ☑ 245 MB or more of hard disk space for a "Typical" Office installation
- ☑ Super VGA or higher-resolution video monitor
- ☑ Printer (laser or ink-jet recommended)
- ☑ Mouse
- ☑ *Optional:* Modem

Software

- ☑ Access 2002 (from Microsoft Office XP)
- ☑ Windows 98 (or later) or Microsoft Windows NT 4.0 with Service Pack 6 installed
- ☑ *Optional:* Browser (and Internet Service Provider), Microsoft Word, Microsoft Excel

Learning about Database Management

There are many ways to learn about database management. In this text, your approach is that of a professional database developer. This approach to learning about database management allows you to better understand someone else's database design, as well as to better design your own database. Some of the basic principles of this approach are described below.

- **You work with one main database with many related tables, queries, forms, and reports.**

  The text uses a realistic relational database that tracks the daily activities of a small company, Carolina Critters. Other texts may use several small databases, so you get the unrealistic impression that a typical database has only one or two tables.

- **You link tables from a secondary database every lesson after Lesson 4.**

  Carolina Critters has two databases, the main one and a secondary database with private and confidential data. You are required to link to the second database in each lesson starting with Lesson 4. This illustrates the typical corporate task of linking to the company's main database at all times. The main database may be on a mainframe or on a client-server system, but you learn that linking is an everyday task. The tables in the secondary database are, of course, related to those in the main database, reinforcing the necessity of good database design.

- **You use the Leszynski Naming Convention.**

  The Leszynski Naming Convention precedes each database object with an identifying prefix, uses no spaces between words, and capitalizes the first character of each word. This system is common in Access and Visual Basic development because it aids in identifying objects when they appear in lists. Although the book does not address programming, use of the naming convention prepares you for a structured, professional approach to naming objects in Access, Visual Basic, or other applications and languages.

- **You base forms and reports on queries, rather than tables.**

  Tables are covered early in the text because they are the foundation of a database. Quickly, though, you base the majority of forms and reports on queries. This is a necessity in the working world. Many forms and reports do not use all the records in a table, because they are designed to show a particular activity, time period, location, or other element. The table may have records from years ago that donít belong in this weekís report. You learn how to build queries for all your work, reinforcing the importance of queries.

- **You "start fresh" at the beginning of each Lesson.**

   You start each Lesson with a new version of each of the database. You work with the database only during the Lesson, the Skills Review Exercises, and the Lesson Applications. When you begin another Lesson, you start fresh with a new version of the database. This approach best accommodates the time and scheduling demands of most students' classes.

- **A current version of your database is available from your instructor at three different points as you work through a Lesson.**

   Your instructor has "Help" versions of the database that can be supplied to you at three different points in the process of working through a Lesson. The "Help" points are: at the mid-way point, at the beginning of Skills Review exercises, and at the beginning of the Lesson Applications. That way, if you miss a class, or work on isolated exercises, you can use the most current version of the database.

CASE STUDY

There's more to learning a database program like Microsoft's Access than keying data in an existing database or running a pre-existing query. You need to know how to use Access in a real-world situation. That's why all these lessons relate to everyday business tasks.

As you work through the lessons, imagine yourself working as an intern for Carolina Critters, a fictional company that manufactures stuffed animals, located in Charlotte, North Carolina.

CAROLINA CRITTERS

1

Carolina Critters, Inc.

Carolina Critters, Inc. was formed in 1946 by Hector Fuentes, upon his return from serving in the U.S. Navy in World War II. Hector's son, Carlos, took over the company in 1962 and ran it until 1997, when his daughter Lisa assumed the presidency.

Originally producing only stuffed "teddy bears," rabbits, squirrels, and other "cuddly" animals, the company has branched out over the years. It now has 5 product lines and 25 products, producing over $25 million in annual sales. Today, the stuffed animals from Carolina Critters—ranging from traditional teddy bears and cats and dogs, to dinosaurs and endangered species—are sold in department stores and toy stores across the nation. The company also sells products on the Internet.

In your work as an intern at Carolina Critters, you will interact primarily with the 4 key people shown in Figure CS-1. The database that you use will relate to Carolina Critters. As you work, take the time to notice the following things:

- Carolina Critters's unusual method for manufacturing its stuffed animals (see page 3).

- The types of database activities required in a small business to carry on day-to-day activities.

If you are unfamiliar with databases, review the diagram on page 4 for a brief introduction to some important database concepts. These are also covered in the text.

FIGURE CS-1
Key Employees

LISA FUENTES
President

FRANCES FALCIGNO
Sales and Marketing Manager

JAMES MCCLUSKIE
Vice-President, Chief Financial Officer

LUIS GUTIERREZ
Manufacturing Manager

Method of Manufacturing

Carolina Critters, Inc. uses an unusual method of manufacturing. Carolina Critters doesn't buy each individual component for a stuffed animal (such as material for the outer shell, plastic joints for arms and legs, felt pads for paws, specially-made eyes, extruded plastic components for the nose or claws, clothes, stuffing, and so on). Instead, it has approached a small number of suppliers and contracted with them for "kits" containing all the pre-cut, pre-weighed, pre-formed materials required to manufacture a specific stuffed animal. For example, Robinson Mills, Inc., a supplier in Passaic, New Jersey, provides the kit for "Professor Bear" (pictured here with some of the components included in the kit).

What Is a Database?

A database is a collection of information (or "data") that is organized to make retrieving specific information easy. Access is a software application used to create and manage a computerized database. In Access, a database consists of the following elements (called "objects"): tables, queries, reports, forms, macros, and modules. The following diagram sketches out the relationships between the first four objects.

FIGURE CS-2
Relationships between Database Objects

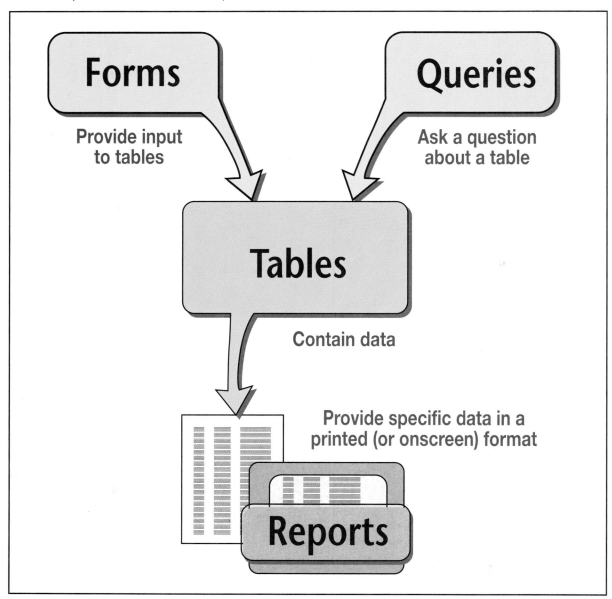

Understanding Access Basics

Getting Started with a Database

After completing this lesson, you will be able to:

1. Copy a database and start Access.
2. Identify parts of the Access screen.
3. Work with objects in the Database window.
4. Work with tables.
5. Work with queries.
6. Open multiple objects.
7. Print a table and a query.
8. Compact and close a database and exit Access.

 Estimated Time: 1¾ hours

Microsoft Access is *database software* that tracks information for businesses or individuals. It's included in the Microsoft Office suite and is also available as a stand-alone program.

You use and are part of many databases. The telephone book is a database that displays information about people, companies, associations, and other groups. You are part of your school's database because the school keeps track of when you enrolled, what courses you've taken, what grades you received, where you live, and other important information.

Access is a *relational database management system* (RDBMS). In a relational database, tables can be linked through a common field such as a part number, invoice number, or social security number. You can eliminate duplication of data and enhance data validity by specifying relationships between tables. A relational database is different from a *flat database*. A flat database is a file that stores data that is not linked by common fields. For example, you can use Excel to create a flat database.

Starting Access

An *object* is an element in a database. The main database objects include tables, queries, forms, reports, pages, macros, and modules. You use these objects to store, display, select, or perform an action in your database.

In this lesson, you work with tables and queries. *Tables* are the basic database objects, similar to the tables created in a word processor or spreadsheet program. *Queries* extract data stored in one or more related tables. *Criteria* (required conditions) can be added to select which fields and records will be extracted.

All data is stored in tables. Within each table, data is stored as a record. A *record* contains data about one entity or activity. Examples of records include an individual, an invoice, or a club event. Each data element within a record is a *field*. Fields are shown in columns in a table.

FIGURE 1-1
Sample table

Field

Record

Guernsey	Anna	888-82-2234	8 Darrydowns Dr.	Charlotte	NC	28204-0008
Handigger	Jane	888-89-0987	43 Wilson Place	Dallas	TX	33779-0043
Hayes	Michael	888-78-2390	345 Owen Boulevard	Los Angeles	CA	90052-0345
Hamsa	Sawsan	888-90-4433	1445 West Lane	Kansas City	KC	43909-1445

Your school has a table of students' names, social security numbers, and addresses. A student's name, social security number, and address, collectively, make up a record of information about a single student. A student's address is a field in the record.

Your school probably has another table that lists courses for each semester. Another table might list the students who are enrolled in specific courses. To make the database manageable, the information is not stored in one big table. Your school's database consists of small, manageable tables that are related to each other. One reason for creating a relational database is to be able to manage data efficiently and effectively.

 TIP: Data is described as "normalized" when it is broken down into separate, smaller tables with no repetition of data from table to table.

EXERCISE **1-1** **Copy a Database and Start Access**

There are several ways to start Access, depending on how your system is installed. For example, you can use the Windows taskbar, the Microsoft Office toolbar, My Computer, or Windows Explorer. If a shortcut is available to start Access, you can double-click the icon on your desktop.

> **NOTE:** Windows provides many ways to start applications. If you have problems, ask your instructor for help. If you are unfamiliar with Windows, see Appendix A: "Windows Tutorial."

In this course, you cannot work directly from a CD. You need to copy the files you need for a particular lesson to a folder on your hard drive or the network. For example, for Lesson 1, you need the files **CC-01**, **CC-E-01**, and the Images folder. If you need help copying files to your computer, ask your instructor or lab manager for assistance.

> **NOTE:** For more information regarding opening, saving, copying, and moving files, see Appendix B: "File Management." For each lesson, you are required to copy and rename the student database. You should be comfortable managing all aspects of a file in the Windows environment.

1. Turn on your computer. Windows loads.

2. Right-click the Start button on the Windows taskbar. A shortcut menu opens.

3. Click Explore. When the Windows Explorer opens, click the Maximize button to maximize the window.

> **NOTE:** When you are told to "click" a menu option or a toolbar button, use the left mouse button. Use the left mouse button unless you are told explicitly to "right-click."

4. In the left pane, open the folder Lesson 01. The files contained in the folder appear in the right pane.

> **NOTE:** Your instructor will tell you where the folders and files for this course are located.

5. In the right pane, point at the filename **CC-01** and right-click. Choose Copy from the shortcut menu. (See Figure 1-2 on the next page.)
6. In the left pane, open the My Documents folder.

FIGURE 1-2
Windows Explorer

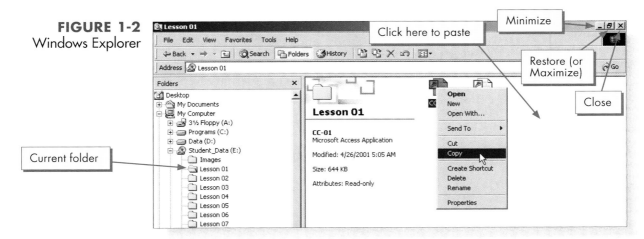

NOTE: Check with your instructor to verify the location where you will store your files. Many times, the My Documents folder is the default folder when you're creating or storing files.

7. In an unused area of the right pane, right-click. Choose **Paste** from the shortcut menu. A file named **CC-01** appears.

8. Right-click the filename **CC-01** and choose **Rename**. Press [Home] and edit the name to *[your initials]*CC-01. Press [Enter] to accept the new name.

9. Right-click *[your initials]*CC-01 and choose **Properties**. Make certain that the **Read-only** attribute check box is not checked.

FIGURE 1-3
Properties
dialog box

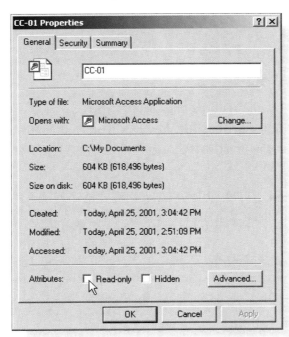

10. Click **OK**. Close the Explorer.

11. With the left mouse button, click the Start button [Start] on the Windows taskbar and point to **Programs**.

12. Click **Microsoft Access 2002**. (You might have to point first to a program group such as **Microsoft Office**.) After the program is loaded, you will see the New File task pane. You can open an existing database, create a blank database, or create a new database from a template.

FIGURE 1-4
Initial Access
window with
New File task pane

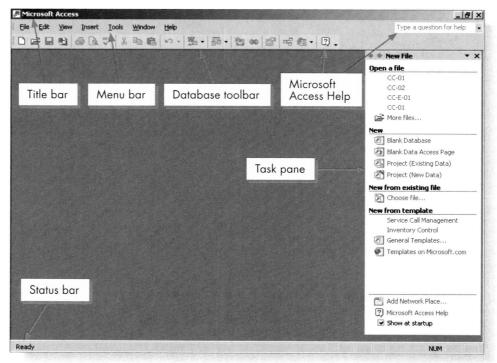

13. In the **Open a file** section, click **More files**.

14. The Open dialog box opens, showing the files in your default folder. Locate the folder containing *[your initials]***CC-01** that you pasted and renamed in steps 5 through 8.

> **NOTE:** At the start of each lesson throughout this course, you copy a template database and rename it, using your initials. This distinguishes your database and work from the original and from other students' databases.

15. Double-click *[your initials]***CC-01** to open the file. Access opens with the Database window. The Database window is the base for operations you perform when working with your database. (See Figure 1-5 on the next page.)

16. Maximize the Database window to remove any scroll bars.

FIGURE 1-5
Access screen with
open database

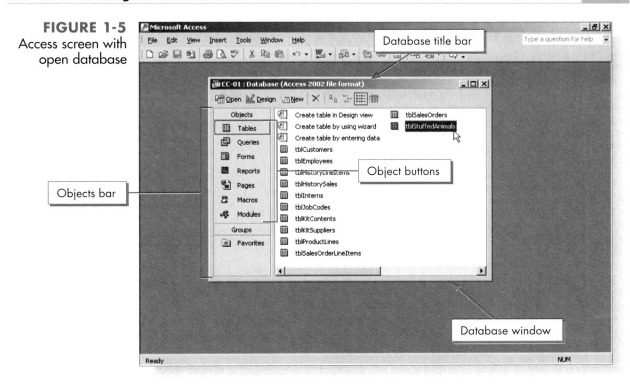

TABLE 1-1   Parts of the Access Screen

PART OF SCREEN	PURPOSE
Title bar	Contains the program name (Microsoft Access).
Database title bar	Contains the name of the database (CC-01).
Menu bar	Displays the names of menus to perform various tasks. You can use the mouse or the keyboard to open menus.
Database toolbar	Displays buttons to execute commands with the mouse. Access opens with the Database toolbar displayed. You learn about other toolbars later.
Database window	Displays a button for each object in the database. Also includes Command buttons to open or design an existing object or create a new one.
Objects bar	Displays buttons for each type of object in the database. By clicking a button, you can work with the database's tables, queries, forms, reports, pages, macros, or modules.

continues

TABLE 1-1   Parts of the Access Screen   *continued*

PART OF SCREEN	PURPOSE
Status bar	Displays information about the current task and shows the current mode of operation.
Microsoft Access Help	Provides online Help and tips as you work.

E X E R C I S E   1-2   Display Database Properties

Database properties are characteristics or attributes that describe and define the database.

1. Move the pointer to <u>F</u>ile on the menu bar. Click to open the menu.

> **NOTE:** Access 2002 has speech recognition capabilities for menu options. If your computer is set up with a microphone, you can use speech recognition for menu commands, toolbar buttons, and text entry. For more information, see Appendix C. Ask your instructor for information regarding the configuration of your workstation.

2. Move the pointer to Da<u>t</u>abase Properties and click to open the Properties dialog box.

> **NOTE:** If you do not see Database Properties in the menu, click the down-pointing arrows at the bottom of the menu to expand the menu. These arrows indicate more options are available.

FIGURE 1-6
Properties
dialog box,
Contents tab

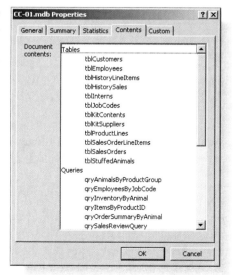

3. Click the Contents tab to see a list of the tables, queries, forms, reports, pages, macros, and modules in the database.

> **NOTE:** There are no macros, modules, or data access pages in your database for Lesson 1.

4. Click OK to close the dialog box.

TABLE 1-2   Properties Dialog Box Tabs

TAB	PURPOSE
General	Contains the date the database was created, last modified, and last opened. Also contains the filename, size, location of the database, and attributes.
Summary	Displays the database title, author, company, category, keywords, and comments.
Statistics	Contains the date the database was created, last modified, printed, and last opened.
Contents	Displays a list of the tables, queries, forms, reports, pages, macros, and modules that the database contains.
Custom	Used to assign a custom property for a file. You can add a name, type, and value for the custom property.

Identifying Parts of the Access Screen

Toolbar buttons are identified by name when you point to them with the mouse.

EXERCISE **1-3**   **Identify Buttons, Menus, and Menu Items**

1. Position the pointer over the New button on the Database toolbar but do not click. A *ScreenTip* (a box with the button name) appears below the button. You choose from a list of sample databases or click the New button to create a blank database.

FIGURE 1-7
Identifying
toolbar button

2. Move the mouse pointer over the Open button (but don't click). You click this button to open an existing database.

NOTE: Some toolbar buttons are light gray, indicating the command is currently not available. You can still identify the button by positioning the mouse pointer over it.

3. Point to other toolbar buttons to identify them.

TIP: The menu shows which commands have keyboard shortcuts. Keyboard shortcuts appear to the right of the menu command. (Your computer might also show the keyboard shortcut in the ScreenTip.)

4. Move the pointer to <u>E</u>dit on the menu bar and click the left mouse button. This opens the <u>E</u>dit menu. Click <u>E</u>dit to close the menu.

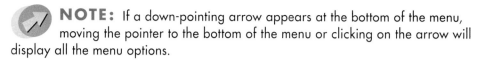 **NOTE:** If a down-pointing arrow appears at the bottom of the menu, moving the pointer to the bottom of the menu or clicking on the arrow will display all the menu options.

5. Click <u>V</u>iew to open the <u>V</u>iew menu. Move the pointer to the **Arrange Icons** menu option. The right-pointing arrow indicates a submenu. This submenu displays options for arranging the icons in the Database window.

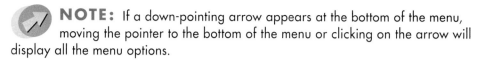 **TIP:** Office 2002 uses *adaptive menus* to display only the most recently used commands. If you wish to always see all commands available on the menu, select <u>T</u>ools, <u>C</u>ustomize. In the Options tab of the dialog box, place a checkmark in the box beside Always show full menus and click OK.

FIGURE 1-8
Displaying
menu options

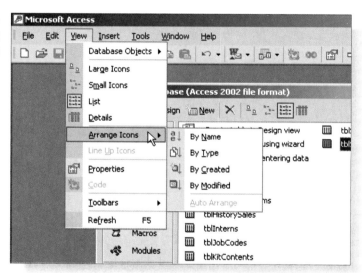

6. Click a blank area of the screen to close the menu. Be careful not to click a menu option or toolbar button.

Looking at Database Objects

At the left of the Database window is an Objects bar showing object buttons. You use these buttons to select the elements with which to work. An object is an item in a database with a specific purpose. It can be a table, a query, or a design element in a form. When you select a button, you see the names of all the objects related to the button that are in the database. For example, if you select the Tables button, the names of all the tables in this database are displayed.

The objects in the databases for this text use *the Leszynski Naming Conventions (LNC)*. These conventions are widely recognized and used by database developers. The object name is preceded by a prefix. Main words are capitalized with no spaces between words.

 NOTE: You can read more about this naming convention in the Preface.

TABLE 1-3   **Naming Conventions**

PREFIX	OBJECT TYPE	EXAMPLE
tbl	Table	tblEmployees
qry	Query	qryKitSuppliers
frm	Form	frmStuffedAnimals
rpt	Report	rptInventoryValue
pge	Page	pgeCustomers
mcr	Macro	mcrPreviewReport
bas	Module	basMyProgram

There are seven types of objects in an Access database:

- Tables store information about a person, place, thing, or event. A table consists of records, which contain fields. The information in a table appears in rows (records) and columns (fields), similar to an Excel worksheet.

- Queries are used to find answers to questions about the data in the database. You can design queries to show fields from one or more tables. You can specify criteria or conditions that must be met for a record to be included. You can use a query to calculate totals or averages from information in the table.

- *Forms* enable you to view, edit, or add records. You can design a form to look like a paper form so people entering the data are familiar with the layout. With most forms, you can see an entire record at one time.

- *Reports* are used to print data. You can group your data, calculate totals, apply different formats, and add graphics to make the report attractive and easy to read.

- *Pages* are HTML documents that are linked to data. They are designed for use in a Web browser and typically require Internet Explorer 5.0 (or later).

- *Macros* run a series of commands. You can write macros for repetitive activities and to automate procedures you use often.
- *Modules* contain Visual Basic for Applications (VBA) functions or procedures.

EXERCISE 1-4 Work in the Database Window

The Table Properties dialog box displays characteristics of a particular table, including the table name, the description, the date the file was created, and the last time the file was updated.

 NOTE: The database you work with in this course relates to the Case Study about Carolina Critters, a fictional company that manufactures stuffed animals (see pages 1 through 4).

1. Click Tables on the Objects bar. All the tables in the current database are shown. The prefix for a table is *tbl*.

2. Click tblCustomers. Click the Properties button 🖼 on the right side of the Database toolbar to open the Customers Properties dialog box. Notice the dates when the file was created and modified. Read the description.

FIGURE 1-9
Customers
Properties
dialog box

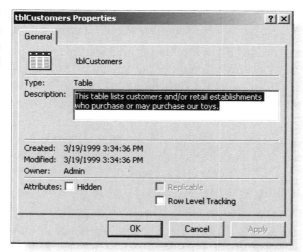

 NOTE: An open object can be referred to without its prefix. For example, the tblCustomers Properties box can be referred to as the "Customers Properties dialog box."

3. Click OK to close the dialog box.

4. Point at tblEmployees and right-click. The shortcut menu is a way to quickly access a table's properties. Choose Properties from the shortcut menu to open the Properties dialog box.

5. Click the Close button in the upper right corner of the Employees Properties dialog box to close the dialog box.

6. Click Queries on the Object bar. All the queries in the database are shown. The prefix for a query is *qry*.

7. Click qryInventoryByAnimal. Click the Properties button on the Database toolbar. There is no description for this query.

8. Click OK to close the dialog box.

9. Click Tables on the Objects bar.

10. Click the Details button in the Database window. Access shows you table descriptions when you set the window to this view.

> **TIP:** Drag the vertical border between column headings to show more of the description.

11. Click Queries on the Objects bar. One of the queries does include a description.

12. Click the Large Icons button and then click the Small Icons button to see what other views are available.

13. Click the List button to return to the original display.

14. Click Tables again. Right-click tblJobCodes. Choose Rename from the shortcut menu.

15. Key **tblMine** and press Enter. The table names are in alphabetical order in List view.

16. Right-click tblMine and choose Rename. Key **tblJobCodes** and press Enter.

> **TIP:** You can rename any database object.

EXERCISE 1-5 Use Datasheet and Design Views

You can look at tables and queries in several views. You can press Ctrl + < to scroll down or Ctrl + > to scroll up through the following table view options.

> **NOTE:** When Keyboard combinations (such as Ctrl + >) are shown in this text, hold down the first key as you press the second key. Release the second key and then release the first key. An example of this entire sequence is: hold down Ctrl, press > , release > , release Ctrl. With practice this sequence becomes easy.

These shortcuts cycle through all four views.

- *Datasheet View.* This view appears when you open a table or query. Datasheet View resembles a worksheet with rows and columns. Each record is displayed in its own row. Each field is shown in its own column. You can enter and edit data, find and sort records, resize rows and columns, and move rows and columns in Datasheet View.

- *Design View.* You use this view to create or modify the layout or structure of a table or query. You do not see the records in this view. In a query, you see a field list and a design grid with sorting directions and criteria. In a table, you see a grid listing field names, the type of data contained in each field (number, text, currency, and so on), and a description of the field. Design View includes field properties with formatting options, default values, validation rules, and other characteristics for each field in the table. (You learn more about data types and field properties in later lessons.)

- *PivotTable View.* You use this view to summarize and analyze data in a table, query, or form. Information is displayed in a table format with columns and rows. You can use different levels of detail or organize data by dragging the fields and items or by showing and hiding items in the drop-down lists for the fields.

- *PivotChart View.* You use this view to summarize and analyze data in a table, query, or form. Information is displayed in a chart form. You can use different levels of detail or organize data by dragging the fields and items or by showing and hiding items in the drop-down lists for the fields.

1. Click tblCustomers. Click the **Open** command button at the top of the Database window to open the Customers table in Datasheet View. Click the Maximize button ▢ to maximize the Table window.

FIGURE 1-10
Customers table
datasheet

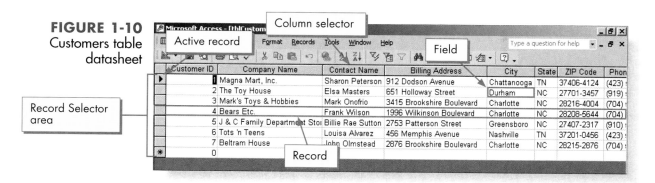

2. With the Customers datasheet displayed, click the down arrow next to the View button on the left side of the Database toolbar. The View shortcut menu appears. (See Figure 1-11 on the next page.)

FIGURE 1-11
Shortcut menu for
View button

Current view

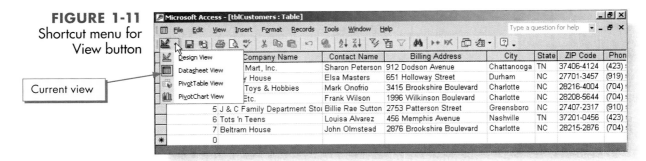

3. Choose Design View from the shortcut menu. This displays the Customers table in Design View. Customer records don't appear in this view. You see the field names, data types, and descriptions.

 NOTE: The buttons on the toolbar change, depending on the current view. You can right-click any toolbar to open a shortcut menu to show which toolbars are active.

FIGURE 1-12
Customers table in
Design View

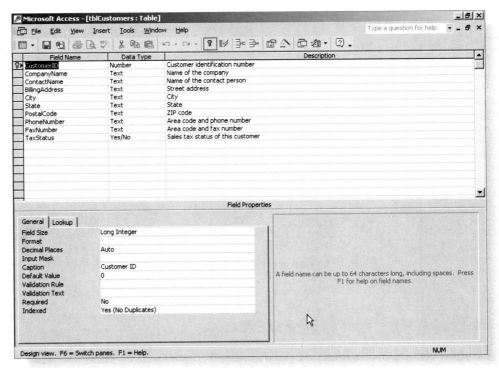

4. Click the Close button ✕ to close the Customers table.
5. Double-click the table icon to the left of tblEmployees. The Employees table opens in Datasheet View.

TIP: You can double-click the table icon to the left of the table name, or the table name itself, to open the table.

6. Click the View button ![icon] (the button, not the down arrow). This displays the Employees table in Design View.

NOTE: The View button is a "toggle" between Design and Datasheet Views. When there are two views for an object, you can click the icon to switch views. The button shows the view that is not currently shown.

7. Click the View button ![icon] to return to Datasheet View. Close the table.

8. Click **Queries** on the Objects bar. Double-click the query icon to the left of qryInventoryByAnimal. The query opens in Datasheet View.

9. Click the View button ![icon] to see Design View for a query.

FIGURE 1-13
Inventory query in
Design View

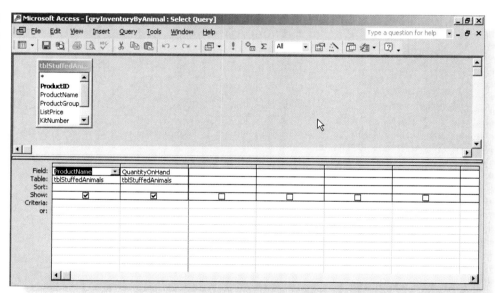

10. Click the Close button ![X].

Working with Tables

The pointer marks the current or active record and where your next action will occur in a table. The pointer appears as a triangle in the narrow empty column to the left of the first field. This column is called the *Record Selector*.

You can use the mouse and the keyboard to move the pointer. You can use navigation buttons to move to a specific record. You can also scroll the records on the screen without moving the pointer.

- Scroll bars frame the right and lower borders of the Table window. You can use the scroll bars to bring different parts of your table into view.

 NOTE: When you scroll a window, you change what you see on the screen. You do not move the pointer.

- Navigation buttons are in the lower left corner of the Table window. These buttons include First Record 〔◄〕, Previous Record 〔◄〕, Next Record 〔►〕, Last Record 〔►〕, and New Record 〔►*〕.
- Press 〔Tab〕 to move from field to field and 〔Shift〕+〔Tab〕 to move backward.

EXERCISE 1-6 Scroll Through a Table

1. With the *[your initials]*CC-01 database open, click Tables on the Objects bar. Double-click tblEmployees and click the Maximize button 〔□〕 to maximize the Employees table window in Datasheet View.

2. On the vertical scroll bar, click below the scroll box to move down one screen. This is the same as pressing 〔PgDn〕.

FIGURE 1-14
Using scroll bars

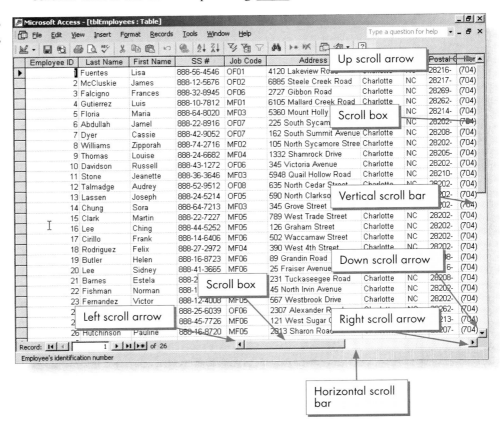

3. Drag the scroll box to the top of the vertical scroll bar.

4. Click the down scroll arrow twice to move down two rows.

5. Click the right scroll arrow on the horizontal scroll bar once; then click the left scroll arrow once to return to the original horizontal position.

6. Click the up scroll arrow on the vertical scroll bar twice. Notice that throughout this scrolling movement, the pointer remains in the first record.

TABLE 1-4   **Scrolling Through a Table**

TO MOVE THE VIEW	DO THIS
Up one line	Click the up scroll arrow.
Down one line	Click the down scroll arrow.
Up one screen	Click the scroll bar above the scroll box.
Down one screen	Click the scroll bar below the scroll box.
To any relative position	Drag the scroll bar up or down.
To the right	Click the right scroll arrow.
To the left	Click the left scroll arrow.

EXERCISE 1-7 Use Navigation Buttons

The navigation buttons are located in the lower left corner of a table in Datasheet View. You can use these buttons to move the pointer to a specific record or form.

FIGURE 1-15
Navigation buttons

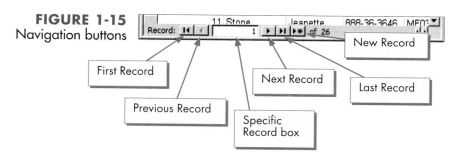

1. With the Employees table open, click the Next Record navigation button once. The next Employee ID is now highlighted. This button moves the pointer one record at a time.

2. Click the Previous Record button once. The pointer moves to the previous record. This button moves one record at a time.

3. Click the Last Record button . The pointer moves to the last record in the table.

4. Click the First Record button . The pointer moves to the first record in the table.

> **TIP:** Press F5 to place the pointer in the Specific Record box (between the navigation buttons). Key the record number, and press Enter to move to that record number.

5. Click the Close button ✕ to close tblEmployees.

6. Open tblCustomers as a maximized window. Click the New Record button . This moves the pointer to the end of the table to enter a new record.

> **TIP:** The New Record button also appears on the toolbar.

7. Press PgUp to move to the top of the current screen.

8. Press Tab twice. This moves the pointer to the Contact Name field. Press Shift + Tab once. This moves the pointer back to the Company Name field.

TABLE 1-5   **Keyboard Navigation Shortcuts**

PRESS	TO DO THIS
Tab	Move to the next field.
Shift + Tab	Move to the previous field.
PgUp	Move up one screen.
PgDn	Move down one screen.
Ctrl + Home	Return to the first record.
Ctrl + End	Move to the last record.

EXERCISE   **1-8**   Change Column Widths, Row Heights, and Fonts

To make your table easier to view, you can increase or decrease column widths. If a field heading or entry is longer than the text, you can adjust the column to accommodate the heading or entry. You can make the column narrower if there is too much blank space.

You can also make the rows appear to be taller. The default font for Datasheet View is 10-point Arial, but you can change that, too. Changes to the column width, the row height, or the font affect the entire table.

1. In the Customers table, place the pointer on the vertical border between the Company Name and Contact Name column selectors at the tops of the second and third columns. Notice that the pointer changes to a two-headed arrow with a wide vertical bar.

FIGURE 1-16
Resizing columns

2. Drag the pointer to the right approximately half an inch to allow enough space for the word "Stores" in Record 5. Release the button.

 TIP: You can set the width of a column to the widest text by double-clicking its column selector's right vertical border.

3. Place the pointer between the Billing Address and City column selectors. Use the scroll bars to bring the columns into view.

4. When the pointer changes to a two-headed arrow with a wide vertical bar, drag the pointer to the left, making the Address column smaller until it just accommodates the longest billing address.

5. From the Format menu, choose Font. Choose Arial as the font and 12 as the size. Click OK.

6. From the Format menu, choose Font again. Choose 10 as the size. Click OK.

7. Place the pointer on the horizontal line between the first and second row in the Record Selector area to the left of the first field.

8. When the pointer changes to a two-headed arrow, drag the pointer down to make the row approximately twice its current height. (See Figure 1-17 on the next page.)

NOTE: The *layout* of a table is the way it appears on the screen. It includes the size of the columns, the height of the rows, the fonts, the arrangement of the columns, the colors, and other settings.

FIGURE 1-17
Adjusting row height

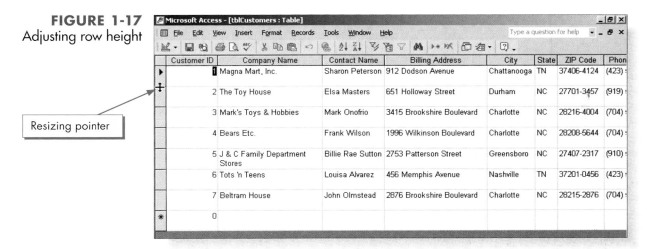

Resizing pointer

9. Place the pointer on the horizontal line between the first and second rows. Drag the pointer up until the row height accommodates the height of all letters.

10. Right-click the Record Selector for row one. From the shortcut menu, choose Row Height.

11. Make certain that a check appears in the **Standard Height** check box.

FIGURE 1-18
Row Height
dialog box

12. Click OK. Close the table. A dialog box appears, prompting you to save the layout of the Customers table. Click Yes to accept the changes.

E X E R C I S E   1-9   Freeze Fields in a Table

Most tables contain more fields than you can view at one time, so you need to scroll the window. If there is a field you want to see onscreen all the time, you can freeze that field at the left edge of the screen.

1. Open tblEmployees in Datasheet View and maximize the window.

2. Move the pointer to the Employee ID column selector. When the pointer changes to a down-pointing arrow, click. The column is selected.

3. Select Format, Freeze Columns. Then click anywhere in the table to deselect the column. Notice that the right vertical border of the frozen column is slightly heavier than the other vertical lines.

4. Click the right scroll arrow several times to move to the last column. The Employee ID column doesn't scroll.

TIP: To select a block of columns, click the first column selector and then hold down Shift while clicking on the last column in the block.

5. To unfreeze all the columns, choose Unfreeze **A**ll Columns from the F**o**rmat menu.

6. Select the SS# column by clicking the SS# column selector when the pointer is a down-pointing arrow.

7. From the F**o**rmat menu, choose Free**z**e Columns. The SS# column moves to the left edge of the table.

TIP: If you freeze a column other than the first column, Access moves that column to be the first column.

8. Click the right scroll arrow several times. The SS# column doesn't scroll.

9. From the F**o**rmat menu, choose Unfreeze **A**ll Columns.

10. Close the Employees table. A dialog box appears, prompting you to save the layout of the Employees table. Click **No**.

NOTE: If you do not save the layout when you close the table, the columns return to their original positions.

Working with Queries

A query has many of the same characteristics as a table. You can look at all the fields from the table, or you can choose to view only specific fields.

All of the navigation commands in a query are the same as those in a table. You can change the font, the column widths, and the row height as well as freeze columns.

EXERCISE **1-10** **Scroll and Navigate in a Query**

1. Click the **Queries** button. Double-click qryInventoryByAnimals. Make certain that the window is maximized. This query shows three fields from the Stuffed Animals table.

2. Click below the vertical scroll box to move down one screen.

3. Drag the scroll box to the top of the vertical scroll bar.

4. Click the down scroll arrow twice to move down two rows.

NOTE: There is no horizontal scroll bar because the query is not wide enough to need one.

5. Click the up scroll arrow on the vertical scroll bar twice.

6. Click the Next Record button ▶ once. The next Product ID is highlighted.

7. Click the Previous Record button ◀ once.

8. Click the Last Record button ▶|. The pointer moves to the last record in the query.

9. Click the First Record button |◀.

10. Press F5 to place the pointer in the Specific Record box. Key **8** and press Enter. The pointer moves to the eighth record.

11. Click the Close button ✕ to close the query.

EXERCISE   1-11   **View a Multiple-Table Query**

1. Double-click qryOrderSummaryByAnimal. Make certain the window is maximized. This query shows fields from more than one table.

2. Click the View button. The top half of the screen shows three table field lists with join lines between them. The join lines connect linked fields holding the same data.

FIGURE 1-19
Order Summary
query in
Design View

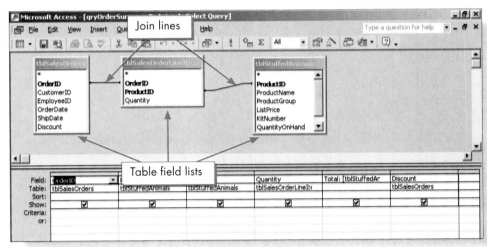

TIP: Join lines are an important concept in a relational database.

3. Click the View button to return to Datasheet View.

4. Place the pointer on the vertical border between the Animal Name and List Price column selectors. The pointer changes to the two-headed arrow with a wide vertical bar.

5. Drag the pointer to the right until there is enough space for the longest animal name.

6. Place the pointer between the Total and Discount field names. When the pointer shows a two-headed arrow, double-click to size the width to the data.

7. Choose F̲ormat and then choose F̲ont. Key **t** and choose Times New Roman. Choose 12 as the size. Click OK.

8. Choose F̲ormat and then **choose Font**. Key **a** and choose Arial. Set 10 as the size. Click OK.

9. Place the pointer on the horizontal line between the first and second rows in the Record Selector.

10. When the pointer changes to a two-headed arrow, drag the pointer down to make the row approximately twice its current height.

11. Close the query. A dialog box appears, prompting you to save the layout. Click No to discard the changes.

Working with Multiple Objects

You can open more than one table to compare or contrast data in the tables. You can also open a query and a table at the same time. When you work with multiple objects, you can see the data better if you tile the windows.

E X E R C I S E   1-12   Open Multiple Tables

1. Click the Tables button. Open tblCustomers.

2. Choose *[your initials]*CC-01 database from the W̲indow menu to return to the Database window.

3. Open tblEmployees.

4. Click the Database Window button 🖻 on the toolbar. This also switches you to the Database window. Click the Minimize button ▬ in the Database window to minimize it.

5. Select W̲indow, Ti̲le Horizontally. The two tables are tiled. (See Figure 1-20 on the next page.)

   NOTE: If you do not minimize the Database window, it is tiled along with the tables.

6. Close both tables.

7. Click the Maximize button ☐ in the minimized Database window.

FIGURE 1-20
Horizontally
tiled tables

EXERCISE 1-13   Open Multiple Queries

1. Click Queries on the Objects bar. Open qryInventoryByAnimal.
2. Click the Database Window button 🗗 on the toolbar.
3. Open qryStuffedAnimals.
4. Click the Database Window button 🗗. Click the Minimize button ▬ in the Database window to minimize it.
5. From the Window menu, choose Tile Vertically. The two queries are tiled.
6. Close both queries.
7. Click the Maximize button ▢ in the minimized Database window.

EXERCISE 1-14   Open a Table and a Query

1. Open qryOrderSummaryByAnimal.
2. Click the Database Window button 🗗.
3. Click Tables on the Objects bar. Open tblStuffedAnimals.
4. Click the Database Window button 🗗. Click the Minimize button ▬.

5. From the <u>W</u>indow menu, choose T<u>i</u>le Horizontally. The table and the query are tiled.

6. Close both objects.

7. Click the Maximize button in the minimized Database window.

Printing a Table and a Query

You can print a table or a query as it appears in Datasheet View. You can use any of these methods:

- Click the Print button 🖨 on the Database toolbar
- Choose <u>F</u>ile, and then choose <u>P</u>rint.
- Press Ctrl + P

🖨 The menu and keyboard methods open the Print dialog box, where you choose printing options. Clicking the Print button 🖨 sends the document directly to the printer, using Access's default settings. It doesn't open the Print dialog box.

EXERCISE **1-15** **Change Page Setup**

You can set the page orientation to portrait (vertical) or landscape (horizontal). Landscape is better if a table or query contains many fields and you want to fit the data on one printed page.

1. Click Tables on the Objects bar. Open tblCustomers.

2. Choose <u>F</u>ile and then choose Page Set<u>u</u>p to open the Page Setup dialog box. The Margins tab opens by default. This dialog box displays the default margin settings.

FIGURE 1-21
Page Setup dialog box with default margin settings

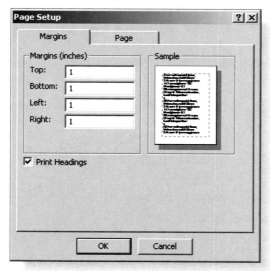

3. Click the Page tab. This dialog box displays the orientation, paper, and printer default settings. Click the <u>L</u>andscape option button. (See Figure 1-22 on the next page.)

4. Click OK to close the dialog box.

 TIP: Check the orientation for each table or query you print.

FIGURE 1-22
Page Setup
dialog box,
Page tab

5. Click the Print Preview button to see how your table will print. You can also see how many pages will print.

FIGURE 1-23
Print Preview of
Customers table

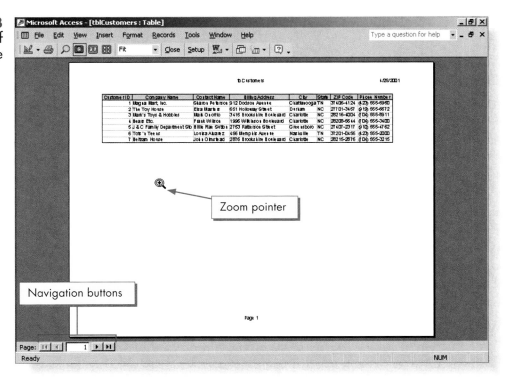

6. Click the Next Page button .

NOTE: Access tiles pages when tables are too wide for the printed page. Only columns that fit on a page print on that page. Columns are not cut in the middle.

7. Click the Close button to close the preview and return to the Customers table.

 TIP: The Close button ☒ closes the table, not just the preview.

EXERCISE 1-16   Print a Table

---

1. To print the Customers table, choose **F**ile and then choose **P**rint. The Print dialog box opens with your default settings.

FIGURE 1-24
Print dialog box

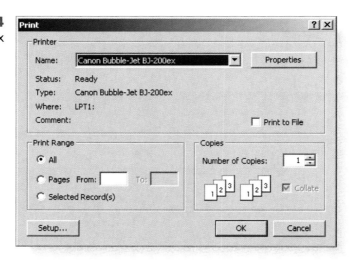

2. Click **OK** or press Enter to accept the settings. A printer icon appears on the taskbar as the table is sent to the printer.

3. Close the table.

EXERCISE 1-17   Preview and Print a Query

---

1. Click **Queries** on the Objects bar and open qryOrderSummaryByAnimal.

2. Click the Print Preview button 🔍. This query will fit in portrait orientation on one page.

3. Click the Print button 🖨. The query is sent to the printer.

TIP: You can print from the Print Preview window.

4. Click <u>C</u>lose to close only the preview.

5. Close qryOrderSummaryByAnimal.

Compacting and Closing a Database and Exiting Access

When you finish working on a database, you should compact it to save disk space. As you work on a database, Access finds and uses space as quickly as it can. The database expands and is usually not as efficiently organized on the disk as it could be. The **Compact and Repair Database** command reclaims unused space and saves the database efficiently. After you compact the database, you can close it and open another database or you can exit the program.

 NOTE: Compacting a database might be compared to running the defragment utility on your hard drive.

There are four ways to close a database and exit Access:

- Use the Close button **X** in the upper right corner of the window when the Database window is maximized.

FIGURE 1-25
Close buttons

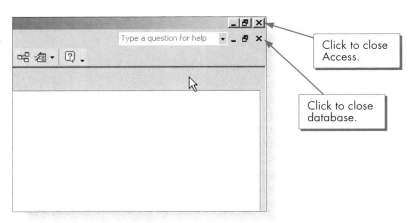

- Use the <u>F</u>ile menu.
- Use the Database Control icon in the upper left corner of the Database window title bar, next to the database name. Choose <u>C</u>lose from the Database Control menu. (See Figure 1-26 on the next page.)

FIGURE 1-26
Control menus

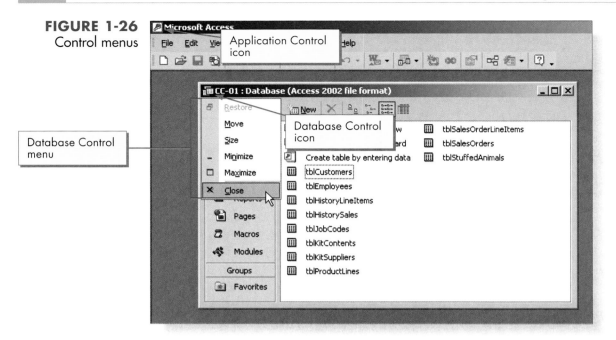

Database Control menu

- Use keyboard shortcuts. Ctrl + W or Ctrl + F4 closes a database and Alt + F4 exits Access.

TIP: You can set Access to automatically compact the database each time it is closed by using Tools, Options.

EXERCISE 1-18 Compact and Close a Database and Exit Access

1. Choose Tools and choose Database Utilities. Then choose Compact and Repair Database. The database is compacted and remains open. (See Figure 1-27 on the next page.)

2. Click the Close button ✖ to close the database.

NOTE: When no database is open, there is no Database window on the screen.

3. Copy your database file from the directory in which you were working. Paste it to your disk. After verifying that your database was properly copied, delete the copy of your database from the directory in which you were working.

FIGURE 1-27
Tools,
Database Utilities
menu

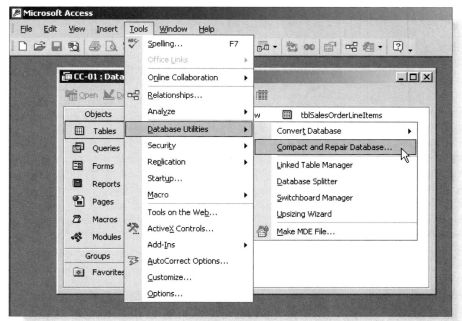

USING HELP

The Microsoft Access Help system is available at all times and is often the quickest and easiest way to determine how to complete a task.

Look up Access commands:

1. From Access, open *[your initials]***CC-01**.

2. Open the <u>H</u>elp menu and choose Show the <u>O</u>ffice Assistant. The Office Assistant opens. If you do not see a text box above the Assistant, click the Assistant icon.

3. In the text box for "What would you like to do?" key **backup and restore**. Click <u>S</u>earch.

4. In the list of topics, click Backup and restore an Access database.

5. The Microsoft Access window opens. Maximize the window. In the right pane, read the information.

6. In the left pane, click on the topic Compact and repair an Access file. Three topic links appear in the right pane.

7. Click on <u>Compact and repair the current Access file</u>. (See Figure 1-28 on the next page.)

FIGURE 1-28
Microsoft
Access Help

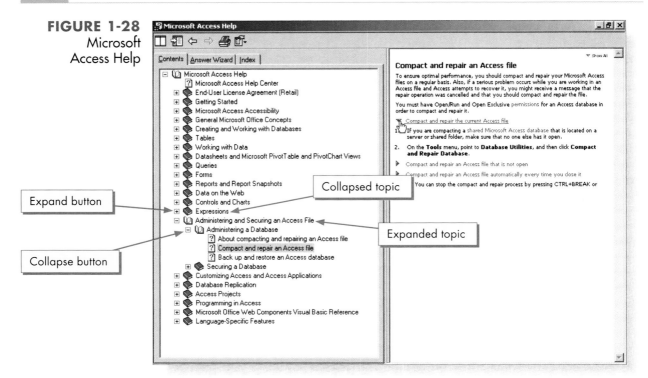

8. Read the Help for the expanded topic. Expand and read the remaining two topics.

9. Close the Help window.

10. Right-click the Office Assistant icon and choose <u>O</u>ptions. Turn off the option to <u>U</u>se the Office Assistant. The next time you use Help, the Office Assistant will not start unless someone else has turned it on.

11. Close the database.

LESSON 1 Summary

➤ After copying a file from a CD, you might need to remove the read-only attribute.

➤ The database properties provide useful information regarding specifications, summary information, statistics, and contents of the file.

➤ You can perform actions on a database through buttons and menus.

➤ You can select database objects through the Database window.

➤ Tables and queries have four different views: Datasheet View, Design View, PivotTable View, and PivotChart View.

➤ You can view records by scrolling through a Datasheet View.

➤ Navigation buttons provide efficient means of moving to different records of a Datasheet View.

➤ You can change column widths, row heights, and fonts in Datasheet View.

➤ Freeze fields in Datasheet View to lock columns on the far left side of the screen.

➤ Linked tables create multiple-table queries.

➤ Multiple tables and queries can be viewed at one time.

➤ Changing the page setup lets you print a table in landscape format.

➤ Printing a table displays the data stored in the table.

➤ You can use Print Preview to look at a table or query prior to actual printing.

➤ Periodically, you should compact your database.

LESSON 1   Command Summary

FEATURE	BUTTON	MENU	KEYBOARD	SPEECH
Close a document	✕	File, Close	Ctrl + W or Ctrl + F4	✓
Column width		Format, Column Width		✓
Compact		Tools, Database Utilities, Compact and Repair Database		✓
Database Properties		File, Database Properties		✓
Datasheet View	▦	View, Datasheet View		✓
Design View	◪	View, Design View		✓
Exit Access	✕	File, Exit	Alt + F4	✓
Freeze Columns		Format, Freeze Columns		✓
Font		Format, Font		✓
Open	☞	File, Open	Ctrl + O	✓

continues

LESSON 1 Command Summary *continued*

FEATURE	BUTTON	MENU	KEYBOARD	SPEECH
Page Setup		File, Page Setup		✓
Print		File, Print	Ctrl + P	✓
Print Preview		File, Print Preview		✓
Query Properties		View, Properties	Alt + Enter	✓
Row Height		Format, Row Height		✓
Save		File, Save	Ctrl + S	✓
Table Properties		View, Properties	Alt + Enter	✓
Tile Windows Horizontally		Window, Tile Horizontally		✓
Tile Windows Vertically		Window, Tile Vertically		✓
Unfreeze Columns		Format, Unfreeze All Columns		✓

Concepts Review

Each of the following statements is either true or false. Indicate your choice by circling T or F.

T   F   *1.* You can have only one object open at a time.

T   F   *2.* An active record can be identified by a triangle in the Record Selector area for that row.

T   F   *3.* A row in a table or query may have a different height than other rows.

T   F   *4.* You can use the navigation buttons to move to a specific record.

T   F   *5.* Records in a table or query do not appear in Datasheet View.

T   F   *6.* A query can use more than one table.

T   F   *7.* You can change the font for individual words in Datasheet View.

T   F   *8.* Freezing fields locks fields to keep them in view.

Write the correct answer in the space provided.

1. What is the Leszynski Naming Convention prefix for table names?

_____

2. Which buttons do you use to move to different records in a table or query?

_____

3. Which view displays the records in columns and rows like an Excel worksheet?

_____

4. What command locks a column on the left in a table?

_____

5. What command compresses or condenses a database file?

_____

6. Which button would move the pointer to Record #2 if it is at Record #3?

_____

7. What dialog box contains the description, creation date, and modification date for a table or query?

_____

8. Which table view displays the field names, data types, and field properties?

_____

CRITICAL THINKING

Answer these questions on a separate page. There are no right or wrong answers. Support your answers with examples from your own experience, if possible.

> **1.** Why might a person want to open more than one table at a time?
>
> **2.** How are navigation buttons different from scroll bars? When would you use scroll bars? When would you use navigation buttons?

Skills Review

EXERCISE 1-19

Copy, rename, and open a database. Identify parts of the Access screen.

> **1.** Copy and rename a database by following these steps:
>
>   **a.** Right-click the Start button  on the Windows taskbar.
>   **b.** Choose Explore and maximize the window.
>   **c.** In the left pane, open folder Lesson 01. Point at the filename **CC-E-01** and right-click.
>   **d.** Choose Copy from the shortcut menu.
>   **e.** In the left pane, open the My Documents folder. Right-click in an unused area of the right pane and choose Paste from the shortcut menu.
>   **f.** Right-click **CC-E-01** and choose Rename. Key *[your initials]***CC-E-01** and press Enter.
>   **g.** Right-click *[your initials]***CC-E-01** and choose Properties. Make certain that the Read-only attribute check box is not checked. Click OK.
>   **h.** Close the Explorer.
>
> **2.** Start Access and open a database by following these steps:
>   **a.** Click the Start button  on the Windows taskbar.
>   **b.** Point to Programs and click Microsoft Access 2002.
>   **c.** Click More Files.
>   **d.** Locate *[your initials]***CC-E-01** and double-click it.

TIP: The **CC-E-01** database contains confidential and private data for the company. The tables can be imported into or linked to the main database and still keep this sensitive information separate from everyday use. You learn about importing in Lesson 4.

3. Move the pointer to the Open button 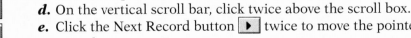 and display the button's ScreenTip. Point to the Print Preview button to identify it.

4. Click <u>V</u>iew on the menu bar. Move the pointer to **Database Objects**.

5. Close the menu by clicking in a blank area of the screen.

EXERCISE 1-20

Select and use objects in a Database window.

1. With *[your initials]***CC-E-01** open, open the Table Properties dialog box by following these steps:

   a. Click the **Tables** button.
   b. Point at tblEmployeeDates and right-click. Choose <u>P</u>roperties.
   c. Click **OK** to close the Properties dialog box.
   d. Click the **Queries** button.
   e. Point at qryEmployeeDates and right-click. Choose <u>P</u>roperties. There is no description.
   f. Click **OK** to close the Properties dialog box.

2. Change from Datasheet View to Design View by following these steps:

   a. Click the **Tables** button. Double-click tblPayroll to open it.
   b. Press Ctrl + < to change to Design View.
   c. Press Ctrl + > to return to Datasheet View.
   d. Click the Close button to close tblPayroll.

3. Navigate through records by following these steps:

   a. Click the **Queries** button. Open qryEmployeeDates and click the Maximize button .
   b. Drag the scroll box on the vertical scroll bar to the bottom of the scroll bar.
   c. Click the up scroll arrow twice to move up two rows.
   d. On the vertical scroll bar, click twice above the scroll box.
   e. Click the Next Record button twice to move the pointer forward two records.
   f. Click the Previous Record button once to move back one record.
   g. Click the Last Record button to move to the last record.
   h. Click the First Record button to move to the first record.

4. Change column widths and row heights by following these steps:

   a. Place the pointer on the vertical border between the Social Security and Employee ID field names.

    b. Drag the pointer to the right until the complete Social Security title fits in the column heading.

    c. Place the pointer between the Date of Birth and Hire Date column selectors.

    d. Double-click to size the Date of Birth field to its longest entry.

    e. Place the pointer on the horizontal line between the first and second rows in the Record Selector.

    f. Drag down the horizontal border to make the rows twice as tall.

    g. Resize all rows to approximately their original height.

    h. Close the query. When the dialog box appears, click No to discard the layout changes.

5. Freeze and unfreeze fields in a table by following these steps:

    a. Click the Tables button and open tblPayroll. Click the Restore button if your window is maximized. The window should not be maximized.

    b. Click the SS# column selector. While holding down the Shift key, click the Employee ID column selector.

    c. Choose Format, Freeze Columns.

    d. Scroll to view the Savings field.

    e. To unfreeze the columns, choose Format and then choose Unfreeze All Columns.

    f. Close the table. Click No in the dialog box to discard layout changes.

EXERCISE 1-21

Open multiple objects.

1. With *[your initials]*CC-E-01 open, open multiple tables by following these steps:

    a. Open tblSickDays.

    b. Choose *[your initials]*CC-E-01 from the Window menu.

    c. Open tblVacDays.

    d. Click the Database Window button. Click the Minimize button to minimize the Database window.

    e. From the Window menu, choose Tile Horizontally.

    f. Close both tables.

    g. Click the Maximize button for your Database window.

2. Open a query and a table by following these steps:

    a. Open tblPayroll.

    b. Click the Database window button.

    c. Click Queries on the Objects bar and open qryEmployeeDates.

    d. Click the Database Window button and minimize the database window.

    e. From the Window menu, choose Tile Horizontally.

f. Close both objects.
     g. Click the Restore button for your Database window.

EXERCISE 1-22

Print a table, compact and close a database, and exit Access.

1. With *[your initials]***CC-E-01** open, right-click tblPayroll and choose Rena**me**.

2. Press End to position the insertion point behind the last letter of the table name.

3. Key *[your last name]*. Press Enter.

4. Open tblPayroll*[your last name]*.

5. Change page orientation by following these steps:
   a. Choose File and then choose **Page Setup**. Click the **Page** tab.
   b. Click the **Landscape** option button.
   c. Click OK to close the dialog box.

6. Preview your table before printing by following these steps:
   a. Click the Print Preview button.
   b. Click **C**lose to return to the table.

7. Print a table by following these steps:
   a. Choose File and then choose **P**rint.
   b. Click OK or press Enter to accept the settings.
   c. Close the table.

8. Right-click **tblPayroll***[your last name]* and choose Rena**me**.

9. Press End. Press Backspace to remove your last name and any blank spaces after "tblPayroll." Press Enter.

10. Compact and close the database and exit Access by following these steps:
   a. Choose **T**ools, choose **D**atabase Utilities, and then choose **C**ompact and Repair Database.
   b. Click the Close button ☒ to close the database.

Lesson Applications

Open a database, add a table description, and print a table.

1. Start Access and open *[your initials]***CC-01**.
2. Rename tblKitSuppliers to show *[your last name]* at the end.
3. Open the Properties dialog box for tblKitSuppliers.
4. Key the following description:

    Table contains the supplier name, contact, address, and phone number of companies supplying kits for Carolina Critters.
5. Close the dialog box.
6. Open the table. Change the page orientation to Landscape.
7. Preview the table. Change the font and column size so the table will print on one page.

 TIP: You can multiple-select all the columns and double-click one of the borders to AutoFit all columns at once.

8. Print the table. Close it without saving the design changes.
9. Rename tblKitSuppliers to remove *[your last name]* and any extra space.

Open multiple tables. Switch views.

1. With *[your initials]***CC-01** open, open tblStuffedAnimals.
2. Open tblProductLines.
3. Minimize the Database window and tile the tables.
4. What is the name of the product group for "Tula Tiger?" What is the product group for "Linda Lamb?" Write your answers on a separate sheet of paper.

 TIP: The Stuffed Animals table includes images that do not display in Datasheet View. Line Code and Product Group represent the same data but have different field captions listed in the column heading.

5. Close both tables.
6. Restore the Database window.
7. Open tblKitContents.

8. Change to Design View. What data type is the Cost field? Write your answer on the same piece of paper you used for your answers in step 4.

9. Close the table. Write your name, class information, and today's date on your answer sheet and turn it in to your instructor.

EXERCISE 1-25

Edit the layout and print a query.

1. With *[your initials]***CC-01** open, rename qryOrderSummaryByAnimal to show *[your last name]* at the end.

2. Open the query.

3. Size each column to fit its longest data.

4. Make the row height approximately twice its current height.

5. Print the query.

6. Close and save the layout changes.

7. Rename the query to remove *[your last name]* and any spaces.

EXERCISE 1-26   *Challenge Yourself*

Switch views. Change the row height, font, and orientation. Print a table. Compact a database.

1. Rename tblStuffedAnimals to include your last name.

2. Open the table. These are the products sold to retailers by Carolina Critters. Notice what type of information is contained in this table.

3. Switch to Design View for the table. What is the name of the field that contains an image of the product? Write your answer on a separate sheet of paper.

4. In Datasheet View, change the row height so the table shows approximately twice as much space between records.

5. Change the font to 11-point Times New Roman. Size the fields to fit the longest data.

6. Preview the table. While in Print Preview, change to Landscape orientation. Write down the number of pages required to print this table. Write your answer on the same piece of paper you used for your answers in step 3.

7. Print the table. Then close it without saving the layout changes.

8. Rename the table to remove *[your last name]* and any spaces.

9. Compact the database, close it, and exit Access. Write your name, class information, and today's date on your answer sheet and turn it in to your instructor.

On Your Own

In these exercises you work on your own, as you would in a real-life work environment. Use the skills you've learned to accomplish the task—and be creative.

 NOTE: The "On Your Own" exercises in this text are all related. They form a single project. To complete the project, you must do *all* the "On Your Own" exercises in *each* lesson.

EXERCISE 1-27

You are forming a new club or professional association. Begin by analyzing your needs on paper. Write one or two paragraphs describing the purpose of your club or association and the information you will need to make your organization run efficiently. After you have completed this exercise, continue to the next exercise.

EXERCISE 1-28

Now think specifically about the kind of information your club or association will need to track membership. Write a bulleted list of information you want to collect for each member (ex: first name, email). You should have no fewer than seven items. Continue to the next exercise.

EXERCISE 1-29

Using the list you created in Exercise 1-28, gather information on five potential members. On a single sheet of paper, record the data you collected. Submit your work for Exercises 1-27 through 1-29 to your instructor.

Adding and Editing Data

OBJECTIVES

After completing this lesson, you will be able to:

1. Add and delete records.
2. Edit data in tables and queries.
3. Use text editing commands.
4. Add records in a form.
5. Change views in a form.
6. Print a form.
7. Edit records in a form.
8. Add a picture to a record.

MOUS
ACTIVITIES

In this lesson:

Ac2002 **1-2**
Ac2002 **1-3**
Ac2002 **2-1**
Ac2002 **3-1**
Ac2002 **4-1**
Ac2002 **4-2**
Ac2002 **5-1**

See Appendix E.

 Estimated Time: 2 hours

In Lesson 1, you were introduced to tables and queries, two types of objects in a database. In this lesson, you continue your work with tables and queries and are introduced to forms. A form is based on a table or query and uses the same underlying data. Forms differ from tables and queries because the data is arranged in a screen format to improve the speed and accuracy of data entry.

In this lesson, you learn how to add and edit data in tables, queries, and forms. You use the duplicate, copy, and paste commands to copy data, which saves time and ensures accuracy. You also learn how to insert images into tables and forms.

A form is used to show data from a table or query. This data is commonly referred to as a *recordset*. A recordset produced from a table is the entire table itself. A recordset produced from a query can be an entire table, a portion of a table, or a combination of one or more tables.

Adding and Deleting Records

It is a simple process to add new records or to delete records that are no longer necessary. When a new student enrolls in your school, for example, a record is added to your school's database. If Carolina Critters discontinues one of their stuffed animals, the company can delete the product information from its database.

 TIP: Before you delete a record, you can copy it into an inactive or "history" table so there is always some record of the data.

EXERCISE **2-1** **Add Records to a Table**

When you are in Datasheet View, you add new records at the end of the table. The row in which the new record will be added is marked by an asterisk in the Record Selector. You move to this new record row by clicking the New Record navigation button or the New Record button ▶* on the toolbar. The two New Record buttons look the same except that the toolbar button is in color.

 REVIEW: The Record Selector is the narrow gray column to the left of the first field in the Datasheet View of a table or query.

You can also enter records by using the Data Entry command. This command hides the existing records while you add new ones.

1. Right-click the Start button 🏁**Start** on the Windows taskbar.
2. Choose **Explore** and click the Maximize button ▫.
3. In the left pane, open folder Lesson 02 from the location where your Student Files are kept. Point at the filename **CC-02** and right-click.
4. Choose **Copy** from the shortcut menu.
5. In the left pane, open the **My Documents** folder. In an unused area of the right pane, right-click. Choose **Paste** from the shortcut menu.
6. Right-click **CC-02** and choose **Rename**. Key *[your initials]***CC-02** and press Enter.
7. Right-click *[your initials]***CC-02** and choose **Properties**. Make certain that the **Read-only** attribute check box is not checked. Click OK.
8. Click the Close button ✕ on the Explorer window.
9. Open Access. Locate and open the *[your initials]***CC-02** database.
10. Open tblCustomers and click the Maximize button ▫. Click the New Record navigation button ▶*.

TIP: The keyboard shortcut to move to the new record is `Ctrl`+`+`.

11. Key the following to create a new record, pressing `Tab` between field entries. You will see a pencil icon in the Record Selector as you add the record.

 TIP: Characters you don't have to key are shown in blue. Access automatically formats these fields to include the characters.

FIGURE 2-1
Pencil icon appears in the Record Selector when adding a record

Customer ID	Company Name	Contact Name	Billing Address	City	State	ZIP Code	Phon
1	Magna Mart, Inc.	Sharon Peterson	912 Dodson Avenue	Chattanooga	TN	37406-4124	(423)
2	The Toy House	Elsa Masters	651 Holloway Street	Durham	NC	27701-3457	(919)
3	Mark's Toys & Hobbies	Mark Onofrio	3415 Brookshire Boulevard	Charlotte	NC	28216-4004	(704)
4	Bears Etc.	Frank Wilson	1996 Wilkinson Boulevard	Charlotte	NC	28208-5644	(704)
5	J & C Family Department Stor	Billie Rae Sutton	2753 Patterson Street	Greensboro	NC	27407-2317	(910)
6	Tots 'n Teens	Louisa Alvarez	456 Memphis Avenue	Nashville	TN	37201-0456	(423)
7	Beltram House	John Olmstead	2876 Brookshire Boulevard	Charlotte	NC	28215-2876	(704)
8	ABC Toys, Inc.						
0							

Record Selector

Customer ID:	8
Company Name:	ABC Toys, Inc.
Contact Name:	Suzanne Parker
Billing Address:	9218 Park West Boulevard
City:	Knoxville
State:	TN
ZIP Code:	39723-9218
Phone Number:	(423) 555-1897
Fax Number:	(423) 555-1899

 NOTE: Depending on the table design, Access formats fields automatically. For example, you don't have to key the hyphen in the ZIP Code field or the parentheses, space, or hyphen in phone numbers.

12. The Tax Exempt field is a Yes/No field. Leaving it blank means "No." Press `Tab` to skip it and leave it blank. Access saves the entry and moves the pointer to the next row so you can add another record.

13. Choose **R**ecords and then choose **D**ata Entry. Key the following to add another record:

 NOTE: In this text, *red italic* indicates specific instructions for that field.

Customer ID:	9
Company Name:	Children's Hospital
Contact Name:	Paul Scheider
Billing Address:	5274 West First Avenue
City:	Durham
State:	NC
ZIP Code:	27702-5274
Phone Number:	(919) 555-1000
Fax Number:	(919) 555-1050
Tax Exempt?:	*Click the box for a check mark to indicate "Yes" and press* Tab.

 TIP: You can toggle back and forth from "yes" to "no" in a check box field by pressing the Spacebar.

14. Open the Records menu and choose Remove Filter/Sort to view all records.

 15. Click the Close button ☒ to close the table tblCustomers.

EXERCISE 2-2   Add Records in a Query

You can enter new records by using a query. Changes made in the query are simultaneously made to data in the underlying table. As you learn more about queries, you will see that many queries create recordsets that do not include all the fields or records in the table.

 1. Click Queries on the Objects bar. Open qryCustomers and click the Maximize button ▢. Press Ctrl + + to move to a new record.

2. Key the following and press Tab between field entries. You will see the pencil icon as you add the record.

Customer ID:	10
Company Name:	New City Circus
Contact Name:	*[your first and last name]*
Billing Address:	501 North Canal Street
City:	Norfolk
State:	VA
ZIP Code:	72723-0501
Phone Number:	(602) 555-1800

Fax Number:	(602) 555-1801
Tax Exempt?:	*Press the* Spacebar *to indicate "Yes" and press* Tab .

3. Click the Close button ☒ to close qryCustomers. Click **Tables** on the Objects bar.

4. Open tblCustomers and look for the New City Circus record. Because the query has all the same fields as the table, the record is complete.

EXERCISE **2-3** **Delete Records from a Table**

There are times when records are no longer needed and can be removed from a table. You also might have records that were entered in error and should be deleted.

You can use Delete , the Delete Record button 🞮 or the **E**dit menu to delete a record. When you use Delete , you must first select the record(s) to delete.

 NOTE: You can delete records from a query the same as in a table.

1. In the Datasheet View of the Customers table, click in the Record Selector to select the row for "Mark's Toys & Hobbies."

FIGURE 2-2
Selecting a record
for deletion

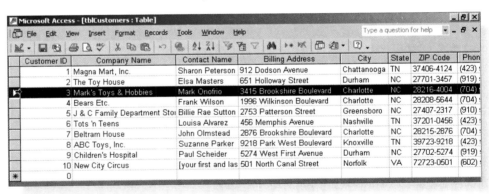

2. Press Delete . The record disappears, and a dialog box opens asking you to confirm the deletion. (See Figure 2-3 on the next page.)

 NOTE: You cannot undo a deleted record.

3. Click **Y**es. Access deletes the record.

4. Click anywhere in the Company Name field for "J & C Family Department Stores" to make it the current record.

FIGURE 2-3
Dialog box
confirming deletion

 NOTE: When you use the keyboard shortcut or the toolbar button to delete a record, you do not need to select the record. Just click anywhere in the record.

5. Press ⎡Ctrl⎤+⎡-⎤ and then click <u>Y</u>es to confirm the deletion.

6. Click the Close button ⎡✕⎤ to close tblCustomers.

Editing Data in a Table or Query

You might have noticed that you do not need to "save" after you insert or delete a record. Access saves changes to a record as soon as you move the insertion point away from that record. If you move to the next record or a previous record, your changes are saved. You do not need to use the Save command when you edit, delete, or add records. You only use the Save command to save changes to the structure of your object.

 TIP: To save your work in a lengthy record while you are editing it, open the <u>R</u>ecords menu and choose Save Rec<u>o</u>rd, or press ⎡Shift⎤+⎡Enter⎤.

You can determine if a record was saved by the shape of pointer in the Record Selector. The Record Selector marks the current record and where the insertion point is located. The Record Selector has three shapes:

● A pencil appears when you add or edit text. This indicates the record changes have not been saved.

● A triangle indicates the record has been saved.

● An asterisk marks a new record.

EXERCISE **2-4** **Delete Text in a Table**

Keyboard shortcuts are available for basic text editing. Table 2-1 summarizes some of the most helpful keyboard shortcuts.

TABLE 2-1 Basic Text Editing

KEY	RESULT
Backspace	Deletes characters to the left of the insertion point.
Ctrl + Backspace	Deletes the word to the left of the insertion point.
Delete	Deletes characters to the right of the insertion point.
Ctrl + Delete	Deletes all the characters to the right of the insertion point to the end of the line.

1. Open tblEmployees in Datasheet View and click the Maximize button ☐ to maximize the window.
2. Move the insertion point to the right of the last name for Employee 8 "Williams." (Use the mouse to position the I-beam and click to place the insertion point.)

TIP: To add or insert text, the insertion point must look like an I-beam. A cross-shaped pointer selects the entire field. You cannot edit individual characters when the entire field is selected.

3. Press Backspace five times to delete five characters and key **son**. The Record Selector changes to a pencil symbol as you edit text. "Williams" is changed to "Wilson."

FIGURE 2-4
Editing data

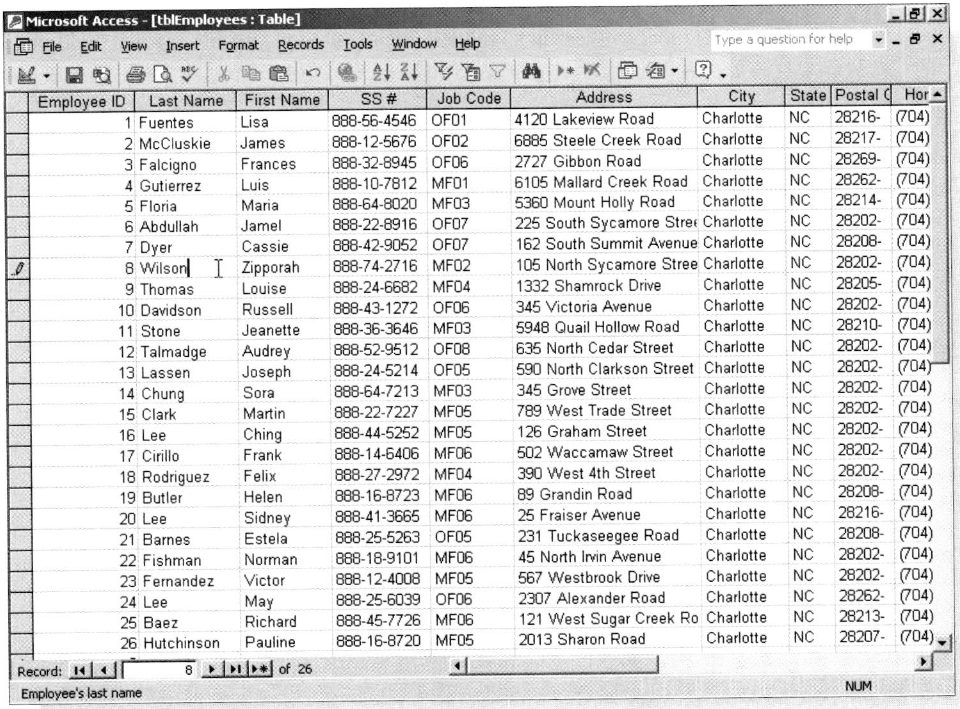

Employee ID	Last Name	First Name	SS #	Job Code	Address	City	State	Postal C	Hor
1	Fuentes	Lisa	888-56-4546	OF01	4120 Lakeview Road	Charlotte	NC	28216-	(704)
2	McCluskie	James	888-12-5676	OF02	6885 Steele Creek Road	Charlotte	NC	28217-	(704)
3	Falcigno	Frances	888-32-8945	OF06	2727 Gibbon Road	Charlotte	NC	28269-	(704)
4	Gutierrez	Luis	888-10-7812	MF01	6105 Mallard Creek Road	Charlotte	NC	28262-	(704)
5	Floria	Maria	888-64-8020	MF03	5360 Mount Holly Road	Charlotte	NC	28214-	(704)
6	Abdullah	Jamel	888-22-8916	OF07	225 South Sycamore Stre	Charlotte	NC	28202-	(704)
7	Dyer	Cassie	888-42-9052	OF07	162 South Summit Avenue	Charlotte	NC	28208-	(704)
8	Wilson	Zipporah	888-74-2716	MF02	105 North Sycamore Stree	Charlotte	NC	28202-	(704)
9	Thomas	Louise	888-24-6682	MF04	1332 Shamrock Drive	Charlotte	NC	28205-	(704)
10	Davidson	Russell	888-43-1272	OF06	345 Victoria Avenue	Charlotte	NC	28202-	(704)
11	Stone	Jeanette	888-36-3646	MF03	5948 Quail Hollow Road	Charlotte	NC	28210-	(704)
12	Talmadge	Audrey	888-52-9512	OF08	635 North Cedar Street	Charlotte	NC	28202-	(704)
13	Lassen	Joseph	888-24-5214	OF05	590 North Clarkson Street	Charlotte	NC	28202-	(704)
14	Chung	Sora	888-64-7213	MF03	345 Grove Street	Charlotte	NC	28202-	(704)
15	Clark	Martin	888-22-7227	MF05	789 West Trade Street	Charlotte	NC	28202-	(704)
16	Lee	Ching	888-44-5252	MF05	126 Graham Street	Charlotte	NC	28202-	(704)
17	Cirillo	Frank	888-14-6406	MF06	502 Waccamaw Street	Charlotte	NC	28202-	(704)
18	Rodriguez	Felix	888-27-2972	MF04	390 West 4th Street	Charlotte	NC	28202-	(704)
19	Butler	Helen	888-16-8723	MF06	89 Grandin Road	Charlotte	NC	28208-	(704)
20	Lee	Sidney	888-41-3665	MF06	25 Fraiser Avenue	Charlotte	NC	28216-	(704)
21	Barnes	Estela	888-25-5263	OF05	231 Tuckaseegee Road	Charlotte	NC	28208-	(704)
22	Fishman	Norman	888-18-9101	MF06	45 North Irvin Avenue	Charlotte	NC	28202-	(704)
23	Fernandez	Victor	888-12-4008	MF05	567 Westbrook Drive	Charlotte	NC	28202-	(704)
24	Lee	May	888-25-6039	OF06	2307 Alexander Road	Charlotte	NC	28262-	(704)
25	Baez	Richard	888-45-7726	MF06	121 West Sugar Creek Ro	Charlotte	NC	28213-	(704)
26	Hutchinson	Pauline	888-16-8720	MF05	2013 Sharon Road	Charlotte	NC	28207-	(704)

4. Use the scroll bar to view the Address field. In Employee #2's record, click between the "6" and the "8" in the Address field.

5. Press Delete once and key **1**. The "6885" changes to "6185."

6. Move to Employee 5's record. In the Address field, click to the left of the word "Holly."

7. Press Ctrl + Backspace. The word "Mount" is deleted.

8. Move to Employee 13's record. In the Address field, click to the right of "Clarkson."

9. Press Ctrl + Delete to delete "Street." Press the spacebar once and key **Road**

10. Click the Close button ⊠ to close tblEmployees.

EXERCISE 2-5 Insert Text in a Query

Queries do not store data. When you use a query to make changes to data, you are making changes to the recordset. You are really editing the same records in both the table and the query. When you edit a record in a query, the data in the underlying table is changed because the query's recordset is a subset of the table.

When editing a table or a query, you can insert text or use Overtype mode to key over existing text. Use Insert to switch between Insert and Overtype mode.

1. Click **Queries** on the Objects bar. Open qryEmployees. Notice that the changes you just made in the Employees table appear in this query.

2. Move to Employee 9's record. In the Last Name field, click to the right of "s" in "Thomas." Key a hyphen and then key **Smith**. As you are keying the name, the beginning of the last name might scroll out of view.

3. Move to Employee 10's record. In the First Name field, click to the left of "Russell."

4. Press Insert to switch to Overtype mode. When you are in Overtype mode, OVR appears on the status bar and the insertion point becomes a block when it is over a character.

FIGURE 2-5
Overtype mode

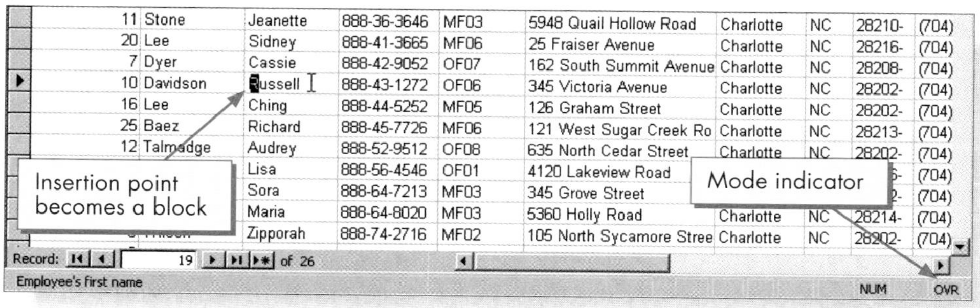

5. Key **Raymond**

6. Click the Close button ☒ to close qryEmployees.

7. Open qryCustomers in Datasheet View. You are still in Overtype mode.

8. In the "Bears Etc." record, click to the left of "Frank Wilson" in the Contact Name field.

9. Key *[your first name & last name]* over the old text. Delete any extra characters.

> **NOTE:** In this text you are often asked to key an identifier such as your name or initials in a field so you can identify your work when you print. The identifier is shown in square brackets, but do not key the brackets.

10. Press Insert to turn off Overtype mode.

11. Click the Close button ☒ to close qryCustomers.

Using Editing Commands

Text editing commands are used to make changes to the data within a record. A feature called *AutoCorrect* corrects commonly misspelled words as you key text—for example, correcting "teh" to "the." It also fixes many capitalization errors. There is an Undo command to undo your most recent edits. There are also Duplicate, Cut, Copy, and Paste commands.

EXERCISE 2-6   Correct Errors with AutoCorrect

1. From the Tools menu, choose AutoCorrect Options and look at the options available.

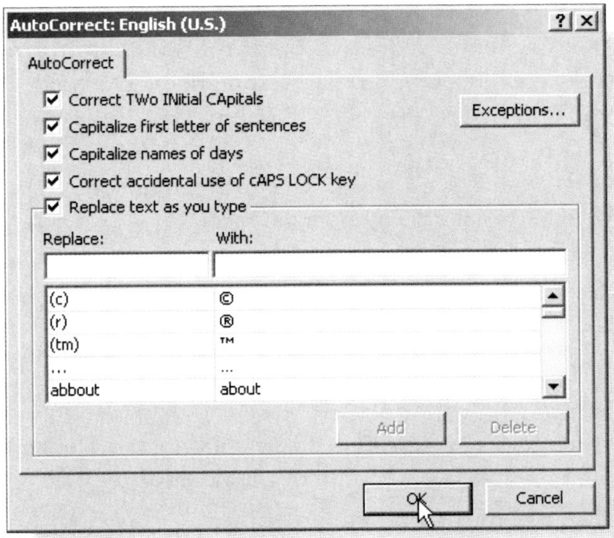

FIGURE 2-6
AutoCorrect
dialog box

2. Scroll down the list of entries to see which words are in the AutoCorrect dictionary. Make sure the **Replace text as you type** option is checked.

 NOTE: Microsoft Office products share AutoCorrect, so changes you make in Access affect Word, Excel, and PowerPoint.

TABLE 2-2   AutoCorrect Options

OPTIONS	DESCRIPTION
Correct TWo INitial CApitals	Corrects words keyed with two initial capital letters, such as "THis."
Capitalize first letter of sentences	Capitalizes the first letter in a sentence.
Capitalize names of days	Capitalizes days of the week and months.
Correct accidental use of cAPS LOCK key	Corrects words keyed with Caps Lock on but [Shift] key pressed, such as cAPS.
Replace text as you type	Makes corrections as you work.

3. Click **Cancel** to close the dialog box.

4. Click **Tables** on the Objects bar. Open tblKitContents and maximize the window. Press [Ctrl] + [+] to open a new record.

5. Key **Zeb002** in the Kit Number field. Press [Tab] three times to move to the Kit Contents field.

6. In the Kit Contents field, key **i want teh kit to contain teh follwoing materials** (key a period after the sentence). The field scrolls as you key the sentence, and Access corrects "i," "teh," and "following."

 TIP: AutoCorrect makes the correction as soon as you press the spacebar or move the pointer away from the record.

7. Next, key this sentence with the errors (include the period): **TOdya is tuesday.** Access fixes the capitalization.

8. Press [CapsLock] to lock capitalization. Key **The**, holding down [Shift] for the "T." Press the spacebar and "tHE" is changed to "The."

 9. Delete the record you just keyed by clicking the Delete Record button ⊠ on the toolbar. Click <u>Y</u>es to confirm the deletion.

10. Press [CapsLock] to turn off capitalization. Close tblKitContents.

EXERCISE 2-7 Duplicate a Field and Use Undo

You can duplicate the data from a field in the previous record to the same field in the next record by pressing Ctrl + ' (apostrophe). The Duplicate command copies one field at a time.

Access remembers changes to the data and lets you undo most edits. If you accidentally delete text in a field, you can use the Undo command to reverse the action. There are three ways to undo an action:

- Click the Undo button ↺ on the toolbar.
- Press Ctrl + Z.
- From the Edit menu, choose Undo.

1. Open tblCustomers and click the Maximize button □ to maximize the window. Click the New Record button ▶* on the toolbar.
2. Key **11** as the Customer ID and press Tab.
3. Press Ctrl + ' to duplicate the company name. Press Tab.
4. Press Ctrl + ' to duplicate the Contact Name and press Tab.
5. Complete the record shown here. Press Ctrl + ' for duplicate fields.

Billing Address:	**123 Orchard Lane**
City:	**Norfolk**
State:	**VA**
ZIP Code:	**72723-0123**
Phone Number:	**(602) 555-1023**
Fax Number:	**(602) 555-1051**
Tax Exempt?:	**Yes**

6. Click to the left of your name in this record. Press Ctrl + Delete.

7. Click the Undo button ↺ on the toolbar to restore your name.

   TIP: The ScreenTip for the Undo button ↺ includes the name of the action, such as "Undo Delete" or "Undo Typing."

8. In the Magna Mart record, click to the left of "Avenue." Press Insert to start Overtype mode. Then key **Road** and press the spacebar. Press Insert to turn off Overtype mode. Delete any remaining characters.
9. Press Ctrl + Z twice to restore "Avenue."
10. Click anywhere in Record 11. Press Ctrl + - and click Yes. Notice that the Undo button ↺ is gray (meaning it is unavailable).

REVIEW: As soon as you move the insertion point away from a record, the record is saved.

11. Close tblCustomers without saving any changes.

EXERCISE | **2-8** | ## Use Copy, Paste, the Office Clipboard, and Paste Append

You can copy a block of text from one part of a table to another. There are several ways to copy and paste text:

- Click the Copy 📋 and Paste 📋 buttons on the toolbar.
- Press `Ctrl`+`C` (copy) and `Ctrl`+`V` (paste).
- Choose <u>C</u>opy and <u>P</u>aste from the <u>E</u>dit menu.
- Right-click and choose <u>C</u>opy and <u>P</u>aste from the shortcut menu.

You can use the Office Clipboard to paste multiple blocks of text. When you paste the second text block, the Office Clipboard pane opens. From that pane, you can select the item you want to paste.

 NOTE: The Windows Clipboard lets you paste one item at a time. Text on the Windows Clipboard can be pasted repeatedly until you place new text on the Clipboard.

You can also paste an entire record from one location to another by using the Paste Append command.

1. Open tblEmployees. Click the New Record button ▸∗. Key the following, leaving the Job Code field blank.

Employee ID:	27
Last Name:	Kwan
First Name:	Sam
SS#:	888-11-2222
Job Code:	*Leave blank.*
Address:	**111 Westbrook Drive**
City:	*Press* `Ctrl`+`'`
State:	*Press* `Ctrl`+`'`
Postal Code:	**28202-3876**
Home Phone:	**(704) 555-1111**
Emergency Contact:	**John Smith**
Emergency Phone:	**(704) 555-1112**
Photograph:	*Press* `Tab` *to skip.*

2. Double-click **MF04** in any record to select it.

3. Click the Copy button on the toolbar to place a copy of the text on the Windows Clipboard. Notice that the selected text remains in its original location.

4. Click in the Job Code field in the record you just added.

5. Click the Paste button . A copy of MF04 is pasted into the field.

6. Double-click "Fishman" in Employee ID 22's record. Click the Copy button . The Office Clipboard pane opens with icons for both copied text blocks. If the Office Clipboard is not open, choose **E**dit and then choose Office Clip**b**oard.

> **TIP:** The first copied text should still be available for pasting and shown on the Office Clipboard pane. The buttons on the Clipboard pane have identifying ScreenTips.

7. Double-click "Helen" in Employee ID 19's record. Click the Copy button .

FIGURE 2-7
Using the
Office Clipboard

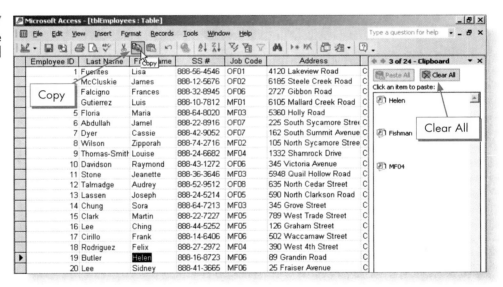

> **REVIEW:** You must use the I-beam pointer to select text.

8. Select "567 Westbrook Drive" in Employee ID 23's record. Click the Copy button . Another icon is added to the Clipboard pane.

9. Click the New Record button ▶✱. Key the following.

Employee ID:	**28**
Last Name:	*Click the last name icon on the Clipboard pane.*
First Name:	*Click the first name icon on the Clipboard pane.*
SS#:	**888-33-1234**

Job Code:	**OF06**
Address:	*Click the address icon on the Clipboard pane.*
City:	*Press* Ctrl + '
State:	*Press* Ctrl + '
Postal Code:	**28202-3576**
Home Phone:	**(704) 555-1137**
Emergency Contact:	**Michael Fishman**
Emergency Phone:	**(704) 555-1137**
Photograph:	*Press* Tab *to skip.*

10. Click the Clear All button . Click the Close button ☒ to close the Clipboard pane.

11. Click in the Record Selector for Employee 28 to select the record. The entire row is highlighted.

12. Click the Copy button ▤. Click the New Record ▸* button.

13. Choose **E**dit and then choose **Paste Append**. The record is copied.

> 🚩 **NOTE:** You must change the Social Security number so you do not duplicate it in the table.

14. Change the Employee ID in the pasted record to **29**. Change the SS# to **888-33-0000**

15. Drag in the Record Selector area to select Employee IDs 28 and 29. Both rows are highlighted.

16. Click the Delete Record button ▨ and click **Yes**.

17. Close tblEmployees.

Adding Records in a Form

A form is an Access object in which you can enter, view, sort, edit, and print data, much as you can with a table or a query. A form, however, is designed for screen work, so it is often easier to use than a table. A form has navigation buttons and scroll bars and the same text editing features as a table. A form is linked to a table or query and can show the same fields of a record—it just shows them in a different layout on the screen.

EXERCISE   2-9   **Navigate in a Form**

You move the insertion point in a form just as you do in a table or query. The navigation buttons are at the bottom of the window. You'll see horizontal and vertical scroll bars when the form is larger than the screen.

Forms

1. Click Forms on the Objects bar. The window lists the forms in the current database. Forms should have a *frm* prefix.

2. Double-click frmEmployeeInformation to open it and maximize the window. The navigation buttons are at the bottom left corner of the form.

 NOTE: To reduce the size of this database, not all records have images. Images can make databases very large.

FIGURE 2-8
Employee
Information Form

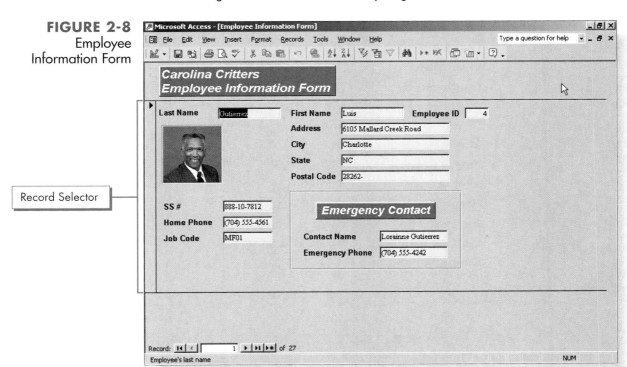

3. Click the Next Record button until James McCluskie's record appears. If you pass the record, click the Previous Record button ◄.

4. Click the Last Record button ►I. The pointer moves to the last employee, Zipporah Wilson.

5. Click the First Record button I◄ to move back to the first record, Luis Gutierrez.

6. Press PgDn several times to move forward through the records. Press PgUp to move backward through the records.

EXERCISE 2-10 Add Records with a Form

Forms make it easier to add records, because they can be designed to reproduce the appearance of a paper document. You see one record at a time, often enabling you to see all the fields at once. The fields on the form are from the table but do not have to be in the same order as in the table.

1. With frmEmployeeInformation open, click the New Record button . A blank form opens.

> **NOTE:** Because you cannot see the previous record when adding a new record, using the Duplicate command Ctrl + ʹ is difficult in a form.

2. Key the following new record, pressing Tab between entries:

Last Name:	**Woodsik**
First Name:	**Sophie**
Employee ID:	**28**
Address:	**456 Victoria Avenue**
City:	**Charlotte**
State:	**NC**
Postal Code:	**28202-7997**
SS#:	**888-55-1111**
Home Phone:	**(704) 555-1601**
Job Code:	**OF06**
Contact Name:	**Howard Woodsik**
Emergency Phone:	**(704) 555-1662**

> **NOTE:** You will insert pictures later in this lesson.

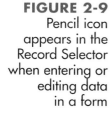

FIGURE 2-9
Pencil icon appears in the Record Selector when entering or editing data in a form

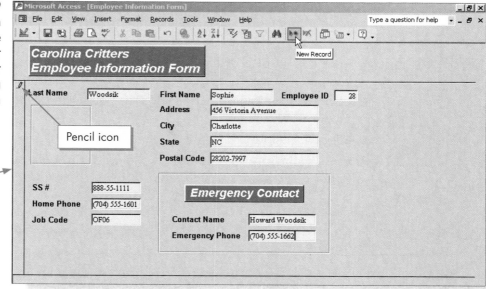

3. Press PgUp several times. The other records are visible, one record per screen.
4. Close the form. Click **Tables** on the Objects bar and open tblEmployees.
5. Click the Last Record button ▶❙ to see Sophie's record.
6. Close tblEmployees.

EXERCISE **2-11** **Add Records with the Data Entry Command**

You can also use the Data Entry command to enter records in a form.

 NOTE: When you're using the Data Entry command, existing records are not displayed in the form. You aren't able to navigate through existing records.

1. Open frmEmployeeInformation.
2. Choose Records and then choose Data Entry. Key the following:

Last Name:	**Willis**
First Name:	**Marjorie**
Employee ID:	**29**
Address:	**7737 Derby Avenue**
City:	**Charlotte**
State:	**NC**
Postal Code:	**28202-6443**
SS#:	**888-77-1135**
Home Phone:	**(704) 555-1828**
Job Code:	**MF03**
Contact Name:	**Ellen Gilroy**
Emergency Phone:	**(704) 555-4998**

3. Press PgUp. Nothing happens, because the other records are hidden.

 NOTE: When you are entering new records, only the current record is visible. Previously entered records can be viewed only by exiting the Data Entry mode.

4. Choose Records and then choose Remove Filter/Sort.
5. Click the Last Record button ▶❙ to see the record you entered.

Changing Views in a Form

As with a table and a query, there are several ways to view a form:

TABLE 2-3 Ways to View a Form

VIEW	DESCRIPTION
Form View	Appears when you open a form. You enter data, edit data, and find records in Form View.
Design View	Lets you create or modify the layout of the form. You don't see records in Design View. You see controls, which include labels and text boxes. *Controls* are objects that display information, perform actions, or enhance the appearance of a form or report. *Labels* display text, such as a title, and *text boxes* show data that is stored in fields.
Datasheet View	Displays the records in the default table style.
PivotTable View	Displays summarized data in a table format with columns and rows. Different levels of detail can be viewed.
PivotChart View	Displays data in a chart form. Different levels of detail can be viewed.

In addition to these basic views, you can set a form to show one record at a time, or as many records as will fit on the screen.

EXERCISE 2-12 Use Form and Design Views

1. With frmEmployeeInformation open, click the drop-down arrow next to the View button 🖳. The shortcut menu includes <u>D</u>esign View, <u>F</u>orm View, and Data<u>s</u>heet View. The highlighted icon indicates the current view 📇.

FIGURE 2-10
View menu

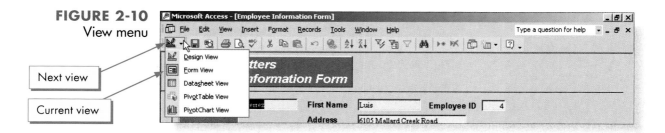

2. Choose <u>D</u>esign View from the shortcut menu to display the Employee Information Form in Design View. This view shows controls for the form's labels and text boxes. Notice that records do not appear in this view.

3. Click the View button 🔲, not the drop-down arrow. The form now appears in Form View.

4. Click the View button 🔲 again to return to Design View.

FIGURE 2-11
Employee
Information Form
in Design View

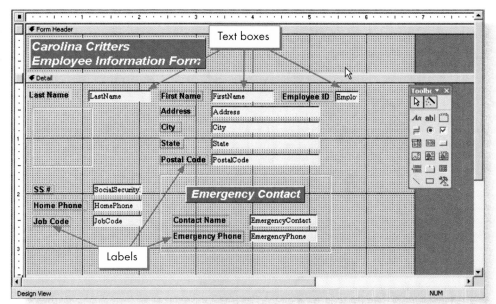

5. Press Ctrl + > to go from Design View to Form View and Ctrl + < to go from Form View to Design View.

> **NOTE:** The View button toggles between Design View and Form View. The button shows the view to which you can switch.

EXERCISE **2-13** **Change the Default View for a Form**

In addition to the basic ways of looking at a form, Access has another setting that determines how many forms you see on the screen at once. All Access objects have a *property sheet* that lists attributes, settings, and formats for that object. A form's property sheet includes a *Default View* setting that controls how many records are shown onscreen at once.

1. In Design View, click the small etched rectangle at the left edge of the horizontal ruler. This is the Form Selector button. When the form is selected, the rectangle shows a small black square. (See Figure 2-12 on the next page.)

FIGURE 2-12
Selected form

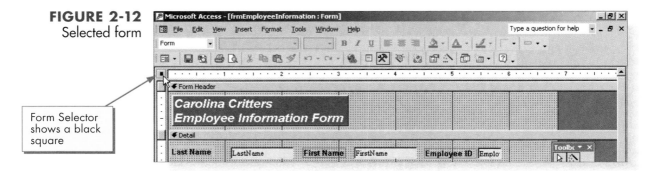

Form Selector
shows a black
square

 2. Click the Properties button on the toolbar. The Form property sheet opens.

NOTE: A property sheet is a window that can be sized and moved.

3. Click the Format tab. The current Default View is Single Form.

4. Click the Default View row and then click the drop-down arrow. Choose Continuous Forms.

FIGURE 2-13
Form property sheet

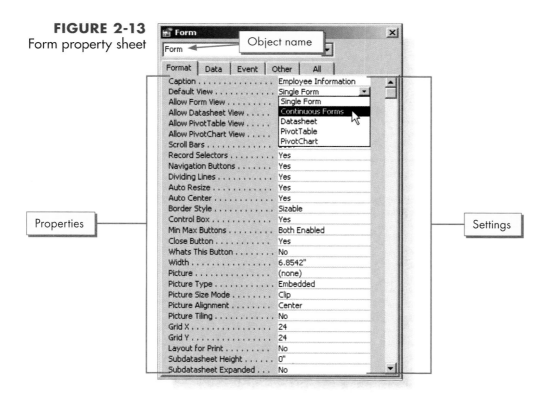

Properties

Settings

5. Click the View button 📧. The form shows as many forms as can fit on your screen. (This depends on your screen size. You might see only one form.)

6. Use the vertical scroll bar to look at several forms.

7. Click the View button 📐.

8. Click the **Default View** row in the property sheet and its drop-down arrow. Choose **Datasheet**.

9. Click the View button 📧. The form now shows the records like a table.

10. Click the View button 📐. Click the **Default View** row and the drop-down arrow. Choose **Single Form**.

11. Click the Close button ✖ to close the Form property sheet.

12. Click the View button 📧.

Printing a Form

The design and layout of a form is optimized for the screen. Although forms are designed for screen work, you can preview and print them. Use any of these methods to print a form:

- Click the Print button 🖶 on the toolbar.
- From the File menu, choose Print.
- Press Ctrl + P.

If you click the Print button 🖶, all the forms are printed with your default print settings. If there are 29 records in the table, 29 forms print. One form prints for each record.

The menu and keyboard commands open the Print dialog box so you can set a print range or change the page setup. A print range designates certain forms for printing.

EXERCISE **2-14** **View a Form in Print Preview**

Print Preview shows how your form will look on paper. You might need to change margins or the orientation before you print.

1. Click the Print Preview button 🔍 to open the Print Preview window. You will probably see a message box that the section width is wider than the page width. This means the form does not fit on the page and requires two or more pages. (See Figure 2-14 on the next page.)

FIGURE 2-14
Page width
message box

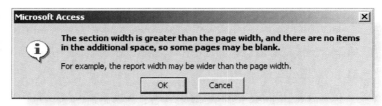

 NOTE: The preview of the Employee Information Form shows two records. The height and width of a form determines the number of records that print per page.

2. Click **OK**. A preview of the Employee Information Form appears.

FIGURE 2-15
Preview of Employee
Information Form

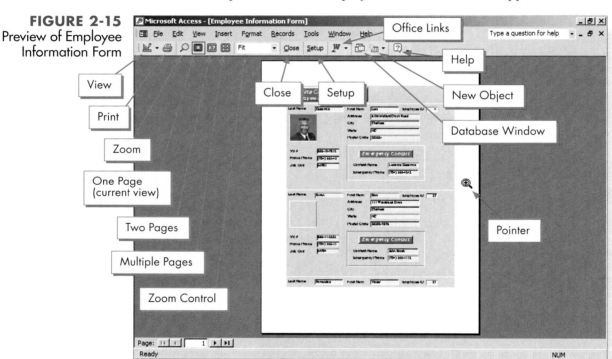

3. Click the Two Pages button. This displays two pages, side by side. The gray vertical bar on the second page is the part of the form that is too wide to fit. It is just part of the form's background. (See Figure 2-16 on the next page.)

4. Click the pointer anywhere on page 1. This enlarges the form, or zooms in. Click the pointer anywhere to reduce the form (zoom out).

 NOTE: The pointer is a magnifying glass with a plus (zoom in) or minus sign (zoom out).

FIGURE 2-16
Viewing two pages

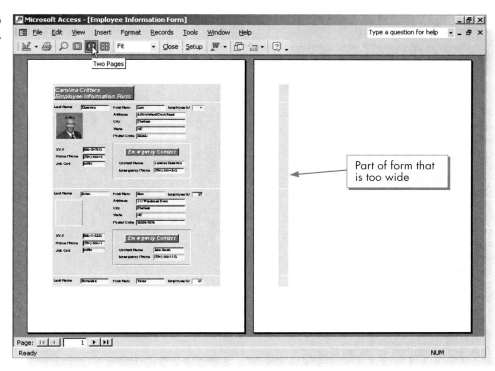

Part of form that
is too wide

TABLE 2-4   Print Preview Toolbar Buttons

BUTTON/NAME	FUNCTION
View	Switches to Design, Form, Datasheet, PivotTable, or PivotChart View.
Print	Prints the form.
Zoom	Enlarges or reduces the view.
One Page	Displays one page.
Two Pages	Displays two pages.
Multiple Pages	Displays a grid of multiple pages.

continues

TABLE 2-4   **Print Preview Toolbar Buttons**   *continued*

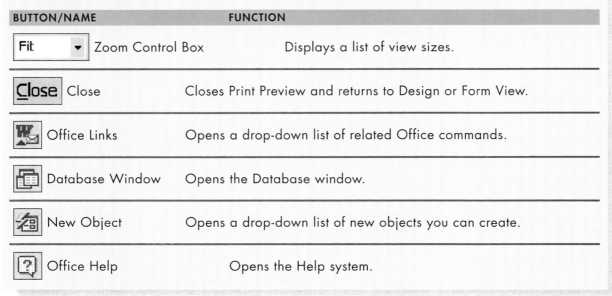

BUTTON/NAME		FUNCTION
Fit ▼	Zoom Control Box	Displays a list of view sizes.
Close	Close	Closes Print Preview and returns to Design or Form View.
(icon)	Office Links	Opens a drop-down list of related Office commands.
(icon)	Database Window	Opens the Database window.
(icon)	New Object	Opens a drop-down list of new objects you can create.
[?]	Office Help	Opens the Help system.

5. Click the drop-down arrow next to the Zoom Control box and choose 50%.

FIGURE 2-17
Zoom Control menu

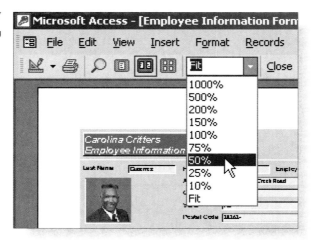

6. Click the One Page button .

7. Close Print Preview by clicking the **Close** button in the middle of the Print Preview toolbar.

TIP: You can use the same Print Preview buttons for a table, query, form, report, or data access pages.

EXERCISE **2-15** **Print a Single Form**

To print the form for one record (employee), you must select that form in Form View on the screen. You must also choose the **Selected Records** option in the Print dialog box.

 NOTE: The default print range for a form is All records. If you want to print only one record, be very certain you select a record and change the Print Range option in the Print dialog box.

You can set the print orientation to landscape for a form just as for a table or query. This is helpful if the form is wide and doesn't fit on one printed page.

1. With frmEmployeeInformation open, choose **File**, and then choose **Page Setup**.

2. Click the **Page** tab to see the orientation, paper size, and printer.

3. Click the **Landscape** option button. Click **OK** to close the dialog box.

4. Click the Print Preview button 🔍. After you view the preview, click the **Close** button **Close** to close the Preview window.

5. Press **PgDn** as many times as necessary to move to Record 4 for James McCluskie.

6. Click in the Record Selector area to select the record.

 REVIEW: The Record Selector is the narrow bar to the left of the labels and text boxes.

7. Choose **File**, **Print** to open the Print dialog box.

 TIP: Make sure you don't press the Print button 🖨 on the toolbar. This will print every record in the table.

8. Click **Selected Record(s)** as the Print Range. (See Figure 2-18 on the next page.)

9. Click **OK** to print the form.

10. Click the Close button **X** to close the form without saving changes.

FIGURE 2-18
Printing selected
records

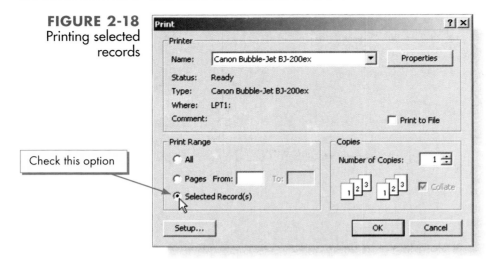

Check this option

Editing Data in a Form

You can edit data in a form with the same shortcuts you use in a table or a query. For example, Backspace deletes a single character and the keyboard combination Ctrl + Delete deletes an entire line.

EXERCISE 2-16 Delete Text in a Form

The data displayed in each field of a form is stored in a table. In the same way that you can delete text from a table by using Datasheet View, you can also delete text from a form.

1. Open frmSalesReviewMain. Click the Next Record button ▶ at the bottom left corner of the screen to move to "The Toy House" record.

2. In the Company Name field, click to the left of "Toy."

3. Press Ctrl + Backspace. Notice that the current record pointer changes to the pencil symbol when you're editing text. "The Toy House" is changed to "Toy House."

4. Click between "0" and "2" in the Order ID field at the top of the form.

5. Press Delete once and key **7**

6. Click to the right of "7" in the Employee ID field. Notice that the Order ID is changed to "20107" in both parts of the form. (See Figure 2-19 on the next page.)

FIGURE 2-19
OrderID changed
in both forms

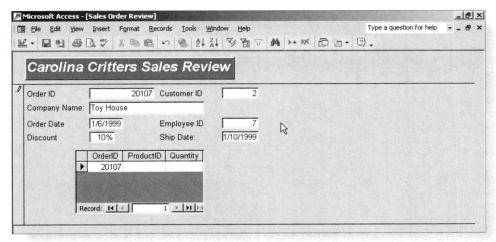

7. Press ⌷Backspace⌷ and key **6**. The Employee ID is now "6."

8. Click to the left of the first character in the Order Date field.

9. Press ⌷Ctrl⌷+⌷Delete⌷. Key *[your birth date]* using the mm/dd/yy format.

 NOTE: You must key a date in mm/dd/yy format. However, Access might use a different display format.

10. Close the form. Click **Tables** on the Objects bar and open tblCustomers. Notice the change to "Toy House." (It was "The Toy House."). Close the table.

11. Open tblSalesOrders. Notice OrderID "20107." There is now no Order ID "20102."

12. Change "20107" to "20102." Close the table.

EXERCISE 2-17 Delete Records in a Form

You can delete records when they become inactive. You can delete the current record by using the **Edit** menu, or you can use the keyboard shortcut, ⌷Ctrl⌷+⌷-⌷. You can also select the record and press ⌷Delete⌷ or use the Delete Record button ⌷✕⌷.

1. Click **Forms** on the Objects bar. Open frmEmployeeInformation. Move to Martin Clark's record. Click the Record Selector to select the record.

2. Press ⌷Delete⌷. Notice the next record is displayed.

NOTE: You cannot use the Undo button 🔙 to restore a deleted record. You can re-key the record if your deletion was in error.

3. Click <u>Y</u>es to confirm the deletion.

EXERCISE 2-18 **Insert Text in a Form**

When editing a form, you can insert text or use Overtype mode to key over existing text. You can also insert text by using the Copy and Paste commands.

1. With frmEmployeeInformation open, move forward to May Lee's record.

2. In the Job Code field, double-click **OF06**. Click the Copy button 📋 on the toolbar.

TIP: Double-clicking selects an entire word.

3. Press PgUp to move back to Estela Barnes' record. Double-click the text in the Job Code field, if it is not already selected.

4. Click the Paste button 📋 on the toolbar. Estela's job code is changed to "OF06."

5. Move back to Jamel Abdullah's record. In the Job Code field, click to the left of **OF07**.

6. Press Insert to switch to Overtype mode. Key **MF04**

7. Make certain that Overtype mode is on. In the Job Code field, select the 4 and key **5**. The Job Code is now "MF05."

8. Press Insert to turn off Overtype mode.

9. Close the form and open tblEmployees. Notice the changes to Estela Barnes' and Jamel Abdullah's records. Close the table.

Adding a Picture to a Record

The records you have added or edited have had text, number, or date fields. Now you will add images. The Stuffed Animals table has a field to show a picture of the animal. The Employees table has a field to show a photograph of the employee. These images are *OLE (Object Linking and Embedding) objects*. Data that was created in another program, such as an illustration or a drawing program, is an OLE object. You cannot see the picture in Datasheet View, but you can see it in the form.

NOTE: OLE objects include pictures, sound clips, movie clips, spreadsheets, or text documents.

When you add a record with an OLE field such as a picture, you use the Insert Object command. You can insert an image in a table, a query, or a form.

EXERCISE 2-19 Insert a Picture

1. Open tblStuffedAnimals. The Illustration field shows Bitmap Image, not the picture.
2. Click the View button 📐. The Product field is an OLE Object data type.

 NOTE: The name of the field is "Product," but it uses a different caption, "Illustration." You will learn about captions in Lesson 4.

3. Click the View button 📰.
4. Click in the Illustration field for Lon Lion.
5. From the Insert menu, choose Object. The Insert Object dialog box opens.
6. In the Object Type window, select Paintbrush Picture.

FIGURE 2-20
Microsoft Access
dialog box used to
insert objects

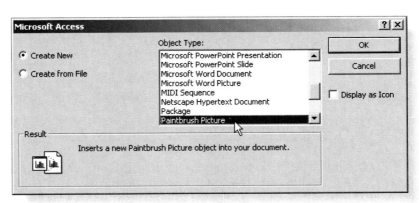

7. Click OK. MS-Paint opens. Click Edit, and then click Paste From.
8. Locate the folder **Images**. Select **Lin003**. (See Figure 2-21 on the next page.)

 NOTE: Your instructor will tell you where the Images folder is stored.

9. Click Open. Click Yes to enlarge the bitmap.

FIGURE 2-21
Using Paintbrush to
insert image

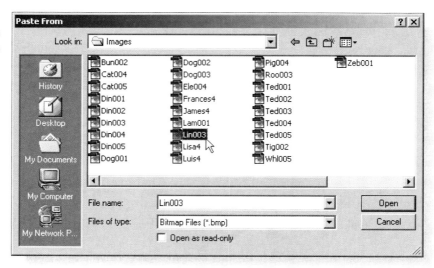

10. Click **Image**, and then click **Attributes**. Click the **Black and white** options button. This makes the file smaller.

FIGURE 2-22
Setting image
attributes

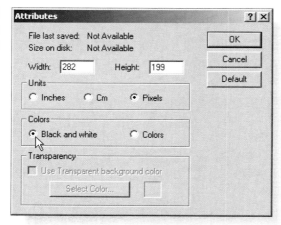

11. Click **OK**. Click **Yes** to convert to black and white. Click **File**, and then click **Exit & Return to tblStuffedAnimals: Table**.

12. Close the table.

13. Click **Forms** on the Objects bar. Open frmStuffedAnimals.

14. Press PgDn until you reach the lion's record and see the image.

15. Press PgDn to move to Elvira Elephant's record.

 TIP: The rectangle that holds the picture is an Access control. You will learn about controls in Lessons 5 and 6.

16. Right-click the empty rectangle where the picture should be. (See Figure 2-23 on the next page.)

FIGURE 2-23
Inserting an Image

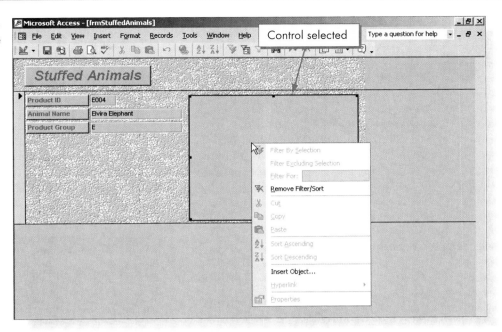

17. Select **Insert Object**. The Insert Object dialog box opens.

18. Select **Paintbrush Picture**. Click **OK**.

19. In MS-Paint, click **Edit**, and then click **Paste From**.

20. Find the image **Ele004** and click **Open**. Click **Yes**.

21. Click **Image**, and then click **Attributes**. Click the **Black and white** options button. Click **OK**. Click **Yes** to convert to black and white.

22. Click anywhere on the form, away from the image.

23. Close the form. Compact and repair the database and then close it.

USING HELP

One way to explore online Help is to display a list of Help topics. You choose a topic and Access displays information or provides a demonstration.

Find Help topics about forms:

1. With *[your initials]***CC-02** open, choose **Help**, and then choose **Microsoft Access Help**. If the Office Assistant starts, click **Options**. Clear the check mark from **Use the Office Assistant** and click **OK**. Then try again.

2. Click the **Contents** tab. Scroll the window and size the panes so you can see the names of the topics in the left pane. Each topic is represented by a book icon.

3. Browse through the list of topics to find **Forms**. Click its Expand button ⊞ 📚.

> **REVIEW:** When a topic is expanded, it shows the Collapse button ⊟ 📖. When a topic is collapsed, it shows the Expand button ⊞ 📚.

4. Expand the **Printing and Previewing Forms** topic and then click **Set page setup options for printing**. Microsoft Access Help jumps to the **Printing and Previewing Reports** topic because previewing is the same for Reports and Forms. The Help text appears in the right pane.

FIGURE 2-24
Help Topics window

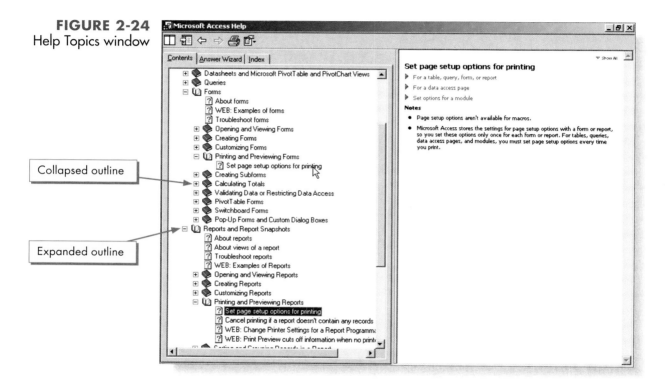

Collapsed outline

Expanded outline

5. Click <u>For a table, query, form or report</u> in the right pane.

6. Read the information, scrolling as necessary.

7. In the left pane, under the topic **Forms**, expand the **Opening and Viewing Forms** topic. Click **About views of a form**.

8. Expand and read <u>Design view</u> and <u>Form view and Datasheet view</u> in the right pane.

9. Click the Close button ✖ when you finish.

LESSON 2 Summary

➤ New records are added and stored in tables.

➤ Add new records to a table through a query. New records can also be added to a table through a form.

➤ Delete records from a table by clicking on the Record Selector and pressing the delete key ⌸Delete⌸.

➤ Delete text from individual fields in either a table or a query.

➤ Add text to individual fields in either a table or a query.

➤ AutoCorrect corrects commonly misspelled words while text is being added.

➤ Press ⌸Ctrl⌸+⌸'⌸ to duplicate the contents in the field from the previous record .

➤ Clicking the Undo button 🔄 will restore the previously deleted text.

➤ Access allows copying, pasting and paste appending of text in a table or query.

➤ A form is an Access object that allows entering, viewing, sorting, editing, and printing of records stored in a table.

➤ When you're using the data entry command in a form, only the current record is visible.

➤ Modify forms in Design View.

➤ Change the Default View of a form through Design View.

➤ Print preview displays on the screen how a form will be printed.

➤ When printing a single form, you must first select the form.

➤ Delete text in individual fields through a form.

➤ You can delete entire records from a table through a form.

➤ Add text in individual fields through a form.

➤ You can insert pictures as a field in a table through a form.

LESSON 2 Command Summary

FEATURE	BUTTON	MENU	KEYBOARD	SPEECH
Copy	📋	Edit, Copy	Ctrl + C	✓
Clipboard		Edit, Office Clipboard	Ctrl + C twice	✓

continues

LESSON 2 Command Summary *continued*

FEATURE	BUTTON	MENU	KEYBOARD	SPEECH
Data Entry		Records, Data Entry		✓
Delete record	✗	Edit, Delete Record	Ctrl + -	✓
Duplicate data			Ctrl + '	
Form Datasheet View	▦	View, Datasheet View		✓
Form Design View	◫	View, Design View		✓
Form View	▤	View, Form View		✓
Insert picture		Insert, Object		✓
Insert current date			Ctrl] + ;	
New record	▢	Insert, New Record	Ctrl + +	✓
Paste	▣	Edit, Paste	Ctrl + V	✓
Print	▤	File, Print	Ctrl + P	✓
Remove Data Entry		Records, Remove Filter/Sort		✓
Save record		Records, Save Record	Shift + Enter	✓
Undo	↶	Edit, Undo	Ctrl + Z	✓

Concepts Review

Each of the following statements is either true or false. Indicate your choice by circling T or F.

T   F   **1.** The pencil icon appears in the Record Selector after the data is saved.

T   F   **2.** You can use the Undo button [↰] to restore a deleted record.

T   F   **3.** When you enter or edit data on a form, you also have to update the underlying table.

T   F   **4.** You can duplicate the data from a field in the previous record to the same field in the next record by pressing [Ctrl]+[D].

T   F   **5.** Forms can be set to show more than one form or record per screen.

T   F   **6.** You can add records in a table, a query, or a form.

T   F   **7.** Access saves changes to the record when you close a form or move to the next record.

T   F   **8.** You can insert various types of objects as data in a table.

Write the correct answer in the space provided.

1. What view of a table lets you add records?

_____

2. What menu and menu command do you use to place an OLE object in a field?

_____

3. What is the keyboard shortcut to delete a record in a table or form?

_____

4. What feature do you use to set 50% magnification in Print Preview?

_____

5. How do you set the number of forms that can appear on the screen at once?

_____

6. How do you print a single form?

_____

7. How do you open a form's property sheet?

_____

8. Which command is carried out by pressing Ctrl + Z ?

_____

CRITICAL THINKING

Answer these questions on a separate page. There are no right or wrong answers. Support your answers with examples from your own experience, if possible.

1. You can insert various types of OLE objects in a table or form. Think about different types of businesses (law firms, real estate agencies, music stores, and others) and what types of objects (pictures, sound clips, video clips) each might use.

2. When you delete a record from a table, it cannot be recovered. Discuss business applications in which you should never completely delete or remove records, even though they might be inactive.

Skills Review

EXERCISE 2-20

Add and delete records in a table and a query.

1. Copy and rename a database by following these steps:

    a. Right-click the Start button on the Windows taskbar.
    b. Choose Explore and maximize the window.
    c. In the left pane, locate the folder "Lesson 02." Open the folder, point to the filename **CC-E-02**, and right-click.
    d. Choose Copy from the shortcut menu.
    e. In the left pane, open the "My Documents" folder. In an unused area of the right pane, right-click. Choose Paste from the shortcut menu.
    f. Right-click the file **CC-E-02** and choose Rename. Key **[your initials]CC-E-02** and press Enter .
    g. Right-click **[your initials]CC-E-02** and choose Properties. Make certain that the **Read-only** attribute check box is not checked.
    h. Click OK and close the Explorer.

2. Open Access. Locate and open the **[your initials]CC-E-02** database.

TIP: Confidential information about employees is typically kept in a separate database.

3. Add a record by following these steps:

   a. Open tblEmployeeDates and maximize the window. Click the New Record button .

TIP: You can key a date without a leading zero if you key the diagonal (forward slash). You can insert the current date by pressing Ctrl + ; .

   b. Key the following, pressing Tab between field entries:

   Social Security Number: 888-11-2222
   Employee ID: 32
   Birth Date: 07/16/72
   Hire Date: *Press* Ctrl + ; *to insert current date.*

   c. Press Tab . Access formats the date based on the field properties.

NOTE: You will learn about field properties later in this course.

   d. Close tblEmployeeDates.
   e. Open tblPayroll.
   f. Choose Records, and then choose Data Entry. Key the following to add another record:

   Social Security Number: 888-11-2222
   Employee ID: 32
   Salary: *Press* Tab *to leave blank.*
   Hourly: $9.75
   Federal Income Tax: $200
   State Tax: $38
   FICA: $116
   Savings: *Press* Tab *to leave blank.*

NOTE: T]he Payroll table shows a default value of 0 for the currency fields. Just key over the zero.

   g. Choose Records, and then choose Remove Filter/Sort. Close tblPayroll.

4. Delete a record by following these steps:

   a. Click Queries on the Objects bar. Open qryEmployeeDates. Maximize the window.
   b. Scroll to find Employee ID 32 and click anywhere in the record.

    c. Choose Edit, and then choose Delete Record. Click Yes to confirm the deletion.

> **NOTE:** When you use the Edit menu to delete a record, you do not need to select the record. Just click anywhere in it.

    d. Close qryEmployeeDates.
    e. Click Tables on the Objects bar. Open tblEmployeeDates. Notice that Employee ID 32 is deleted. Close the table.
    f. Open tblPayroll and maximize the window.
    g. Scroll to find the record for Employee ID 32.
    h. Click in the Record Selector to select the record.
    i. Press Delete. Click Yes to confirm the deletion.
    j. Close tblPayroll.

EXERCISE 2-21

Edit data.

    1. Delete text by following these steps:

        a. Open tblTimeCards and maximize the window. In the second record, click to the right of the hyphen after "888-14."
        b. Press Ctrl + Delete to delete "6406." Key **4444**
        c. In the fourth record, click between the decimal point and "2" in "$8.25."
        d. Press Delete once and key **5**. "$8.25" is changed to "$8.55."
        e. Click after "32" in the third record.
        f. Press Ctrl + Backspace to delete "32." Key **35**
        g. Close tblTimeCards.

    2. Insert text by following these steps:

        a. Open tblSalesReps and maximize the window.
        b. Press Insert to switch to Overtype mode.
        c. In the first record, click to the left of the "N" in "North." Key **Central**
        d. In the third record, click to the left of "East." Key **West**
        e. Press Insert to turn off Overtype mode.
        f. Close tblSalesReps.

    3. Compact and repair the database before closing it.

EXERCISE 2-22

Use text editing commands.

    1. Correct errors automatically by following these steps:

        a. Open your file *[your initials]*CC-02.
        b. Open tblCustomers and click the New Record button ▶*.
        c. Key **11** in the Customer ID field.

d. Press Tab to move to the Company Name field.

e. Key **Teh Hobby Comany** and press Tab.

f. Press CapsLock to lock capitalization. In the Contact Name field, hold down Shift for the first character and key **Tony**. Press the Spacebar. Capitalization is reversed from what it should be. Press CapsLock to turn off the Caps Lock. Key **Greenfield**. Press Tab. "tONY" becomes Tony.

2. Duplicate data from the previous record by following these steps:

a. Key the following to finish the record, duplicating the fields as shown.

Billing Address:	**3258 Bolton Boulevard**
City:	*Press* Ctrl + ´ .
State:	*Press* Ctrl + ´ .
ZIP Code:	**72723-3258**
Phone Number:	**(602) 555-8011**
Fax Number:	**(602) 555-8012**
Tax exempt?:	*Press* Ctrl + ´ .

b. Close the table.

3. Undo editing actions by following these steps:

a. Open tblProductLines.

b. Double-click "Endangered" to select it and press Delete.

c. Click the Undo button .

 REVIEW: The insertion point must be an I-beam when you select text.

d. In the first record, click to the left of "Dogs." Press Insert and key **Critters**. Turn off Overtype mode.

e. Press Ctrl + Z to restore "Dogs."

f. Close tblProductLines.

4. Copy and paste to edit records by following these steps:

 a. Open tblCustomers. Click the New Record button ▶✳ and key the following, leaving the Company Name and City fields blank:

Customer ID:	**12**
Company Name:	*Leave blank.*
Contact Name:	**Frank Davis**
Billing Address:	**1012 Dobson Avenue**
City:	*Leave blank.*
State:	**TN**
ZIP Code:	**37406-1012**
Phone Number:	**(423) 555-7765**

 Fax Number: **(423) 555-7766**
 Tax Exempt?: *Leave blank.*

b. Select "Magna Mart, Inc." in the Company Name field of the first record and click the Copy button . In the City field, double-click "Chattanooga" and press Ctrl + C.

REVIEW: From the Edit menu, you can open the Clipboard pane.

c. Click in the Company Name field in the new record. Click the Company Name in the Clipboard pane.

d. Click in the City field in the new record. Click the city in the Clipboard pane.

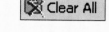

e. Click the Clear All button . Close the Clipboard pane.

f. Close tblCustomers.

EXERCISE 2-23

Add records with a form. Change form views. Preview and print a form. Add a picture.

1. Add records with a form by following these steps:

a. Click Forms on the Objects bar and open frmEmployeeInformation.

b. Click the New Record button and key the following:

 Last Name: **Adams**
 First Name: **William**
 Employee ID: **30**
 Address: **6825 Steele Creek Road**
 City: **Charlotte**
 State: **NC**
 Postal Code: **28217-3599**
 SS#: **888-22-5554**
 Home Phone: **(704) 555-5122**
 Job Code: **MF04**
 Contact Name: **Cynthia Adams**
 Emergency Phone: **(704) 555-5122**

2. Navigate in a form by following these steps:

a. Click the First Record button to move to the first record, Luis Gutierrez.

b. Press PgDn to move to the fourth record.

TIP: Depending on your screen size and settings, you might have to press PgDn twice to move to the next form.

    c. Press PgUp to move back two records.

    d. Click the Last Record button 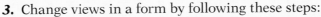 to move to the last employee, William Adams.

    e. Press Ctrl + Home to move to the first record.

    f. Press Ctrl + End to move to the last record.

    g. Click the First Record button.

    h. Close the form.

3. Change views in a form by following these steps:

    a. Open frmStuffedAnimals.

    b. Click the drop-down arrow of the View button  and choose **D**esign View from the shortcut menu.

    c. Click the View button 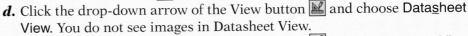 to return to Form View.

    d. Click the drop-down arrow of the View button  and choose Data**s**heet View. You do not see images in Datasheet View.

    e. Click the drop-down arrow of the View button  and choose **F**orm View.

    f. Click the View button 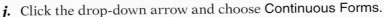 to switch to Design View.

    g. Click the **Form Selector** button to select the entire form.

    h. Click the Properties button to open the form's property sheet.

    i. Click the **Format** tab and the **Default View** row.

    j. Click the drop-down arrow and choose **Continuous Forms**.

    k. Click the View button to switch to Form View.

    l. Click the View button to switch to Design View.

 TIP: You can double-click the item in the list to cycle through the choices.

    m. Display the Default View list in the property sheet and choose **Single Form**. Close the property sheet.

    n. Close the form without saving the design changes.

4. Change the page setup and preview a form by following these steps:

    a. Open frmSalesReviewMain and maximize the window.

    b. Choose **F**ile, and then chose **Page Set**u**p**. Click the **Page** tab.

    c. Click the **L**andscape option button. Close the dialog box.

    d. Click the Print Preview button.

    e. Click anywhere on the page to zoom in. Click again to zoom out.

    f. Click the drop-down arrow next to the Zoom Control box and choose 75%.

    g. Close Print Preview by clicking the **C**lose button.

5. Print a form for one record by following these steps:

    a. Move to the Magna Mart record.

    b. Click in the Record Selector to select the form.

    c. Choose File, and then choose Print. Click Selected Record(s) to print the selected form.

    d. Click OK. Close frmSalesReviewMain.

6. Edit data in a form by following these steps:

    a. Open frmEmployeeInformation and maximize the window. Move to Norman Fishman's record.

    b. Click to the right of "North" in the Address field.

    c. Press Ctrl + Backspace . "45 North Irvin Avenue" changes to "45 Irvin Avenue." Delete the extra space between "45" and "Irvin."

    d. Click to the left of "Fishman" in the Contact Name field.

    e. Press Ctrl + Delete and key **Taylor.** "Fishman" changes to "Taylor."

    f. Press PgUp to move to Helen Butler's record.

    g. Click in the Record Selector to select the record. Click the Delete Record button.

    h. Click Yes to confirm the deletion.

    i. Close tblEmployeeInformation.

7. Insert a picture in a form by following these steps:

    a. Open frmStuffedAnimals.

    b. Locate the record for Tyrannosaurus Tommy.

    c. Click the empty rectangle for the picture.

    d. Choose Insert, and then choose Object. The Insert Object dialog box opens.

    e. Select Paintbrush Picture. Click OK.

    f. In MS-Paint, click Edit, and then click Paste From.

    g. Find the image file **Din002** and click Open. Click Yes.

    h. Click Image, and then click Attributes. Click the Black and white options button. Click Yes.

    i. Click anywhere on the form outside the image.

    j. Close the form.

8. Compact and repair the database before closing it.

Lesson Applications

EXERCISE 2-24

Add records in a table.

1. Open tblKitSuppliers in *[your initials]*CC-02 and maximize the window. Add the following new suppliers:

Supplier #:	5
Supplier ID:	EE-05
Supplier Name:	Northeast Fabric Supply
Contact Name:	[your first and last name]
Address:	562 Industrial Parkway
City:	Wallingford
ZIP Code:	06492-5223
Phone Number:	(203) 555-6332
Fax Number:	(203) 555-6331

Supplier #:	6
Supplier ID:	FF-06
Supplier Name:	Southern Fabrics, Inc.
Contact Name:	Randolph Peterson
Address:	2600 Patterson Street
City:	Greensboro
ZIP Code:	27407-2600
Phone Number:	(910) 555-6625
Fax Number:	(910) 555-6626

2. Preview the table. From the Preview window, change to Landscape orientation. Print and close the table.

EXERCISE 2-25

Edit records in a table.

1. Open frmStuffedAnimals and make the corrections shown in Figure 2-25 on the next page. Use navigation commands to find the records to be changed.

    TIP: To select a word in a field, double-click it. To select the entire field, press F2 .

FIGURE 2-25

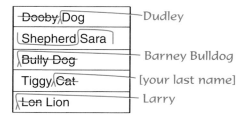

 NOTE: Refer to Appendix D to review proofreaders' marks.

2. Close the form and open tblStuffedAnimals. Print the table in portrait orientation.

EXERCISE 2-26

Edit records in a table.

1. Open tblEmployees. Make the Postal Code column wider to display the postal entries in the last few records of the table.

2. Freeze the Employee ID, Last Name, and First Name. Scroll the window to position the Postal Code field next to the names.

3. Using the ⬇ and ⬆, move from one record to another. Move to the Postal Code field and press F2 to edit the text. Use the ➡ and ⬅ to position the insertion point. Add the additional postal code numbers to each record. Add text as indicated in Figure 2-26. (Not all the columns appear in the following figure.)

FIGURE 2-26

Employee ID	Last Name	First Name	Postal Code
1	Fuentes	Lisa	28216-1933
2	McCluskie	James	28217-5324
3	Falcigno	Frances	28269-3024
4	Gutierrez	Luis	28262-2202
5	Floria	Maria	28214-1807
6	Abdullah	Jamel	28202-1121
7	Dyer	Cassie	28208-4411

continues

FIGURE 2-26   *continued*

Employee ID	Last Name	First Name	Postal Code
8	Wilson	Zipporah	28202-1141
9	Thomas-Smith	Louise	28205-2546
10	Davidson	Russell	28202-1051
11	Stone	Jeanette	28210-5006
12	Talmadge	Audrey	28202-1212
13	Lassen	Joseph	28202-1216
14	Chung	Sora	28202-1114
15	Clark	Martin	28202-1452
16	Lee	Ching	28202-1330
17	Cirillo	Frank	28202-1133
18	Rodriguez	Felix	28202-1548
20	Lee	Sidney	28216-5572
21	Barnes	Estela	28208-4417
22	Fishman	Norman	28202-1321
23	Fernandez	Victor	28202-1044
24	Lee	May	28262-9712
25	Baez	Richard	28213-6649
26	Hutchinson	Pauline	28207-2642

 NOTE: F2 starts Edit mode when the entire field is selected and selects an entire field when there is only an insertion point in the field.

4. Change the name in the last record to your name.
5. Unfreeze all columns.
6. Change the page orientation to landscape. Print the table.
7. Close the table without saving changes to the layout.

EXERCISE 2-27 *Challenge Yourself*

Add pictures to records.

1. Open tblStuffedAnimals.

2. Move to the Professor Bear record and insert the **Ted001** bitmap image. Close the table.

3. Open frmStuffedAnimals. Move to the Professor Bear record and print it.

 TIP: Click the rectangle for the picture to insert an image.

4. Insert the **Din004** bitmap image for Triceratops Tony.

5. Select and print this record in landscape format.

6. Compact and repair the database before closing it.

On Your Own

In these exercises you work on your own, as you would in a real-life work environment. Use the skills you've learned to accomplish the task—and be creative.

EXERCISE 2-28

Search the Web for companies that would sell products of interest to members of the club you formed in Lesson 1. If you are unable to locate any companies, search the Web for companies selling clothing that appeals to you. Write down at least five URLs (Web page addresses). Continue to the next exercise.

EXERCISE 2-29

On each of the five Web sites, determine what information the company asks a person when that person places an order or requests a catalog. Write a bulleted list of different information collected by each company on potential customers (for example: first name, email) on the same sheet of paper where you wrote down the five URLs. Continue to the next exercise.

EXERCISE 2-30

On a second sheet of paper, create a new field list by combining the list you created in Exercise 1-28 (in Lesson 1) with the list you created in Exercise 2-29. On a third sheet of paper, organize the items from your new list to sketch a form layout. You might want to refer to Figure 2-8. Submit your work for Exercises 2-28 through 2-30 to your instructor.

Finding and Sorting Records

3

OBJECTIVES

After completing this lesson, you will be able to:

1. **Find specific text.**
2. **Use the Replace command.**
3. **Sort records.**
4. **Use filters.**
5. **Create an advanced filter/sort.**
6. **Use AND/OR criteria.**
7. **Build a query.**

MOUS
ACTIVITIES

In this lesson:
Ac2002 **2-1**
Ac2002 **3-1**
Ac2002 **5-2**
Ac2002 **5-3**
Ac2002 **5-4**

See Appendix E.

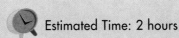 Estimated Time: 2 hours

The Find, Replace, Sort, and Filter commands in Access are similar to the Find, Replace, Sort, and Filter commands in other software programs.

- Find and Replace commands search the records for data you specify. To search for a particular employee, for example, you key the employee's name in the dialog box, and Access finds the record.

- Sort commands arrange records in a particular sequence. For instance, you can sort employee records alphabetically by last name or numerically by ID number.

- Filter commands display only records that meet conditions you specify. For example, you can display only customers in Charlotte, North Carolina.

Finding Specific Text

Finding records can be time-consuming if you have to scroll through several thousand of them. You can use the Find command to locate a record quickly.

There are two ways to use Find:

- Choose <u>E</u>dit and then choose <u>F</u>ind.
- Press Ctrl + F.

The Find command can search an entire field or part of a field. Searches are not case sensitive, which means Access finds uppercase and lowercase versions of the text.

E X E R C I S E   **3-1**   **Find Records**

---

1. Copy **CC-03** and rename it *[your initials]***CC-03**. Make certain it is not a Read-only copy.

 REVIEW: If you need help copying and renaming the database, refer to the beginning of Lesson 2.

2. Open tblCustomers and maximize the window.
3. Click <u>E</u>dit and then click <u>F</u>ind. Make certain you are on the **Find** tab.
4. Key **charlotte** in the **Find What** text box.
5. To search all fields in the table, click the down arrow next to the **Look In** box and choose "tblCustomers: Table."
6. Click the down arrow next to the **Match** box and choose **Whole Field**.
7. Make certain the **Search** drop-down list is set to **All**. The **All** option starts at the current record, continues to the end of the table, and wraps back to records that precede the current record.
8. Make certain that the **Match Case** option is not selected.

FIGURE 3-1
Find and Replace
dialog box

Find and Replace	? X
Find / Replace	
Find What:	charlotte ▼	Find Next
		Cancel
Look In:	tblCustomers : Table ▼	
Match:	Whole Field ▼	
Search:	All ▼	
	☐ Match Case ☑ Search Fields As Formatted	

NOTE: To see the results of a search, you can drag the Find and Replace dialog box by its title bar to a location on the screen where it doesn't obscure the results of the search.

TABLE 3-1   **Find and Replace Dialog Box Options**

OPTION	DESCRIPTION
Look In	Sets the search for the current field or the entire table.
Match: Any Part of Field	Finds records with matching characters anywhere in the field.
Match: Whole Field	Finds records in which an entire field matches the value in the Find What text box.
Match: Start of Field	Finds records in which the beginning of a field matches the Find What entry.
Search: All	Searches forward to the end of the table and wraps back to the beginning.
Search: Up	Searches in the Up (backward) direction only.
Search: Down	Searches in the Down (forward) direction only.
Match Case	Finds exact uppercase and lowercase matches.
Search Fields As Formatted	Enables you to key data in its display format. To find a date that is stored as 1/25/01, you can key 25-Jan-01. This is the slowest search.

9. Click Find Next. Access moves the pointer to the first occurrence of "Charlotte."

10. Click Find Next to move to the next occurrence of "Charlotte."

11. Continue clicking Find Next until Access displays a message that it has finished searching the records.

12. Click OK in the message box. Close the Find and Replace dialog box.

 NOTE: The Find and Replace dialog box remains open until you close it.

EXERCISE **3-2** **Find Records with Match Case and Match Any Part of a Field**

The Find command includes options for fine-tuning how words or phrases are matched. One of these options, Match Case, is used to conduct a case-sensitive search. Another option enables you to look for matches in any part of a field.

1. Move to the end of the table by pressing Ctrl + End.

2. Click the Find button .

> **NOTE:** The text from the prior search Access performed might be in the Find What text box. You can simply key the new search string over it.

3. In the Find What text box, key **durham**

4. Click the Match Case check box. From the Search list box, choose Up to search backward from the current record.

FIGURE 3-2
Choosing options in the Find and Replace dialog box

5. Click Find Next to begin the search. There are no matches.

6. Click OK in the message box that says the search is finished.

7. Click anywhere in the Billing Address field of any record.

8. Key **boulevard** in the Find What text box.

9. Choose "Billing Address" for the Look In entry.

> **TIP:** Searches are faster if you use a single field instead of an entire table.

10. In the Match list box, choose Any Part of Field.

11. Deselect the Match Case check box. Set the Search direction to All. Click Find Next. The first match is highlighted.

12. Continue to click Find Next until the message box opens. Click OK.

13. Close the Find and Replace dialog box. Close tblCustomers.

EXERCISE   3-3   Find Records by Using the Asterisk (*)

When you use the Find command, you are actually specifying criteria. *Criteria* are text strings or expressions that Access uses to find matching records. Up to this point, you have used text as criteria (the words "Charlotte" and "Durham").

When you use text as criteria, you can use *wildcards*. These are characters used to represent one or more alphabetical or numerical characters. They are helpful when you are not quite sure of the complete spelling or value.

- A question mark (?) represents a single character. **Mar?** is a criterion that would find "Mary," "Mark," or "Mart"—four-character words that start with "Mar."

- An asterisk (*) represents any number of characters. **Mar*** is a criterion that would find "March," "Martin," "Marigold," or "Marblestone"—words that start with "Mar" regardless of how many letters follow.

- The number sign (#) represents a single numerical character. If you are looking for numbers less than 100, you can key **##** as criteria to eliminate any numbers with three or more digits.

1. Open frmEmployeeInformation.

2. Click the Find button .

3. Key **mf*** in the Find What text box.

4. Set the Look In box to "Employee Information Form." Set the Match criteria to Any Part of Field.

5. From the Search drop-down list box, choose All.

6. Make certain that the Match Case check box is deselected.

7. Click Find Next to find the first occurrence of an "MF" job code.

> **TIP:** Move the Find and Replace dialog box if it is in the way of the Job Code field.

8. Continue clicking Find Next until the message box opens. Notice that records for employees with any "MF" job code are displayed ("MF02," "MF03," and so on).

9. Click OK in the message box.

10. Click anywhere in the Last Name field in the form.

11. In the Find What text box, key **f*.** In the Look In box, choose Last Name.

12. Verify that the search will be for All records with no Match Case. Click Find Next.

13. Click Find Next again to see each employee whose last name begins with "F."

14. Close the message box and the Find and Replace dialog box.

15. Close frmEmployeeInformation.

EXERCISE 3-4 **Find Records by Using the Question Mark (?)**

1. Open frmStuffedAnimals and click in the Animal Name field.

2. Click the Find button . The **Look In** box shows "Animal Name" because you clicked in that field.

3. Key **T????** in the **Find What** text box. Each question mark represents one character.

4. Click the down arrow next to the **Match** list box and choose **Start of Field**.

5. Click the **Match Case** check box to select it. In the **Search** list box, choose **All**.

6. Click **Find Next** to begin and continue to click **Find Next**. Access moves the pointer to each record that begins with a "T" followed by any four characters in the Animal Name field.

> **TIP:** A space is considered a character in Find and Replace activities; therefore, "Tula Tiger" is included in these matches.

7. Click **OK** to close the message box.

8. In the **Find What** text box, key **C???**

9. Click in the Product ID field in the form. Click anywhere in the Find and Replace dialog box to update the **Look In** entry.

10. Click **Match Case** and choose **Search: All**. Click **Find Next**. Access displays the records for animals in the "C" category.

11. Continue clicking **Find Next** until Access tells you that no additional search items are found.

12. Click **OK** in the message box and close the Find and Replace dialog box.

13. Close frmStuffedAnimals.

Using the Replace Command

The Replace command finds matching text and substitutes replacement text. You can replace all instances of matching text at once, or you can find and confirm each replacement.

There are two ways to use the Replace command:

- Choose <u>E</u>dit and then choose <u>R</u>eplace.
- Press Ctrl + H.

EXERCISE   **3-5**   **Replace Text by Using Find Next**

1. Open tblCustomers.
2. Click the Find button 🔍. Click the **Replace** tab. The value in the first field in the first record is shown.
3. In the **Find What** text box, key **boulevard**. Click in the Billing Address field in the first record.
4. Set the **Look In** box to Billing Address.
5. Click in the **Replace With** text box and key **Avenue**
6. In the **Match** list box, choose **Any Part of Field**. Use **Search: All**.
7. Make certain the **Match Case** check box is not selected.

FIGURE 3-3
Replacing text

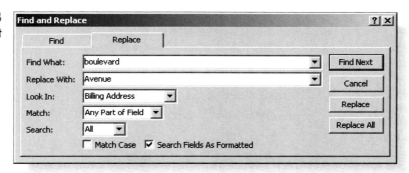

NOTE: If you choose Whole Field in the Match list box, Access matches the entire contents of the field. In this case, the search string "boulevard" would not match "3415 Brookshire Boulevard."

8. Click **Find Next** to start the search.
9. Click **Replace** to replace the first occurrence of "Boulevard" with "Avenue" and to find the next occurrence.
10. Click **Replace** again to replace the next occurrence. Continue clicking **Replace** until Access indicates that it can't find the text you specified.
11. Click **OK** in the message box.
12. Close the Find and Replace dialog box and tblCustomers.

EXERCISE   **3-6**   **Replace Text by Using Replace All**

The **Replace All** option in the Replace dialog box replaces all occurrences of text in a table or form without confirmation.

1. Open tblKitSuppliers.

2. Click anywhere in the Address field. Look for the word "Street."

3. Click the Find button and then click the **Replace** tab.

> ✦ **TIP:** Ctrl + H opens the Replace tab on the Find and Replace dialog box.

4. In the Find What text box, key **street** and press Tab. In the **Replace With** text box, key **Road**. Use Match: Any Part of Field, no Match Case, and Search: All.

> ↗ **NOTE:** If you search all fields and all records of the table and use Any Part of Field, you change all occurrences of "street" to "road." An employee named "Mary Ann Street" would become "Mary Ann Road." A town named "Streeter" would become "Roader."

5. Click the **Replace All** button. Access warns that you cannot undo a Replace activity.

FIGURE 3-4
Access warns that you cannot undo the Replace

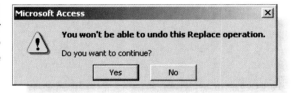

6. Click Yes. All occurrences of "Street" in the Address field are changed to "Road." Close the Find and Replace dialog box.

7. Close tblKitSuppliers.

Sorting Records

Records are displayed in some type of alphabetical or numerical order. By default, Access displays records based on the primary key if that field is first. The *primary key* is a field in which data is unique for every record. If there is no primary key, Access displays records based on the order in which they were entered.

> ✦ **TIP:** A table does not need to have a primary key. However, you do give up database integrity (the stability and soundness of the data) when there is no primary key. You will learn more about this as you continue through the lessons.

You can arrange records in other orders to find information more quickly. For example, records in the Customers table are arranged by CustomerID number, but when you plan sales calls it may be more helpful to see them in order by ZIP code.

The Stuffed Animals table is arranged by ProductID, but you may need to see them in order by price or inventory if you are planning a sales campaign.

You can sort data in three ways:

- Choose Records and then choose Sort.
- Click the Sort Ascending button or Sort Descending button .
- Click the right mouse button and select Sort Ascending or Sort Descending from the shortcut menu.

EXERCISE 3-7   Sort a Single Field

A simple sort uses one field. You can sort records in a table, a query, a form, or a data access page.

1. Open qryEmployees and make certain the window is maximized. Click anywhere in the Last Name field.

> **TIP:** The sort buttons on the toolbar are known as the QuickSort buttons.

2. Click the Sort Ascending button on the toolbar to sort the records by Last Name in ascending order (A to Z).

3. Click the Sort Descending button to sort in descending order (Z to A).

4. Close qryEmployees. Click No when Access asks if you want to save design changes.

> **NOTE:** If you save the design changes after sorting a table or query, the records are saved in the new order.

5. Click Forms on the Objects bar and open frmStuffedAnimals. Click anywhere in the Animal Name field.

6. From the Records menu, choose Sort and then choose Sort Ascending.

FIGURE 3-5
Records menu

7. Press PgDn to scroll through the records. The records are sorted alphabetically, in ascending order, by animal name.

 NOTE: Sorts in a form are not considered design changes, so you are not asked to save the changes.

8. Close frmStuffedAnimals.

EXERCISE **3-8** **Sort by Multiple Fields in Datasheet View**

You can sort a table or query by more than one field. For example, you might want to view customers by city and alphabetically by customer name within each city. In a datasheet, Access requires that sorted fields be next to each other on the screen. The sorting priority goes from left to right, so the first sort is the leftmost column, the second sort is the next column, and so on.

 REVIEW: The top border of a field or column is its column selector.

1. Open tblCustomers. Place the pointer at the top of the State field, on the column selector, and click when the pointer changes to a down-pointing arrow. This selects the column.

2. Click the State field name and drag the column to the left. As you drag, a wide vertical line shows where the column will be dropped. When the vertical line is to the left of the Company Name field, release the mouse button. The State column, still selected, is now to the left of the Company Name column.

FIGURE 3-6
A vertical line shows where the field will be dropped

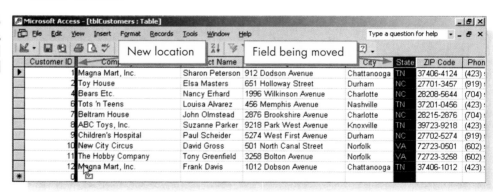

3. Hold down Shift, point to the Company Name column selector, and click when the pointer changes to a down-pointing arrow. This selects both columns.

4. Click the Sort Ascending button ⬇. The records are sorted first by state and then by company name within each state.

5. Close tblCustomers without saving changes.

EXERCISE 3-9 Sort a Query in Design View

You can sort a query in Datasheet View by using the QuickSort buttons. This type of sort is part of the layout and is temporary if you do not save the layout changes. You can also sort by one or more fields in Design View. This becomes a permanent sort when you save the query.

To sort a query in Design View, you add the fields to be used in sorting to the design grid. You can add fields to the design grid by double-clicking the field name or by dragging the field name into position.

1. Open qryCustomers. Click the View button . The design grid is on the lower half of the screen. The field list is in the top pane.

FIGURE 3-7
Query Design
window

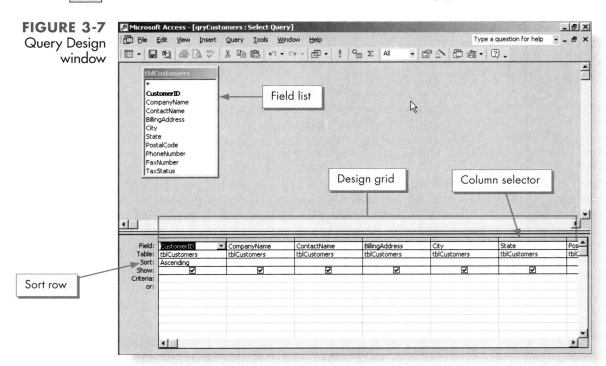

2. Make certain the window is maximized. Notice that the query sorts the records by CustomerID.

3. Click the **Sort** row for CustomerID. Click the drop-down arrow and choose (**not sorted**).

4. In the State field column, click the **Sort** row. Choose **Ascending**.

5. Click the View button 🔳. The records are sorted by state.

6. Click the View button 🔳.

7. In the CompanyName column, click the Sort row. Choose Ascending. The design grid now shows two sorts.

8. Click the View button 🔳. The records are sorted by the leftmost column in the design grid, the Company Name. The State sort order does not matter in this case.

9. Click the View button 🔳.

10. Place the pointer on the column selector for the State field. Click when the pointer changes to a down-pointing arrow.

11. With the column selected, click and drag the column to the left of the Company Name column. Release the mouse button.

12. Click the View button 🔳. The records are sorted first by state and then by company name.

13. Close the query and do not save the changes.

Using Filters

A *filter* shows a subset of records (a recordset) matching a criteria you set. You can apply filters in tables, queries, and forms. For example, if you want to find all stuffed animals in the D Product Group, you can create a filter that removes the other records.

There are four types of filters:

- Filter By Selection displays only those records that include selected text. This filter is available as a button, as a menu command, and as an option from a shortcut menu.

- Filter By Form displays records that match criteria on a form. In a blank datasheet or form, you specify a field (or fields), how the field (or fields) are to be sorted, and any additional criteria. Use the Apply Filter/Sort command (or the Apply Filter button 🔽) to run the filter. This filter also is available as a button and as a menu command.

- Filter By Input displays records that match a keyed value. It is available only from a shortcut menu. The shortcut menu command is Filter For.

- Filter Excluding Selection excludes all records that match a selected value. This filter is available as a menu command and as an option from a shortcut menu.

NOTE: After you use the Apply Filter button 🔽, it turns into the Remove Filter button 🔽. Clicking the Remove Filter button 🔽 displays all records in the table again.

EXERCISE 3-10 Use Filter By Selection

When you create a Filter By Selection, you highlight text to establish it as criteria.

TABLE 3-2   Selecting Text for a Filter By Selection

SELECT	TO DISPLAY
Entire field	Records containing an exact match of the text selected
Start of a field	Records that start with the same character(s) as the selected text
Characters anywhere in the field	Records in which all or part of the field matches the selected text

 1. Open tblStuffedAnimals and make certain the window is maximized.

 2. Click anywhere in the List Price field for the first record. Press F2 to select the entire field.

 3. Click the Filter By Selection button. Access displays only products with list prices of $12.50.

FIGURE 3-8
Products with a list price of $12.50

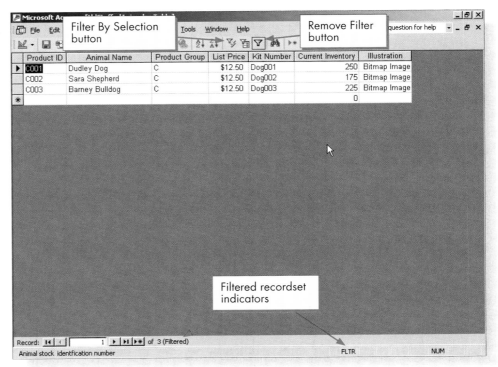

4. Click the Remove Filter button ▽ to display all the records again.

5. In the Kit Number field, select "Dog" but not the numbers.

6. From the <u>R</u>ecords menu, choose Filter By <u>S</u>election. Only the records with Kit Numbers beginning with "Dog" are displayed.

7. From the <u>R</u>ecords menu, choose <u>R</u>emove Filter/Sort.

8. Close tblStuffedAnimals. Click **Yes** to save the changes to the table. This saves the last filter you used.

EXERCISE **3-11** **Look at the Filter Property**

If you save the design changes after applying a filter, that filter is saved as part of the design. You can see it as part of the Table Properties sheet.

1. Open tblStuffedAnimals. Click the Apply Filter button ▽. The "Dog" filter is reapplied.

2. Click the View button 🖾 to switch to the Table Design window.

3. Click the Properties button 📑. The Table Properties dialog box shows the filter that has been saved.

> **NOTE:** You can click the Filter row and open the Zoom window [Shift] + [F2].

FIGURE 3-9
Table Properties
dialog box

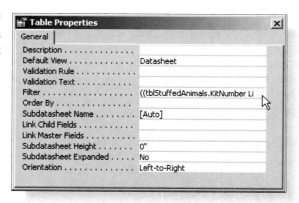

4. Close the Table Properties dialog box and the table.

EXERCISE **3-12** **Use an Additive Filter By Selection**

After you apply a Filter By Selection, you can apply another Filter By Selection to the filtered records.

1. Open tblEmployees.
2. In the JobCode field, select "MF" (not the number) in any record.
3. Click the Filter By Selection button . The "MF" job code employees are filtered and displayed.
4. In the JobCode field, double-click "MF06" in any record.
5. Click the Filter By Selection button . The records are further filtered.

> **NOTE:** When you click the Filter By Selection button ![icon], the filter is automatically applied. You do not need to click the Apply Filter ![icon] button.

6. Click the Remove Filter button ![icon]. The filter is no longer applied; however, the filter definition is stored if you save the design changes.
7. Close the table and do not save the design changes.

EXERCISE **3-13** **Use Filter By Form**

A Filter By Form is more flexible than a Filter By Selection because you can set criteria for more than one field. When you use a Filter By Form, a blank datasheet or form is opened. You key an expression or choose from a drop-down list of values.

> **TIP:** Filter By Form is similar to the AutoFilter command in Microsoft Excel.

1. Open tblEmployees and click the Filter By Form button ![icon]. A blank Filter By Form datasheet opens.
2. Click in the Job Code field. A drop-down list arrow appears.
3. Press F4 to list the values in the field. Choose "MF05" from the list. Quotation marks appear around "MF05," and the value is entered in the field. (See Figure 3-10 on the next page.)
4. Click the Apply Filter button ![icon]. The records with job code "MF05" are shown.
5. Click the Remove Filter button ![icon].
6. Click the Filter By Form button ![icon]. Your most recent filter is shown.

7. Click the Clear Grid button ![icon]. The filter is cleared.
8. Click in the Job Code field and display the list.
9. Choose "MF05" from the list.

FIGURE 3-10
Criteria in a
Filter By Form

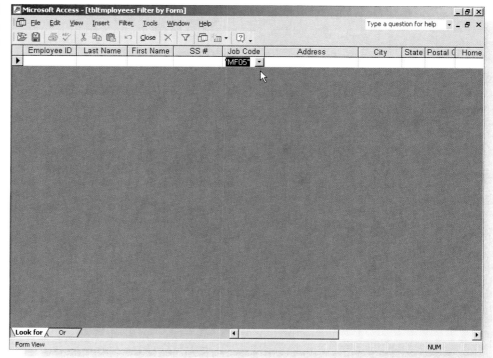

10. Click in the Address field, but do not display the list.

11. Key ***street**

TIP: In a Filter By Form, you can use the same wildcards as were used in Find and Replace.

FIGURE 3-11
Two criteria in
Filter By Form

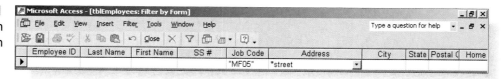

NOTE: When you use two criteria on the same Filter By Form, both criteria must exist for each record displayed. You will learn more about this type of criteria in Exercise 3-17.

12. Click the Apply Filter button ▽. The records with job code "MF05" and "street" at the end of the address are shown.

13. Click the Remove Filter button ▽.

14. Close tblEmployees. Do not save the design changes.

EXERCISE 3-14 **Use Wildcards and Null Values in Criteria**

Wildcards are used to locate records when only part of the information stored in a field is known or to locate a group of records containing common text or numbers.

A *null value* identifies fields that do not contain data. A null value is not the same as the number zero or a space character created by pressing the spacebar. The number zero and a space character are both actual values. Only fields that do not contain any text, numbers, or values are null values.

 Forms

1. Click Forms on the Object bar. Open frmStuffedAnimals. Make certain the window is maximized.

2. Click the Filter By Form button. A blank form opens.

3. Click in the Animal Name field and key ***dog***

4. Click the Apply Filter button. Two records are filtered, both with the word "Dog" in the name.

 NOTE: You can see how many records are filtered by looking at the status bar at the bottom left corner of the screen.

5. Press PgDn to see the other record that fits the criteria.

6. Click the Filter By Form button.

7. Click the Clear Grid button.

8. Click in the Picture field and display the drop-down list. Because this is on OLE data type, your choices are either that the field has something in it (Is Not Null) or does not have anything in it (Is Null).

 REVIEW: The picture field is the large rectangle to the right of the three text fields.

9. Choose Is Null.

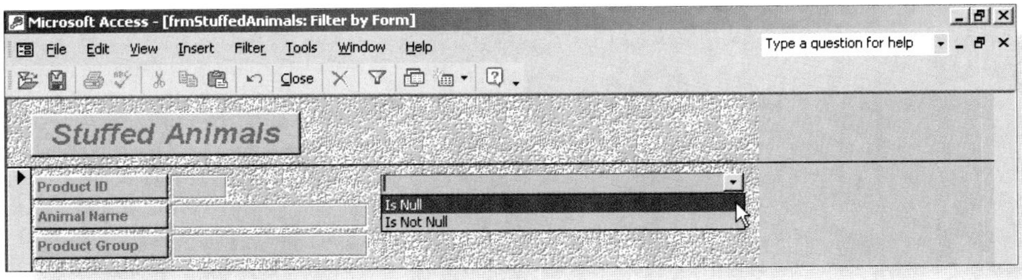

FIGURE 3-12
Using Is Null
as a condition

10. Click the Apply Filter button . The records that do not have pictures are displayed in the recordset. Only the record for Rodney Rooster does not have an image.

11. Close the form.

12. Open frmStuffedAnimals and click the Apply Filter button . The same filter is applied because it was saved with the form.

13. Click the View button . Click the Properties button . The form's property sheet opens.

14. Click the **Data** tab. Notice the **Filter** row and its entry.

15. Close the property sheet and the form.

EXERCISE **3-15** **Use Filter By Input and Filter Excluding Selection**

The Filter By Input command is available from a shortcut menu displayed by clicking the right mouse button in a field. Although it is called a "Filter By Input," you key your input in the <u>F</u>ilter For text box in the shortcut menu.

Use Filter <u>E</u>xcluding Selection to exclude records that match a value. For example, you can filter the records to show all kits except those from a certain supplier.

1. Open tblCustomers.

2. Right-click anywhere in the Company Name field. Choose the <u>F</u>ilter For text box.

3. Key **children***

FIGURE 3-13
Use Filter By Input

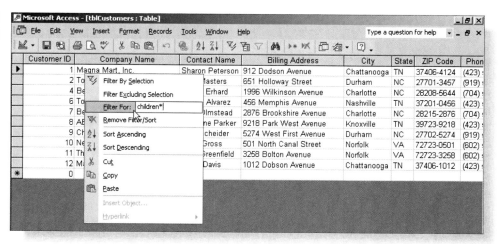

NOTE: You must key the exact spelling in the Filter For text box, and the insertion point must be in the field used for filtering.

4. Press Enter to apply the filter. The Children's Hospital record is displayed.

5. Click the Remove Filter button ▽ and close the table. Do not save the changes.

6. Open tblKitContents.

7. Select "AA-01" in any record and right-click.

 REVIEW: Point at the selected text as you right-click.

8. Choose Filter Excluding Selection.

FIGURE 3-14
Use Filter
Excluding Selection

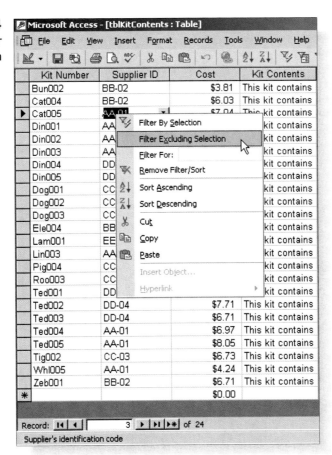

9. All records but those for Supplier AA-01 are shown. Click the Remove Filter button ▽ and close the table. Do not save the changes.

Creating an Advanced Filter or Sort

The Filter window enables you to build an Advanced Filter or Sort. You can use several fields and sophisticated expressions by making choices and entering criteria. The top pane in the Filter window displays a list of fields in the table. The bottom pane shows a design grid in which you add field names, sort orders, and criteria expressions. You add only those field names that should be used in the filtering.

 TIP: Many of the filters you design in a Filter window can be built in a Filter By Form when you know how to enter the expressions.

EXERCISE **3-16** **Create an Advanced Filter**

1. Open tblHistorySales and maximize the window.

2. From the Records menu, choose Filter. Then choose Advanced Filter/Sort.

3. If you can't see all the names in the Field Name list box, you can adjust the height of the top pane to provide more space. Place the pointer on the horizontal border between the two panes. It changes to the split pointer.

4. Drag the pointer down to make the top pane taller than the lower pane. Then drag the border of the Field Name list box to make it taller so you can see all the field names.

FIGURE 3-15
Resizing the Filter window panes

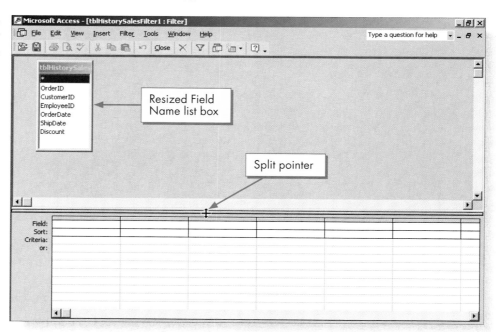

5. Click the EmployeeID field in the Field Name list box in the top pane. Drag it to the **Field** row of the first column in the lower pane. (When the pointer reaches the lower pane, it shows a field icon.)

6. Click the **Criteria** row under the EmployeeID field in the lower pane. Key **7**. This filter will find records in which the EmployeeID is "7."

7. Click the Apply Filter button [▽]. The records are filtered, and the status bar shows the number of records that are displayed.

8. Choose <u>R</u>ecords and then choose <u>F</u>ilter. Click <u>A</u>dvanced Filter/Sort.

9. Double-click the Discount field in the Field Name list box. It is added to the design grid in the next available column.

FIGURE 3-16
Adding fields and
criteria to the
Filter window

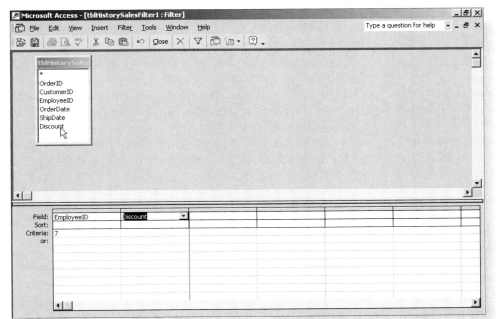

10. Click the Criteria row for the Discount field. Key **.1**

11. Click the Apply Filter button [▽]. The records are filtered to show those in which the EmployeeID is "7" and the Discount is 10%.

 REVIEW: [Ctrl] + [F6] is a Windows command to toggle between open windows.

12. Press [Ctrl] + [F6] to return to the Design window.

13. Double-click the ShipDate field in the Field Name list box. It is added to the design grid.

14. Click the Sort row for the ShipDate field and choose Descending.

15. Click the Apply Filter button . The filtered records are sorted with most recent date first.

> **TIP:** You do not need to remove the filter if you do not plan to save the design changes.

16. Close the table. Do not save the design changes.

Using AND/OR Criteria

You have already used more than one condition in some of your filters. Multiple criteria fall into one of two categories—AND or OR. *AND conditions* are database criteria that combine two or more requirements.

An *OR condition* finds records that match any of the criteria you specify. The record needs to match only one of your requirements.

Suppose that you need to list all the stuffed animals in Product Group D and E. Although you might say "D and E," this is actually an OR condition. You want all the products that are in D along with all the products that are in E. This is an OR criteria. It lists products in either Group D or Group E.

Now think about this situation. Suppose you need to list all the stuffed animals in Group D that cost $10.75. A record would have to meet both criteria; this is an AND condition. AND conditions are more restrictive and usually find fewer matching records than OR conditions.

You can use AND/OR conditions in a Filter By Form or in the Filter window.

EXERCISE 3-17   **Create an AND/OR Filter By Form**

---

1. Open tblStuffedAnimals and maximize the window.

2. Click the Filter By Form button and click the Clear Grid button .

3. Click in the Product Group field and choose "D" from the list.

4. Click the Apply Filter button .

5. Click the Filter By Form button .

6. Click the Or tab at the bottom left of the window. This opens a blank form for the next criteria.

FIGURE 3-17
Click the Or tab
to open a new
blank form

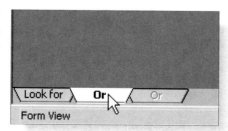

7. For the Product Group field, choose "E."

8. Click the Apply Filter button . The stuffed animals from either Group D or E are listed.

9. Click the Filter By Form button and click the Clear Grid button .

10. For the Product Group field, choose "E."

11. Click the List Price field and choose 10.75. An AND condition shows all the criteria on the same row.

FIGURE 3-18
An AND condition uses only one form

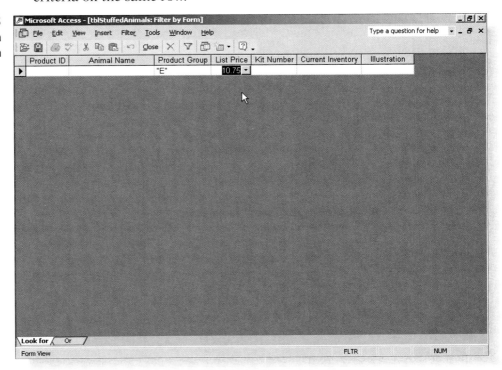

12. Click the Apply Filter button 🟥. Stuffed animals from Group E with a list price of $10.75 are listed. Both conditions must be met for the record to be listed.

13. Close the table and do not save the changes.

EXERCISE 3-18 Create an AND/OR Advanced Filter

Filters are very useful for locating and displaying records. When working with large databases, using advanced filters for your searches reduces the time it takes for you to locate important data.

1. Open tblHistorySales and maximize the window.

2. Choose Records and then choose Filter. Click Advanced Filter/Sort.

3. Place the pointer on the horizontal border between the two panes to display the split pointer.

4. Drag the border down to make the top pane taller. Then drag the border for the Field Name list box so you can see more of the field names.

5. Double-click the OrderDate field in the Field Name list box. It is added to the design grid in the first column.

6. Click the **Criteria** row for the Order Date field. Key **>2/1/98**

7. Click the Apply Filter button ▽. The records are filtered to show those in which the OrderDate is later than 2/1/98.

8. Press Ctrl + F6.

 NOTE: When you use a date in a filter or query, Access applies its standard formatting, which encloses the date in # symbols.

9. Double-click the Discount field to add it to the design grid.

10. For the Discount field, click in the **Criteria** row. Key **>0** This is an AND condition; the criteria are entered on the same row.

FIGURE 3-19
An AND condition in the Filter window uses the same row

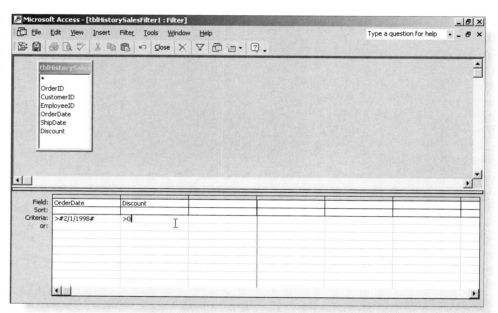

11. Click the Apply Filter button ▽. The records have an OrderDate after 2/1/98 AND a discount.

12. Press Ctrl + F6. Click the Clear Grid button ✕.

13. Double-click the CustomerID field in the Field Name list box.

14. Click the **Criteria** row for the field and key **1**

15. Click the first **or** row for the field and key **3**. OR conditions are keyed on separate rows. (See Figure 3-20 on the next page.)

16. Click the Apply Filter button ▽. The filtered records are for Customers 1 OR 3.

FIGURE 3-20
Using OR criteria in
the Filter window

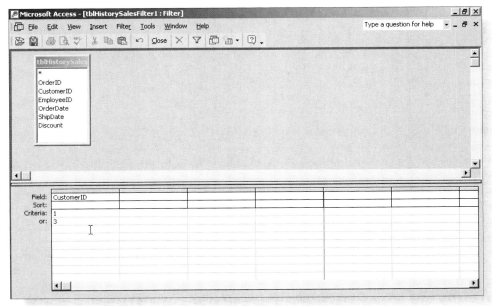

17. Close the table and do not save the changes.

Building a Query

You have already opened several queries in both Datasheet and Design View. A query has many of the same features and properties as an advanced filter, including the field list and the design grid.

With a table, you can save only one filter at a time. A filter is a table property. It is not a database object (like tables, queries, forms, and reports). Only one filter definition can be stored per object.

Queries are more powerful than filters. A query is a database object and appears in the Queries window. You can save as many different queries as necessary, each with a separate name. Unlike a filter, a table can have multiple queries associated to it.

EXERCISE 3-19 Create a Query by Using the Wizard

In Access, the Query Wizard provides simplified steps for designing a query. A *wizard* is a feature that asks questions and uses your answers to create an object automatically. Objects created through a wizard include tables, queries, forms, reports and even databases. Through the wizard, you select the source table, the fields to include, and the order in which the fields appear.

After selecting the fields, you name and run the query. The results of the query you create appear in a Datasheet View. This Datasheet View is a dynaset. A *dynaset* is a dynamic recordset. Changes you make to data in a dynaset are automatically made to the records in the source table.

TABLE 3-3   **Wizard Buttons**

BUTTON	PURPOSE
>	Adds the selected sample field to the Fields in my new table list.
>>	Adds all the sample fields to the Fields in my new table list.
<	Removes the selected sample field from the Fields in my new table list.
<<	Removes all the sample fields from the Fields in my new table list.

 Queries

1. Click **Query** on the Objects bar. Double-click **Create query by using wizard**.
2. Choose "Table: tblEmployees" from the drop-down list.
3. Double-click on FirstName, LastName, HomePhone, EmergencyContact, and EmergencyPhone.
4. Click <u>N</u>ext. Name the query **qryEmergencyContact**

REVIEW: The "qry" prefix is used to identify queries.

5. Click <u>F</u>inish.
6. Move to Sam Kwan's record. Change "Sam" to **Samuel**
7. Close qryEmergencyContact.
8. Open tblEmployees. Move to Samuel Kwan's record. Notice that the changes made in the dynaset were automatically made to the data in the underlying table.
9. Close tblEmployees.

EXERCISE  **Create and Save a Query by Using Design View**

You can create a query by using Design View. You have the option of selecting the source table, the fields to include, and the order in which the fields appear, just as you did when using the wizard. Additionally, you can define the criteria used in the query.

1. Click tblHistorySales but do not open it.

2. Click the drop-down arrow next to the New Object button 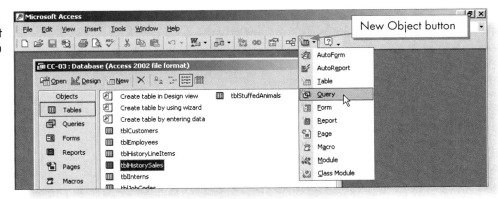. Choose **Query**.

FIGURE 3-21
New Object
shortcut menu

3. The New Query dialog box provides several ways to build a query. Choose **Design View**.

FIGURE 3-22
New Query
dialog box

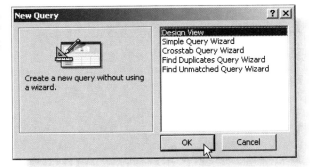

4. Click **OK**. Make certain the window is maximized.

5. Place the pointer on the border between the two panes and make the top pane taller. Then make the Field Name list box taller.

6. In the Field Name list box, double-click the OrderDate field. It is added to the design grid in the first column.

7. Click the **Criteria** row for the OrderDate field. Key **>2/1/98**

8. Click the View button . Only the Order Date field is shown, and only those records in which the OrderDate is after 2/1/98.

REVIEW: You can press Ctrl + > to switch to Datasheet View and then press Ctrl + < to return to Design View.

9. Click the Save button. The Save As dialog box opens.

10. Key **qryHistorySales** as the name and press Enter.

EXERCISE 3-21 **Modify a Query**

Having created a query either though the wizard or Design View, you can modify the field list, field order, or criteria for the query. You can also add advanced criteria such as AND/OR conditions.

1. Click the View button 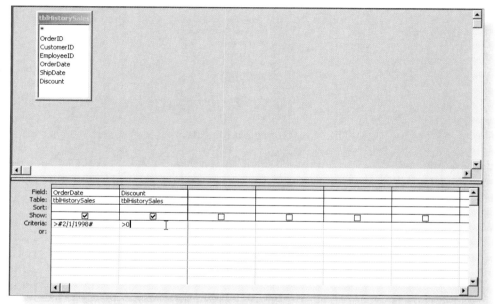 to return to the design grid.

2. Double-click the Discount field to add it to the design grid.

3. Click on the same Criteria row for the Discount field. Key **>0** This is an AND condition; the criteria are entered on the same row.

FIGURE 3-23
An AND condition in the Query Design window uses the same row

4. Click the View button 🔲. Both fields are shown, and the records have an OrderDate after 2/1/98 and a discount.

5. Click the View button 🔳. Choose **E**dit, and then choose Clear **G**rid.

6. Double-click the OrderID field and the CustomerID field in the field list to add them to the design grid.

7. For the CustomerID field, click the Criteria row and key **1**

8. Click the View button 🔲. This criteria shows all orders from Customer 1.

9. Return to the design grid.

10. Click the first **or** row for the CustomerID field and key **3**. (See Figure 3-24 on the next page.)

11. Click the View button 🔲. The criteria shows all orders from either Customer 1 or 3.

FIGURE 3-24
OR conditions
in a query use
different rows

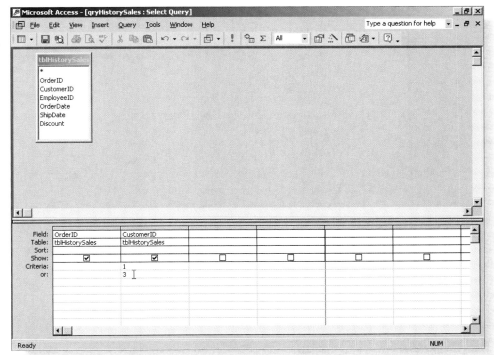

12. Close and save the query.

13. Compact and repair the database; then close it.

USING HELP

A special type of Help called "What's This?" is available for toolbar buttons and many options in a dialog box. When you use "What's This?" the mouse pointer changes to a question mark. You can then point at a button or command name and click to display a ScreenTip. You can also use the Answer Wizard, similar to the Office Assistant, from the Microsoft Access Help window.

Use What's This? and the Answer Wizard:

1. Open tblEmployees in *[your initials]***CC-03**.

2. Choose **Help**, and then choose **What's This?**

3. Point at the Filter By Selection button and click. A ScreenTip opens with a description of the button.

4. To print the ScreenTip, point at it and click the right mouse button. Choose **Print Topic** from the shortcut menu. (Click **Cancel** if you do not want to print the topic.)

5. Click the ScreenTip to close it.

6. Click the What's This? button .

7. Click the <u>F</u>ile menu and choose Page Set<u>u</u>p. A description of the Page Setup feature appears.

8. Click the ScreenTip to remove it.

9. Click the View button 🔽. Press `Shift` + `F1` to start the What's This? Help feature.

10. Point at the Primary Key button 🔑 and click. Read the description of "Primary Key" and then click the ScreenTip to close it.

11. Close the table.

12. Choose <u>H</u>elp and then choose Microsoft Access <u>H</u>elp. If the Office Assistant starts, turn it off.

13. Click the Answer Wizard tab. Triple-click in the <u>W</u>hat would you like to do? text box.

14. Key **sort records** and press `Enter`.

FIGURE 3-25
Using the
Answer Wizard

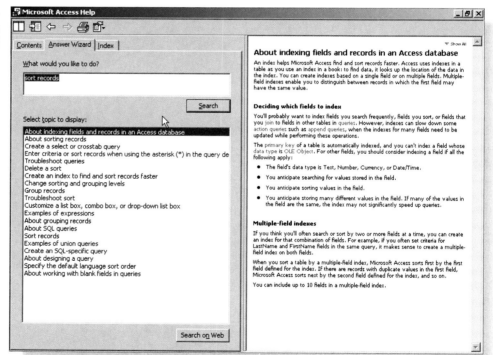

15. Click Delete a sort in the Select a <u>t</u>opic to display list box. In the right pane, click <u>Delete a sort order in Form view or Datasheet view</u>. Read the Help window.

16. Triple-click in the <u>W</u>hat would you like to do? text box.

17. Key **filters and queries** and press [Enter].

18. Click About using criteria to retrieve certain records**.**

19. Click <u>Combining criteria with the And or the Or operator</u> and read all subtopics.

20. Close the Help windows when you have finished.

LESSON 3 Summary

➤ The <u>F</u>ind command helps locate specific records by searching up and down a recordset.

➤ You can fine-tune searches by matching case and by searching for parts of a field.

➤ The asterisk (*) wildcard represents any number of characters in a search. The question mark (?) wildcard represents a single character in a search.

➤ The <u>R</u>eplace command matches text and replaces it with other text. The Replace All command replaces text without prompting the user.

➤ QuickSorts provide easy ways to sort a recordset by a single field in Datasheet View. QuickSorts can sort a recordset by several adjacent fields in Datasheet View.

➤ You can sort queries in Design View.

➤ You can use Filter By Selection to filter by selected text in a field. You can combine Filter By Selections.

➤ You save filters as a table property.

➤ A Filter By Form is more flexible than a Filter By Selection.

➤ You can apply wildcards and Is Null criteria to filters.

➤ The Filter By Input and Filter Excluding Selection provide flexible methods of creating recordsets.

➤ You can use several fields and sophisticated expressions in Advanced Filters and Sorts.

➤ You can use AND conditions and OR conditions in a Filter By Form.

➤ You can use AND conditions and OR conditions in Advanced Filters.

➤ The Query Wizard creates simple queries.

➤ You can create and modify queries by using Design View.

LESSON 3 Command Summary

FEATURE	BUTTON	MENU	KEYBOARD	SPEECH
Apply Filter	▽	Records, Apply Filter/Sort		✓
Display List			F4	
Filter By Selection	▽⁄	Records, Filter, Filter By Selection		✓
Filter By Form	▽▤	Records, Filter, Filter By Form		✓
Filter Excluding Selection		Records, Filter, Filter Excluding Selection		✓
Find	🔍	Edit, Find	Ctrl + F	✓
Next Window			Ctrl + F6	
Remove Filter	▽	Records, Remove Filter/Sort		✓
Replace	🔍	Edit, Replace	Ctrl + H	✓
Select Field			F2	
Sort, Ascending	A↓Z	Records, Sort, Ascending		✓
Sort, Descending	Z↓A	Records, Sort, Descending		✓
What's This Help	▶?	Help, What's This?	Shift + F1	✓
Zoom Window		View, Properties	Shift + F2	✓

Concepts Review

TRUE/FALSE QUESTIONS

Each of the following statements is either true or false. Indicate your choice by circling T or F.

T F **1.** The results of a Filter By Form created in a table are displayed in a form.

T F **2.** The keyboard command to find text is Ctrl + H .

T F **3.** You can use filters or queries to apply multiple criteria or conditions.

T F **4.** The asterisk (*) wildcard finds exact matches for a single character anywhere in the field.

T F **5.** To narrow your search, you can use the **Match Case** option to find words with the same capitalization.

T F **6.** When using the **Sort** command to sort multiple columns in Datasheet View, the columns must be next to each other.

T F **7.** In a query, OR conditions are keyed on separate rows.

T F **8.** A query can be sorted in Datasheet View or Design View.

SHORT ANSWER QUESTIONS

Write the correct answer in the space provided.

1. Why might you need to move the Find and Replace dialog box?

_____

2. What command updates all occurrences of data without confirmation?

_____

3. What word describes a sort from lowest to highest number or from A to Z?

_____

4. How do you add fields to the design grid in the Filter window or Query Design window?

_____

5. What is a "dynaset"?

_____

6. What criteria is used to find empty records in an OLE field?

_____

7. What wildcard character can you use to find a name when you remember only its first three characters?

_____

8. What Search option do you select when you want to search an entire table?

_____

CRITICAL THINKING

Answer these questions on a separate page. There are no right or wrong answers. Support your answers with examples from your own experience, if possible.

1. The Replace All option can create problems if you haven't thought through a specific Replace All operation. Describe what types of problems or issues might occur and discuss precautions you might take when using Replace All.

2. Filters and queries show only the records that meet your conditions. Give some examples of when and why you might use filters or queries for different tables.

Skills Review

EXERCISE 3-22

Find and replace specific text and use wildcards. Sort records.

1. Copy **CC-E-03** and rename it *[your initials]*CC-E-03. Make certain it is not a Read-only copy.

 REVIEW: If you need help copying and renaming the database, refer to the beginning of Lesson 2.

2. Use Match: Any Part of Field and Search Fields As Formatted to find a record by following these steps:
   a. Open tblEmployeeDates and click in the Date of Birth field.
   b. From the Edit menu, choose Find. Make sure Date of Birth is selected in the Look In list box.
   c. Key **apr** in the Find What text box. Choose Any Part of Field in the Match list box. Also, click the Match Case and Search Fields As Formatted to deselect them.

    d. Click Find Next. Access searches the records without finding a match. Click OK.

    e. Click to select Search Fields As Formatted to search the formatted dates. Click Find Next.

    f. Continue clicking Find Next. How many employees have birthdays in April?

 NOTE: When you are asked a question in this exercise, write your answers on a piece of paper to hand in. Include your name, class information, and date.

    g. Click OK when Access finishes searching the table. Close the Find and Replace dialog box and the table.

3. Use wildcards to find a record by following these steps:

    a. Open tblPayroll. Click in the SS# field.

    b. Choose Edit and then choose Find.

    c. Key ***9052** in the Find What text box. Choose Any Part of Field from the Match list box. Choose All from the Search list box. Deselect Search Fields As Formatted.

    d. Click Find Next. Is this employee salaried or hourly? Write your answer on your answer sheet.

    e. Key ***-22-*** in the Find What text box. Click Find Next.

    f. Continue clicking Find Next. How many employees have "22" in the middle of their social security numbers? Write your answer on your answer sheet.

    g. Click OK when Access finishes searching the table.

    h. Click in the Hourly field in the table.

    i. Edit the Find What text box by keying **$1#.##**. From the Match list box, choose the Whole Field option. Click Search Fields As Formatted to select it.

    j. Click Find Next. Continue clicking Find Next. How many employees make $10 or more an hour? Write your answer on your answer sheet. Click OK when Access finishes searching.

    k. Close the Find and Replace dialog box and close tblPayroll.

4. Use Find Next to replace data by following these steps:

    a. Open tblTimeCards. Click in the Regular field of the first record.

    b. Choose Edit and then choose Find. Click the Replace tab.

    c. Key **30** in the Find What text box. Press Tab and key **35** in the Replace With text box.

    d. From the Match list box, choose Whole Field. From the Search list box, choose Down.

    e. Click Find Next to start the search.

    f. Click Replace to replace the first occurrence and to find the next occurrence.

   g. Click Find Next to skip this occurrence and find the next one.

   h. Click Replace to replace the third occurrence. Continue clicking Replace. Click OK when Access can't find the text you specified.

   i. Close the Find and Replace dialog box and tblTimeCards.

5. Use multiple fields to sort by following these steps:

   a. Open tblSalesReps.

   b. Point at the Rate field name and click when the pointer changes to a down-pointing arrow. Point at the field name. Click and drag the column to the right of the Salary field.

   c. Press and hold Shift, point to the Salary field name, and click when the pointer changes to a down-pointing arrow.

    d. Click the Sort Ascending button.

   e. Close tblSalesReps and do not save the changes.

EXERCISE 3-23

Use filters to display records.

1. Use Filter By Selection by following these steps:

    a. Click Queries on the Objects bar and open qryEmployeeDates.

   b. Select "Feb" anywhere in the Date of Birth field.

   c. Click the Filter By Selection button. How many employees have birthdays in February?

> **NOTE:** When you are asked a question in this exercise, write your answers on a piece of paper to hand in. Include your name, class information, and date.

    d. Click the Remove Filter button.

2. Use Filter By Form by following these steps:

   a. Click the Filter By Form button.

   b. Click in the Date of Birth field and display the list. Choose 9/7/51.

   c. Click the Apply Filter button.

   d. Click the Filter By Form button.

    e. Click the Clear Grid button.

   f. Click in the Date of Birth field and key **>1/1/65**

   g. Click the Apply Filter button. How many employees were born after January 1, 1965? Write your answer on your answer sheet.

   h. Click in the Date of Birth field and click the Sort Ascending button.

    i. Click the Remove Filter button. Close qryEmployeeDates and do not save the design changes.

3. Use Filter By Input by following these steps:

   a. Open tblSalesReps. Right-click in the Region field.

   b. In the Filter For text box, key **west** and then press Enter.

c. Click the Remove Filter button .
    d. Right-click in the Rate field.

    TIP: You must key the decimal equivalent for percentages.

    e. In the **Filter For** text box, key **.05** and then press ⌷Enter⌷.
    f. Click the Remove Filter button 🔽.
    g. Close the table and do not save the changes.

4. Use Filter Excluding Selection by following these steps:
    a. Open tblTimeCards.
    b. Select 1/8/99 in any record. Point at the selection and right-click.
    c. Click Filter E**x**cluding Selection.

    d. Click the Remove Filter button 🔽.
    e. Select $8.25 in any record. Point at the selection and right-click. Click Filter E**x**cluding Selection.
    f. Click the Remove Filter button 🔽.
    g. Close the table and do not save the changes.

EXERCISE 3-24

Create advanced filters with AND/OR conditions.

1. Use the Filter window by following these steps:
    a. Open tblTimeCards.
    b. Choose **R**ecords and then choose **F**ilter. Click **A**dvanced Filter/Sort and maximize the window.
    c. Place the pointer on the border between the two panes and make the top pane taller. Make the Field Name list box taller.
    d. Double-click the OT Hours field in the Field Name list box.
    e. Click in the **Criteria** row for the OTHours field and key **>0**

    f. Click the Apply Filter button 🔽. These are the employees who have worked overtime.
    g. Click the Remove Filter button 🔽.

2. Create an AND condition by following these steps:
    a. Press ⌷Ctrl⌷ + ⌷F6⌷ to return to the **A**dvanced Filter/Sort grid.
    b. Double-click the WeekEnding field in the Field Name list box to add it to the grid.
    c. Click in the **Criteria** row for the WeekEnding field and key **1/8/99**

    d. Click the Apply Filter button 🔽. These are the employees who have worked overtime during the week ending 1/8/99. Why is this an AND condition?

NOTE: When you are asked a question in this exercise, write your answers on a piece of paper to hand in. Include your name, class information, and date.

     e. Click the Remove Filter button 🔽.

3. Create an OR condition by following these steps:

    a. Press [Ctrl] + [F6].

    b. Click the column selector for the WeekEnding field.

    c. Press [Delete]. The field is deleted from the design grid.

    d. Select and delete the OTHours field.

    e. Double-click the HourlyRate field to add it to the grid.

    f. Click in the Criteria row for the HourlyRate field and key **8.5**

 TIP: For currency amounts, you need to key only the numbers (and some-times a decimal point). Key the decimal point when there are numbers other than zero to its right.

    g. Click the Apply Filter button 🔽.

    h. Press [Ctrl] + [F6].

    i. Click in the OR criteria row directly below the 8.5. Key **12**

    j. Click the Apply Filter button 🔽. The employees who earn either $8.50 or $12 are listed.

    k. Close the table and do not save the changes.

EXERCISE 3-25

Build a query with the Query Wizard. Build a query by using Design View. Modify a query.

1. Build and save a query with the Query Wizard by following these steps:

    a. Click the Queries button. Double-click Create query by using wizard.

    b. From the <u>T</u>ables/Queries drop-down list box, select Table: tblTimeCards.

    c. Double-click on SocialSecurityNumber, WeekEnding, and OTHours.

    d. Click <u>N</u>ext twice. Name the query **qryOTHours***[your last name]*.

    e. Click <u>F</u>inish. Display the query in Datasheet View.

    f. Close qryOTHours*[your last name]*.

2. Build and save a query in Design View by following these steps:

    a. Click tblTimeCards but do not open it.

     b. Click the drop-down arrow with the New Object button 📇. Choose Query.

    c. Choose Design View and click OK.

    d. Size the top pane and the Field Name list box so you see all the field names.

    e. Double-click the SocialSecurityNumber field in the Field Name list box.

f. Double-click WeekEnding and OTHours to add them to the design grid.

  g. Click the View button . Return to Design View.

  h. Click the **Criteria** row for the OTHours column. Key **>0**

  i. Click the View button .

  j. Click the Save button 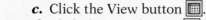. Key **qryTimeCards*[your last name]*** and press Enter .

 3. Modify a query by following these steps:

  a. Click the View button .

  b. Click the **Criteria** row for the WeekEnding column. Key **1/8/99**

  c. Click the View button .

  d. Click the Save button .

  e. Close **qryTimeCards*[your last name]***

  f. Click <u>T</u>ools and choose <u>D</u>atabase Utilities. Click <u>C</u>ompact and Repair Database and then close the database.

Lesson Applications

EXERCISE 3-26

Sort records. Find and replace data in a table.

1. Start Access and open the file *[your initials]*CC-03. Open tblKitContents.

    TIP: Check the options in the Replace dialog box for each activity.

2. Sort the records by Kit Number in descending order.
3. Click in the Kit Number field.
4. Find all occurrences of "pig" within the Kit Number field. Match any part of the word without using a case-sensitive search.
5. Use the Replace command to replace all occurrences of "Ted" with "Bear." Set the Match option to Any Part of Field.
6. Close tblKitContents and do not save the changes.
7. Open tblStuffedAnimals. It includes data related to tblKitContents.
8. Sort by Kit Number in descending order and then use the Replace command to change all occurrences of "Ted" to "Bear."
9. Key your initials in uppercase letters after "Zebra" in the first record.
10. Print the table using landscape orientation.
11. Close the tblStuffedAnimals table and do not save the changes.

     REVIEW: Data changes are saved automatically. The design changes were the sort orders.

EXERCISE 3-27

Use filters to display records.

1. Open tblHistoryLineItems.
2. Use Filter By Selection to show all the items for Order 20006. How many product types were ordered? How many total products were ordered? Remove the filter.

    NOTE: When you are asked a question in this exercise, write your answers on a piece of paper to hand in. Include your name, class information, and date.

3. Use Filter By Selection to show all the orders that included ProductID F002. How many of this product were sold? Write your answer on your answer sheet. Remove the filter. Notice how many records are in this table.

4. Use Filter Excluding Selection to show orders that did not include ProductID T005. How many orders did not include this item? Write your answer on your answer sheet. Remove the filter.

5. Close tblHistoryLineItems and do not save the changes.

6. Open frmEmployeeInformation.

7. Right-click in the Last Name field and use Filter For to find Maria Floria's record. Remove the filter.

8. How many records are there? Write your answer on your answer sheet.

9. Create a Filter By Form and clear the grid. Add criteria to find records in which the picture field has a picture. How many records do not have a picture? Write your answer on your answer sheet.

10. Remove the filter and close the form.

EXERCISE 3-28

Use AND and OR conditions in a Filter By Form. Use an Advanced Filter.

1. Open tblKitContents.

2. Use a Filter By Form to find the kits from Suppliers BB-02 or DD-04. How many kits fit the criteria? Remove the filter.

NOTE: When you are asked a question in this exercise, write your answers on a piece of paper to hand in. Include your name, class information, and date.

3. Use a Filter By Form and clear the grid. Find records from Supplier AA-01 that cost more than $5. The cost criteria is >5 with no dollar sign or decimal point. How many kits fit the criteria? Write your answer on your answer sheet.

REVIEW: OR conditions are entered on separate forms. AND conditions are entered on the same form.

4. Close tblKitContents and do not save the changes.

5. Open qryCustomers and create and apply an Advanced Filter. First use the City field to find customers in Chattanooga. Then add the Billing Address field to the filter design so you can find customers in Chattanooga with the word "Dobson" in the address.

TIP: Use wildcards in front of and behind the search string to find matching addresses.

6. Change the Contact name to *[your first and last name]*.

7. Print the results of the filter; use Landscape orientation.

8. Close the query and do not save changes.

EXERCISE 3-29 *Challenge Yourself*

Build a query.

1. Choose tblKitSuppliers and use the New Object button 🔲 to build a query in Design View.

2. Size the panes in the Query Design window.

3. Add the SupplierID, SupplierName, and PhoneNumber fields to the design grid.

4. Add criteria in the SupplierName field to find companies that have any form of the word "fabric" in their names.

5. Save the query as **qrySuppliers***[your last name]*.

6. Print the query.

7. Compact the database and exit Access.

On Your Own

In these exercises you work on your own, as you would in a real-life work environment. Use the skills you've learned to accomplish the task—and be creative.

EXERCISE 3-30
Review the Web sites you located in Exercises 2-28 and 2-29 of the companies that sell products of interest to members of the club you formed. Determine which companies allow products to be sorted or displayed by different conditions. On a sheet of paper, write down the fields that can be sorted or selected. Continue to the next exercise.

EXERCISE 3-31
For one of the Web sites, print three lists of products sorted or filtered by various methods. Write a brief description of the sort or filter being applied on each of the three printouts. Continue to the next exercise.

EXERCISE 3-32

Refer to the form you created in Exercise 2-30. Write down the fields that may be used to sort or filter the information displayed on the form. Sketch two new forms based on your sorting and filtering parameters. Submit your work for Exercises 3-30 through 3-32 to your instructor.

Unit 1 Applications

UNIT APPLICATION 1-1

Edit and sort records in a table. Change the font and row height. Print a table. Add and delete records in a form. Print a single form. Duplicate text in a table.

1. Copy the file **CC-U01** and rename it *[your initials]***CC-U01**. Open *[your initials]***CC-U01**.

2. Open tblEmployees as a maximized window. Size all the columns so they are wide enough to show the longest text for each field.

3. Check the record order and make certain the table is sorted by Employee ID. Freeze the Employee ID and Last Name fields.

4. Make the changes shown in Figure U1-1. (Not all the columns or rows of the table are shown in the figure.)

FIGURE U1-1

Emp ID	Last Name	First Name	Job Code	Address	Contact Name
5	Floria	Maria	~~MF03~~ MF05	5260 Holly Road	Chet Floria
6	Abdullah	Jamel	MF05	225 ~~South~~ Sycamore Road	Martha Abdullah
7	Dyer	~~Cassandra~~ Cassie	OF07	162 North Summit Avenue	Jane Anderson
8	Wilson	Zipporah	MF02	105 North ~~Sycamore~~ Oak Street	Estella Williams
9	Thomas-Smith	Louise	OF05	1332 Shamrock Street	James ~~Thomas~~ Smith

5. Unfreeze the columns.

6. Change the font size to **9** and resize the columns so they are wide enough to show the longest text for each field in the new font.

    TIP: Select several or all columns at once and choose F̲ormat, C̲olumn W̲idth, Best Fit.

7. Print the table in Landscape orientation. Write your name on the bottom of each sheet.

8. Close tblEmployees without saving the layout changes.

9. Open tblStuffedAnimals and sort by Product ID in descending order.

10. Make the changes shown in Figure U1-2 on the next page. (Not all the columns or rows of the table are shown in the figure.)

FIGURE U1-2

Product ID	Animal Name	List Price	Kit Number	Current Inventory
T005	~~Sleepy~~ Bear *(Night Time)*	~~$14.50~~ 12.75	Bear005	~~250~~ 225
T004	Santa Bear	$13.~~00~~ .75	Bear004	150
T003	*(Mr.)* Theodore Bear	$14.50	Bear003	275

11. Make the row height slightly taller and change the font to Times New Roman 10 point.

12. Size the fields so you can see all the data and so the records fit on one page in Portrait orientation. Print the table in Portrait orientation.

13. Close the table without saving the changes.

14. Open frmEmployeeInformation.

15. Find and delete Raymond Davidson's record.

16. Add the following new record:

Last Name:	**Jacobs-[your last name]**
First Name:	**Cynthia**
Employee ID:	**33**
Address:	**152 Grandin Road**
City:	**Charlotte**
State:	**NC**
Postal Code:	**28208-4679**
SS#:	**888-72-4852**
Home Phone:	**(704) 555-2266**
Job Code:	**MF04**
Contact Name:	**Dorothy Jacobs**
Emergency Phone:	**(704) 555-2266**

17. Select and print only this record in Portrait orientation.

18. Close frmEmployeeInformation.

19. Open tblEmployees.

20. Add a record for yourself as Employee 34. Duplicate all the fields from the previous record, except your name, your social security number, and the Emergency Contact Name. Key your first and last name. Key **888-99-0000** as your social security number. Key the name of your mother, father, or friend as the Emergency Contact.

21. Close tblEmployees. Open frmEmployeeInformation as a maximized window.

22. Select and print only the employee record that you added for yourself.

23. Close the table.

UNIT APPLICATION 1-2

Copy and paste text in a table. Copy and paste a picture in a table. Delete and insert a picture in a form. Find and replace text. Use filters and wildcards.

1. Open tblStuffedAnimals as a maximized window.

2. Add the following new record, leaving fields blank as shown.

Product ID:	**F006**
Animal Name:	*Leave blank.*
Product Group:	**F**
List Price:	*Leave blank.*
Kit Number:	**Shp001**
Current Inventory:	**200**
Illustration:	*Leave blank.*

3. Copy and paste the Animal Name and List Price fields from the Linda Lamb record to the new record. Copy and paste the bitmap image from the Illustration field of the Gary Gecko record to the new record.

4. Change the Animal Name to **Linda Lizard.**

5. Close the table.

6. Open frmStuffedAnimals.

7. Find the record for Linda Lizard. Delete the picture and insert **Lam001** from the Images folder.

8. Change the Animal Name to **Sherry Sheep**. Add your initials after the animal name. Print only the form for the new record.

9. Close the form.

10. Open tblKitSuppliers and tblKitContents. Tile the tables horizontally.

11. In tblKitSuppliers, edit Robinson Mills, Inc. to show **GG-07** as the Supplier ID.

12. In tblKitContents, replace all occurrences of "DD-04" with **GG-07.**

 TIP: Always verify the options in the Find and Replace dialog box.

13. In tblKitContents, key **GG-07** in a Filter by Form to list all Kit Numbers from Robinson Mills, Inc.

14. Print the filter results in Portrait orientation.

15. Close both tables without saving design changes.

 TIP: Clear the grid before starting a new filter.

16. Open frmEmployeeInformation as a maximized window.

17. Use a wildcard in a Filter By Form to find employees with any "OF" job code. How many employees are in this category?

 NOTE: When you are asked a question in this application, write your answer on a piece of paper to hand in. Include your name, class information, and date.

18. Create another Filter By Form to find all employees in postal codes that start with 28208. How many employees live in this postal code? Write your answer on your answer sheet.

19. Create a Filter by Input to find all employees with an "MF" job code.

20. From the filter results, create a Filter Excluding Selection to find all employees except those in job code MF05. How many employees have an "MF" job code other than MF05? Write your answer on your answer sheet.

21. Close the form.

UNIT APPLICATION 1-3

Create an advanced filter. Use AND/OR criteria.

1. Open tblCustomers as a maximized window.

2. Create an advanced filter/sort. Add the Company Name and Tax Status fields to the design grid. Sort by the company name in ascending order.

3. Enter criteria to find those customers who are tax exempt. This is a Yes/No field, and your criteria is either "yes" or "no," depending on what you are looking for. How many customers meet this criteria?

 NOTE: When you are asked a question in this application, write your answer on a piece of paper to hand in. Include your name, class information, and date.

4. Create another advanced filter/sort.

 TIP: Press Ctrl + F6 to return to the Filter window.

5. Add the Company Name and City fields to the grid and sort by the name in ascending order.

6. Add critieria to find customers who are in Chattanooga or Durham. How many customers meet this criteria? Write your answer on your answer sheet.

7. Create another advanced filter that finds Charlotte customers who are tax exempt. Who are they? Write your answer on your answer sheet.

8. Close the table without saving the changes.

9. Open tblHistorySales as a maximized window.

10. Create a new query named **qrySalesFirstHalf98-[your initials]** with the fields CustomerID and OrderDate.

11. Modify the query to display the records for orders that occurred in the first six months of 1998.

12. Sort the records in ascending order by CustomerID. Print the dynaset.

13. Create another query named **qrySalesLastHalf98-[your initials]** for sales that occurred in the last six months of 1998.

14. Sort the records in ascending order by OrderDate. Print the dynaset.

15. Close the query and the table.

UNIT APPLICATION 1-4 *Using the Internet*

Add data to a table and print it. Add records to a form and print it.

1. Using the search engine of your choice, locate a company that sells children's toys. Find the company name, address, phone number, and fax number.

2. Open tblKitSuppliers as a maximized window.

3. Key the company information. Use your name for the contact name. Use the Supplier ID **HH-08** and the Supplier #7.

4. Print the table in Landscape orientation. At the bottom of the page, write the Web address (URL) of the company you located.

5. Using the search engine of your choice, locate a person who lives in a different state or who has a last name similar to yours.

6. Open frmEmployeeInformation. Key the information you found on the Web as the information for the new employee. Assign the employee number **99** and the social security number **555-99-1212**

7. Add your name as the contact name. Use the phone number **(101) 555-1212**

8. Print only this form in Landscape orientation.

9. Close the database and compact it.

Building a Database

4

Creating Databases and Tables

OBJECTIVES

MOUS
ACTIVITIES
In this lesson:
Ac2002 **1-1**
Ac2002 **2-1**
Ac2002 **2-4**
Ac2002 **5-1**
Ac2002 **8-1**

See Appendix E.

After completing this lesson, you will be able to:

1. **Create a new database.**
2. **Create a table by using the Table Wizard.**
3. **Edit field properties.**
4. **Insert and delete fields.**
5. **Create a table in Datasheet View.**
6. **Import data.**

 Estimated Time: 1½ hours

In the previous unit, you worked with data in tables, with queries, and with forms in an existing database. You learned how to navigate through records, how to edit data, and how to add records. In this lesson, you learn how to create a new database. Then you learn how to add tables to a database by using:

- The Table Wizard
- Design View
- Datasheet View
- Import

Creating a New Database

In the previous lessons, you worked with two existing databases that included objects and data. Most people work with existing databases rather than creating totally new ones. However, on some occasions you might need to create a new database.

There are two methods for creating databases. One method develops a structure containing major objects (tables, queries, forms, or reports), but no data. The other method creates a blank database without any objects or data.

Prior to creating a new database, you should analyze the needs of the people who will use it. You should plan for the type of data that will be entered, stored, and displayed. Most database designers have had extensive prior experience working with data and databases.

EXERCISE 4-1 Create a Database by Using the Database Wizard

Access provides many database templates that use a wizard to step you through the creation of a new database. A *database template* is a wizard that creates a functional database structure based on user selections. Using the wizard is only valuable when there is a template that closely matches your needs. Each template has a predefined list of fields from which you must select.

When you use a Database Wizard, a main switchboard is created. A *main switchboard* is a form that helps a user navigate around a database. When the database is launched, the main switchboard automatically opens. You then can use the main switchboard to navigate within the database.

 NOTE: The databases you create and modify in this course relate to the Case Study (see pages 1–8) about Carolina Critters, a fictional company that manufactures stuffed animals.

1. Click the Start button on the Windows taskbar and point to Programs.

2. Click Microsoft Access 2002. (You might have to point first to a program group such as Microsoft Office.) Access loads.

3. After Access is loaded, click the New button . The New File Task Pane appears on the right side of the screen. (See Figure 4-1 on the next page.)

4. In the **New from template** section, click General Templates.

5. Click the **Databases** tab.

6. Choose the Asset Tracking wizard and click **OK**.

7. The File New Database dialog box asks you to name the new database and indicate where to save it. The dialog box shows a default name based on the wizard you specified.

FIGURE 4-1
New File Task Pane

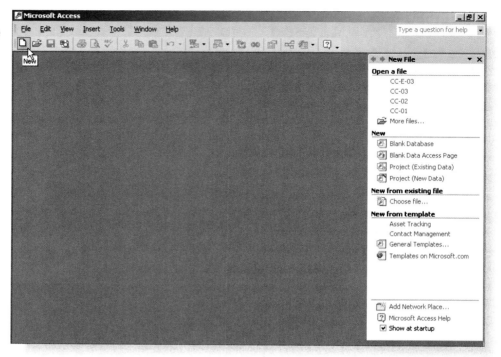

8. Save the new database to your desktop. Click <u>C</u>reate to use the default file name, **Asset Tracking1**.

 NOTE: At the end of this exercise, you will delete this database. It is used only to demonstrate the Database Wizard. You will not need to keep a copy of the file.

9. The first dialog box explains what this database will store. Click <u>N</u>ext.

10. This dialog box lists the tables on the left and the fields for each table on the right. Click each table name on the left and review the field names. A check mark next to the field name indicates that the field will be included in the new database. Access shows optional field names in italic. You can see an optional Home Phone field in the Information about employees table.

11. Click the check box to select the Home Phone field. (See Figure 4-2 on the next page.)

12. Click <u>N</u>ext. In the next dialog box, you select the style to be used for all forms. Choose SandStone and click <u>N</u>ext.

13. Next you select the report style. Choose Formal and click <u>N</u>ext.

14. Title this database **Asset Control** and click <u>F</u>inish. After the database is built, the title appears on the Main Switchboard of the **Asset Tracking1** database. (See Figure 4-3 on the next page.)

FIGURE 4-2
Selecting fields to include in the new database

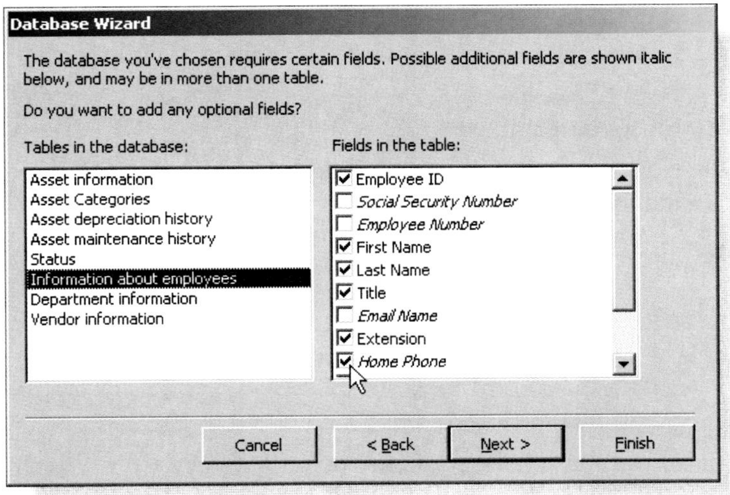

FIGURE 4-3
Main Switchboard and database window

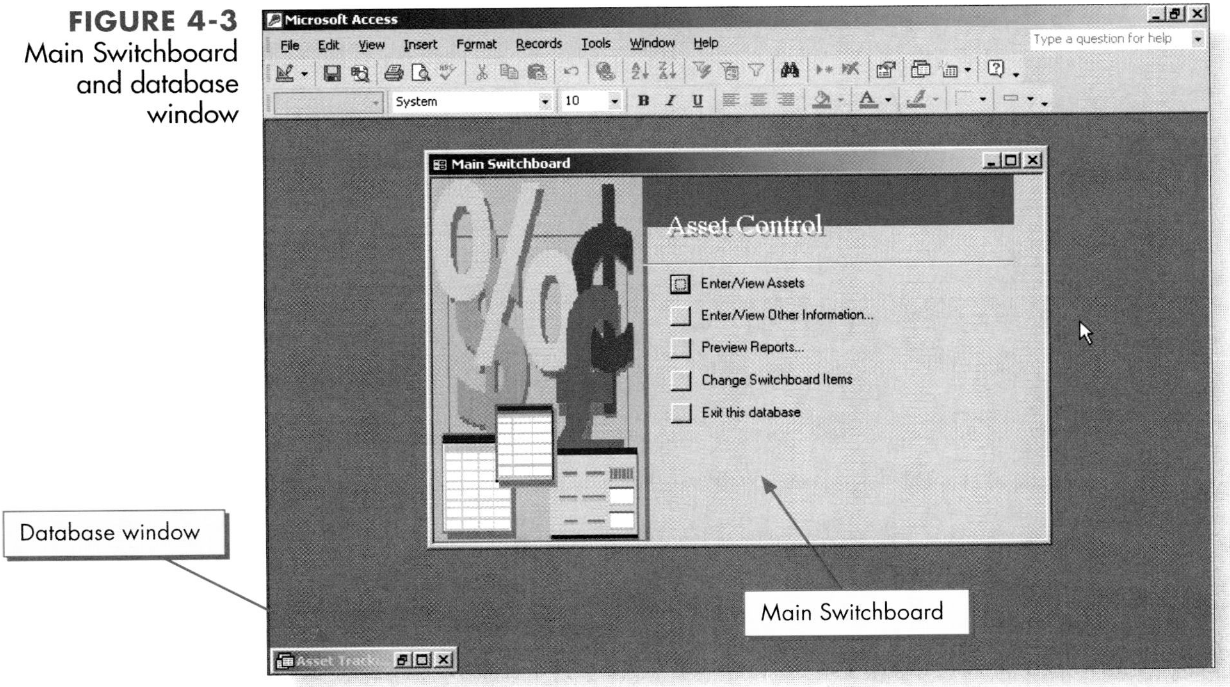

NOTE: Whenever the Main Switchboard is open, the database window is minimized.

15. Close the Main Switchboard Form.

16. Maximize the database window located in the lower left corner of the screen.

17. Notice that the Database Wizard created seven tables, eleven forms, and five reports. However, if you open a table, you will see that it does not contain any data.

18. Close the database.

19. Now that you have seen how the wizard works, delete the Asset Tracking1 database from your desktop.

EXERCISE **4-2** **Create a Blank Database**

If you cannot find a database template to meet your needs, you must create a blank database from scratch. You only will be required to name the database and specify a location in which to save it. After you have saved the blank database, you must create new tables so you can add data. You will be able to add other major objects such as queries, reports, and forms at a later time.

1. Click the **New** button . The New File Task Pane appears on the right side of the screen.

2. In the **New** section, click Blank Database.

3. The File New Database dialog box asks you to name the new database and indicate where it should be saved. It shows a default file name of **db1**.

4. Verify your Save in location.

> **REVIEW:** Your instructor will tell you where to save the database. In this course, do not work on a database from a floppy drive.

5. Triple-click **db1** to select it. Key *[your first and last name]* (do not include a space between your names) as the File name.

6. Click **C**reate. A blank database window opens with no objects. Notice the name of the database in the title bar and its file format.

Creating Tables by Using a Wizard

The Table Wizard is a quick and easy way to produce tables containing commonly used fields. In the Table Wizard, you select the type of table (such as customer lists, employee lists, invoices sent, or new projects). The Table Wizard then provides a list of suggested fields. After selecting the fields and naming the table, you can start adding records. Tables created by using the wizard provide a structure you can later modify.

EXERCISE **4-3** **Choose Fields in the Table Wizard**

The Table Wizard displays predefined table lists in two groups, Personal and Business. Each table has a predefined list of fields. From these lists you select which fields will be used and the order in which they will appear in the new table. After you have finished using the Wizard, you can change the field names and the order in which they appear in the table.

1. With your database window open, click the **Tables** button. Click the **New** command button. The **New Table** dialog box opens.

FIGURE 4-4
New Table
dialog box

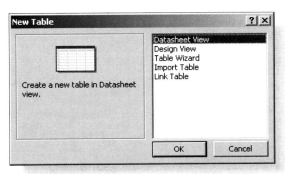

2. Click Table Wizard and OK. The first dialog box of the Table Wizard opens, with sample tables on the left and related sample fields in the middle. The sample tables relate to either business or personal activities.

3. Above the list of Sample Tables, click the Business option button.

4. In the Sample Tables list, select Customers.

FIGURE 4-5
Table Wizard
dialog box

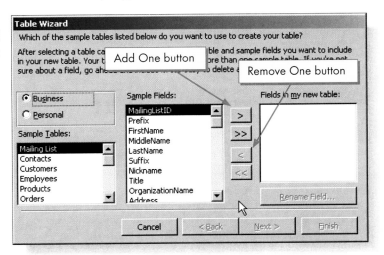

NOTE: The Sample Tables and Sample Fields lists are not in alphabetical order. The field names follow the Leszynski Naming Conventions.

5. Select the CustomerID field and click the Add One button ⟩ . The CustomerID field is added to the Fields in my new table list.

REVIEW: If you add a sample field to your field list by mistake, select the name and move it back to the Sample Fields list by clicking the Remove One button < .

6. Add the following sample fields to the **Fields in my new table** list by double-clicking the field in the **Sample Field** list. (You can also select the name and click the Add One button > .)

CompanyName
ContactFirstName
BillingAddress
StateOrProvince
PostalCode
ContactTitle
PhoneNumber
FaxNumber

NOTE: You can create a custom table by choosing sample fields from more than one table.

FIGURE 4-6
Table Wizard
dialog box with
added fields

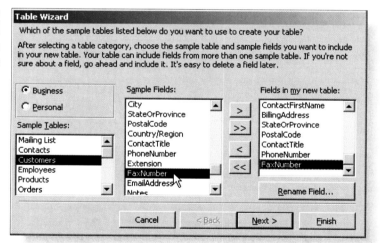

EXERCISE **4-4** **Rename Fields in the Table Wizard**

While in the Table Wizard, you can rename the selected fields to make the names more descriptive of the data. For example, if your company has customers only in the United States, you might wish to rename the field PostalCode to ZIPCode.

TIP: You can rename a field in Table Design View.

1. Select the CompanyName field in your list.

2. Click the <u>R</u>ename Field command button in the Table Wizard dialog box. The Rename field dialog box opens with the field name highlighted.

3. Key **Customer** in the Rename field text box. Click OK. Customer replaces CompanyName in the Fields in <u>m</u>y new table list.

FIGURE 4-7
Renamed field appears in the Fields In My New Table list

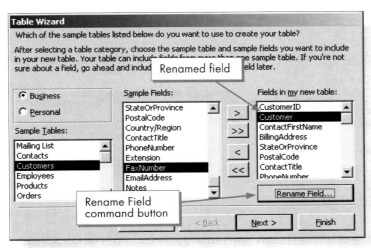

4. Select the ContactFirstName field in your list. Click <u>R</u>ename Field.

5. In the Rename field dialog box, edit the name to **ContactName**. Click OK.

6. Rename StateOrProvince to **State** and click OK.

7. Rename ContactTitle to **EmployeeID** and click OK.

EXERCISE 4-5 Name the Table and Enter Records

When using the wizard to create a table, in addition to selecting the fields for the table, you will be asked to define a primary key. Remember that a primary key is a field containing unique data that is used to identify each record in a table. Many business processes use some form of unique identifier such as a check number, an employee social security number, or a customer number.

1. After renaming the fields, click <u>N</u>ext. The dialog box asks what you want to name your new table. Access enters a default name based on the sample table you selected.

REVIEW: When creating new tables, you should use the Leszynski Naming Conventions. This means tables are preceded by the prefix "tbl" and the first letter of main words are capitalized with no spaces between words.

2. Key **tblCustomers** in the <u>W</u>hat do you want to name your table? text box.

3. Read the paragraph about the primary key. Then select N<u>o</u>, I'll set the primary key.

FIGURE 4-8
Naming the table

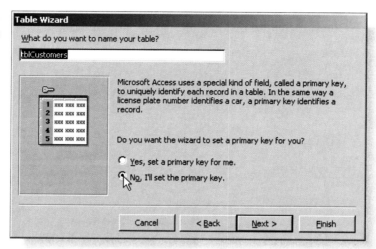

> **NOTE:** When a wizard dialog box has a <u>B</u>ack command button, you can use it to return to the previous dialog box to view or change your choices.

4. Click <u>N</u>ext. CustomerID will hold unique data for each record, making it the primary key. Select Numbers I enter when I <u>a</u>dd new records.

FIGURE 4-9
Setting the primary key

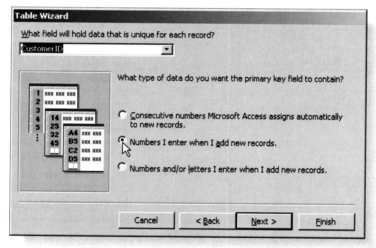

5. Click <u>N</u>ext. Access now has the information it needs to create the table. You have the option to modify the table design, enter data directly into the table, or enter data through a form created by a wizard.

6. Select Enter data directly into the table. Click Finish. The table opens, ready for you to enter data. The columns have a default width so you might not see the complete field names.

7. Maximize the window and add the following three records to the table.

 REVIEW: Use the Tab key to move from one field to another.

Customer ID:	1
Customer:	**Crafts & More**
ContactName:	**Caroline Morgan**
Billing Address:	**22651 45th Avenue**
State:	**WA**
Postal Code:	**98032-2265**
EmployeeID:	**6**
Phone Number:	**(206) 555-1919**
Fax Number:	**(206) 555-1199**

Customer ID:	2
Customer:	**Bears & Such**
ContactName:	**Wayne Fitch**
Billing Address:	**141 Route 1**
State:	**VA**
Postal Code:	**24472-0141**
EmployeeID:	**7**
Phone Number:	**(703) 555-2734**
Fax Number:	**(703) 555-2735**

Customer ID:	3
Customer:	**The Doll and Bear Barn**
ContactName:	**Theodora Alexander**
Billing Address:	**365 Main Street**
State:	**CT**
Postal Code:	**06085-0365**
EmployeeID:	**7**
Phone Number:	**(860) 555-9116**
Fax Number:	**(860) 555-9117**

8. Close the table.

Editing Field Properties

You use Design View to modify the design or structure of a table. Design View shows the following:

- *Field name* describes the information in the field (a column).
- *Data type* identifies the type of information in the field (such as alphabetic or numeric data.)
- *Field description* is optional and further clarifies the purpose of the field.
- *Field properties* are settings that affect how a field looks and acts. Each data type has a specific list of properties that you can change.

NOTE: Spaces in field names are not recommended in the Access' object naming rules and in the Leszynski Naming Conventions. Spaces create additional requirements for advanced features such as macros and VBA modules.

EXERCISE **4-6** **View Table Design**

After creating a table by using the Table Wizard, you should check the table design to determine if you need to modify field properties such as Field Size. In Design View, field names are listed on the top half of the screen. The properties for the selected field are displayed on the bottom half of the screen.

You also might need to modify Captions or add field descriptions to make your table more useful. A *Caption* is a field property that controls the column selector in Datasheet View. The field description for a selected field displays in the status bar of objects such as forms or queries.

 A key icon to the left of the field indicates which field is the primary key. For each selected property, a short Help message appears in the lower right portion of the screen.

TABLE 4-1 Access Data Types

SETTING	TYPE OF DATA
Text	Alphanumeric data. A text field can be up to 255 characters long. Use Text as the Data Type for numbers that aren't used in calculations (addresses, phone numbers).
Memo	Descriptive text such as sentences and paragraphs. Use a memo field for comments and notes that do not fit other Data Types. A memo field cannot be sorted or used in filters. It can store up to 64,000 characters.

continues

TABLE 4-1   Access Data Types   *continued*

SETTING	TYPE OF DATA
Number	Numbers with or without a decimal point. Data in a number field can be used in arithmetic calculations.
Date/Time	Formatted dates or times that can be used in date and time calculations.
Currency	Money values that include the symbol and can be used in arithmetic calculations.
AutoNumber	Consecutive numbers assigned automatically as you add a record. It is also known as a "counter" and often used as the primary key.
Yes/No	Either "Yes" or "No," "True" or "False," or "0" or "−1." Known as a logical field.
OLE Object	Pictures, sound or video clips, or other files created in another application. An OLE field cannot be sorted and is limited in filters.
Hyperlink	Internet site, e-mail address, or file pathname. The data is displayed as hyperlink text. When you click it, Access searches for the Internet site or address or opens the file.

1. Open tblCustomers and maximize the window.

2. Click the View button to switch to Design View. A window with two panes opens. The top pane lists the field names, Data Types, and descriptions. The wizard does not set descriptions for any field. Notice the small key symbol in the row selector next to the CustomerID field, indicating that this field is the primary key. (See Figure 4-10 on the next page.)

3. Press F6. The insertion point moves to the lower pane. The lower pane displays the field properties of the current field. It includes two tabs, **General** and **Lookup**. In the lower right corner of the screen, a Help window displays definitions and hints related to any field property selected on the left.

4. Press F6 again to move the insertion point to the top pane. Click on the field name Customer. The Customer field properties are now listed in the lower pane.

5. Click the PostalCode row in the top pane and press F6. This field has a Caption that shows a space between the words.

6. Click the PhoneNumber row in the top pane. Notice the Caption for this field in the bottom pane.

7. Click the State row. This text field has no Caption and has a Field Size of 20 spaces.

FIGURE 4-10
Customers table in
Design View

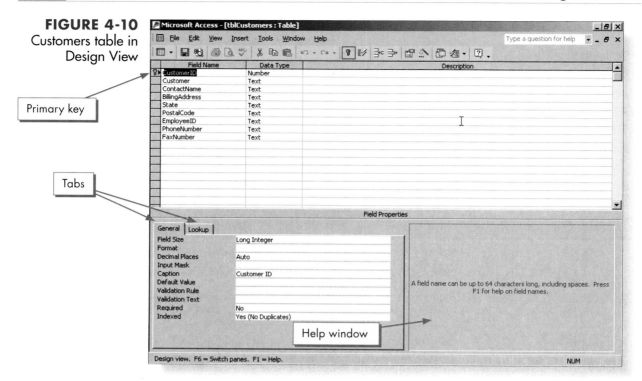

EXERCISE 4-7 **Edit Field Properties**

At this stage you can use Design View to edit the table structure. Changes to the
table design might affect the data already stored in the table. For example, if you
have a long title stored as a text field, reducing the size of the field might cut off
characters from some records.

TABLE 4-2 Text Field Properties

PROPERTY	PURPOSE
Field Size	Sets the size of a text field and can be up to 255 characters. Access uses only the space it needs for the data when the size is larger than the data. Data that does not fit is cut off.
Format	Defines the appearance of data. You can use a Format to force characters to upper- or lowercase, or you can format dates to appear as "May 5, 2002" even though you key "05/05/02."

continues

TABLE 4-2   Text Field Properties   *continued*

PROPERTY	PURPOSE
Input Mask	Displays a model or pattern for entering the data. Examples are the parentheses around an area code or the hyphen in a social security number.
Caption	Sets a label or title for the field other than the field name. The Caption appears as the column title in the table and as the label for the controls in forms and reports.
Default Value	Enters a value for new records. If all employees live in Illinois, you can set "IL" as the Default Value for the State field.
Validation Rule	Expression that specifies criteria or requirements for entering data. The following is an example of a Validation Rule: ">100." This rule would not allow you to enter a number less than 100 in the field.
Validation Text	Text that displays if you violate the Validation Rule. For the rule ">100," you might use the Validation Text "You must enter a value greater than 100."
Required	Requires an entry in the field when set to "Yes."
Allow Zero Length	Used in combination with the Required field to determine if blank text fields can be assigned a zero length string ("") or Null. Blank fields are assigned a "Null" value which is different from zero or no text.
Indexed	Increases the speed of searches and queries, but might slow general operations. Set this to "Yes" for fields that you use to find or sort records.
Unicode Compression	Two-byte character representation for the Jet 4.0 database engine. This format requires more space so this option compresses the data.
IME Mode	Property applies to all East Asian languages.
IME Sentence Mode	Property applies to Japanese only.

1. Select the State field name in the top pane. Press F6. In the Field Size property, key **2** to make the field narrower.

2. Click the BillingAddress field name in the top pane. This text field has a Caption and a Field Size of 255 spaces.

3. In the Field Size property, key **50**

 TIP: Text fields should be wide enough to hold most data, but not so wide that they waste space.

4. Click in the Description row for ContactName. Key **Person to call at this location**.

5. Close the table. Because you changed the design of the table, Access reminds you to save it. Click Yes to save the new design.

FIGURE 4-11
Save Table
dialog box

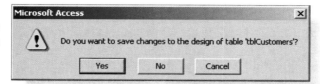

6. Because you changed the Field Size, Access warns that some data might be lost. It would be cut off or truncated if you make the Field Size too small. That will not happen in this case, so click Yes to continue.

FIGURE 4-12
Access warns
that some data
might be lost

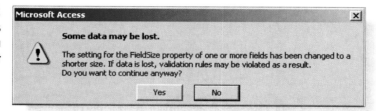

7. Open tblCustomers and maximize the window.

8. Click anywhere in the ContactName column. Read the description in the status bar in the lower left corner of the screen.

9. Close the table.

NOTE: When you changed the Field Size of the State field, you changed the design size, not the display size. The field requires less space in the database file but can be displayed in any width.

Inserting and Deleting Fields

Maintaining a database requires making periodic adjustments to table structures. As user requirements for company information change, so should your database. You might find that you will need to add or remove fields from one or more tables.

Before adding any field to a table, you should make certain that it does not duplicate an existing field's data. You should never design a database that stores redundant information.

Deleting a field is much more dangerous than adding one. Before deleting a field from a table, make certain that the data contained in the field will never be needed in the future. Good practice is to make a backup copy of the working database prior to modifying any table.

You can add fields to a table at any time. You might need to do so if you forgot a field while designing a table or discover that you have new data requirements. You can insert new fields in either Design View or Datasheet View.

On occasion, you might create a wide text field or a memo field. It will be difficult to see the entire contents of the field in Datasheet View. You will need to use the Zoom dialog box to display the contents of the field. A *Zoom dialog box* is a text-editing window for lengthy text.

1. Open tblCustomers and click the View button to return to the Design window.

2. Click the State field name. Click the Insert Rows button .

   NOTE: When you insert a row, the new row is placed above the selected field.

FIGURE 4-13
Inserting a row

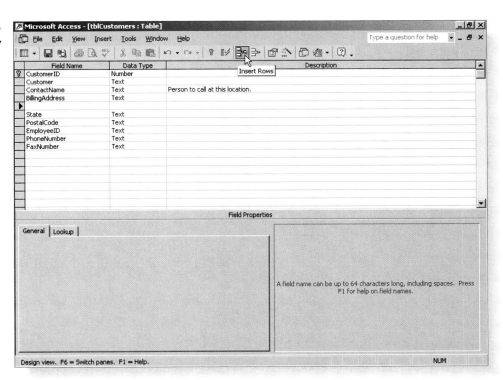

3. Key **City** as the Field Name. Press Tab. Text is the default Data Type.

4. Press Tab again. In the Description column, key **City where customer's corporate office is located**.

5. Click the EmployeeID field name. Choose Insert, Rows.

6. Key **EMailAddress** as the Field Name. Press Tab. Click the Data Type drop-down arrow and select Hyperlink.

7. Press Tab again. In the Description column, key **Company's E-mail address**

8. For the Caption property of the EMailAddress field, key **E-Mail**

9. In the top pane, click the first blank row after FaxNumber. Key **Comments** as the Field Name.

10. Press Tab. Select Memo as the Data Type.

11. Press Tab. Key **General notes** as the Description.

 REVIEW: Changes to the data are saved automatically; however, you must save design changes.

 12. Click the View button to return to the datasheet. Access asks you to save the table because you made design changes. Click Yes.

 TIP: To edit text in a Hyperlink field, click in the previous field, press Tab to reach the hyperlink field, and then press F2 to display a text cursor.

13. Key the following cities and E-mail addresses in the appropriate columns. Text in a Hyperlink field is formatted as an Internet address. (These addresses are not real, so do not try to access them.)

Crafts & More:	Seattle	**mailto:craftsmore@mail.com**
Bears & Such:	Norfolk	**mailto:bears@animals.net**
The Doll and Bear Barn:	Hartford	**mailto:dollbear@stores.org**

 NOTE: The Hyperlink Data Type in Access defaults to a Web address. You must key **mailto:** before the email address to generate an email message rather than launch a Web browser.

14. Scroll the window and click in the Comments field for Record #1.

15. Press Shift + F2 to open the Zoom dialog box.

16. Key **This company will order all small stuffed animals**. (See Figure 4-14 on the next page.)

17. Click OK to close the dialog box. Click in the Comments field for Record #2 and press Shift + F2.

18. Key **This company will order only small teddy bears**. Do not click OK.

NOTE: If you click OK and close the Zoom dialog box before you are ready, press Shift + F2 to open it again.

FIGURE 4-14
Entering text in the
Zoom dialog box

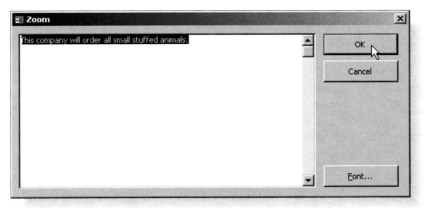

19. Select all the text in the Zoom dialog box. Press Ctrl + C to copy the text. Click **OK** to close the window.

20. Right-click the Comments field of Record #3 and select <u>P</u>aste. You do not have to open the Zoom dialog box for lengthy text.

EXERCISE **4-9** **Insert and Delete a Field in Datasheet View**

You also can insert fields in Datasheet View. Access inserts text fields with a default width of 50 spaces. Each field will be named Field*n*, where *n* is a sequential number. You can also delete a field in Datasheet View.

1. Click anywhere in the Billing Address column.

2. From the <u>I</u>nsert menu, select <u>C</u>olumn. A new column named Field1 is inserted before the Billing Address column.

3. Click the View button. Field1 is a Text Data Type.

4. Return to Datasheet View.

5. Click anywhere in the Fax Number column.

6. Click <u>E</u>dit, Delete Colu<u>m</u>n.

7. A dialog box asks if you want to delete the field and all the data.

FIGURE 4-15
A message warns
that data will
be deleted

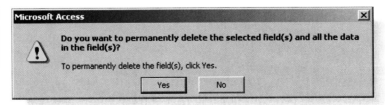

8. Click Yes to delete the field. Close the table.

Creating Tables in Datasheet View

In addition to using the Table Wizard to create new tables, you can also create new tables in Design View or Datasheet View.

You can create a table by simply entering data into columns and rows. Access evaluates your entries and determines Field Sizes and Data Types. The field names are generic, but you can rename them in Design View. Although it is easy to create a table in Datasheet View, most likely you will need to customize the table in Design View.

EXERCISE 4-10 Create a Table in Datasheet View

If you have the data available to enter into a table, you might choose to create a table by using Datasheet View. Access evaluates the data you key to determine the Data Type for the newly created field.

When you key letters or a combination of letters and numbers, Access defines a text field. When you key only numbers, Access defines a number field. When you key numbers with symbols such as the decimal point (.), the dollar sign ($), or the percent sign (%), Access defines the field as a number field and assigns specific properties to the field. When you key numbers with the forward slash (/) or the colon (:), Access defines the field as a Date/Time field. If your entry is not recognized as a valid number, date, or time, Access defines the field as Text.

1. Click the **Tables** button. Double-click **Create table by entering data**. A blank datasheet opens, and the field names are Field1, Field2, and so on.

2. In Field1 for the first row, key **7**

3. Press `Tab`. Key *[your last name]* in Field2.

4. Press `Tab`. Key **5%** in Field3.

5. Press `Tab`. Press `Ctrl`+`;` to enter today's date in Field4.

 NOTE: If you see an error message when you give the current date command, enter the date in this format: *mm/dd/yy*

6. Press `Tab`. Key **West** in Field5.

7. Key **$6.25** in Field6.

8. Click the Save button . The **Save As** dialog box opens with a default name.

9. Key **tblReps** as the table name and click **OK**.

10. A dialog box reminds you that you have not set a primary key. If you choose **Yes**, Access will create an AutoNumber field. (See Figure 4-16 on the next page.)

FIGURE 4-16
Message box telling
you there is no
primary key

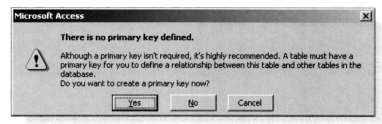

11. Click **No**. The datasheet displays only the records and fields you entered.

EXERCISE 4-11 **Set Captions and Set a Primary Key**

You have already viewed how the Table Wizard creates default Captions for fields. Through the Table Design View, you can change existing Captions or add new Captions.

You also learned about the primary key. The primary key is the field that holds unique or different data for each record. When you set a primary key, Access requires that values for this field be unique in each record. For example, if the social security number is the primary key for an employee database, each employee must have a unique social security number. If you attempt to use the same social security number for more than one record, an error will occur.

1. Click the View button . Access analyzed the data you entered and selected an appropriate field type.

2. In the top pane, change the name of Field1 to **EmployeeID**. Click the Caption row in the bottom pane and key **Rep's ID** with a space.

3. Change Field2 to **LastName** and change its Caption to **Last Name**

4. Change Field3 to **CommissionRate** and change its Caption to **Commission Rate**

5. Change Field4 to **HireDate** and set the Caption to **Hire Date**

6. Change Field5 to **Region**. Leave the Caption row blank.

7. Change Field6 to **BasePay** and set the Caption to **Base Pay**

TIP: When a Field Name is one word, you do not need a Caption.

8. Click the EmployeeID row. Click the Primary Key button 🔑.

9. Save the table and return to Datasheet View.

10. Enter the following new record. You must enter the date in mm/dd/yy format.

Rep's ID: **6**
Last Name: **Gleason**

Commission Rate:	.04
Hire Date:	6/6/01
Region:	**North**
Base Pay:	**$6.50**

11. Close the table.

Importing Data

As a database administrator, a goal of yours should be to avoid requiring users to re-enter data already stored in an electronic format. You should transfer the data by importing it into your database. Each time you import data, you make a copy of the original data. The original data is maintained in the source application while you work with a copy of it in your database.

You can import data into an Access database from many different applications, including Excel, Lotus, dBase, Word, or a mainframe database system. After being imported, the table behaves just like any other table.

EXERCISE 4-12 Import Access Data

Data can be imported from other Access databases, including previous versions of Access. In addition to importing tables, Access can import other objects, such as queries, forms, and reports. However, only tables contain data.

1. Right-click the Start button 🏁Start on the Windows taskbar. A shortcut menu opens.

2. Click Explore. When the Explorer opens, click the Maximize button 🔲 to maximize the window.

3. In the left pane, open folder Lesson 04. The files contained in the folder appear in the right pane.

> **NOTE:** Check with your instructor to verify the location of your student data files and the folder in which you will be working. The folder "My Documents" is often the default folder when you're creating or storing files.

4. In the right pane, point to the filename **CC-E-04** and right-click. Choose Copy from the shortcut menu.

5. In the left pane, open the My Documents folder.

6. Right-click in an unused area of the right pane. Choose Paste from the shortcut menu. A file named **CC-E-04** appears.

7. Close the Explorer.

8. With your *[your first name and last name]* database window maximized, click the **Tables** button.

9. From the **File** menu, choose **Get External Data** and then choose **Import**.

10. In the **Import** dialog box, find the folder with **CC-E-04** and select the filename. Click **Import**.

11. In the **Import Objects** dialog box, click the **Tables** tab. You can import all major objects (tables, queries, forms, reports, pages, macros, and modules).

12. Select tblSalesReps.

FIGURE 4-17
Importing a table

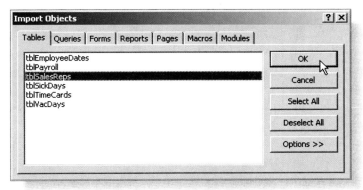

13. Click **OK**. The table is added to your database. Open tblSalesReps in Design View.

14. Click the first empty **Field Name** row after Rate and key **Supervisor**. Make the **Data Type** Text, **25** spaces wide.

15. Save the changes and switch to Datasheet View. The table has a new field. Close the table.

EXERCISE **4-13** **Import Excel Data**

For most non-Access applications, a wizard steps you through the import process. When importing from a worksheet, you may select all the data from the worksheet or just a range of cells. Your ease in importing data depends greatly on how the information is stored in the application. Use of blank columns and rows in the worksheet adds unnecessary fields and records to your database.

1. In the Tables window, right-click in a white, unused area. Choose **Import** from the shortcut menu.

2. Click the drop-down arrow for **Files of type** and choose **Microsoft Excel**.

3. Set the **Look In** location to the Lesson 04 folder.

4. Select the **Employees** workbook. (This is a Microsoft Excel worksheet.) Click **Import**.

5. A wizard starts to help you import the Excel worksheet. Click Show Worksheets.

FIGURE 4-18
Selecting data
to import

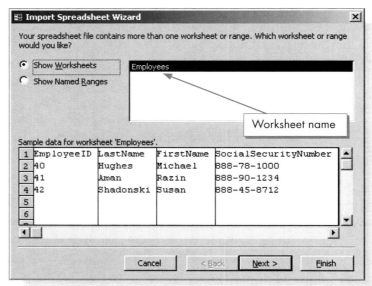

6. Click <u>N</u>ext. Click the check box to indicate that the F<u>i</u>rst Row Contains Column Headings.

7. Click <u>N</u>ext. You can import the data into a new table, or you can add the records to an existing table.

 NOTE: So you can add records, the fields in the imported table must be the same data type and size and in the same order as in the target table.

8. Click the option button for In a Ne<u>w</u> Table. Click <u>N</u>ext.

9. For each field in the new table, you can change the Field Name, indicate whether it should be indexed, or skip the field altogether.

10. Click in the SocialSecurityNumber column. Click the drop-down arrow for Indexed and choose Yes (No Duplicates). (See Figure 4-19 on the next page.)

11. Click <u>N</u>ext. In the next dialog box, you can set the primary key.

12. Click the option <u>C</u>hoose my own primary key. Choose SocialSecurityNumber from the drop-down list. Click <u>N</u>ext.

13. In the <u>I</u>mport to Table entry box, key **tblNewEmployees**

14. Click <u>F</u>inish. The message box tells you that the table has been imported. Click OK in the message box.

15. Open tblNewEmployees in Datasheet View. Switch to Design View. Text fields are all 255 spaces wide. Close the table.

FIGURE 4-19
Setting a
field's options

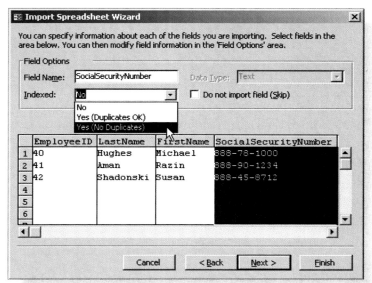

EXERCISE **4-14** **Delete Tables**

No matter how you created the table, you can delete it from your database. When you delete an imported table, the data is still in the original location from which you imported it. When you delete a table you created from the Wizard or Datasheet View, it is deleted along with any data it contains.

 TIP: You can only Undo a deleted table immediately after deleting it.

1. Click tblSalesReps in the Database window. Press Delete .
2. A dialog box verifies that you want to delete this table. Click Yes.
3. Delete tblNewEmployees from the database.
4. Compact and close your database.

USING HELP

After you open the Microsoft Access Help dialog box, you can locate a topic by using the **Contents** or **Index** tabs.

- Use the **Contents** tab like a table of contents in a book. The **Contents** tab displays Help topics in outline form.
- Use the **Index** tab like a search command. Key a topic and then scroll through the alphabetical list of topics.

Display Help windows to learn about primary keys by using the Contents tab.

1. Choose <u>H</u>elp and Microsoft Access <u>H</u>elp. Click the <u>C</u>ontents tab.
2. Scroll to find the Tables topic. Click the Expand icon ⊞ 📖.
3. Scroll to find Primary Keys and Indexes. Expand the topic.
4. Click the topic to Set or change the primary key.
5. Maximize the Help Window. Read the information in the right panel.
6. Click the topic About primary keys.
7. In the right pane, click each of the three primary key types and read the information shown.
8. Close the Help window.
9. Compact and close your database.

LESSON Summary

➤ The Database Wizard creates a new database from an existing template.

➤ A new database created through the Database Wizard contains major objects such as tables, forms, and reports, but does not contain data.

➤ A new database created as a blank database does not contain objects or data.

➤ The Table Wizard creates a new table based on commonly used fields.

➤ When using the Table Wizard, you can rename selected fields.

➤ You can enter data directly into the table after creating and naming a table by using the Table Wizard.

➤ The properties of any field can be edited after a table is created.

➤ You can insert fields into and delete them from an existing table through either Design View or Datasheet View.

➤ When tables are created by using Datasheet View, Access evaluates the data entered to determine the data type for the field to create.

➤ A Caption is a field property that displays as a column heading in Datasheet View.

➤ The data contained in a field defined as the primary key of a table must be unique.

➤ Data imported from another Access database, a non-Access database, or a non-database application can be added to an existing table or used to create a new table.

➤ Tables can be deleted from an Access database.

LESSON 4 Command Summary

FEATURE	BUTTON	MENU	KEYBOARD	SPEECH
New Database		<u>F</u>ile, <u>N</u>ew	Ctrl + N	✓
Insert Row		<u>I</u>nsert, <u>R</u>ows		✓
Delete Row		<u>E</u>dit, Delete <u>R</u>ows		✓
Primary Key		<u>E</u>dit, Primary <u>K</u>ey		✓
Table Properties		<u>V</u>iew, <u>P</u>roperties		✓
Import		<u>F</u>ile, <u>G</u>et External Data, Import		✓
Delete Table		<u>E</u>dit, <u>D</u>elete	Delete	✓

Concepts Review

Each of the following statements is either true or false. Indicate your choice by circling T or F.

T F **1.** After you create a table, you can rename fields and change the data type of fields in Design View.

T F **2.** When you're creating a table in Datasheet View, all fields are Text data types.

T F **3.** The Table Wizard can create a new database.

T F **4.** The primary key field of a table must contain unique data.

T F **5.** Fields can be deleted only through Datasheet View.

T F **6.** Access can import tables, queries, forms, and reports from previous versions of Access.

T F **7.** In Datasheet View, the Description property of a field displays at the top of the column instead of the Field Name.

T F **8.** The field properties of a table created through a wizard cannot be modified through Design View.

Write the correct answer in the space provided.

1. When is it useful to use the Database Wizard to create a database?

_____

2. When using the Leszynski Naming Conventions, what would you rename a table called Management Profiles?

_____

3. Name the four ways to add a table to a database.

_____

4. What kind of data type does the Table Wizard assign to a street address?

_____

5. What field data type can store more than 255 characters?

_____

6. In what view can you change the data type or description of a field?

_____

7. In Design View, which function key toggles the insertion point between the lower and upper panes?

_____

8. What kind of field must store unique or different data for each record?

_____

CRITICAL THINKING

Answer these questions on a separate page. There are no right or wrong answers. Support your answers with examples from your own experience, if possible.

1. The Access Table Wizard uses field names such as StateOrProvince and PostalCode instead of State or ZIPCode. Why do you think Access does this?

2. Many businesses find it necessary to import tables into Access. Why do you think this is true?

Skills Review

EXERCISE 4-15

Create a blank database. Set a primary key. Choose and rename fields in the Table Wizard.

1. Create a new database by following these steps:

    a. With Access running and no database open, click the New button 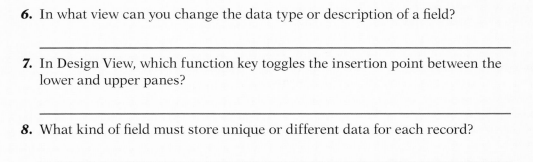.
    b. Click the Blank Database in the New File task pane.
    c. Verify your Save in location.
    d. Key *[your first name, middle initial, and your last name]* as the File name. Click Create.

2. Create a table, using the Table Wizard, by following these steps:
    a. Click the Tables button and the New button.
    b. Click Table Wizard and click OK.
    c. Select Business. In the Sample Tables list, click Suppliers.

    d. Click the SupplierID field and click the Add One button > .
    e. Add the following sample fields by double-clicking the field name.
      ● SupplierName
      ● EmailAddress

3. Rename table fields, using the Wizard, by following these steps:

   a. In the Fields in my new table list, select the SupplierID field.
   b. Click the Rename Field button.
   c. Edit the name to **CarrierID** and click OK.
   d. Rename the SupplierName field as **Name**.

4. Set the primary key and name the table by following these steps:

   a. Click Next. Key **tblCarriers** to name your table.
   b. Select No, I'll set the primary key. Click Next.
   c. Choose Carrier ID as the field for the primary key.
   d. Choose Numbers and/or letters I enter when I add new records. Click Next.
   e. Select Enter data directly into the table. Click Finish.
   f. Close the table.

EXERCISE 4-16

Edit field properties. Add records.

1. Make design changes to a table by following these steps:

   a. Open tblCarriers. Switch to Design View.
   b. In the top pane, click in the CarrierID row.
   c. Click in the Caption row in the bottom pane.
   d. Key **Carrier ID** as the Caption.
   e. Click in the EmailAddress in the top pane.
   f. Change the Data Type to Hyperlink.
   g. While in the EmailAddress row in the top pane, click the Insert Rows button .
   h. Key **Region** as the new field name. Press Tab.
   i. Choose Text as the Data Type. Press Tab.
   j. For the Description, key **Carrier delivery area**
   k. Press F6. Set the Field Size at **20**
   l. Click the first empty row in the top pane below EmailAddress. Key **Phone** as the Field Name.
   m. Press Tab and choose Text.
   n. Press F6 and make the Field Size **15**
   o. Save the table.

2. Add records by following these steps:

   a. Click the View button ▦. Maximize the window.

Carrier ID:	**A101**
Name:	**Southtown Transportation**
Region:	**State**

Email Address:	**mailto:southtown@me.com**
Phone:	**(312) 555-6114**
Carrier ID:	**B202**
Name:	**Federal Parcel Systems**
Region:	**Country**
Email Address:	**mailto:fps@downtown.com**
Phone:	**(773) 555-1234**
Carrier ID:	**C303**
Name:	**Bell Shipping**
Region:	**City**
Email Address:	**mailto:bell@shipping.net**
Phone:	**(602) 555-7777**

b. Close the table.

EXERCISE 4-17

Edit field properties. Add records.

1. Create a table in Datasheet View by following these steps:

   a. In the Tables window, double-click Create table by entering data.

   b. In Field1, click in the first row. Key **2001**.

   c. Press Tab. Key **1/1/02** in Field2.

   d. Press Tab. Key **1** in Field3.

   e. Press Tab. Key **A101** in Field4.

    f. Click the Save button 🖫. Key **tblSales** as the table name and click OK.

   g. A dialog box reminds you that you have not set a primary key. Click No.

2. Make design changes by following these steps:

    a. Click the View button 📐.

   b. Key **OrderID** as the first Field Name. Press Tab.

   c. Choose Number as the Data Type. Press Tab.

   d. Key **Order ID #** in the Description column.

   e. Press F6. Click in the Caption row and key **Order ID**

   f. Double-click Field Name Field2. Key **OrderDate**. Press Tab.

   g. Choose Date/Time as the Data Type. Press Tab.

   h. Key **Order date** in the Description column.

   i. Press F6. Click in the Caption row and key **Order Date**

    j. Click in the OrderID row in the top pane and click the Primary Key button 🗝.

   k. Change the Field Name for Field3 to **CustomerID**.

   l. Press Tab. Use a Number Data Type and Long Integer as the Field Size.

   m. Key **Customer ID #** in the Description column.

   n. Click in the Caption row and key **Customer ID**

   o. Change Field4 to **CarrierID**

   p. Press Tab . Select Text as the Data Type and 4 as the Field Size. Set the Caption to **Carrier ID**

   q. Key **Carrier ID #** in the Description column.

   r. Click the Save button 💾. Click Yes.

3. Insert a field by following these steps:

   a. Click the Carrier ID row in the top pane.

   b. Click Insert, Rows.

   c. Key **ExpressShip** as the field name. Select Yes/No as the Data Type.

   d. Save the table and click the View button 🖼.

4. Add two new records.

Order ID:	**2002**
Order Date:	**1/1/02**
Customer ID:	**2**
Express Ship:	*Press* Spacebar *to place a check mark.*
Carrier ID:	**B202**
Order ID:	**2003**
Order Date:	**2/1/02**
Customer ID:	**3**
Express Ship:	*Press* Tab *to leave check box empty.*
Carrier ID:	**C303**

5. Close the table.

EXERCISE 4-18

Import Excel Data

1. Import Excel data by following these steps:

   a. Right-click in the white unused area of the Tables window. Choose Import.

   b. Click the drop-down arrow for **Files of type** and choose **Microsoft Excel**.

   c. Set the **Look in** control to the Lesson 04 folder. Select MoreSales and click Import.

   d. Click **Show Named Ranges** in the dialog box. Select NewSales.

   e. Click Next. Set the check box to select the **First Row Contains Column Headings**.

   f. Click Next. Click the option button for **In an Existing Table**. Then choose tblSales from the drop-down list box and click Next.

   g. Verify that the **Import to Table** entry box shows **tblSales**. Click Finish.

   h. The message box tells you that the table has been imported. Click OK.

   i. Open tblSales in Datasheet View to see the new records. Close the table.

   j. Compact and close the database.

Lesson Applications

Create a blank database. Create a table, edit field properties, and enter records.

1. Open a blank database and name it *[your first, middle, and last initials]*.

2. Using the Table Wizard, add the following fields from the Payments sample table:

   PaymentID

   CustomerID

   OrderID

   PaymentAmount

   PaymentDate

3. Name the table **tblPayments***[your last name]*.

4. Choose the option to set the primary key yourself and use the PaymentID field with consecutive numbers assigned by Access.

5. Select the option to enter records directly in the table.

6. Enter the following record:

Payment ID:	*Press* `Tab`
Customer ID:	**1**
Order ID:	**20101**
Payment Amount:	**500**
Payment Date:	**1/1/02**

7. In Design View, change the Field Size of the OrderID field to Double.

8. Change to Datasheet View and save the table. Add the following records:

Payment ID:	*Press* `Tab`
Customer ID:	**2**
Order ID:	**20102**
Payment Amount:	**750**
Payment Date:	**10/1/02**

Payment ID:	*Press* `Tab`
Customer ID:	**5**
Order ID:	**20103**
Payment Amount:	**1000**
Payment Date:	**2/7/02**

TIP: If you key the diagonals in a date, you do not need to key leading zeros for the date or month.

9. Size the columns to the widest text or title.

10. Print the table in portrait orientation.

EXERCISE 4-20

Delete a field in Datasheet View. Change field properties. Rename a table.

1. Open tblPayments in Datasheet View.

2. Delete the CustomerID field.

3. Change to Design View.

4. Change the Caption for Order ID to **Order Number**

5. Change the Caption for Payment Amount to **Amount Paid**

6. Change the Caption for Payment Date to **Date Paid**

7. Resize the columns appropriately.

8. Rename the table as **tblNewPayments**

9. Print the table in portrait orientation.

10. Close the table.

EXERCISE 4-21

Create a table in Datasheet View. Set Captions and Field Sizes. Set a primary key.

1. Create a new table by entering data.

2. Add the following record:

Field1:	**464-23-4824**
Field2:	**Supplies**
Field3:	**10/15/02**
Field4:	**$14.85**
Field5:	**Cleaning Supplies**
Field6:	**Trash Bags, Soap, and Paper Towels**

3. Save the table as **tblEmployeeExpenses***[your first and last name].*

4. Set Field1 as the primary key.

5. Rename the field names to the following:

Field1:	**EmployeeID**
Field2:	**ExpenseType**

Field3:	DatePurchased
Field4:	AmountSpent
Field5:	Purpose
Field6:	Description

6. Set the Caption for EmployeeID to EmployeeSSN.

7. Add appropriate Captions to the other fields.

8. Enter the following record:

EmployeeID:	234-45-7890
ExpenseType:	Supplies
DatePurchased:	10/22/02
AmountSpent:	$25.34
PurposeOfExpense:	Office Supplies
Description:	Pens, Staples, Memo Pads

9. Based on the data you have just entered; resize the four text fields to an appropriate width.

10. Resize columns so all data is visible.

11. Print the table in landscape orientation.

12. Save and close the table.

EXERCISE 4-22 Challenge Yourself

Create a new database. Import data. Enter data.

1. Use the Database Wizard to create a database that will keep track of expenses for a company. Name it **Expenses[your initials]**

2. Make sure you include a field to store the date an employee is hired.

3. The company is only concerned with domestic expenses, so there is no need to store what country an employee is from.

4. Change the names of fields StateOrProvince and PostalCode to better fit a company located in the United States.

5. Import payroll information from **CC-E-04** into the new database.

6. Add one new record in the table Employees. Use your real name in the record, but make up the rest of the data.

7. Print the new record in landscape orientation.

8. Compact and close your database.

On Your Own

In these exercises you work on your own, as you would in a real-life work environment. Use the skills you've learned to accomplish the task—and be creative.

EXERCISE 4-23

Using the Database Wizard, select a template that will assist you in creating a database to store the member information you collected and organized for the On Your Own exercises of Lessons 1 through 3. Enter the member information. Print the table. On the first sheet of your printout, write the name of the template you selected. Continue to Exercise 4-24.

EXERCISE 4-24

Review the structure of the main table in the database you created in the Exercise 4-23. On a blank sheet of paper, list the fields, data types, and field sizes from the table that are most appropriate for your organization's needs. Add any additional fields that would improve the usability of the table. Without using the Database Wizard, create a blank database. Create a table to store the data. Enter the member information. Print the table. Continue to Exercise 4-25.

EXERCISE 4-25

Search the Web for Microsoft Access Templates. Locate a template that will enhance the database you created in the previous exercise. Using the template you located on the Internet, create a new database. Enter appropriate data for at least five records. Print the table. Submit to your instructor the printouts from Exercises 4-23 through 4-25 along with your field list from 4-24. Make sure your name, the date, and the class are written on the printouts. Keep a copy of the three databases you created in Exercises 4-23 through 4-25. They will be used in subsequent lessons.

Managing Data Integrity

After completing this lesson, you will be able to:

1. **Create relationships between tables.**
2. **Work with referential integrity.**
3. **Work with subdatasheets.**
4. **Use default values, formats, and input masks.**
5. **Use the Lookup Wizard.**

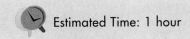 Estimated Time: 1 hour

A *relationship* is a link or connection between two tables sharing a common field. Relationships are critical for properly designed databases. They change a flat database, containing isolated data, into a relational database, containing linked data. For tables to relate to each other, they must share common data. In an integrated database, tables can link to one or more other tables.

Relationships must be planned; they do not just happen. Understanding them—and how to set them—takes time and practice. As you work more extensively with databases, you will learn more about their subtleties.

Creating Relationships Between Tables

Relationships between tables can be graphically viewed in the Relationships window. Tables display as field lists. Related fields from each table are connected by a join line. A *join line* graphically represents the relationship between two tables. Each end of the join line connects to the related fields of two tables.

The related field between the two tables must be of the same data type and the same size. The related fields do not need to use the same name. However, you will find it much easier to create and recognize relationships when the common fields use the same field name in both tables.

EXERCISE 5-1 Look at an Existing Relationship

The Relationships window shows existing relationships in the current database. One or more relationships can be displayed at a time. When more than two tables are displayed, it is advantageous to arrange the tables to allow optimum viewing of all join lines.

1. Find the **Asset Tracking** database located in the folder Lesson 05. This is a copy of the database you created in Lesson 4.

 NOTE: Ask your instructor where files for this Lesson are saved. They might be located on your computer, on the network, or on a student disk.

2. Make a copy of this file on your hard drive and name it **Asset Tracking*[your initials]***. Open **Asset Tracking*[your initials]***.

 3. Close the Main Switchboard. Click the Relationships button and maximize the Relationships window.

FIGURE 5-1
Relationships
window

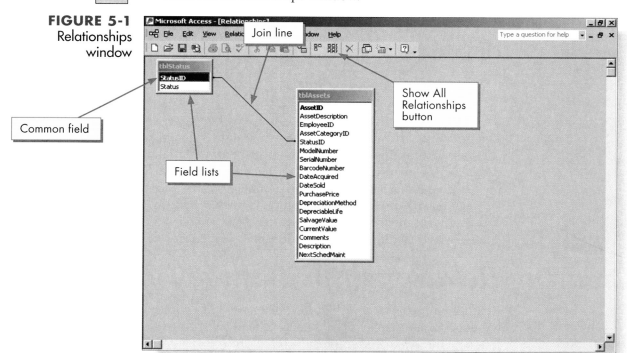

REVIEW: In a field list, the key field for a table is bold.

 4. Click the Show All Relationships button . All tables that have a relationship with other tables will open. The line connecting two tables represents the relationship between the tables.

5. Resize the field lists so all field names are visible.

 REVIEW: Click and drag the bottom or right edge of a list box to resize it.

6. Click and drag the title bar of each field list and rearrange them to appear as shown in Figure 5-2.

FIGURE 5-2
Relationships window
with field lists
rearranged

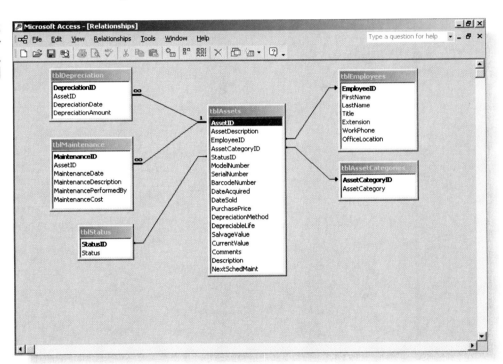

7. Right-click the sloping part of the join line between tblAssets and tblStatus to open the shortcut menu for a join line. (See Figure 5-3 on the next page.)

 NOTE: Make sure you open the shortcut menu for a join line. It will enable you to edit relationships or to delete the join line. You might accidentally open the shortcut menu for the Relationships window or for a field list. Neither of these menus offers you the option to edit relationships or to delete the join line.

FIGURE 5-3
Shortcut menu

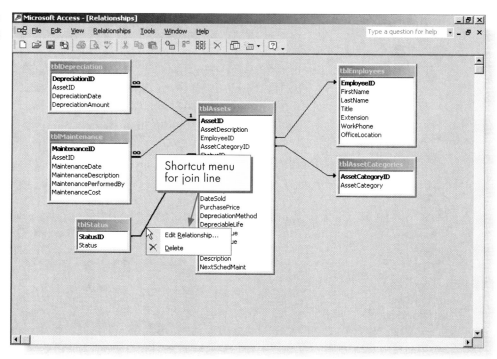

FIGURE 5-4
Edit Relationships
dialog box

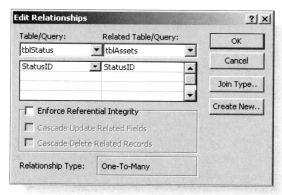

8. Choose Edit Relationship.

NOTE: You will learn more about the types of relationships later in this lesson.

9. Click Cancel to close the dialog box.

<hr>

EXERCISE **5-2** **Print Relationships**

Printing relationships helps a database administrator document and troubleshoot database integrity. Access creates a graphical report showing field lists and join lines. (You will learn more about reports in the next lesson.)

1. Choose File, Print Relationships. Access generates a report and opens it in Print Preview.

2. Change to a Landscape orientation. Click the Print button 🖨.

3. Click the Close button ✖ without saving the report.

4. Close the Relationships window. A message box might ask if you want to save the new layout. Click **Yes**.

5. Close the database without closing Access.

EXERCISE **5-3** **Create a Relationship in the Relationships Window**

You have just looked at a relational database with integrated tables. You will now build a relationship between isolated tables by creating a relationship directly in the Relationships window. You create relationships by dragging or drawing a line between the two common field names.

Different relationships can be produced depending on whether the common fields are primary key fields or foreign key fields. A *foreign key field* is the field that refers to the primary key field in a related table.

Access provides various types of relationships between two tables. If the common field is a primary key in the first table and not a primary key in the second table, the relationship is a *One-To-Many relationship*. This means one record in the first table can connect to one or more records in the second table.

If the common fields in both the first and the second tables are primary keys, the relationship is a *One-To-One relationship*. This means one record in the first table can connect to only one record in the second table.

If the common fields in the first or the second table are not primary keys, an *Indeterminate relationship* is created. Access does not have enough information to determine the relationship between the two tables.

1. Make a copy of CC-05 and rename it *[your initials]*CC-05. Open *[your initials]*CC-05.

2. Click the Relationships button . This window shows no relationships.

3. Click the Show All Relationships button 🔡. Nothing happens. This proves that the entire database has no relationships set up.

4. Click the Show Table button 🔳. The Show Table dialog box lists the tables and queries that are in the database.

> 🕐 **NOTE:** The Show Table dialog box sometimes opens automatically when no relationships are present in the database.

5. Click the **Tables** tab. Double-click **tblCustomers** to add its field list to the window.

TIP: If you cannot see the field lists, move the Show Table dialog box.

6. Double-click tblHistorySales.

FIGURE 5-5
Show Table
dialog box

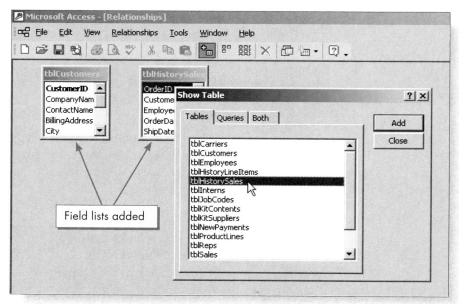

NOTE: If a field list is added more than once, the title bar of the duplicate field list shows a number after the table name. You can delete duplicates by clicking in the field list and pressing Delete.

7. Close the **Show Table** dialog box. Maximize the Relationships window.

8. Size and position the field lists so you can see all the field names.

9. In the tblCustomers list, click the CustomerID field. The field name is bold because it is the primary key in this table.

10. Click and drag the CustomerID field from the tblCustomers field list to the CustomerID field in the tblHistorySales field list.

11. The **Edit Relationships** dialog box opens. The **Relationship Type** is one-to-many because the CustomerID (primary key) appears only once in the table tblCustomers but can appear many times in the table tblHistorySales.

12. Click **Create**. A join line links the common field names.

 13. Click the Clear Layout button ⊠.

14. Click **Yes** to clear the layout.

15. Click the Show All Relationships button ⊞.

NOTE: The Clear Layout button ⊠ clears the way tables are arranged but does not delete the relationships between them.

16. Resize each field list so all field names are visible.

 17. Click the Save button 🖬. Close the Relationships window.

Working with Referential Integrity

When a relationship is one-to-many and the tables are in the same database, you can use additional database rules known as *referential integrity*. These rules keep track of changes in related tables and help eliminate mistakes, accidental deletions, and other common errors. Referential integrity cannot be set for Indeterminate relationships.

EXERCISE   5-4   Enforce Referential Integrity

1. Open tblHistorySales. Change the Customer ID in the first record to **15**. Close the table.

2. Open tblCustomers. Notice that there is no Customer ID 15. Referential integrity would prevent this type of error from being made. Close the table.

3. Open tblHistorySales. Change the Customer ID 15 back to **1**. Close the table.

4. Click the Relationships button 🖼.

5. Right-click the sloping join line between the two field lists. Select Edit <u>R</u>elationship. The Relationship Type is One-To-Many.

6. Click the check box to select Enforce Referential Integrity.

FIGURE 5-6
Enforcing
referential integrity

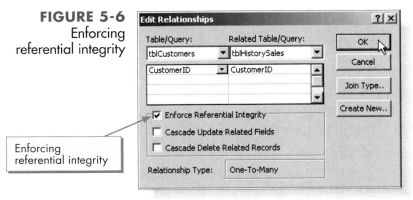

Enforcing
referential integrity

7. The Relationship Type remains a One-To-Many relationship. Click OK. The join line represents referential integrity because it now displays a 1 for the "one" side of the relationship and an infinity symbol (∞) for the "many" side.

FIGURE 5-7
One-To-Many
relationship

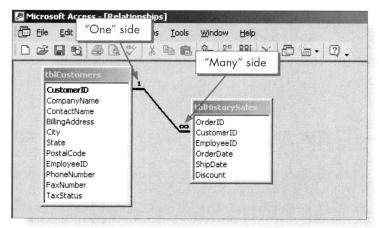

8. Save and close the Relationships window.

9. Open tblHistorySales. Change the Customer ID in the first record to **15**. Press ⬇ to save the record.

10. A message box alerts you to a problem. Click **OK**.

FIGURE 5-8
Referential Integrity
finds an error

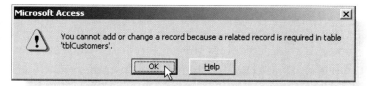

11. Change the Customer ID back to **1**. Close the table.

EXERCISE **5-5** **Remove Referential Integrity**

Removing referential integrity can be relatively easy. When you delete the join line between two field lists in the Relationships window, you delete the relationship between the two corresponding tables.

1. Click the Relationships button 🔲.

2. Right-click the join line between tblCustomers and tblHistorySales.

3. Choose **D**elete from the shortcut menu. Click **Yes** in the warning dialog box. The One-To-Many relationship and the rules for Referential Integrity have been deleted.

4. Save the changes to the layout and close the Relationships window.

Working with Subdatasheets

When a table viewed in Datasheet View is on the "one" side of a One-To-Many relationship, a subdatasheet is generated. A *subdatasheet* is a datasheet nested inside another datasheet. You can see records from the related table while in Datasheet View of the primary table. The common field will be the primary key field in the main table and a foreign key field in the related table.

EXERCISE   **5-6**   **Insert a Subdatasheet**

---

1. Open tblCustomers and maximize the window.

2. From the <u>I</u>nsert menu, choose <u>S</u>ubdatasheet. The Insert Subdatasheet dialog box lists the tables in the database.

3. Click the Tables tab and choose tblHistorySales.

4. In the Link Child Fields box, Access displays a common field of CustomerID in the table tblHistorySales. In the Link Master Fields box, Access has found a common field of CustomerID in the main table tblCustomers. Click OK.

FIGURE 5-9
Inserting a
subdatasheet

> **Insert Subdatasheet**   ? X
>
> Tables | Queries | Both | [OK]
>   [Cancel]
>
>   tblCarriers
>   tblCustomers
>   tblEmployees
>   tblHistoryLineItems
>   tblHistorySales
>   tblInterns
>   tblJobCodes
>   tblKitContents
>   tblKitSuppliers
>   tblNewPayments
>   tblProductLines
>   tblReps
>   tblSales
>
> Link Child Fields: [CustomerID   ▼]
> Link Master Fields: [CustomerID   ▼]

5. The message box alerts you that there are no relationships between these two tables. Click Yes. Access creates the relationship for you and a subdatasheet appears.

6. The subdatasheet shows an Expand icon ✚ in the first column. Click the Expand icon ✚ in the fourth record to expand the subdatasheet. It displays information about the customer's purchases.

FIGURE 5-10
Expanded
subdatasheets

Customer ID	Company Name	Contact Name	Billing Address	City	State	ZIP Code	
1 Magna Mart, Inc.		Sharon Peterson	912 Dodson Avenue	Chattanooga	TN	37406-4124	7
2 Toy House		Elsa Masters	651 Holloway Street	Durham	NC	27701-3457	7
3 The Doll and Bear Barn		Theodora Alexanc	365 Main Street	Hartford	CT	06085-0365	7
4 Bears Etc.		Nancy Erhard	1996 Wilkinson Avenue	Charlotte	NC	28208-5644	6

	OrderID	EmployeeID	OrderDate	ShipDate	Discount
	20003	6	2/8/1998	2/15/1998	0%
	20008	6	5/20/1998	5/23/1998	0%
	20013	6	8/1/1998	8/5/1998	0%
	20018	6	10/7/1998	10/15/1998	0%
*					

5 Crafts & More		Carolina Morgan	22651 45th Avenue	Seattle	WA	98032-2265	6
6 Tots 'n Teens		Louisa Alvarez	456 Memphis Avenue	Nashville	TN	37201-0456	6
7 Beltram House		John Olmstead	2876 Brookshire Avenue	Charlotte	NC	28215-2876	6
8 ABC Toys, Inc.		Suzanne Parker	9218 Park West Avenue	Knoxville	TN	39723-9218	7
9 Children's Hospital		Paul Scheider	5274 West First Avenue	Durham	NC	27702-5274	7
10 New City Circus		David Gross	501 North Canal Street	Norfolk	VA	72723-0501	6
11 The Hobby Company		Tony Greenfield	3258 Bolton Avenue	Norfolk	VA	72723-3258	7
12 Bears & Such		Bob Jones	1012 Dobson Avenue	Chattanooga	TN	37406-1012	6
13 Best 4 U		[your first and las	1000 Washington Avenue	Chicago	IL	60032-1000	7
0							7

7. Click the Collapse icon ▬ to collapse the subdatasheet.

8. Expand and collapse the subdatasheet for another customer.

NOTE: You can expand or collapse all subdatasheets in a table by choosing Format, Subdatasheet, Expand All or Collapse All.

9. Save and close the table.

EXERCISE 5-7 Remove a Subdatasheet

If the database users will not need to see the subdatasheet, you might decide to remove it from the main datasheet. You can remove the displayed subdatasheet in Design View. Although the subdatasheet no longer displays, the relationship between the two tables remains.

1. Open tblCustomers.

2. Click Format, Subdatasheet, and Remove.

3. Save and close the table.

Using Default Values, Formats, and Input Masks

As you improve the design of your database, you will want to add features to improve the speed at which users can enter data. The field properties that can speed data entry are default values, formats, and input masks. In addition to enabling users to work faster, these properties also increase accuracy and consistency.

EXERCISE 5-8 Set Default Values

A *default value* sets the same field value for all new records. For example, if the majority of your employees live in the same state, you can set the default value of the state field to appear automatically in each new record.

Previously entered records will not be changed. The default value displays only when a user is entering new records. If the data being entered is not the same as the default value, the user can key over the default value.

1. Select tblCustomers. Click the <u>D</u>esign button to open the table in Design View. Maximize the window.

2. Click on the **Field Name** EmployeeID.

3. Click in the **Default Value** row and key **7**

FIGURE 5-11
Setting
default values

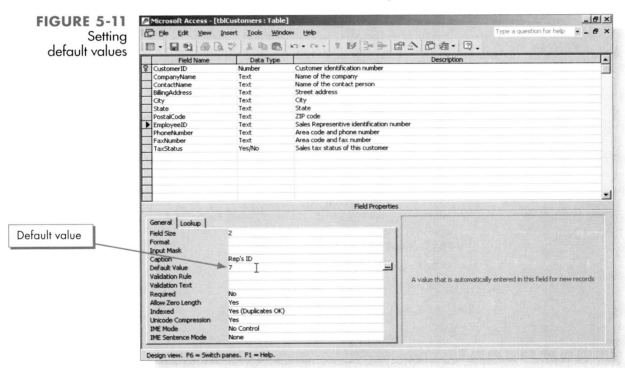

Default value

4. Click the View button to return to Datasheet View. Click **Yes** to save the design changes.

5. Add the following record. The Rep's ID is entered for you.

Customer ID:	**13**
Company Name:	**Best 4 U**
Contact Name:	***[your first and last name]***
Billing Address:	**1000 Washington Avenue**
City:	**Chicago**
State:	**il**
ZIP Code:	**60032-1000**
Rep's ID:	*Press* Tab
Phone Number:	**(312) 555-1000**
Fax Number:	**(312) 555-1199**
Tax Exempt?:	*Press* Tab

EXERCISE **5-9** Add a Field, Set Formats, and Change the Data Type

You can assist database users when entering data by specifying formats. A *format* determines the way data is displayed. For example, you can set the format for a date to show the month spelled out. You can set the format for currency amounts to show dollar signs. You can set the format for text to show only uppercase letters. For some data types, you can select from predefined formats. For others, you enter a custom format.

NOTE: You should not key formatting symbols such as the dollar sign. They can be misinterpreted as text data by Access.

1. Click the View button 📐 to return to Design View.

2. In the top pane, click in the blank row after TaxStatus. Key **InitialOrderDate** as the field name.

3. Press Tab and key **d** to choose Date/Time. Press F6 .

4. In the Format row, click the drop-down arrow and select Long Date.

5. Click the Caption row and key **Initial Order**.

6. Click the View button 🖩 and save the changes.

7. Click on the Customer ID column selector to select the first column.

8. Hold down Shift and click the Company Name column selector to select the second column.

9. Choose F̲ormat, Free̲ze Columns. Scroll right to see the customer name and the Initial Order column.

10. Add the following dates to the existing records:

Doll and Bear Barn: **7/7/02**

Crafts & More: **5/1/01**

Bears & Such: **6/1/01**

Best 4 U: **12/01/02**

 TIP: Size the column so you can see the formatted date.

11. Choose F̲ormat, Unfreeze A̲ll Columns.

12. Return to Design View and click in the State row in the top pane.

13. Click the Format row in the bottom panel. Click the drop-down arrow. There are no predefined formats for a text field.

14. Press F1 to open a Help window regarding formats.

15. Read about the Format property. Click <u>Text and Memo Data Types</u>.

16. Read the explanation of the greater-than symbol (>). Close the Help window.

17. In the Format row for the State field, key **>**

FIGURE 5-12
Setting a format
for a text field

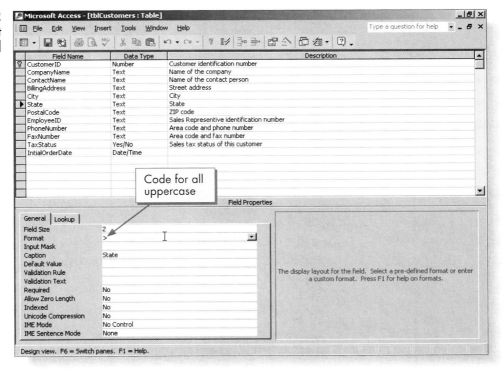

18. In the top pane, click on EmployeeID.

19. Press Tab and key **n** to change the Data Type to Number.

NOTE: Text fields are left-aligned; numbers are right-aligned.

20. Press F6 and set the Default Value to **7**

21. Click the Save button 🖫 and switch to Datasheet View.

22. Enter the following new record. The EmployeeID is again entered for you. The state will be capitalized when you move to the next field. The date also will be formatted when you move to the next record.

Customer ID:	**14**
Company Name:	**Caroline's Crib**
Contact Name:	**Laurie Roberts**
Billing Address:	**20200 West Governors Drive**
City:	*Press* Ctrl + ´
State:	**il**
ZIP Code:	**60682-0200**
Rep's ID:	*Press* Tab
Phone Number:	**(312) 555-2234**
Fax Number:	**(312) 555-2232**
Tax Exempt?:	*Press* Tab
Initial Order:	**12/15/02**

EXERCISE 5-10 Insert a Field with an Input Mask

An *input mask* is a field property that displays a pattern for entering data. In Datasheet View, the input mask would display as (__) __-__ where the underlines are placeholders for entering numbers. An Input Mask Wizard exists for telephone numbers, social security numbers, and other common fields.

In Design View, an input mask for a telephone number is !\(999") "000\-0000. The number nine (9) is used as a placeholder for optional numbers and the number zero (0) is used as a placeholder for required numbers.

1. Switch to Design View for tblCustomers.

2. Click on the Field Name TaxStatus. Click the Insert Rows button ꒢.

3. Key **NightNumber** as the Field Name. Press Tab. This is a Text data type.

4. Press Tab. Key **After hours phone number** as the Description.

5. In the Field Size row, double-click 50. Key **14**

6. In the Caption row, key **After Hours**

7. Click the Input Mask row.

8. Click the Build button ▣.

9. Before the Input Mask Wizard starts, you must save the table design. Click Yes.

10. The Input Mask Wizard lists several common masks and shows how the data is displayed. Select the Phone Number mask.

FIGURE 5-13
Input Mask Wizard
dialog box

Input Mask Wizard

Which input mask matches how you want data to look?

To see how a selected mask works, use the Try It box.

To change the Input Mask list, click the Edit List button.

Input Mask:	Data Look:
Phone Number	(206) 555-1212
Social Security Number	531-86-7180
Zip Code	98052-6399
Extension	63215
Password	*******
Long Time	1:12:00 PM

Try It: [   ]

[Edit List] [Cancel] [< Back] [Next >] [Finish]

11. Click **Next**. The wizard asks if you want to change the input mask. Click in the Try It entry box.

12. Click at the beginning of the mask and key your phone number.

FIGURE 5-14
Change Input Mask
dialog box

Input Mask Wizard

Do you want to change the input mask?

Input Mask Name: Phone Number

Input Mask: [!(999) 000-0000   ]

What placeholder character do you want the field to display?

Placeholders are replaced as you enter data into the field.

Placeholder character: [_   ▼]

Try It: [(555) 314-3344|]

[Cancel] [< Back] [Next >] [Finish]

13. Click **Next**. The wizard asks how you want to store the data. Select With the symbols in the mask, like this.

FIGURE 5-15
Storage option
dialog box

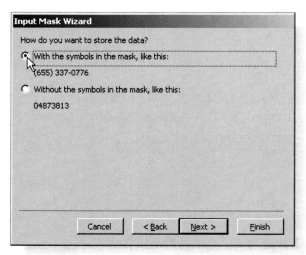

14. Click <u>N</u>ext. Read the final message and click <u>F</u>inish.

15. Change to Datasheet View and save the table.

16. Click on the Customer ID column selector to select the first column.

17. Hold the Shift and click the Company Name column selector to select the second column.

18. Choose F<u>o</u>rmat, Free<u>z</u>e Columns. Scroll right to see the Customer Name and the After Hours column.

19. Add the following phone numbers to the existing records:

 TIP: If the input mask does not appear, press F2 .

The Doll and Bear Barn:	**(860) 555-6576**
Crafts & More:	**(206) 555-3130**
Bears & Such:	**(703) 555-1470**
Best 4 U:	**(312) 555-9523**
Caroline's Crib:	**(312) 555-8281**

20. Choose F<u>o</u>rmat, Unfreeze <u>A</u>ll Columns.

21. Close the table and save the changes.

Using the Lookup Wizard

Relationships let you use lookup fields. A *lookup field* displays input choices from another table so you can enter data by choosing from a list. Instead of keying a product group in tblStuffedAnimals, for example, you can "look it up" from tblProductLines.

Companies often use codes within their databases. For the casual observer, the codes might appear meaningless. However, data entry operators quickly become familiar with the codes and their associated meanings. Codes are used because they use less space than lengthy text describing the record.

You can create a lookup field for the ProductGroup field in tblStuffedAnimals. The Lookup Wizard, listed as a Data Type, guides you step-by-step through the process of creating the lookup field.

EXERCISE 5-11 Modify Field Size and Data Type

TblStuffedAnimals and tblProductLines share the common field ProductGroup. For a lookup field to work as expected, the fields should be the same size and must be of the same Data Type.

1. Open tblProductLines. The ProductGroup field lists a one-character code for each product category.

 NOTE: The Caption for ProductGroup is "Line Code."

2. Click the View button ☒. Click the field named ProductGroup. It is a Text data type, one space wide, and is the primary key. Close the table.

3. Open tblStuffedAnimals. This table also has a field named ProductGroup. Maximize the window.

4. Click the View button ☒. Click the **ProductGroup** row. It is Text, 30 spaces wide, and is not the primary key.

5. Press F6 and change the field size to **1** to match tblProductLines.

6. Click the Save button ☐. Click **Yes**. No data will be lost.

7. Switch to Datasheet View to verify that the data is still there.

8. Return to Design View. Click in the Data Type column for the **ProductGroup** row. Click the drop-down arrow and select Lookup Wizard.

 NOTE: You can use Insert, Lookup Column to start the Lookup Wizard.

9. In the first dialog box, choose I want the lookup column to look up the values in a table or query. Click Next.

10. In the next dialog box, select the related table. Choose tblProductLines and click Next.

11. Double-click ProductGroup to transfer it to the **Selected Fields** list. Click Next.

12. The next dialog box shows the ProductGroup field with all its values from the tblProductLines. Double-click the right border of the column selector. Click <u>N</u>ext.

13. Insert a space in the label for your lookup column. Click <u>F</u>inish.

14. A message box tells you that the table must be saved before relationships can be created. Click Yes.

15. Click the Lookup tab in the Field Properties section. The Display Control for this field should now show a combo box. The Row Source Type is Table/Query. The Row Source row shows the complex code that the wizard created to link these two tables.

 NOTE: A combo box control has a drop-down arrow and expands to show a list when you click the arrow.

FIGURE 5-16
Lookup tab for
ProductGroup field

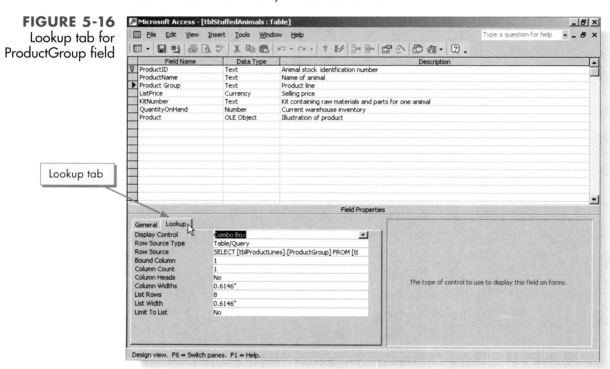

16. Save the table and switch to Datasheet View.

EXERCISE **5-12** **Add Data with a Lookup Field**

A lookup field ensures accuracy and consistency because the user can only select a value from a predefined list. Users enter data in a lookup field by clicking the drop-down arrow and selecting a value from the list.

1. Click the New Record button ▶＊.

2. Add the following record:

Product ID:	**T006**
Animal Name:	**Easter Bear**
Product Group:	*From the drop-down list, select T.*
List Price:	**14.5**
Kit Number:	**Bear006**
Inventory:	**200**
Illustration:	*Leave blank.*

FIGURE 5-17
Choose the value from the lookup column

```
Microsoft Access - [tblStuffedAnimals : Table]                              _ 8 X
 File  Edit  View  Insert  Format  Records  Tools  Window  Help    Type a question for help  _ 8 X
```

Product ID	Animal Name	Product Group	List Price	Kit Number	Current Inventory	Illustration
C002	Sara Shepherd	C	$12.50	Dog002	175	Bitmap Image
C003	Barney Bulldog	C	$12.50	Dog003	225	Bitmap Image
C004	Siamese Sally	C	$13.00	Cat004	255	Bitmap Image
C005	Tiggy Cat	C	$13.00	Cat005	240	Bitmap Image
D001	Gary Gecko	D	$11.00	Din001	300	Bitmap Image
D002	Tyrannosaurus Tommy	D	$10.75	Din002	295	Bitmap Image
D003	Brontosaurus Barry	D	$10.75	Din003	150	Bitmap Image
D004	Triceratops Tony	D	$11.00	Din004	125	Bitmap Image
D005	Stegosaurus Sue	D	$11.00	Din005	200	Bitmap Image
E001	Ziggy Zebra	E	$13.75	Zeb001	150	Bitmap Image
E002	Tula Tiger	E	$13.75	Tig002	235	Bitmap Image
E003	Larry Lion	E	$14.00	Lin003	225	Bitmap Image
E004	Elvira Elephant	E	$10.75	Ele004	175	Bitmap Image
E005	Whitey Whale	E	$10.75	Whl005	200	Bitmap Image
F001	Linda Lamb	F	$10.75	Lam001	175	Bitmap Image
F002	Biffy Bunny	F	$9.50	Bun002	125	Bitmap Image
F003	Rodney Rooster	F	$9.50	Roo003	135	
F004	Penelope Pig	F	$9.50	Pig004	275	Bitmap Image
F006	Sherry Sheep	F	$10.75	Shp001	200	Bitmap Image
T001	Professor Bear	C	$14.00	Bear001	325	Bitmap Image
T002	Valentine Bear	D	$14.25	Bear002	175	Bitmap Image
T003	Mr. Theodore Bear	E	$12.50	Bear003	275	Bitmap Image
T004	Santa Bear	F	$13.75	Bear004	150	Bitmap Image
T005	Night Time Bear	T	$12.75	Bear005	225	Bitmap Image
T006	Easter Bear					
*					0	

```
Record: 14 ◄ [   26  ] ► ►1 ►＊ of 26
Product line
```

3. Close the table.

EXERCISE 5-13 View the Created Relationship

When you created the lookup field, Access identified a relationship between tblProductLines and tblStuffedAnimals based on the common field ProductGroup. You can now view that relationship in the Relationships window.

1. Click the Relationships button ⊞.

2. The Relationships window shows the last layout you saved. Click the Clear Layout button ☒ and click **Yes**.

3. Click the Show Table button .

4. Double-click tblProductLines and tblStuffedAnimals. Close the **Show Table** dialog box. Resize and rearrange the field lists so all field names and the join line are visible.

5. Double-click the join line to open the **Edit Relationships** dialog box. This is a One-To-Many relationship. The main table is tblProductLines; it has the primary key. Click **OK**.

6. Close the Relationships window. A message box asks if you want to save the changes to the layout. Click **Yes**.

7. Compact and close the database.

USING HELP

In the Microsoft Access Help dialog box, you can locate a topic by using the **Contents** or **Index** tabs.

● Use the **Contents** tab like a table of contents in a book. The **Contents** tab displays Help topics in an outline form.

● Use the **Index** tab like a Search command. Key a topic and then scroll through the alphabetical list of topics.

Display Help windows to learn about input masks and subdatasheets.

1. Choose <u>H</u>elp and Microsoft Access <u>H</u>elp. Click the <u>C</u>ontents tab.

2. Scroll to find the **Tables** topic. Click the Expand icon ⊞.

3. Expand the **Customizing Fields** topic.

4. Scroll to find **Restricting or Validating Data**. Expand the topic.

5. Click the topic **About creating input masks to control how data is entered in a field or control**.

6. Maximize the Help window. Read the information in the right panel.

7. Click the topic and read Choosing between using a mask and a display format.

8. Click the Collapse icon ⊟ next to the topic **Tables**.

9. Click the <u>I</u>ndex tab.

10. Key **subdatasheet**. Click **Search**.

11. In the C<u>h</u>oose a topic section, click **About subdatasheets**. Read the information in the right panel.

12. In the C<u>h</u>oose a topic section, click **Show or hide the foreign key in a subdatasheet**. Read the information in the right panel.

13. Close the Help window. Compact and close the database.

LESSON 5 Summary

➤ The current relationship layout displays in the Relationships window.

➤ Clicking the Show All Relationships button ▦ shows the currently viewed relationship and all other relationships in the database.

➤ Print relationships to troubleshoot and document portions of your database structure.

➤ Clicking and dragging from one common field in a field list to the other common field in another field list creates a relationship.

➤ Referential integrity can be enforced in a One-To-Many relationship or a One-To-One relationship, but not in an Indeterminate relationship.

➤ Deleting the line between two field lists in the Relationships window will remove the relationship between the two tables.

➤ Records from the related table can display as a subdatasheet within the datasheet of the primary table.

➤ When you add a default value to a field, values in previously entered records do not change.

➤ Formats help standardize how data will be displayed in Datasheet View.

➤ Input masks help standardize how data is entered.

➤ Lookup fields help standardize data entry by displaying input choices from another table.

LESSON 5 Command Summary

FEATURE	BUTTON	MENU	KEYBOARD	SPEECH
Insert Row		Insert, Rows		✓
Delete Row		Edit, Delete Rows		✓
Insert Subdatasheet		Insert, Subdatasheet		✓
Expand Subdatasheet	+	Format, Subdatasheet, Expand All		✓

continues

LESSON 5 Command Summary *continued*

FEATURE	BUTTON	MENU	KEYBOARD	SPEECH
Collapse Subdatasheet	—	Format, Subdatasheet, Collapse All		✓
Show Table		Relationships, Show Table		✓
View Relationships		Tools, Relationships		✓
Print Relationships		File, Print Relationships		✓

Concepts Review

TRUE/FALSE QUESTIONS

Each of the following statements is either true or false. Indicate your choice by circling T or F.

T F *1.* A lookup field lets you select a value from a list instead of keying the value.

T F *2.* When you clear the Relationships window, you also delete the relationships.

T F *3.* The set of database rules for relationships is known as validation norms.

T F *4.* A subdatasheet is a nested datasheet inside a main datasheet and shows records from a related table.

T F *5.* Using a default value can improve the speed, accuracy, and consistency of data entry.

T F *6.* Deleting the join line between two field lists in the Relationships window deletes the corresponding tables.

T F *7.* The Relationships window can display more than one relationship at a time.

T F *8.* You must use an input mask for data entry when a field has a Date/Time data type.

SHORT ANSWER QUESTIONS

Write the correct answer in the space provided.

1. What field property can you use to display data in a particular style?

2. What graphic represents the relationship between two tables in the Relationships window?

3. In a One-To-Many relationship with referential integrity, how can you identify the table on the "many" side of the relationship?

4. How do you delete a relationship in the Relationships window?

5. What button do you click to start the Input Mask Wizard?

_____

6. In the Format property, what symbol is used to capitalize all data in a field?

_____

7. How do you start the Lookup Wizard?

_____

8. What field property automatically enters a value for each new record?

_____

CRITICAL THINKING

Answer these questions on a separate page. There are no right or wrong answers. Support your answers with examples from your own experience, if possible.

1. The One-To-Many relationship is the most commonly used relationship in business databases. Why do you think this is true?

2. Input masks and default values are very useful when controlling data entry. When would it not be appropriate to use an input mask or default value?

Skills Review

EXERCISE 5-14

Set default values, formats, and input masks.

1. Set a default value and an input mask by following these steps:
   a. Open *[your initials]*CC-05.
   b. In Design View for tblCarriers, click in the Region row in the top pane.
   c. Key **state** in the Default Value row in the bottom pane.
   d. Click on the Field Name Phone in the top pane.
   e. Click the Input Mask row and the Build button ⬚.
   f. Click Yes to save the table.
   g. Select the Phone Number mask and click Finish.
   h. Change to Datasheet View. Click Yes to continue.

2. Set a format for a field by following these steps:
   a. Return to Design View.
   b. Click the Region row and its Format row.
   c. Key > to force the text to uppercase.
   d. Save the table and close the table.

3. Add a custom format by following these steps:
   a. Open the table tblSales in Design View.
   b. Click on the **Field Name** OrderDate in the top pane.
   c. Click its **Format** row in the lower pane.
   d. Key **mmmm d, yyyy** to spell out the month, show one or two digits for the date, a comma, and four digits for the year.
   e. Change to Datasheet View and click **Yes** to save the table.

4. Add two new records.

Order ID:	**2011**
Order Date:	**12/5/02**
Customer ID:	**2**
ExpressShip:	*Press* Tab
Carrier ID:	**B202**
Order ID:	**2012**
Order Date:	**12/10/02**
Customer ID:	**3**
ExpressShip:	*Press* Spacebar
Carrier ID:	**C303**

5. Close the table.

EXERCISE 5-15

Insert a subdatasheet. Create a relationship in the Relationships window.

1. Insert a subdatasheet by following these steps:
   a. Open tblSales and maximize the window.
   b. Choose I̲nsert, S̲ubdatasheet. Choose tblCarriers.
   c. In the **Link Child Field** and **Link Master Fields** boxes, select CarrierID. Click **OK**.
   d. The message box about relationships opens. Click **Yes** so Access creates the relationship for you.

   e. Click the Expand button ⊞ in the second record.

   f. Click the Collapse button ⊟. Close the table and save the layout.

2. Look at a relationship by following these steps:

   a. Click the Relationships button.
   b. Click the Show All Relationships button.
   c. Rearrange the field list so you can see all fields and join lines.
   d. Right-click the sloping part of the join line. Choose **Edit** R̲elationship. Notice that the main table is tblSales on the left. The related table is tblCarriers on the right. The common field is CarrierID. The relationship is Indeterminate, because CarrierID is not the primary key in the main table.

      e. Click Cancel to close the dialog box.

      f. Close the Relationships window and save the layout.

  3. Delete a subdatasheet and a relationship by following these steps:

      a. Open tblSales.

      b. Choose Format, Subdatasheet, and Remove.

      c. Save and close the table.

      d. Click the Relationships button .

      e. Right-click the sloping part of the join line between tblSales and tblCarriers. Choose Delete and click Yes.

EXERCISE 5-16

Create a relationship with enforced referential integrity. Print a relationship.

  1. Create a relationship in the Relationships window by following these steps:

      a. In the Relationships window, point at CarrierID in the tblCarriers field list and click.

      b. Hold down the left mouse button and drag to CarrierID in tblSales. Release the mouse button.

      c. The Edit Relationships dialog box opens. The Relationship Type is One-To-Many because CarrierID appears once in the tblCarriers table but could appear many times in the table tblSales.

      d. Click Create.

  2. Set referential integrity by following these steps:

      a. Double-click the sloping part of the join line between tblSales and tblCarriers.

      b. Click the check box to select Enforce Referential Integrity.

      c. Click OK.

  3. Print the relationship by following these steps:

      a. Save the layout.

      b. Click File, Print Relationships.

      c. Click File, Page Setup. Click the Page tab. Set the Orientation to Landscape.

      d. Click the print button ⊟.

      e. Click the close button ☒. Click No when asked to save.

EXERCISE 5-17

Create and use a lookup field.

  1. Create a lookup field by following these steps:

      a. Delete the join line between tblSales and tblCarriers and click the Yes button to verify the deletion. Close the Relationships window and save.

b. Open tblSales in Design View.

c. Click in the **Data Type** column for the CarrierID row. Click the drop-down arrow and select **Lookup Wizard**.

d. Choose **I want the lookup column to look up the values in a table or query**. Click **Next**.

e. In the next dialog box, select **Tables** from the View option group. Choose tblCarriers and click **Next**.

f. Double-click CarrierID. Click **Next**.

g. Adjust the column width and click **Next**.

h. Insert a space in the label for your lookup column. Click **Finish**.

i. Click **Yes** to save the table. Switch to Datasheet View.

2. Add data with a lookup field by following these steps:

a. With tblSales open in Datasheet View, add the following records. Use the lookup column to choose the carrier.

 TIP: Press F4 to display the choices in a drop-down list.

Order ID:	**2004**
Order Date:	**5/1/02**
Customer ID:	**4**
ExpressShip:	*Press* Tab
Carrier ID:	**A101**

Order ID:	**2005**
Order Date:	**6/1/02**
Customer ID:	**3**
ExpressShip:	*Press* Spacebar
Carrier ID:	**C303**

b. Close the table.

 c. Click the Relationships button.

d. Notice that Access has created a relationship between tblSales and tblCarriers. Close the Relationships window.

Lesson Applications

Create a relationship between tables. Set referential integrity. Print relationships.

1. In *[your initials]*CC-05, open the Relationships window and clear the layout.

2. Add tblNewPayments and tblSalesOrders to the window. Size the field lists to see the field names. Determine which is the common field.

3. Create a One-To-Many relationship with referential integrity between the tables. Save and close the layout.

 TIP: The fields used for a relationship must be the same size and data type.

4. Open tblNewPayments and enter another payment from Customer #4. Use OrderID **20500** and key an amount and date. Press [Enter] after the last field to see the error message.

5. Click OK in the message box.

6. Close the table and click OK in the message box again. Then click Yes. The record is not added to tblNewPayments, because there is no Order #20500 in tblSalesOrders.

7. From the Relationships window, print the relationship between these two tables.

8. Close the report without saving.

9. Save and close the Relationships window.

Add a field. Set a format. Add data.

1. Open *[your initials]*CC-05, if it is not already open.

2. Open the tblKitSuppliers table in Design View.

3. Insert a field between the City and PostalCode fields. Name the field **State** and choose Text as the data type. Set the Field Size at **2**. Set the Format to uppercase characters.

4. Change to Datasheet View and save the table.

5. Key the following states in the appropriate rows:

Mills Fabric & Notion Supply:	**il**
Laramie Fabric Works:	**co**
Colby Manufacturing Company:	**nc**
Northeast Fabric Supply:	**ct**
Southern Fabrics, Inc:	**nc**
Robinson Mills, Inc.:	**nj**

6. Change the contact name in the first record to *[your first and last name]*.

7. Print the table in landscape orientation. Close the table.

EXERCISE 5-20

Insert a subdatasheet. View the relationship. Print and then delete the relationship.

1. Open tblEmployees in Datasheet View.

2. Insert a subdatasheet that shows the job title of each employee. Use the table tblJobCodes with the common field JobCode.

3. Allow Access to create the relationship.

4. Print only the relationship between tblEmployees and tblJobCodes.

5. Delete the relationship between tblEmployees and tblJobCodes.

6. Save and close the Relationships window.

EXERCISE 5-21   ✚   *Challenge Yourself*

Create a new table. Add fields, input masks, and a lookup field. Create relationships. Enforce referential integrity. Add data. Print tables and relationships.

1. Create a new table named tblEmployeeAwards. Create a unique AwardID field. Create a field that acts as a foreign key field and links to the table tblEmployees.

2. In the new table, add a date field and a comment field.

3. Add an input mask for the date field and make the foreign key field a lookup field.

4. Modify the relationship between the two tables to enforce referential integrity.

5. Add at least five records to tblEmployeeAwards to test your structure.

6. Print each table in a landscape orientation.

7. Print the relationship.

8. Compact and close your database.

On Your Own

In these exercises you work on your own, as you would in a real-life work environment. Use the skills you've learned to accomplish the task—and be creative.

EXERCISE 5-22

Review the designs for the three databases you created in Exercises 4-23
through 4-25. Select one of the three databases to continue developing. Identify
two additional tables you might need to make your database designs more
useful. The relationships between the main table and the two additional tables
should be One-To-Many. On a blank sheet of paper, list the field names, data
types, field sizes, and attributes for the two new tables. Identify the common
fields among the three tables. Continue to Exercise 5-23.

EXERCISE 5-23

Create the two tables you designed in Exercise 5-22. Add appropriate field
properties to each table to make your design more useful. Create One-To-Many
relationships with referential integrity between the tables. Test the referential
integrity of the tables. Add at least five records to each empty table. Print each
table and its relationships. Continue to Exercise 5-24.

EXERCISE 5-24

Search the Internet for images or graphics you might wish to use in your
database. Design and create a new table to store the images. Create an appropriate relationship between this new table and the main table. Insert the images
into the new table. Print the relationship. Keep a copy of the database you
modified in Exercises 5-22 through 5-24. It might be used in subsequent lessons.
Submit to your instructor the printouts from Exercises 5-22 through 5-24, along
with your field list from 5-22.

Adding Forms to a Database

OBJECTIVES

After completing this lesson, you will be able to:

1. Create AutoForms.
2. Create a form using the Form Wizard.
3. Work with form sections.
4. Work with controls on a form.
5. Add a calculated control to a form.
6. Modify format properties.
7. Use the Web to display data.

MOUS
ACTIVITIES

In this lesson:

Ac2002 **3-1**
Ac2002 **3-2**
Ac2002 **4-1**
Ac2002 **4-2**
Ac2002 **8-2**
Ac2002 **8-3**

See Appendix E.

 Estimated Time: 2 hours

Y ou have already used tables, queries, and forms to enter and edit data. When you use a table or a query, the records are displayed in rows. If a table or query has many fields, you cannot see the entire record at once and need to scroll. Instead of scrolling, it's often better to view one record at a time by using a form.

There are other advantages to using forms:

- You can arrange data in an attractive format that may include special fonts, colors, shading, and images.
- You can design a form to match a paper source document.
- You can determine totals and make other calculations.
- You can display data from more than one table.

Creating AutoForms

The quickest way to create a form for any table or query is to use an *AutoForm*, a form layout that includes all fields in a specified arrangement. After you specify a recordset, Access creates an AutoForm that includes all the fields. You can create an AutoForm from the Tables or the Queries window by selecting the table or query and clicking the New Object button. From the Forms window and the New Form dialog box, you can choose between a columnar and a tabular AutoForm. A columnar AutoForm shows one record at a time with the fields in columns or lists. A tabular AutoForm displays each record in a row with fields in separate columns.

NOTE: When you use the New Object button, the AutoForm style is the same as the last AutoForm used at your computer.

EXERCISE **6-1** ## Create an AutoForm by Using the New Object Button

The New Object button is available on the Tables and Queries toolbars. You click the table or query you want to use and then choose what object you want to create from the New Object drop-down list.

1. Make a copy of **CC-06** and **CC-E-06**. Rename them to *[your initials]*CC-06 and *[your initials]*CC-E-06. Make sure neither new file is Read-only. Open *[your initials]*CC-06.

2. Click the Tables button. Click tblStuffedAnimals to highlight the name.

3. Click the drop-down arrow for the New Object button.

FIGURE 6-1
New Object
drop-down menu

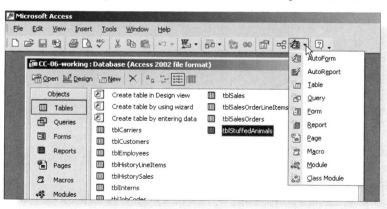

4. Choose AutoForm. A simple form opens, showing the first record from tblStuffedAnimals. The navigation buttons are at the bottom left corner of the form.

FIGURE 6-2
AutoForm with fields
displayed in a
single column

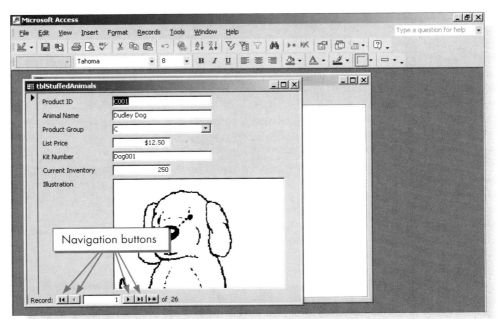

5. Click the Next Record button . Click the Last Record button. Click the Previous Record button. Click the First Record button.

6. Close the form without saving it.

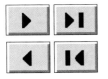

EXERCISE   6-2   Create a Multiple-Table Query

Forms are based on recordsets (tables or queries). If two tables are linked by a common field, you can build a query that uses fields from both tables.

REVIEW: A query is a database object that extracts information from the table or from other queries.

1. Click tblStuffedAnimals to highlight the name.

2. Click the drop-down arrow for the New Object button.

3. Choose Query. The New Query dialog box opens so you can choose how to build your query.

TIP: The face of the New Object button shows the most recently used choice.

4. Choose Design View and click OK. Maximize the window. The window shows one field list.

5. Place the pointer on the border between the top and bottom panes. Size the panes and the field list so you can see the field names.

6. Click the Show Table button 🔲. You can add tables to the query design.

7. Double-click tblProductLines. The field list appears in the top pane with an automatic join line for the common field.

FIGURE 6-3
Show Table
dialog box in
Query Design
window

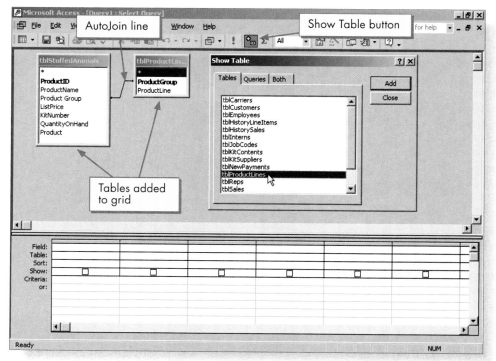

> **NOTE:** When two tables are placed in a query and no relationships have been defined, Access creates an AutoJoin if each table has a field with the same name and data type and one of these fields is a primary key.

8. Close the Show Table dialog box. Adjust the size of the field lists so you can see them both.

9. In the tblStuffedAnimals field list, double-click these field names:

ProductID

ProductName

ProductGroup

KitNumber

Product

10. In the tblProductLines list, double-click ProductLine.

11. Click the View button to see the results.

12. Click the Save button 🖫. Name the query **qryProductLines**

13. Close the query.

EXERCISE Create an AutoForm from the Forms Window

When you create a form from the Forms window, you need to choose the query or table in the drop-down list in the New Form dialog box.

1. Click the Forms button and the <u>New</u> button. The New Form dialog box opens.

2. Click AutoForm: Columnar in the list.

3. Click the drop-down arrow for Choose the table or query where the object's data comes from. The list displays the names of tables and queries in the database. Choose qryProductLines.

> **REVIEW:** Press F4 to display a drop-down list when the cursor is in the field.

FIGURE 6-4
Drop-down list displaying existing tables and queries

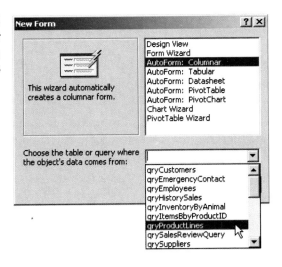

4. Click OK. Access creates a form with the fields in columns. Access displays the first record from the Product Lines query. (See Figure 6-5 on the next page.)

> **NOTE:** The appearance of your form might differ slightly from that of the form shown in Figure 6-5 if it has a different style applied to it.

5. Press PgDn several times to navigate through the records, and then press PgUp. Press Ctrl + End to move to the last record. Press Ctrl + Home to return to the first record.

6. Click the Save button 🖫. Change the name to **frmProductLines** and click OK. Close the form.

FIGURE 6-5
AutoForm with
fields in columns

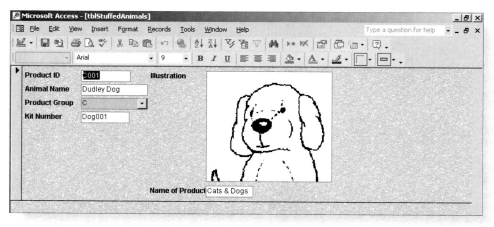

Using the Form Wizard

You can create a similar form by using the Form Wizard. The Form Wizard lets you select fields, a layout, and a style. The layout determines if the records are arranged in columns or rows. A style selects colors, backgrounds, and fonts automatically.

 NOTE: A form is created from a recordset and does not have to include all the fields from the query or table.

EXERCISE 6-4 Create a Form by Using the Form Wizard

Designing user-friendly input screens can be a time-consuming task. Database designers often use the Form Wizard to create a template they can modify to enhance the speed and accuracy of data entry.

1. Click the Forms button and then click **N**ew.

2. In the New Form dialog box, select Form Wizard.

3. Display the drop-down list of tables and queries. Select tblStuffedAnimals and click OK.

 NOTE: If you make a mistake selecting the table or query, you can select it in the first Form Wizard dialog box.

4. The dialog box asks which fields to use on the form. Click the Add All button >> to choose all fields.

5. Click KitNumber in the <u>S</u>elected Fields list. Click the Remove One button <u><</u> to move it back to the list on the left.

FIGURE 6-6
Selected fields
to be included
on the form

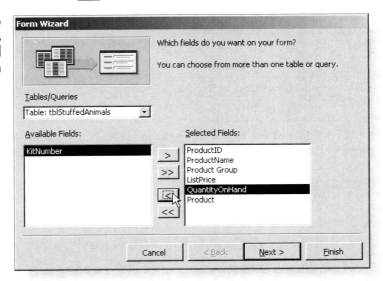

6. Click <u>N</u>ext. The dialog box asks you to choose a layout. Select <u>C</u>olumnar.

7. Click <u>N</u>ext. The next dialog box lists several styles. Click each style to see a preview.

8. Click Standard as the style for your form. Then click <u>N</u>ext.

9. The dialog box asks for a title for the form. This is the name used to save the form; it does not appear anywhere on the form. Key **frmAnimals**

10. Select <u>O</u>pen the form to view or enter information and then click <u>F</u>inish.

Working with Form Sections

Forms are designed to be viewed on a screen, but they can be printed. A form is divided into sections; some are visible on the screen and others on the printed page. You see the sections when you change to Design View.

 NOTE: The sections that initially appear in a form depend on how you created it.

Almost all forms have a *Detail section* to display one record. The *Form Header* appears once at the top of a form and is used to display such things as titles, images, and photographs. The *Form Footer* is similar to the Form Header, but appears at the bottom of a form. The *Page Header* is a section that prints at the top of each printed page. The *Page Footer* prints at the bottom of each page. A Page Header or Page Footer is often used for page numbers or dates.

TABLE 6-1   Sections of a Form

NAME OF SECTION	PURPOSE
Detail	Displays each record in a separate form.
Form Header	Appears once at the top of the form; typically includes a title, logo, date, or other similar data.
Form Footer	Appears once at the bottom of the form; typically includes a company name, logo, date, or other similar data.
Page Header	Prints at the top of each page.
Page Footer	Prints at the bottom of each page.

EXERCISE 6-5   **Open and Size the Form Header**

When you scroll through a form, the Form Header always displays at the top of the Form window. If the information in the Detail section is too large to display on one screen, it is good practice to place relevant information such as the title of the form in the Form Header.

1. Click the View button . Design View shows the sections and the objects in those sections. You also see a Standard toolbar, a Formatting toolbar, and the Toolbox.

> **NOTE:** The Toolbox might be floating; you can anchor it with the other toolbars by double-clicking its title bar.

FIGURE 6-7
Form Design View

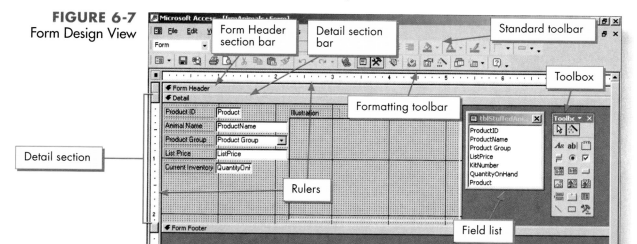

2. Place the pointer on the border between the **Form Header** and **Detail** section bars. The pointer changes to a two-headed arrow.

3. Drag the pointer down below the CurrentInventory field. This makes the **Form Header** section about 1.5 inches tall.

FIGURE 6-8
Opening the
Form Header

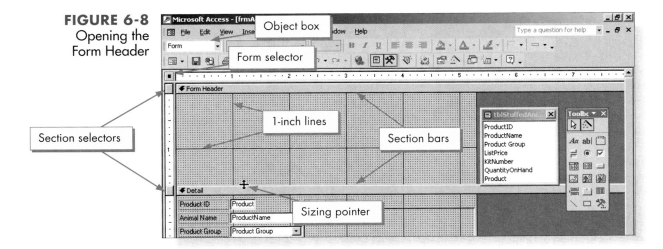

4. Drag the **Detail** border up to the 1-inch mark on the vertical ruler. (Notice the line that extends vertically and horizontally on the design grid. You should drag the border until it meets the line extending horizontally in the design grid from the 1-inch mark on the vertical ruler.)

 TIP: Each square of the design grid is 1 inch by 1 inch.

5. Double-click the **Form Header** section bar. The Form Header property sheet opens, listing the settings for this section. Click the **Format** tab. Change the **Height** to **.75**. (See Figure 6-9 on the next page.)

 6. Click the Close button ⊠. The **Form Header** section is now precisely sized.

7. Move the pointer to the right edge of the form (the gray area with dots.) When the pointer changes to a two-headed arrow, drag to the right until the edge of the form reaches the 6-inch mark on the horizontal ruler.

 8. Click the Form Selector ■ to the left of the horizontal ruler. A small black rectangle means the entire form is selected. The Object box on the Formatting toolbar shows that the Form is selected.

 NOTE: All objects in a form, as well as all parts of the form, have a property sheet. Select an object and press F4 to open its property sheet.

FIGURE 6-9
Form Header
property sheet

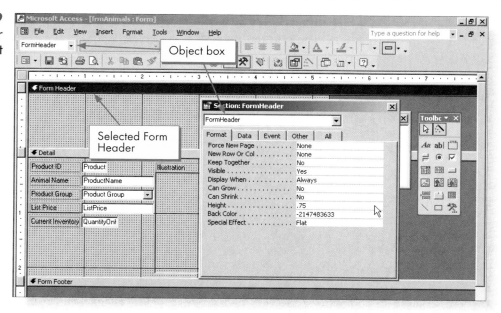

EXERCISE 6-6 Add a Label to the Form Header

The Label tool in the Toolbox is used to enter text or titles in a form. A label appears on all forms and does not change from record to record.

You can format a label much as you format text in a word processor. You can select the font, color, weight, and size of type. The Formatting toolbar includes buttons for most of these settings. Changes you make from the toolbar automatically are recorded in the label's property sheet. Changes to the position or size of an object are also recorded automatically in the label's property sheet.

When you select a label or any other object eight small black squares known as *selection handles* appear around the object. Selecting the top left selection handle moves the object. The other seven selection handles are also known as *sizing handles*. You can use them to adjust the size of the object.

1. Click the Label button Aa in the toolbox. The pointer changes to a crosshair cursor with the letter A.

2. Place the pointer in the **Form Header** section at the left edge. Click and then drag down and to the right to draw a box about 2 inches wide and .5 inch tall. When you release the mouse button, you see the box and a text insertion point.

3. Key **Stuffed Animals** and press Enter . The label box is selected and displays the eight selection handles around its edges.

NOTE: Pressing Enter does not move the cursor to the next line in a label. It finishes the label and selects it.

FIGURE 6-10
Adding a label to
the Form Header

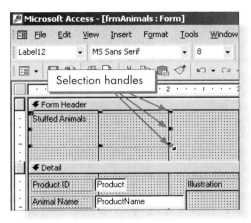

4. The Formatting toolbar displays the font name and size. Click the drop-down arrow next to the Font list box. Key **t** to move to the first font name that begins with "T." Select Times New Roman.

5. Click the drop-down arrow next to the **Font Size** list box. Click **18**.

6. Place the pointer on any selection handle except the top left one to display a two-headed arrow. Double-click. This sizes the label box to fit the text.

7. Place the pointer on the middle right selection handle to display a two-headed arrow. Drag to the right about 1 inch. This resizes the label box to a custom size.

FIGURE 6-11
Sizing the label box

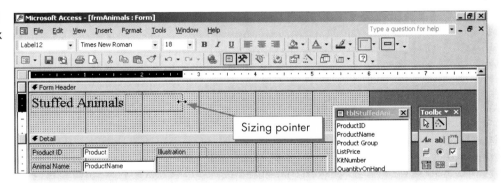

 8. Click the Center button ▤ on the Formatting toolbar. This centers the text within the box.

9. Double-click any sizing handle again.

 10. Click the drop-down arrow next to the Font/Fore Color button **A** on the Formatting toolbar to open a palette.

11. Click a medium blue color tile to change the text. (See Figure 6-12 on the next page.)

 12. Click the drop-down arrow next to the Fill/Back Color button ▧. Select white from the color palette.

 13. Click the View button ▤ to see the changes. Close and save the form.

FIGURE 6-12
Changing the
font color

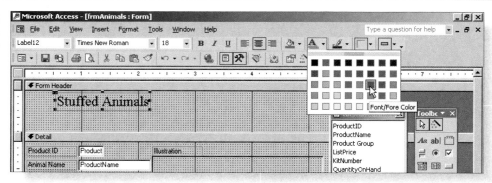

Working with Controls on a Form

When you view a form in Design View, you see its controls. A *control* displays data, performs an action, or adds a design element. A control can be bound, unbound, or calculated.

- A *bound control* is linked to a recordset; it has a data source. Use bound controls to enter or change data. The data in a bound control changes from record to record.

- An *unbound control* displays labels, titles, lines, rectangles, or other design elements. It has no data source and isn't linked to a recordset.

- A *calculated control* uses an expression as its source of data. A calculated control can use field names, arithmetic operators, constant numbers, or functions. It is not a field in a recordset.

To change any control, you first select it. Many controls initially include a text box and an attached label. To select the control as a whole, click the text box. Labels are unbound and do not affect the information in a recordset.

As you move the pointer over the top or bottom borders of a selected control, the Move pointer (an open-hand pointer) appears. The Move pointer moves the text box and its label.

When you place the pointer on the top left selection handle of a control, a hand with a pointing finger appears. This pointer moves the individual bound part of a control (a text box) or unbound part of a control (a label). You can size either part of a control by placing the pointer on a handle other than the top left one and displaying a two-headed arrow.

TABLE 6-2 Special Pointers

NAME	POINTER	USED TO
Open-hand	✋	Move a control and its label.
Upward-pointing hand	☝	Move a label or text box separately.
Two-headed arrow	↕ ↗ ↔	Resize a control vertically, diagonally, or horizontally.

EXERCISE **6-7** **Select and Move Controls**

In the form you are going to view, text boxes have a white background. Labels have black text and a background matching the rest of the form.

1. In the Forms window, select frmAnimals and click <u>D</u>esign.

 NOTE: An attached label shows the caption from the field as a default.

2. Click the ProductName text box; its label shows "Animal Name." Handles appear around the borders of the text box. The name of the selected object appears in the Object box at the left edge of the Formatting toolbar.

3. Click the QuantityOnHand text box; its label is "Current Inventory." Its name appears in the Object box.

4. Click the List Price label, not the text box. The Object box indicates this is a label.

5. Click the large box for the picture. The Object name box shows "Product," the name of the field. The label "Illustration" displays above the box.

6. Double-click the Detail section bar to open its property sheet.

 TIP: You do not need to type the quotation mark (") to show inches when entering a size in a property sheet.

7. Click the Format tab and set the Height to **4** inches. Close the property sheet.

8. Click the large picture box. This is the Product control.

9. Place the pointer on either the top or bottom edge of the box (but not on a handle). The pointer changes to an open-hand pointer.

10. Drag the control below the other controls and to the left to align under the Current Inventory label. (See Figure 6-13 on the next page.)

  REVIEW: If you make an error sizing or moving a control, click the Undo button and try again.

11. Click the ProductName text box. Place the pointer on the top or bottom edge of the text box (but not on a handle). The pointer changes to an open-hand pointer.

12. Drag the control to the right and up to align with the ProductID control. Place the left edge of the Animal Name label at the 2-inch mark on the horizontal ruler.

 NOTE: When you select a text box, the label is included in the selection.

FIGURE 6-13
Moving a control

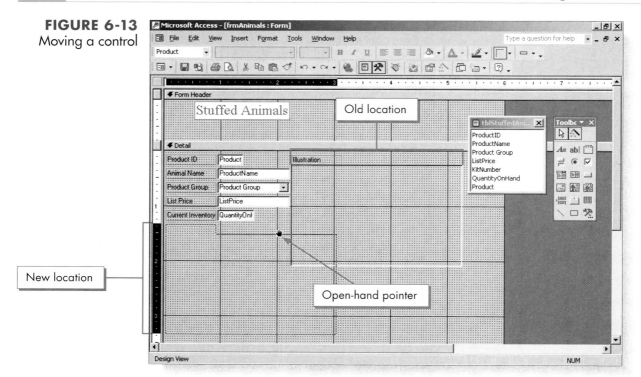

New location

13. Select the ProductGroup text box. Hold down Ctrl and press → to nudge the control to the right. Repeat this step several times.

14. Hold down Ctrl and press ↑ to nudge the control up. Nudging moves the control one pixel at a time.

15. Drag the ProductGroup control beneath the ProductName control. Nudge it until one row of grid dots shows between it and the ProductName text box.

16. Select the ListPrice text box. Press Shift and select the QuantityOnHand text box. Both controls are selected.

17. Point at the top or bottom edge of either control until you see the open-hand pointer. Drag both controls below the ProductGroup control, leaving a space of one row of grid dots.

18. Click an unused part of the form to deselect all controls.

19. Click the View button ▣ to see your changes.

EXERCISE   6-8   Adjust the Size of Controls

You can adjust the width and height of the text box or the label box. You can select multiple controls and change them all at once.

1. Click the View button to return to Design View.

2. Select the QuantityOnHand text box. Point at the middle sizing handle on the right edge. The pointer changes to a horizontal two-headed arrow.

3. Drag the pointer to the right to make the box the same width as the ListPrice text box.

4. Press Shift and click the ListPrice text box to add it to the selection. Repeat the steps to add the ProductGroup, ProductName, and ProductID text boxes to the selection. All the text boxes show handles.

5. Click the Properties button on the Standard toolbar. The property sheet shows that this is a multiple selection.

6. Click the **Format** tab. Set the **Width** to **1** inch. Press ↑ to see your changes.

FIGURE 6-14
Multiple selections of controls

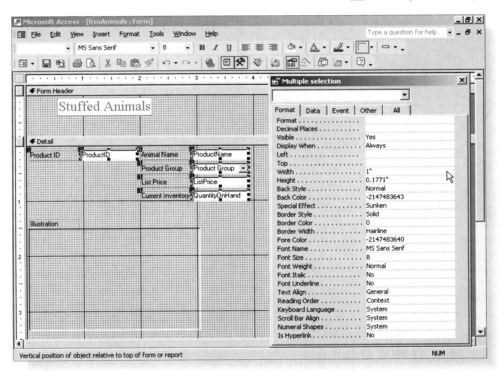

7. Close the property sheet and deselect the controls. Switch to Form View to see your changes. Then return to Design View.

8. Point at the bottom edge of the horizontal ruler, close to the 3.5-inch mark, directly above the text boxes in the **Detail** section. When the pointer is a solid black arrow, click to select the controls in a column. (See Figure 6-15 on the next page.)

9. From the **Format** menu, choose **Vertical Spacing, Make Equal**. Access evens the spacing between the controls.

FIGURE 6-15
Selecting multiple
controls in a column

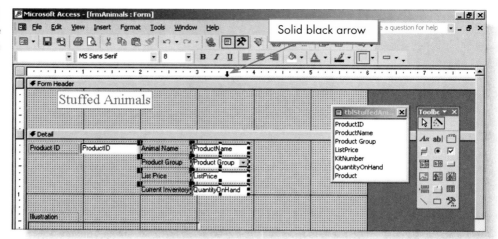

FIGURE 6-15
Selecting multiple
controls in a column

 NOTE: The Vertical Spacing command uses the space between the first two controls as a guide for the others.

10. While the controls are still selected, choose Format, Vertical Spacing, and Increase. More space is added between each set of controls.

11. Click the ProductID text box. Hold down ⇧Shift and press ← to size the control in small increments. Repeat this several times.

12. Click the View button ▣ to see the changes.

13. Save the form and return to Design View.

 TIP: You can save a form in either Design or Form View.

EXERCISE **6-9** **Align and Move Controls**

As you move and size controls, you might place them so they are no longer vertically or horizontally aligned. The Align command lines up controls at the top, bottom, left, or right. You can align both text boxes and labels.

1. Select the ProductID text box. Press ⇧Shift and select the Product ID label, the ProductName text box, and the Animal Name label.

2. Choose Format, Align, Top to align the top borders of the controls. Deselect the controls.

3. Select the labels Animal Name, Product Group, List Price, and Current Inventory. Choose Format, Align, Left. Deselect the labels.

4. Select the ProductName text box. Point at the move handle (top left). The pointer changes to an upward pointing hand.

5. Drag the text box to the right until its left edge is about at the 3-inch mark, moving it away from its label.

6. Select the ProductGroup text box and display the upward pointing hand pointer. Drag the box to the 3-inch mark. Repeat for the ListPrice and QuantityOnHand text boxes.

 NOTE: You cannot move multiple controls with the move handle (upward pointing hand pointer).

TABLE 6-3   **Alignment Options**

CHOOSE	TO DO THIS
Left	Vertically align the left edges of the controls with the control that is the farthest to the left.
Right	Vertically align the right edges of the controls with the control that is the farthest to the right.
Top	Horizontally align the top edges of the controls with the control that is the highest.
Bottom	Horizontally align the bottom edges of the controls with the control that is the lowest.
To Grid	Align the uppermost corner of the selected control to the design grid.

7. Click anywhere in the unused portion of the form to deselect the controls.

8. Save the changes. Switch to Form View to see your form.

EXERCISE   6-10   Use the Property Sheet

Each control, object, and section on a form has its own *property sheet*. A property sheet lists all the characteristics or attributes for that object.

Properties depend on the type of object. Properties for a label, for example, include such things as font size, font name, and font color. Properties for a text box include a format setting, a data source, and whether the data is visible. When you're selecting a property, a short description of what the property will control appears in the status bar.

For a bound control, many properties are inherited from the table. For example, if you used the Yes/No check box for a field in the table, that control is a Yes/No check box in the form. If you set the Currency format in the table, the control inherits the Currency format in the form.

 NOTE: A form inherits the field properties of the table. Changes to the form's properties do not affect the table's properties.

1. Click the View button to return to Design View.

2. Right-click the ProductName text box (not the label). Choose <u>P</u>roperties from the shortcut menu. The **Text Box** property sheet for ProductName opens. It has five tabs and shows the name of the control in the title bar and the drop-down list box.

3. Click the **All** tab. The property sheet is a window that you can size and move. Drag the border of the window to make it taller. Scroll to view the list of properties for the text box.

FIGURE 6-16
Text Box
property sheet
for ProductName

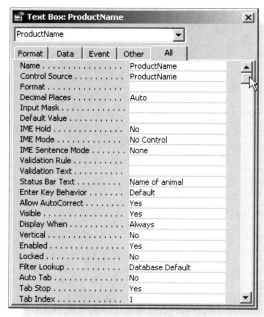

4. Select ListPrice_Label from the drop-down list box. The title bar shows the name and type of property sheet.

5. Scroll through the properties on the **All** tab. Notice that the properties for a label are different from the properties for a text box.

 TIP: You can double-click an unselected control to open its property sheet.

6. Click the **Format** tab. Change the Width to **3**. This makes the label 3 inches wide. Close the property sheet.

7. Because the label is too wide, click the Undo button.

8. Double-click the box for the picture to open its property sheet. The title bar shows that this control is a Bound Object Frame.

9. Pictures have a property called **Size Mode** (on the **Format** tab) that specifies how the picture fits in the box.

10. Click the **Size Mode** row and its drop-down arrow. Choose **Stretch**. (See Figure 6-17 on the next page.)

FIGURE 6-17
Bound Object Frame
property sheet

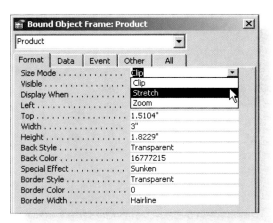

11. Close the property sheet.

12. Switch to Form View. The picture is resized to fit the box.

13. Save your form.

EXERCISE 6-11   Set Tab Order

Tab order determines where the insertion point goes when you press Tab in Form View. The usual order is left-to-right, top-to-bottom. When you move controls in Design View, the tab order might be changed and might not be what you expect.

1. Press Tab to move from field to field. The order is left-to-right, top-to-bottom. Finish so the pointer is in the Product ID field on any record.

 NOTE: If your tab order is not left-to-right, top-to-bottom, you might have already made a change that adjusted the tab order.

2. Switch to Design View.

3. Drag the ProductID control to the right of the QuantityOnHand control.

4. Select the ProductName control and drag it where the ProductID control was.

5. Switch to Form View.

6. Press Tab to move from field to field. With the controls rearranged, the tab order is no longer left-to-right, top-to-bottom.

7. Switch to Design View.

8. Click the **Detail** section bar to select the section. Choose **View, Tab Order**. The **Tab Order** dialog box opens.

9. Click **Auto Order** to set the tab order left-to-right, top-to-bottom. (See Figure 6-18 on the next page.)

10. Click **OK**. Return to Form View.

11. Check the tab order. Close the form without saving the changes.

FIGURE 6-18
Tab Order
dialog box

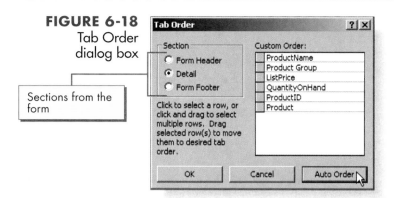

Sections from the
form

Adding a Calculated Control to a Form

A calculated control uses an expression instead of a field. An expression might combine arithmetic operators (+ – * /), constants, field names, or functions.

EXERCISE 6-12 Create a Form from the Query Window

Your next form includes the name of a stuffed animal product and the number of units in inventory. After creating and saving the form, you use an unbound control to calculate a new cost.

1. Click the **Queries** button. Click **qryInventorybyAnimal** to select it.

2. Click the **New Object** drop-down arrow. Select **F**orm.

3. The New Form dialog box opens with the query name.

4. Click **Form Wizard** and click **OK**.

5. The dialog box asks which fields to use on the form. Click the Add All button **>>** .

6. Click **N**ext. Select **C**olumnar for the layout.

7. Click **N**ext. Click **Stone** as the style, and then click **N**ext.

8. Edit the title to show **frmNewInventory**. Select **O**pen the form to view or enter information and then click **F**inish.

9. Maximize the window.

EXERCISE 6-13 Add a Calculated Control

You add calculated controls by using the Text Box button **ab** in the toolbox. You can add expressions to the **Control Source** row by using the Expression Builder. An *expression* is any legal combination of text, numbers, or symbols that represents a value. The *Expression Builder* lets you build an expression by selecting field names, operators, functions, constants, and other elements. Because a calculated control has no inherited format, you will need to specify the format after you create the control.

1. Click the View button .

2. Click the Field List button 🔲. This turns the field list on and off. Finish with the Field List displayed.

3. Place the pointer on the right edge of the form and drag to the 5-inch mark.

4. Click the Text Box button **ab** in the toolbox. The pointer shows a crosshair and the text box icon.

5. Click at the 4-inch mark on the design grid on the same row as the QuantityOnHand text box. A new unbound text box with a label appears on the form.

FIGURE 6-19
Adding a text box

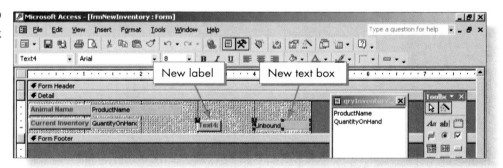

NOTE: The default label for new text boxes is "Text" followed by a number and a colon.

6. Click the new label. Click again within its text to display an I-beam.

7. Click and drag to select the whole default label "Text##:" (Access uses ## to indicate that this could be any number.) Key **New Quantity** as the new label and delete the colon.

TIP: When you click twice to display an I-beam, you might accidentally open the property sheet if you click too fast. If you do, close the property sheet and try again.

8. Double-click the unbound text box. Click the **Data** tab.

9. Click the **Control Source** row; read the status bar. There is a drop-down list and a Build button 🔳. The drop-down arrow displays a list of the fields in the underlying query. (See Figure 6-20 on the next page.)

FIGURE 6-20
Control Source row

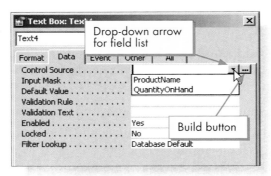

 TIP: Press Esc to close the field list if you open it.

10. Click the Build button ... to open the Expression Builder. In the left panel, your frmNew-Inventory form is shown as the current object at the top of the list.

TABLE 6-4   **Parts of the Expression Builder**

PART	PURPOSE
Expression box	White area at the top of the window that shows the formula as you build it. (Also called the preview area.)
Operator row	Set of buttons with common arithmetic and logical symbols below the preview area.
Left panel	List of folders with objects available for use.
Middle panel	Contents of the folder selected in the left panel.
Right panel	Details or properties of the object selected in the middle panel.
Paste button	Copies selected object or command into the preview area.

11. In the middle panel, click <Field List>. The right panel shows the fields in the form.

12. Double-click QuantityOnHand in the right panel. It is pasted into the preview area with square brackets. Access applies its standard formatting for expressions you build in the Expression Builder.

 NOTE: You can double-click the field names or select them and click the Paste button.

 13. Click the multiplication button * in the operator row. It appears in the Preview window after [QuantityOnHand].

14. Key **1.1**

FIGURE 6-21
Expression Builder
with an expression

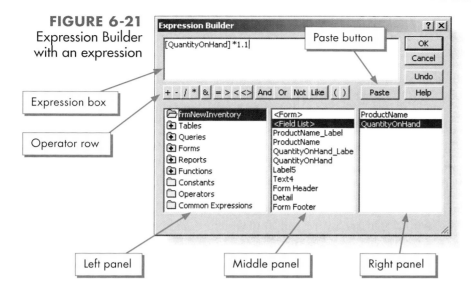

Expression box

Operator row

Left panel   Middle panel   Right panel

15. Click **OK** to close the Expression Builder. The expression is entered in standard Access format in the **Control Source** row of the property sheet.

 TIP: You must click the OK button to accept the changes in the Expression Builder.

16. Click the **Format** tab in the property sheet. Click the **Format** row and its drop-down arrow. Choose **Fixed**.

17. Click the **Decimal Places** row and choose **0**.

18. Click the **Other** tab. Key **NewQuantity** in the **Name** property; this is the name of the control.

19. Click on another property; notice that the title bar has changed to show the new name of the control.

20. Close the property sheet. The calculated control appears on the form.

21. Change to Form View. Press PgDn to view a few records.

22. Close and save the form. You are returned to the Queries window where you started when you began creating this form.

Modifying Format Properties

No matter how you create a form, you can apply styles, colors, and fonts to give the form an attractive and professional look. You can change border styles and background colors for controls. You can even change the background color for an entire section. In addition to your own formatting, you can use a predefined style template for the form.

EXERCISE **6-14** **Create a Multiple-Table Query with a Calculated Field**

Multiple table queries are created when two or more tables are combined to create a unique recordset. Each table must relate to another table through a common field.

You can create a multiple-table query that uses a calculated field. The calculated field will display as a new column in the recordset. Using calculated fields saves storage space by displaying numerical results only at the time that you need the information. For example, it would not be necessary to store the total cost of items ordered if you had already stored the quantity ordered and the price of each item.

1. In the Tables window, click tblKitContents to highlight the name.

2. Click the drop-down arrow for the New Object button . Choose **Query.**

3. Choose Design View and click **OK.** Maximize the window. Adjust the size of the panes and the field list.

4. Click the Show Table button . Double-click tblKitSuppliers and then double-click tblStuffedAnimals. Notice the join lines for the common fields.

> **TIP:** You can arrange field lists in the Queries window to eliminate crisscrossed join lines just as in the Relationships window.

5. Close the Show Table dialog box. Adjust the size of the new field lists.

6. In the tblStuffedAnimals list, double-click ProductName.

7. In the tblKitContents list, double-click these field names:

   KitNumber

   Cost

8. In the tblKitSuppliers list, double-click SupplierName. (See Figure 6-22 on the next page.)

9. Click the Save button . Name the query **qryKitCosts**

10. Click the Field row for the first empty column (the fifth column). Then click the Build button to open the Expression Builder.

11. Double-click Cost in the middle panel. Key **+.75** to increase the cost by 75 cents. Click **OK** to close the Expression Builder.

12. Click the View button to see the results. Return to Design View.

13. In the new calculated field, drag across Expr1 and key **NewCost**. Leave the colon.

> **NOTE:** The colon separates the caption from the actual expression.

14. Click the Properties button. Set the **Format** to Currency.

15. Set the **Caption** to **New Cost**. Close the property sheet.

FIGURE 6-22
Multiple-table query
in Design View

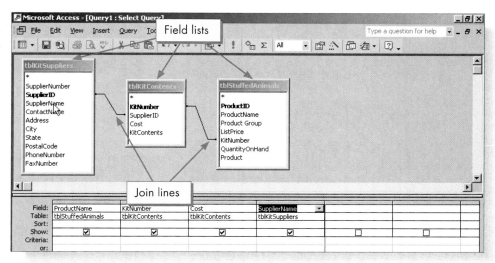

16. View the results. Then save and close the query.

17. Click the **Queries** tab. Click qryKitCosts. Click the drop-down arrow for New Object ⚎. Select Auto**F**orm.

18. Click the Save button 🖫 and name the form **frmKitCosts**

EXERCISE 6-15 Open the Form Header/Footer

When you create an AutoForm, the Form Header is not open. You need to turn it on from the View menu. When you turn on the **Form Header/Footer** option, both the header and footer sections open.

1. In form frmKitCosts, switch to Design View.

2. Choose **V**iew, Form **H**eader/Footer. The **Form Header** and **Form Footer** sections open.

3. Drag the bottom border of the **Form Header** to make the section about 1 inch tall.

4. Click the Label button 🄰𝘢. Draw a label about 1.5 inches wide and .5 inch tall near the left edge of the **Form Header**.

5. Key **Increased Kit Costs** and press Enter.

6. Change the font and size to 20-point Arial. Click the Bold button **B** and the Italic button _I_.

7. Double-click a sizing handle to adjust the size of the label to show the title.

8. Place the pointer on the bottom edge of the form. Drag the edge up to the bottom of the **Form Footer** section bar. This closes the **Form Footer**.

9. Save the form.

EXERCISE 6-16 *Move, Align, and Space Controls*

When you design a form, you should align controls and space them appropriately.

 REVIEW: The Form Selector is the etched rectangle to the left of the horizontal ruler.

1. Click the Field List button 🔲 to close the field list.
2. Double-click the Form Selector to open the form's property sheet.
3. Click the **Format** tab and make the form **6.25** inches wide. Close the property sheet.
4. Select the SupplierName text box and drag it and its label to the right of the ProductName text box.
5. Select the NewCost text box and drag it up, closer to the Cost text box.
6. Select the ProductName text box. Place the pointer on the move handle (the top left selection handle) to display the upward-pointing hand pointer. Drag the text box closer to its label. Leave about four columns of dots between the text box and the label.
7. Repeat these steps for the KitNumber text box.

 TIP: You cannot nudge a single label or text box by using Ctrl and an arrow key. You must drag the label or text box.

8. Select the ProductName, KitNumber, Cost, and NewCost text boxes.
9. Click the Properties button 🔳. Click the **Format** tab.
10. Click the **Left** row and set the left position for all the selected controls at **1** inch. Then set the **Width** at **1.25** inches. Close the property sheet.

FIGURE 6-23
Labels positioned closer to text boxes and resized

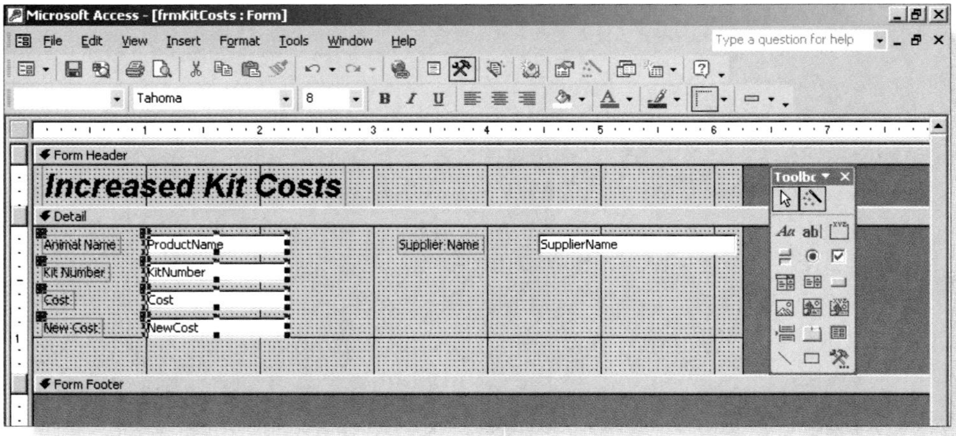

![Microsoft Access screenshot showing the frmKitCosts form in design view with the "Increased Kit Costs" header and fields for Animal Name (ProductName), Kit Number (KitNumber), Cost (Cost), New Cost (NewCost), and Supplier Name (SupplierName).]

11. Select the SupplierName text box and drag it until the label starts at the 3-inch mark. Then drag the text box closer to its label, showing about four columns of dots.

12. Set the width of the SupplierName text box at **2** inches.

13. Position the pointer at the left edge of the form, on the right border of the vertical ruler, on the row for the **Name** controls. The pointer displays a solid black arrow. Click to select all the controls in the row.

FIGURE 6-24
Selecting a row
of controls

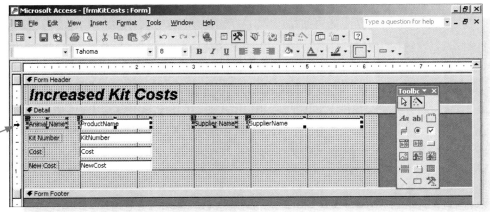

Solid black arrow

 TIP: You can also click the bottom edge of the horizontal ruler to select a column of controls.

14. Choose F**or**mat, **A**lign, **T**op to align the controls on their top edges.

15. Position the pointer on the bottom border of the horizontal ruler, above the Animal Name and other labels. Click to select all the controls in the column, including the main title.

16. Point at the label in the **Form Header** and press Shift and click to deselect the control.

17. Choose F**or**mat, **A**lign, and **L**eft to align the labels in the **Detail** section on their left edges. Leave the labels selected.

18. Position the pointer on the bottom border of the horizontal ruler, above the ProductName and other text boxes. Press Shift and click to add the text boxes to the selection. The main title is included again.

19. Point at the label in the **Form Header** and press Shift and click.

20. Choose F**or**mat, **V**ertical Spacing, and Make E**q**ual. While the controls are selected, choose F**or**mat, **V**ertical Spacing, and **I**ncrease.

21. Save the form and switch to Form View.

22. Press Tab to determine how the insertion point moves through the form.

23. Return to Design View.

24. Click the Detail section bar. Choose <u>V</u>iew and then Ta<u>b</u> Order. Click AutoOrder. Click OK.

25. Return to Form View and check the tab order.

26. Return to Design View and save the form.

EXERCISE **6-17** **Change the Font and Set a Special Effect**

You can quickly change the font and font size to make the text easier to read. You can also apply special effects to a control. Special effects change the appearance of the border around the control.

1. With frmKitCosts open in Design View, position the pointer at the left edge of the form, on the first row of name controls in the Detail section. With the solid black arrow, drag down to select all controls in the Detail section.

 TIP: You can select one row of controls and add others by pressing Shift and clicking.

2. Click the Font arrow and choose Arial. Click the Font Size arrow and choose 11.

3. While the controls are selected, choose F<u>o</u>rmat, <u>S</u>ize, and To <u>F</u>it. The controls are sized to fit the font.

 TIP: The <u>S</u>ize, To <u>F</u>it command is helpful but might not make the controls wide enough for all the text. Always preview your form.

4. Deselect the controls and switch to Form View. Several controls are now not wide enough, because the font is larger.

5. Return to Design View and select the ProductName text box.

6. Place the pointer on the top left handle and drag the text box to the right until you see the complete Animal Name label.

7. Make the ProductName text box slightly wider.

8. Preview the form to see if the text box is wide enough. Return to Design View. Adjust the size of the text box and move it until you can see all the animal names.

9. Open the property sheet for the ProductName text box. Check the Width property.

10. Click the KitNumber text box and make it the same width as the ProductName text box. Repeat these steps for the Cost and New Cost text boxes.

11. Select the KitNumber, Cost, New Cost, and ProductName text boxes. Choose F<u>o</u>rmat, <u>A</u>lign, <u>R</u>ight.

12. Select the Supplier Name label (not the text box).

13. Drag the label by itself to the left until you see all of it.

14. Press Shift and click to add the Animal Name label to the selection. Repeat these steps to add the other labels in the Detail section.

 15. Click the drop-down arrow for the Special Effect button in the toolbar. Place the pointer on each button in the palette to see its name.

> **NOTE:** If you click a button that has a drop-down arrow, you apply the current color or style. You must click the drop-down arrow to see the choices.

16. Select Etched for the labels. Save the form.

EXERCISE 6-18 Change Colors

Controls have a fill or background color and a border or outline color. The font can also have a color. Each section on a form has a fill or background color, too.

1. With frmKitCosts open in Design View, select the label in the Form Header.

2. Click the drop-down arrow for the Fill/Back Color button . Choose red.

3. While the label is selected, click the drop-down arrow for the Font/Fore Color button [A]. Choose white.

> **TIP:** Some special effects cannot have Fill/Back colors.

4. While the label is selected, click the drop-down arrow for the Special Effects button [□]. Select Raised.

5. Click the Detail section bar to select the section.

6. Because red is the current Fill/Back color, you do not need to display the palette. Click the Fill/Back Color button [□].

7. Change to Form View. As you might guess, red is not a good background color for a form. It would be tiresome to look at it all day. Return to Design View.

8. Click the Undo button [↺].

9. Select all the text boxes, not the labels.

 10. Click the drop-down arrow for the Line/Border Color button [✎]. Select red.

11. Change to Form View. The border color overrides the special effect. Return to Design View.

12. With the text boxes selected, apply a Sunken special effect. The Sunken effect cannot have a border color.

13. View and save the form. Return to Design View. Click anywhere in an unused part of the form to deselect all controls.

EXERCISE 6-19   **Apply an AutoFormat**

An *AutoFormat* is a style template or preformatted design. A template applies font sizes and colors, border colors, and background colors to the entire form or to parts of the form.

1. With frmKitCosts open in Design View, click the **Form Selector**. The Object box shows Form.

2. Choose F**o**rmat, Auto**F**ormat.

3. The AutoFormat dialog box lists the names of the style templates. As you click each name, the preview appears. Click each A**u**toFormat name. Choose Blends.

 NOTE: You can apply your own local formatting after using an AutoFormat.

FIGURE 6-25
AutoFormat
dialog box

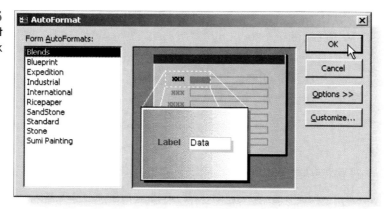

4. Click **OK**. The form is reformatted. Change to Form View to see the changes.

5. Return to Design View. Click the **Form Header** section bar to select only that section.

 6. Click the AutoFormat button. Click **Industrial** and click **OK**. Only the label in the **Form Header** is reformatted.

7. Use the AutoFormat to change the **Form Header** back to **Blend**.

8. Click the **Form Selector**.

9. Click the AutoFormat button. Click **International**.

10. Click the **Options** button.

11. Turn off the **Font** and the **Color** so only the **Border** is changed. Click **OK**. (See Figure 6-26 on the next page.)

12. Close the form without saving the changes.

FIGURE 6-26
AutoFormat options

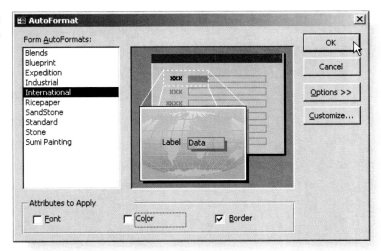

Using the Web to Display Data

You can save tables, queries, forms, or reports as Web pages. This allows you or others to look at your work by using a browser that can display the HTML format. *HTML* (Hypertext Markup Language) is the standard formatting language for Web documents. HTML documents are stored separately from the database.

You can share data through the Internet with Data Access Pages. To users, the Data Access Pages appear similar to forms. However, instead of viewing and changing data directly through the database, the user connects through an Internet browser.

EXERCISE 6-20 Save a Form as a Web Page

When you save a form as a Web page, the Web document shows the data in a tabular arrangement, like the table or query. However, it does not show any of the formatting or arrangement of controls from your form.

1. Click the Forms button. Click frmKitCosts to highlight it.

2. Choose File, Export. The Export Form To dialog box opens.

3. Set the Save in folder to your usual working folder.

4. Click the Save as type drop-down arrow. Choose HTML Documents. The default file name is the same as your form.

5. Click Export. (See Figure 6-27 on the next page.)

6. The HTML Output Options dialog box lets you choose a style sheet for Web pages. Click OK.

 NOTE: You can preview your Web document in Word or in your browser. You can choose File, Web Page Preview in Word to launch your browser.

FIGURE 6-27
Exporting a form as
a Web document

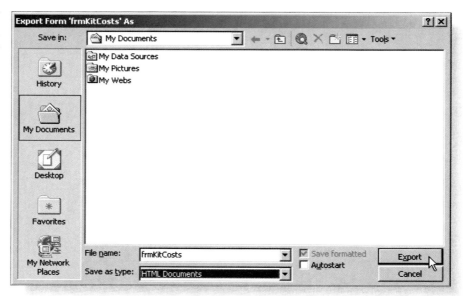

7. Start Word and open the HTML file **frmKitCosts**. Although the data displayed as a form in your database, the HTML document displays the raw data as a table.

FIGURE 6-28
Viewing the
Web document
in Word

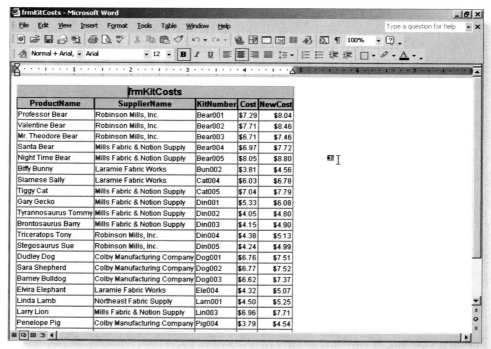

8. Exit Word without saving and return to Access.

EXERCISE 6-21 Create a Data Access Page

When a company wants to share Access information with customers or employees through the Internet, the company needs to create a Data Access Page and place it on the Web server. A *Data Access Page* is an object that acts like a form but whose controls are Internet compatible. A direct link is established between the Data Access Page and the source recordset.

1. Click the Pages button. Double-click Create data access page by using wizard.
2. Click the drop-down arrow for Tables/Queries and choose tblSalesOrders.
3. Click the Add All button >> . Click Next.
4. Do not use any grouping. Click Next.
5. Sort by OrderID in ascending order. Click Next.
6. Edit the name of the page to **pgeSalesOrders**. This will be the name of the page inside Access.
7. Choose the option to Open the page. Click Finish. The page opens in Page View, similar to Form View.

FIGURE 6-29
Data Access Page in
Page View

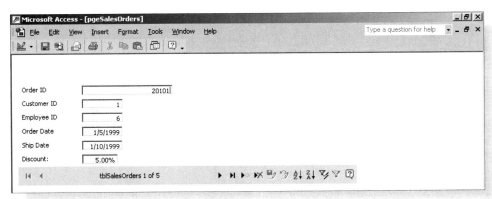

8. Click the Save button . Save the page using the same name.
9. Close the page. Notice that the page icon is a shortcut. The main page is located outside the database.
10. Compact and repair the database and exit Access.
11. Start Internet Explorer.

NOTE: So you can view data in Access 2002 Data Access Pages, your workstation must have an active Internet connection.

12. Choose File, Open. Click the Browse button. Set the Look in folder to the location where your files are stored.

13. Choose **pgeSalesOrders**. Click Open.

14. Click OK. This is a current view of the table. The Data Access Page has a row of navigation buttons.

15. Close Internet Explorer.

USING HELP

To learn more about many tasks or commands, you can ask the Office Assistant. Ask a question in your own words, and the Office Assistant provides a list of relevant topics.

Use the Office Assistant to learn about modifying a control:

1. Choose Help, Show the Office Assistant. If your Office Assistant is already active, your menu shows Hide the Office Assistant. Close the menu and press F1 to start the Assistant.

2. Key **modify a control** in the What would you like to do? box.

3. Press Enter. Access displays a list of related topics.

4. Click About types of controls in Access. Maximize the Microsoft Access Help window. Read the Help pane on the right.

5. Click Text boxes. Read the Help pane.

6. Read any topics that interest you.

7. Close Help.

LESSON 6 Summary

➤ You can create simple forms by using the New Object button and selecting AutoForm.

➤ Tables in a multiple-table query are linked by common fields.

➤ The Form Wizard guides you through the process of creating a form.

➤ Form Headers display at the top of each form window and Form Footers display at the bottom of each form window.

➤ You can resize labels by repositioning the selection handles.

➤ Text boxes are distinct from labels in appearance and purpose.

➤ The width and height of text boxes and label boxes can be changed individually or as a group.

➤ You can reposition multiple objects in a form by using the <u>A</u>lign command.

➤ The property sheet for each object in a form lists all the characteristics or attributes for that object.

➤ The tab order determines the sequence of the insertion point.

➤ Calculated fields are arithmetic expressions based on one or more fields in a recordset.

➤ The Expression Builder guides you in the creation of a calculated field.

➤ Calculated fields can be created in any type of query, including multiple table queries.

➤ Well-designed forms have controls that are aligned and spaced properly.

➤ The font type, font size, special effects, background color, border color, and outline color change the appearance of objects.

➤ AutoFormat applies font sizes, font colors, border colors, and background colors to an entire form or parts of a form.

➤ Web pages allow Access forms to be displayed as HTML pages. The data can be viewed using the Internet, but cannot be modified.

➤ Data Access Pages enable records to be viewed, entered, and modified through the Internet.

LESSON 6 Command Summary

FEATURE	BUTTON	MENU	KEYBOARD	SPEECH
View Properties	🗔	<u>V</u>iew, <u>P</u>roperties	F4	✓
AutoFormat	🗎	F<u>o</u>rmat, Auto<u>F</u>ormat		✓
Field List	▤	<u>V</u>iew, Field <u>L</u>ist		✓
Fill/Back Color	🪣			
Font/Fore Color	A			

continues

LESSON 6 Command Summary *continued*

FEATURE	BUTTON	MENU	KEYBOARD	SPEECH
Line/Border Color				
Special Effect				
Tab Order		View, Tab Order		✓
Label				
Text Box				
Align		Format, Align		✓
Web Page		File, Export		✓

Concepts Review

Each of the following statements is either true or false. Indicate your choice by circling T or F.

T F **1.** As you move controls on a form, the tab order adjusts so controls are always in left-to-right and top-to-bottom order.

T F **2.** Every form contains a main section and a subsection.

T F **3.** You can export a form to the World Wide Web.

T F **4.** An AutoForm creates a form that includes all the fields in a selected table.

T F **5.** The pointer changes to an open hand when you place it on the top left selection handle.

T F **6.** You can use AutoFormat to select a style template for a form.

T F **7.** You can change the background color of a **Form Header** section in Form View.

T F **8.** Field properties from the table are inherited when a form is created.

Write the correct answer in the space provided.

1. What section on a form shows different data for each record?

_____

2. What type of information might be displayed in the **Form Header** section?

_____

3. Which button do you use when adding a calculated control to a form?

_____

4. What opens when you click the Build button [...] in a query?

_____

5. What is the name of the list of characteristics or settings for every object in a form?

_____

6. What determines where the insertion pointer moves when you press Tab or Enter in a form?

_____

7. What button changes the text color in a label or a text box?

_____

8. What does your pointer look like while you are moving a label or text box separately?

_____

CRITICAL THINKING

Answer these questions on a separate page. There are no right or wrong answers. Support your answers with examples from your own experience, if possible.

1. You have edited, added, and searched records in a table and in a form. What commands are the same? What commands are different? Describe differences or similarities between a table and a form.

2. In this lesson you were introduced to some ideas about designing forms. What design principles might be effective for forms? How would the design ideas be different from printed reports?

Skills Review

EXERCISE 6-22

Create an AutoForm. Create a form by using the Wizard.

1. Create an AutoForm from the Forms window by following these steps:
   a. Open *[your initials]*CC-E-06.
   b. Click the Forms button and the <u>N</u>ew button.
   c. Click AutoForm: Columnar.
   d. Click the drop-down arrow for Choose the table or query where the object's data comes from.
   e. Choose tblEmployeeDates. Click OK.

 NOTE: The AutoForm uses one of the AutoFormat styles.

   f. Save the form as **frmEmployeeDates**
   g. Close the form.

2. Create a form with the Form Wizard by following these steps:

   a. Click the **Forms** button and <u>N</u>ew. In the New Form dialog box, select Form Wizard.

   b. Select tblSalesReps from the list. Click **OK**.

   c. Click the Add All button **>>**.

   d. Click <u>N</u>ext and select <u>C</u>olumnar as the layout.

   e. Click <u>N</u>ext. Click **Standard** as the style. Then click <u>N</u>ext.

   f. Key **frmSalesReps** as the title. Select <u>O</u>pen the form to view or enter information. Click <u>F</u>inish.

EXERCISE 6-23

Work with form sections. Work with controls.

1. Open and size the **Form Header** by following these steps:

   a. Switch to Design View for frmSalesReps and maximize the window.

   b. Place the pointer at the right edge of the form and drag to the 5-inch mark.

   c. Place the pointer at the top edge of the **Detail** section bar. When the pointer is a horizontal bar with a two-headed arrow, drag the bar down until the **Form Header** section is 1 inch tall.

   d. Double-click the **Form Header** section bar to open its property sheet.

   e. Click the **Format** tab. Set the Height to **.75**. Close the property sheet.

2. Add a label to the **Form Header** by following these steps:

   a. Click the Label button ⒜. Position the pointer at the top left corner of the **Form Header**.

   b. Draw a label box about .5 inch tall and as wide as the form.

   c. Key **Sales Representatives Rates** and press ⏎.

   d. Click the drop-down arrow for the **Font** box and select **Arial**. Click the drop-down arrow for the **Font Size** and select **20**. Click the Center button ▤.

> **TIP:** When a control is as wide as the form, the Center button ▤ gives the appearance of centering the text on the form or page.

   e. Double-click a sizing handle in the label box to size the control to fit the text.

   f. Switch to Form View to see the changes. Save the form.

3. Move, size, and align controls by following these steps:

   a. Select the Salary text box and display the open-hand pointer.

   b. Drag the control until the left edge of the label is at the 2-inch mark on the horizontal ruler, next to the SS# control.

   c. Drag the Rate control below the Salary control.

d. Select the Salary and Rate text boxes and choose F<u>o</u>rmat, <u>A</u>lign, and <u>R</u>ight.

e. Select the Rate label and position the pointer on the top left selection handle. Drag the label to the 3-inch mark.

 f. Select the Rate and Salary text boxes. Click the Properties button.

g. Set the Width for both controls to **1** inch. Set the Left position at **4**. Close the property sheet.

h. Press Shift and click to select the Salary and Rate labels. Choose F<u>o</u>rmat, <u>A</u>lign, and <u>L</u>eft.

i. While the labels are selected, position the mouse pointer on either of the middle right handles to display a two-headed arrow and drag to the left to make the labels slightly narrower.

j. Select the Region text box. Press Ctrl and ↑ as many times as needed to nudge the control below the SS# control on the same row as the Rate controls.

k. Position the pointer at the left edge of the vertical ruler to select the first row of controls in the Detail section. Choose F<u>o</u>rmat, <u>A</u>lign, and <u>T</u>op. Repeat for the second row.

l. Save the form.

4. Change and set the tab order by following these steps:

a. Choose <u>V</u>iew, Ta<u>b</u> Order.

b. Select the Detail section.

c. When the pointer displays a solid black arrow, select the Region field. Drag the row to be second in the list. Click OK.

d. Change to Form View. Press Tab to move from field to field.

e. Save and close the form.

EXERCISE 6-24

Create a form from the Queries window. Add a calculated control. Modify format properties.

1. Create a form from the Queries window by following these steps:

a. In *[your initials]***CC-E-06**, click the Queries button. Click qryEmployeeDates to select it.

 b. Click the drop-down arrow for the New Object button. Select <u>F</u>orm. Select Form Wizard and click OK.

c. Double-click the following fields to add them to the Selected Fields list: EmployeeID, BirthDate, HireDate.

d. Click <u>N</u>ext and choose <u>C</u>olumnar for the layout.

e. Click <u>N</u>ext and choose Blends as the style.

f. Click <u>N</u>ext and name the form **frmAnniversary**. Click <u>F</u>inish. Maximize the window.

2. Add a calculated control to a form by following these steps:

 a. Switch to Design View.

 b. Double-click the Form Selector button to open the form property sheet.

 c. Set the Width to **5** and close the property sheet.

 d. Click the Text Box button [ab].

 e. Draw a text box that starts at the 4-inch mark on the same row as the HireDate control. Make the box about 1 inch wide.

 f. Select the default text in the label. Key **20-Year Dates** as the new label and delete the colon.

 g. Right-click the Unbound control and open its property sheet. Click the **Data** tab.

 h. Click the Control Source row and the Build button [...].

 i. Click <Field List> in the middle panel. Double-click HireDate in the right panel.

 j. Click the addition button [+] in the operator row.

 k. Key **365.25*20** in the preview box after the plus sign. Click **OK**.

> **REVIEW:** You must use 365.25 to account for leap years.

 l. Click the **Format** tab and the **Format** row. Click the drop-down arrow and choose Medium Date.

> **TIP:** The name of the control is what you see in the field list.

 m. Click the **Other** tab. Key **AnnivDate** as the **Name**. Close the property sheet.

 n. Change to Form View to check your work. Move, align, and size the controls to make them all visible. Then save and close the form.

3. Move, size, and align controls by following these steps:

 a. Open **frmAnniversary** in Design View.

 b. Drag the EmployeeID text box without the label to the 1.5-inch mark on the horizontal ruler.

 c. Drag the BirthDate and HireDate text boxes to the 1.5-inch mark.

 d. Click at the bottom edge of the horizontal ruler, above the three text boxes. Choose F**o**rmat, **A**lign, and **L**eft.

 e. Place the pointer at the left edge of the first row of controls in the **Detail** section to display a black arrow. Drag to select all controls.

 f. Click the Font arrow. Key **t** and choose Times New Roman.

 g. Click the Font Size arrow and choose 12.

 h. Choose F**o**rmat, **S**ize, and To **F**it. Deselect the controls.

> **NOTE:** Move individual controls with the upward-pointing hand pointer.

i. Move the EmployeeID label to the .25-inch mark on the horizontal ruler.

j. Use [Shift] and click to add the Date of Birth and Hire Date labels to the selection. Choose F̲ormat, A̲lign, and R̲ight.

k. Click the vertical ruler to select the Hire Date and calculated control. Choose F̲ormat, A̲lign, and T̲op.

l. Switch to Form View to see your changes. Return to Design View. Save the form.

4. Change colors by following these steps:

a. Click the Form Selector button and then the AutoFormat button 🗟.

b. Choose **Industrial**. Click the **O̲ptions** button and turn off the **Font** and the **Border** so only the **Color** is applied. Click **OK**.

c. Select all the text boxes. Use the Line/Border Color button 🖊 to match the labels' back color.

d. Drag the top edge of the **Form Footer** bar down to show about six rows of dots below the controls in the **Detail** section.

e. Select the Employee ID, Date of Birth, and Hire Date text boxes. Choose **F̲ormat, V̲ertical Spacing**, and **Make E̲qual**.

f. While the controls are selected, choose **F̲ormat, V̲ertical Spacing**, and **I̲ncrease**. Increase the spacing again.

g. Align the 20-Year Date control with the Hire Date control.

h. Switch to Form View to view your work.

i. Save and close the form.

EXERCISE 6-25

Save a form as a Web page. Create a Data Access Page.

1. Save a form as a Web page by following these steps:

a. Click frmAnniversary to highlight it.

b. Choose F̲ile, E̲xport.

c. In the Export Form To dialog box, set the **Save i̲n** location to your working folder.

d. Click the **Save as t̲ype** arrow. Choose **HTML Documents** and use the default filename.

e. Click E̲xport.

f. Leave the HTML Template entry box empty and click **OK**.

g. Start Word or your browser and open the HTML file **frmAnniversary**. Exit Word or your browser and return to Access.

2. Create a Data Access Page by following these steps:

a. Click the Pages button. Click the N̲ew button. Choose the Page Wizard.

b. Select tblTimeCards. Click **OK**.

c. Use the following fields: WeekEnding, HourlyRate, RegHours, and OTHours. Click N̲ext twice.

d. Sort by WeekEnding. Click <u>N</u>ext.

e. Name the Page **pgeTimeCards**. Click <u>F</u>inish.

f. Click the View button .

g. Save and use the default name.

h. Close the page. Compact and close the database.

Lesson Applications

EXERCISE 6-26

Create an AutoForm. Modify controls and properties. Open the Form Header and add a label.

1. Open *[your initials]***CC-06**.

    REVIEW: Use the New Form dialog box to create a columnar AutoForm.

2. Create a columnar AutoForm for tblKitSuppliers. Save the form as **frmSuppliers**.

    REVIEW: Ctrl + A is a Windows shortcut to select all.

3. Make the form 6 inches wide and apply the SandStone AutoFormat.

4. Press Ctrl + A to select all the controls and change them to 10 point. Size them to fit.

5. Select the State label and press Delete. Move the State text box to the 3.25-inch mark on the same line as the City text box.

    REVIEW: If you delete a text box by mistake, drag it back to the Detail section from the Field List.

6. Delete the ZIP Code label. Move the PostalCode text box next to the State text box. Delete the City label.

7. Select all the text boxes except the State and PostalCode. Open the property sheet and make the text boxes **2** inches wide. Deselect the controls.

    REVIEW: You can select all controls in a "column" from the horizontal ruler or you can press Shift and click.

8. Move the Phone and Fax Number controls closer to the address so everything is consistently spaced.

9. View your form and return to Design View. Make any adjustments you feel would help visibility.

10. Open the Form Header property sheet and make it **.75** inches high.

11. Draw a label in the Form Header about 3 inches wide. Key **Carolina Critters** on the first line. Press Shift + Enter for a line break, and key **Approved Suppliers**. Press Enter.

12. Make the label 18-point Arial bold italic, and adjust the size to fit the text on two lines as you keyed it.

13. Change the label text color to white. Change the Fill/Back color to black and apply the raised special effect.

14. Position the header label to align on the left with the controls in the Detail section. Move the label and size the section so there is a row of dots above and below the label.

15. Size the Detail section to show one row of grid dots below the last control.

16. Select all the text boxes and apply the Etched effect. Save the form.

17. Add a new record:

 REVIEW: The current field might change background color as you are adding/editing data.

Supplier #:	**7**
Supplier ID:	**HH-08**
Supplier Name:	*Key your last name and then key* **& Associates**
Contact Name:	*Key your first and last name*
Address:	*Key your address*
City:	*Key your city*
State:	*Key your state, using two characters*
Postal Code:	*Key your ZIP code*
Phone Number:	**(123)-555-0000**
Fax Number:	**(123)-555-0001**

 REVIEW: To print a single form, choose File, Print.

 18. Click the Print Preview button 🔍. Make sure no text is cut off. Close the preview.

19. Select your record and print it.

20. Save and close the form. Compact and close the database.

EXERCISE 6-27

Create a form by using the wizard. Filter the records in a form. Replace data in a form. Save the form as an HTML file.

1. Open *[your initials]*CC-E-06.

2. Create a form for tblSickDays by using the Form Wizard. Use all fields and make it a justified layout. Use the Industrial style and name the form **frmSickDays**

 NOTE: A justified layout places controls left to right, stacked in rows, with no spacing between rows.

3. Open the Form Header and add a label for **Employee Sick Days**. Make it 14-point Arial bold italic. Size the box to fit the label. Save the form.

4. Create a Filter By Form to determine how many employees took 2/5/01 as a sick day. Apply and remove the filter. Write your answer on a piece of paper.

5. Create an Advanced Filter that shows how many employees took 2/5/01 or 2/14/01 as a sick day. Remove the filter. Write your answer.

6. Create a Filter By Form to determine how many employees took 9/1/01 as a sick day. Write your answer.

7. While the records are filtered, replace all occurrences of 9/1/01 with your birthday in 2002. Use the *mm/dd/yy* format for both dates. Remove the filter.

  REVIEW: You can click the drop-down arrow for the View button ⬚ and switch to Datasheet View to see all records in a table layout.

8. Close and save the form.
9. Export the form frmSickDays as an HTML file.
10. Open the HTML file **frmSickDays** in Internet Explorer and print.

EXERCISE 6-28

Create a form with the Form Wizard. Modify form controls. Add a form header with a label.

1. Import tblEmployees from *[your initials]*CC-06 into *[your initials]*CC-E-06.

2. Create a new form for tblEmployees by using the Form Wizard. Use these fields:
    *   EmployeeID
    *   LastName
    *   FirstName
    *   EmergencyContact
    *   EmergencyPhone

3. Use a columnar layout and the Standard style. Name the form **frmEmerInfo**

4. Maximize the window. Make the form 6 inches wide.

5. Change all the controls (labels and text boxes) to 10-point Arial. Size them to fit.

6. Select all the controls except the EmployeeID and drag them to the right side of the form to get them out of the way as you reposition them.

7. Position the FirstName control two rows of dots below the EmployeeID control. Position the LastName control to the right of the FirstName control, with the label aligned left at the 3.25-inch mark.

8. Position the EmergencyContact control below the FirstName control. Position the EmergencyPhone control to the right of the EmergencyContact control and aligned with the LastName control. Use consistent spacing.

9. Select the EmployeeID text box and open its property sheet. Set its Left position and its Width at **1.5** inches. Leave the property sheet open.

10. Click the FirstName text box and change its Left position and Width to **1.5**. Do the same for the EmergencyContact text box.

11. Align the labels for Employee ID, First Name, and Emergency Contact on the left.

12. Use the Move handle to position the EmergencyPhone text box at the 4.5-inch mark. Do the same for the LastName text box. Align the labels on the left.

13. Make both of these text boxes **1.5** inches wide to match the others. Then make the form slightly wider.

14. Set the tab order. Close the Field List window.

 TIP: A form is easy to use when the controls are the same size and aligned well.

15. Open the Form Header and make it 1 inch tall. Add a label with **Emergency Information**. Make it 24-point Arial bold italic. Show the label on a single line. Select colors and a special effect for this label.

16. Save the form.

17. Find the record for Joseph Lassen. Change the first and last names to yours.

18. Print your record and close the form.

EXERCISE 6-29 *Challenge Yourself*

Create a multiple-table query. Create an AutoForm. Add a calculated control.

1. Create a new query in Design View for tblEmployees and tblPayroll.

REVIEW: The join line is on the SocialSecurityNumber field.

2. Add the fields FirstName and LastName from tblEmployees. From tblPay-roll, add SocialSecurityNumber and HourlyRate.

3. In the Criteria row for HourlyRate, key **is not null**

4. Save the query as **qryHrWages**. View the dynaset and close the query.

5. Create a columnar AutoForm for qryHrWages.

6. Make all controls 10-point Arial. Size them to fit.

7. Increase the vertical spacing between controls twice.

8. Change the form width to **6** inches.

9. Set all text box widths to **1.5** inches.

 TIP: You can click to place a text box instead of drawing the control.

10. Add a Text box at the 4-inch mark on the same row as HourlyRate. Edit the new label to show **Monthly Pay** with no colon. Format it as 10-point Arial and size it to fit.

 11. Use the Build button to set the control source for the unbound text box to **HourlyRate*140**.

 NOTE: The number "140" is a constant that you must key in the preview area.

12. Set the format for Monthly Pay text box to Currency and its width to **1.5** inches.

13. Change its Name property to **Pay**

14. Format the font for this control to match the others.

15. Save the form as **frmHrWages**

 TIP: Press [Shift] + [Enter] or [Ctrl] + [Enter] to create a line break in a label.

16. In the Form Header, add a label. Key **Carolina Critters** on the first line. Key **Hourly Employee Wages** on the second line. Key **Confidential** *[your last name]* on the third line.

17. Format the label as 16-point Arial bold italic. Size the label and the form header as needed, and keep the label as a three-line title. Save the form.

 18. Click the Print Preview button . Several forms will print per page, depending on your printer. Size the Detail section so all the records fit on two pages.

NOTE: You often need to check a printed form to verify the sizes of controls.

19. Print the records. Save the form and close it.

20. Compact and close your database. Exit Access.

On Your Own

In these exercises you work on your own, as you would in a real-life work environment. Use the skills you've learned to accomplish the task—and be creative.

EXERCISE 6-30
Using the Form Wizard, create a form for the main table of the database you modified in Exercise 5-24. Include all fields from the table in your form. On the form printout, sketch changes that will improve each form. Using the Form Wizard, create forms for each additional table in your database. Print a copy of each form. On each form printout, sketch changes that will improve each form. On each form, write your name and "Exercise 6-30." Continue to Exercise 6-31.

EXERCISE 6-31
Modify your forms to incorporate the improvements you sketched. In the Form Footer of each form, include your name and **Exercise 6-31**. In the Form Header, include the name of the form and the current date. Print the data contained in each of your tables. Print a copy of each form. Test your redesigned forms by having another person enter the data. On each form printout, sketch changes that will improve your form. Continue to Exercise 6-32.

EXERCISE 6-32
Modify your forms appropriately. Analyze your database design. Determine if any additional forms might be required for queries or recordsets. Create any additional forms you might need. On each form, include your name and **Exercise 6-32** in the Form Footer. Print a copy of each form. Submit the copies of the forms you printed in Exercises 6-30 through 6-32 to your instructor. Keep a copy of the database you modified in Exercise 6-32. It will be used in subsequent lessons.

Adding Reports to a Database

OBJECTIVES

After completing this lesson, you will be able to:

1. **Create a report by using a wizard.**
2. **Work with report sections.**
3. **Work with controls in a report.**
4. **Create and modify AutoReports.**
5. **Add a calculation to a report.**
6. **Use Format Painter and conditional formatting.**
7. **Create a multicolumn report and mailing labels.**
8. **Export data to Excel and Word.**

MOUS
ACTIVITIES
In this lesson:
Ac2002 **7-1**
Ac2002 **7-2**
Ac2002 **7-3**
Ac2002 **8-2**

See Appendix E.

 Estimated Time: 2 hours

Forms are the best way to view data on your screen. If you want a well-designed printed page, however, you should use a report. Although you can print a table or form, reports are best suited for a printed format. In a report you can:

- Show data in an attractive format that may include variations in fonts, colors, shading, and borders.
- Show certain fields or records rather than the entire table.
- Group and sort records with summaries and totals.
- Add images.
- Display fields from more than one table.

In this lesson you learn how to create reports by using the Report Wizard and AutoReports. You will work with Design View for a report (which has the same types of controls as Design View for a form). Working with controls will also be very similar to working with controls in a form. However, the design considerations for a report are different, because reports are usually printed to a black-and-white printer.

Creating a Report by Using the Report Wizard

The Report Wizard lets you choose the fields, the layout, and the style for a report. The style selects fonts, lines, and colors automatically. You can also choose whether to group records and how to sort them.

EXERCISE **7-1** **Create a Report with the Wizard**

1. Make a copy of **CC-07** and **CC-E-07**. Rename them as *[your initials]*CC-07 and *[your initials]*CC-E-07. Make sure neither new file is Read-Only. Open *[your initials]*CC-07.
2. Click the Tables button and select tblEmployees.
3. Click the New Object drop-down arrow and choose Report.
4. In the New Report dialog box, select Report Wizard.

FIGURE 7-1
New Report
dialog box

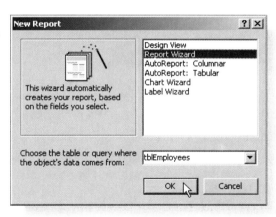

5. Click OK. The first Report Wizard dialog box asks which fields to use in the report. Click the EmployeeID field and then click the Add One button to move the field to the Selected Fields list.

REVIEW: If you move a field to the right by mistake, click the Remove One button `<` to move it back.

6. Double-click the following field names to move them to the Selected Fields list:

LastName

FirstName

SocialSecurityNumber

JobCode

7. Click Next. The dialog box asks if you want to group the records. You will add the groups later. Click Next.

8. The next dialog box asks if you want to sort the records. You can use up to four fields for sorting in ascending or descending order.

 NOTE: The Ascending/Descending button switches between ascending and descending order.

9. Click the drop-down arrow for the first sort field and choose LastName.

10. Click the drop-down arrow for the second sort field and choose JobCode.

FIGURE 7-2
Sorting in the
Report Wizard

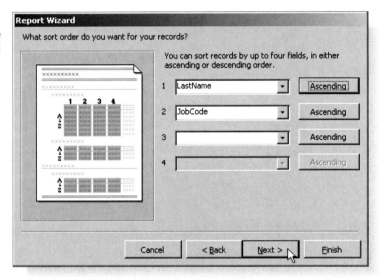

11. Click Next. The dialog box asks which layout and orientation you want. Select Tabular. (A tabular report prints the records in rows.)

12. Select Portrait. (Portrait orientation is taller than it is wide.)

13. Make sure there is a check mark for Adjust the field width so all fields fit on a page. This forces all the fields to fit on the page, but it can make them too small to show all the data.

14. Click Next to see the available styles. The Preview window simulates the appearance of each style. Click each style name to preview it.

15. Choose Formal. (See Figure 7-3 on the next page.)

16. Click Next. The dialog box asks for a title. This becomes the name of the report and appears as a title on the printed page. Key **rptEmpByCode[your initials]**

17. You can choose here to preview the report or modify the design. Select Preview the report and click Finish.

FIGURE 7-3
Selecting the
report style

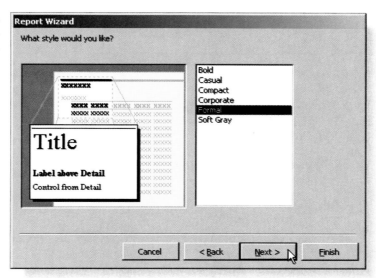

NOTE: Report names are preceded by **rpt** in the Leszynski Naming Conventions.

18. The report opens in Print Preview. Maximize the window.

FIGURE 7-4
Report maximized
in Print Preview

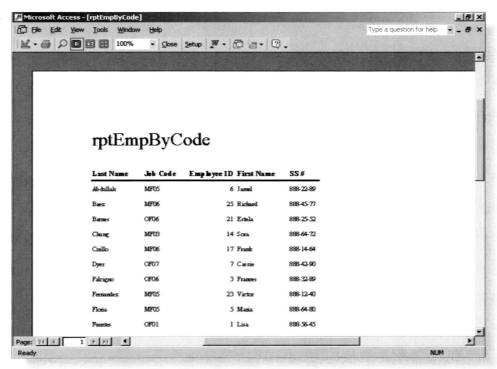

EXERCISE **7-2** **Use Print Preview**

Reports open in a 100% size, which attempts to show the report at the size it will print. You can change to different zoom sizes to get an overall impression of the layout or to zoom in and enlarge the data. The Zoom box in the toolbar shows the current size. The pointer displays a magnifying glass with a minus sign when you are in 100% view.

1. Click anywhere in the report to zoom out and view the entire page. The viewing size is Fit, and the pointer shows a plus sign.

2. Point anywhere on the page and click to zoom in. The pointer switches between 100% and Fit views.

3. Click the drop-down arrow for the Zoom box and try other sizes. Finish with the Zoom size at 100%.

 TIP: The pointer switches between the two most recently used sizes.

 4. Click the Close button on the toolbar to switch to Design View. The wizard arranges the fields left to right based on the order in which you selected the fields.

Working with Report Sections

In Design View, you can see the Standard toolbar, the Formatting toolbar, the Toolbox, and the report sections. A report has a Detail section that shows a row or column for each record, depending on the layout. The *Report Header* section prints once at the beginning of the report (on the first page) and the *Report Footer* section prints once at the end of the report (on the last page). Headers and footers can contain main titles, summary calculations, design lines, and even images. The *Report Page Header* section, which prints at the top of every page, and the *Report Page Footer* section, which prints at the bottom of every page, are often used for page numbers and the date. Reports may also have one or more *Group Header* or *Group Footer* sections. These sections are used for group titles and summaries.

 NOTE: Your toolbars might be in a different order. You can anchor the Toolbox with the other toolbars by double-clicking its title bar.

FIGURE 7-5
Design View
for the report

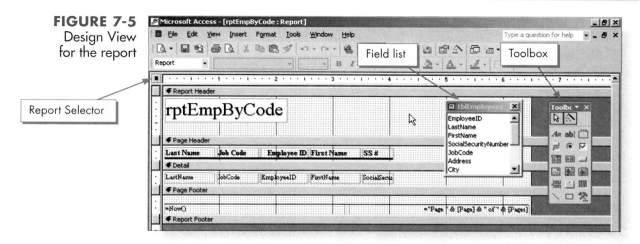

Report Selector

TABLE 7-1   Sections of a Report

NAME OF SECTION	PURPOSE
Report Header	Prints once at the top of the report (first page). It might include a title, logo, or image.
Page Header	Prints once at the top of every page. It might include column headings, page numbers, or a date.
Group Header	Prints once at the start of each group. It might display a group title.
Detail Section	Prints each record from the table or query.
Report Header	Prints once at the bottom of the report (last page). It might include summaries or totals.
Page Footer	Prints once at the bottom of every page. It might include page numbers or a date.
Group Footer	Prints once at the end of each group. It might include a total or other calculation for the group.

EXERCISE **7-3** **Change Section and Report Properties**

You can change section properties from the property sheet or from the Formatting toolbar.

1. Click the **Report Header** section bar. The **Object** box shows that the "Report-Header" is selected.

2. Click the Properties button . The Report Header property sheet opens.

3. Click the **Format** tab. Change the **Height** to **.75** and press Enter. The **Back Color** row shows a numeric code to represent the current color.

FIGURE 7-6
Report Header
property sheet

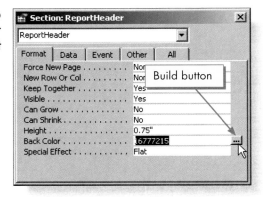

4. Click the Build button . A color palette opens.

NOTE: The Build button opens different dialog boxes for the different rows in the property sheet.

5. Choose any light color and click **OK**. The new code is shown. Close the property sheet.

6. Click the Undo button to remove the background color.

7. Double-click the **Page Header** section bar to open its property sheet.

8. Click the **Format** tab. Change the **Height** to **.75** and press Enter. Leave the property sheet open.

9. Click the **Detail** section bar. The property sheet updates to show the current section.

10. Click the **Format** tab and choose a different back color. Close the property sheet.

11. While the **Detail** section is selected, click the Fill/Back Color button. The current color is applied to the section.

REVIEW: The current Fill/Back color appears beneath the bucket on the icon.

12. Click the drop-down arrow for the Fill/Back Color button. Select white.

13. Click the Report Selector button ■ to display a solid black square. Click the Properties button. This property sheet lists settings for the report.

14. Click the **All** tab. Review the report properties and then close the property sheet.

15. Position the pointer on the top edge of the **Detail** section bar to display a double-ended arrow. Drag upward to size the **Page Header** section to show one row of dots below the horizontal line.

16. Save the report.

EXERCISE **7-4** **Add a Group Section**

A *group* organizes or categorizes the records by a particular field. For example, you can group the records by job code in rptEmpByCode. All the employees who are tailors would be listed together, all the assemblers/finishers would be listed together, and so on. As you establish groups, you can also indicate how the records should be sorted.

To use groups, you add a Group Header/Footer to the report, creating Group sections.

TABLE 7-2 **Group Section Properties**

GROUP SECTION	OPTION	PURPOSE
Group Header	Yes or No	Display or hide a Group Header section.
Group Footer	Yes or No	Display or hide a Group Footer section.
Group On	(Depends on data type)	Identifies what value, or range of values, makes a group.
Group Interval	(Enter a number)	Interval or number of characters to use in identifying the group.
Keep Together	Yes or No	Keeps group together on one page.

1. With rptEmpByCode open in Design View, click the Sorting and Grouping button . The Sorting and Grouping dialog box shows the sorting choices you made in the Report Wizard.

2. Click in the Field/Expression column for the LastName row. The Group Properties show that no Group Header or Group Footer is used.

3. Click in the Field/Expression column for the JobCode row. No Group Header or Group Footer is used here, either.

4. Click the Group Header box for the JobCode field. Click the arrow and select Yes. The Group icon appears to the left of the field name. (See Figure 7-7 on the next page.)

5. Close the dialog box. The report now has a JobCode Header section.

6. Click the Print Preview button . The records are not grouped by job code. Close the preview.

7. Click the Sorting and Grouping button .

8. Point at the row selector for the JobCode row to display a black arrow. Click to select the row.

FIGURE 7-7
Sorting and
Grouping
dialog box

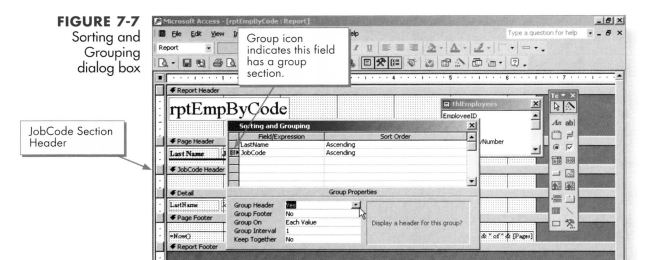

JobCode Section
Header

9. Point at the row selector to display a white arrow, and then drag the row to be first. Close the dialog box.

 NOTE: The field used for grouping must be first in the Sorting and Grouping dialog box.

10. Preview the report. Notice that the records are now grouped by Job Code.

11. Close the preview and save the report.

EXERCISE **7-5** **Create a Non-Breaking Group**

The default page break for a report occurs when the text reaches the bottom margin. You can control how groups are kept together so they are not split between pages. Of course, some groups are too large to print on a single page.

1. Drag the top of the Page Footer bar down to show three rows of dots below the controls in the Detail section. Preview the report. Notice if any groups split between pages.

2. Return to Design View.

3. Click the Sorting and Grouping button [≣]. Click the JobCode row in the top part of the dialog box.

4. Click the Keep Together row in the bottom part of the dialog box. Display the list and choose Whole Group.

5. Close the dialog box.

 6. Preview the report. Click the Two Pages button [目目]. Then click the One Page button [目].

Working with Controls on a Report

Just as with forms, reports have bound controls (such as text boxes), unbound controls (such as labels), and calculated controls. You can move, size, align, and format controls in a report just as you do in a form.

EXERCISE | **7-6** | **Move and Delete Controls**

Depending on the number of changes you need to make to a report, you might find that it is faster for you to delete controls and reinsert them instead of moving them.

> **1.** With rptEmpByCode open in Design View, select the Job Code label in the **Page Header** section. Drag the control into the **JobCode Header** at the left edge.

FIGURE 7-8
Moving controls into
the Group Header

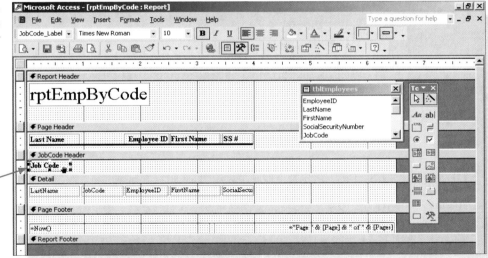

Label that has
been moved

> **2.** Select the JobCode text box in the **Detail** section and drag it into the **JobCode Header**, next to the label.

> **TIP:** When you move controls from one section to another, move one control at a time.

> **3.** Select the SS# label in the **Page Header** section and the SocialSecurityNumber text box in the **Detail** section. Press Delete.

> **4.** Select the Employee ID label in the **Page Header** section and the Employee ID text box in the **Detail** section.

5. Drag both controls to the right, across the First Name controls to the 3.5-inch mark.

6. Hold down Shift and add the First Name label and the First Name text box to the selection so four controls are selected.

7. Move all four controls left to the 1.25-inch mark.

 TIP: You can click the View button 🔍 or the Print Preview button 🔍 to view a report.

8. Preview the report to see if all the data is visible.

 **TIP:** You can click the View button 📐 or the Close button Close to return to Design View.

9. To return to Design View, click the View 📐 button.

10. Save your changes.

EXERCISE 7-7 Add a Field to a Report

When you add a field to a report, the field label and field text box are inserted as a unit. Each control can then be sized and moved individually or together.

 1. Click the Field List button 🔲 to open the Field List window, if it is not visible.

2. Size or scroll the window until you see the City field.

3. Drag the City field to the **Detail** section at the 4.5-inch mark.

FIGURE 7-9
Adding a field
to the report

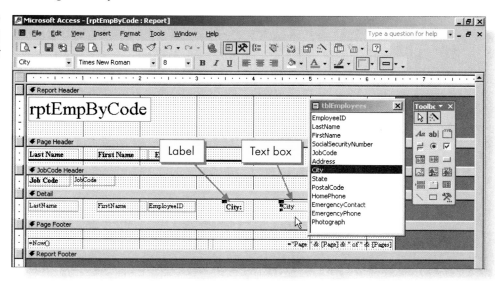

4. Select the City label (not the text box). Press Delete.

5. Drag the City text box to the 3.5-inch mark.

 REVIEW: Use the grid dots as an aid when you size and align controls.

6. Close the Field List window and save the report.

EXERCISE **7-8** **Copy a Label, Size a Line, and Size a Section**

You now need a new label for the city field. One way to enter the label so it uses the same format as the other labels is to copy and edit an existing label. You also need to resize the horizontal line in the **Page Header** section to match your new field.

1. Select the Employee ID label in the **Page Header** section.

2. Click Ctrl + C to copy. Then click Ctrl + V to paste. The copy is placed below the original, and the section expands.

FIGURE 7-10
Copying a control

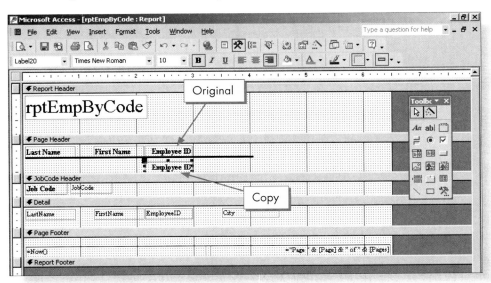

3. Drag the copied label to the 3.5-inch mark above the horizontal line, in the same section.

 NOTE: The wizard added horizontal lines to the Page Header and Page Footer. These design elements make the report more attractive.

4. Click in the copied label to display an I-beam. Delete the text. Then key **City** and press Enter.

5. Double-click a sizing handle to size the label. Press Ctrl + ← to nudge the control close to the 3.75-inch mark.

6. Click the horizontal line below the controls in the **Page Header**. The Object box shows that a line is selected.

7. Position the pointer on the far right selection handle to display an angled two-headed arrow.

8. Hold down Shift and drag the end of the line to the 6.5-inch mark.

 TIP: Holding down Shift keeps the line straight.

9. Place the pointer on the top edge of the **JobCode Header** bar. Drag the bar up to show two rows of dots below the horizontal line.

10. Size the **Detail** section to show one row of dots below the controls.

 NOTE: Designing a report is a matter of trial and error. Switch back and forth between Print Preview and Design View often.

11. Preview the report. Then return to Design View and save it.

EXERCISE **7-9** **Change Font Size and Align Controls**

Most printed reports use a 10-, 11-, or 12-point font size for the body of the report. This is easier to read than the default 8-point font size.

After making various edits to the controls, you should align them. To align controls, you must have at least two controls selected.

1. Place the pointer to the right of the vertical ruler, next to the row of controls in the **Page Header**. The pointer changes to a black arrow.

 NOTE: A Group Header can be identified by the field name in the section bar. The records are grouped by this field.

2. Drag down to select all the controls in the **Page Header**, the JobCode Header, and the **Detail** sections. (See Figure 7-11 on the next page.)

3. Click the drop-down arrow next to **Font Size** and choose **11**.

4. While the controls are selected, choose **F**ormat, **S**ize, and To **F**it.

5. Click in a blank area of any section to deselect the controls.

6. Select the First Name label in the **Page Header** and the FirstName text box in the **Detail** section.

7. Press Ctrl + ← to nudge them to the 1-inch mark.

FIGURE 7-11
Selecting several
rows of controls

Drag from here

To here

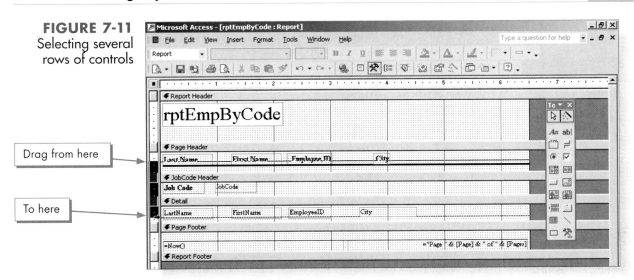

8. Place the pointer to the right of the vertical ruler for the JobCode Header section to display the black arrow. Click to select the controls.

9. Choose F̲ormat, Ali̲gn, and B̲ottom.

10. Select the row of controls in the Detail section and align them on the top.

11. Show one row of dots below the controls in the JobCode Header. Do the same for the Detail section.

12. Preview both pages of the report and return to Design View.

13. Save the report and then return to Print Preview.

EXERCISE **7-10** **Edit Common Expression Controls**

The wizard added two controls to the Page Footer. Both controls use common expressions to display the date and the page number. A *common expression* is a pre-defined control with built-in commands. Common expressions display frequently-used controls such as current date, current time, current page number, or total pages.

1. In Print Preview for rptEmpByCode, zoom until you can see the entire page.

2. Point at the Footer text at the left and click. This zooms in on that part of the page. The Footer displays the current date.

3. Scroll to the right to see the page number.

4. Zoom out and return to Design View.

5. Right-click the =Now() control in the Page Footer and select P̲roperties. The property sheet title bar shows that this is a text box.

NOTE: If the property sheet shows that this is a line, you selected the horizontal line above the controls. Click again to select the text box.

6. Click the **Data** tab. The **Control Source** for this control is an Access common expression that displays the current date.

FIGURE 7-12
Current date
expression

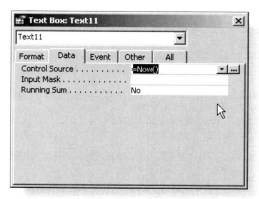

7. Click the **Format** tab. Click the **Format** row and choose **Medium Date**.

8. Change the **Width** to **1.5**. Close the property sheet.

9. Right-click the page number control and open its property sheet.

10. Click the **Data** tab. Click the **Control Source** row and the Build button. The Expression Builder shows the Access code for this control.

 TIP: You can select common expressions in the Expression Builder.

11. Close the Expression Builder and click the **Format** tab. Change the **Width** to **1.5**. Close the property sheet.

12. Drag the page number control to the right edge of the report.

13. Preview both pages. Close and save the report.

Creating and Modifying AutoReports

An *AutoReport* is a default, standard report that includes all the fields and a style. Your only decision is to select the query or table used as the basis for the report. An AutoReport that you create from the New Report dialog box usually has **Report**, **Detail**, and **Page** sections. It does not include Group sections. An AutoReport can be either columnar or tabular.

 TIP: You can print a tabular report one record to a page.

EXERCISE **7-11** **Create a Columnar AutoReport**

A columnar AutoReport prints each field on a separate line in one or more columns. The field may have a label to its left or perhaps above it. The columnar style is also known as a vertical report. Columnar style can be used when the report has many fields that would not fit across the page in a tabular arrangement. You might use a columnar report when you want each record to print on a separate page. You can print a columnar report in portrait or landscape orientation.

1. Click the Queries button and open **qryStuffedAnimals** in Design View. The query uses one table and has no criteria.

2. Add, but do not show, the ProductGroup field. Add the criteria **d** to show only records from the D (Dinosaur) category. Turn off the Show checkbox for this field. Save and close the query.

3. Click the New Object drop-down arrow and choose Report. Choose AutoReport: Columnar.

4. Click OK. View the report in Fit and 100% sizes. The records might be separated by horizontal lines, depending on the last style used on your computer.

5. Click the Last Page button to determine the page length of the report.

> **TIP:** When the report is in a Fit view, you can press PgUp and PgDn to navigate through the pages.

6. Click the First Page button to return to page 1.

7. Click Close to switch to Design View.

8. Save the report as **rptColAnimals**.

EXERCISE 7-12 Apply an AutoFormat

An AutoReport might not use the style you prefer. Generally, Access uses the last style that was selected on your computer. You can apply an AutoFormat instead of using the style Access uses.

1. With **rptColAnimals** open in Design View, click the Report Selector button ■, the square to the left of the horizontal ruler. A black rectangle appears in the box to show that the entire report is selected.

> **REVIEW:** The Object box in the Standard toolbar says "Report" when the entire report is selected.

2. Click the AutoFormat button and choose Bold. Click OK and preview the report.

3. Return to Design View.

> **NOTE:** An AutoReport created directly from the New Object list includes a Detail section and empty Page Footers and Page Headers.

EXERCISE **7-13** | **Modify Control Properties**

You can edit controls in any report section, as well as add group sections. Each section can include bound controls (such as text boxes), unbound controls (such as labels), and calculated controls. A field control consists of its unbound label, if any, and its bound control.

This report has a bound object frame for the picture. A *bound object frame* is a control that displays an OLE data type field from the table. Its properties are similar to those for a text box.

The Text Align property determines how a label is positioned within its box. It is similar to the Alignment commands in Word and Excel.

1. In Design View for rptColAnimals, select the large Illustration frame and drag it with its label to the 3.5-inch mark, aligned at the top with the ProductID controls.

2. Right-click the Illustration frame and open its property sheet. Notice that the control is a bound object frame. Make it **2** inches wide and **1.5** inches high. Set the **Size Mode** to **Zoom**. Close the property sheet.

3. Drag the top edge of the **Page Footer** bar up to show two rows of dots below the bound object frame.

4. Place the pointer on the right edge of the vertical ruler to display a black arrow. Drag to select the controls in the **Detail** section, but not the horizontal line.

FIGURE 7-13
Selecting controls

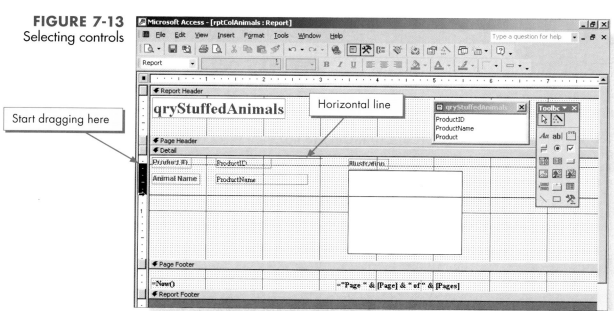

5. Press [Ctrl] + [↓] three times to nudge all the controls lower in the section.

6. While the controls are selected, change them to 10-point Arial. Choose Format, Size, and To Fit. Deselect the controls.

 REVIEW: The solid lines in the design layout grid are at 1-inch intervals.

7. Delete the Illustration label and drag the frame to align at the top with the ProductID controls.

8. Drag the Page Footer bar to show two rows of dots below the frame.

 TIP: You can edit a label from the property sheet by changing the Caption. You can also change a label, using the label box in Design View.

9. Change the Main Title to **Stuffed Animals**

10. Attempt to drag the right edge of the report to the 6-inch mark. Notice that you cannot do this because the Page Number control in the Page Footer extends past that mark.

11. Select the Page Number text box and drag the right middle handle to the 5.5-inch mark.

12. Drag the right edge of the report to the 6-inch mark.

13. Preview the report to see the date and page numbers. You might see a message box telling you that the section width is greater than the page width. Click **OK** if the message box appears. The Page Number control might be too close or even overlap the Date control. Return to Design View.

 NOTE: The right middle handle for the Date control is close to or possibly inside the Page Number control.

14. Select the Date control. Drag its right middle handle to the 3-inch mark.

 15. Click the Align Left button .

TIP: The Text Align command is listed near the bottom of the Format tab in the property sheet.

 16. Select the Page Number control and click the Align Right button ▤. Align this control on the right with the bound object frame. (See Figure 7-14 on the next page.)

17. Preview the report. Return to Design View and save it.

18. Select the bound object frame.

 19. Click the drop-down arrow for the Line/Border Color button ▨. Choose the color that matches the title and the labels.

 20. Click the drop-down arrow for the Line/Border Width button ▢. Select **4** pt.

FIGURE 7-14
Report
(in Design View)

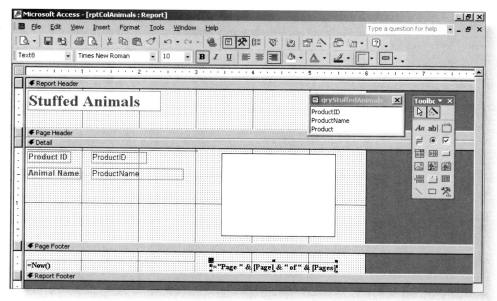

21. View the report in 100% and Fit sizes. Return to Design View.

22. Select the label in the **Report Header**. Apply a Shadowed special effect.

23. Open the property sheet for the label. Click the **Border Color** row and the Build button 	[...]. Choose the color that matches the label text.

24. Click **OK** and close the property sheet.

25. Preview the report. Return to Design View and save.

EXERCISE 7-14 **Modify a Horizontal Line Control**

This AutoReport displays a horizontal line near the top of the **Detail** section. Anything in the **Detail** section prints with each record, so the line repeats with each record. You can delete this line and add a new vertical dotted line.

You can adjust the setting of the *selection marquee* (the dotted line indicating that an object is selected). If the setting is full, you must click and drag over the entire object to select it. However, the default setting for the selection marquee is partial. You only need to click and drag over a portion of an object to select it.

1. Select the horizontal line at the top of the **Detail** section in Design View. Press [Delete].

2. Click in an unused area of the window to deselect all controls. Point to the intersection of the 3-inch horizontal line and 1-inch vertical line in the **Detail** Section. Click and drag up and to the left until you have part of the ProductID label in the selection marquee.

FIGURE 7-15
Drawing a
selection marquee

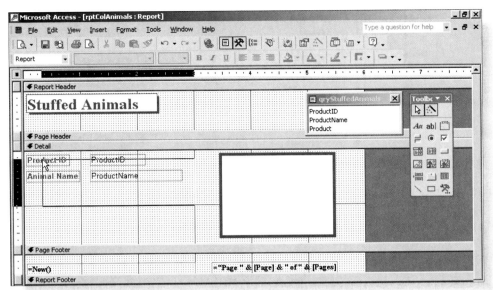

TIP: You can start the selection marquee from any corner of your planned
selection; start where you have the most room.

3. Drag the selected controls to the right until the labels start at the .25-inch
mark on the horizontal ruler.

4. Click the Line button in the Toolbox.

5. Point midway between the Product ID label and the left edge of the report.
Hold down [Shift] and draw a vertical line that is the same height as the
bound object frame.

FIGURE 7-16
Adding a
vertical line

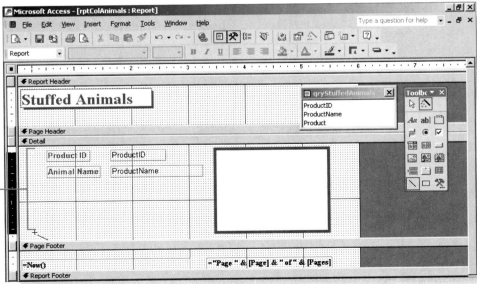

The line doesn't
appear until you
release the mouse
button.

6. Double-click the line to open its property sheet. Click the Format tab and the Border Style row.

7. Choose Dots. Click the Border Width row and choose **4 pt**.

8. Set the Height at **1.5**. Close the property sheet.

9. Align this line at the top with the bound object frame.

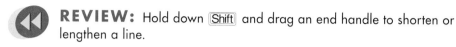

REVIEW: Hold down ⬚Shift⬚ and drag an end handle to shorten or lengthen a line.

10. Preview the report. Save and close it.

EXERCISE 7-15 Create a Tabular AutoReport

A tabular AutoReport shows each record on a separate line, usually with labels at the top of the column. Tabular reports are best for printing many records on the same page. You can print a tabular report in portrait or landscape orientation.

1. Create a query using tblCustomers and tblSalesOrders. The join line appears for the CustomerID field.

2. From tblCustomers, add CompanyName to the grid. From tblSalesOrders, add OrderID and OrderDate. Sort by OrderID in ascending order.

3. Save the query as **qryReminder**

4. Click the Field row for the fourth column and click the Build button 🛠.

5. Double-click OrderDate in the middle panel. Key **+365** and click OK.

6. View the query and return to Design View.

7. Change Expr1 to **OneYear**, leaving the colon.

8. Set the caption to **One Year Later**.

9. Save and close the query.

10. Select qryReminder in the Queries window, click the New Object drop-down arrow, and choose Report. Choose AutoReport: Tabular and click OK.

11. Maximize the window and view the report in a Fit size. (See Figure 7-17 on the next page.)

12. Return to Design View.

13. Double-click the Page Number control and set the Left property at **4**. Make the control **1.5** inches wide. Do not close the property sheet.

14. Click the Date control and make it **2** inches wide. Close the property sheet.

15. Delete the horizontal line in the Page Footer.

16. Click the Line button ⬚ in the Toolbox. Position the pointer at the left edge in the Page Footer, on the second row of dots.

FIGURE 7-17
Tabular AutoReport
in Print Preview

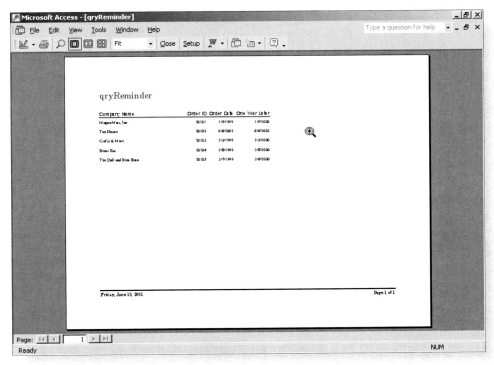

17. Hold down [Shift] and drag to draw a line that ends at the 9.5-inch mark on the horizontal ruler.

   TIP: If you aren't satisfied with the line, select it, press [Delete], and try again.

18. Preview the report. You might see the section-width error message box. Click **OK** if you do.

FIGURE 7-18
Section-width error
message box

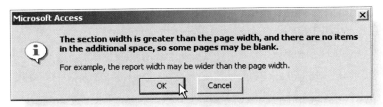

19. Click the Two Pages button [⊞]. Blank pages mean that the report is too wide. Return to Design View.

20. In the **Page Footer**, the solid line is too wide; resize it so the right margin ends at the 6.5-inch mark.

21. Drag the right edge of the report to the 6.5-inch mark. Drag the page number control to align on the right with the horizontal line.

22. Select the Date and Page controls in the Page Footer and choose Format, Align, and Top.

23. Save the report as **rptRemDates**. Preview and close the report.

Adding a Calculated Control

Calculated fields should not be keyed into a table. Instead, they should be calculated when they are needed in a query, form, or a report. In the Stuffed Animals report, for example, you can compute the total inventory value for each product by multiplying the list price by the quantity on hand.

EXERCISE **7-16** **Add a Calculated Control in a Report**

You will now modify an existing report to calculate the inventory value of the stuffed animals based on the number of units in inventory and on the list price. You will use an unbound control to calculate a new cost.

1. Open **rptStuffedAnimals** in Design View.

2. Click the Text Box button . Click at the 5.5-inch mark in the Detail section.

> **REVIEW:** You can click to place a text box or label at a default size.

3. Select and delete the label, not the unbound control.

4. Open the property sheet for the unbound control.

5. Click the Other tab. Change the Name to **CurrentValue**.

6. Click the Data tab. In the Control Source row, click the Build button [...].

7. In the middle panel, click <Field List> to show only the table fields in the right panel.

> **REVIEW:** The middle panel in the Expression Builder lists all objects in the folder or in the object selected in the left panel.

8. Double-click ListPrice in the right panel.

9. Click symbol once for multiplication.

10. Double-click QuantityOnHand in the right panel. (See Figure 7-19 on the next page.)

11. Click OK. Click the Format tab and the Format row. Choose Currency and close the property sheet.

12. Position the control so that its left edge aligns at the 5-inch mark.

FIGURE 7-19
Expression Builder
with an expression

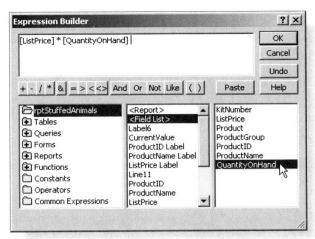

13. Click the List Price label in the Page Header. Press Ctrl + C and then press Ctrl + V.

14. Drag the copied label to be the title for the calculated control. Change the label to **Value**

15. Align the Value label and the calculated control on the right.

16. Align the labels in the Page Header on the top.

17. Drag the top edge of the Detail bar up to show two rows of dots below the line in the Page Header.

18. Select and extend the horizontal line.

19. Save the report.

Using Format Painter and Conditional Formatting

The *Format Painter* is a tool that copies the font, size, color, and alignment from one control to another. It saves you from having to set the individual properties for each control. To use the Format Painter, you select the control that has the formatting, click the Format Painter button, and then click the control to be changed.

You can also apply *conditional formatting*. Conditional formatting is a style, color, or other setting that displays under certain conditions. For example, you can set conditional formatting to show values over $15,000 in a different color, in bold, or underlined.

EXERCISE 7-17 Use the Format Painter

You use the Format Painter to give the calculated control the same format as the other controls in the Detail section of the report.

1. With rptStuffedAnimals open in Design View, select the ListPrice text box.

2. Click the Format Painter button. The pointer changes to an arrow with a paintbrush.

3. Click the calculated control. The font and size are copied.

4. Double-click each text box in the Detail section to autofit its height. Align the controls on the top.

5. Select one of the labels in the Page Header.

6. Click the Format Painter button .

7. Click the Date control in the Page Footer. Double-click a handle to autofit the height.

> **REVIEW:** Double-clicking a sizing handle for a text box autofits only the height, not the width.

8. Move the Date to align with the Value controls at the right.

9. Preview the report and size the Date control so you can see the entire Date.

10. Size the Detail section so there are two rows of grid dots below the controls.

EXERCISE 7-18 Use Conditional Formatting

Often managers use reports to track sales, production, and inventory levels. Many database designers use conditional formatting to call attention to records that are outside a specified parameter. Conditional formatting helps to quickly identify action that might need to be taken.

1. Click the calculated control in the Detail section.

2. Choose Format, Conditional Formatting. The top half of the dialog box shows the current formatting.

3. Click the first drop-down arrow for Condition 1. Select Field Value Is.

4. Click the second drop-down arrow and select between as the operator.

5. Click in the third box and key **3000**

6. Click in the last box and key **3500**. The condition is that the value in the calculated control is between 3000 and 3500.

7. In the Condition 1 area, set the Fill/Back Color to a dark blue and the Font/Fore Color to white. This sets the color for the value if it is between 3000 and 3500. (See Figure 7-20 on the next page.)

> **NOTE:** You can choose a different color by clicking the drop-down arrow to display the palette.

8. Click OK.

9. Preview, save, and close the report.

FIGURE 7-20
Conditional
Formatting
dialog box

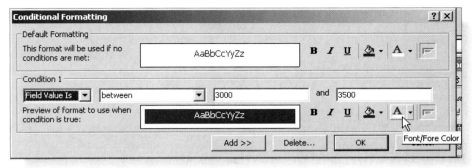

Creating a Multicolumn Report and Labels

In addition to columnar and tabular reports, you can format a report to show the data in more than one column. You can use either a wizard or Design View to lay out the fields, usually in a single column. Then use the **Page Setup** command to set the number and width of the printed columns.

You can also create labels by using the Label Wizard, an option in the New Report dialog box. The wizard lists common label brands and sizes, including mailing labels, package labels, CD and cassette labels, and more.

EXERCISE **7-19** **Create a Multicolumn Report for a Query**

In addition to creating reports by selecting predefined labels, you can create custom multicolumn reports to fit nonstandard labels.

1. Open qryStuffedAnimals in Design View. Delete the fourth field. Save and close the query.

2. With qryStuffedAnimals highlighted, click the New Object drop-down arrow. Select **R**eport.

3. Choose **AutoReport: Columnar** and click **OK**. The AutoReport shows all the fields in a single column.

4. Return to Design View.

 NOTE: The AutoFormats for reports are different from the AutoFormats for forms because the report AutoFormats are designed for printing.

5. Click the AutoFormat button ⊞. Choose **Formal** and click **OK**.

6. Select all the controls in the Detail section. Choose Format, Vertical Spacing, and Decrease.

7. Select the controls in the Page Footer and delete them. Close the Page Footer.

8. Preview the report in a Fit size. While in Print Preview, choose File, Page Setup.

9. Click the Page tab and choose Landscape.

10. Click the Columns tab. Set the Number of Columns to **2**. Set the Row Spacing to **.15** and the Column Spacing to **.25**.

11. Set the Column Size Width to **3.5** inches.

12. Choose Across, then Down for the Column Layout.

FIGURE 7-21
Setting up a
multicolumn report

13. Click OK. The records are shown in two columns across the page.

14. Preview several pages of the report. Return to Design View.

 NOTE: You do not see two columns in Design View. The first page might also show fewer records because of the space the title requires.

15. Save the report as **rptMultiCol** and close it.

EXERCISE 7-20 Create Package Labels

The Label Wizard assists you in creating package labels. After you select a label type and size, the Label Wizard asks which fields to place on the label, which font to use, and how to sort the labels.

1. In the Reports window, click <u>N</u>ew. Choose Label Wizard and tblStuffedAni-mals. Click OK.

2. In the first wizard dialog box, choose **Avery** as the manufacturer. Choose **English** as the **Unit of Measure** and **Sheet Feed** as the **Label Type**. Choose **5388** as the product number for labels that measure 3 inches by 5 inches, 1 label across the page. Click <u>N</u>ext.

3. Set the font as 18-point Times New Roman, Normal weight, with a black text color. Click <u>N</u>ext.

4. Press Enter once to insert a blank line in the prototype.

5. Key **Product ID:** and press the spacebar twice.

6. Double-click ProductID to place it in the prototype.

7. Press Enter twice to leave a blank line in the prototype.

8. Key **Product Name:** and press the spacebar twice. Double-click Product-Name to place it in the prototype. Press Enter twice.

9. Key **Kit Number:** and press the spacebar twice. Double-click KitNumber to place it in the prototype.

FIGURE 7-22
Prototype for
large labels

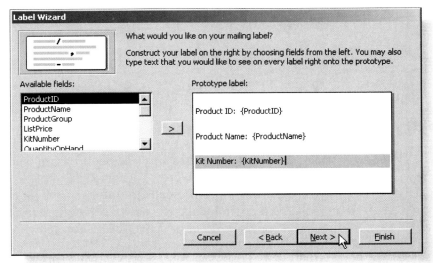

10. Click <u>N</u>ext. In the next dialog box, choose ProductID for the **Sort Order** and click <u>N</u>ext.

11. In the last wizard dialog box, change the name to **rptAnimalLabels**. Select the option **See the labels as they will look printed**. Click <u>F</u>inish.

12. The labels are one across. The report is eight pages long. Maximize the window and view several pages in a Fit size.

13. Return to Design View. The "&" joins the text you keyed to the data on the same line. The blank lines show an equal sign and two quotation marks surrounding a blank space.

FIGURE 7-23
Design View for
large labels

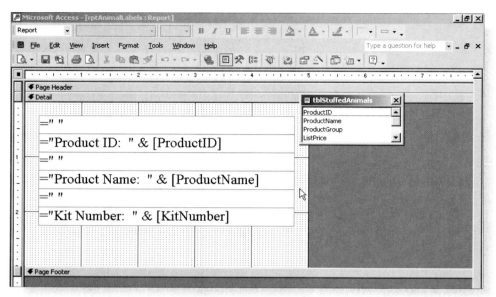

14. Close and save the report.

Exporting Data to Excel or Word

A recordset can be exported to a spreadsheet program (such as Excel) or a word processing program (such as Word). You can also export to several other formats. When you export a table, you create an unformatted file for the other program. You can, of course, then format the new file in the other application.

When you export a form or a report, the results show the underlying data and not the design of the form or report.

EXERCISE 7-21 Export a Table to Excel

When you export a table to Excel, Access attempts to match the table's field type and properties to create a similar worksheet. Field types such as currency are directly converted.

1. Right-click tblCustomers and choose Export.

2. Click the drop-down arrow for Save as type and choose Microsoft Excel 97-2002.

3. The default filename is the name of the table. The file extension for an Excel workbook is automatically entered. Click Export.

4. Start Excel and open the spreadsheet **tblCustomers**.

5. Maximize Excel and the workbook. The fields are set to default Excel screen width. Notice the Yes/No field shows true or false rather than a check mark. This is how Excel interprets that data.

FIGURE 7-24
Exported table
in Excel

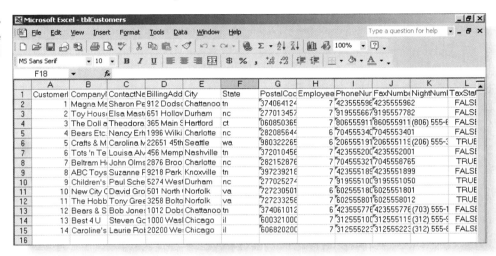

6. Close the workbook, but not Excel.

EXERCISE 7-22 Drag and Drop a Table to Excel

By opening both Excel and Access, you can drag and drop a table from Access to a blank worksheet in Excel. A new worksheet is automatically created, showing the table's data.

 TIP: If you drag and drop a query to Excel, you see the dynaset in Excel.

1. Click Excel's New button [□].

2. Close all applications other than Access and Excel.

3. Right-click on an open area of the taskbar.

4. Choose Tile Windows Vertically from the shortcut menu. Excel and Access are tiled side-by-side on the desktop.

5. Arrange the application windows so you can see tblCustomers in the Access window and Cell A1 in the Excel window.

6. Click and drag tblCustomers from the Access window to Cell A1 in the Excel window. Release the mouse button when it shows the plus sign with the pointer.

FIGURE 7-25
Dragging and
dropping the table

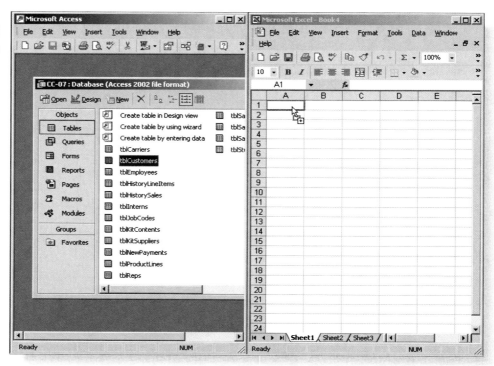

7. Maximize the Excel application window and the workbook. Review the table. You can widen columns and change the colors in Excel.

8. Exit Excel without saving the table.

9. Maximize the Access window.

EXERCISE 7-23 Export a Query to Word

Word does not have a database-type structure like Excel. To create a file that is recognized by Word, Access converts the query's dynaset to a comma-delimited file. This means the raw data is exported with commas separating ("delimiting") each field in a record. When you export a query, you create a file that includes the records displayed in the query's Datasheet View.

TIP: You cannot export a parameter query because it requires an entry from the keyboard to display a dynaset.

1. Click the Queries button. Right-click qryKitCosts and choose <u>E</u>xport.

2. Click the drop-down arrow for **Save as <u>t</u>ype** and choose **Text Files.**

3. The default filename is the name of the query. Click E<u>x</u>port.

4. The **Export Text Wizard** guides you through exporting the file. The wizard has determined that the fields are delimited. In this case, the delimiter is a comma.

FIGURE 7-26
Delimiter is
a comma for
the query

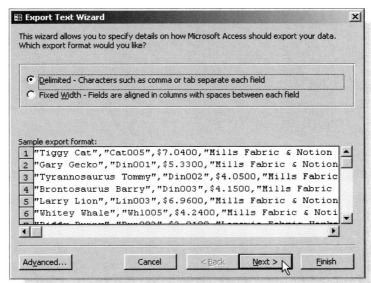

5. Click <u>N</u>ext. Click the Comma button to mark the character used to separate the fields. Click <u>I</u>nclude Field Names on First Row. Click <u>N</u>ext.

6. In the **Export to File** name box, verify the folder and filename. Click <u>F</u>inish. Click **OK** in the message box that confirms the export is completed and indicates the file location.

TIP: To find the document in Word, set the Files of <u>T</u>ype in the Open dialog box to show All Files.

7. Start Word and open the text file **qryKitCosts**.

8. Click OK.

FIGURE 7-27
Exported data
in Word

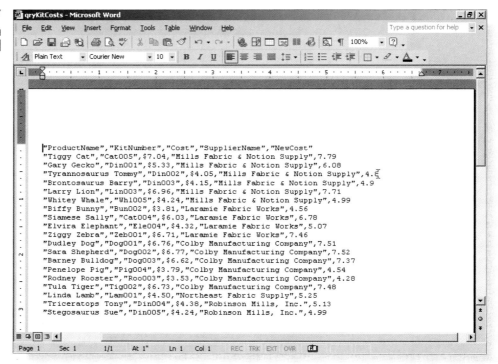

9. Exit Word. Compact your database and close it. Exit Access.

USING HELP

Use Help Contents to view information about sections in a report.

Find out more about using Help:

1. Turn off the Office Assistant. Choose <u>H</u>elp and Microsoft Access <u>H</u>elp. Click the <u>C</u>ontents tab.
2. Find and click Reports and Report Snapshots.
3. Expand Customizing Reports.
4. Expand Report Sections.
5. Click and read the topic About sections of a report.
6. In the left panel, click Resize a section. In the right panel, click and read Resize a form or report section.
7. Close the Help window.

LESSON 7 Summary

➤ You can create simple reports by using the Report Wizard.

➤ Before printing a report, a good practice is to view the report in Print Preview.

➤ You can view and modify section properties in the property sheet.

➤ You can use group sections to organize and summarize information based on categories.

➤ You can keep groups together on a page.

➤ You can move, size, align, and format controls in reports in much the same way as in forms.

➤ You can add fields to a report by using the Field List window.

➤ When adding fields to a report, take care to align other controls in the **Report Header** or **Report Footer** to match the **Detail** section.

➤ Controls should be sized and aligned to make the report easier to read.

➤ The Date and Page Number are common controls created by the Report Wizard.

➤ Columnar-style reports are most commonly used when the length of the data is too wide to properly display in tabular format.

➤ AutoFormat applies font sizes, font colors, border styles, and border colors to an entire report or parts of a report.

➤ The property sheet for each object in a report lists all the characteristics or attributes for that object.

➤ Horizontal lines in a report can be move or resized just as any other object.

➤ In a tabular report, each record displays on a separate line.

➤ Calculated controls display the results of a numeric expression based on one or more fields in a record.

➤ You can set the properties of multiple objects simultaneously by using the Format Painter.

➤ Conditional formatting applies a property only when certain conditions are met.

➤ Records in a multicolumn report or label display in two or more columns.

➤ The Label Wizard can create nonstandard package labels.

➤ You can easily export an Access table to Excel by dragging and dropping the table from Access into Excel.

➤ Comma-delimited files can be created to transfer data from Access to Word.

LESSON 7 Command Summary

FEATURE	BUTTON	MENU	KEYBOARD	SPEECH
AutoFormat		Format, AutoFormat		✓
Conditional Formatting		Format, Conditional Formatting		✓
Field List		View, Field List		✓
Format Painter				
Multicolumn Report		File, Page Setup		
One Page		View, Pages, One Page		✓
Print Preview		View, Print Preview		✓
Sorting and Grouping		View, Sorting and Grouping		✓
Two Pages		View, Pages, Two Pages		✓
Zoom		View, Zoom		✓

Concepts Review

TRUE/FALSE QUESTIONS

Each of the following statements is either true or false. Indicate your choice by circling **T** or **F**.

T F **1.** A tabular report displays data in rows with column headings, similar to a worksheet.

T F **2.** Use the Text Box button to add a calculated control to a report.

T F **3.** Conditional formatting depends on criteria you enter in the dialog box.

T F **4.** You can move controls from one section to another in a report.

T F **5.** A Report Header prints at the top of every page.

T F **6.** You cannot change the name of a control.

T F **7.** Common expressions include calculations such as [HourlyRate]+[Bonus].

T F **8.** You add a new section to a report when you group records.

SHORT ANSWER QUESTIONS

Write the correct answer in the space provided.

1. What section of a report includes the data from the records?

_____

2. How do you create a multicolumn report?

_____

3. In what menu are the Page Header and Report Header options listed?

_____

4. What is the name of the dialog box you use to select fields, common expressions, or arithmetic operators?

_____

5. What does the expression =Now() do?

_____

6. What tool should you use to add a calculated control to a report?

_____

7. Is a label a bound or an unbound control?

_____

8. What button on the toolbar copies the font and colors from one control to another?

_____

Answer these questions on a separate page. There are no right or wrong answers. Support your answers with examples from your own experience, if possible.

1. You used the Line tool in this lesson to add a design element to a report. What other tools might be good design ideas for a printed report?

2. In this lesson you learned how to change the size, position, and color of labels and text boxes by using the property sheet. What are the advantages of using the property sheet instead of the mouse and toolbars?

Skills Review

Create a report by using the Report Wizard. Work with sections and controls.

1. Create a report with the Report Wizard by following these steps:
   a. Open *[your initials]*CC-E-07.
   b. Click the Tables button and select tblEmployeeDates.
   c. Click the New Object drop-down arrow and choose Report. Choose Report Wizard and then click OK.
   d. Add the following field names to the Selected Fields:

   SocialSecurityNumber

   EmployeeID

   HireDate

   e. Click Next. Do not add grouping. Click Next.
   f. Click the drop-down arrow for the first sort level. Choose HireDate and click Next.
   g. For the layout, choose Tabular. For the orientation, choose Portrait. Click Next.
   h. For the style, choose Soft Gray. Click Next.
   i. Key **rptHireDates** as the title for the report.
   j. Select the option to Preview the report. Click Finish.

NOTE: The Hire Date field is farthest left in the report because it is the sort field.

    k. Maximize the window and click anywhere to change to a Fit zoom size.

2. Work with report sections by following these steps:
    a. In Design View, double-click the **Report Header** bar to open its property sheet.
    b. Click the **Format** tab. Set the **Height** at **.75** inches, but do not close the property sheet.
    c. Click the **Page Header** bar to switch to its property sheet.
    d. Change its **Height** to **.35**. Close the property sheet.

3. Add a group by following these steps:
    a. Click the Sorting and Grouping button .

 NOTE: The HireDate field is in the Grouping and Sorting dialog box because you selected it for sorting in the wizard.

    b. Click the **Group Header** row for the HireDate field and choose **Yes**.
    c. Click the **Group On** row for the HireDate field and choose **Year**. Close the dialog box. The **HireDate Header** is added to the report.
    d. Click the Print Preview button to see the grouping. The records are grouped, but there are no titles for the groups.
    e. Return to Design View and save.

4. Add a field to a report by following these steps:
    a. Display the field list by clicking the Field List button , if it is not already displayed.
    b. Drag the HireDate field from the field list to the **HireDate Header** section.
    c. Delete the label with the new field and save the report.

5. Work with controls and sections by following these steps:
    a. Right-click the HireDate text box in the **HireDate Header** and open its property sheet.
    b. Click the **Format** tab and the **Format** row.
    c. Key **yyyy** as a custom format to display only four-digit years and replace any preset formats. Close the property sheet.
    d. Double-click a sizing handle to autofit the height.
    e. Select the HireDate text box in the **HireDate Header** and the HireDate text box in the **Detail** section. Choose F**ormat**, **Align**, and **Left**.
    f. Format the text box in the **HireDate Header** as bold and italic.

 TIP: For alignment to be accurate, controls should be the same height and width and use the same data type and font.

    g. Preview the report and return to Design View.
    h. Select all three HireDate controls and click the Align Left button .
    i. Show one row of dots below the control in the **HireDate Header**.

j. Double-click the label in the **Report Header**. Click the **Format** tab. Key **Employee Hire Dates** as the **Caption**.

k. Autofit the label.

l. Save the report and preview it.

m. Print the first page of the report, and then close the report.

EXERCISE 7-25

Create and modify AutoReports.

1. Create an AutoReport by following these steps:

    a. Click the **Tables** button and select tblEmployeeDates.

    b. Click the New Object drop-down arrow and choose **R**eport. Choose Auto-Report: **Columnar** and click **OK**.

> **NOTE:** If you are continuing from the previous exercise, this AutoReport will use the Soft Gray style.

    c. Click the AutoFormat button and apply the **Casual** style.

    d. Save the report as **rptAges**

2. Modify controls and sections by following these steps:

    a. With **rptAges** open in Design View, drag the BirthDate control and label until the label is at the 3-inch mark and the controls are aligned at the top with the SocialSecurity # field.

    b. Select and delete the HireDate text box and label.

    c. Drag down the edge of the horizontal ruler to select all the controls in the **D**etail section. Change them to **11** points and choose F**o**rmat, **S**ize, and To **F**it.

    d. Make the SocialSecurity# text box the same width as the EmployeeID text box.

    e. Open the property sheet for the **D**etail section and make it **.75** inch high.

    f. Edit the label in the **Report Header** to show **Employee Ages**

    g. Format the label as 16-point Arial, bold italic, and double-click a sizing handle.

    h. Double-click the **Report Header** bar and make the section **.5** inch high.

    i. Resize the date and page number controls in the **Page Footer** so each is about 2 inches wide. Place the date control near the left margin and the page number control near the right margin.

    j. Click the Label button and click at the 2.5-inch mark in the **Page Footer**.

    k. Key *[your first and last name]* and press Enter.

    l. Preview and save the report.

EXERCISE 7-26

Add calculated controls to a report. Use the Format Painter and conditional formatting.

1. Add a calculated control with a common expression by following these steps:

    a. With **rptAges** open in Design View, click the Text Box button . Click at the 4.25-inch mark below the BirthDate text box.

    b. Double-click the new label. Change its Caption to **Age**

    c. Click the unbound text box to switch to its property sheet. Click the Data tab, the Control Source row, and the Build button .

    d. Click the Common Expressions folder in the left panel. Double-click Current Date/Time in the middle panel.

    e. Key - for subtraction in the operator row.

    f. Click the rptAges folder in the left panel. Click <Field List> in the middle panel. Double-click BirthDate.

    g. Click OK and leave the property sheet open. Preview the report.

> **NOTE:** Dates use serial numbers, so the ages are shown in days, not years.

    h. Return to Design View and open the Expression Builder for the calculated field.

    i. Key a left parenthesis after the equals sign. Press End and key a right parenthesis after the right square bracket of [BirthDate]. This groups the first part of the formula.

    j. Click ⑦, the operator for division. Key **365.25** and then click OK.

    k. Click the Format tab. Use a Standard number with **2** decimal places.

    l. Click the Other tab and name the control **Age**

    m. Close the property sheet. Preview and save the report.

> **TIP:** To convert the age to a whole number, key **\1** at the end of your expression. The backward slash is the integer operator in Visual Basic. You can also use the INT() function.

2. Use Format Painter and conditional formatting by following these steps:

    a. With **rptAges** open in Design View, click the BirthDate text field.

    b. Click the Format Painter button .

    c. Click the calculated text box. Double-click a sizing handle to autofit the height.

    d. Line up the calculated control under the Date of Birth text box and label.

    e. Click the calculated control and choose Format, Conditional Formatting.

    f. Click the first arrow for Condition 1 and choose Field Value Is.

    g. Click the second arrow and select greater than as the operator.

h. Click in the third box and key **45**

i. Click the Bold **B** and Italic **I** buttons. Change the font color to red. Click **OK**.

j. Preview the report. Click the Two Pages button. Then return to a one-page display.

k. Save, print the first page, and close the report.

EXERCISE 7-27

Create a multicolumn report. Export a table to Excel.

1. Create a multicolumn report by following these steps:

    a. Click the **Tables** button and select tblTimeCards. Click the New Object drop-down arrow and choose **R**eport.

    b. Choose **AutoReport: Columnar**. Click **OK**.

    c. Maximize the window and switch to a Fit zoom size.

    d. Click the **C**lose button and go to Design View.

    e. Click the Report Selector button ■ next to the horizontal ruler.

    f. Click the AutoFormat button. Choose **Compact** and click **OK**.

    g. Preview the report. In Print Preview, choose **F**ile, Page Set**u**p.

    h. Click the **Columns** tab. Set the **Number of Columns** to **2**. Set the **Row and Column Spacing** to **.25**.

    i. Set the **Column Size Width** to **3**. Choose **Across, then Down** for the **Column Layout**. Click **OK**.

    j. In Design View, edit the label in the **Report Header** to show **Time Cards**

    k. Resize the Date and Page Number controls in the **Page Footer** so each is about 2 inches wide. Place the Date control near the left margin and the Page Number control near the right margin.

    l. Click the Label button in the middle of the **Page Footer**.

    m. Key *[your first and last name]* and press Enter.

    n. Format your name to match the Date control.

    o. Save the report as **rptTimeCards**. Print the first page of the report.

    p. Close the report.

2. Export a table to Excel by following these steps.

    a. Right-click on the table tblTimeCards. Choose **E**xport from the shortcut menu.

    b. In the Export Table dialog box, for **Save as type** select Microsoft Excel 97-2002.

    c. Verify the **Save in** location and use the default name, **tblTimeCards**.

    d. Click E**x**port.

    e. Compact and close the database.

    f. Open Excel and load the spreadsheet **tblTimeCards**.

    g. View your data and then close your file and Excel.

Lesson Applications

Create a multicolumn report by using the Report Wizard. Size controls. Add a label. Export a query.

1. Open *[your initials]*CC-07.
2. Use the Report Wizard to create a report for qryInventoryByAnimal.
3. In the wizard, choose both fields, but do not add grouping. Sort by Product-Name in ascending order.
4. Use justified layout, portrait orientation, and Bold style.
5. Title the report **rptCurrInv**. Preview each page in Fit and 100% sizes.
6. Select the Current Inventory label and the QuantityOnHand text box. Drag either right middle handle until the right edges align at the 2.75 inch mark.

 NOTE: The rectangle gives the appearance of a border. Click any edge of the rectangle to select it.

7. Select the black rectangle. Size it to match the QuantityOnHand controls.
8. Change the report to use two columns that are 3 inches wide. Determine your own row and column spacing so all the records fit on one page. The columns should run across and then down.
9. Delete the Page Number control. Add a label in its place and key *[your first and last name]*.
10. Use the Format Painter to copy the format from the Date text box to the new label.
11. Edit the label in the Report Header to read **Current Inventory**
12. Save and print the report. Close the report.
13. Export the data used to create rptCurrInv to a text file.
14. Using Microsoft Word, print the text file.

Create an AutoReport. Modify controls. Add labels and common expressions.

1. Create a tabular AutoReport for qryCustomers.
2. Apply the Compact AutoFormat to the entire report.

REVIEW: Controls must be selected to adjust the horizontal or vertical spacing.

3. Delete the FaxNumber text box and its label.

4. Select all the labels in the **Page Header**. Make the horizontal spacing equal.

5. Select all the text boxes in the **Detail** section and make the horizontal spacing equal.

6. Preview the report and then move individual labels or text boxes so each label is positioned well over its column.

7. Select and position the controls in the **Detail** section so there is one row of dots above and below the controls in the section. You might need to resize the section.

8. Preview the report; it might be too wide. Check for blank pages.

9. Change the left and right margins to **.75** inch.

10. Preview again. Check all text boxes to see if they are wide enough, and make adjustments. Move and resize to make the report attractive.

11. Save the report as **rptCustomers**

12. Edit the label in the **Report Header** to show **Carolina Critters Customers**. Align it on the left with the labels in the **Page Header** section.

13. Add a label with your name in the **Page Footer**. Move and position the Date and Page Number controls to make the report attractive.

14. Preview, print, and save the report. Close the report.

EXERCISE 7-30

Sort and group records in a report. Add a calculated control for the group.

1. Open **rptCustomers** in Design View. Maximize the window.

2. Open the Sorting and Grouping dialog box and place State in the **Field/Expression** list. Turn on the **Group Header** and the **Group Footer** for State. Set the **Keep Together** property to **Whole Group**. Show CompanyName as the second **Field/Expression**, but do not turn on its **Group Header** or **Group Footer**.

3. Drag the State label from the **Page Header** into the **State Header** at the left edge. Drag the State text box from the **Detail** section into the **State Header** next to the State label.

4. Use the **Format Painter** to copy the format from the label in the **Page Header** to the State text box.

5. Size, move, and align the labels and text boxes so nothing is cut off.

6. Add a new text box so its label starts at the 1-inch mark in the **State Footer**.

7. Change the label to **# of Customers**

8. Open the property sheet for the unbound text box. Open the Expression Builder.

9. Click in the preview area and key **count(** to start the expression.

10. Click <Field List> and double-click CustomerID. Then key a closing parenthesis to finish the expression. Your expression should show:

    =count([CustomerID])

 REVIEW: Name a control on the Other tab of the property sheet.

11. Change the name of this control to **StateTotal**

12. Copy the format from the label in the State Footer to the calculated control.

13. Size, move, and align the controls if you feel it is needed. Size the sections so there is space between groups of customers.

14. Save, print, and close the report.

EXERCISE 7-31 *Challenge Yourself*

Create a report based on a query.

1. Double-click **qryEmployeesByJobCode** to open it. The Enter Parameter Value dialog box asks for a job code.

2. Key **of06** and press Enter. The query shows only those people in the OF06 job category. Close the query.

3. Use the Report Wizard to create a report for qryEmployeesByJobCode.

4. Use all the fields, do no grouping, and sort by last name. Use a tabular layout and portrait orientation. Use the Casual style. Title the report **rptCodeGroup**

5. In the Enter Parameter Value dialog box, key **mf06** and press Enter. The report is filtered to show employees in the MF06 category.

6. In Design View, add a label for your name in the Report Header.

7. Change the title of the report to **Employee Code Group**

8. Print the report and close it.

9. Compact the database and close it.

On Your Own

In these exercises you work on your own, as you would in a real-life work environment. Use the skills you've learned to accomplish the task—and be creative.

EXERCISE 7-32

Review the design of the database you modified in Exercise 6-32. On a sheet of paper, sketch three reports that will enhance the usability of this database. On each sketched report, describe who would use the report, the reason the information on the report is valuable, and the frequency at which the report will be printed. Name each report and give it a title that best describes the purpose for the report. Write your name and "Exercise 7-32" on each sketch. Continue to Exercise 7-33.

EXERCISE 7-33

Based on the sketches you created in Exercise 7-32, create three reports. Select the style and layout most appropriate for each report. Arrange the controls in a way that you feel is appropriate. In the **Page Footer**, include your name and "Exercise 7-33." In the **Report Header**, include the title of the report. Print a copy of each report. Continue to Exercise 7-34.

EXERCISE 7-34

Create a Group for your report. Depending on your design, you might need to add a field to a table and enter appropriate data. Select a name, title, style, and layout appropriate for the report. Arrange the controls appropriately. In the **Page Footer**, include your name and "Exercise 7-34." Test your report in Print Preview. You might need to sort the records for the grouping to work correctly. Print the report. Submit the copies, the sketches, and the reports you printed in Exercises 7-32 through 7-34 to your instructor. Keep a copy of the database you modified in Exercise 7-34. It will be used in subsequent lessons.

Unit Applications 2

UNIT APPLICATION 2-1

Add a table using the Table Wizard. Create a relationship. Print a table and a relationship.

1. Make a copy of **CC-U02**. Rename it to *[your initials]***CC-U02**. Make sure the file is not Read-only. Open *[your initials]***CC-U02**.

2. Create a new table using the Table Wizard. Use all the fields from the Tasks sample table in the Business category. Rename the TaskID field as **Campaign#**. Rename TaskDescription as **Name**

3. Name the table tblCampaigns and select Yes, set a primary key for me. Do not assign any relationships. Modify the table design before entering records.

4. Change the Data Type for the Campaign# field to Text with a Field Size of **10**. For the Caption, key **Campaign**. Use Text as the Data Type for the Name field and set the Field Size to **35**.

5. After the Notes field, add a field named **Supplier**. Make it a Text field with a Field Size of **10**. Format the field to show uppercase.

 TIP: An uppercase format command does not affect numbers and symbols.

6. Save the table and key the following records.

Campaign:	**Jan 01**
Campaign Name:	**New Year, New Toys**
StartDate:	**1/1/01**
EndDate:	**1/31/01**
Notes:	**This sales campaign announces a new line of toys purchased from Animals 'N Me. Jeffrey Harrison will be in charge of the campaign.**

 TIP: Use [Shift]+[F2] to open the Zoom window for the "Notes" field.

Supplier:	**aa-01**
Campaign:	**Mar 01**
Campaign Name:	**Easter Critters**
StartDate:	**3/1/01**
EndDate:	**4/4/01**
Notes:	**This is our usual Easter sales promotion. The new sales rep in the Midwest region will take charge in mid-February.**

Supplier: **aa-01**

Campaign: **May 01**

Campaign Name: **Memorial Day Special**

StartDate: **5/1/01**

EndDate: **5/31/01**

Notes: **This is a red, white, and blue campaign that will highlight animals who wear those colors. Sales rep will be assigned in mid-April.**

Supplier: **bb-02**

7. Close the table.

8. Add a validation rule in Design View that will allow you to add supplies with only the following numbers: AA-01, BB-02, and CC-03.

9. Add one more record to the table tblCampaigns:

Campaign: **Sept 01**

Campaign Name: **Back To School Critters**

StartDate: **8/1/01**

EndDate: **9/4/01**

Notes: **We will have a new line of animals for this campaign. They will include Eddie Einstein Elephant and Alexander Graham Bear. Others to be developed by** *[your first and last name]*.

Supplier: **cc-01** *(see Note)*

 NOTE: You won't be able to complete the third record because it violates the Validation Rule.

10. Change the Supplier to **cc-03**

11. Size all the fields except the Notes field so you can see the data. Print the Datasheet View in Landscape orientation.

UNIT APPLICATION 2-2

Using a Wizard to create a form and a grouped report. Modify controls in both.

1. Using the Form Wizard, create a form that displays all the fields from tblCampaigns. Use a columnar layout with the Standard style. Name the form **frmCampaigns**

2. Add a label to the Form Header containing the text **Carolina Critters Sales Campaigns**. Format the label as 14-point Arial bold, with red text on a white background. Size the label to show the text on one line.

3. Move the Name controls to the right of the Campaign# controls at the 2-inch mark on the horizontal ruler. Align the controls at the top.

4. Move the StartDate up, leaving 2 rows of grid dots under Campaign. Move the EndDate to the right of StartDate on the 2-inch mark. Align these controls. Move the Notes and Supplier controls up, leaving 2 rows of dots above each.

5. View the form and save it.

6. Change the main title to white letters on a red background with a Raised special effect. Size the Form Header to .5 inch tall.

 TIP: Use the property sheet to set a specific width, height, or position.

7. Make the Name text box 1.5 inches wide.

8. Set the width of the labels in the first column to .65 inch. Move the Campaign# text box until its left edge is on the .75-inch mark on the horizontal ruler. Align the StartDate, Notes, and Supplier text boxes on the left with the Campaign# text box.

9. Change the labels in the Detail section to the Etched special effect.

10. Switch the Supplier and Notes controls so Supplier is under StartDate and Notes is under Supplier. Align controls appropriately and check the tab order.

11. Size the Notes text box so its right edge rests on the 4.5-inch mark on the horizontal ruler.

12. Save the form. Print Record #4 and close the form.

 13. Using the Report Wizard, create a report for all the fields in tblCampaigns. Click the Remove One button <kbd><</kbd> to remove the Supplier group, and sort by StartDate from earliest to latest. Make it a tabular report in Landscape orientation with a Corporate style. Name the report **rptCampaigns**

14. Delete the Campaign# text box and its label.

15. Change the Name label to read **Campaign Name**. Size this label and its text box to be 1.35 inches wide. Drag the controls to align the left edges at the 1-inch mark.

 NOTE: Multiple-select a label and text box and move them together.

16. Move the left edges of the EndDate controls to the 2.5-inch mark. Move the left edge of the Notes control to the 3.5-inch mark. Make the Notes text box 4 inches wide.

17. Add a Group Header for Supplier and make it the first Field/Expression, sorted in ascending order. This will remove any existing sort.

18. Add the Supplier field from the Field List to the Supplier Header. Format the text box to be the same font, size, and color as the label. Align the controls appropriately.

19. Edit the main title to read **Sales Campaigns**. Add a label in the Report Header with your first and last name in 10-point Arial. Align the label at the right edge of the report.

20. Preview, print, save, and close the report.

UNIT APPLICATION 2-3

Create a multicolumn report with conditional formatting.

1. Make a copy of **CC-E-U02**. Rename it to *[your initials]*CC-E-U02. Make sure the file is not Read-only. Open *[your initials]*CC-E-U02.

2. Use the New Report dialog box to create a columnar AutoReport for tblPayroll. Apply a different AutoFormat and save the report as **rptPayCols**

3. Use at least an 11-point font for the text boxes and align them on the right. Set the currency amounts to show no decimal places. Use Text Align Right for the SocialSecurityNumber and EmployeeID text boxes and make these two the same width. Line up all numbers in the text box column.

 NOTE: The Text Align property is in the property sheet and on the Formatting toolbar.

4. Set up the page to show 2 columns. Decide how much space to leave between rows and columns and how wide to make the columns.

5. Set the Savings field to appear bold italic if the amount is greater than $100.

6. Change the label in the Report Header to show **Deductions Summary**. Resize the controls in the Page Footer to make room for a label with your name. Then add a label with your name.

7. Print the first two pages of the report. Save and close it.

UNIT APPLICATION 2-4 *Using the Internet*

Carolina Critters is planning to add life insurance coverage for its employees. First, search the Internet for life insurance rates. Then create a new table and form. Enter the life insurance data.

Create a relationship and query between the new table and the employees table so you can create a report that displays the name of the employee, the address of the employee, the age of the employee, the name of the insurance company, and the monthly insurance rate.

Print the table, form, and report. Make sure your name is shown in an appropriate location on the table, form, and report.

Create a new report that lists the current rate and an anticipated next year's rate (calculated as 10% above the current rate). Print this report. Make sure your name is shown in an appropriate location on the report.

Getting Information from a Database

Designing Queries

OBJECTIVES

After completing this lesson, you will be able to:

1. Link and import data from another database.
2. Create and modify a select query.
3. Modify field properties in a query.
4. Use criteria and operators in a query.
5. Use AND and OR criteria.
6. Use query properties.
7. Add a calculated field to a query.

MOUS
ACTIVITIES
In this lesson:
Ac2002e **1-2**
Ac2002e **3-1**
Ac2002e **3-2**
Ac2002e **4-1**

See Appendix E.

 Estimated Time: 2 hours

As you know, a query is a database object that extracts information from one or more tables. When you design a query, you select fields, sort records, and specify criteria to find information you need. You can save a query and name it. You can use it as the source of records for a form or a report.

Queries form the basis for most reports and forms because they make the data more manageable. For example, a report simply based on an employees table with 2,000 employees would show each of those 2,000 records. A report based on a query shows a subset of those records. By using queries, forms or reports can show specific information about employees, such as who is eligible for retirement, who is scheduled for evaluation, or who is on vacation this week.

TIP: A query is similar to a filter in some respects. However, only one filter is saved automatically with a table, but you can create and save as many queries as necessary.

Linking and Importing Data from Another Database

Databases are upwardly compatible. That means an Access 2000 database can be opened in Access 2002. Most software, however, is not downwardly compatible. You cannot, for example, open an Access 2002 database in Access 2000.

Access 2002 does have a tool that allows you to save a database in a previous version. You might do this if you need to give a copy of your work to someone who is still using Access 2000.

EXERCISE 8-1 Convert a Database

There are two ways to convert databases written in an older version of Access to Access 2002. You can:

- Open a database and then convert it to Access 2002.
- Convert a database without opening it (that's the method used in this exercise).

In either case you are required to provide a new database name.

 NOTE: You cannot use the same database name if you intend to save the current version and the new version in the same folder.

1. Start Access, but do not open a database.
2. Choose Tools, Database Utilities, Convert Database.
3. Choose To Access 2002 Format. The Database to Convert From dialog box opens. Choose **CC-08-2000** from your student CD (or a location indicated by your instructor). Click Convert.
4. The Convert Database Into dialog box opens. Verify the folder where the database will be saved. Key **[your initials]CC-08**. Click Save.
5. Read the information given in the dialog box and click OK.

EXERCISE 8-2 Link Access Tables

When you link a table, it is connected to your database. You can use the table in your database just as any other table. However, a linked table does not become part of your database. You can edit the data of the table, but you cannot make design changes.

1. Rename the **CC-E-08** database to *[your initials]*CC-E-08
2. Open *[your initials]*CC-08.
3. Choose File, Get External Data, Link Tables. In the Link dialog box, select *[your initials]*CC-E-08 and click Link.
4. Click Select All.

FIGURE 8-1
Link Tables
dialog box

5. Click OK. The tables linked to *[your initials]*CC-08 display, with right-pointing arrows before the object names.

EXERCISE 8-3   Link Excel Tables

You can link Excel workbooks to your database the same way you link Access tables. You can link entire Excel worksheets or you can link ranges from a worksheet.

1. Copy the spreadsheet **MoreSales** from your student CD (or the location indicated by your instructor) and save it in the same location as your databases.
2. Right-click in the white space in the Tables window. Choose Link Tables.
3. For Files of type, select Microsoft Excel.
4. Select the worksheet **MoreSales** and click Link.
5. In the Link Spreadsheet Wizard dialog box, click Show Named Ranges. A list of range names in the worksheet **MoreSales** appears.
6. Select NewSales and click Next.
7. The next dialog box lets you specify whether the first row of the range contains column headings. If the first row contains column headings, Access uses the column heading as the field names.

8. Deselect First Row Contains Column Headings. The headings now look like data.

9. Select First Row Contains Column Headings. The column headings are again used as field names.

FIGURE 8-2
Selecting the
First Row Contains
Column Headings
option

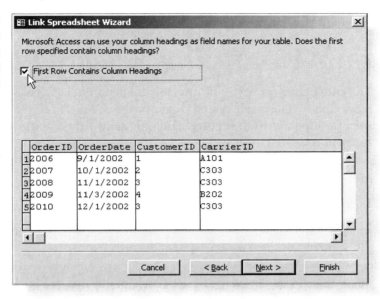

10. Click Next.

11. Key **tblNewSales** as the Linked Table Name.

12. Click Finish and then click OK to finish linking the new table. Notice the icon for the new object.

EXERCISE 8-4   Import Queries and Reports

You can import a query or a report from another Access database in the same way you import a table. Sometimes importing a query or report is easier than creating it. For you to import a query or report, both databases must have a similar structure. If a report you wish to duplicate is based on a query, the report will run only if you import the underlying query.

 TIP: A query is similar to a filter in some respects. However, only one filter is associated with a table at a time. You can create and save as many queries as you need.

1. Right-click in the white space and choose Import. Select *[your initials]* **CC-E-08** and click Import.

2. Click the Queries tab and then click Select All to select all the queries. Click the Reports tab and click Select All to select all the reports. Click OK. All the queries and reports are imported.

3. Check to make sure the reports and queries have been imported. Look for rptEmployeeBirthDate and rptEmployeeHireDate. Click Queries and look for qryBirthDates and qryHireDates.

Creating and Modifying Select Queries

The most common type of query is a select query. A select query locates data from one or more tables and displays the results in a datasheet. You can use a select query to group records and calculate sums, counts, averages, and other types of totals.

As with tables, forms, and reports, queries have a Design View. You can use a wizard to design some types of queries, but most queries are quickly built in Design View.

The Query Design window has two panes. The upper pane shows the Field List(s). The lower pane is the design grid, where you specify the fields and criteria for queries.

FIGURE 8-3
Query Design window

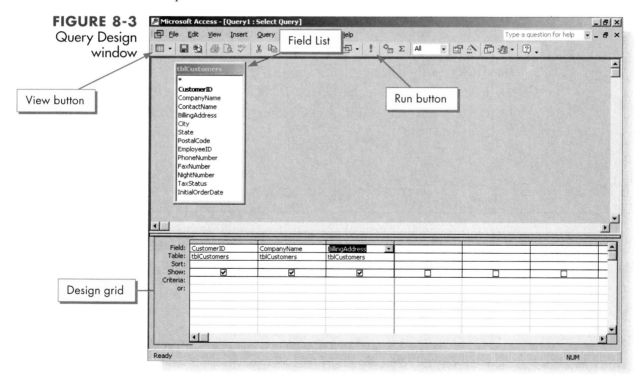

 TIP: The design grid is sometimes called the *QBE (Query by Example) grid,* because you key an example as criteria for a query.

After you design a query, you switch to Datasheet View to see the results. Queries form the basis for most reports and forms because they make the data more manageable. For example, a report simply based on an employees table with 2,000 employees would display 2,000 records. A report based on a query shows a subset of those records.

EXERCISE 8-5 View a Select Query and Its Report

Select queries can be simple. For example, you can create a select query that includes fields from a few records of a large table. The field names are placed on the design grid. When you view the results, the dynaset shows only the fields for the specified records.

NOTE: Imported queries, forms, and reports become part of your database. There is no linking symbol when these are imported.

1. Double-click qryBirthDates. This runs the query and displays the dynaset. The dynaset shows the employee's first and last name and date of birth.

NOTE: To use two tables in a query, the tables must have a common field.

2. Click the View button ![] and maximize the window. This query uses two tables. Each table has a Field List in the top pane of the window. You can see a join line between the common fields named SocialSecurityNumber. The three fields shown as the result of the query appear in the lower pane.

FIGURE 8-4
Query Design
window

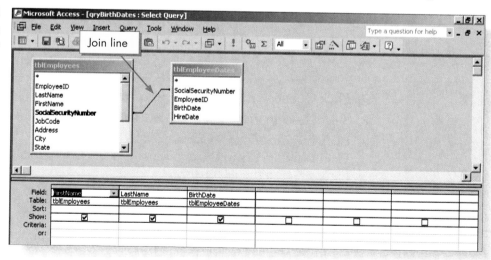

3. Close the query.

4. Click **Reports**. Double-click rptEmployeeBirthDate to open the report in Print Preview. Zoom to Fit and then choose **100%**. This report has a graphic image, shown twice.

5. Press [Ctrl]+[>] to open the report in Design View.

6. Double-click the **Report Selector** button ■ to the left of the horizontal ruler to open the report's property sheet.

 NOTE: The report's property sheet might already be open.

7. Click the **Data** tab. The **Record Source** for this report is qryBirthDates. The Record Source is the basis for the data shown in the report.

FIGURE 8-5
Report's
property sheet

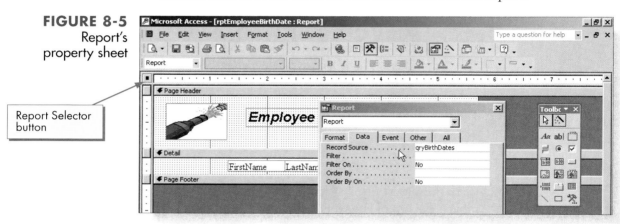

8. Close the property sheet and the report.

EXERCISE **8-6**   **Create a Select Query**

1. Click **Queries** and the **New** button. The New Query dialog box opens.

2. Select **Design View** and click **OK**. The Show Table dialog box opens.

3. Click the **Tables** tab. Double-click tblStuffedAnimals. The Stuffed Animals Field List appears in the upper pane of the Query Design window. (See Figure 8-6 on the next page.)

REVIEW: If you accidentally open two copies of a Field List, right-click the second one and choose Remove Table. You can also click the title bar of the Field List window and press [Delete] to remove the extra copy.

4. Click the **Close** button in the Show Table dialog box.

FIGURE 8-6
Show Table
dialog box

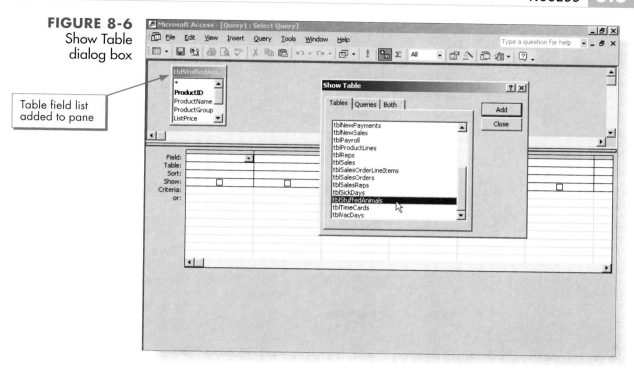

Table field list
added to pane

5. Size the panes and Field List.

 6. Click the Save button 🖫. Name the query **qryAnimalPrices** and click OK.

EXERCISE 8-7 Add Fields to the Query

There are three ways to add fields to the design grid. You can:

- Double-click the field name.
- Drag the field to a cell in the Field row.
- Click the Field row and choose from the list.

1. Double-click ProductName in the Field List. It appears as the first field in the Field row. The Table row shows the name of the source table. This is useful if you use multiple tables. The Show row shows a check box, indicating the field will be shown in the dynaset.

2. Drag the ProductGroup field from the Field List to the Field row, second column.

3. In the third column, click the Field row, and then click its drop-down arrow. Choose ListPrice from the list of field names. (See Figure 8-7 on the next page.)

FIGURE 8-7
Adding fields
to the design grid

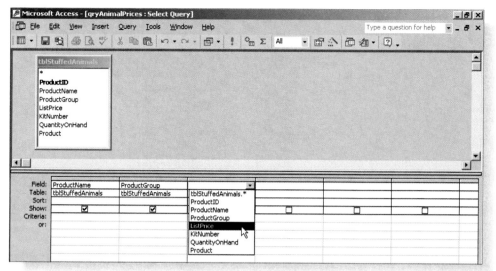

4. Click the Save button .

EXERCISE 8-8 View and Print a Query

There are two ways to view the dynaset for a select query. You can:

- Click the View button .
- Click the Run button [!].

1. Click the View button . The dynaset shows all the records but only the three fields in the design grid.

2. Click the View button [✎].

3. Click the Run button [!]. As you can see, there is no difference between the View button and the Run button [!] for a select query.

> **NOTE:** The View button and the Run button [!] act differently with other types of queries.

4. Click the Print Preview button [🔍]. Notice that the Print Preview for a dynaset is the same as for a table. Close the preview.

5. Click the Print button . The dynaset prints like a table.

6. Save and close the query.

EXERCISE 8-9 **Apply Filters to a Query**

Filters can be applied to queries in the same way they are applied to tables.

 TIP: Applying a temporary filter to a query is a fast way to get specific information.

 1. Open qryBirthDates in the Datasheet View and click the Filter By Form button .

2. Click in the Last Name column and then click the drop-down arrow. Choose Lee from the list of field names.

 3. Click the Apply Filter button . Only the three employees whose last names are "Lee" appear.

4. Close without saving the query.

Modifying Field Properties in a Query

A dynaset is a live link to data in a table. It is a dynamic picture of the table. If you add a new record in a dynaset, the record is added to the underlying table. If you edit an existing record, the changes are saved in the underlying table.

 NOTE: If a query does not include all the fields from a table and you add a record, that record in the table will be missing fields not included in the dynaset.

EXERCISE 8-10 **Modify Query Field Properties**

In a query, you can modify the field properties. When you move fields in the Design View of a query, the fields display in the new order in the Datasheet View of that query.

1. Click qryAnimalPrices and click <u>D</u>esign.

2. Place the pointer on the border between the column selectors for the ProductName and ProductGroup fields in the design grid. (The column selector is the thin bar at the top of each column.) The pointer shows a double-ended arrow (the column-sizing pointer).

3. Drag the border to the left, but don't release the mouse button. As you drag, a vertical black line shows the new width. Return the pointer to its original position and release the button.

FIGURE 8-8
Sizing a field

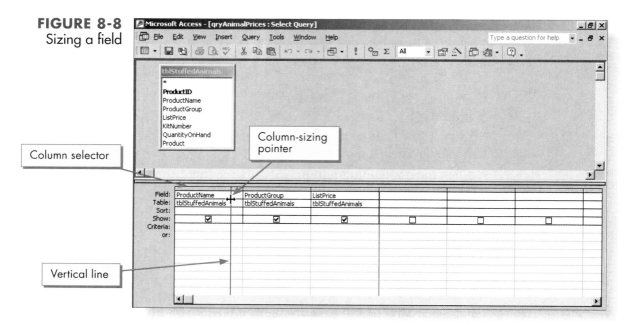

4. Between the ProductGroup and ListPrice column selectors, drag the border to the left to make the ProductGroup column too narrow to display the complete table name.

 TIP: Size fields in the design grid the same way you size columns in a datasheet.

5. Double-click the border to size the column to fit the complete table name.
6. Double-click KitNumber in the Field List. It is placed in the fourth column.

 TIP: If you make a mistake and want to start from scratch, choose <u>E</u>dit, Clear <u>G</u>rid.

7. Drag the ProductID field from the Field List directly on top of the ProductGroup field name in the design grid. ProductID is inserted as the second column, and the ProductGroup moves to the third column.
8. Click the View button 🔲. The dynaset shows the new fields.
9. Return to Design View. Click the column selector for ProductID when the pointer is a black arrow.

FIGURE 8-9
Selecting a column

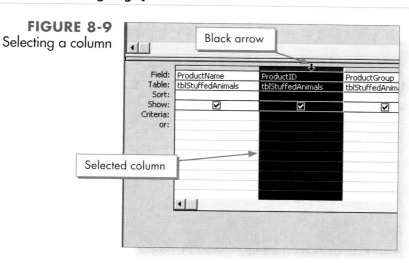

Black arrow

Selected column

10. Press Delete to delete the ProductID field from the query.

11. Click the column selector for KitNumber to select the column.

12. Point at the column selector to display the move pointer (a white arrow). Drag the field into position as the second column. The thick vertical line marks where the column will be dropped.

FIGURE 8-10
Moving a column

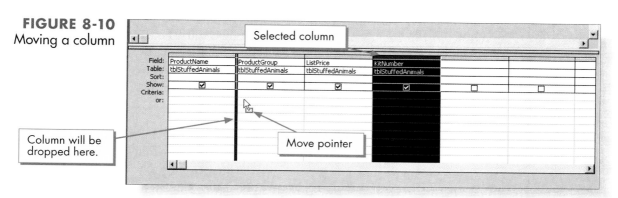

Selected column

Column will be dropped here.

Move pointer

13. View the dynaset and return to Design View.

14. Select and delete the KitNumber field.

15. Click the Save button 🖫.

EXERCISE 8-11 Sort by a Single Field

You can use the **Sort** row in the query design window to specify sorting arrangements for the records in the dynaset.

1. Click in the **Sort** row of the ProductName column.

2. Click the arrow and select **Ascending**. (See Figure 8-11 on the next page.)

3. View the dynaset. Notice that Access alphabetizes the Animal Name field.

 NOTE: The ProductName field has a caption of "Animal Name." You see the caption in the dynaset.

FIGURE 8-11
Select a Sort option
in the design grid

Field:	ProductName	ProductGroup	ListPrice			
Table:	tblStuffedAnimals	tblStuffedAnimals	tblStuffedAnimals			
Sort:						
Show:	Ascending	☑	☑	☐	☐	☐
Criteria:	Descending					
or:	(not sorted)					

EXERCISE 8-12 Sort by Multiple Fields

Suppose you want to sort by product group and then alphabetically by animal name within each group. The main sort field must be the column at the left side of the design grid. Additional fields used for the sort do not need to be next to the first field, but they must be in left-to-right order, reflecting their desired sort order.

1. Return to Design View.

2. Click the **Sort** row for the ProductGroup field and choose **Ascending**.

3. View the dynaset. The products are sorted first by name, but the group is not correct.

4. Return to Design View. Move the pointer to the column selector for Product-Group. When the pointer is a black arrow, click.

5. Point at the column selector to display a white arrow. Drag the column to the first column position. The left-to-right order is now ProductGroup, ProductName, ListPrice.

6. View the dynaset. Notice that the query is now sorted first by Product Group and then by Animal Name within the Product Group.

 TIP: You can save a query in Datasheet View or Design View.

7. Save and close the query.

EXERCISE 8-13 Create a Report Based on a Query

You can use a query to build reports by using a wizard or by using Design View.

1. With qryAnimalPrices selected, click the New Object arrow. Choose **R**eport.

2. In the New Report dialog box, choose **Report Wizard** and click **OK**.

3. Click the Add All button to use all the fields. Click **Next**.

4. Click **Next** to bypass the Grouping dialog box.

5. Click **Next** to bypass the Sorting dialog box. (The query already has the sorting instructions.)

6. Select a **Tabular** layout and **Portrait** orientation. Click **Next**.

7. Use the Bold style and click **Next**.

8. Edit the report name to show **rptAnimalPrices**. Click **Finish**.

9. Maximize the window. View the report in both **Fit** and **100%** Zoom sizes.

10. Close Print Preview and return to Design View for the report.

11. Double-click the Report Selector button ■ next to the horizontal ruler to open the report's property sheet.

12. Click the **Data** tab. The Record Source for the report is your query.

13. Save and close the report.

Using Criteria and Operators in a Query

You enter criteria in a query to select certain records and exclude others. When you view the results of a query with selection criteria, you see only those records that match the criteria. You might, for example, set criteria that limit the records to products in Group C only. Or you might set criteria that produce a list of stuffed animals with a list price of greater than $10. Criteria can be text, numbers, or expressions.

EXERCISE 8-14 Use a Single Criteria

Criteria can be as simple as one condition in one field. You might, for example, list products in a particular group, such as cats and dogs. Because the product code for cats and dogs is "C," you key **c** in the **Criteria** row for the ProductGroup field. The **Criteria** row is below the **Sort** row.

1. Open qryAnimalPrices in Design View.

2. Click the **Criteria** row for ProductGroup. Key **c**. (See Figure 8-12 on the next page.)

TIP: Text criteria are not case-sensitive. You also do not need to key formatting characters such as the dollar sign.

FIGURE 8-12
Entering criteria

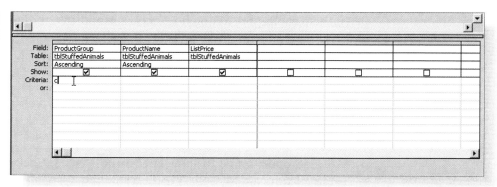

3. Click the View button [▦]. Notice that only those products in Product Group C (the cats and dogs) are shown.

4. Return to Design View. Access formats text used in criteria with quotation marks.

5. Click in the **Criteria** row for ProductGroup and press [F2] to select the criteria. Then press [Delete].

6. In the **Criteria** row for ListPrice, key **between 9.5 and 11**

7. View the dynaset. Notice that only those products with prices between and including $9.50 and $11 are shown.

8. Return to Design View. Notice that Access formats its reserved words with initial caps.

9. Click in the **Criteria** row for ListPrice and press [F2]. Press [Delete].

EXERCISE 8-15 Use Relational Operators

You have already used mathematical operators. The same symbols are used as relational operators. Relational operators are operators that compare two values. You can use relational operators in setting criteria.

TABLE 8-1 **Relational Operators**

OPERATOR	MEANING
=	Equal
<>	Not equal

continues

TABLE 8-1 Relational Operators *continued*

OPERATOR	MEANING
<	Less than
<=	Less than or equal to
>	Greater than
>=	Greater than or equal to

1. In the **Criteria** row for ListPrice, key **>10**
2. Click the View button 🔳. The products shown are priced over $10. Return to Design View.
3. Edit the criteria to show **>10 and <12**

FIGURE 8-13
Edited criteria with relational operators

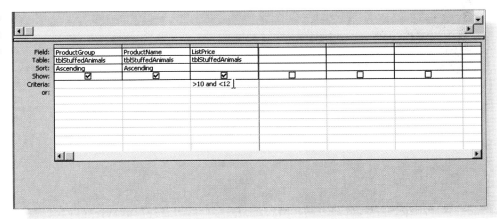

4. View the dynaset. The products are priced over $10 but less than $12. Return to Design View.
5. Press F2 and delete the criteria.
6. In the **Criteria** row for ProductName, key **>m**
7. View the dynaset. Only those products whose name begins with an "M" or higher letter in the alphabet are shown. Return to Design View.
8. Delete the criteria. In the **Criteria** row for ProductGroup, key **<>d**
9. View the dynaset. All products except those in the D group are shown. Return to Design View.
10. Delete the criteria. Save and close the query.

EXERCISE **8-16** **Use the Like Operator, Wildcards, and the Is NULL Criteria**

You already know how to use wildcards with the <u>F</u>ind command. In much the same way, you can use wildcards in a query to match records. Access uses the Like operator to compare your criteria with each record when you key a wildcard in a query.

NULL is a reserved word in Access that means "blank" or "empty." It is different from zero (0).

1. Double-click **qrySalesReview** to open it in Datasheet View. It shows general information about sales orders.

2. Click the View button . This query uses two tables, and you can see the join line between the common field, named CustomerID.

3. In the Criteria row for CompanyName, key **the***

> **REVIEW:** The wildcard * represents any number of characters. Thus, the criteria "the*" specifies the word "the" followed by any number of characters.

FIGURE 8-14
Using the * wildcard

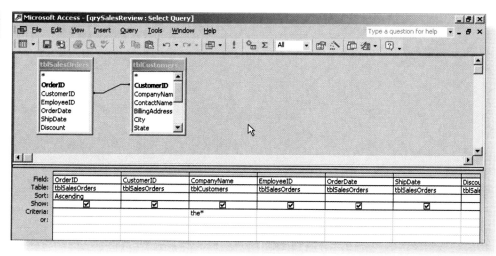

4. Click the View button. Only company names that start with the word "the" are listed.

5. Return to Design View. Access inserts the Like operator and formats the text with quotes.

6. Press F2 and Delete.

7. In the Criteria row for CompanyName, key ***inc***

8. View the dynaset. Companies that have "inc" somewhere in the name are shown.

9. Return to Design View. Delete the criteria.

10. Key ***m???*** in the CompanyName Criteria row. This means that somewhere in the company name is a four letter word that starts with "M."

 REVIEW: The wildcard ? represents a single character.

11. View the dynaset. Two records are displayed.

12. Return to Design View and delete the criteria.

13. Close the query without saving the changes.

14. Open qryEmployees to see its dynaset. Switch to Design View.

15. In the Criteria row for Photograph, key **is null**

16. View the dynaset. These are the employees without pictures.

17. Return to Design View. Notice that Access capitalizes reserved words.

18. Edit the criteria to show **is not null**

19. View the dynaset. These are the records with pictures.

 REVIEW: You cannot see an image in Datasheet View.

20. Close the query without saving.

Using AND and OR Criteria

An AND criteria or an OR criteria uses more than one specification or requirement. You use an AND criteria when two or more things must occur at the same time for the criteria to be true. You use an OR criteria when either of two or more things must occur for the criteria to be true. When you use AND criteria, you enter the conditions on the same Criteria row in the design grid. When you use OR criteria, you enter the conditions on different Criteria rows in the design grid.

EXERCISE   **8-17**   **Use AND Criteria**

Suppose you need to list only customers who live on Brookshire Avenue in Charlotte. You would use an AND criteria, because the two conditions must be met for the record to display. The first is that the city be Charlotte. The second condition is that the address include the word "Brookshire."

1. Click the Queries and click <u>N</u>ew.

2. In the New Query dialog box, choose Simple Query Wizard and click OK.

3. Click the drop-down Tables/Queries arrow and choose Table: tblCustomers.

 TIP: Tables are listed before queries in the drop-down list.

4. Click the Add All button >> . Click Next.

5. Choose Detail as the type of query and click Next.

6. Name the query **qryCustomers** and click Finish. The query opens in Data-sheet View.

 NOTE: You might need to scroll through the window to see all the fields in the design grid.

7. Return to Design View. Access lists all the fields in the design grid.

8. Size the panes and the Field List.

9. In the City column, key **charlotte** in the Criteria row.

10. View the dynaset to see how many customers are in Charlotte. Return to Design View.

11. In the BillingAddress column, key ***brookshire** in the same Criteria row.

FIGURE 8-15
AND criteria
on the same row
in the design grid

Field:	CustomerID	CompanyName	ContactName	BillingAddress	City	State	Postal
Table:	tblCustomers	tblCustomers	tblCustomers	tblCustomers	tblCustomers	tblCustomers	tblCus
Sort:	Ascending						
Show:	☑	☑	☑	☑	☑	☑	
Criteria:				Like "*brookshire*"	charlotte		
or:							

12. View the dynaset and return to Design View.

EXERCISE 8-18 Use OR Criteria

Suppose you need a list of customers in Connecticut as well as customers in Tennessee. This is an OR criteria, because only one condition needs to be true for the record to be listed. You want to include customers whose state is CT. You also want those whose state is TN. If a customer matches one or the other condition, the customer is listed. If a customer met both conditions (not likely in this case), the customer would also be included.

1. Point to the right of the word "Criteria" in the Criteria row to display a black arrow pointing right. Click to select the Criteria row and press Delete . (See Figure 8-16 on the next page.)

FIGURE 8-16
Selecting a
Criteria row

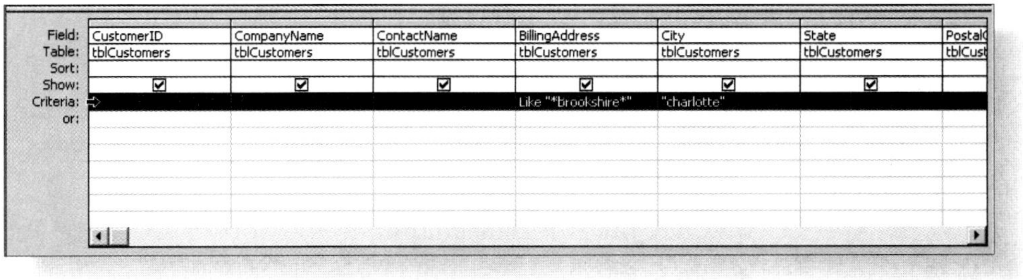

2. In the State column, key **tn** in the **Criteria** row. View the dynaset to see four matching records. Return to Design View.

3. Key **ct** in the row below "tn" to enter a second condition. The first **Or** row is directly below the **Criteria** row.

FIGURE 8-17
OR criteria
on separate rows
in the design grid

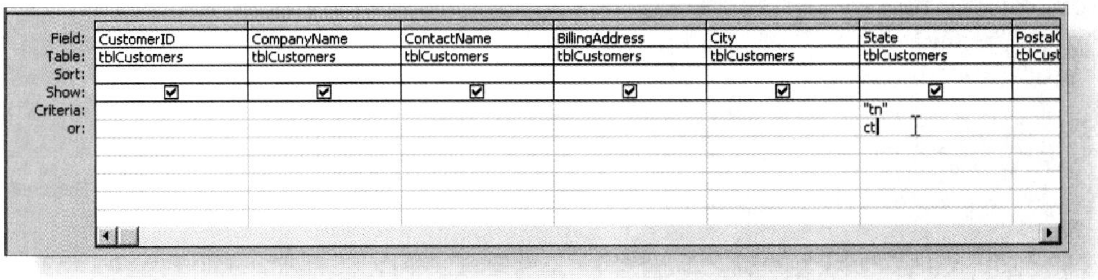

4. View the dynaset. Each record meets one of the OR conditions. Return to Design View.

5. Point to the right of the word "Criteria" in the **Criteria** row to display a black arrow. Drag to select both **Criteria** rows. Press ⌊Delete⌋.

6. Save and close the query.

Using Query Properties

You might need to determine such criteria as the best and worst, highest and lowest, or youngest and oldest. In the Stuffed Animals table, for example, you might need to list the five highest or lowest list prices. In a Customers table, you might want to find the customers who generate the most revenue. To display the highest or lowest values, you use the Top Value property in a query.

EXERCISE 8-19 Find the Top and Bottom Values

The Top Values property finds a certain number of records (the top 5, for instance) or a percentage (the top 5%). Depending on the sort order, Top Values can display either the highest (top) or lowest (bottom) values. For example, when you use an ascending sort with numbers, the "top" of the list shows the lowest numbers. In a descending sort, the "top" represents the highest numbers.

1. Open qryHireDates. It shows the first and last name and date of hire.

2. Return to Design View. This query uses two tables. SocialSecurityNumber is the common field.

3. Click the HireDate column in the Sort row. Choose Ascending.

4. View the dynaset. At the top of the list are the employees who have worked at Carolina Critters the longest.

5. Return to Design View.

6. Click the Top Values arrow on the toolbar and choose 5

FIGURE 8-18
Top Values property
set from a
drop-down list box

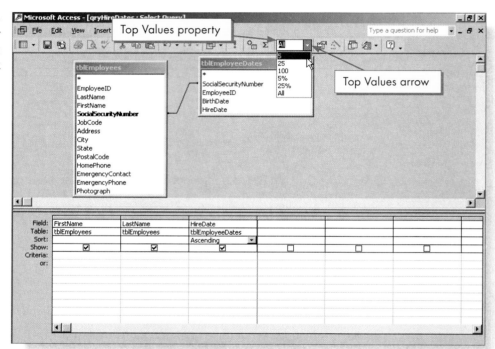

7. View the dynaset. These are the five workers with the most seniority. Return to Design View.

8. Click in the Sort row for HireDate and choose Descending. The Top Values property still shows 5.

9. View the dynaset. These are the five most recently hired workers. Return to Design View.

 NOTE: The Top Values property can also be used for the highest or lowest percent. The Top Values property is also listed on the query property sheet.

10. Reset the Top Values box to All.

 NOTE: Remember to reset the Top Values property to All. If you forget to reset it and later prepare a query to show employees hired after 1984, you would still see only the five most recent hires.

11. Close and save the query.

EXERCISE 8-20 Display a Subdatasheet in the Dynaset

You are already familiar with subdatasheets that show a related table while viewing a table. You can use the same feature in a query to see a related table. The Subdatasheet Name is a query property.

1. Open qrySalesReview in Design View.

 2. Click anywhere in the top pane, but not in a Field List. Click the Properties button 📇.

 NOTE: If the property sheet shows "Field Properties," click again in the top pane.

3. Size the property sheet to see all choices.

4. Click the Subdatasheet Name row and choose Table.tblSalesOrdersLineItems.

FIGURE 8-19
Choosing a subdatasheet in the property sheet

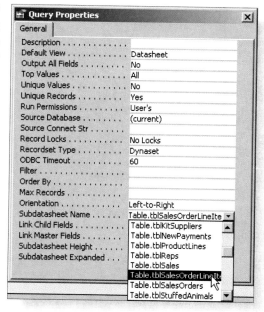

5. Click the Link Child Fields row and key **OrderID**

6. Click the Link Master Fields row and key **OrderID**

7. Close the property sheet. View the dynaset. Click the Expand button ➕ for any record to see which items were ordered.

8. Collapse the subdatasheet.

9. Close the query and do not save the changes.

Adding a Calculated Field to a Query

You have already used calculated fields in forms and reports. You can also use a calculated field in a query.

 TIP: You can key expressions directly in the Field row and do not need to use the Expression Builder.

EXERCISE 8-21 **Create a Calculated Field**

A calculated field is an unbound field that uses an expression or formula as its data source. The definition and properties of the calculated field are stored in the query object. A calculated field does not store data in a table. The data contained in the calculated field is created every time you run the query.

1. Open qryAnimalPrices in Design View.

2. Right-click the empty Field row in the fourth column. Choose Build.

3. The left panel shows that your query is the open folder. Notice that QuantityOnHand is not listed in the middle panel because it is not shown in the design grid of the query.

4. Double-click ListPrice in the middle panel to paste it.

 5. Click ■ (the * operator in the Expression Builder).

6. Double-click the Tables folder in the left panel. It expands to show the tables in the database.

7. Click tblStuffedAnimals. Double-click QuantityOnHand in the middle panel. Note that Access adds an identifier indicating the source of the field.

FIGURE 8-20
Building an
expression
for the query

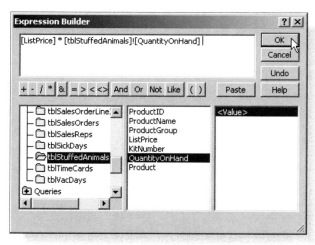

8. Click OK to close the Expression Builder.

9. View the dynaset. Notice that the last column shows the value of the current inventory, or the list price multiplied by the quantity on hand. The caption is "Expr1."

10. Return to Design View.

 REVIEW: To see the calculation more easily, you can open the Zoom window by using [Shift] + [F2].

11. Replace "Expr1" with **WholesaleValue**. Be certain to leave the colon after the field name.

 NOTE: The colon identifies the preceding text as the field name.

12. Click the Properties button and set the field caption to **Wholesales Value**

13. View the dynaset. Widen the last column so you can see the name.

14. Save and close the query.

15. Select and delete each linked table in the database.

16. Compact and close the database.

USING HELP

Once you open the Microsoft Access Help dialog box, you can have Access search for a topic by using the Answer Wizard tabs.

Use the Answer Wizard to learn about query types.

1. With your database open, press F1.

2. Click the Answer Wizard tab. Key **select query** and press [Enter].

3. Click the topic About a select query or crosstab queries.

4. In the right pane, click Select queries. Then click What is a select query?

5. Read the information on select queries. Click the keyword criteria and read its definition. (See Figure 8-21 on the next page.)

6. Click Creating a select query.

7. In the left pane, click the subject About types of queries.

8. There are five types of queries. Explore the right pane and read about each type.

9. Close the Help window.

FIGURE 8-21
Microsoft Access
Help

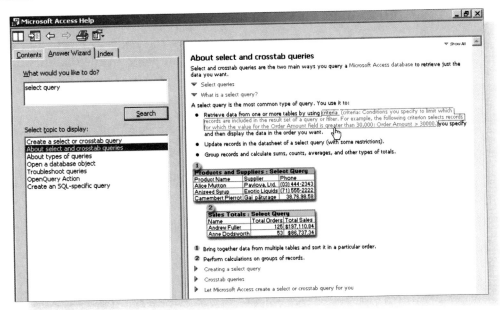

LESSON 8 Summary

➤ A select query shows a dynaset of a table. Select queries can be printed and used as the basis for reports.

➤ In Design View, panes and Field Lists can be sized to better see the fields. Fields can be added or deleted from the query design. The order of the fields can be changed. Records can be sorted by one or more fields.

➤ When editing data in a dynaset, the data is changed in the underlying table.

➤ Criteria in a query sets the conditions for which records are shown in the dynaset. You can use a single criteria, multiple criteria with AND and OR, relational operators, and wildcards.

➤ The criteria IS NULL locates fields that do not contain any data. This criteria is not the same as the zero value in a numeric field. The criteria IS NOT NULL locates fields that contain data.

➤ An AND criteria uses two or more fields on the same row and requires that all conditions be true for the record to display.

➤ An OR criteria uses two or more rows and requires that either condition be true for the record to display.

➤ The Top Values property finds a specified number of the top or bottom values.

LESSON 8 Command Summary

FEATURE	BUTTON	MENU	KEYBOARD	SPEECH
Run query		<u>V</u>iew, Data<u>s</u>heet View		✓
Design View		<u>V</u>iew, <u>D</u>esign View		✓
Delete field		<u>E</u>dit, Delete Colu<u>m</u>ns	Delete	✓
Subdatasheet		<u>V</u>iew, <u>P</u>roperties		✓
Change View			Ctrl + < or Ctrl + >	

Concepts Review

Each of the following statements is either true or false. Indicate your choice by circling T or F.

T F   **1.** You cannot add records in a dynaset.

T F   **2.** You can build criteria by using logical and relational operators.

T F   **3.** You cannot use a query as the source of records for a report.

T F   **4.** You can add a field to a query in Design View by double-clicking the field name in the Field List window.

T F   **5.** To sort on two fields in a query, the main sort field should be to the right of the field that is sorted second.

T F   **6.** You can use the Top Values property to find the bottom 5% of values for any field.

T F   **7.** In the design grid, OR criteria are entered in the same row.

T F   **8.** The criteria "is not null" finds records with a blank or empty field.

Write the correct answer in the space provided.

1. What is the name of the grid in which you sort data and enter criteria?

_____

2. In what view do you see the dynaset of a query?

_____

3. What property can display the highest or lowest values?

_____

4. What type of criteria do you use when you want two conditions to be true at the same time?

_____

5. What type of sort displays names in alphabetical order?

_____

6. What reserved word in Access means "blank" or "empty"?

_____

7. When you key a wildcard in a query, what operator does Access use to compare your criteria with each record?

8. What symbol represents "not equal?

CRITICAL THINKING

Answer these questions on a separate page. There are no right or wrong answers. Support your answers with examples from your own experience, if possible.

1. Think about a database of music titles, sports teams and players, or movies. Give examples of how you could use queries to find something you want to know.

2. AND and OR criteria are common to database, programming, and spread-sheets. You can build a logic table to help you visualize what happens with two criteria in these situations. Complete this table (on a separate sheet of paper) to show if the result is True or False (a match or no match).

FIGURE 8-22
Logic table

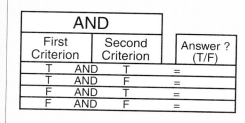

Skills Review

EXERCISE 8-22

Import a table, delete a table, and link tables.

1. Import a table by the following these steps:
  a. Open *[your initials]*CC-E-08.
  b. Choose File, Get External Data, and Import.
  c. Select *[your initials]*CC-08 and click Import.
  d. Select the table tblEmployees.

   e. Click **OK** to import the table.
   f. Compact and close the database, but not Access.

2. Delete a table by using the following steps:

   a. Open *[your initials]***CC-08**.
   b. Select the table tblEmployees.
   c. Press ⌈Delete⌉. Choose **Y**es.

3. Link all the tables from one database to another by using the following steps:

   a. Choose **F**ile, **G**et External Data, and **L**ink Tables.
   b. Select *[your initials]***CC-E-08** and click Lin**k**.
   c. Click **Select All** and then **OK**.

EXERCISE 8-23

Create a select query. Add a field to a query. Edit data in a dynaset. Sort a query. Use a query for a report.

1. Make changes in the dynaset by following these steps:

   a. Click the **Queries**. Double-click qryInventoryByAnimal.
   b. Double-click Sara in the second record and key *[your last name]*
   c. Click the record selector for Whitey Whale and press ⌈Delete⌉. Choose **Y**es.

2. Make changes in Design View by following these steps:

   a. Click the View button .
   b. Double-click the ProductGroup field in the Field List.
   c. Click the column selector for the ProductGroup field.
   d. Point at the column selector and drag the field to be the first column.
   e. Click the View button 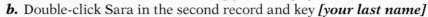.

3. Sort by a single field by following these steps:

   a. With qryInventoryByAnimal in Design View, maximize the window.
   b. Click in the Sort row for the ProductGroup field. Choose **Descending**.
   c. View the dynaset. Return to Design View.

4. Sort by multiple fields by following these steps:

   a. Click in the **Sort** row for the ProductName field and select **Ascending**.
   b. View the dynaset. Return to Design View.
   c. Change the sort order for the ProductGroup field to **Ascending**.
   d. View the dynaset. Save the query.

5. Use a query for a report by following these steps:

   a. With qryInventorybyAnimal open in Datasheet View, click the New Object arrow and choose **R**eport.
   b. Choose **Report Wizard** and click **OK**.
   c. Add all the fields. Click **Next**. Double-click ProductGroup to use it for grouping. Bypass the Sort Order dialog box, because the query sorts the records.

   d. Use a <u>S</u>tepped layout, <u>P</u>ortrait orientation, and <u>F</u>ormal style.
   e. Name the report **rptNewInv**
   f. View the report at several zoom levels. Close the report.
   g. Close the query.

EXERCISE 8-24

Use criteria in a query. Use AND and OR criteria.

   1. Create a query in Design View by following these steps:

   a. Click the Tables button and click tblKitSuppliers.
   b. Click the New Object arrow and choose **Query**. Select Design View and click OK. Maximize the window.
   c. Place the pointer on the horizontal bar between the top and bottom panes. Drag down to make both panes the same height.
   d. Drag the bottom border of the Field List window to make it taller.
   e. Double-click SupplierName, ContactName, and PhoneNumber in the Field List to add them to the design grid.

   f. Click the Save button ▣ and name the query **qrySupplierContacts**
   g. Click the View button ▦. Return to Design View.

   2. Add and delete fields by following these steps:

   a. Double-click SupplierID.
   b. Drag the SupplierID field on top of the SupplierName field in the design grid, placing SupplierID in the first column.
   c. View the dynaset.
   d. Save the query.

   ✎ **NOTE:** Write your answers for the following questions on a piece of paper. Make sure to include your name, the date, your class, and the exercise number.

   3. Set criteria in a query by following these steps:

   a. Make sure qrySupplierContacts is open in Design View.
   b. Key **j*** in the Criteria row for ContactName.
   c. View the dynaset. How many records are displayed? Describe the records the criteria selected.
   d. Return to Design View. Press F2 to select the criteria and press Delete.
   e. Key **206*** in the Criteria row for PhoneNumber. View the dynaset. How many suppliers are in this area code?
   f. Return to Design View. Delete the criteria.
   g. Key ***fabric*** in the Criteria row for SupplierName. View the dynaset. How many suppliers include a variation of the word "fabric" in their names?
   h. Return to Design View. Delete the criteria.
   i. Close the query without saving.

4. Use AND criteria by following these steps:

    a. Open qrySalesReview in Design View. Maximize the window.

    b. Key **6** in the **Criteria** row for EmployeeID.

    c. View the dynaset. How many records are displayed? Describe the records the criteria selected.

    d. Return to Design View. Key **>2/1/2001** in the **OrderDate** criteria row. View the dynaset. How many records are displayed? Describe the records the criteria selected.

    e. Return to Design View. Point to the right of the word "Criteria" in the **Criteria** row to display a black arrow.

    f. Click to select the **Criteria** row and press Delete.

5. Use OR criteria by following these steps:

    a. View the dynaset. How many records are shown when no criteria is used?

    b. Switch to Design View. Key **>.04** in the **Criteria** row for Discount. View the dynaset. How many records meet this criteria?

 TIP: The discounts are entered as decimals.

    c. Return to Design View.

    d. Click in the **Or** row for Employee ID. Key **6** and then view the dynaset. How many records meet either of the criteria? Describe the records the criteria selected.

    e. Return to Design View. Point to the right of the word "Criteria" in the **Criteria** row to display a black arrow.

    f. Drag to select both **Criteria** rows and press Delete.

    g. Close the query without saving.

EXERCISE 8-25

Set query properties. Add a calculation to a query.

 NOTE: Write your answers for this exercise on a piece of paper. Make sure to include your name, the date, your class, and the exercise number.

1. Set a query property by following these steps:

    a. Open **qryAnimalPrices** in Design View. Maximize the window.

    b. Delete any criteria on the design grid.

    c. Click in the **Sort** row for ProductGroup and choose (**not sorted**).

    d. Remove the sort order for the ProductName field.

    e. Click in the **Sort** row for WholesaleValue and choose **Descending**.

    f. View the dynaset. Describe how the products are listed. Return to Design View.

    g. Click the Top Values box and key **10**

TIP: When you key **10** Access will assume that you are trying to key 100. To correct this, key **10** and press ⌊Delete⌋ and then ⌊Enter⌋.

    h. View the dynaset. Describe which products are listed.

    i. Return to Design View. Change the Top Values property to 25% and view the dynaset. How many products are shown?

    j. Return to Design View. Change the Top Values property to All.

    k. Remove the sort order for WholesaleValue.

2. Add a calculation by following these steps:

    a. Right-click the Field row for the empty fifth column. Choose **Build**.

TIP: You can left-click an empty column and click the Build button on the toolbar to open the Expression Builder.

    b. Double-click ListPrice in the middle panel.

    c. Click ⊞ in the operator row.

    d. Key **.1**. Click **OK** to close the Expression Builder.

NOTE: This expression calculates additional revenue from a product if the price is increased by 10%.

    e. View the dynaset.

    f. Return to Design View. Replace the field name "Expr1" with **PriceIn-crease**. Make sure not to delete the colon.

    g. Right-click the PriceIncrease column and choose **Properties**. Click the General tab and click the **Format** row. Choose **Currency**. Set its caption to **Price Increase**. Close the property sheet.

    h. Select the PriceIncrease column and move it to the right of the ListPrice column.

    i. View the dynaset. Save and close the query.

    j. Compact and repair the database. Close the database.

Lesson Applications

EXERCISE 8-26

Create and sort a query. Specify selection criteria. Create a report.

1. Start Access and open *[your initials]*CC-08. Delete any linked tables. Link the tables from *[your initials]*CC-E-08 and the "NewSales" range of the **MoreSales** worksheet.

2. Create a query for tblStuffedAnimals. Use these fields: ProductName, ProductGroup, ListPrice, and QuantityOnHand.

3. Sort the query in ascending order by ProductName. Save the query as **qryProdInfo**

4. Add criteria to list animals with a list price greater than $11 and with more than 200 units in stock.

5. With the dynaset open, create an AutoReport. Add your name in a label in the report's Page Header. Format the page to use two columns and to fit on one page.

6. Print the report. Close it without saving.

7. Return to the query design grid and delete the criteria.

8. Add criteria to list animals with a list price of $10.75 or greater than 200 units in stock. Save the query.

9. Create an AutoReport and add your name to the report's Page Header. Format the page to use two columns and to fit on one page.

10. Print the report. Close it without saving. Save and close the query.

EXERCISE 8-27

Create and sort a query. Specify selection criteria. Set query properties.

 NOTE: Write your answers for this exercise on a piece of paper. Make sure to include your name, the date, your class, and the exercise number.

1. Create a query for tblPayroll. Add the EmployeeID and MonthlySalary fields to the grid.

2. Sort in ascending order by EmployeeID. Save the query as **qryPayInfo**

3. Add criteria to eliminate the hourly employees from the dynaset.

4. Edit the query properties to use qryEmployees as a subdatasheet. EmployeeID is the Link Child and Master Child field.

5. Display the subdatasheet for Employee #3. Who is Employee #3? Write the name on a piece of paper. Collapse the subdatasheet.

REVIEW: To create a tabular AutoReport, you must use the New Report dialog box.

6. Create a tabular AutoReport for the dynaset. Apply an AutoFormat that will print well at your printer. Add your name to the Report Header.

7. Adjust the report to fit on one page. Print the report and close it without saving.

8. Delete the MonthlySalary field from the query and add HourlyRate.

9. Add criteria to eliminate the salaried employees from the dynaset.

10. Display the subdatasheet for Employee #18. Write the name of Employee #18 on your paper. Collapse the subdatasheet.

11. Create a tabular AutoReport and apply an AutoFormat that will print. Add your name to the Report Header.

12. Print the report and close it without saving.

13. Close and save the query.

EXERCISE 8-28

Copy and modify a query. Add a calculation.

1. Right-click qryStuffedAnimals. Choose Save As.

2. Name the copied query **qryDinoInv**. Open qryDinoInv in Design View.

3. Select and delete the Product fields. Add the ListPrice and QuantityOnHand fields. Save the query.

4. Add criteria in the ProductID field that will show only the dinosaur animals. Sort by animal name in ascending order.

 TIP: The decimal equivalent of 20% is 0.2.

5. Add a calculated field to multiply the quantity on hand by 20%. Name this new column **ReorderAmt** and set a new caption.

 NOTE: If you do not see ListPrice and QuantityOnHand in the Expression Builder, close it and save the query. Then reopen the Expression Builder.

6. Create a report by using the Report Wizard to show all the fields. Use a tabular landscape layout with the Soft Gray style. Name the report **rptDinos**

7. Move, size, and align the controls to prepare a professional-looking report. Make sure the ListPrice field is formatted to show two decimal places and Currency.

8. Delete the Page control in the Page Footer and add your name in its place.

9. Print the report and close it.

10. Save and close the query.

EXERCISE 8-29 *Challenge Yourself*

Create a query. Specify criteria. Print a report.

1. Use the Simple Query Wizard to create a detail query for tblCustomers named **qryExempt**. Use the ID, CompanyName, City, and TaxStatus fields. Modify the query to show only the tax-exempt customers.

 TIP: The TaxStatus field is a "yes/no" data type; keep that in mind to figure out what to enter as criteria.

2. Create and print a tabular portrait report by using the Report Wizard. Add your name in the page footer. You can delete a page number control if the report has only one page.

3. Compact and close the database.

On Your Own

In these exercises you work on your own, as you would in a real-life work environment. Use the skills you've learned to accomplish the task—and be creative.

EXERCISE 8-30

You will create a database that you will use for the On Your Own exercises in this lesson and in all subsequent lessons. The database structure should be sufficiently complex, requiring at least three related tables. On a sheet of paper, describe the purpose of the database, who will use it, and the type of information it will store. List the fields that will be stored in each table. Draw the relationships among the tables. List at least two records to be stored in each table. On the first sheet of each sketch, write your name and **Exercise 8-30**. Before proceeding to the next exercise, have your instructor approve your database design and intentions.

EXERCISE 8-31

Create the database you designed in Exercise 8-30. Enter at least five records into each table. Print the tables. Review the design of the database. On a sheet of paper, sketch a report that incorporates data from two or more tables. Identify the type of query needed to create the report. On a sheet of paper, list all fields to be used in the query. For each field, include the name of the table from which the field originates. Identify the key field and any foreign key fields. Describe the criteria that might be required. Name the report and query appropriately. Write your name and **Exercise 8-31** on each sketch. Continue to the next exercise.

EXERCISE 8-32

Based on the sketches you created in Exercise 8-31, create the query and report. Select the style and layout most appropriate for the report. Arrange the controls appropriately. In the Page Footer, include your name and **Exercise 8-32**. In the Report Header, include the title of the report. Print a copy of the query dynaset. Print a copy of the report. Submit to your instructor your sketches and printouts you created for Exercises 8-30 through 8-32. Keep a copy of the database you created and modified in Exercises 8-30 through 8-32. You will use it in the On Your Own exercises in subsequent lessons.

Using Joins and Relationships

OBJECTIVES

After completing this lesson, you will be able to:

1. **Refresh linked tables**
2. **Create a multiple-table query.**
3. **Create and edit joins in a query.**
4. **Create relationships.**
5. **Use referential integrity and cascade options.**
6. **Use a Lookup Field.**
7. **View and print a relationship report.**
8. **Create and edit an index.**

MOUS
ACTIVITIES

In this lesson:
Ac2002e 1-2
Ac2002e 1-3
Ac2002e 3-2
Ac2002e 5-1
Ac2002e 5-2

See Appendix E.

 Estimated Time: 2 hours

As a relational database, Access can assemble information from many tables when you follow certain rules. The main rule is that related tables must have a common field. A *common field* is a field in each table with the same data type and size (and usually the same field name).

 NOTE: Common fields do not need to have the same name; however, they are easier to identify if the names are consistent.

Relationships are essential for good database management. In this lesson you learn about joins and relationships between tables. You can create, edit, and delete joins and relationships. You also learn some basic relationship rules in Access.

Refreshing Linked Tables

Access maintains links to external tables as long as it can locate those tables. The Linked Table Manager lists linked tables and the location where they were when they were last used.

EXERCISE 9-1 **Use the Linked Table Manager**

When you work with linked tables, you need to know where the linked database is located. If the linked database has been moved to another folder or renamed, you need to update the links.

1. Make a copy of the **CC-09** database and rename it *[your initials]*CC-09

2. Rename **CC-E-09** database as *[your initials]*CC-E-09

3. Open *[your initials]*CC-09. The linked tables are shown by the icons.

4. Double-click tblEmployeeDates. An error message appears because Access cannot find the database or table.

5. Click OK to remove the message.

6. Choose Tools, Database Utilities, Linked Table Manager. The linked tables are listed. They were originally in **CC-E-09**, but you renamed that database to include your initials.

7. Click Select All. Click the check box for the Excel file to deselect it.

FIGURE 9-1
Linked Table
Manager

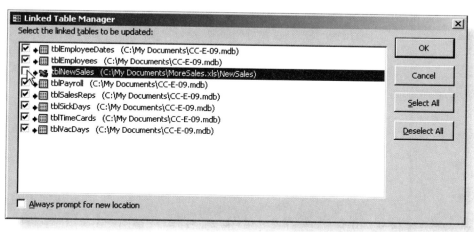

8. Click OK. The Select New Location dialog box enables you to find the correct database.

 NOTE: If the linked tables are in a different location or have been renamed, Access opens the Select New Location dialog box.

9. Choose *[your initials]*CC-E-09 and click Open. The links have been refreshed. Close the message box.

10. Repeat the preceding steps to update the link for the Excel file. Close the Linked Table Manager dialog box.

11. Double-click one of the linked tables. Notice that Access knows its location. Close it.

Creating a Multiple-Table Query

Good database management requires that you use small, manageable tables rather than large, unmanageable ones. That's why Carolina Critters uses a Kit Contents table with information about kits and codes for the suppliers. This table doesn't include the names and addresses of the suppliers. If it did, you would need to enter that name and address many times. Not only would that be a lot of extra work, but you would be more likely to make an error. If a supplier's address changed, you would have to change many records.

The Kit Suppliers table lists the names and addresses of suppliers. You only need to key supplier information once in this table. If the address changes, you only need to change it here. Suppose you need a report that shows the kit number, the kit cost, and the supplier's name. Two of those fields are in the Kit Contents table, but the actual supplier's name is in the Kit Suppliers table. You need to create a query that uses both tables.

FIGURE 9-2
Required fields
are in two
separate tables

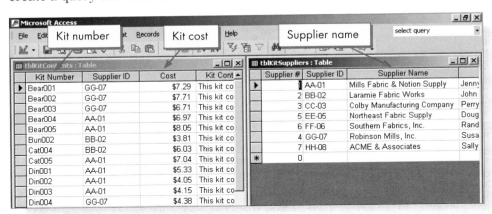

EXERCISE   9-2   Create a Query with Two Tables

To create a query with two tables, you add both tables to the query design grid, add fields to the grid, set the sort option, and enter criteria.

1. Click the Queries button and click **New**. Select Design View and click OK. The Show Table dialog box opens.

2. Double-click tblKitContents to add it to the grid. Double-click tblKitSuppliers. Close the Show Table dialog box.

 NOTE: The join line appears because AutoJoin is on by default. If you do not see a join line, choose Tools, Options. Click the Tables/Queries tab and turn on Enable AutoJoin.

3. Maximize the window. The join line connects the common field in the tables, the SupplierID field. Access sets a join line when the common field is the primary key in one table but not the primary key in the other table.

4. Size the panes to be the same height. Size the Field Lists to show all the names.

5. Double-click the KitNumber field to add it as the first field in the design grid.

6. Add SupplierName and Cost to the grid. The **Table** row identifies the source of the field.

 NOTE: Choose View, Table Names if you do not see the Table row in your design window.

7. Click the Sort row for KitNumber and choose Ascending.

FIGURE 9-3
Join line shows relationship between two tables

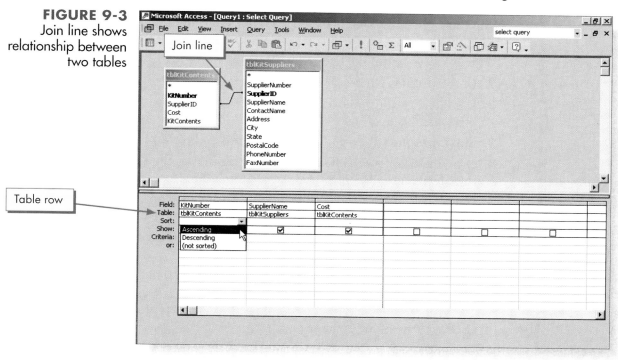

8. Click the View button to see the dynaset.

9. Save the query as **qrySuppliers&Costs.** Close the query.

Creating and Editing Joins

A *join* is a temporary link made in a query. It is available only for that query. If the primary key in one table does not match a non-primary key in the other table, Access does not establish a join, even though there might be common field names in both tables. If a join is not automatically established, you can set the join by dragging from one common field to the other.

An *inner join* displays records that have the same value in the common field. This is the default and most common type of join and what you have seen so far in your queries. There are two other types of joins. A *right outer join* shows all the records from one table (the left) and only those fields from the table on the right where the joined fields are equal. A right outer join shows a join line with an arrow pointing to the right. A *left outer join* shows all the records from the right table and only those fields from the left table where the joined fields are equal. A left outer join shows a join line with an arrow pointing to the left.

EXERCISE 9-3 **Create and Edit Joins in a Query**

Join lines can be created between two tables through the Design View of a query. As in the Relationships window, you identify the common field between two field lists and drag a join line from one list to the other.

1. In the Queries window, click **New**, select **Design View**, and click **OK**.

2. Double-click tblEmployees and tblSalesOrders. Close the Show Table dialog box. There is no join line, but the tables have a common field.

3. Maximize the window and size the panes and Field Lists.

4. Drag the EmployeeID field from tblEmployees to the EmployeeID field in tblSalesOrders. When you release the mouse button, the join line appears.

5. In the tblEmployees Field List, double-click FirstName, LastName, and EmployeeID. In the tblSalesOrders Field List, double-click OrderID.

6. View the dynaset. This is an inner join. It shows eight records with all four fields for each record. Return to the design grid.

7. Right-click the sloping portion of the join line and choose **Join Properties**. The dialog box indicates that the join displays only those records in which the EmployeeID field matches. This is the default type of join—an inner join. (See Figure 9-4 on the next page.)

8. Select the second join type and click **OK**. An arrow now points to the secondary table; the main table does not have an arrow. View the dynaset. This is a right outer join, showing all the records from tblEmployees and only those from tblSalesOrders that have a match. (See Figure 9-5 on the next page.)

FIGURE 9-4
Join Properties
dialog box

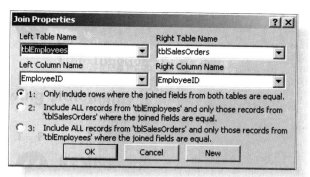

FIGURE 9-5
Right outer join

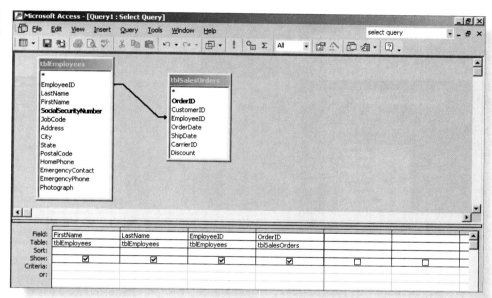

TIP: You can double-click the join line to open the Join Properties dialog box.

9. Return to Design View and edit the join properties.

10. Select the third join type and click **OK**. The arrow points left. View the dynaset. This is a left outer join, listing all records from tblSalesOrders and only matches from tblEmployees. In this case, the results are the same as the inner join.

11. Close the query without saving it.

Creating Relationships

A *relationship* is a permanent link or join made at the table level. It is available for any query, form, or report. Different types of relationships can exist between or among tables in a database. The most common type of relationship is One-to-Many. In a *One-to-Many relationship*, a value occurs once in the primary table and many times in the related table.

The Customers and Sales Orders tables have this type of relationship. The Customers table has a unique field for each customer, Customer ID. Each customer can have only one ID, and an ID number can be used only once in that table. The Customer ID field is the primary key in this table. This is the "One" side of the relationship to the Sales Orders table.

The Sales Orders table has a record for every order. The record includes a field for the Customer ID. If a customer orders many times, his or her ID can appear several times in the Sales Orders table: the "many" side of the relationship. A non-primary key that is common to a related table is called a *foreign key*, so the Customer ID field is a foreign key in the related table tblSalesOrders.

FIGURE 9-6
Comparing
Customer ID fields
in two tables

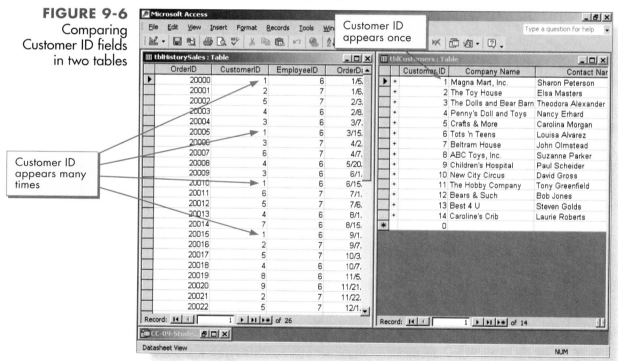

EXERCISE 9-4 Establish a One-to-Many Relationship

You create relationships in the Relationships window by dragging the common field name from one table to another. As soon as you release the mouse button, the Relationships dialog box opens so you can define the relationship.

1. Click the Relationships button 🔲. There should be no relationships shown in the window. Maximize the window.

NOTE: If you see Field Lists in the Relationships window, click the Clear Layout button and click Yes.

2. If the Show Table dialog box is not open, click the Show Table button 📇.

3. Click tblCustomers and click Add. Double-click tblSalesOrders. Click Close.

4. Drag the bottom border of each Field List until you can see all the field names.

5. Drag the CustomerID field from tblCustomers to the CustomerID field in tblSalesOrders. You dragged the primary key to the foreign key. Release the mouse button.

6. The Edit Relationships dialog box opens. The primary table is on the left; the related table is on the right. The Relationship Type is **One-To-Many**, shown near the bottom of the dialog box. Access determines the type of relationship based on the primary and foreign keys.

FIGURE 9-7
Edit Relationships
dialog box

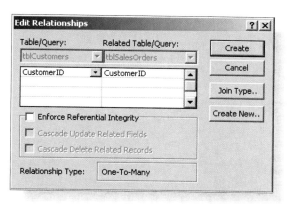

7. Do not check any box. Click **Create**. The join line appears in the window.

8. Click the Close button . Click **Yes** to save the window layout.

FIGURE 9-8
Relationship join line

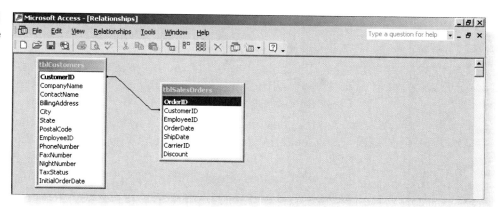

EXERCISE **9-5** **Use the Simple Query Wizard**

Because a relationship exists between tblCustomers and tblSalesOrders, you can now use the Simple Query Wizard to build a query that uses both tables.

To use the Simple Query Wizard with multiple tables, the relationships must already be established. If you select unrelated tables in the wizard, an error message informs you that the tables are not related. You need to cancel the wizard, set the relationships, and start over.

1. Click the Queries button and click <u>N</u>ew.
2. Choose **Simple Query Wizard**. Click OK.
3. Choose Table:tblCustomers from the <u>T</u>ables/Queries list.
4. Double-click CustomerID, CompanyName, and PhoneNumber.
5. Click the <u>T</u>ables/Queries drop-down arrow and choose tblSalesOrders. Its Field List appears in the window.
6. Double-click OrderID and OrderDate. Click <u>N</u>ext.
7. Choose <u>D</u>etail and click <u>N</u>ext.
8. Name the query **qrySales&Cust**. Click <u>F</u>inish. The dynaset includes fields from both tables.
9. Switch to Design View. The grid shows the relationship line.

EXERCISE **9-6** **Edit Data in a Multiple-Table Query**

You can make many edits in a dynaset that is based on more than one table. Some edits, however, are not possible, because the relationship and primary key are verifying your work.

1. Return to the dynaset. Select and delete the record for Penny's Dolls and Toys.
2. Replace the word "Toy" with your last name in the Company Name field of CustomerID 2. Close the dynaset.

3. Click the Tables button. Open tblCustomers. Penny's Dolls and Toys was not deleted from the main table, but your name appears in the second record. Close the table.
4. Open tblSalesOders. Order 20104 was deleted from the related table when you deleted the Penny's Dolls and Toys record from the dynaset. Close the table.
5. Click the Queries button and double-click qrySales&Cust. Try to edit the CustomerID in one of the records. You cannot do so because this is the

primary key in the table. That is also why Penny's Dolls and Toys was not deleted from the table containing the primary key. Close the dynaset.

6. Click the Tables button. Select tblCustomers and press ⌈Delete⌋. Click Yes. A message box alerts you to the relationships between this table and another table.

FIGURE 9-9
Message box when trying to delete a table with relationships

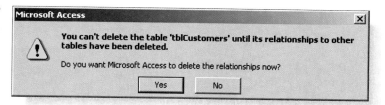

7. Click No and then click OK in the next message box.

EXERCISE **9-7** **Create a One-to-One Relationship**

A One-to-One relationship between tables means that the primary key in the main or primary table matches the primary key value in one record in the related table. A One-to-One type of relationship is unusual but can be useful. You can establish a One-to-One relationship between the Employees table and the EmployeeDates table by using social security numbers. An individual social security number can appear only once in each table.

For this relationship to be created, you first need to make the social security number field the primary key in the related table.

1. In the Tables window, right-click in the white space and choose Import. You will import a copy of tblEmployeeDates for this exercise because you cannot set the primary key in a linked table.

2. In the Import dialog box, find and click the *[your initials]*CC-E-09 database. Click Import.

3. In the Import Objects dialog box, click tblEmployeeDates and then click OK. Your database now has a linked copy of tblEmployeeDates and an imported copy. The imported copy is named tblEmployeeDates1. (See Figure 9-10 on the next page.)

4. Open tblEmployeeDates1 in Design View. Click the SocialSecurityNumber row and click the Primary Key button ⎘.

5. Close the table and save the changes.

6. Click the Relationships button 🔠. Click the Clear Layout button ⌧ and click Yes. This does not delete the relationship in the window; it just removes it from view.

FIGURE 9-10
Two copies of
tblEmployeeDates

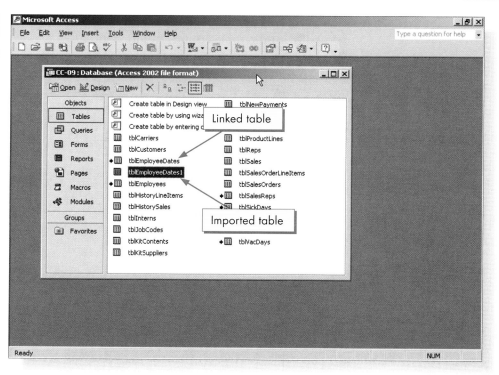

7. Click the Show Table button . Double-click tblEmployees. Double-click tblEmployeeDates1. Click <u>C</u>lose.

8. Size each Field List to see all the field names.

REVIEW: The primary key appears in bold in each Field List.

9. Drag the SocialSecurityNumber field from tblEmployees to the SocialSecurityNumber field in tblEmployeeDates1 and release the mouse button.

10. The Relationships dialog box identifies the primary table on the left and the related table on the right. The **Relationships Type** is One-to-One because the field is the primary key in both tables. Click **Create**. (See Figure 9-11 on the next page.)

11. Close the Relationships window and do not save the layout. The relationship is saved even though you do not save the picture of it in the window.

12. Click the **Queries** button and click <u>N</u>ew. Choose **Simple Query Wizard**. Click **OK**.

13. Choose Table:tblEmployees from the <u>T</u>ables/Queries list.

14. Double-click FirstName and LastName.

15. Click the <u>T</u>ables/Queries drop-down arrow and choose tblEmployeeDates1. Double-click BirthDate and HireDate. Click <u>N</u>ext.

FIGURE 9-11
Creating a
One-to-One
relationship

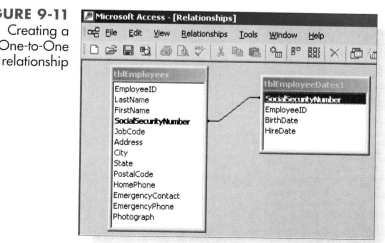

16. Name the query **qryEmp&Dates**. Click Finish. The dynaset includes fields from both tables.

17. Switch to Design View. The grid shows the relationship line. Close the query.

18. Select qryEmp&Dates and press [Delete]. Click Yes.

19. Return to the **Tables** tab and delete tblEm-ployeeDates1. You see the same message box about deleting the relationship before the table can be deleted. Click Yes.

EXERCISE   9-8   Create a Many-to-Many Relationship

A *Many-to-Many* relationship allows you to link two tables that do not share a common field and could not otherwise be linked. You do so by using a third table, called a *junction table*.

1. Click the Relationships button 🗗. It shows the last relationship layout that you saved. Click the Clear Layout button ✕ and click Yes.

2. Click the Show Table button 🗗. Double-click tblSalesOrders. Double-click tblStuffedAnimals. Click Close.

3. Size the Field Lists to see all the names. There is no common field between these two tables, but you might want to relate them to see the name of animals ordered on each Order ID. You can relate these two tables through tblSalesOrderLineItems.

4. Click the Show Table button 🗗. Double-click tblSalesOrderLineItems. Click Close. This table includes a two-field primary key. One of the fields is a primary key in tblSalesOrders; the other is the primary key in tblStuffed-Animals.

5. Arrange the Field Lists so tblSalesOrderLineItems is between tblSalesOrders and tblStuffedAnimals.

6. Drag the OrderID field from tblSalesOrders to the OrderID field in tbl-SalesOrderLineItems. A One-to-Many relationship is identified because the

OrderID is the primary key in the primary table and a foreign key in the related table. Click <u>C</u>reate.

7. Drag the ProductID field from tblStuffedAnimals to the ProductID field in tblSalesOrderLineItems. A One-to-Many relationship is identified because ProductID is the primary key in the primary table and a foreign key in the related table. Click <u>C</u>reate.

 NOTE: The term "Many-to-Many" does not appear in the Relationships dialog box.

FIGURE 9-12
Creating a
Many-to-Many
relationship

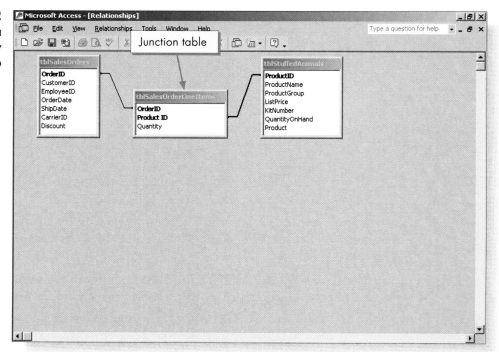

8. Close the Relationships window and do not save the layout. The relationship was saved when you clicked **Create** in the Relationships dialog box.

9. Click the **Tables** button and click tblSalesOrders to highlight it. Click the New Object arrow. Choose <u>Q</u>uery.

10. In the New Query dialog box, click **Design View** and then click **OK**. The query design grid includes a Field List for tblSalesOrders.

11. Click the Show Table button 🖼. Add tblSalesOrderLineItems and tblStuffed-Animals to the grid. Close the Show Table dialog box.

12. Size the panes and Field Lists.

13. From tblSalesOrders, double-click OrderID and OrderDate. From tblSales-OrderLineItems, double-click ProductID and Quantity. From tblStuffedAni-mals, add ProductName to the grid. (See Figure 9-13 on the next page.)

FIGURE 9-13
Building a query
for a Many-to-Many
relationship

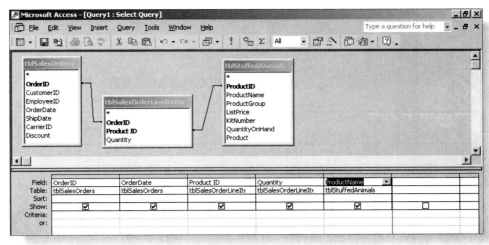

14. View the dynaset and close the query without saving it.

EXERCISE **9-9** **Delete a Relationship**

When you delete the join line between two tables, you delete the relationship between them.

1. Click the Relationships button. Click the Clear Layout button ⊠ and click Yes.

 TIP: You can open the Relationships window by choosing Tools, Relationships.

2. Click the Show Table button. Double-click tblSalesOrders, tblSalesOrder-LineItems, and tblStuffedAnimals. Click Close.

3. Right-click one of the join lines.

4. Choose Delete. A confirmation message box appears.

5. Click Yes to delete the relationship.

6. Right-click the other join line and delete the relationship.

7. Close the Relationships window and do not save the layout.

8. Compact and repair the database. Close the database.

Using Referential Integrity and Cascade Options

As you know, referential integrity is a set of relationship rules. You can turn these rules on or off in the Relationships dialog box. These rules verify your editing so you don't delete data that shouldn't be deleted or change information that shouldn't be changed.

Here's an example of what referential integrity does for the relationship between tblCustomers and tblSalesOrders. You cannot add a sales order in tblSalesOrders that uses a nonexistent customer ID. The customer ID must already be in tblCustomers (primary table) before you can complete the related record in tblSalesOrders. If you could add orders and ship products without customer IDs, the company would not know who to bill.

Here's another example of referential integrity for these two tables. You cannot delete a customer from tblCustomers if the customer has outstanding orders in tblSalesOrders. If you could delete this customer, you might delete customer information before getting paid for the order.

E X E R C I S E **9-10** **Enforce and Test Referential Integrity**

You can enable referential integrity for two tables if:

- The related fields have the same type of data (Text, Number, and so on).
- The tables are in the same database.
- The common field in the primary table is the primary key for that table.

 NOTE: You cannot set referential integrity between two tables if one of the tables is linked. The only relationship that can be set in this case is "Indeterminate."

1. Open *[your initials]*CC-09. Refresh the linked tables in *[your initials]*CC-E-09.

2. Click the Relationships button 🔲. It shows the relationships layout you saved in Exercise 9-4.

3. Double-click the sloping portion of the join line. The Edit Relationships dialog box opens.

 TIP: You can right-click the join line and choose Edit Relationship.

4. Check the Enforce Referential Integrity box and click OK.

5. The relationship line shows a "1" on the "one" side (tblCustomers) and an infinity sign on the "many" side (tblSalesOrders). (See Figure 9-14 on the next page.)

6. Close the Relationships window.

 7. Open tblCustomers. Click the Database Window button 🔲. Open tblSalesOrders.

FIGURE 9-14
One-to-Many
relationship with
referential integrity

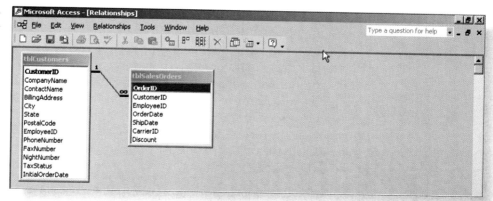

8. Minimize the Database window. Choose Window, Tile Vertically. Notice that there is no Customer ID 15 in tblCustomers.

9. Click in tblSalesOrders and try to add a new record:

Order ID:	**20110**
Customer ID:	**15**
Employee ID:	**7**
Order Date:	**8/1/01**
Ship Date:	**8/5/01**
Carrier ID:	**B202**
Discount:	**.1**

10. Press [Tab] to move past the new record. You cannot complete the record until you fix the problem. Click OK in the error box.

FIGURE 9-15
Error message
for violation of
referential integrity

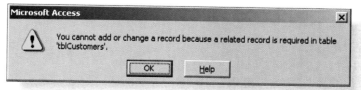

11. Press [Shift]+[Tab] to move the insertion point back to the Customer ID field. Change the ID to **3**

12. Press [↑] to move away from the new record. The record is now added to the table.

13. Close both tables. Restore the Database window.

EXERCISE 9-11 Enable Cascade Update Related Fields

When you enable referential integrity, you cannot make certain types of changes. Suppose you change the customer ID numbering system and need to update all

IDs. Referential integrity won't allow it. (You could, of course, turn off referential integrity and make the changes in both tblCustomers and tblSalesOrders.) You can override this rule about changing related records if you enable the **Cascade Update Related Fields** option. Then you can edit the ID in tblCustomers, and Access automatically changes all the related records in tblSalesOrders.

Suppose you want to delete a record in tblCustomers and the customer has outstanding orders in tblSalesOrders. Under the rules of referential integrity, you cannot delete the record. If you enable the **Cascade Delete Related Records** option, you can delete the record in tblCustomers. All the related orders in tblSalesOrders are deleted as well.

1. Click the Relationships button 🔲. Double-click the sloping part of the join line.

2. Click the **Cascade Update Related Fields** box to turn on the option.

3. Click **OK** and close the Relationships window.

 NOTE: You cannot edit relationships while the table is open.

4. Open tblCustomers. Click the Database Window button 🔲. Open tblSales-Orders.

 REVIEW: If you click a window to make it active, it is tiled on the top or left, depending on the tile option.

5. Minimize the Database window. Choose <u>W</u>indow, <u>T</u>ile Vertically.

6. In tblCustomers, double-click **2** in the Customer ID field and key **15**. Press 🔽 to move past the record. Look for the related change in tblSalesOrders.

7. In tblCustomers, double-click **15** in the Customer ID field. Key **2** and press 🔽. Look for the change in tblSalesOrders.

8. In tblSalesOrders, double-click **8** in the Customer ID field. Key **6** and press 🔽. The related record in tblCustomers is not changed, because a cascade update goes from the primary table in the relationship to the related table.

9. Change the **6** for Order 20106 to **8**

10. Close both tables and restore the Database window.

EXERCISE **9-12** **Enable Cascade Delete Related Records**

The **Cascade Delete Related Records** option is dangerous. If you delete a customer from tblCustomers, all the customer's orders are deleted from tblSalesOrders. This might be acceptable if the customer is up-to-date with payments, but it's certainly not acceptable if the customer owes money! Suppose your school keeps your records in two related tables: Students and Classes. The **Cascade Delete**

Related Records option would allow someone to delete you from the Students database, thus deleting all the classes you have taken.

1. Click the Relationships button and double-click the join line.

2. Turn on **Cascade Delete Related Records**. Click **OK** and close the Relationships window.

3. Open tblCustomers. Click the Database Window button 🔲. Open tblSalesOrders.

4. Minimize the Database window. Choose <u>W</u>indow, <u>T</u>ile Vertically.

5. In tblCustomers, expand the subdatasheet for Tots 'n Teens. There is one sales order for this customer in tblSalesOrders: 20107.

6. In the subdatasheet, select order 20107 and click the Delete Record button 🗙. A warning message box appears.

FIGURE 9-16
Warning message
for Cascade Delete
option

7. Click <u>Y</u>es. The record in tblSalesOrders is marked #Deleted. This indicator and the record are removed when you close or refresh the table.

8. Close both tables.

9. Restore the Database window and open tblSalesOrders table. Order ID 20107 is deleted. Close the table.

Using a Lookup Field

Relationships enable you to use Lookup Fields. A *Lookup Field* looks up selections from another table so you can enter data by choosing from a list. Rather than keying text to describe the type of payment made, you can list all possible choices and have the user select from the list.

EXERCISE 9-13 **Add a Field to a Table**

The first step to creating a Lookup Field is to create a field to store the data. This field will contain the text from which the user selects.

1. Double-click tblNewPayments. Notice that no method of payment is indicated.

2. Click the View button . Click on PaymentDate in the **Field Name** column.

3. Click the Insert Rows button . In the new row, key **PaymentType**. For the Data Type, choose Text with a field size of **20**. Set the caption to **Paid With**

4. Save the table.

EXERCISE 9-14 Create a Lookup Field

You can create a Lookup Field for the Payment Type field in tblNewPayments. Because the Payment Type field is already in the table, you need to edit the table design and use the Lookup Wizard (listed as a Data Type). The Lookup Wizard guides you step-by-step through the process of creating the Lookup Field.

> **NOTE:** You can use Insert, Lookup Column to insert a new column with the Lookup Wizard.

1. With tblNewPayments open in Design View, click in the Data Type column for the PaymentType row. Click the drop-down arrow and select Lookup Wizard.

2. In the first dialog box, choose I will type in the values that I want. Click Next.

3. In the next dialog box you are asked to key in your options. In the first row of Col1, key the following, using ↓ between each.

American Express

Cash

Check

Discover

Master Card

Visa

FIGURE 9-17
Lookup column
containing
payment types

Lookup Wizard

What values do you want to see in your lookup column? Enter the number of columns you want in the list, and then type the values you want in each cell.

To adjust the width of a column, drag its right edge to the width you want, or double-click the right edge of the column heading to get the best fit.

Number of columns: | 1 |

Col1
American Express
Cash
Check
Discover
Master Card
Visa

Cancel | < Back | Next > | Finish

4. Size the column to fit all entries. Click Next.

5. Use the default label for your Lookup column. Click Finish.

6. Click the Lookup tab in the Field Properties section. The Display Control for this field now shows "Combo Box." It uses a "Value List" as its Row Source Type. The Row Source row shows the values in that list.

7. Click in the Row Source row and press [Shift] + [F2] to open the Zoom window.

FIGURE 9-18
Row Source in
Zoom dialog box

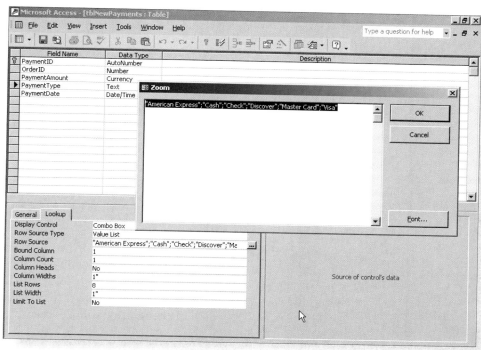

8. Close the Zoom window. Save the table and switch to Datasheet View.

EXERCISE 9-15 Enter a Record by Using a Lookup Field

A Lookup Field ensures accuracy and consistency because you select a value from a list. To enter data in a Lookup Field, click the drop-down arrow and select the value from the list.

1. Click the New Record button ▶*.

2. Enter the data for the new record, but don't key the Paid With value. Click the drop-down arrow that appears and select the payment type from the list.

Payment ID: *Press* [Tab]

Order Number: **20104**

Amount Paid:	**750**
Paid With:	**Visa**
Date Paid:	**6/11/02**

FIGURE 9-19
Choosing the value
from the
Lookup column

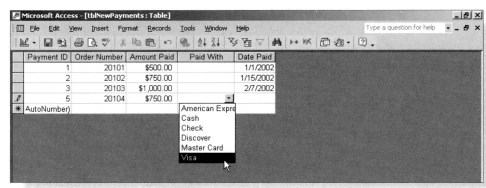

3. Close the table.

Viewing and Printing Relationships

You can see the relationships in a database in the Relationships window. You can select to see all relationships in the window, or just some of them.

By printing the relationships in a database, you can document your work. This enables you and others to know what relationships exist without having to look at the window. When you print the relationships, Access generates a report that can be saved and edited. If you edit the relationships, however, you should regenerate the report so it is current.

EXERCISE **9-16** **View Relationships**

In Exercise 9-3 you created a join line between tblEmployees and tblSalesOrders in a query. Relationships created in a query exist only for that query, not for the whole database.

1. Click the Relationships button 🔲. The Relationships window shows the last layout that you saved.

2. Click the Show All Relationships button 🔲. Only one relationship is shown.

3. Click the Show Table button 🔲.

4. Double-click tblKitContents and tblKitSuppliers. Close the Show Table dialog box.

TIP: You can add several tables at once to the Relationships window. Hold down [Ctrl] and click each table name and then click Add.

5. Create a relationship between tblKitSuppliers and tblKitContents. Use the common field SupplierID.

6. This is a One-to-Many relationship. The main table is tblKitSuppliers, which has the primary key. Click Create.

7. Click the Clear Layout button ⊠. Click Yes to remove the layout.

8. Close the Relationships window. A message box asks if you want to save the changes to the layout. Click Yes.

EXERCISE 9-17 **Create a Relationships Report**

1. Click the Relationships button 🔡.

2. Click the Show All Relationships button 🔳. Four Field Lists are shown with join lines.

3. Size each list to show all the field names. Arrange the Field Lists neatly in the window.

4. Choose File, Print Relationships. A report opens in Print Preview.

5. Zoom to Fit size and then 100%.

6. Click the View button 📷. The report has a Report Header with labels.

7. Add your name in the Report Header.

8. Save the Report and name it **rptLayout*[today's date]***. You can print this report like any other report.

9. Close the report and the Relationships window.

Creating and Editing an Index

Access uses indexes to speed up searching and sorting. An *index* is a sort order for records that is identified in the table design. Indexes can be based on one or more fields. You should create indexes for fields that you use often in searching or sorting. You can create indexes for a field if its Data Type is Text, Number, Currency, or Date/Time.

EXERCISE 9-18 **View Properties of a Linked Table**

An index for a table can be compared to an index for a book. When Access needs to find data, it first looks to the index, which points to the actual location of the data.

1. Open tblEmployees and maximize the window.
2. Click the View button 🔳 to see the table design.
3. Access will not allow you to change properties in a linked table. Click <u>Y</u>es.

FIGURE 9-20
Properties cannot
be changed

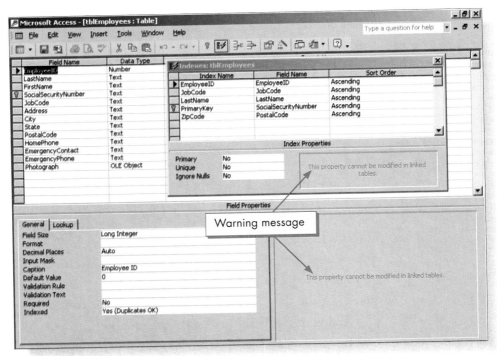

4. Click the Indexes button 🗐. The Indexes dialog box opens, listing five existing indexes.
5. Close the Indexes dialog box and the table.
6. Compact and repair the database, and then close it.

EXERCISE 9-19 View and Edit an Index

Too many indexes can slow down editing. Every time you make a change in an indexed field, Access must update the indexes to include the new information entered. At times you might need to change your index structure to make your database more efficient.

1. Open *[your initials]*CC-E-09.
2. Open tblEmployees in Design View.
3. Click the Indexes button 🗐.

4. Click the row for the LastName index. This is the name of the index. It uses the LastName field and keeps the names in ascending order.

   REVIEW: You can see a Help message in the Index Properties pane as you click each property.

5. Click the **Primary property** row in the lower part of the dialog box. This is not the primary key for this table.

6. Click the **Unique property** row. The values (the last names) do not have to be unique or different for each person.

   REVIEW: A null value in a database means "blank," "nothing," "empty." This is not the same as zero (0).

7. Click the **Ignore Nulls** property row. If the field is blank or empty, it is still included in the index.

8. Click the row selector for the PrimaryKey **Index Name** in the top pane to select that row.

FIGURE 9-21
Indexes dialog box

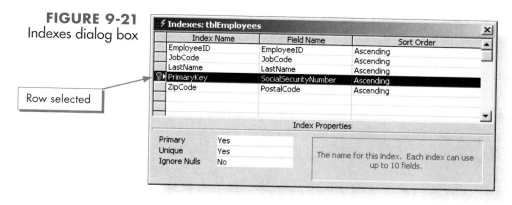

Row selected

9. Press Insert to insert a blank row. You are going to add the FirstName field after the LastName index definition.

10. Key **FirstName** in the **Index Name** column.

11. Press Tab to move the insertion point to the Field Name column for the new row. Key **f** to choose the FirstName field.

12. Press Tab and choose **Ascending** as the **Sort Order**.

13. Click anywhere in the PrimaryKey index row. This index is the primary key, and each value must be different or unique.

14. Click anywhere in the ZipCode row. This is not the primary key, and the values do not need to be unique.

FIGURE 9-22
Editing an index

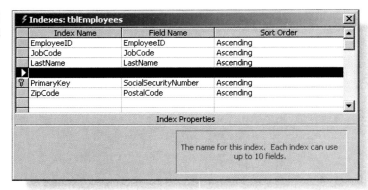

15. Close the Indexes dialog box.

16. Click anywhere in the PostalCode row in the top pane of the Design window. The Index properties in the lower pane show that the field has an index and that duplicates are acceptable.

 NOTE: You can create a single-field index from the Field Properties in the Table Design window.

17. Close the table and save the design changes.

18. Double-click tblEmployees. Indexes do not control the sort order that you see. They are used only to make your searching and sorting faster.

 19. Click anywhere in the Employee ID field. Click the Sort Ascending button to make sure your records are sorted.

20. Close the table and save the design changes. Now your table is sorted by Employee ID number again.

21. Compact and repair the database, and then close it.

USING HELP

Use the Contents tab to learn more about relationships:

1. Choose Help, Microsoft Access Help. If the Assistant starts, choose Options and turn off Use the Office Assistant.

2. Click the Contents tab.

3. Maximize the window and size the panes so you can see the topics in the left pane.

4. Expand the Tables topic.

5. Expand the Relationships and Referential Integrity topic.

6. Click the first topic About relationships in an Access database. Scroll and read the information in the right pane.

FIGURE 9-23
Microsoft Access Help

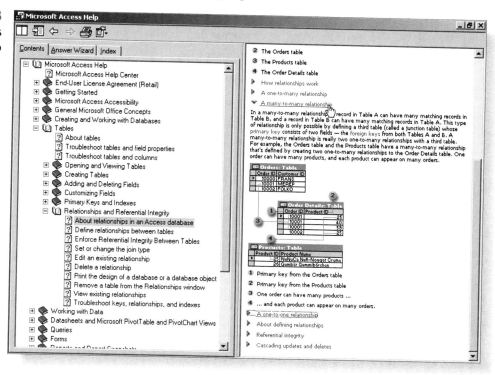

7. Click each remaining topic for Relationships and Referential Integrity in the left pane and read the corresponding Help window.

8. Collapse any expanded topics.

9. Close the Help window.

LESSON 9 Summary

➤ Linked tables must be refreshed if the related database is moved or renamed.

➤ Multiple-table queries use data from two or more tables, and they must be joined with common fields.

➤ Joined tables produce dynasets.

➤ A relationship is a permanent join at the table level.

➤ Joins can be One-to-One or One-to-Many.

➤ In a One-to-Many join, the "one" side of the relationship refers to the table joining a primary key and the "many" side of the relationship refers to the table joining a non-primary key.

➤ Referential integrity prevents accidental deletion of related information.

➤ Referential integrity allows only certain types of changes when the Cascade Update Related Fields option or the Cascade Delete Related Records is selected.

➤ Lookup Fields control data entry by requiring users to select from a list box.

➤ Viewing and printing relationships helps you track how tables are related.

➤ Indexes improve the performance of viewing and sorting records in tables.

LESSON 9 Command Summary

FEATURE	BUTTON	MENU	KEYBOARD	SPEECH
Clear Layout	✗	Edit, Clear Layout		✓
Delete Field List		Relationships, Hide Table	Delete	✓
Index	≣✐	View, Indexes		✓
Lookup column		Insert, Lookup Column		✓
Print Relationships		File, Print Relationships		✓
Relationships	⬚	Tools, Relationships		✓
Show All Relationships	⬚	Relationships, Show All		✓
Show Table	⬚	Relationships, Show Table		✓

Concepts Review

TRUE/FALSE QUESTIONS

Each of the following statements is either true or false. Indicate your choice by circling **T** or **F**.

T F *1.* When you clear the Relationships window, you also delete the relationships.

T F *2.* The most common type of relationship is One-to-One.

T F *3.* You can use the Cascade Delete Related Records option only when you enforce referential integrity.

T F *4.* Access shows a join line in a query if the primary key in one table matches a foreign key in the second table.

T F *5.* A join in a query is available for all queries.

T F *6.* Common fields must have the same data type.

T F *7.* A Lookup Field enables you to select values for data entry rather than keying them.

T F *8.* When you create a query with more than one table, you add the tables from the Show Table window.

SHORT ANSWER QUESTIONS

Write the correct answer in the space provided.

1. In a One-to-Many relationship, what do you call the field with matching data in the related table?

_____

2. What is the name of the set of Access rules governing relationships?

_____

3. Name two types of joins.

_____

4. Where can you learn what relationships already exist among tables?

_____

5. What option enables you to change records in related tables, even with referential integrity?

_____

6. In a One-to-Many relationship with referential integrity, how can you iden-tify the table on the "many" side of the relationship?

_____

7. How can you determine the primary field in a Field List in the Relationships window?

_____

8. How do you create a lookup column?

_____

CRITICAL THINKING

Answer these questions on a separate page. There are no right or wrong answers. Support your answers with examples from your own experience, if possible.

1. Why use a relational database? Why are tables broken down into subsec-tions of data? Why not place all information about a company in one large table?

2. Discuss how referential integrity would be helpful in managing a database. What problems or issues are connected with using referential integrity?

Skills Review

EXERCISE 9-20

Check a linked table. Create a multiple-table query.

 NOTE: Write your answers for this exercise on a piece of paper. Make sure to include your name, the date, your class, the exercise number, and the step number.

1. Rename a table by using the following steps.
    a. Open *[your initials]*CC-09.
    b. Right-click the table tblEmployees. Choose Rename.
    c. Key **tblEmployeesData**. Press ⌨Enter.
    d. Double-click tblEmployeesData. Check to make sure the link works.
    e. Rename the table **tblEmployees**. Click the link. Check to make sure the link works.

2. Create a query by using the following steps.
    a. Click the Queries button and click New. Choose Design View and click OK.
    b. In the Show Table dialog box, double-click tblCustomers. Double-click tbl-SalesOrders. Close the Show Table dialog box and maximize the window.

c. Size the panes to be the same height. Size the Field Lists to show all fields. What is the common field? Has referential integrity been enforced?
d. Double-click CompanyName in tblCustomers to add it to the design grid. Double-click OrderID and ShipDate in tblSalesOrders.
e. Click the column selector for the OrderID field to select the column.
f. Drag the OrderID column so it is the first column.
g. Click in the **Sort** row for the OrderID column and choose **Ascending**.
h. Click the View button . The orders are listed in ascending order by order number with the customer name and ship date.
i. Save the query as **qryDelDates**

EXERCISE 9-21

Create and edit joins. Create relationships.

> **NOTE:** Write your answers for this exercise on a piece of paper. Make sure to include your name, the date, your class, the exercise number, and the step number.

1. View and edit joins in a query by following these steps:
   a. Return to Design View. Right-click the sloping portion of the join line.
   b. Choose **J**oin Properties.
   c. Select the second join type for a right outer join to show all records from tblCustomers. Click **OK**.

> **NOTE:** See the direction of the arrow on the join line; it points to the "many" side.

   d. View the dynaset. How many customers have not ordered?
   e. Return to Design View. Double-click the sloping portion of the join line.
   f. Select the third join type to show all records from tblSalesOrders and click **OK**.

> **NOTE:** The join line points to the "one" side.

   g. View the dynaset. Are there any OrderIDs without a customer?
   h. Return to Design View and double-click the join line.
   i. Select the first inner join and click **OK**.
   j. Save the query and close it.

2. Create a relationship by following these steps:
   a. Click the Relationships button .
   b. Click the Clear Layout button and click **Y**es.
   c. Click the Show Table button . Double-click tblSalesOrderLineItems. Double-click tblSalesOrders. Click **C**lose.

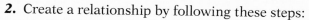

    d. Size the Field Lists to show all the field names. Show the table name in the title bar.

    e. Drag the OrderID field from tblSalesOrders to the OrderID field in tbl-SalesOrderLineItems. Which table is the primary table? Which is the related table? What type of relationship is identified?

    f. Make sure the Enforce Referential Integrity option is not on. Click Create.

    g. Save the layout.

EXERCISE 9-22

Set and test referential integrity. Use cascade options.

 NOTE: Write your answers for this exercise on a piece of paper. Make sure to include your name, the date, your class, the exercise number, and the step number.

    1. Edit and delete a relationship by following these steps:

        a. Right-click the join line and choose Edit Relationship.

        b. Click the Enforce Referential Integrity check box. Click OK. A message box tells you that the data types must be the same.

        c. Click OK in the message box. Click Cancel in the Edit Relationships dialog box.

 REVIEW: You need to delete the relationship to change the data type in one of the tables.

        d. Right-click the join line and choose Delete. Choose Yes.

        e. Close the Relationships window and save the layout.

        f. Open tblSalesOrdersLineItems in Design View. Click the OrderID field. What is its Data Type and Field Size? Close the table.

        g. Open tblSalesOrder in Design View. Click the OrderID field. Change its field type and size to match the field in tblSalesOrderLineItems. Save and close the table.

 REVIEW: Press F1 when the pointer is in the Field Size row to learn about field sizes for the Number Data Type.

    2. Test referential integrity by using the following steps:

        a. Click the Relationships button ⊞. The window opens displaying tblSalesOrders and tblSalesOrderLineItems.

        b. Drag the OrderID field from tblSalesOrders to tblSalesOrderLineItems.

        c. Click the Enforce Referential Integrity check box. Click Create. What marks the primary table? What marks the related table?

        d. Close the Relationships window without saving the layout.

3. Use the Cascade Update and Delete options by following these steps:
   a. Click the Relationships button . Double-click the join line.

> **REVIEW:** If you do not see tblSalesOrders and tblSalesOrderLineItems in the Relationships window, click the Show Table button and add them to the layout.

   b. Click Cascade Update Related Fields to turn on the option.
   c. Click Cascade Delete Related Records to turn on the option. Click OK.
   d. Close the Relationships window.
   e. Open tblSalesOrders. Open tblSalesOrderLineItems. Minimize the Database window and tile the windows vertically.
   f. In tblSalesOrders, double-click **20106** and change it to **20111**. Press ⬇ to move the insertion point away from the record. Look for the cascade update in tblSalesOrderLineItems.
   g. In tblSalesOrders, click the Record Selector for Order ID **20105** to select that record. Verify that there is one line item for this order in tblSalesOrderLineItems.

   h. Click the Delete Record button to delete OrderID 20105. The message reminds you about the cascade delete.
   i. Click Yes. The cascade delete appears in tblSalesOrderLineItems, and the records are marked as deleted.
   j. Sort both tables by Order ID in ascending order.

> **NOTE:** Deleted marks are removed when you sort, because you refreshed the window of the related table.

   k. Close both tables and save the changes. Restore the Database window.

EXERCISE 9-23

Create a Lookup Field. Print relationships. Edit an index.

> **NOTE:** Write your answers for this exercise on a piece of paper. Make sure to include your name, the date, your class, the exercise number, and the step number.

1. Create a Lookup Field by following these steps:
   a. Open tblCarriers in Datasheet View. Notice that the Carrier ID file is a code for the Name field.
   b. Switch to Design View. Notice the data types for these two fields. Which field is the primary key? Close the table.
   c. Open tblSalesOrders in Design View and maximize the window. What field matches a field in tblCarriers?

d. Click in the Data Type column for CarrierID. Click the drop-down arrow and select Lookup Wizard.

e. Choose I want the lookup column to look up the values in a table or query. Click Next.

f. Choose Tables in the View group. Choose tblCarriers. Click Next.

g. In the next dialog box, double-click CarrierID and Name. Click Next.

h. The next dialog box shows only the Name field. Click to remove the check mark from Hide key column (recommended). Both fields are visible, but only the Name field is needed. Click to select the check box again.

i. Widen the column until all data is visible. Click Next.

j. Use **CarrierID** as a label for the Lookup Field. Click Finish.

k. The message box reminds you to save the table. Click Yes.

l. Switch to Datasheet View.

m. Click in the Carrier ID column. Notice that all the old CarrierID codes are gone and replaced by the Carrier Names.

2. Enter a record, using a Lookup Field, by following these steps:

  a. Click the New Record button .

  b. Key the following data for the new record. For the Carrier ID, click the drop-down arrow and choose the ID from the list.

Order ID:	**20112**
Customer ID:	**9**
Employee ID:	**30**
Order Date:	**12/12/02**
Ship Date:	**12/15/02**
Carrier ID:	**F** *Press* Tab
Discount:	**0**

  c. Close the table.

3. Print relationships by following these steps:

  a. Click the Relationships button .

  b. Click the Show All Relationships button.

  c. Size the Field Lists to show the complete table name in the title bar and all the field names.

  d. Arrange the Field Lists to eliminate crisscrossed lines.

  e. Choose File, Print Relationships.

  f. Change the report so it prints in a landscape orientation.

  g. Add your name in the Report Footer.

  h. Print the report.

  i. Close the report without saving.

  j. Close the Relationships window.

4. Edit an index by following these steps:

  a. Open tblHistorySales. Click the View button .

b. Click the Indexes button .

c. Key **OrderDate** as the second Index Name.

d. Press Tab and choose OrderDate from the drop-down list.

e. Select Descending Order.

f. Press Tab. Key **ShipDate** as the third Index Name.

g. Choose ShipDate from the drop-down list.

h. Select Descending Order.

i. Close the Indexes dialog box.

j. Close the table and save the changes.

k. Compact and close the database.

Lesson Applications

EXERCISE 9-24

Create a multiple-table query with a calculation. Create an AutoReport.

1. Open *[your initials]*CC-09. Link and refresh the tables.

2. Click the Queries button and create a new query in Design View for tblCustomers and tblSalesOrders.

3. Maximize the window. Size the panes and Field Lists so you can see all the fields.

4. From tblCustomers, add CompanyName and State to the design grid. From tblSalesOrders, add OrderID and Discount.

5. Sort by OrderID in ascending order.

6. View the dynaset. Return to Design View and save the query as **qryTNDiscounts**

7. Right-click the Field row for the first empty column and choose Build.

8. Create this expression: **[Discount]*2**. Then click OK.

9. View the dynaset and return to Design View.

10. Select Expr1 and replace it with **DoubleDiscount**. Remember to leave the colon.

11. Right-click just below DoubleDiscount and open the property sheet.

12. Click the General tab. Format the field to **Percent** and set Decimal Places to 0. Set the Caption to **Double Discount**. Close the property sheet.

 NOTE: If you do not see Format on the property sheet, view the dynaset and then return to Design View and try again.

13. In the Discount field, key **>0** as criteria to show only customers who get a discount.

14. Turn off the Show option for the State field. In the State field, key **tn** as criteria to use the double discount only for customers in Tennessee Both criteria are on the same row.

15. View the dynaset. Widen the Double Discount column so you can see the title.

16. Create an AutoReport for the dynaset and add your name in a label in the Page Header. Print and close the report without saving.

 REVIEW: You need to save the query before you can create an AutoReport.

17. Save and close the query.

EXERCISE 9-25

Create a relationship with referential integrity. Test referential integrity.

1. Open tblStuffedAnimals and tblSalesOrderLineItems. Minimize the Database window and vertically tile the windows. The Product ID field is the primary key in tblStuffedAnimals and a foreign key in tblSalesOrderLineItems.

 NOTE: TblSalesOrderLineItems has a multiple-field primary key, using both OrderID and ProductID. Either of those fields alone can be repeated, but a combination of the two cannot.

2. Close both tables and restore the Database window.
3. Open the Relationships window and clear the layout.
4. Add tblStuffedAnimals and tblSalesOrderLineItems to the window.
5. Size the Field Lists to show the field names.
6. Create the relationship with referential integrity but no cascade options.
7. Print the Relationship. Add your name to the **Report Header**. Do not save the report.
8. Close the Relationships window and save the layout.
9. Open tblStuffedAnimals and tblSalesOrderLineItems. Minimize the Database window and vertically tile the windows.
10. Add the following record to tblSalesOrderLineItems:

Order ID:	**20112**
Product ID:	**Q001**
Quantity:	*Press* Ctrl + ´

11. Press Tab to move away from the record. Click **OK** in the error box.
12. Press Shift + Tab to move the insertion point back to the Product ID field. Change the ID for the new record to **F004**. Move the pointer to any other record.
13. Close both tables and restore the Database window.

EXERCISE 9-26

Enforce Cascade Update and Cascade Delete options. Delete and modify records.

 NOTE: This Exercise assumes you completed Exercises 9-24 and 9-25.

1. Open tblStuffedAnimals.
2. Select and delete the record for Product ID C003. You cannot delete the record because of its referential integrity with tblSalesOrderLineItems. Click **OK** and close the table.

3. Edit the relationship between the tables to turn on Cascade Update Related Fields and Cascade Delete Related Records.

4. Open tblStuffedAnimals. Open tblSalesOrderLineItems. Minimize the Database window and vertically tile the windows.

5. Click the record selector for Product ID C003 in tblStuffedAnimals. Click the Delete Record button and click **Yes**. Access deletes the record and its related records in tblSalesOrderLineItems.

6. In tblSalesOrderLineItems, note which orders include Product ID T005. Find that Product ID in tblStuffedAnimals.

7. In tblStuffedAnimals, change T005 to **T006**. Move the insertion point away from the record.

8. Print the table tblSalesOrderLineItems.

9. Sort tblSalesOrderLineItems by Product ID in descending order.

10. Print the table tblSalesOrderLineItems.

11. Close both tables, save changes, and restore the Database window.

12. Compact and repair the database and then close it.

EXERCISE 9-27 ✚ *Challenge Yourself*

Create a Lookup Field. Add a record. View the relationship created by a Lookup Field.

1. Open *[your initials]*CC-E-09. Import tblJobCodes from *[your initials]*CC-09.

2. Use the Lookup Wizard for the JobCode field in tblEmployees, looking up the values in tblJobCodes. Use both fields and turn off the Hide Key Column option. Store the JobCode field. Label the column JobCode.

3. Add the following record. Use the drop-down list to choose the Job Code.

Employee ID:	**32**
Last Name:	*Key [your last name]*
First Name:	*Key [your first name]*
SS #:	**888-55-5555**
Job Code:	**OF06**
Address:	*Press* Ctrl + '
City:	*Press* Ctrl + '
State:	*Press* Ctrl + '
Postal Code:	*Press* Ctrl + '
Home Phone:	*Press* Ctrl + '
Emergency Contact:	*Press* Ctrl + '
Emergency Phone:	*Press* Ctrl + '
Photograph:	*Leave blank.*

4. Create a stepped report in landscape orientation by using the Report Wizard. Do not show the Home Phone, Emergency Contact, Emergency Phone, or Photograph fields. Group by Job Code and sort by Last Name. Use the Corporate style and name the report **rptJobLookup**

5. Add your name in the Report Header. Edit the main title to **Job Code Groups** and print the report.

6. Remove all other tables from the Relationships window and add tblJob-Codes and tblEmployees.

7. Print the layout with your name in the Report Header.

On Your Own

In these exercises you work on your own, as you would in a real-life work environment. Use the skills you've learned to accomplish the task—and be creative.

EXERCISE 9-28
Review the design of the database that you created and modified in Exercises 8-30 through 8-32. Identify at least two additional tables requiring referential integrity that will enhance your database design. Consider adding tables that will keep cumulative or historical information. On a sheet of paper, list the fields that will be stored in each table. Draw the relationships among all the tables in your database. Identify the type of integrity and cascade options to be used for each relationship. On each sheet, write your name, the date, your class, and the exercise number. Continue to the next exercise.

EXERCISE 9-29
Create each table you designed in Exercise 9-28. Create the relationships and enforce the proper integrity and cascade options. Enter at least five records into each new table. Test the integrity and cascade options for each relationship. Identify any errors in your design and make the appropriate corrections. Continue to the next exercise.

EXERCISE 9-30
On separate printouts, print each relationship between all tables. For each relationship printout, write the type of referential integrity used and the cascade option applied. Print the Relationships window, showing all relationships for the entire database. On each printout, write your name, the date, your class, and the exercise number. Submit to your instructor the sheets from Exercise 9-28 and the printouts from Exercise 9-30. Keep a copy of the database you modified in Exercises 9-28 through 9-30. You will use it in subsequent lessons.

LESSON

10

Designing Advanced Queries

OBJECTIVES

After completing this lesson, you will be able to:

1. **Create summary queries.**
2. **Create a crosstab query.**
3. **Design a parameter query.**
4. **Create an update query.**
5. **Use a make-table query.**
6. **Create a delete query.**
7. **Create an append query.**
8. **Use specialized query wizards.**

MOUS
ACTIVITIES

In this lesson:
Ac2002e **3-2**
Ac2002e **3-3**
Ac2002e **3-4**
Ac2002e **3-5**

See Appendix E.

 Estimated Time: 1½ hours

Although tables are the foundation of a database, queries are the basis of most reports and forms. Queries give you the ability to accomplish business tasks by combining data, calculating summaries and totals, making mass changes, deleting inactive records, and more.

Creating Summary Queries

The queries you have created so far were detail queries. They showed each record on a separate row, similar to a table. A *summary query* shows totals, averages, or counts, rather than each detail. Using a summary query, you first create a group of records based on one of the fields and then use an aggregate function on the group of records. An *aggregate function* is a sum, average, maximum, minimum, or count for a group of records.

EXERCISE **10-1** **Create a Summary Query by Using a Wizard**

A *history table* keeps track of past sales or other activities. The history table tbl-HistoryLineItems includes line items for sales orders from another year.

1. Copy the database **CC-E-10** and rename it to *[your initials]***CC-E-10**. Copy the CC-10 database and rename it to *[your initials]***CC-10**. Copy the **More-Sales** worksheet. Open *[your initials]***CC-10**. Refresh all linked tables.

2. Using *[your initials]***CC-10**, click the Queries button and click <u>N</u>ew. Choose Simple Query Wizard.

 REVIEW: Tables precede queries in the Tables/Queries list.

3. In the <u>T</u>able/Queries list, choose Table:tblHistoryLineItems. Add ProductID and Quantity to the <u>S</u>elected Fields list. Click <u>N</u>ext.

4. Click <u>S</u>ummary in the dialog box. Then click Summary <u>O</u>ptions. The numeric fields are listed, with values you can calculate.

 NOTE: This query has only one number field.

5. Click <u>S</u>um to select it.

FIGURE 10-1
Summary options

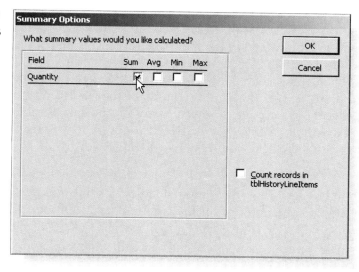

6. Click OK. Click <u>N</u>ext. Key **qrySalesCount** as the title and then click <u>F</u>inish. The dynaset shows each product ID and the quantity sold during the year. Maximize the window.

7. Click the View button . The design grid shows a Total row below the Table row in the lower pane. The aggregate functions in the Total row group the records by Product ID and then sum the quantity.

FIGURE 10-2
Design grid for
summary query

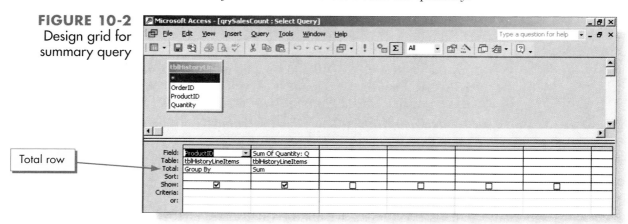

Total row

8. Close the query.

EXERCISE 10-2 Create a Summary Query in Design View

To create a summary query on your own, you add the Total row to the design grid and choose from the list of aggregate functions. Set the Group By function for the field for which you want to see a count, sum, or average. You can use the Count function for any field in the table that represents one of the entities. Use the Sum and Avg functions for number fields.

When you set the Group By function, Access creates a caption for each field based on the function and the name of the field to which you are applying the function. For example, if you were to sum the field TotalSale, the caption for the field would be "SumOfTotal Sale." If you were to average the field UnitsSold, the caption for the field would be "AvgOfUnitsSold."

1. Click the **Queries** button and click <u>N</u>ew. Choose **Design View** and click OK.

2. In the Show Table dialog box, double-click tblEmployees and tblJobCodes. You should see a join line for the common field, JobCode. Close the dialog box.

3. Size the panes and the Field Lists.

4. From tblEmployees, add SocialSecurityNumber and JobCode to the design grid.

5. From tblJobCodes, add JobTitle to the grid.

6. Click the View button . At this point, you have a simple select query.

7. Return to Design View.

8. Click the Totals button Σ. The **Total** row appears below the **Table** row in the design grid. All fields show Group By as a default.

> **NOTE:** The Totals button Σ toggles the Total row off and on. You can also toggle the Total row off and on from the <u>V</u>iew menu.

9. Click the **Total** row for the SocialSecurityNumber field. Choose **Count** from the drop-down list. Your query now counts the SocialSecurityNumber field and groups records by job code and title.

FIGURE 10-3
Counting and
grouping

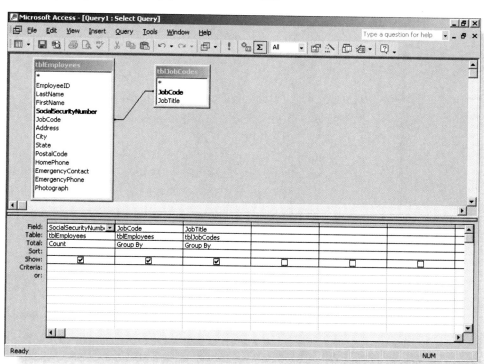

10. View the dynaset. Save the query as **qryCodeCount**. Close the query.

Creating a Crosstab Query

A *crosstab query* displays information similar to a spreadsheet with rows and columns. You group data by two fields, one listed on the left and the other listed across the top.

EXERCISE 10-3 **Design a Crosstab Query**

You use the **Total** row and the **Crosstab** row in the design grid. In a crosstab query, you calculate a sum, average, count, or other total for the data.

1. Click the **Queries** button and click **New**. Choose **Design View** and click **OK**.

2. Double-click tblStuffedAnimals to add it to the grid and close the Show Table dialog box.

3. Size the panes and the Field List.

 NOTE: Crosstab queries require that you have data suitable for summarizing. Many tables do not have fields that make sense in a crosstab.

4. Double-click ListPrice, ProductGroup, and ProductID to add them to the design grid.

5. Click the Totals button Σ. All the rows display Group By.

6. Click the **Total** row for ProductID and choose **Count**.

7. Choose **Query** and then choose **Crosstab** Query. The **Crosstab** row opens below the **Total** row.

8. Click the **Crosstab** row for ListPrice and choose **Row Heading**. The list prices are shown down the left side of the datasheet as row labels.

9. Click the **Crosstab** row for ProductGroup and choose **Column Heading**. The group letters are shown across the top of the datasheet as column labels.

10. Click the **Crosstab** row for ProductID and choose **Value**. The value is the field that is summed, counted, or averaged.

FIGURE 10-4
Crosstab query in
Design View

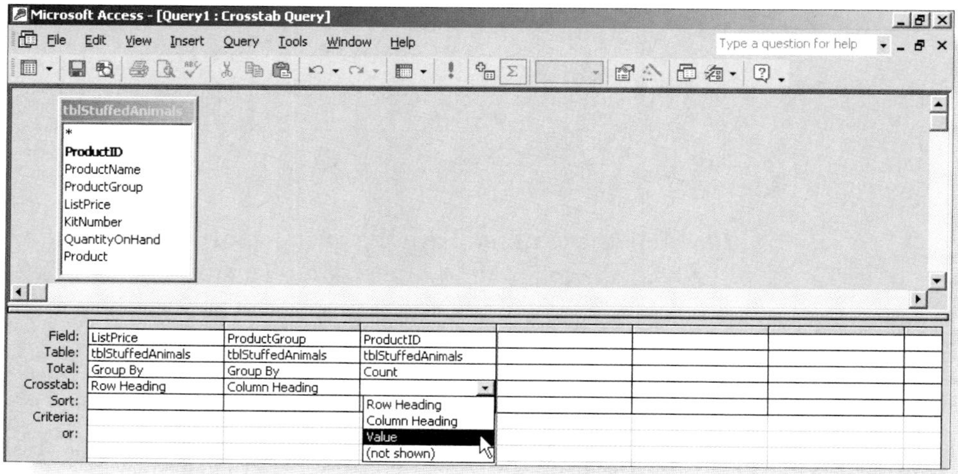

11. View the dynaset. There are three products that sell for $9.50, all of them in the F group. There are five products that sell for $10.75; two in group D, two in group E, and one in group F.

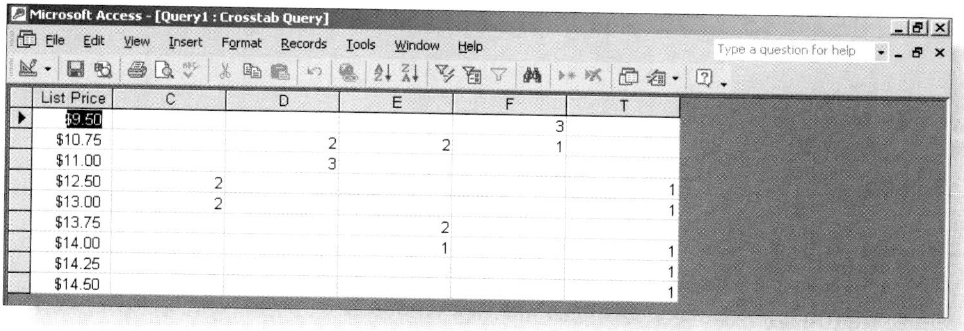

FIGURE 10-5
Crosstab query results

List Price	C	D	E	F	T
$9.50				3	
$10.75		2	2	1	
$11.00		3			
$12.50	2				1
$13.00	2				1
$13.75			2		
$14.00			1		
$14.25					1
$14.50					1

12. Save the query as **qryPricing** and close it.

EXERCISE **10-4** **Use PivotTable View**

A PivotTable View displays the same information as a crosstab query, including counts and sums of numeric fields. A *PivotTable* is an interactive table that can quickly summarize large amounts of data. For example, a PivotTable can display field values horizontally or vertically. These values can then be totaled, based on the row or column. Individual values are calculated at the intersection of each row and column heading. Subtotals and grand totals can also be calculated. You can rotate the rows and columns to see different summaries of the same data, or you can filter the data to show only certain fields.

1. Click the Queries button and click <u>New</u>. Choose Design View and click OK.
2. Double-click tblStuffedAnimals to add it to the grid and then close the Show Table dialog box.
3. Size the panes and the Field List.
4. Double-click ListPrice, ProductGroup, and ProductID to add them to the design grid.
5. Click the drop-down arrow for the View button ▦ and choose PivotTable View. The PivotTable window and a smaller PivotTable Field List window appear.
6. Drag the Product Group field from the PivotTable Field List to the Drop Column Fields Here row. (See Figure 10-6 on the next page.)

FIGURE 10-6
Dropping Product
Group field into
Column Heading

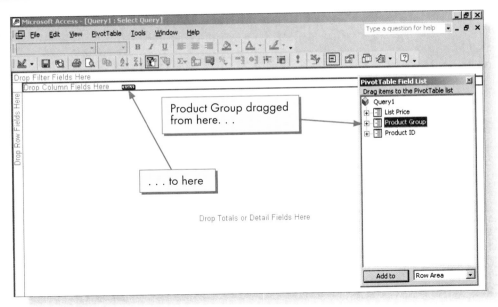

7. Drag the Product ID into the Drop Totals or Detail Fields Here section of the PivotTable. The Product ID fields are listed under each Product Group heading.

8. Click the drop-down arrow for Product Group. Deselect C, E, and T. Click OK. Only the Product ID fields for Product Groups D and F are now visible.

FIGURE 10-7
Product Groups
D and F

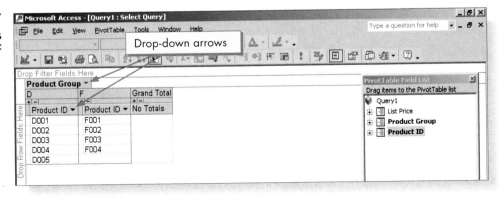

9. Click the plus sign just below the column title Grand Total. This shows all ProductIDs for Product Groups D and F.

10. Save the query as **qryProductGroupsD&F** and then close the query.

Designing Parameter Queries

A *parameter* is a determining factor or characteristic. A *parameter query* prompts you for selection criteria each time the query is run. A parameter query prompts you to enter criteria in a separate dialog box rather than in Design View. For example, you could use the criteria "nc" to show customers from a particular state.

Suppose you run reports based on a query for each product group. The criteria for the query would be "C" for the first report, "D" for the second, "E" for the third, and so on. You could open the query in Design View and edit the criteria for each report. A parameter query lets you enter the criteria each time the report is run.

EXERCISE **10-5** **Run a Parameter Query**

There are two parameter queries in your database. You can run and examine them before you create your own parameter queries.

1. Click the **Queries** button. Double-click qryEmployeesByJobCode.

2. The Enter Parameter Value dialog box opens as the query runs.

3. Key **mf04** in the dialog box.

FIGURE 10-8
Enter Parameter
Value dialog box

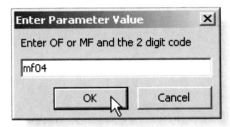

4. Press [Enter] or click **OK**. The dynaset shows employees who work as "MF04," the job code for designers. You would enter **mf04** in the **Criteria** row of a regular select query to see the same results.

5. Click the View button ▨ and maximize the window.

6. Click the **Criteria** row for the JobCode field. The criteria is the prompt you see in the Parameter Value dialog box.

7. Press [Shift]+[F2]. The prompt is enclosed in square brackets. Click **Cancel**.

8. Click the View button ▦. The query runs again and displays the Parameter Value dialog box.

9. Key **mf03** and press [Enter] or click **OK**. This dynaset shows the tailors who work at Carolina Critters.

10. Close the query.

11. Double-click qryAnimalsByProductGroup. Key **c** and press [Enter].

12. Click the View button ▨. Click **Query** and then click **Parameters**. The dialog box lists the parameter and its data type. Click **Cancel**.

13. Close the query without saving changes.

EXERCISE **10-6** **Create a Parameter Query**

When you create a parameter query, you must first choose the field or fields on which the comparisons are to be made. If you are looking for information about a particular sales date, you would use an order date field. If you are looking for data about the location of a company, you might use city and state fields.

1. Create a new query in Design View for tblCustomers and tblSalesOrders. You should see the join line with referential integrity for the CustomerID field.

 TIP: A parameter query is a type of select query.

2. Size the panes and the Field Lists.
3. Double-click these field names in the order shown: CompanyName, Contact-Name, City, State, and OrderDate.
4. Click the Criteria row for the State field.
5. Key **[Enter State]** (include the square brackets but do not key a period).

 TIP: You cannot use a period in a parameter, because a period is an Access operator.

6. Press F2 to select the prompt. Press Ctrl+C to copy the prompt to the Office Clipboard.
7. From the Query menu, choose Parameters. Click in the Parameter column for the first row.
8. Press Ctrl+V to paste the text from the Clipboard.
9. Click in the Data Type column and select Text.

FIGURE 10-9
Choose a
Data Type in the
Query Parameters
dialog box

Query Parameters	? X
Parameter	Data Type
[Enter State]	Text
OK	Cancel

10. Click OK to close the Query Parameters dialog box.
11. Click the View button. Key **nc** and click OK.
12. Save the query as **qryCust&Orders** and return to the design grid.

EXERCISE 10-7 **Use AND and OR Criteria in a Parameter Query**

Often, users need to select data based on two or more fields. Just as you can create a single-parameter query, you can create a query using one or more parameters. If the parameters are on the same Criteria row, the query is an AND query. If parameters are listed on separate rows, the query is an OR query.

1. With qryCust&Orders open in Design View, click the Criteria row for OrderDate.

2. Key >[Enter Date] to create AND criteria.

3. Drag to select the parameter without the greater-than symbol. Press Ctrl + C .

4. Choose Query and then choose Parameters. Click in the second Parameter row.

5. Press Ctrl + V and press Tab .

6. Select Date/Time in the Data Type column. Click OK.

FIGURE 10-10
AND parameters

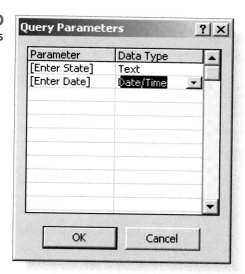

7. Run the query. Key **nc** and click OK. Key **4/1/01** and click OK. These are the North Carolina customers who ordered after the first quarter in 2001.

8. Return to the design grid.

9. Select the parameter >[Enter Date] and press Ctrl + X to cut it.

10. Click the Or row just below the row you cut. Press Ctrl + V to paste. This creates an OR criteria. (See Figure 10-11 on the next page.)

FIGURE 10-11
OR parameters

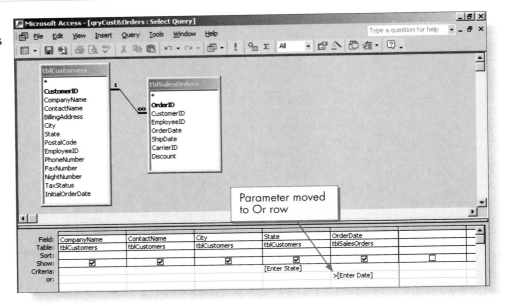

> Parameter moved
> to Or row

11. Run the query. Key **nc** and click OK. Key **4/1/01** and click OK. These are all the North Carolina customers or any customers who ordered after the first quarter of 2001.

12. Save and close the query.

Creating an Update Query

You have been using select queries, which select and display records. You can edit the dynaset, but the query does not make any changes to the records. An *action query* changes the data in a table. Action queries carry out commands that you choose in the design grid. An action query might change the area code for all customers in a particular city, delete all kits made by a certain supplier, or add records from one table to another.

An *update query* is an action query that edits the data in a field for many records with one command. You can, for example, update all prices to be lower or higher, replace an old area code with a new one, or revise employee office locations when a department moves.

EXERCISE **10-8** **Create an Update Query**

You can see how an update query works by changing the job code for all designers in the Employees table. Then you can run another update query to return it to the original code. In the design grid for an update query, you add the field that is to be updated or changed and any fields that are needed to set criteria.

1. Create a new query in Design View for tblEmployees.

2. Size the panes and the Field List.

3. Double-click JobCode to add it to the grid.

4. Click the drop-down arrow for the Query Type button and choose Update Query. The Update To row appears below the Table row.

> **TIP:** The Update To row is case-sensitive. Exactly what you key will appear in the record.

5. On the Update To row, key **MF14**, the new job code.

6. On the Criteria row, key **mf04**, the current job code.

FIGURE 10-12
Update query with criteria

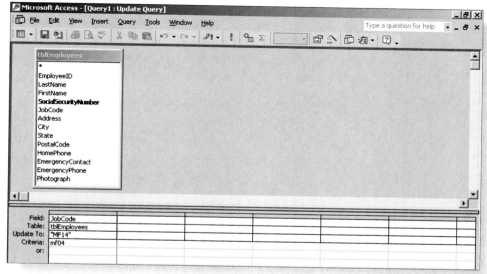

7. Click the View button. The dynaset shows the fields from the records that will be changed; they have not yet been updated. Five records will be updated.

8. Return to the design grid. Click the Run button to run the update. A warning box tells you how many records will be changed. Click **Yes**.

9. Click the View button again. No records are shown because they have been updated and no longer meet the criteria.

10. Save the query as **qryCodeUpdate**

11. Close the query. The update query displays a pencil and an exclamation point as a reminder that this is an action query.

> **TIP:** All action queries show an exclamation point with a corresponding icon.

12. Double-click qryCodeUpdate. A dialog box reminds you about changing data.

13. Click **Yes**. Because you have already updated the records, none will be changed this time. Click **No**.

14. Open tblEmployees.

 15. Click anywhere in the JobCode column and click the Find button 🔍. Search for **mf14**, the new code for designers. Close the Find dialog box and the table.

EXERCISE **10-9** **Edit an Update Query**

You often do not need to save an update query because it is a one-time change. Update queries are often one-time changes and do not need to be saved. In this case you saved your update query, so you can open it in Design View, edit the Update and Criteria rows, and reset the original job code.

1. Click qryCodeUpdate and click <u>D</u>esign.

2. Edit the Update To row to show **MF04**, the original job code.

3. Edit the Criteria row to show **mf14**, the code now in the table.

4. Click the View button 🔲 to see how many records will be changed.

5. Return to Design View. Click the Run button 🔳. The warning box opens. Click **Yes**.

6. Close and save the query.

Using a Make-Table Query

A *make-table query* is an action query that builds a new table from an existing one. In the query you can choose fields for the new table and enter criteria to select only certain records. You might make a table, for example, of all records that show sales from last year. Then you could delete last year's records from the current table so it shows only this year's sales. Most companies do not delete records without a trace, however. They often make a separate table (a "history table" or "archive table") with the old records and then delete them from the active table.

EXERCISE **10-10** **Create a Make-Table Query**

Use tblPayroll and a make-table query to create a table that shows only salaried employees.

1. Click the Tables button and select tblPayroll. Click the drop-down arrow for the New Object button and choose **Q**uery. Choose Design View and click OK.

2. Maximize the window; size the design grid and the Field List.

3. Click the drop-down arrow for the Query Type button 🖼 and choose Ma**k**e-Table Query. The Make Table dialog box opens.

4. Key **tblSalaried** in the Table Name box. Choose Current Database.

FIGURE 10-13
A make-table query creates a new table from existing records

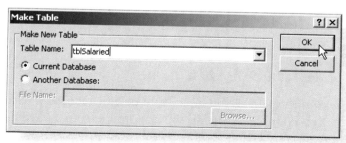

5. Click OK. Double-click the asterisk at the top of the Field List to add all the fields to the grid. Double-click MonthlySalary to add it to the second column.

 NOTE: The asterisk uses one column in the design grid but shows all fields in the dynaset.

6. Key **>0** on the Criteria row for MonthlySalary. Click to deselect the Show check box in the same column.

FIGURE 10-14
Choosing all fields and setting criteria for new table

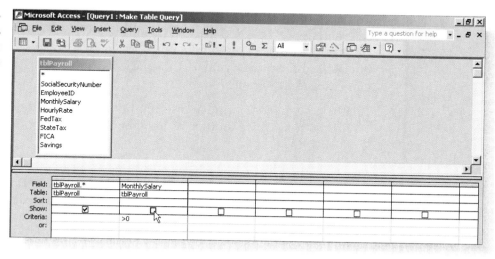

 NOTE: The MonthlySalary field is included in the new table because you selected all fields with the asterisk.

7. Click the View button 🔳 to preview the records for the new table. The new table is not made until you click the Run button ❗.

8. Return to Design View, click the Run button ❗, and click **Yes** in the message box.

9. Close the query without saving it.

10. Open tblSalaried. Click the View button 🖾. The fields do not inherit the field properties (captions, input masks, and so on), and the primary key is not copied.

11. Close the table.

Creating a Delete Query

A *delete query* is an action query that deletes records that match the criteria. You might, for example, delete all the customers from a particular state because they have been assigned to a new distributor. If you stop making a stuffed animal category, you can delete those records. You can delete sales orders from a particular date forward or from a range of dates. A company would typically make a new table with the deleted sales orders and make it a "history table."

 TIP: Frequent backups of your database file can help you recover from accidental deletions.

EXERCISE `10-11` **Create a Delete Query**

You need to be cautious with delete queries if you have created relationships with referential integrity. You learned in a previous lesson about the **Cascade Delete Related Records** option for referential integrity. If you delete records with a delete query from the primary table (the "one" side of the relationship), those deletions can cascade from table to table.

1. Click the **Tables** button and select tblPayroll. Click the drop-down arrow for the New Object button 🗐 and choose **Query**. Choose **Design View** and click **OK**.

2. Size the design grid and the Field List.

3. Double-click the asterisk at the top of the Field List. Double-click Monthly-Salary to add it to the second column. You need this field for your criteria.

 TIP: You need only one field in a delete query to specify the records to delete. Showing other fields, however, helps you check which records will be deleted.

4. Key **>0** on the **Criteria** row for MonthlySalary.

5. Click the drop-down arrow for the Query Type button 🖻 and choose <u>D</u>elete Query. The Delete row appears in the grid below the Table row. The first column shows "From" in the Delete row to show where you are deleting records from. The MonthlySalary column shows "Where." Access is building an expression similar to this one: "Delete all records from tblPayroll where the MonthlySalary>0."

FIGURE 10-15
Delete query uses
the Delete row

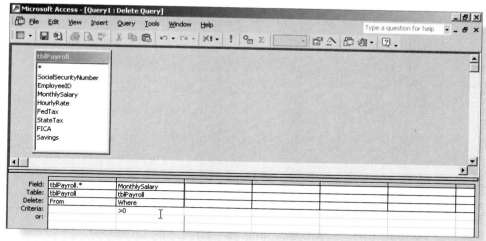

6. Click the View button 🖩 to preview the records to be deleted. These are the same records you just made into a new table.

7. Click the View button 🔣 and then click the Run button 〔!〕. Click Yes in the warning box.

8. Close the query without saving its design.

9. Open tblPayroll. The salaried workers have been deleted. Close the table.

Creating an Append Query

An *append query* is an action query that adds records from one table to another. Both tables must have the same fields in the same order. The target table can be in the same database or another database. When you build an append query, you use the table to be appended as your target table when you start your query. The table that is appended is copied into the target table but also remains in its original location. Appended records are added at the bottom of the target table.

EXERCISE 10-12 Create an Append Query

Because you created a table of salaried workers, you can add them back to the main payroll table.

1. Select tblSalaried. Click the drop-down arrow for the New Object button and choose Query. Choose Design View and click OK.

2. Size the design grid and the Field List.

3. Click the drop-down arrow for the Query Type button and choose Append Query. The Append dialog box opens.

4. Click the Table Name drop-down arrow and choose tblPayroll.

5. You can append records from a table in the current or another database. Choose Current Database.

FIGURE 10-16
Append dialog box

6. Click OK. An Append To row appears in the grid.

7. Double-click the asterisk to add all the fields to the grid. The grid shows that all the fields from tblSalaried will be added to tblPayroll.

FIGURE 10-17
Append query
adds records to
existing table

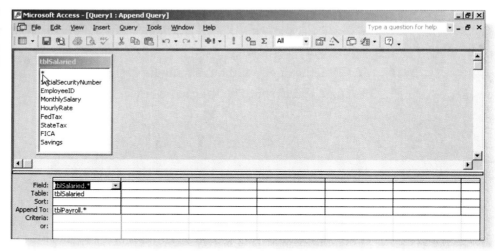

8. Click the View button to preview the records to be appended.

9. Return to Design View, click the Run button , and click Yes.

10. Close the query without saving it.

11. Open tblPayroll to see that it includes all employees again. Close the table.

12. Right-click tblSalaried and choose Delete. Choose Yes.

Using Specialized Query Wizards

You have seen how relationships and referential integrity can help you check the soundness of your work. Many times, however, you receive data from other sources, such as a mainframe, an online source, or a purchased list. These tables might have duplicate records or might not follow your relationship rules. Two query wizards serve special purposes and help you verify the accuracy of your data. They are the Find Unmatched Records Query Wizard and the Find Duplicate Records Query Wizard.

EXERCISE 10-13 Find Unmatched Records

The tables in your database do not have any redundant or unnecessary field names or any other duplication issues. This is because they have been normalized. *Normalization* is the process of separating data into tables so they do not have redundant fields. To test the Find Unmatched Records Query Wizard, you first need to add a deliberate error (an unmatched record) for it to catch.

1. Open tblJobCodes and add a new record for job code **MF07** with a title of **Student**. There are, of course, no employees with this job code. It is a deliberate error. Close the table.

2. Click the Queries button and **N**ew. Choose Find Unmatched Query Wizard and click OK.

3. The first dialog box asks you to choose a table that might have records with no match. You created the error in tblJobCodes, so choose it.

FIGURE 10-18
Choose the table that might have records with no match

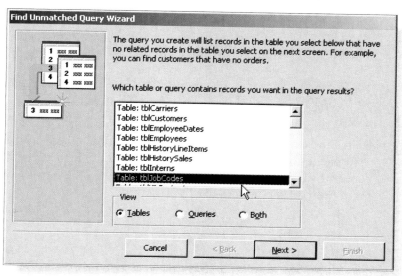

TIP: Records with no match are sometimes called "orphan records."

4. Click **Next**. The next dialog box asks you to choose the table that should have the matching records. Choose tblEmployees and click **Next**.

5. In both Field Lists, choose the common field JobCode. Click the <=> button <=> .

FIGURE 10-19
Choose the common field

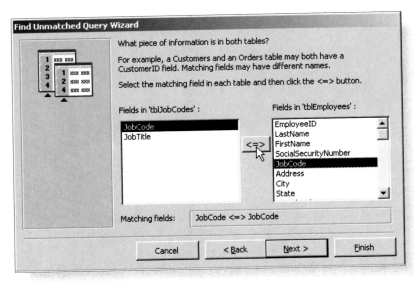

6. Click **Next**. Click the Add All button >> to show both fields in the query results. Click **Next**.

7. Save your query as **qryNoCode** and click **Finish**. The records in tblJobCodes with no matches in tblEmployees are listed. (They are OF03, OF04, and MF07.) The query shows you the problem records; you still have to decide how to solve the problem. Close the dynaset.

E X E R C I S E **Find Duplicate Records**

The Find Unmatched Query Wizard finds unmatched, or orphan, records. The Find Duplicates Query Wizard checks a table for duplicate data. Perhaps a company has several sites and is listed many times in the table. You can find these duplicates and then decide how to list the company.

NOTE: Again you will need to create an error to see how the wizard works.

1. Open tblCustomers. Copy the contents of the CompanyName field for record 9.

2. Locate the record for the customer named Magna Mart, Inc. Paste over Magna Mart, Inc. Both records now have the same company name (your deliberate error). Close the table.

3. Click the Queries button and click New. Choose Find Duplicates Query Wizard and click OK.

4. The first dialog box asks you to choose the table that might have duplicates. Choose tblCustomers and click Next.

5. The next dialog box asks you to choose the field that might have duplicates. Choose CompanyName and click Next.

FIGURE 10-20
Choose the field
that might have
duplicates

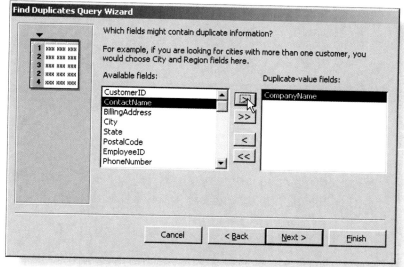

6. Click the Add All button [>>] to show all fields in the resulting dynaset. Click Next.

7. Save your query as **qryDuplicates** and click Finish. The duplicate records are listed. The query shows the problem records. You could delete one now if that were the appropriate thing to do; however, do not delete anything. Close the dynaset.

EXERCISE 10-15 Use the Documenter

Access has a tool that lets you print information about any of the objects in your database. It's called the Documenter and it provides a way for you to document all your work. The Documenter generates (creates) a report that can be printed. These generated reports do not have a Design View and cannot be edited or saved.

1. From the Database window, choose Tools and then choose Analyze, Documenter. The Documenter dialog box opens, with tabs for all objects in your database.

2. Click the **Queries** tab to print documentation for a query.

3. Click the check box for qryCodeCount to select it for documentation. Click qryCodeUpdate, qryCust&Orders, qryDuplicates, qryNoCode, qryPricing, and qrySalesCount. These are all the queries you saved in this lesson.

FIGURE 10-21
Choosing queries to
be documented

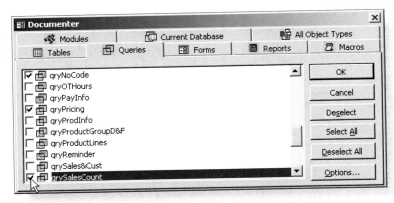

4. Click **Options**. The Print Query Definition dialog box opens.

5. In the **Include for Query** group, select only **Parameters**.

6. In the **Include for Fields** group, select **Names, Data Types, and Sizes**.

7. In the **Include for Indexes** group, select **Nothing**. Click **OK**.

FIGURE 10-22
Making selections
in the
Print Query Definition
dialog box

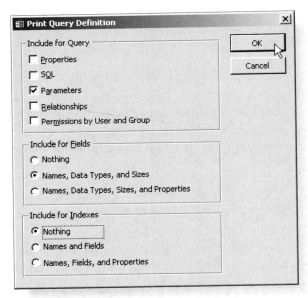

8. Click **OK** in the Document dialog box. Access generates a report with information about each of your queries on a separate page.

9. View each page of the report in a Fit and Zoom size. (If you close Print Preview before printing the Documenter's report, you need to run the Documenter again.)

  NOTE: At this point you could click the Print button to print the generated report. However, before printing, ask your instructor whether to print.

10. Close the report.

11. Compact and repair the database. Close the database.

USING HELP

As you learned in this lesson, normalization is the process of breaking data into manageable, unduplicated tables. A normalized table is one that does not have repetitive data.

Use the Assistant to learn more about normalization:

1. Choose Help. Show the Office Assistant.

2. Click the Office Assistant icon if its dialog box does not open.

3. Key **normalize** and press Enter.

4. Click Split a table into related tables.

5. Read the Help window and then close it.

6. Choose Options in the Assistant dialog box.

7. Deselect the option to Use the Office Assistant and click OK.

FIGURE 10-23
Deselecting the
option to use the
Office Assistant

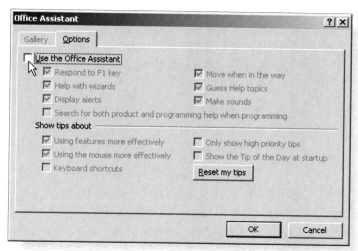

LESSON Summary

➤ A summary query shows aggregate information from a group of records rather than just details from individual records. Aggregate functions include sum, average, maximum, minimum, and count information. You can create a summary query in Design View or by using a Wizard.

➤ A crosstab query displays aggregate information based on values displayed in columns and rows (similar to a spreadsheet).

➤ A PivotTable is a quick way to summarize large amounts of information in a query.

➤ A parameter query prompts a user for one or more criteria. Double-clicking a parameter query runs the query. AND and OR criteria can be used in a parameter query.

➤ An action query carries out one or more commands from the design grid. Update queries, make-table queries, delete queries, and append queries are all action queries.

➤ An update query modifies the data in one or more fields from one or more tables.

➤ A make-table query creates a new table.

➤ A delete query deletes records from one or more tables.

➤ An append query adds records to an existing table.

➤ A find unmatched query locates unmatched ("orphaned") records.

➤ A find duplicates query checks for duplicate records within a table.

➤ The Documenter prints information about any object within the database.

LESSON 10 Command Summary

FEATURE	BUTTON	MENU	KEYBOARD	SPEECH
Show Total row	Σ	View, Totals		✓
Crosstab query		Query, Crosstab Query		✓
Update query		Query, Update Query		✓
Append query		Query, Append Query		✓

continues

LESSON 10 Command Summary *continued*

FEATURE	BUTTON	MENU	KEYBOARD	SPEECH
Delete query		Query, Delete Query		✓
Make-table query		Query, Make-Table Query		✓
Document object		Tools, Analyze, Documenter		✓

Concepts Review

Each of the following statements is either true or false. Indicate your choice by circling **T** or **F**.

T F **1.** You use an append query to edit many records at once.

T F **2.** When you use a delete query, records from more than one table might be deleted.

T F **3.** You can find orphan records with the Simple Query Wizard.

T F **4.** In Query Design View, you can select all fields in a Field List by double-clicking the primary key.

T F **5.** An aggregate function might use Count or Sum.

T F **6.** A summary query shows each record for a particular group.

T F **7.** In a parameter query, you make changes in Design View to run the query with different criteria.

T F **8.** You use an update query to add records from one table to another table.

Write the correct answer in the space provided.

1. What kind of action query would you use to remove records from a table?

_____

2. How do you enter parameters in Query Design View?

_____

3. What is a fast way to add all the fields to the design grid?

_____

4. What row might show "Group By" or "Count" in Query Design View?

_____

5. What happens when you run a parameter query?

_____

6. What button do you click to preview the records that will be changed in an update query?

_____

7. What symbol appears as part of the icon for all action queries in the Database window?

_____

8. Name the two specialized query wizards.

_____

CRITICAL THINKING

Answer these questions on a separate page. There are no right or wrong answers. Support your answers with examples from your own experience, if possible.

1. Think about the database your school maintains for student records. Discuss when you might use an update query, a delete query, or an append query to manage the tables.

2. The aggregate functions show a sum, count, or average. Using your school database again, what types of summary queries would be valuable?

Skills Review

EXERCISE 10-16

Create a summary query in Design View. Create a summary query by using a wizard.

1. Create a summary query in Design View by following these steps:

a. Open *[your initials]*CC-10 and refresh the link in the tables in *[your initials]*CC-E-10.

b. Click the Queries button and click New. Choose Design View and click OK.

c. Double-click tblEmployees and tblPayroll. Close the Show Table dialog box.

d. Maximize the window, and size the panes and Field Lists. Drag a join line between the common fields if you do not see the line.

 REVIEW: The join line is shown automatically for the SocialSecurityNumber field if your computer is set for Enable AutoJoin under Options on the Tools menu.

e. Double-click JobCode, FedTax, StateTax, and FICA to add them to the design grid.

f. Click the Totals button Σ.

g. Click the Total row for FedTax and choose Avg. Also choose Avg for StateTax and FICA. The JobCode field now shows Group By.

h. View the dynaset.

i. Return to the design grid. Right-click the FedTax column and choose Properties. Change the caption to **Average Federal Tax**

j. Change the caption for StateTax to **Average State Tax**. Change the caption for FICA to **Average Social Security Tax**

k. View the dynaset. Save the query as **qryTaxRpt**

 REVIEW: Create an AutoReport from the New Object drop-down list.

l. Create an AutoReport for the dynaset.

m. In Design View, align the currency fields on the right at the 3-inch mark. Size the labels to fit.

 NOTE: Use the Move handle (top left) to move the text boxes without moving the labels.

n. Format the page to use two columns. If you see an error message that data might not display or fit, adjust the column width or the column spacing.

o. Add your name in the Page Footer and print the report.

p. Close the report without saving. Close the query.

2. Create a summary query by using the Simple Query Wizard by following these steps:

a. Click the Queries button and click New. Choose Simple Query Wizard and click OK.

b. In the Tables/Queries list, choose Table:tblStuffedAnimals.

c. Double-click ProductGroup, ListPrice, and QuantityOnHand. Click Next.

d. Click Summary and then click Summary Options.

e. Calculate the minimum list price and the maximum quantity on hand. Click OK and click Next.

f. Name the query **qryMinMax** and click Finish.

g. Return to the design grid and view the options on the Total row.

h. Change the caption for the MinOfListPrice field to **Minimum List** Change the caption for the MaxOfQuantityOnHand field to **Maximum Stock**

i. Save the query and create an AutoReport. Add your name in the Page Header, print the report, and close it without saving it.

j. Close the query.

EXERCISE 10-17

Create a crosstab query. Create a parameter query.

1. Create a crosstab query by following these steps:
   a. Click the Queries button and click <u>N</u>ew. Choose Crosstab Query Wizard and click OK.
   b. Choose tblHistorySales in the list of tables and click <u>N</u>ext.
   c. Choose CustomerID to use it as the row heading and click <u>N</u>ext.
   d. Choose EmployeeID to use it as the column heading and click <u>N</u>ext.
   e. From the Fields list, click the OrderID. From the Functions list, click Count. Click <u>N</u>ext.
   f. Name the query **qrySalesHistory**

 REVIEW: To create a tabular AutoReport, you must use the New Report dialog box.

   g. Without closing the query, create a tabular AutoReport for the dynaset. Add your name in the Report Header and print the report.
   h. Close the report without saving. Close the query.

2. Create a parameter query by following these steps:
   a. Select tblHistorySales and click the New Object drop-down arrow. Choose Query and Design View. Click OK.
   b. Size the window, the panes, and the Field List.
   c. Double-click the asterisk to add all fields to the grid.
   d. Double-click OrderDate to add it again as the second column. Click the Show box to turn off display of this column.
   e. Click the Criteria row for OrderDate and press Shift + F2.
   f. Key **between [Enter beginning date] and [Enter ending date]** as the parameter with operators. Click OK to close the Zoom window.

 TIP: You cannot enter operators in the Query Parameters dialog box, but you should specify the data type.

   g. Choose Query, and then choose Para<u>m</u>eters. Leave the Parameter column empty and click in the Data Type column. Choose Date/Time. Click in the second Data Type row and choose Date/Time. Click OK.

 NOTE: A parameter with the BETWEEN/AND operator is really two parameters.

 h. Click the View button . Key **1/1/98** in the first dialog box and click OK.
   i. Key **3/31/98** in the second parameter box and click OK. These are the first quarter orders for 1998.
   j. Save the query as **qryQtrSales**

NOTE: You must enter parameters each time you view the report.

> **k.** Create a tabular AutoReport and use the same parameters. Add your name in the **Report Header** and print the report.
>
> **l.** Close the report without saving. Close the query.

EXERCISE 10-18

Create an update query, a make-table query, a delete query, and an append query.

> **1.** Create an update query by following these steps:
>
> **a.** Select tblStuffedAnimals and create a new query in Design View.
>
> **b.** Size the window, the panes, and the Field List.
>
> **c.** Click the Query Type drop-down arrow and choose **Update Query.**
>
> **d.** Double-click ListPrice and ProductGroup.
>
> **e.** On the Update To row for ListPrice, key **[listprice]*1.1** to increase the price by 10%.
>
> **f.** On the Criteria row for ProductGroup, key **d** to apply this price increase to the Dinosaur category.

  TIP: You can run an action query to preview the data by using the View button .

> **g.** Click the Run button . Five records will be updated. Click **Yes.**
>
> **h.** Click the Save button and name the query **qryPriceIncrease**. Close the query.
>
> **i.** Open tblStuffedAnimals. Double-click the first occurrence of **D** in the Product Group column and click the Filter by Selection button . These are the increased prices.
>
> **j.** Print the table in landscape orientation, remove the filter, and close the table without saving changes.
>
> **k.** Click the **Queries** button. Double-click qryPriceIncrease. Click **Yes** in the first warning box. Click **Yes** again in the second warning box.
>
> **l.** Open tblStuffedAnimals and apply a filter by selection for the **D** group. What has happened to the prices?
>
> **m.** Remove the filter. Close the table without saving.
>
> **2.** Create a make-table query by following these steps:
>
> **a.** Select tblStuffedAnimals and create a new query in Design View.
>
> **b.** Maximize the window and size the panes and the Field List.
>
> **c.** Click the Query Type drop-down arrow and choose **Make-Table Query.**
>
> **d.** Key **tblBears** in the Table Name box. Click the **Current Database** button and click OK.

e. Double-click the asterisk to use all the fields from tblStuffedAnimals for the new table.

f. Double-click ProductGroup to add it to the second column for criteria.

g. On the Criteria row for ProductGroup, key **t**, the code for bears. Deselect the Show check box.

h. Click the View button  to preview the records.

i. Return to Design View, click the Run button 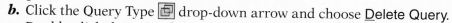, and click Yes.

j. Close the query without saving it.

k. Open, review, and close tblBears.

3. Create a delete query by following these steps:

a. Select tblStuffedAnimals and create a new query in Design View. Size the grid and the Field List.

b. Click the Query Type drop-down arrow and choose Delete Query.

c. Double-click the asterisk to add all the fields from tblStuffedAnimals.

d. Double-click ProductGroup to add it to the grid for criteria.

e. Key **t** on the Criteria row for ProductGroup.

f. Click the View button to preview the records that will be deleted.

g. Return to Design View. Click the Run button to delete the records and click Yes.

h. Close the query without saving the changes.

i. Open tblStuffedAnimals. Notice that the teddy bear group has been deleted. Close the table.

4. Create an append query by following these steps:

a. Select tblBears and create a new query in Design View. Size the grid and the Field List.

b. Click the Query Type drop-down arrow and choose Append Query.

c. Click the drop-down arrow for the Table Name and choose tblStuffed-Animals. Choose Current Database and click OK.

d. Double-click the asterisk to add all the fields to the grid.

e. Click the View button to preview the records that will be added to tblStuffedAnimals.

f. Return to Design View. Click the Run button and click Yes.

g. Close the query without saving.

h. Open tblStuffedAnimals to see that the teddy bear records have been appended. Close the table.

EXERCISE 10-19

Create a specialized query.

1. Create a Find Unmatched Records query by following these steps:

a. Click the Queries button and click New. Choose Find Unmatched Query Wizard and click OK.

b. Choose tblCustomers as the table that might have records with no match. Click <u>N</u>ext.

c. Choose tblSalesOrders as the table that should have the matching records. Click <u>N</u>ext.

d. In both Field Lists, choose the common field CustomerID. Click <u>N</u>ext.

 e. Click the Add All button <u>>></u>. Click <u>N</u>ext.

f. Save your query as **qryNoSales** and click <u>F</u>inish. These are customers who have not yet ordered. Close the dynaset.

g. Choose <u>T</u>ools, Ana<u>l</u>yze, and <u>D</u>ocumenter.

h. Click the Queries tab. Click to place a check mark for qryNoSales.

i. Click <u>O</u>ptions.

j. Turn on SQL only for the query. Show Names, Data Types, and Sizes for the fields. Show Nothing for the Indexes. Click OK.

k. Click OK again to generate the report.

l. Preview and print the report. Do not save the report.

m. Compact and repair the database. Close the database.

Lesson Applications

EXERCISE 10-20

Create a summary query.

1. Create a new query for tblKitContents and tblKitSuppliers in Design View. Maximize the window and size the panes and Field Lists. Drag a join line if you do not see one. The common field is SupplierID.

2. Add KitNumber and SupplierName to the design grid. Add the Total row to the grid.

3. Count the kit numbers and group by SupplierName. Change the caption for the KitNumber field to **Kits Supplied**

4. For SupplierName, add the criteria **not *supply** to eliminate companies with the word "supply" in the name.

    NOTE: The word "not" is an Access operator used with text fields, similar to <>.

5. Save the query as **qry#OfKits** and view the dynaset.

6. Create a tabular AutoReport for the query. Edit the title to show **Number of Kits per Supplier**. Delete the page number control and add a label with your name in its place. Print the report and close it without saving.

7. Close the query.

EXERCISE 10-21

Create an update query.

1. Open tblSalesOrders and print it in landscape orientation.

2. Create a query for tblSalesOrders, using the Discount and CarrierID fields. Make this an update query.

3. On the Update To row for Discount, key an expression to double the discount. Enclose the field name in square brackets.

4. On the Criteria row for CarrierID, key **not c303** to exclude those records.

5. Preview the dynaset. Five records will be updated.

    TIP: Multiplying any number by zero results in zero.

6. Run the query and close it without saving.

7. Create a tabular AutoReport for tblSalesOrders. Add your name in the Report Header and print it.

8. Close the report without saving.

9. Create another update query to return the records to the original discount. The expression for the Update To row is **[discount]*.5**. The criteria are the same.

10. Run the query and do not save it.

EXERCISE 10-22

Create make-table and append queries.

1. Create a query for tblSalesOrders. Make it a make-table query.

2. Name the new table **tbl1stQtr** and choose Current Database.

3. Add all the fields to the first grid column. Add OrderDate to the second column, but do not show it.

4. Set criteria to show records from the first quarter with dates between **1/1/2001** and **3/31/2001**

5. Preview the records for the new table and then run the query. Close it without saving.

6. Open tblHistorySales. Note the field names and the order in which they appear. Close the table.

7. Open tbl1stQtr to check it. It has a CarrierID field. Before you can append tbl1stQtr to tblHistorySales, you need to delete that field. It is not in the history table.

8. Switch to Design View. Select and delete the CarrierID field. Save and close the table.

9. Create an append query for tbl1stQtr. Append this table to tblHistorySales, using all the fields.

10. Preview the records to be appended. Run the query and append the records. Close the query without saving it.

11. Open tblHistorySales and sort by OrderID in ascending order. Change the Order Date in the first record to your birthday.

 REVIEW: Enter dates as mm/dd/yy.

12. Print the table in landscape orientation. Close the table and save the changes.

EXERCISE 10-23 Challenge Yourself

Create a parameter query.

1. Create a new query for tblEmployees and tblSickDays. Drag a join line if you do not see one.

2. Add these fields to the design grid: FirstName, LastName, and SickDay.

3. View the dynaset without any criteria and return to Design View.

4. Open the Zoom window for the SickDay Criteria row. Key **>=[Enter beginning date] and <=[Enter ending date]** and then close the Zoom window.

5. In the Query Parameters dialog box, set the Data type to Date/Time for the first two rows, but do not copy any parameters.

6. Save the query as **qrySickDays**

7. Find the employees who took sick days between **6/1/01** and **8/31/01**

8. Create a tabular AutoReport for the same dates. Add your name in the Report Header and print the report.

9. Close the report without saving it. Close the query.

10. Compact and repair your database and exit Access.

On Your Own

In these exercises you work on your own, as you would in a real-life work environment. Use the skills you've learned to accomplish the task—and be creative.

EXERCISE 10-24

Review the design of the database you created and modified in Exercises 9-28 through 9-30. Identify at least two summary queries, two parameter queries, and one append query that will enhance your database design. For each query, write the name of the query on a sheet of paper, describe its purpose, and list the fields that will be used in the query. On each sheet of paper, write your name and "Exercise 10-24." Continue to the next exercise.

EXERCISE 10-25

Design and create each query that you identified in Exercise 10-24. Before testing the queries, create a backup copy of your database. Modify your designs appropriately. Continue to the next exercise.

EXERCISE 10-26

Print the dynaset of the five queries you created in Exercise 10-25. On the printouts, write your name and "Exercise 10-25." Submit these printouts to your instructor. Keep a copy of the database you modified in Exercise 10-25. You will use it in subsequent lessons.

Unit 3 Applications

UNIT APPLICATION 3-1

Create a multiple table query. Add new records in the dynaset. Run an update query. Print a report and a form from a query. Create a summary make-table query.

1. Copy **CC-E-U3** and rename it *[your initials]*CC-E-U3. Copy the **CC-U3** database and rename it to *[your initials]*CC-U3. Open *[your initials]*CC-U3 and link the tables from *[your initials]*CC-E-U3.

2. Create a new query in Design View for tblKitContents and tblStuffedAnimals. Size the window, grid, and Field Lists.

3. Add all the fields from both tables. View the dynaset.

 REVIEW: You can press F4 to display a drop-down list in a lookup field.

4. Add the following new record. Create and use the lookup field for the SupplierID. The second occurrence of the KitNumber field in the dynaset is filled in automatically.

KitNumber	**Cat006**
SupplierID	**FF-06**
Cost	**4.26**
Kit Contents	**This kit contains brown and yellow striped acrylic, a velvet collar, feline eyes/nose, and pellet fill.**
ProductID	**C006**
AnimalName	**Kaliko Kat**
ProductGroup	**C**
ListPrice	**10.5**
KitNumber	*Press* Tab.
Current Inventory	**100**
Illustration	*Leave blank.*

5. Move the pointer away from the new record. Save the query as **qryAnimals&Kits**.

 TIP: The Page Header for a form prints but does not show in Form View.

6. Create an AutoForm for the dynaset. Add your name to the Page Header. Print this new record. Close the form without saving it, and close the query.

NOTE: As you add a record in the dynaset, records are added to both tables.

7. Open tblKitContents and find the record for KitNumber Cat006. Close the table. Do the same for tblStuffedAnimals.

8. Open the query in Design View. Add criteria to find kits that cost between $6 and $8 and are supplied by SupplierID BB-02.

9. Change this to an update query to increase the cost of *all* kits from Supplier BB-02 by 15%. Follow the onscreen messages and make the update. Close the query without saving the changes.

10. Open tblKitContents and apply a filter by selection to show the products from Supplier BB-02. Create an AutoForm for the filtered records. Open the Page Header for the form and add your name. Print the filtered records.

11. Close the form without saving it. Remove the filter and close the table.

12. Create a summary query for tblEmployees and tblVacDays. Link the tables by social security number. Add FirstName, LastName, and VacationDay to the grid.

13. Group by the name fields and count the vacation days. Sort by LastName.

14. Make this a make-table query, naming the new table **tblCountVacDays**. Create the new table and close the query without saving it.

15. Open the new table, change the first name to your name, and print the table.

16. Close the table.

UNIT APPLICATION 3-2

View a relationship. Create a summary query. Create a multiple-table parameter query. Add a calculated field.

1. Open the Relationships window and clear the layout.

2. Add tblEmployees and tblVacDays to the Relationships window. Create a relationship between the two tables. Close the window and save the layout.

3. Use the Documenter for these two tables. Select both tables on the Tables tab. Choose Options to print only relationships for the table. Print names, data types, and sizes for the fields. Print nothing for the indexes. Print the generated report.

4. Create a query for tblProductLines and tblStuffedAnimals. Add Product-Line, ProductID, and ListPrice to the grid and make this a summary query.

5. Group by ProductLine, count by ProductID, and show the average list price. Save the query as **qryAvgPrice**

6. Create a tabular AutoReport for the dynaset.

7. Change the label for the Count field to **# of Items**. Change the label for the price field to **Average Price**. Change the main title to **Average Price by Group**. Add your name in the Report Header and print the report. Close the report without saving.

8. Close the query.

9. Create a query for tblEmployees and tblTimeCards. Add FirstName, Last-Name, WeekEnding, HourlyRate, and RegHours to the grid.

10. Save the query as **qryWeeklyPay**

11. Add a calculated field that multiplies HourlyRate by RegHours. Name this calculated field **Gross Pay**

12. Drag OTHours directly on top of the calculated field in the grid. Save the query again.

 NOTE: If you do not see the OTHours field in the Expression Builder, close the Expression Builder and re-save the query to write the change.

13. Edit the calculation to include overtime pay at time-and-a-half. Format the field for Currency.

14. Add a parameter for the WeekEnding field that allows you to specify the date. Test the parameter with **1/8/01**.

15. Prepare a tabular AutoReport for the week ending **1/15/01**. Position and size the controls, change the title to **Weekly Pay**, add your name in the header, and print the report. Close it without saving.

16. Close the query.

UNIT APPLICATION 3-3

Create make-table, delete, and append queries. Use the Top Values property.

1. Create a make-table query for tblEmployeeDates.

2. Name the new table **tblLate80s** and include it in the current database. The new table should contain all fields. Use criteria to find employees hired between January 1, 1985, and December 31, 1989. Preview the table before you create it. Do not save the query.

3. Open tblLate80s and print it. Close the table.

4. Create and run a delete query for tblEmployeeDates to delete employees hired between January 1, 1985, and December 31, 1989. Do not save this query.

5. Open tblEmployeeDates and sort by HireDate. Print the table. Save and close the table.

6. Create and run an append query to append the records in tblLate80s to tblEmployeeDates. Do not save this query.

7. Open tblEmployeeDates. Create a filter by form to find employees hired between January 1, 1985 and December 31, 1989. Remove the filter and close the table without saving changes.

 REVIEW: You can key any number in the Top Value entry box.

8. Create a select query for tblEmployeeDates. Add SocialSecurityNumber and HireDate to the grid. Use a sort and the **Top Values** property to show the 15 most recent hires.

9. Save the query as **qryRecentHires**. Create a tabular AutoReport for the dynaset. Make your own design changes. Add your name in a header. Print the report and do not save it.

10. Close the query.

11. Compact and repair your database. Exit Access.

UNIT APPLICATION 3-4 *Using the Internet*

Using the Internet.

Make a list of five states close to where you live, including your home state. Find the capital, the state bird, and two other statistics or data about each state. Decide which two statistics or data you will use for each state before you start searching. For each state, list three cities and their populations. One of the cities can be the capital. Estimate or find the distance in miles from your hometown to each of these three cities.

Create a new database following these guidelines:

- Create a table that lists state names and their two-letter abbreviations. Make the state abbreviation the primary key.

- Create one table that lists cities in each state, the city's population, and the distance from your hometown. Use a Yes/No field to indicate if the city is the capital of its state. The city name and the state together should be the primary key. (Select both rows and then click the Primary Key button.)

- Create a table that lists the state abbreviation, the state bird, and the other two pieces of data that you researched.

- Create a query to show the state name, its abbreviation, the capital, and the state bird. Create an AutoReport for this query.

- Create a query to show the state name, cities in the state, the population of each city, and the distance of each city from your hometown. Sort descending by the distance. Create an AutoReport for this query.

Adding Objects and Data to a Database

Building Tables, Forms, and Reports

After completing this lesson, you will be able to:

1. Create a table in Design View.
2. Add a validation rule and text.
3. Create a form in Design View.
4. Refine the appearance of a form.
5. Create a report in Design View.
6. Use multiple groups in a report.
7. Use page breaks in a report.
8. Add images to a report.

 Estimated Time: 2 hours

Y ou have already used wizards, AutoForms, and AutoReports to add tables, forms, and reports to your database. In this lesson, you learn how to start from scratch to create each of these database objects. You also learn how to enhance forms and reports.

Creating a Table in Design View

You create a table in Design View by entering field names, data types, descriptions, and field properties. Use the naming conventions you have learned so far to name fields (that is, capitalize the first letter of main words and don't use spaces). Field names should be short and descriptive.

> **TIP:** You can use two keys as a primary key. For example, you can use LastName and FirstName as a primary key. A table with a two-field primary key often serves as a junction table, relating many other tables.

EXERCISE 11-1 Create a Table in Design View

When you design a table, you should determine a primary key. This is the field whose values are unique for each record. No two records can have the same data in this field. Social security numbers are often used as a primary key for people, because no two people have the same number. Last names are not good as primary key fields, because people can have the same last name.

1. Create a copy of **CC-11** and call it *[your initials]***CC-11**
2. Open *[your initials]***CC-11**. Click the Tables button. Double-click Create table in Design view.
3. Maximize the window. The design grid is empty, and the insertion point is in the first row in the Field Name column.
4. Key **EmployeeID** and press Tab.
5. Text is the default data type. Key **n** and press Tab.
6. In the Description field, key **Rep's ID**
7. Press F6 to move to the General tab in the property sheet.

> **REVIEW:** In all Windows applications, you can move from one pane to another by pressing F6.

8. Click in the Caption row and key **Employee ID** with a space between the words.
9. Press F6 and Tab or click in the Field Name column in the second row in the top pane.

10. Click the Build button ▨. The Field Builder opens with the sample tables and field names used in the Table Wizard.
11. In the Sample Tables list, choose Mailing List. In the Sample Fields list, double-click LastName. The field is listed as a Text data type, 50 spaces wide, with a caption. It is also indexed. (See Figure 11-1 on the next page.)

> **TIP:** You can use any sample table in the Field Builder that has the field name you want.

FIGURE 11-1
Field Builder in
Table Design View

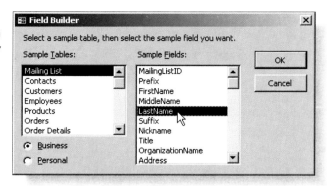

12. Set the Field Size for LastName to **25**

13. Press F6 and Tab or click in the Field Name column in the third row in the top pane.

14. Key **CommissionRate** as the Field Name and press Tab.

15. Key **n** for the Data Type. Press F6. Long Integer is the default because it is the most efficient. Number fields automatically have a default value of 0.

16. Set the caption to **Commission Rate**

17. Click in the EmployeeID row in the top pane.

18. Click the Primary Key button ⬚. Primary key here means that no two records can have the same EmployeeID value.

 REVIEW: The primary key field cannot be left empty or null in a record.

19. Click the fourth row in the top pane. Click the Build button ⬚.

20. Choose Mailing List as the sample table and Region as the field. The field is Text, 50 spaces wide, with a caption. It does not have an index.

21. Make the Region field 15 spaces wide.

22. Click the fifth row in the top pane. Click the Build button ⬚.

23. Choose Contacts as the sample table and MobilePhone as the field. The field is Text, 30 spaces wide, with a caption. It does not have an index or input mask.

24. Click the Input Mask row, and then click the Build button ⬚.

25. Click OK and save the table as **tblSalesStaff.** The Input Mask Wizard dialog box appears.

26. Choose Phone Number and click Finish.

27. Click the sixth row in the top pane and key **AutoPlate**. Make this a Text field that is **15** spaces wide. Set the caption to **License Plate**

28. Save the table. (See Figure 11-2 on the next page.)

FIGURE 11-2
Completed
tblSalesStaff table

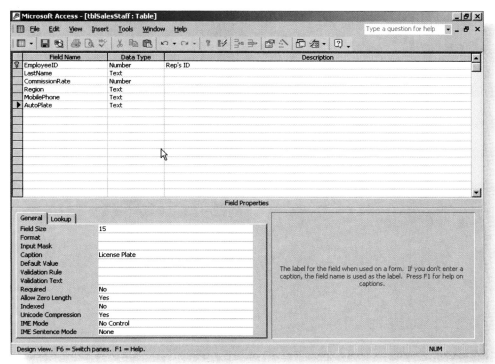

EXERCISE **11-2** **Optimize Data Types and Set Field Properties**

The default size for a Number field is Long Integer. This field size is not always the most appropriate for your data. Choosing the best field size optimizes the size of the database file and makes sure that calculations in queries and reports are accurate. You can determine the best size for a number field by asking two questions:

- Will the field store decimal values?
- How large or how small are the values to be stored?

TABLE 11-1   Number Field Size Settings

SETTING	STORES NUMBER FROM	DECIMAL PRECISION	STORAGE SIZE
Byte	0 to 255	(None)	1 byte
Integer	–32,768 to 32,767	(None)	2 bytes

continues

TABLE 11-1 Number Field Size Settings *continued*

SETTING	STORES NUMBER FROM	DECIMAL PRECISION	STORAGE SIZE
Long Integer	–2,147,483,648 to 2,147,483,647	(None)	4 bytes
Single	–3.4028E38 to –1.4013E-45 and 1.4013E-45 to 3.4028E38	7	4 bytes
Double	–1.7977E308 to –4.9407E-324 and 4.9407E-324 to 1.7977E308	15	8 bytes
Decimal	–10^28-1 to 10^28-1	28	12 bytes

1. With tblSalesStaff open in Design View, click the CommissionRate row in the top pane.
2. Press F6 and key **d** The Field Size is changed to Double.
3. Click the Format row and display its list. Choose Percent.
4. Set the Decimal Places for CommissionRate to **0**
5. Delete the Default Value for CommissionRate.
6. Click the AutoPlate row in the top pane. Click its Format row. Key **>** to force alphabetic characters to uppercase.
7. Click the Input Mask row for AutoPlate. Key **LL0000** to require an entry to start with two alphabetic characters, followed by four digits.

FIGURE 11-3
Format and Input
Mask for
AutoPlate field

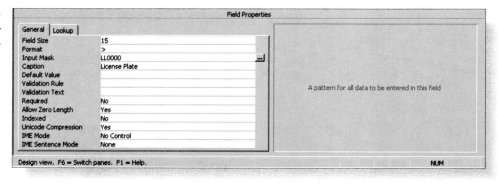

8. Save the table.

NOTE: The license plates all contain CC (for Carolina Critters) and four digits.

EXERCISE 11-3 Modify an Input Mask

The MobilePhone field has an input mask for a telephone field, **!\(999") "000\-0000;;_**. The exclamation point (!) makes the mask appear in Datasheet View from right to left. The first backslash (\) causes the character that follows it (the left parenthesis) to display. The three nines (999) allow an optional entry of numbers or spaces. If you press Spacebar in this position, you show no area code.

The next four characters are quotation marks, a right parenthesis, a space, and quotation marks. Everything between the quotes displays as *literal characters*; that is, the characters are exactly what you see on the screen. Three zeros (000) require that you enter three digits between 0 and 9 in these positions. The second backslash displays the hyphen. Then you must enter four more digits.

TABLE 11-2 Input Mask Symbols

SYMBOL	DESCRIPTION
0	Digit (0 to 9, entry required)
9	Digit or space (entry optional)
#	Digit or space (entry optional; spaces are displayed as blanks while in Edit mode, but blanks are removed when data is saved)
L	Letter (A to Z, entry required)
A	Letter (A to Z, entry required)
?	Letter (A to Z, entry optional)
a	Letter (A to Z, entry optional)
&	Any character or a space (entry required)
C	Any character or a space (entry optional)
<	Causes all characters to be converted to lowercase
>	Causes all characters to be converted to uppercase
!	Causes the input mask to display from right to left, rather than from left to right
\	Causes the character that follows to be displayed as the literal character
"abc"	Displays exactly what is between the quotation marks
. , : ; - /	Placeholders (decimal, thousand, date and time separators)

NOTE: Use the backslash in an input mask for a single literal character.

1. With tblSalesStaff open in Design View, click the MobilePhone row in the top pane.

2. Press F6 and click the **Input Mask** row.

3. Delete the exclamation point.

4. Edit the input mask to show **999\-000\-0000** This will show an optional area code, a hyphen, the exchange or first three digits of a phone number, a hyphen, and then the rest of the numbers.

FIGURE 11-4
Input Mask for
MobilePhone field

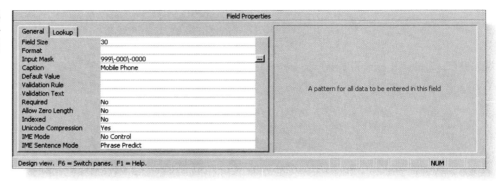

5. Save the table.

Adding Validation Rules and Text

A *validation rule* sets a rule or requirement for the data you enter in a field. For example, you could set a validation rule in an Inventory field that doesn't allow you to enter a number greater than 100. If you key 105 in that field, you break the rule and cannot complete the record. You see an error message when you try to move the insertion point away from the record.

Validation text is the message you see when you break a validation rule. If you do not enter your own validation text, Access displays a default message.

 NOTE: Some validation rules are automatic. For example, you cannot enter alphabetic characters in a Number field.

EXERCISE 11-4 Add Validation Criteria

Validation criteria can be placed on text, number, date/time, and currency fields. When validating numbers, date/time, and currency, you can create criteria that limit both the lower and the upper ranges of entries. When validating text, however, you need to list all valid entries. Therefore, you should add validation criteria on text fields only if the possible choices for entry are limited.

1. With tblSalesStaff open in Design View, click in the Region row in the top pane.

2. Click in the Validation Rule row in the lower pane. You can key a validation rule or enter an expression with the Build button . You will be keying the validation rule.

3. Key **north or south or east** in the Validation Rule row.

4. Click in the Validation Text row. When the focus is no longer on the Validation Rule row, Access enters quotation marks around the text, but not around the word "or." Access recognizes "or" as a logical operator and capitalizes it.

5. Save the table.

> **NOTE:** Text is enclosed in quotation marks in Access expressions. A logical operator is a reserved word that Access uses in its expressions.

EXERCISE **11-5** **Add Validation Text and Test the Rule**

When defining validation criteria, you should always include validation text. Validation text assists the data entry operator by displaying a message that tells the operator what should be entered.

1. With tblSalesStaff open in Design View, click the Validation Text row for the Region field.

2. Key **You must enter North, South or East for the region.** (Key the period.) Validation text is not an expression and does not have any quotation marks.

FIGURE 11-5
Validation rule and text for Region field

Field Properties	
General Lookup	
Field Size	15
Format	
Input Mask	
Caption	Region
Default Value	
Validation Rule	"north" Or "south" Or "east"
Validation Text	er North, South or East for the region.
Required	No
Allow Zero Length	No
Indexed	No
Unicode Compression	Yes
IME Mode	No Control
IME Sentence Mode	Phrase Predict

The error message that appears when you enter a value prohibited by the validation rule. Press F1 for help on validation text.

Design view. F6 = Switch panes. F1 = Help.   NUM

3. Switch to Datasheet View. Click **Yes** to save the changes.

4. Add the following records, one with a deliberate error, to check your validation rule.

Employee ID:	**6**
Last Name:	**Abdullah**
Commission Rate:	**5%**

 NOTE: Because the CommissionRate field is formatted for Percent, you can key the digit with the percent sign. You can also key the decimal equivalent (5%=.05).

Region:	**North**
Mobile Phone:	**709-555-4567**
License Plate:	**cc0001**

 NOTE: The characters in the license plate field are capitalized when you move the insertion point away from the field.

Employee ID:	**7**
Last Name:	**Dyer**
Commission Rate:	**5%**
Region:	**West**

5. Access displays the validation text because your region ("West") violates the validation rule. It is not North, South, or East. Click **OK** in the message box.

FIGURE 11-6
Validation text
appears

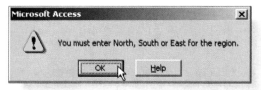

6. Change West to **South** and then complete the record.

Mobile Phone:	**308-555-8765**
License Plate:	**cc0002**

7. Press **Enter** to finish the second record.

 REVIEW: Press **Ctrl**+**'** to duplicate data from the previous field.

8. Add one more record:

Employee ID:	**28**
Last Name:	**Stewart**
Commission Rate:	**8%**
Region:	**South**
Mobile Phone:	**708-555-7350**
License Plate:	**cc0003**

9. Close the table.

Creating a Form in Design View

Most database designers create forms by first using the Form wizard and then modifying the controls on the form. However, on occasion, you might need to create a form so unique that the Form wizard does not have a template similar to your needs. This might be the case when you are copying the layout of a printed form already in use by the company.

EXERCISE 11-6   Create a Form in Design View

When you create a form in Design View, you start with a blank form window with only the **Detail** section open. You then place fields anywhere on the form, open other sections, and add design elements.

1. Click the Tables tab and click tblSalesStaff to select it. Click the New Object drop-down arrow and choose **F**orm.

2. The New Form dialog box opens with the table name. Choose Design View.

3. Click OK. A blank form opens with an empty **Detail** section. The Field List should be open. Maximize the window.

> ◀◀ **REVIEW:** Move the Field List and the toolbox by dragging the title bar.

4. Click the Field List button 📄. This toggles the Field List on and off. Show the Field List.

5. Select the EmployeeID field in the Field List window. Drag the field name from the window to the 1-inch mark, two rows of dots down. The pointer changes to a small field-box icon as you drag.

6. Repeat these steps to place the LastName field at the 1-inch mark, leaving two rows of dots between it and the EmployeeID controls.

FIGURE 11-7
Dragging the
LastName field

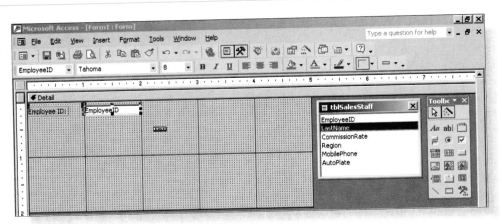

7. Place the CommissionRate field at the 1-inch mark, leaving two rows of dots between it and the LastName controls.

8. Select the Region field in the Field List window. Drag it to the 3.5-inch mark, two rows of dots down, aligned at the top with the EmployeeID controls.

9. Drag MobilePhone two rows below Region. Drag AutoPlate two rows below MobilePhone, leaving two rows of dots between it and MobilePhone.

FIGURE 11-8
Placement of
six fields

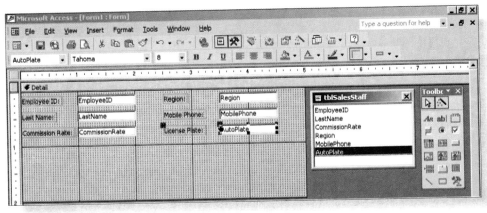

10. Click the Save button ▣. Name the form **frmSalesStaff**

EXERCISE 11-7 Modify Form Properties

Empty space below the controls in the Detail section appears as space between records when the form in displayed in Continuous Forms View. The Default View is a form property.

1. Double-click the Form Selector button to open the form's property sheet.

TIP: You can select the Form Selector button by pressing Ctrl + R if another control is selected.

FIGURE 11-9
Changing the
Default View

Form Selector
button

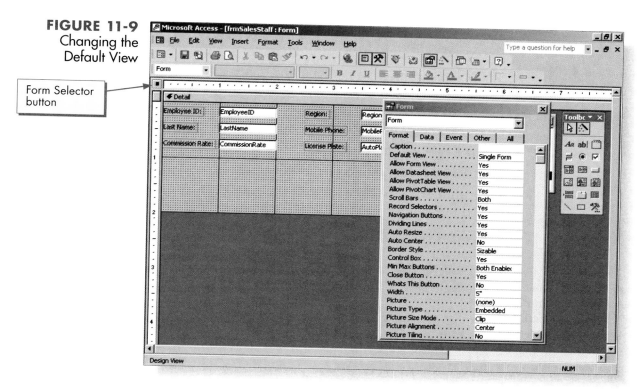

2. Click the Format tab and the Default View row. Choose Continuous Forms. Leave the property sheet open.

3. Click the View button 📧. Notice how many forms appear on screen.

4. Click the View button 📐.

5. Place the pointer on the bottom edge of the Detail section. Size the section to show two rows of dots below the controls.

6. Click the View button 📧. Notice how many forms appear now. Return to Design View.

7. Close the property sheet. Click the Save button 🖫.

EXERCISE 11-8 Work with Form Sections and Controls

The Detail section contains the fields from the table or query. The Form Header often contains a main title. The Page Header in a form is a print element; you do not see it in Form View.

1. With frmSalesStaff open in Design View, choose <u>V</u>iew and then choose Form <u>H</u>eader/Footer.

2. Click the Label tool . Click at the left edge of the Form Header.

3. Key **Sales Staff Information** and press (Enter).

4. Change the font to 16-point Arial italic. Double-click a sizing handle.

5. Size and position the label and the Header section so there is a row of dots above and below the label.

6. Switch to Form View. The Form Header appears once even though the form is still in Continuous Forms View. Return to Design View.

7. Click the Text Box tool ab and click at the 1-inch mark in the Form Footer.

8. Delete the label and move the unbound control to the left edge.

9. Open the property sheet for the unbound control. Click the Data tab, the Control Source row, and the Build button.

10. Open the Common Expressions folder. Double-click Current Date/Time.

FIGURE 11-10
Adding a common
expression in the
Expression Builder

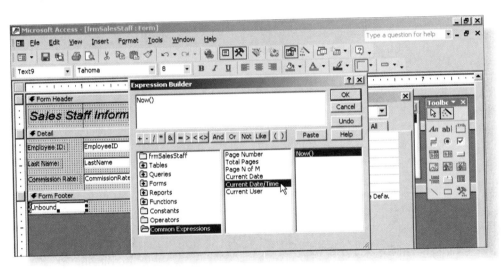

11. Click OK. Close the property sheet. View and save the form.

Refining the Appearance of a Form

Forms in a well-designed database should be consistent. The look and feel of each form should be similar to all other forms. When forms are consistent, the time it takes for data entry operators to learn how to use each form is greatly reduced.

EXERCISE 11-9 Modify Controls

A form is easy to use when the controls have been sized, colored, and arranged in a logical way. Keep the user in mind when you design a form. Design the form to increase the accuracy and efficiency of data entry.

1. With frmSalesStaff open in Design View, drag down the edge of the vertical ruler to select all the controls in the Detail section.

FIGURE 11-11
Selecting multiple controls horizontally

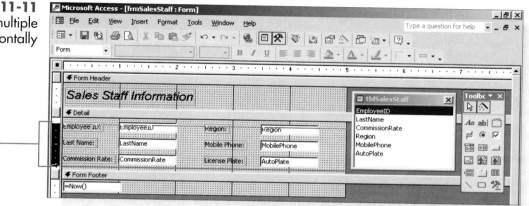

2. Change all the controls to 11-point Tahoma. Choose Format and then Size, to Fit. Deselect the controls.

REVIEW: The solid lines in the design layout grid are at 1-inch intervals.

3. Click on the horizontal ruler just above the EmployeeID, LastName, and CommissionRate text boxes.

4. Point at the label in the Form Header and press Shift + click to deselect the title.

5. Open the property sheet for the selected controls. Set the Left position at **1.35**. Press ↓ to accept the change. Leave the property sheet open.

6. Move the property sheet and the toolbox so you can see the Region, MobilePhone, and AutoPlate text boxes.

7. Click on the horizontal ruler just above the Region, MobilePhone, and AutoPlate text boxes. Set the Left position to **3.85**, press ↓, and leave the property sheet open. (See Figure 11-12 on the next page.)

8. Click somewhere in the form to deselect the text boxes. Select the first column of labels. Set the Left position at **.1** and the Font Size to **10**

FIGURE 11-12
Selecting a column
of text boxes

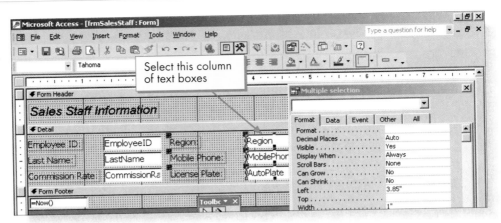

9. Click the **Font Weight** row in the property sheet and choose **Bold**. Double-click a sizing handle for one of the labels. Leave the property sheet open.

 NOTE: By default, the text boxes are the same width.

10. Set the **Left** position for the second column of labels at **2.75**. Make them bold, with a **Font Size** of 10. Close the property sheet.

11. Click the =Now() control in the **Form Footer**. Click the drop-down arrow for the Fill/Back Color button and choose **Transparent**. Set the **Special Effect** to **Flat**.

12. Select the first row of controls in the **Detail** section. Choose F**ormat**, **Align**, and **Top**.

13. Repeat these steps for the remaining two rows of controls.

14. View and save the form.

EXERCISE 11-10 Set and Copy Conditional Formatting

The active control in a form is where the insertion point is located. The active control is described as "having the *focus*." You can set conditional formats based on the control that has the focus.

1. With frmSalesStaff open in Form View, click in the first text box, EmployeeID. It now has the focus (indicated by a flashing I-bar).

 NOTE: You can set conditional formatting in Form View or Design View.

2. Choose F**ormat** and then **Con**ditional Formatting.

3. Click the drop-down arrow for Condition 1 and choose Field Has Focus.

4. Click the drop-down arrow for the Fill/Back Color button 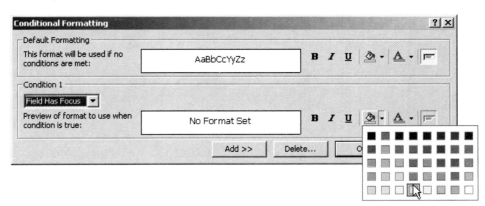 and choose a light color.

FIGURE 11-13
Setting a
conditional format

FIGURE 11-13

5. Click OK. Press [Tab] to move the insertion point through the first form and to the second form.

6. Return to Design View and click the EmployeeID text box to select it. You do not see the color in Design View.

 7. Double-click the Format Painter button to lock it on.

8. Click each of the remaining text boxes to copy the conditional formatting.

9. Click the Format Painter button to turn it off.

10. Return to Form View and press [Tab] to move through the fields. Set the Tab Order to move through the fields top-to-bottom, left-to-right.

REVIEW: Tab Order is listed in the <u>V</u>iew menu in Design View.

11. Save the form.

EXERCISE 11-11 **Insert an Image on a Form**

You can size an image in a report or form in three ways or modes. *Clip mode* shows the picture at the original size it was drawn or scanned. If the image is bigger than the frame, it is cut off. *Stretch mode* sizes the picture to fit the control and can distort the image by changing its proportions. *Zoom mode* sizes the image to fill the height or width of the control, without changing the proportions.

You can insert images in a form as design elements. This is different from using an OLE field in a form to show images that change with each record. An image might be used in the Form Header to show the company logo or slogan at the top of each form. Images might also be placed in the Form Footer to display at the bottom of the form. Access can use most popular graphics formats, such as JPG, TIF, and BMP.

 TIP: Your software must recognize the graphic format being used and be able to display it.

1. With frmSalesStaff open in Design View, make the **Form Footer** section about 1 inch high.

 2. Click the Image tool in the toolbox.

 NOTE: You need access to the Images folder to complete this exercise.

3. Click at the 3-inch mark in the **Form Footer**. The Insert Picture dialog box opens.

FIGURE 11-14
Insert Picture
dialog box

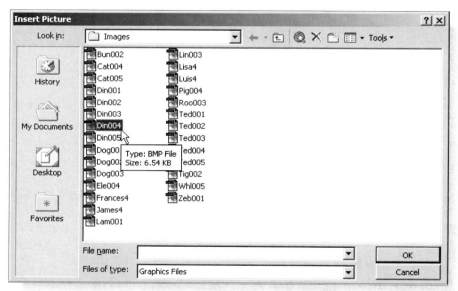

4. Find the Images folder and open it. Double-click **Din004.** The image is placed at a default size.

 5. Click the Properties button . Make the image **1.5** inches wide and **1** inch high.

6. Arrange the property sheet and the Toolbox so you can see the resized image control. The control is sized, but the picture is still at its default size.

7. Click the **Size Mode** row in the property sheet, and choose **Stretch**. This makes the picture fill the control. (See Figure 11-15 on the next page.)

FIGURE 11-15
Resized control

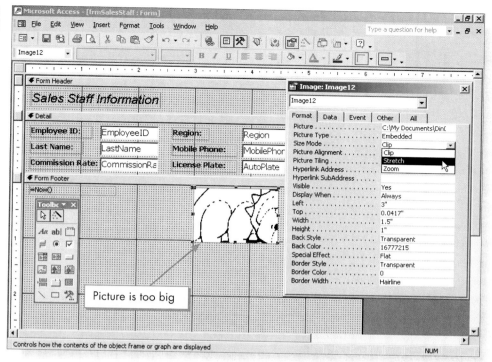

8. Choose **Zoom** as the **Size Mode**. This makes the picture fill either the width or the height of the control and sizes the other dimension proportionally.

9. Choose **Stretch** and close the property sheet.

10. Make the form 5 inches wide and show one row of dots below the picture.

11. View the form and return to Design View.

NOTE: The picture has a white background that cannot be changed in Access. You can change the background in graphic design software.

12. Size the date control so you see all the data. Align it left.

13. Open the form's property sheet and set the **Default View** to **Single Form**.

14. Click the **Form Header** bar. Click the down arrow for the Fill/Back Color button and choose **White**.

15. Click the **Detail** bar. Click the Fill/Back Color button .

REVIEW: If the face of a button shows the color you want, just click the button to apply that color.

16. Click the **Form Footer** bar and give it a white background color.

17. Save the form and enter these two records:

Employee ID:	**29**
Last Name:	**Gleason**
Commission Rate:	**7%**
Region:	**East**
Mobile Phone:	**847-555-6300**
License Plate:	**cc0004**

Employee ID:	**31**
Last Name:	**Alvarez**
Commission Rate:	**6%**
Region:	**West**

18. The validation rule is inherited in the form. Change West to **North** and complete the record.

Mobile Phone:	**212-555-0055**
License Plate:	**cc0005**

19. Close the form and save the design changes.

Creating a Report in Design View

Most often, database designers modify reports that were first created by using the Report Wizard. On occasion, just as with forms, it might be necessary to create a report from scratch.

EXERCISE 11-12 Create a Report in Design View

You have been using Design View to edit AutoReports and wizard reports. When you use Design View to create a report, the report opens with blank Detail and Page sections. You can then add fields from a query or table, open additional sections, and add other design elements.

1. Click the Tables button. Click tblSalesStaff to select it. Click the drop-down arrow for the New Object button 🖅 and select Report.

2. Choose Design View in the New Report dialog box. Click OK.

3. A blank report opens with empty Page Header/Footer and Detail sections. Maximize the window.

4. Size the Field List window to show all the fields.

5. Click the LastName field in the Field List window. Press Ctrl and click CommissionRate and then click Region to add them to the selection. Drag the fields to the 1-inch mark in the **Detail** section. Deselect the controls.

> **NOTE:** All new text boxes have an attached label. When you drag fields from the Field List, the location where you release the mouse marks the left edge of the text box, not the label.

6. Click on the horizontal ruler above the labels to select the column of labels. Press Delete.

FIGURE 11-16
Column of
labels selected

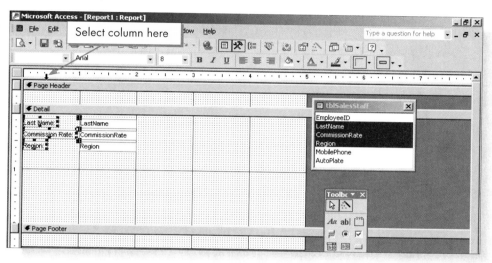

7. Click the Save button 🔲. Name the report **rptSalesCom** and click OK.

EXERCISE **11-13** **Format Controls**

You should format controls on a report to improve the usefulness of the report. Always keep the user in mind when designing a report. The report should be easy to read and provide enough detail to satisfy the requirements of the end user.

1. With rptSalesCom open in Design View, right-click the LastName text box and open its property sheet. Click the **Format** tab.

2. Set the **Left** position at **.1** Set the **Top** position at **.125**

3. Set the **Width** at **1** inch. Set the **Height** at **.1667** Do not close the property sheet.

4. Click the CommissionRate text box. The property sheet updates to the newly selected control.

5. Key the following settings for the CommissionRate control.

Left   **1.25**
Top   **.125**

Width	1
Height	.1667

6. Click the Region control and key these settings.

Left	2.5
Top	.125
Width	1
Height	.1667

7. Close the property sheet and change to Print Preview. In the Fit zoom size, you can see that there is too much space between records. Return to Design View.

8. Save your report.

EXERCISE 11-14 Size and Open Report Sections

Empty space below the controls in the **Detail** section appears as space between records. By adjusting the height of the **Detail** section, you adjust the vertical space between records.

1. With rptSalesCom open in Design View, place the pointer at the top edge of the **Page Footer** section bar. Drag up to show two rows of dots below the controls in the **Detail** section.

2. Choose <u>V</u>iew, and then choose Report <u>H</u>eader/Footer. Both sections open.

3. Make the **Report Header** about 1 inch tall.

FIGURE 11-17
Resized
Report Header

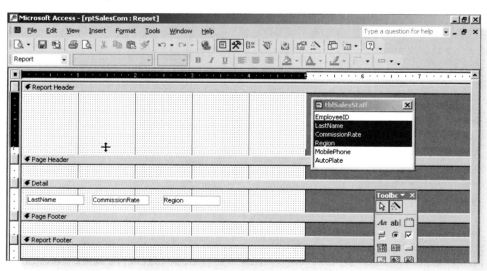

4. Save the report.

EXERCISE **11-15** Add, Copy, Paste, and Format Labels

You can enter and format one column title and then copy or edit it for the other labels. The main title in the **Report Header** will be formatted differently than the column titles.

1. With rptSalesCom open in Design View, click the Label button . Draw a label box in the **Report Header** that is about 3 inches wide and as tall as the **Report Header** section.

2. Key **Projected Commissions** and press Enter.

3. Format the label as 18-point Arial bold italic. Double-click a sizing handle in the label. If the label is more than one line, drag a handle to manually fit the label on one line.

4. Click the Label button and click in the **Page Header** above the LastName text box.

5. Key **Name** and press Enter. Format the label as 12-point Arial bold italic.

6. Double-click a sizing handle in the label to size it. The **Page Header** section expands to accommodate the label.

> **NOTE:** The Edit and Duplicate commands are the same as Copy and Paste.

7. Make sure the Name label is selected. Choose Edit, and then choose Duplicate. A copy is placed below the original.

8. Choose Edit, Duplicate again. Another copy is placed below the first one.

9. Drag one of the copied labels in position to be the title for the CommissionRate text box, aligned with the Name label.

10. Click in the label to display an I-beam, and delete Name. Key **Rate** and press Enter.

11. Drag the other copy to be the title for the Region text box. Replace the text in the copied label with **Territory**

12. Click on the vertical ruler to select this row of controls. Align these labels at the top.

13. Drag the **Detail** bar up until there are two rows of dots below the controls in the **Page Header** section. (See Figure 11-18 on the next page.)

14. Add a new label at the left edge of the **Page Footer**. Key *[your first and last name]* Format it as 11-point Times New Roman and size it.

15. Save the report.

FIGURE 11-18
Label added to
report

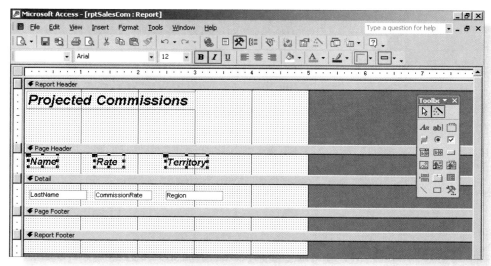

EXERCISE **11-16** Size and Align Controls

You should assume that many people will see and use your reports. Always take time to make these reports look professional by sizing and aligning all controls.

1. With rptSalesCom open in Design View, click the vertical ruler to select the text boxes in the Detail section. Change them to 12-point Times New Roman. Choose Format, Size, To Fit.

TIP: Text boxes can be autofit only for the height. You must check the width.

2. Make the CommissionRate Text box .**5** inches wide. It will be easier to align with its label.

3. Select the Rate label and the CommissionRate text box. Choose Format, Align, Right.

4. Drag the two controls until their right borders are near the 2.25-inch mark on the horizontal ruler. Click the Right Align button ▤.

NOTE: Using Format, Align, Right aligns the borders of the controls, but the Right Align button ▤ moves the content of the controls to the right.

5. Preview the report. Resize any controls that are not wide enough.

6. Size the Name label to fit the text. Align the Name label, the LastName text box, the main title, and your name on the left.

7. Drag the controls to show three columns of dots to the left of the controls.

8. Align the Territory label and the Region text box on the left. Drag them until the left edges are at the 2.75-inch mark.

9. Align the text boxes in the Detail section on the top.

10. View the report in Print Preview. Return to Design View and save the report.

EXERCISE 11-17 Key a Common Expression and Use a Custom Format

You have used common expressions in forms and reports. A common expression is a control that uses built-in commands to enter dates, times, and page numbers. You can key them in an unbound control when you know the expressions, or you can use the Expression Builder.

1. With rptSalesCom open in Design View, click the Text Box button ab. Click at the 4-inch mark in the Page Footer.

2. Select and delete the label.

 NOTE: If you accidentally draw a label instead of a text box, delete it and draw a text box.

3. Click in the unbound control to show a text insertion point.

4. Key **=now()** and press Enter.

FIGURE 11-19
Keying a common expression

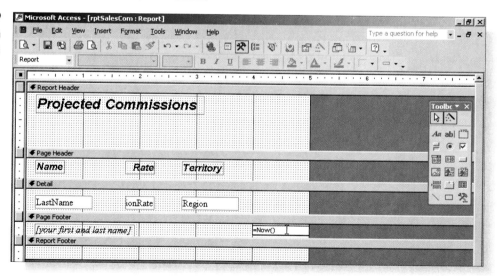

 TIP: Access has a Date() expression and a Now() expression. Both can be formatted to show the date or the time.

5. Preview the report in a Fit size. The date is formatted in a default size. Return to Design View.

6. Open the property sheet for the =Now() control.

TABLE 11-3 **Custom Formats**

SYMBOL	DESCRIPTION
:	Time separator
/	Date separator
d	Day of the month in one or two digits (1 to 31)
dd	Day of the month in two digits (01 to 31)
ddd	First three letters of the weekday (Sun to Sat)
dddd	Full name of the weekday (Sunday to Saturday)
w	Day of the week (1 to 7)
ww	Week of the year (1 to 53)
m	Month of the year in one or two digits (1 to 12)
mm	Month of the year in two digits (01 to 12)
mmm	First three letters of the month (Jan to Dec)
mmmm	Full name of the month (January to December)
q	Date displayed as quarter of the year (1 to 4)
y	Number of the day of the year (1 to 366)
yy	Last two digits of the year (01 to 99)
yyyy	Full year (0100 to 9999)
h	Hour in one or two digits (0 to 23)
hh	Hours in two digits (00 to 23)
n	Minute in one or two digits (0 to 59)
nn	Minute in two digits (00 to 59)
s	Second in one or two digits (0 to 59)
ss	Second in two digits (00 to 59)

continues

TABLE 11-3 Custom Formats *continued*

SYMBOL	DESCRIPTION
AM/PM	Twelve-hour clock with the uppercase letters "AM" or "PM"
am/pm	Twelve-hour clock with the lowercase letters "am" or "pm"

7. Click the Format tab and the Format row. Key **mmmm yyyy**

8. Click the Other tab. Change the Name of the control to **ReportDate** Close the property sheet.

 REVIEW: Use the Format Painter to copy a font from one control to another.

9. Match the font in the date control to the one in your name and size it. Align the controls in the Page Footer on the bottom.

10. Size the Report Header section to show two rows of dots below the label.

11. Preview and save the report.

EXERCISE **11-18** **Apply an AutoFormat with Options**

Because you have spent some time formatting your controls, you might want to apply only a portion of the design from an AutoFormat.

1. With rptSalesCom open in Design View, click the Report Selector button.

2. Click the AutoFormat button 🗐.

3. Choose Soft Gray and click Options.

FIGURE 11-20
Changing
AutoFormat options

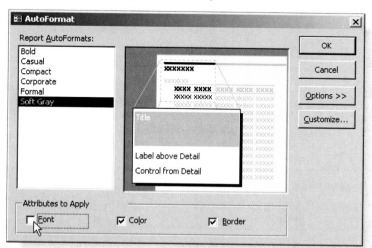

4. Deselect Font and click OK. The colors are used, but the font names and sizes are unchanged.

5. Click the label in the Report Header and make the text black.

6. Save the report.

EXERCISE 11-19 Adjust the Page Setup

Widths of reports vary greatly. Before printing, you often need to adjust the margins and center the controls.

1. With rptSalesCom open in Design View, drag the right edge of the report to the 6.5-inch mark. The colors for the Header and Footer sections expand, too.

2. Preview the report. In Print Preview, choose File, Page Setup.

3. Change the left and right margins to 2 inches. Click OK.

4. Click the Two Pages button. Although the report looks better in the center of the portrait page, it is too wide to fit.

5. Click the One Page button. Return to Design View.

6. Drag the date control until its right edge rests on the 4.5-inch mark.

7. Drag the right edge of the report to the 4.5-inch mark. With 2-inch margins on a portrait page, your report should be 4.5 inches wide to appear centered.

8. Click the label in the Report Header. Drag each middle sizing handle to make the label as wide as the report.

> **TIP:** If you make a control as wide as the report or form and center-align it, the data in the control will appear to be centered on the page.

FIGURE 11-21
Label as wide as report

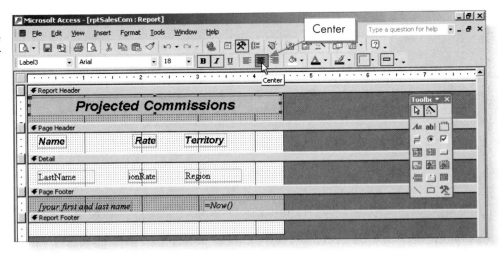

9. Click the Center button ▤.

10. Preview, save, and close the report.

Creating a Summary Report with Multiple Groups

As you know, you can use a group in a report to arrange records by a single field. You can also use more than one group. For example, you might group employees first by job code and then by city. Or you could group the stuffed animals first by product group and then by prices.

EXERCISE **Use Multiple Groups in the Report Wizard**

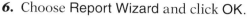

For each field you add to the Grouping and Sorting dialog box, you can display the Group Header and the Group Footer. You can also use the Grouping and Sorting dialog box to sort by a field without using it for grouping.

1. Create a new query in Design View for tblHistorySales and tblHistoryLineItems.

2. Size the grid and the Field Lists. Drag a join line between the common fields.

3. Add the CustomerID and OrderID fields from tblHistorySales to the grid. Add ProductID and Quantity from tblHistoryLineItems.

4. View the dynaset and save the query as **qrySalesHistory**

> **NOTE:** There is no sorting in the query.

5. From the dynaset, click the drop-down arrow for the New Object button 🗗 and choose <u>R</u>eport.

6. Choose Report Wizard and click OK.

7. Click the Add All button >> to select all fields. Click <u>N</u>ext.

8. Double-click CustomerID to make it the first group. Double-click OrderID to make it the second group. (See Figure 11-22 on the next page.)

> **NOTE:** If you choose the wrong field for grouping, select it in the preview area on the right and click the Remove One button < . You can also use the Priority buttons to rearrange the groups.

FIGURE 11-22
Using two groups
in the wizard

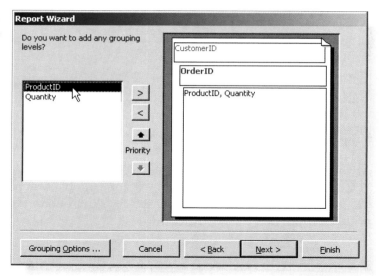

9. Click <u>N</u>ext. Sort by ProductID in ascending order. Click Summary <u>O</u>ptions.

 NOTE: Summary options are available only for Number fields.

FIGURE 11-23
Choosing
summary calculation

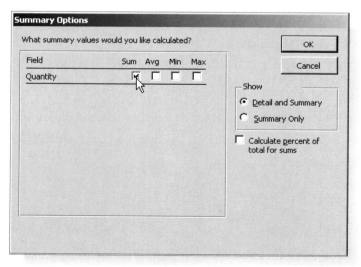

10. Click the Sum check box to sum the quantity. For the Show group, choose <u>D</u>etail and Summary. Click OK and click <u>N</u>ext.

11. Choose <u>O</u>utline 1 as the layout and choose Portrait. Click <u>N</u>ext.

12. Choose the Corporate style and click <u>N</u>ext.

13. Name the report **rptSalesHistory** and click <u>F</u>inish.

14. View several pages in Fit and 100% sizes. Return to Design View.

EXERCISE 11-21 Format the Group Headers

This report has two group headers and two group footers, for the CustomerID and OrderID fields. The OrderID group frames the Detail section. The CustomerID group frames the OrderID group.

FIGURE 11-24
Two groups in
Design View

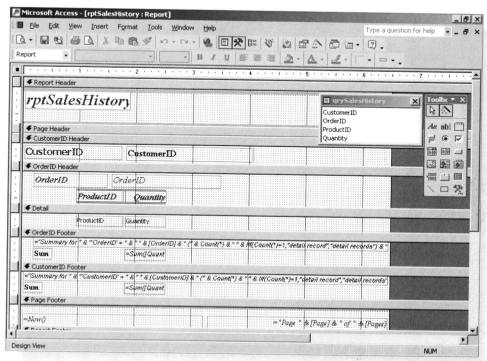

 REVIEW: Check the Object box in the Formatting toolbar to determine which control is the label and which is the text box.

1. With rptSalesHistory open in Design View, double-click a sizing handle for the CustomerID label in the CustomerID Header to size it to fit.

 REVIEW: All handles except the top left (move) handle act as sizing handles.

2. Size the CustomerID text box to be about 1 inch wide. Use the move handle to move it next to the label.

 3. Click the Align Left button ▤ to align the number within the box. (In Design View, the text alignment for a text box doesn't appear.)

4. Double-click a sizing handle for the OrderID label in the OrderID Header to size the label to fit. Do not move the label.

5. Size the OrderID text box to be about 1 inch wide. Move it next to the label.

6. Click the Align Left button ▤.

7. Preview the report.

EXERCISE **11-22** **Format the Group Footers**

Both group footers include a summary control that counts how many records are in that particular group. The OrderID footer shows how many products were ordered on each order. The CustomerID footer shows the total number of products bought by that customer.

1. In Print Preview for rptSalesHistory, find the summary section for Order ID 20015. Find the summary section for CustomerID 1.

FIGURE 11-25
Summary sections
for each group

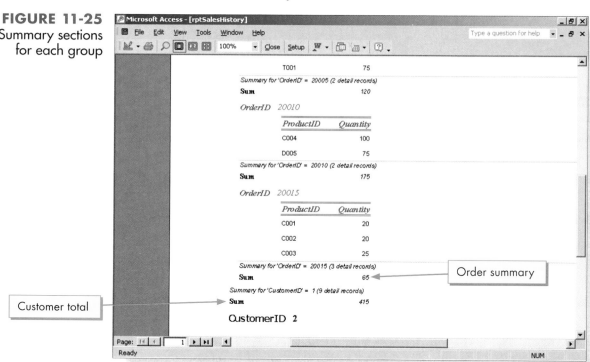

2. Click the Last Page button and look at the grand total in the Report Footer.

 NOTE: The Report Footer appears once at the end of the report.

3. Return to Design View.

4. In the OrderID Footer, delete the control ="Summary for"...

5. Move the Sum label in the OrderID Footer to align beneath the ProductID text box in the Detail section. Align these two controls on the left.

6. Move the =Sum calculated control to align beneath the Quantity text box. Align these controls on the right.

> **TIP:** You can use either the upward-pointing-finger or open-hand pointer to move these controls because they were added as separate objects by the wizard. You can also nudge them.

7. Size the OrderID Footer to show 3 rows of dots below the controls.

8. In the CustomerID Footer, delete the control that counts the detail records (="Summary for"...).

9. Move the Sum label in the CustomerID Footer to align beneath the Sum label in the OrderID Footer. Align these two controls on the left.

10. Edit this label to show **Total Purchases**

11. Move the calculated control to align beneath the calculated control in the OrderID Footer. Align the calculated controls on the right.

12. Size the CustomerID Footer to show one row of dots below the controls.

13. In the Report Footer, edit the label to show **Total Products Sold**. Align this control on the right with the label in the CustomerID Footer.

14. Select the calculated control in the Report Footer and open its property sheet.

15. Click the Format tab and change the Border Style to Transparent.

16. Save the report, preview it, and return to Design View.

Using Page Breaks in a Report

Access places a page break at the end of a printed page, based on the margins, paper size, and orientation in the Page Setup dialog box. You have control over page breaks through the properties for each section and through the grouping options. You can, for example, set a property to start a new page for each group. In the Grouping and Sorting dialog box, you can specify that a group be kept together on a page.

EXERCISE **11-23** **Use Page Break and Keep Together**

A likely location for a page break is as each new CustomerID starts. You would not want to place each OrderID on a separate page, although you might want to keep each OrderID together on a page.

1. In Design View for rptSalesHistory, double-click the CustomerID Header bar to open its property sheet.

2. Click the Format tab. Click the Force New Page row and display its drop-down list.

FIGURE 11-26
Forcing a new page
for each group

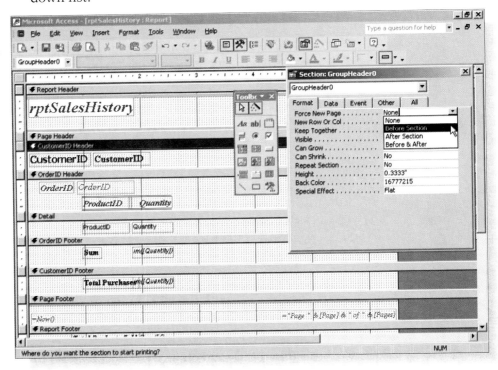

3. Choose Before Section. This forces a new page each time a new CustomerID is encountered. Close the property sheet.

4. Click the Sorting and Grouping button.

FIGURE 11-27
Setting the
Keep Together
property

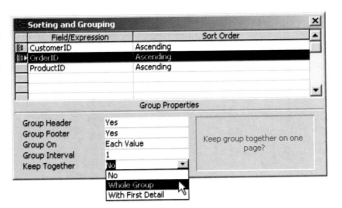

5. Click the OrderID row and set **Keep Together** to **Whole Group**. Close the dialog box.

6. Preview several pages of the report in a **Fit** size. Each Customer ID group is on a separate page and no OrderID is split between pages. The first group, however, does not start on page 1; it starts on page 2.

7. Return to Design View. Double-click the **Page Header** bar.

8. Click the **Format** tab. Set the **Height** at **.05** and close the property sheet.

9. Preview the report in a **Fit** size. The **Page Header** must have a height, no matter how small, for the **Force New Page** property to work properly.

10. Return to Design View and save the report.

EXERCISE **11-24** Create a Custom Page

You can use the **Force New Page** property in any section. When you force a page break after the **Report Header**, you create a blank title page as the first page of your report.

1. In Design View for rptSalesHistory, double-click the **Report Header** bar to open its property sheet. Click the **Format** tab.

2. Set the **Force New Page** row to **After Section**.

3. Set the section **Height** at **3** and close the property sheet.

4. Drag the title until its bottom edge rests on the 2-inch horizontal grid line.

5. Drag the left and right handles to make the label as wide as the report.

6. Click the Center button ▤. The title appears centered on the page because the control is as wide as the page.

7. Change the font size to **48**. Double-click a sizing handle. The control is resized to fit the text, but still appears centered.

8. Edit the title to **Sales History** (See Figure 11-28 on the next page.)

 TIP: You can create a custom page for the Report Footer to show a separate summary page.

9. Preview the report. Return to Design View and save it.

FIGURE 11-28
New title for
custom page

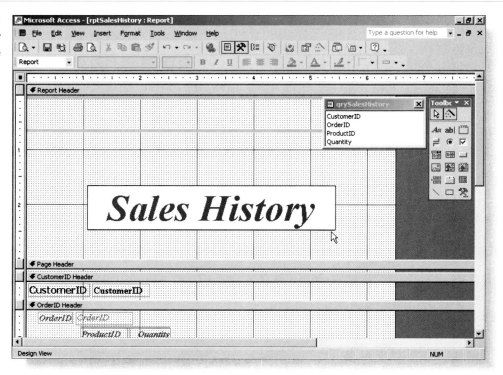

Adding Images to a Report

An OLE field in the table displays an image in a form or report in a bound object frame. This type of control changes from record to record. In many forms and reports, however, you use an image as a design element that does not change from record to record. A company logo is an example.

 NOTE: Images in a table substantially increase the size of a database.

As you have seen in your SalesStaff form, you can place an image as a separate control with a property sheet. This type of picture is a *foreground image*. A foreground image is one that appears exactly where you place it in the report or form.

 NOTE: You need access to the Images folder to complete the next exercise.

EXERCISE **11-25** **Add an Image Frame to the Report**

You can place a foreground picture in an image frame or an unbound object frame. You used an *image frame* earlier in this lesson. It is a control structure that allows the placement of an image on a report or form. It is best for pictures that are placed once and not changed.

If the picture is one that you will often need to edit in another application, such as Paint, you should use an *unbound object frame* to place the foreground picture. You can double-click this type of control and launch the application you will use for editing.

1. In Design View for rptSalesHistory, double-click the **Report Header** bar and make the section 5 inches high. Close the property sheet.

2. Click the Image button in the toolbox.

3. Position the pointer at the 3-inch horizontal grid line and the 3-inch vertical line. Click to open the Insert Picture dialog box.

> **REVIEW:** You can click to place any control at a default size; you do not need to drag to size it.

4. In the Images folder, click **Din002**.

5. Click OK. The image is added at a default size.

6. Double-click the image control to open the property sheet. It is identified in the title bar as an image control.

7. Click the Format tab. The default size mode is Clip to show the picture at its original size.

8. Set the Width of the image control to **2**

9. Click another row in the property sheet to write the change without closing the property sheet. The image control is resized, but the picture is not.

FIGURE 11-29
Image
property sheet

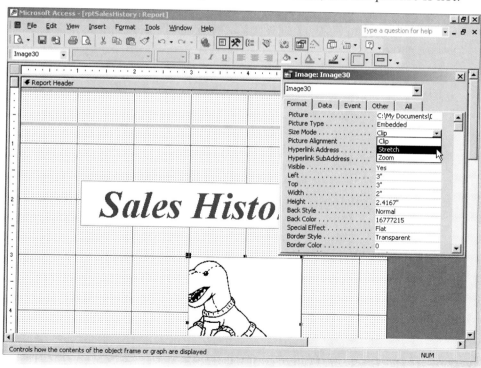

10. Choose **Stretch** as the **Size Mode**. The picture is sized to fit the control and is distorted.

11. Choose **Zoom** as the **Size Mode**. The picture is sized to the width of the control, but its original proportions are maintained.

12. Choose **Clip** as the **Size Mode** and close the property sheet.

13. Double-click a sizing handle to size the control to fit the picture.

14. Move the image to align its left edge at the 2.5-inch mark.

15. Preview the report in a **Fit** size. Return to Design View.

16. Save the report.

EXERCISE **11-26** **Add a Background Image to a Report**

A *background image* is like a watermark. It prints behind the data on each page of the report. It is set as a Report property.

1. In Design View for rptSalesHistory, click the image and press Delete.

2. Double-click the **Report Header** bar and make the section 3 inches high. Close the property sheet.

3. Double-click the **Report Selector** button. Click the **Format** tab.

FIGURE 11-30
Setting a
background image

4. Click the Picture row and the Build button . The Insert Picture dialog box opens.

5. In the Images folder, double-click **Din002.** The path and filename are shown on the Picture row, and the image appears on the design grid. Close the property sheet.

6. Preview several pages in a Fit size. The image is part of the background for each page.

 NOTE: You can use a background image in a form.

7. Return to Design View and double-click the Report Selector button.

8. Choose Stretch as the Picture Size Mode. The picture is sized to fit the page and is distorted. Do not close the property sheet.

9. Preview several pages again and return to Design View.

10. Choose Zoom as the Size Mode. The picture is sized to the width of the page, and its proportions are maintained.

 TIP: A background image is not a control. It is a property.

11. Close the property sheet.

12. Preview the report in a Fit size. Return to Design View.

EXERCISE 11-27 Save a Report with a Different Name

You can keep your first report unchanged and keep this version as a separate copy.

1. Choose File, Save As. The current report name is shown in the dialog box.

2. Click after the last character and key **2** to change the name to **rptSalesHistory2**

3. Click OK and close the report.

 TIP: You can also right-click a report name in the Database window and save it as another report.

4. Close the query if it is still open.

USING HELP

Access has a page-break tool. You can use it to insert a break wherever you want.

1. With *[your initials]*CC-11 open, press F1 to start Help. Click the Contents tab. If the Office Assistant starts, turn it off and try again.

2. Expand the Reports and Report Snapshots folder. Expand the Customizing Reports folder. Expand the Page Breaks and Page Numbers topic.

3. Click the topic Add a page break to a report. Read the Help window.

4. In the right pane, click Add a page break by using the page break control.

FIGURE 11-31
Microsoft Access
Help

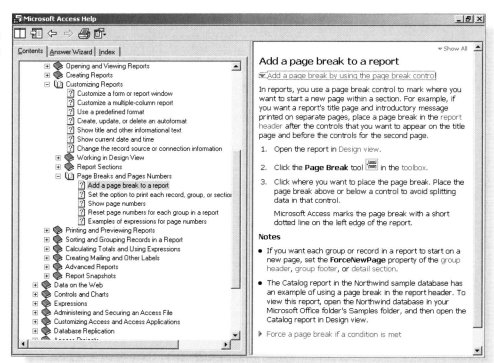

5. Read and close the Help window.

LESSON Summary

➤ Add field names, sizes, and properties in Design View to build a table from scratch.

➤ Use a validation rule in a table to manage what data can be entered in a field. You can key your own validation message or use the default.

➤ When you build a form or report in Design View, drag fields from the Field List to where you want them on the grid. Modify labels and text boxes by selecting the control and opening the property sheet.

➤ You can apply most format settings for a control on the Formatting toolbar or from the property sheet.

➤ Conditional formatting is applied when the control meets the criteria you set. You can apply conditional formatting in a form or a report.

➤ A form or a report can display an image that prints once in a certain location. These images are controls that can be sized and positioned.

➤ Forms and reports have a property that allows an image to appear as a water-mark, or background, on each page or form.

➤ Common expressions show the date, page number, or time. You place them by using a Text Box control.

➤ A report can have multiple groups that show summaries. Each group has its own header and footer section.

➤ Each section on a report has a **Force New Page** property to control where a new page starts. You can also keep groups together on a page.

LESSON 11   Command Summary

FEATURE	BUTTON	MENU	KEYBOARD	SPEECH
Insert Image		Insert, Picture		✓
Select Form		Edit, Select Form	Ctrl + R	✓
Select Report		Edit, Select Report	Ctrl + R	✓
Save As		File, Save As	F12	✓
Duplicate		Edit, Duplicate		✓
Build				
Conditional Formatting		Format, Conditional Formatting		✓
Field List		View, Field List		✓
Keep Together		View, Sorting and Grouping		✓

Concepts Review

Each of the following statements is either true or false. Indicate your choice by circling T or F.

T F   **1.** A validation rule does not allow you to enter text in a Number field.

T F   **2.** The Field Builder adds captions and input masks, depending on which field you choose.

T F   **3.** You can group by more than one field in a report.

T F   **4.** You can use a page break in the **Page Header** to print each group on a separate page.

T F   **5.** You cannot set conditional formats based on the control that has the focus.

T F   **6.** A summary report can show details as well as sums, averages, or other calculations.

T F   **7.** A background image appears in an unbound object frame.

T F   **8.** An AutoFormat will not overwrite formatting you have already applied.

Write the correct answer in the space provided.

1. Name three sections that appear in both forms and reports.

_____

2. Which field cannot be left empty (null) in a table?

_____

3. What input mask symbol requires that you enter a letter?

_____

4. What should you do if there is no Field List in Design View for a form?

_____

5. Name two ways to control where or how a group or section ends on the page.

_____

6. How would you keep two slightly different versions of a report on disk?

_____

7. How do you add a background image to a form or report?

_____

8. Where does Align Left set text alignment?

_____

CRITICAL THINKING

Answer these questions on a separate page. There are no right or wrong answers. Support your answers with examples from your own experience, if possible.

    1. Designing a professional, good-looking report or form can be tedious. Explain how creating and saving a weekly report can increase your productivity.

    2. An image has three size modes: Clip, Stretch, and Zoom. In what situation would Clip be best? What about Stretch and Zoom? When might Stretch be a poor choice?

Skills Review

EXERCISE 11-28

Create a table in Design View. Add a validation rule and text. Add a custom format.

    1. Create a table in Design View by following these steps:

        a. In the Tables window in *[your initial]*CC-11, click New. Select Design View and click OK.

        b. Key **AssetID** as the first field name. Press Tab.

        c. Choose Text as the Data Type. Press Tab.

        d. Key **Asset ID #** in the Description column.

        e. Make the field 10 spaces wide. For the Format, enter > to force uppercase. As an Input Mask, key **LL000**. Key the Caption **Asset ID**

        f. Press F6 and Tab.

        g. In the second Field Name row, click the Build button . Choose Assets as the sample table. Double-click DateAcquired as the field.

        TIP: The Assets sample table is in the Business group.

h. Click in the Field Name column for the third row and click the Build button . Choose Assets as the sample table. Double-click EmployeeID.

> **NOTE:** The EmployeeID field is the same data type and size as EmployeeID in tblEmployees.

i. Use the Field Builder in the fourth row to choose AssetDescription from the Assets table.

j. Change the field name to **AssetName**. Make the field 50 spaces wide and change the Caption to **Asset Name**

k. Click in the AssetID row in the top pane and click the Primary Key button .

l. Click the Save button 🖫 and key **tblAssets** as the table name. Click OK.

2. Add a validation rule and validation text by following these steps:

   a. Click the EmployeeID row in the top pane.

   b. Click its Validation Rule row in the lower pane. Key **<35** as the rule.

   c. Click the Validation Text row. Key **The Employee ID must be below 35.** (Include the period.)

   d. Change to Datasheet View and click Yes to save the table.

   e. Size the columns to show the captions for each column, if they are not shown.

   f. Return to Design View.

   g. Click the DateAcquired row in the top pane.

   h. Click its Format row in the lower pane.

   i. Key **mmmm d, yyyy** to spell out the month and show one or two digits for the date, a comma, and four digits for the year.

   j. Change to Datasheet View and click Yes to save the table.

3. Check the Validation Rule by following these steps:

   a. Add these records, one with an error.

Asset ID:	**cp303**
Date Acquired:	**1/1/02**
Employee ID:	**30**
Asset Name:	**Color copier**
Asset ID:	**lp201**
Date Acquired:	**1/1/02**
Employee ID:	**40**

   b. Click OK in the message box and change the Employee ID to **24**

Asset Name:	**Laser printer**

   c. Size the columns to show the data. Close and save the table.

EXERCISE 11-29

Create a form in Design View. Modify controls. Add a label and a common expression. Add an image.

1. Create a form in Design View by following these steps:
   a. Click tblAssets and click the drop-down arrow for New Object. Choose F̲orm.
   b. Choose Design View. Click OK. Maximize the window.
   c. Select the AssetID field in the Field List window. Drag it to the 1-inch mark, two rows of dots down.
   d. Repeat these steps to place the AssetName field at the 1-inch mark, two rows of dots below the AssetID controls.
   e. Select DateAcquired in the Field List window. Drag it to the 3.5-inch mark, two rows of dots down, aligned vertically with the AssetID controls.
   f. Repeat these steps to place EmployeeID below DateAcquired.
   g. Click the Save button . Name the form **frmAssets**

2. Modify controls by following these steps:
   a. Point at the vertical ruler, near the top control in the Detail section. Drag down to select all the controls.
   b. Set the controls to 11-point Arial. Choose F̲ormat, S̲ize, To F̲it.
   c. Deselect the controls and use the horizontal ruler to select the AssetID and AssetName text boxes.
   d. Open the property sheet for the two controls and set the Left position at **1** and the Width at **1.5**
   e. Select the DateAcquired and EmployeeID text boxes. Set their Left positions at **3.75** and the Width at **1.5**. Close the property sheet.
   f. Use the vertical ruler to select the AssetID and DateAcquired controls. Align them at the top.
   g. Do the same for the other two controls.
   h. Select all the controls and increase the Vertical Spacing two times.

   REVIEW: Vertical Spacing is in the F̲ormat menu.

   i. Show three rows of dots below the controls. Save the form.

3. Add a label and a common expression by following these steps:
   a. Choose V̲iew, Form Header/Footer.
   b. Select the Label tool . Click at the left edge of the Form Header.
   c. Key **Asset List** and make it 18-point Arial bold italic. Adjust the size.
   d. Select the Text Box tool . Click at the 4-inch mark in the Form Footer.
   e. Delete the label and open the property sheet for the unbound control.
   f. Click the Data tab, the Control Source row, and the Build button .

    g. Open the Common Expressions folder and double-click Current Date/ Time. Click OK.

    h. Set the format to **mmmm yyyy** and close the property sheet. View the form.

    i. In Design View, size the date control. Align it at the right edge of the form. Set Special Effect to Flat. Save the form.

4. Insert an image by following these steps:

NOTE: You need access to the Images folder to complete this exercise.

    a. Make the Form Header section about 1 inch high.

    b. Click the Image tool . Click at the 3-inch mark in the Form Header. Find the Images folder and double-click Dog003.

    c. Click the Properties button . Make the image **1.75** inches wide and **1.5** inches high.

    d. Click the Size Mode row and choose Stretch. Close the property sheet.

    e. Show one row of dots below the picture. View the form and return to Design View.

    f. Select the four text boxes and the date control. Click the Fill/Back Color arrow and choose Transparent.

    g. Save the form and enter these two records:

REVIEW: Click the New Record button ▶* before starting a new record.

Asset ID:	**dc307**
Asset Name:	**Digital camera**
Date Acquired:	**5/1/02**
Employee ID:	**28**
Asset ID:	**cd701**
Asset Name:	**Read/Write CD drive**
Date Acquired:	**7/1/02**
Employee ID:	**52**

REVIEW: The Validation Rule is inherited in the form.

    h. Click OK in the message box and change the Employee ID to **8**

    i. Print only Employee number 8 and then close the form.

    j. Compact the database.

EXERCISE 11-30

Create a report based on a query in Design View. Add and modify controls. Print the report as multiple columns.

1. Create a report in Design View by following these steps:

   a. Make a copy of **CC-E-11** and rename it *[your initials]***CC-E-11**

   b. Open *[your initials]***CC-11**. Refresh all linked tables.

   c. Create a query in Design View for tblEmployees and tblEmployeeDates. Make sure there is a join line.

   d. Add FirstName, LastName, and BirthDate to the design grid.

   e. Format the BirthDate field as **mmmm dd, yyyy**

   f. View the dynaset and widen the columns to see the data.

   g. Save the query as **qryEmpDates**

   h. From the dynaset, click the drop-down arrow for New Object and choose Report.

   i. Choose Design View and click OK. Maximize the window.

   j. Double-click the Field List window title bar. Drag all the fields to the 1-inch mark.

   k. Save the report as **rptEmpDates**

2. Add and modify controls by following these steps:

   a. In Design View for rptEmpDates, double-click the Detail bar and make the section **1.1** inches high. Close the property sheet.

   b. Place the pointer on the vertical ruler and drag to select the controls in the Detail section.

   c. Press Ctrl + ↓ seven times to nudge the controls lower in the section. View the report and return to Design View.

   d. Use the horizontal ruler to select the text boxes (not the labels).

    REVIEW: The property sheet for multiple controls shows Multiple selection in its title bar.

   e. Click the Properties button 🗐.

   f. Click the Format tab and the Text Align row. Choose Left.

   g. Set the Width of the multiple controls to **1.5**. Close the property sheet. Deselect the controls.

   h. Click the Label tool [Aa] and click at the left edge of the Page Header.

   i. Key **Employee Birthdays** and format the label as 14-point Arial bold italic. Adjust the size. Align the label with the labels in the Detail section.

   j. Select all the controls in the Detail section and make them 11-point Arial. Size them to fit, and increase the vertical spacing.

3. Print the report as multiple columns by following these steps:

   a. Preview the report. While in Print Preview, choose File, Page Setup.

   b. Click the Columns tab. Set two columns, each three inches wide. Click OK.

    c. Add a label with your name in the Page Footer.

    d. Save and print the report.

    e. Close the report and the query.

EXERCISE 11-31

Use multiple groups in a report. Insert page breaks. Add an image to the report.

1. Create a summary report with multiple groups by following these steps:

    a. Click the Queries button and right-click qryInventoryByAnimal. Choose Save <u>A</u>s and name the copy **qryInvCount**

    b. Open qryInvCount in Design View.

    c. Double-click ListPrice. View the dynaset. Save and close the query.

    d. Using qryInvCount, click the drop-down arrow for New Object and choose <u>R</u>eport. Choose Report Wizard and click OK.

    e. Click the Add All button <u>>></u> and click <u>N</u>ext.

    f. Double-click ProductGroup as the first grouping level. Double-click List-Price as the second level. Click <u>N</u>ext.

    g. Sort by ProductName. Click Summary <u>O</u>ptions.

    h. Click the Sum check box. For the Show group, choose <u>D</u>etail and Summary. Click OK and click <u>N</u>ext.

    i. Choose <u>A</u>lign Left 1 as the layout and choose <u>P</u>ortrait. Click <u>N</u>ext.

    j. Choose Formal as the style and click <u>N</u>ext.

    k. Name the report **rptInvCount** and click <u>F</u>inish.

    l. Maximize the window and use a Fit size.

    m. Look at the groups and summaries on the report.

2. Modify controls by following these steps:

    a. Return to Design View. Change the main title to **Totals by Group and Price**

    b. In the ListPrice Header, double-click the ListPrice text box.

    TIP: When Decimal Places is set at 0, the amounts are rounded to the nearest dollar.

    c. Click the Format tab and set Decimal Places to **2**. Close the property sheet.

    d. Point at the vertical ruler, just below the ListPrice controls. When the pointer is a black arrow, drag down to select the horizontal lines, the Animal Name and Current Inventory labels in the ListPrice Header, and the controls in the Detail section.

    e. Drag the selected controls until the right edges align on the **4**-inch mark. If you miss a control or line, drag it separately into position.

    f. In the ListPrice Footer, select and delete the control that sums and counts the ListPrice.

g. Drag the calculated control for QuantityOnHand in the ListPrice Footer to align on the right with the QuantityOnHand text box in the Detail section.

h. Change the label in the ListPrice Footer to show **Total Count at This Price**. Move the label to align on the left with the ProductName text box in the Detail section.

i. Select the control that sums and counts the ProductGroup in the ProductGroup Footer. Set it to bold and Text, Right Align.

  REVIEW: You can click the Align Right button ▤ or open the property sheet to set Text Align, Right.

j. Drag the right middle handle until this control ends at the same position as the controls above it.

k. Drag the calculated control for QuantityOnHand in the ProductGroup Footer to align on the right with the QuantityOnHand text box in the Detail section.

l. Change the label in the ProductGroup Footer to show **Total Count in This Group**. Move the label to align on the left with the ProductName text box in the Detail section.

m. Point just below the ListPrice Footer bar and click to select the horizontal line. Press Delete .

 TIP: Check the Object box in the Formatting toolbar to verify that the line is selected.

n. Align the controls in the Report Footer with those in the group footers.

o. Save the report and preview it. Look at the end of a price group and product group to see the calculations.

3. Insert page breaks by following these steps:

a. Return to Design View.

b. Double-click the ProductGroup Header bar and click the Format tab.

c. Set the Force New Page property to Before Section.

d. Drag the top of the ProductGroup Header bar as little as possible to open the Page Header. Show a minimum of white space in the Page Header.

e. Preview the report.

f. Delete the date control in the Page Footer and add your name in a label. Insert spaces in any labels that do not show a space between words.

g. Print pages for Groups C and D. Save and close the report.

4. Add an image to a report by following these steps:

a. Open rptSalesCampaigns. View the report in Fit and 100% sizes. Return to Design View.

b. Double-click the Report Footer bar and make it 1.75 inches high. Close the property sheet.

c. Click the Image button  in the Toolbox.

d. Position the pointer at the gridline 1 inch from the left in the **Report Footer** about two rows of dots down and click.

e. Find the appropriate folder and double-click any one of the images.

f. Double-click the image control to open the property sheet.

g. Click the **Format** tab. Set the **Width** and **Height** of the image to **1.5**

h. Choose **Zoom** as the **Size Mode** and close the property sheet.

i. Click the Image button in the Toolbox and position the pointer at the 5-inch horizontal grid line, aligned at the top with your existing image.

j. Find the appropriate folder and double-click a different image.

k. Double-click the image and set the **Width** and **Height** to **1.5**

l. Choose **Zoom** as the **Size Mode** and close the property sheet.

m. Preview the report in a **Fit** size. Return to Design View. Move the images so they appear balanced and centered on the page.

n. Reduce the size of the Report Footer so two rows of dots appear below the image.

o. Add your name in the **Report Header**.

p. Print, save, and close the report.

Lesson Applications

EXERCISE 11-32

Create a table in Design View. Use a custom format, an input mask, and a validation rule.

 NOTE: To complete this exercise as directed, you need to have completed tblAssets in Skills Review Exercises 11-28 and 11-29.

1. With *[your initials]*CC-11 open, create a new table named **tblServiceRecords** in Design View.

 TIP: There is a sample table in the Field Builder for Service Records.

2. Add the following fields, with the data types and field properties shown:

Field Name	Data Type	Field Size	Properties
ServiceRecordID	Number	Long Integer	Primary Key Caption: Service Call # No Default Value
AssetID	LookupWizard Text *(Look up the AssetID field in the tblAssets)*	10	Format: > Input Mask: LL000 Caption: Asset ID Required: Yes
ServiceDate	Date/Time		Format: Short Date Input Mask: 99/99/00 Caption: Service Date
EmployeeID	Number	Long Integer	Caption: Employee ID
ProblemDescription	Memo		Caption: Description
EstimatedCost	Currency		Caption: Estimated Cost
			Validation Rule: <250 Validation Text: See your supervisor if the estimated cost is more than $250.

NOTE: The AssetID field is a foreign key in this table; it is the primary key in tblAssets. It is good practice to set the Required property to Yes for foreign keys.

3. Add the following records. Use the drop-down list to choose the Asset ID. Test your Validation Rule in the second record by first keying **300** Correct the entry to **225**

Service Call #:	**12**
Asset ID:	**dc307**
Service Date:	**08/01/02**
Employee ID:	**28**
Description:	**Not taking pictures**
Estimated Cost:	**225**

REVIEW: Press Shift + F2 to open the Zoom window for the Memo field.

Service Call #:	**13**
Asset ID:	**cd701**
Service Date:	**12/02/02**
Employee ID:	**8**
Description:	*[your last name]* **cannot write to drive**
Estimated Cost:	**300**

4. Size the fields to show all the data, including the Memo field. Print the table in landscape orientation. You can identify your copy by your name in the Description field in the second record.

EXERCISE 11-33

Create a form in Design View. Modify sections and controls.

1. Create a new form for tblServiceRecords in Design View.

NOTE: To complete this exercise as directed, you need to have completed Exercise 11-32.

2. Double-click the Field List title bar and drag all the fields into the Detail section. While the controls are all selected, make them 10 points and double-click any sizing handle. Repeat for the labels.

3. Set control properties as shown on the next page.

Service Call # label	Left	.2
	Top	.2
	Width	1.0
	Height	.2
ServiceRecordID text box	Left	1.2
	Top	.2
	Width	1.0
	Height	.2
Service Date label	Left	2.375
	Top	.2
	Width	1.0
	Height	.2
ServiceDate text box	Left	3.5
	Top	.2
	Width	1.0
	Height	.2
Asset ID label	Left	.2
	Top	.55
	Width	1.0
	Height	.2
AssetID text box	Left	1.2
	Top	.55
	Width	1.0
	Height	.2
Employee ID label	Left	2.375
	Top	.55
	Width	1.0
	Height	.2

continues

continued

EmployeeID text box	Left	3.5
	Top	.55
	Width	1.0
	Height	.2
Description label	Left	.2
	Top	.9
	Width	1.0
	Height	.2
ProblemDescription text box	Left	1.2
	Top	.9
	Width	3.3
	Height	.5
Estimated Cost label	Left	.2
	Top	1.55
	Width	1.0
	Height	.2
EstimatedCost text box	Left	1.2
	Top	1.55
	Width	1.0
	Height	.2

4. Preview the form and save it as **frmServiceRecords**

5. Add a label in the Form Header and key **Service Records**. Make it 16-point bold italic. Align it left with the first column of labels in the Detail section.

6. Add your name in a label in the form's Page Footer.

NOTE: You do not see a form's Page Footer in Form View. You see it in Print Preview and on the printed page.

7. Save the form and add these two records.

Service Call #:	14
Asset ID:	cp303
Service Date:	08/03/02
Employee ID:	30
Description:	**Color toner needs replacement**
Estimated Cost:	200

Service Call #:	15
Asset ID:	lp201
Service Date:	09/15/02
Employee ID:	24
Description:	**Add the PostScript software**
Estimated Cost:	300

8. The Validation Rule is inherited in the form. Change the cost to **235**

9. Close the Page Header and the Form Footer.

10. Preview and print the forms. Save and close the form.

EXERCISE 11-34

Create a report in Design View. Add an image to a report.

 NOTE: To complete this exercise as directed, you need to have completed tblAssets (Exercises 11-28 and 11-29) and tblServiceRecords (Exercises 11-33 and 11-34).

1. Create a query for tblAssets, tblServiceRecords, and tblEmployees. There should be a join line on the AssetID field. Drag a join line on EmployeeID.

2. From tblAssets, add AssetName to the design grid. From tblServiceRecords, add ServiceDate and ProblemDescription. From tblEmployees, add LastName. View the dynaset. Save the query as **qryServiceCards**

3. Create a report in Design View for qryServiceCards. Make the report 5 inches wide. Close all the sections except the Detail section. Make the Detail section 3 inches high.

 NOTE: You are formatting this report as if it were being printed on index cards that are 5 inches wide and 3 inches high.

4. Drag all the fields from the Field List to the Detail section.

5. Make all the text in the text boxes and labels 10 points and make all the labels bold.

6. Move, size, and align the controls attractively (again remembering that you are formatting the report as if it were being printed on 5 x 3-inch index cards). Left-align the ServiceDate text box.

7. Sort the cards by ServiceDate.

8. Save the report as **rptServiceCards**

9. Add the image **Dog001** in the lower right corner of the card. Size and position the image, keeping in mind that the card must be 5 inches wide by 3 inches high.

10. Preview the report in a Fit size. Use a Two Pages view and check for blank or tiled pages. Return to Design View.

11. In Print Preview, set the cards to print in landscape orientation with two columns. Adjust the margins and column spacing to fit two columns of cards on a page.

12. Print, save, and close the report.

EXERCISE 11-35 *Challenge Yourself*

Create a report with multiple groups. Modify controls and sections.

1. Create a query for tblStuffedAnimals with the ProductID, ProductName, ListPrice, and ProductGroup fields. Show only the records from Product Groups C, D, or E. Save the query as **qryPromo**

2. Use the Report Wizard to build a report for qryPromo with all the fields. Group first by ProductGroup and second by ListPrice. Sort by Product-Name. Choose a layout and style and name the report **rptPromo**

3. In Design View, delete everything in the Page Header. If the section remains open, close it.

 TIP: There might be horizontal design lines in the Page Header that need to be deleted.

4. In the ProductGroup Header, size the ProductGroup text box to be about 1 inch wide.

5. In the ListPrice Header, size the ListPrice text box to be about .75 inch wide and move the text box to the 1-inch mark. Format it to match the text box in the ProductGroup Header and to show two decimal places.

6. Move the controls in the Detail section to start at the 2-inch mark. Make the text boxes 12-point Times New Roman. Size and position them as necessary.

7. Make all other necessary changes to make the report look professional.

8. Edit the main title to **Promotional Items**. Add your name in a label in the Report Header. Print the report.

9. Compact your database and exit Access.

On Your Own

In these exercises you work on your own, as you would in a real-life work environment. Use the skills you've learned to accomplish the task—and be creative.

EXERCISE 11-36

Review the design of the database you modified in Exercises 10-26. Print the structure of your tables. Review the data stored in the tables. On the printout, note any optimization changes you should make to field data types and sizes. Identify at least two different input masks and two different validation rules that will enhance your database design. Modify your tables appropriately. Reprint the table structures. On each sheet of paper, write your name and "Exercise 11-36." Continue to the next exercise.

EXERCISE 11-37

Add an image field to one of your tables. Locate and insert at least two images. On a sheet of paper, sketch a form for the table that contains the image field. On separate sheets of paper, sketch two additional forms for your queries or other tables. For each form, include an appropriate header and include your name in the footer. Create the forms. Make certain they are consistent in their appearance. Print a copy of each form. On each sketch and printout, write your name and "Exercise 11-37." Continue to the next exercise.

EXERCISE 11-38

On separate sheets of paper, design two grouped reports and one summary report. Identify the fields, their table source, and any sort order you will apply. On each sketch, write your name and "Exercise 11-38." Create the reports. Include your name and "Exercise 11-38" in the header of each report. If your tables don't have records, add data to your tables to make your reports more meaningful. Submit the sketches and printouts from Exercise 11-36 through 11-38 to your instructor. Keep a copy of this database. It will be used in subsequent lessons.

12

Working with Subreports

OBJECTIVES

MOUS
ACTIVITIES
In this lesson:
Ac2002e **4-1**
Ac2002e **4-2**
Ac2002e **4-3**
Ac2002e **5-1**

See Appendix E.

After completing this lesson, you will be able to:

1. **Build main and subreport queries.**
2. **Create a main report.**
3. **Add text expressions to a report.**
4. **Create a subreport.**
5. **Add a subreport to a main report.**
6. **Edit a subreport.**
7. **Add calculations to a main report.**
8. **Create a subreport by using the wizard.**

 Estimated time: 2 hours

Y ou have seen how to use several tables in a query as the basis for a report. Another approach to combining data from multiple tables is to use a report within a report. For example, you could prepare a report with basic information about each stuffed animal, using fields from tblStuffedAnimals and tblKitContents. Each record could be printed on a separate page. This would be the main report, based on a query using the two tables. A *main report* is a report that acts as a container or holder for other reports.

As a separate section on each page of this report, you could include the supplier's name and address from tblKitSuppliers. The supplier's information would change on each page, depending on the Kit Number. This separate section is a subreport. A *subreport* is a report often based on its own query that is inserted into another report. When you insert the subreport into the main report, it appears as an object you can select and edit.

Creating Queries for Main and Subreports

The Carolina Critters sales invoice is a report because it is printed. Because it is an invoice, each record prints on a separate page so you can mail an invoice to each customer with only that customer's data.

The top section of an invoice usually includes the customer's name and address as well as general information about the order. Most invoices have a separate section that lists each item ordered, the extended price, discounts, and other details. As you show each customer in the top section of an invoice, the detail section should show that customer's order information. Main and subreports generally use a One-to-Many relationship, so there is one order with many items per order.

Your first step is to create a query to show basic sales order information using tblCustomers and tblSalesOrders. This query will be the basis for the main report.

EXERCISE 12-1 Establish Relationships

Your first step toward creating customer invoices is to create a relationship to show basic sales order information using tblCustomers, tblSalesOrders, and tblSalesOrderLineItems. These relationships will be the basis for the dynasets needed by the main report and subreport.

1. Copy the file **CC-12** from your student disk and name it *[your initials]* **CC-12**. Copy **CC-E-12** and name it *[your initials]***CC-E-12**. Open *[your initials]***CC-12** and refresh the linked tables from *[your initials]***CC-E-12**.

2. Click the Relationships button . If any tables are displayed, clear the layout.

3. Click the Show Table button .

4. Double-click tblCustomers, tblSalesOrders, tblSalesOrderLineItems, and tblStuffedAnimals. Close the dialog box.

5. Size the Field Lists to see all the field names.

6. Drag the CustomerID field from tblCustomers to the CustomerID field in tblSalesOrders. The relationship is identified as One-to-Many because CustomerID is the primary key in tblCustomers and a foreign key in tblSalesOrders.

7. Click <u>C</u>reate. The join line shows the relationship, with no referential integrity.

NOTE: There are multiple primary keys in tblSalesOrderLineItems, but OrderID or ProductID, by itself, is a foreign key.

8. Drag the OrderID field from tblSalesOrders to the OrderID field in tblSalesOrderLineItems. The relationship is One-to-Many because OrderID is the primary key in tblSalesOrders and a foreign key in tblSalesOrderLineItems.

9. Click <u>C</u>reate.

10. Drag the ProductID field from tblStuffedAnimals to the ProductID field in tblSalesOrderLineItems. The relationship is One-to-Many because ProductID is the primary key in tblStuffedAnimals and a foreign key in tblSalesOrderLineItems.

 NOTE: The primary table can be on the left or the right in the Relationships window.

11. Click <u>C</u>reate.

FIGURE 12-1
Relationships for the
Sales Invoice

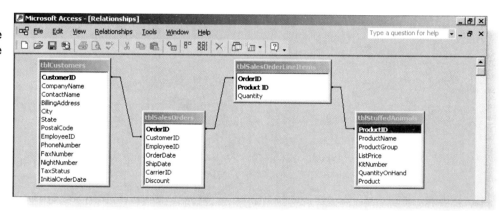

12. Close the Relationships window and save the layout.

EXERCISE 12-2 Create a Query for the Main Report

Now that the relationship has been created, you need to generate the dynaset the main report will be based on.

1. Click the Queries button and <u>N</u>ew. Choose Simple Query Wizard and click OK.

2. From the Tables/Queries drop-down list, select Table:tblSalesOrders.

3. Double-click each of the following fields: OrderID, CustomerID, OrderDate, ShipDate, and Discount.

4. From the Tables/Queries drop-down list, select Table:tblCustomers.

5. Double-click each of the following fields: CompanyName, BillingAddress, City, State, and PostalCode. Click Next.

 REVIEW: If you forget to make a selection in a wizard dialog box, click the Back button.

6. Choose a Detail query and click Next.

7. Name the query **qryMainInvoice** and click Finish.

8. Notice the record order. Switch to Design View. The relationship is now shown in the top pane.

9. Click the Sort row for OrderID and choose Ascending.

10. Save the query and close it.

EXERCISE 12-3 Create a Query for the Subreport

The main report for the invoice includes OrderID. The subreport for the invoice shows the product ID, product name, quantity ordered, list price, and extended price for each item ordered. Access links the main report and the subreport because OrderID is a field in both the query for the main report and the query for the subreport.

1. Create a new query by using the Simple Query Wizard, starting with Table:tblSalesOrderLineItems.

 2. Click the Add All button >> to select all the fields.

3. Add Table:tblStuffedAnimals to the query. Move ProductName and ListPrice to the Selected Fields list.

4. Click Next and choose a Detail query. Click Next.

5. Name the query **qrySubInvoice** and click Finish.

6. In Design View, sort by OrderID in ascending order.

 7. Click in the Field row for the first empty column and click the Build button in the toolbar.

 REVIEW: You can right-click an empty row and choose Build from the shortcut menu.

 8. The qrySubInvoice folder is open in the left panel. Double-click Quantity in the middle panel. Click the multiplication button and double-click ListPrice.

9. Press [Home] to position the insertion point in front of the left bracket in the preview.

10. Key **Total:** (including the colon).

FIGURE 12-2
Expression
to compute
extended sales price

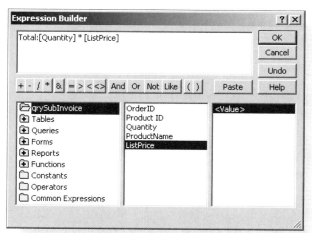

11. Click **OK** to close the Expression Builder.

12. Right-click the second row for this field and choose Properties. Change the format to **Currency** and close the property sheet.

13. Click the column selector for the ProductName field and drag it to the right of the ProductID field.

14. View the dynaset. Save and close the query.

Creating the Main Report

The main report, based on qryMainInvoice, is the top part of the invoice. A main report is designed and formatted like any other report.

EXERCISE 12-4 Create a Report in Design View

A main report is designed to allow the subreport to be embedded as a control.

1. Click qryMainInvoice in the Queries window. Click the New Object button drop-down arrow and choose Report. Choose Design View and click OK.

2. If you don't see the list of field names, click the Field List button. Size the Field List so you can see all the field names. Maximize the window.

3. Drag the top border of the Detail bar to make the Page Header section about 1 inch tall.

4. Click the Label button . Click at the 0.25-inch horizontal mark in the Page Header, about two rows of dots down.

5. Key **Carolina Critters Sales Invoice** and press Enter.

6. Change the font to 18-point bold italic. Double-click a sizing handle to size the box to the text.

> **REVIEW:** If you accidentally double-click the control instead of a sizing handle, the property sheet opens. Close it and try again.

7. Click the drop-down arrow for the Font/Fore Color button and choose dark blue from the first row in the palette.

8. Click the drop-down arrow for the Special Effect button and choose Shadowed.

9. Click the drop-down arrow for the Line/Border Color button and choose the same blue.

> **NOTE:** The Line/Border Color button sets the shadow color in this case.

10. Click the drop-down arrow for the Fill/Back Color button and choose light gray.

11. Choose CompanyName in the Field List. Hold down Ctrl and click to add BillingAddress to the selection.

FIGURE 12-3
Two fields selected in Field List

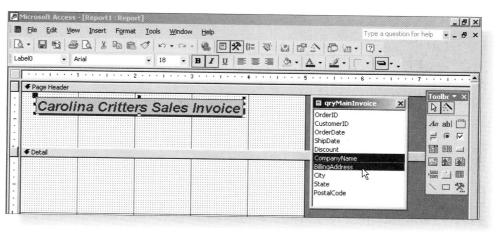

12. Drag both fields to the 2-inch horizontal mark, two dot rows from the top, in the Detail section. Deselect the controls.

13. Position the pointer above the first label and drag it below the second label to marquee both labels.

FIGURE 12-4
Marquee
selecting labels

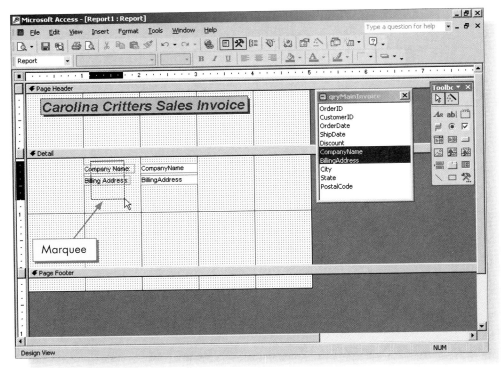

14. Press Delete to delete both labels.
15. Move the CompanyName text box one row of dots down in the Detail section, aligned left with the main title.
16. Move the BillingAddress text box two dot rows beneath CompanyName.
17. Align the controls on the left.

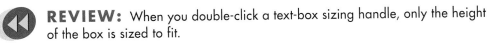

REVIEW: When you double-click a text-box sizing handle, only the height of the box is sized to fit.

18. Select both text boxes and set them to 11-point Times New Roman. Drag the right edges to the 2.5-inch horizontal mark. Double-click a sizing handle.
19. View the report to determine if the controls need to be sized.
20. Save the report as **rptMainInvoice**

Using Text Expressions

A *text expression* is similar to the calculations you have used. A text expression is entered in a text box control, not a label. Rather than multiplying or dividing numbers, a text expression displays text. You could, for example, create a simple text expression to say "Not available." To create a text expression, you use the

Expression Builder and enter the text in the Preview area, enclosed in quotation marks.

A *concatenated expression* joins fields so they appear to be one field. The city, state, and ZIP codes are separate fields in all the tables. When you use these fields in a form or a report, you can position the controls as close together as possible, but it still doesn't quite look like a normal envelope address. You can make these three fields appear to be one field in a printed report if you concatenate them.

EXERCISE 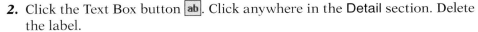 **Create a Concatenated Expression**

When you concatenate text fields, you use the ampersand (&) between fields to connect the fields. Literal text in a concatenated expression is enclosed in quotation marks. *Literal text* is the characters, words, or phrases you want to see onscreen or on paper. The comma and the space between the city and the state are literal text in a concatenated expression for the address.

1. Make sure that rptMainInvoice is open in Design View.
2. Click the Text Box button . Click anywhere in the **Detail** section. Delete the label.
3. Double-click the unbound control. Click the **Data** tab and click the Build button for the **Control Source** row.
4. Click <Field List> in the middle panel. The right panel lists the fields in the underlying query.
5. Double-click "City" in the right panel.
6. Click the ampersand button in the row of operators. This joins the next element in the expression.

> ✸ **TIP:** You can key the ampersand if you want to.

7. Key "**,**" (quote, comma, space, quote). This displays a comma and a space after the city. It is literal text enclosed in quotes.

> ⟋ **NOTE:** The comma between the city and state is not necessary for U.S. Post Office delivery.

8. Click the Ampersand button & again.
9. Double-click "State" in the right panel. Click the Ampersand button &.
10. Key "** **" (quote, space, quote). This displays one space after the state.
11. Click the Ampersand button & and double-click "PostalCode." (See Figure 12-5 on the next page.)

FIGURE 12-5
Expression Builder
with concatenated
fields

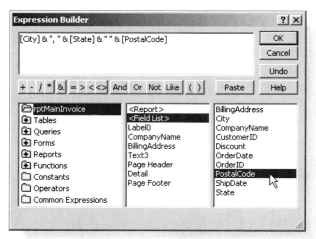

12. Click OK. Click the **Other** tab, name the text box **FullAddress**

13. Close the property sheet.

14. Position, format, and align the control to complete the address.

  REVIEW: Use the Format Painter button to copy the font from one control to another.

15. Save the report.

EXERCISE **12-6** **Add an IIF Expression to the Main Report**

Some of the customers get a discount; others don't. If the customers do not receive a discount, you can create an expression to show the word "None" instead of a zero. An *IIF expression* checks a condition that you specify and then shows one or the other of your choices.

🌟 **TIP:** "IIF" represents "Intermediate IF."

1. Drag the right border of the report to the 6.5-inch horizontal mark.

2. Select the OrderID field in the Field List. Hold down Ctrl and click to add OrderDate and ShipDate to the selection. Drag all three fields to the 5-inch horizontal mark in the **Detail** section.

3. Change the labels and text boxes to 11-point Times New Roman. Size the controls to fit.

4. Align OrderID vertically with CompanyName. Align OrderDate with Billing-Address. Align ShipDate with the FullAddress control.

5. Click the Text Box button [ab] and click below ShipDate. Change the label to **Discount**. Size and align this control to match the others.

6. Select the unbound control. Press [Ctrl] + [C] and then [Ctrl] + [V].

7. Change the label for the copied control to **Total Due**. Size and align this control to match the others.

FIGURE 12-6
Completing the
main report

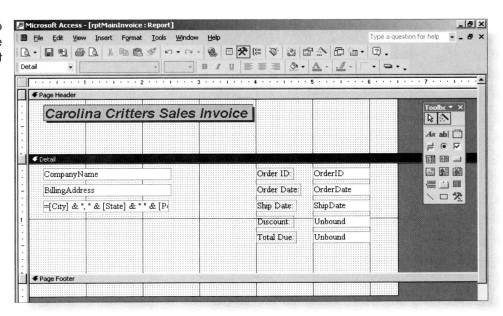

8. Double-click the first unbound control to open its property sheet. Click the Data tab, the Control Source row, and the Build button [...].

9. Double-click the Functions folder in the left panel. Click Built-in Functions in the left panel.

10. Click Program Flow in the middle panel. Double-click IIf in the right panel. The function is pasted in the preview box with placeholders.

11. Click once in the middle of <<expr>> in the Preview area to select it.

12. Click rptMainInvoice in the left panel. Click <Field List> in the middle panel. Double-click Discount in the right panel. The field name replaces <<expr>>.

13. Key **=0**

14. Click once in the middle of <<truepart>> to select it.

15. Key **"None"** (including the quotes). The literal text replaces <<truepart>>.

16. Click once in the middle of <<falsepart>> to select it.

17. Double-click Discount in the right panel. (See Figure 12-7 on the next page.)

FIGURE 12-7
IIF expression

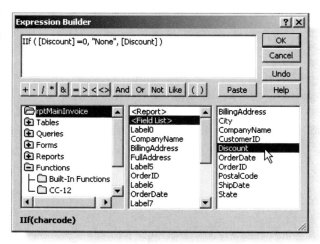

18. Click **OK** to close the Expression Builder.
19. Click the **Format** tab and format the expression to **Percent** with 0 decimal places.

 NOTE: You cannot name the expression "Discount," because that name is already used in the query.

20. Click the **Other** tab and name this control **Disc**
21. Preview and save the report.

EXERCISE 12-7 **Complete the Main Report**

The report you have created will be used instead of preprinted customer invoices. Therefore, it is important that the report maintains a professional appearance.

 1. Click the Rectangle button in the toolbox. The pointer changes to a plus sign with a small rectangle.

2. Using the new pointer, draw a rectangle around the name and address fields, leaving the same amount of space between the edge of the rectangle and the controls.

 NOTE: A rectangle is an object with properties. You can size and move it like a control.

3. The rectangle is on top of the controls. While the rectangle is selected, choose F**o**rmat, Send to Ba**c**k. This places the rectangle behind the controls.

REVIEW: If an icon shows the color you want on its face, just click the icon rather than the arrow.

4. While the rectangle is selected, change its Fill/Back Color to light gray to match the label in the **Report Header**. Change its Special Effect to **Shadowed** and the Line/Border Color to the same blue used in the main title.

5. Deselect the rectangle. Select the three controls in the rectangle and click the Fill/Back Color button ![icon] drop-down arrow. Choose <u>T</u>ransparent.

FIGURE 12-8
Sales Invoice
main report

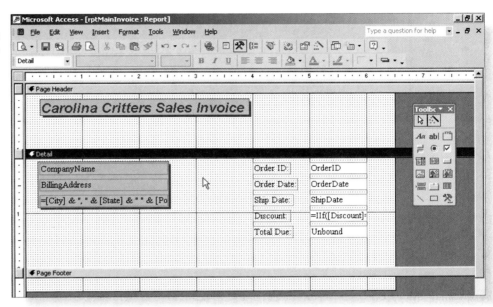

6. Preview, save, and close the main report.

7. Compact and repair the Database.

Creating a Subreport

Subreports are embedded—or placed—as objects in main reports. The subreport becomes a control with properties within the main report. A main report and its subreport are linked by a common field. Although you can use any report as a subreport, it must have an established relationship with the main report.

EXERCISE **12-8** **Create a Subreport**

A subreport is not really a subreport until it is inserted into a main report. Up to that point, it is just a report like any other report. You can use the Report Wizard, one of the AutoReports, or Design View to create a subreport.

1. Create a new report in Design View for qrySubInvoice. Maximize the window and click the Field List button 🔲 to display the Field List, if it is not already displayed.

 TIP: If you start at the Queries window with the query highlighted and choose Report from the New Object list, the Field List appears.

2. Drag the right border of the design grid to the 6.5-inch horizontal mark.

3. Drag the ProductID field to the 1-inch horizontal mark in the Detail section, three rows of grid dots down.

4. Delete the label and double-click the text box.

5. Click the Format tab and set the Left property at **0.125** inch and the Top at **.1667** inch. Close the property sheet.

6. Choose these four fields in the Field List: ProductName, Quantity, ListPrice, and Total. Drag them to the Detail section. Deselect the controls.

7. Draw a marquee to select the labels and delete them.

8. Drag the ProductName text box to the right of the ProductID text box.

9. Drag the remaining text boxes in this order—Quantity, ListPrice, and Total—to create a horizontal row of controls. Set them side-by-side, with no space between them but not overlapping.

10. Press Ctrl + A to select all the text boxes. Choose Format, Align, Top. Then choose Format, Horizontal Spacing, Increase.

11. Click the Label button 🅰 and click in the Page Header above the ProductID text box.

12. Key **Product ID** and press Enter.

 NOTE: The result of the number of items multiplied by unit cost is an "extended price."

13. Press Ctrl + C and Ctrl + V. Drag the copied label to be the title for the ProductName text box.

14. Press Ctrl + V three times to paste three more labels.

15. Edit the copied labels for the corresponding text boxes to show **Animal Name**, **Quantity**, **List Price**, and **Extended Price**

16. Align the labels at the top. Show one row of grid dots above and below the labels.

17. While the labels are selected, apply bold formatting. Double-click any selection handle to size the labels to fit. If data is still cut off, widen the labels.

18. Preview the report. Because numbers are right-aligned and text is left-aligned, a label might not align well with the text box.

19. In Design View, size the Quantity text box to be the same width as its label.

20. Select the label and text box and choose Format, Align, Right.

21. While the controls are selected, click the Align Right button ▤. Repeat these steps for the List Price and Extended Price/Total controls.

22. Size the Detail section to show two rows of dots below the controls.

FIGURE 12-9
Invoice subreport in
Design View

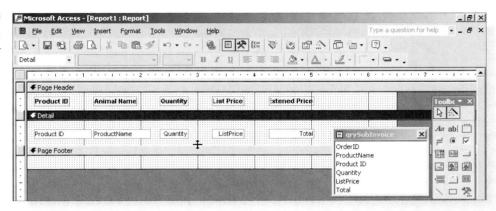

23. Preview the report. Save it as **rptSubInvoice**

EXERCISE 12-9 Group Records in a Subreport

The subreport lists each product, how many were ordered, and the cost. These are the sales line items. For your invoice, you need to know which products belong with which order. The OrderID field is not shown in the report, but you can use it for grouping. The OrderID field is also the common field between the subreport and the main report.

1. With rptSubInvoice open in Design View, click the Sorting and Grouping button ▤.

2. Click the drop-down arrow for the first Field/Expression row and choose OrderID. The default sort order is ascending.

3. Set the Group Header property to Yes. Close the dialog box.

4. Preview the report. You can see the grouping, even though there is not a heading for each group. Return to Design View.

NOTE: You do not need a group header label in the subreport because the OrderID is identified in the main report.

5. Drag the top border of the Detail bar up until it meets the OrderID Header bar. This closes the OrderID Header section, but leaves the grouping in effect.

6. Close the Page Footer section.

7. Save the report.

EXERCISE **12-10** **Add the Sum Function to a Subreport**

Because a subreport is a report like any other, you can use calculated fields as well as all Access functions and common expressions.

In your invoice subreport, you need to calculate the sum of all the extended prices. In the subreport itself, this totals the amounts for all orders. When the subreport is embedded in the main report, however, the link on the OrderID field causes the subreport to display the total for each order.

1. With rptSubInvoice open in Design View, choose View, Report Header/ Footer.

2. Draw a text box in the Report Footer that aligns beneath the Total text box in the Detail section.

3. Double-click the label. Change the caption to **Total Sales**. Close the property sheet.

4. Double-click a sizing handle to size the label to fit.

5. Double-click the unbound control and in the Control Source row, open the Expression Builder.

6. Double-click the Functions folder.

7. Click Built-in Functions once. Click SQL Aggregate in the middle panel.

8. Double-click Sum in the right panel.

9. Click in the middle of <<expr>> in the preview to select it.

10. Click the rptSubInvoice folder in the left panel. Click <Field List> in the middle panel.

11. Double-click Total in the right panel. The expression Sum([Total]) totals the extended prices for each order number in the final report.

12. Click OK to close the Expression Builder dialog box.

13. Click the Format tab and change the format to Currency.

14. Click the Other tab and name the control **TotalSales**. Close the property sheet.

 NOTE: It is important to name calculated controls so you can find and reference them in other forms or reports.

15. Align the calculated control and the Total text box on the right. Do the same to their labels.

16. Drag the top of the Page Header bar up until it meets the Report Header bar; this closes the section.

FIGURE 12-10
Subreport with
calculation

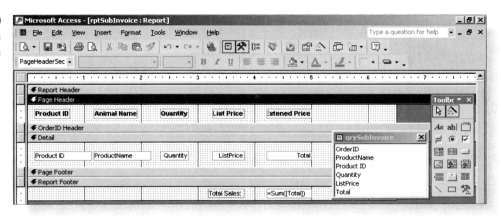

17. Save and close the report.

Adding a Subreport to the Main Report

You embed a subreport in the main report by using a control wizard. The Control Wizards button in the toolbox must be pressed or activated.

NOTE: Subforms and subreports are built and embedded similarly.

EXERCISE 12-11 **Embed a Subreport in a Main Report**

When you place a subreport in a main report, you can click a starting point or draw a box for the location of the subreport. The Subreport/Subform Wizard asks you to identify the subreport and the link. After the subreport is placed in the main report, it appears as a separate object that can be moved, sized, and edited.

1. Open rptMainInvoice in Design View and maximize the window.

2. Double-click the Detail bar and make the section **3** inches high.

3. Make sure the Control Wizards button is activated.

4. Click the Subform/Subreport button 🔲. The insertion point displays a crosshair cursor with a Form icon.

5. Position the pointer at the 4-inch mark on the horizontal ruler, a couple of rows of dots below the Total Due label. Click to start the wizard.

6. The first wizard dialog box asks if you want to use an existing table or query to build a new report. You can also use an existing report. Choose Use an existing report or form.

7. Choose rptSubInvoice in the list.

FIGURE 12-11
Choosing an
existing report

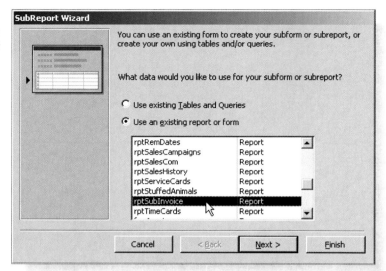

8. Click Next. The dialog box asks about linking the subreport to the main report. You can define your own link if the appropriate relationships were not created. Access also lists links based on the controls in the two reports. Choose Choose from a list. Then choose Show qrySubInvoice for each record in qryMainInvoice using OrderID.

FIGURE 12-12
Choosing a link for
the subreport

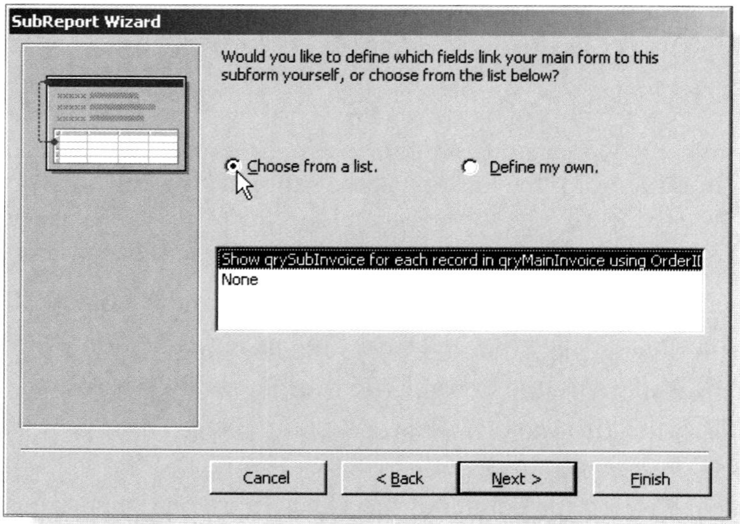

9. Click <u>Next</u>. The next wizard asks for the name of the subreport object. The default name is the name of the report you are embedding. Click <u>F</u>inish.

10. The subreport appears as an object in the main report. It is not sized or positioned well at this point.

11. Maximize the window and close the Field List.

 NOTE: If you see the section width error message, click OK.

12. Preview the report in Fit and 100% sizes. Preview several pages.

13. Return to Design View. Save the main report.

FIGURE 12-13
Main Invoice report after embedding subreport

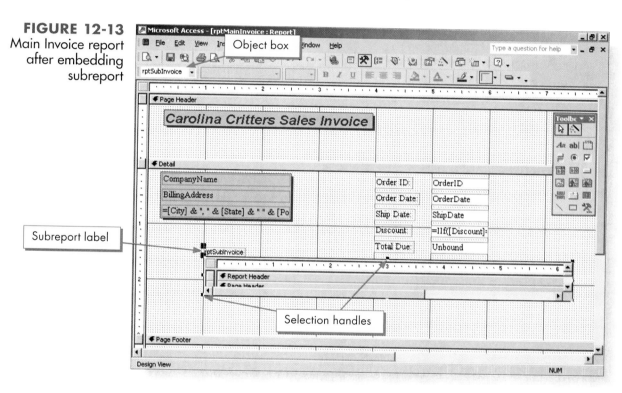

Editing Subreports

You might notice that something is missing from a subreport after you place it in the main report. You might see that the controls aren't sized properly, or you might decide to change the label, delete an existing field, or add a new field.

EXERCISE 12-12 Edit a Subreport Object

You can edit a subreport from the Reports window like any report. You can also edit a subreport from within the main report to see the changes in the main report more quickly.

1. With rptMainInvoice open in Design View, arrange the screen so you can see the subreport. Click anywhere in the **Page Header** to deselect all controls.

2. Click the top edge of the subreport to select it.

 NOTE: You can click any edge of the subreport to select it. It is easy to accidentally click a scroll bar in the subreport. The selection handles might not be fully visible, but you can see them.

3. Place the pointer on an edge to display the open-hand pointer. Drag the subreport until its left edge aligns with the rectangle.

 4. Click the Properties button [icon]. Verify that it is the property sheet for the subreport.

FIGURE 12-14
Subreport
property sheet

5. Make the subreport **2** inches high. Close the property sheet.

TIP: The size of the subreport object does not accurately reflect the data shown in Print Preview.

6. Display the Line/Border Color palette and choose <u>T</u>ransparent. This removes the border around the subreport.

7. Select the label at the top left edge of the subreport.
8. Change the label's caption to **Items Ordered** and press Enter.
9. Set the font to 18-point Times New Roman. Size the control to fit and position it.
10. Select the label and the subreport. Press Ctrl + ↓ to nudge them down, just below the Total Due controls. The Items Ordered label should start on the grid row below Total Due. Deselect the label.

 REVIEW: To deselect one control, hold down Shift and click.

11. Find the right middle sizing handle for the subreport. Drag it to the 6-inch horizontal mark.

FIGURE 12-15
Sizing the
subreport control

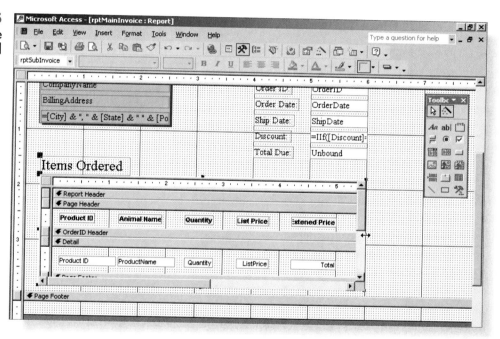

12. Drag the right edge of the main report to the 6.5-inch horizontal mark.
13. Preview the report and return to Design View.
14. In the subreport, drag the right edge of the subreport to the 5.25-inch horizontal mark.
15. Move the subreport and its label to align left at the .75-inch horizontal mark.
16. Save the main report.

EXERCISE 12-13 Edit Subreport Controls

Notice that the labels in the **Page Header** of the subreport do not appear in the combined report. To edit controls in the subreport, click the **Report Selector** button for the subreport and make changes as usual. You can also close the main report and edit the subreport from the Reports window. A third option is to choose <u>V</u>iew, Subreport in New <u>W</u>indow. This opens the subreport in its own window.

1. Make the OrderID Header height .5 inch. Select all labels in the **Page** Header; drag them into the **OrderID Header**.

2. Size the OrderID Header to show one row of dots below the labels. Close the **Page Header**.

3. Click the **Report Selector** button in the subreport.

FIGURE 12-16
Clicking subreport
Report Selector
button

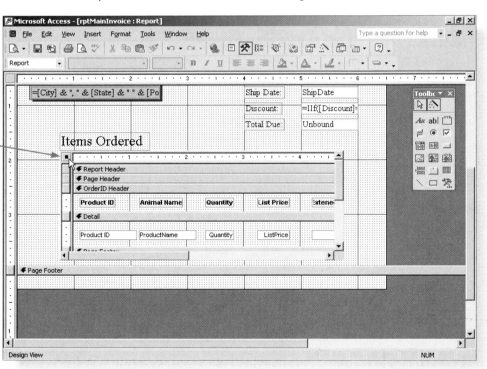

Report Selector
button for subreport

4. Press Ctrl+A. Change the font to 11-point Times New Roman. Choose Format, Size, To Fit. Move the controls as needed to see everything.

5. Scroll in the subreport to find the Total Sales label in the **Report Footer**. Select and delete it.

NOTE: If you see the section width error message, click OK. You fix that later.

6. Save the subreport.

7. Preview the report. Return to Design View and save the main report.

Adding Calculations to the Main Report

Often the data displayed in a subreport is summarized in the main report. Calculated fields are used in the main report to show totals, counts, or averages of records displayed in the subreport.

EXERCISE 12-14 Calculate the Total Due in the Main Report

Your main report now shows the total sales in the subreport. It does not show the total amount due after the discount. You can use the TotalSales calculated control in the subreport to calculate the total due in the main report. The total due is the total sales minus the discount.

1. With rptMainInvoice open in Design View, double-click the unbound control. Use the Expression Builder for the **Control Source** row.

2. Double-click the rptMainInvoice folder in the left panel. The rptSubInvoice folder is part of the main folder.

3. Click the rptSubInvoice folder to open it. Its fields and controls appear in the middle panel.

FIGURE 12-17
Using the
subreport folder

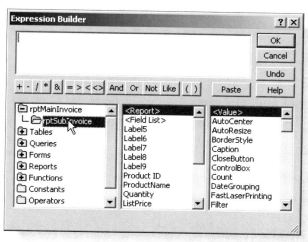

4. In the middle panel, double-click TotalSales. The control appears with a complete identifier [rptSubInvoice].Report![TotalSales]. It is the name of the report object and the control.

NOTE: Access adds an identifier when you select a control from a folder other than the current report or form in the Expression Builder.

5. The insertion point should be after the right bracket. If it is not located there, click to place it there.

6. Click ✱ for multiplication. Then click (for the left parenthesis.

7. Key **1** after the left parenthesis. Key **-** to subtract.

8. Click rptMainInvoice in the left panel. Click <Field List> in the middle panel.

9. Double-click Discount in the right panel.

10. Click) for the right parenthesis. The expression should read [rptSubInvoice].Report![TotalSales]*(1-[Discount]) This computes the total due, including the discount.

FIGURE 12-18
Expression Builder
with discount
calculation

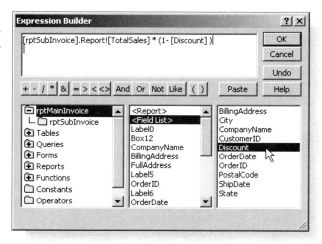

11. Click OK to close the Expression Builder dialog box.

12. Click the Format tab and change the format to Currency. Close the property sheet.

13. Double-click the Detail bar. Set the Force New Page property to After Section.

14. Preview the report. Return to Design View. Save and close the report.

Creating a Subreport in the Wizard

As long as a relationship exists between tables, you can build a subreport from within the Subform/Subreport Wizard. When you use this method, you do not design the subreport before embedding it.

EXERCISE 12-15 Create Table Relationships

All subreports (and subforms) assume there is a relationship between the underlying dynasets. You can use tblHistorySales and tblHistoryLineItems to create a similar report for past sales.

1. Click the Relationships button . Clear the layout.
2. Click the Show Table button.
3. Double-click tblHistorySales and tblHistoryLineItems. Close the dialog box.
4. Size the Field Lists to see all the field names.
5. Drag a join line from the OrderID field in tblHistorySales to the same field in tblHistoryLineItems. The relationship is identified as indeterminate because neither table has a primary key and the OrderID field data size is different.
6. Click Create. The join line shows the relationship.

⭐ **TIP:** Archive or history tables generally do not need a primary key.

7. Close the Relationships window and save the layout.

EXERCISE 12-16 Create the Main Report

The main report shows the basic sales information.

1. Click tblHistorySales in the Tables window. Click the New Object arrow and choose Report.
2. Choose AutoReport: Columnar and click OK. Return to Design View.

3. Click the AutoFormat button and choose Casual. Click OK.
4. Show five rows of dots below the Discount control in the Detail section.

5. Click the Save button and name the report **rptHistorySales**

⭐ **TIP:** Don't retype the filename; just edit the prefix.

EXERCISE 12-17 Create the Subreport

The subreport shows the line items. It does not include the extended price because that is not a field in the table. In your first subreport, the extended price was a calculated field in your query.

1. With rptHistorySales open in Design View, click the Subform/Subreport button 🖼 in the toolbox.

2. Position the pointer at the horizontal 3.5-inch horizontal mark, aligned with the OrderID controls. Click to start the wizard.

3. Choose Use existing Tables and Queries and click Next.

4. Click the drop-down arrow for the Tables/Queries list and choose tblHistoryLineItems.

5. Click the Add All button >> .

6. Click Next. Choose Define my own to set the correct link between tables.

7. Click the drop-down arrow for Form/reports fields. Choose OrderID. Notice that its number size is Double.

8. Click the drop-down arrow for Subform/subreports fields. Choose OrderID. Notice that its number size is Long Integer. These are two different field sizes—one of the reasons for the indeterminate relationship.

FIGURE 12-19
Defining the link for
the subreport

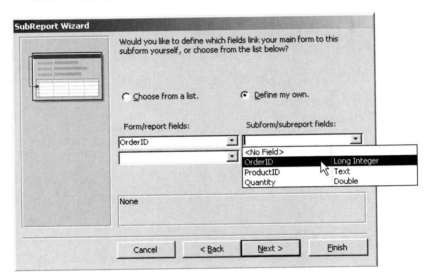

9. Click Next. Change the prefix of the default name to **rpt** and click Finish.

10. Maximize the window and preview the report.

11. Return to Design View. You can now edit this report like any report or subreport.

 NOTE: The subreport needs editing to show all the fields.

12. Save and close the main report.

13. Compact and close your database.

USING HELP

Most subreports (and subforms) use a One-to-Many relationship between the main report and the subreport. There are, however, subreports that use other types of relationships.

Learn about subreports that do not use One-to-Many relationships. Also learn how to make a control invisible:

1. Start <u>H</u>elp and click the Contents tab. Turn off the Office Assistant if it pops up.

2. Expand the Reports and Report Snapshots topic. Expand the Advanced Reports topic. Expand the Subreports topic.

3. Click the About subreports topic. Click each jump term in the Help window to view the sample reports.

FIGURE 12-20
Microsoft Access
Help

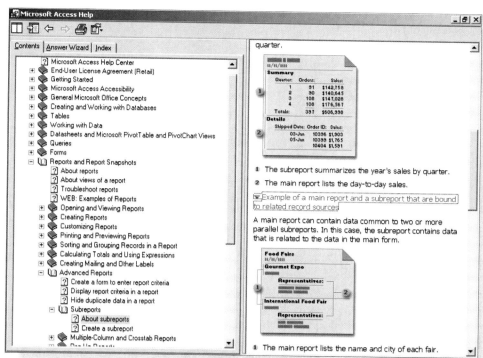

4. Read the rest of the Help window.

5. Click the <u>A</u>nswer Wizard tab and key **make a control invisible**. Press [Enter].

6. Click Show or hide a control in the list of topics and read the Help window.

7. Close Help.

LESSON Summary

➤ Tables must have a common field to create a relationship.

➤ A query for a subreport must include a common field with the planned main report.

➤ When you create a report from a query, the only fields you have to work with are the ones in the query. Some fields from the underlying tables might not be available.

➤ Concatenating two or more fields together lets you control the spacing between fields.

➤ By using the IIF expression, you can have two different outcomes based on the value of one field.

➤ Controls can be layered in a form, one on top of the others.

➤ By using copy and paste, you can shorten the time it takes to place controls on a report.

➤ When setting grouping for a field in a subreport, you should use the field that is common between the main and subreports.

➤ If you group a calculated field in the Report Footer, the calculated field will show its results at the end of each grouping.

➤ Use the Control Wizard to create and embed a subreport in a main report.

➤ If you create a link between the main and subreports, the information in the subreport can be unique for each record in the main report.

➤ In the main report, you can change the properties for the subreport object, including size, borders, and location.

➤ You can edit a subreport from inside the main report.

➤ Certain report sections will not show when the report is embedded in another report.

➤ You can change a calculated field's content by using the Expression Builder.

➤ To use a wizard to create a subreport, you must have already established the relationships between the underlying dynasets.

➤ The linked fields in a One-to-Many relationship must have the same data type and size.

LESSON 12　Command Summary

FEATURE	BUTTON	MENU	KEYBOARD	SPEECH
Control Wizards				
Rectangle				
Subform/Subreport				
Arrange controls		Format, Bring to Front/ Send to Back		✓

Concepts Review

Each of the following statements is either true or false. Indicate your choice by circling T or F.

T F **1.** Relationships are established automatically when you create a subreport.

T F **2.** A main report is embedded in a subreport.

T F **3.** A main report and a subreport must always be linked by concatenated fields.

T F **4.** You can use an IIF expression to show text or a field based on a condition you specify.

T F **5.** You can select all controls by pressing Ctrl + D .

T F **6.** The ampersand (&) in an expression joins one element to the next one.

T F **7.** To place a comma or other literal text in an expression, enclose it in brackets.

T F **8.** The results of a Sum function are the same in both the subreport and the main report.

Write the correct answers in the space provided.

1. In a report that actually consists of two reports, what is each part called?

_____

2. To edit controls in a subreport from within the main report, what should you do first?

_____

3. What term describes an expression that causes multiple fields to look like one field?

_____

4. How can you include literal text in an expression?

_____

5. What command places one object in back of another in the Design window?

_____

6. What causes the right side of a report to print on the next page?

_____

7. Where is a text expression entered?

_____

8. What symbol represents concatenation?

_____

CRITICAL THINKING

Answer these questions on a separate page. There are no right or wrong answers. Support your answers with examples from your own experience, if possible.

1. Describe how you would create a concatenated expression to build this salutation for a letter: "Dear Mr. Smith." Assume that your table has fields for Fname, Lname, and Title.

2. Describe the various types of commands you can use to design an attractive report. What types of changes do you use for the controls? What objects can you add to the report?

Skills Review

EXERCISE 12-18

Build main and subreport queries.

1. Build a query for a main report by following these steps:

  a. Open the file *[your initials]*CC-12. Refresh the linked tables to *[your initials]*CC-E-12.

  b. Click the Relationships button 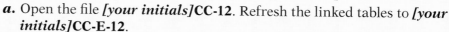 and clear the layout. Maximize the window. Click the Show Table button .

  c. Add the following tables to the layout: tblCarriers, tblSalesOrders, tblEmployees, tblStuffedAnimals, and tblSalesOrderLineItems. Close the dialog box. Size and move the Field Lists to see all the field names and join lines.

 REVIEW: Drag the common field from one table to the same field name in the other table.

d. Drag the CarrierID field from tblCarriers to tblSalesOrders. Create the One-to-Many relationship without referential integrity.

e. Drag the EmployeeID field from tbEmployees to tblSalesOrders. Do not enforce referential integrity. This is an indeterminate relationship because neither table uses EmployeeID as its primary key.

 REVIEW: You can rearrange Field Lists in the Relationships window to eliminate crossed lines or better see the join lines.

f. Close the Relationships window and save the layout.

g. Create a new query by using the Simple Query Wizard.

h. From the **Tables/Queries** drop-down list, choose Table:tblSalesOrders. Double-click OrderID.

i. From the **Tables/Queries** drop-down list, choose Table:tblEmployees. Double-click EmployeeID.

j. From the **Tables/Queries** drop-down list, choose Table:tblCarriers.

k. Double-click each of the following fields: CarrierName, DeliveryMethod, and NextDayDelivery. Click **N**ext.

l. Choose **D**etail query and click **N**ext.

m. Name the query **qryMainShip**. Click **F**inish.

n. In Design View, sort by OrderID.

 TIP: You sort by OrderID so new orders added later are still shown in ascending order.

o. Save the query and close it.

2. Build a query for a subreport by following these steps:

a. Create a new query by using the Simple Query Wizard for tblStuffedAnimals.

b. Add ProductID, ProductName, and ListPrice to the **S**elected Fields list.

c. From the **Tables/Queries** list, choose Table:tblSalesOrderLineItems. Add OrderID to the selected fields.

d. Click **N**ext and choose a **D**etail query. Click **N**ext.

e. Name the query **qrySubShip**. Click **F**inish.

f. In Design View, move the OrderID field to be the first column. Sort by OrderID in ascending order.

g. Save the query and close it.

EXERCISE 12-19

Create a main report. Use a text expression. Create a subreport. Add a subreport to the main report.

1. Create a main report by following these steps:

 a. Click qryMainShip and then click the drop-down arrow for the New Object button . Choose **R**eport and **Design View**. Click OK.

b. Make the Page Header section 1 inch tall.

c. Click at the 0.25-inch horizontal mark in the Page Header section with the Label button .

d. Key **Shipments** and press [Enter]. Set the font to 18-point bold italic. Double-click a sizing handle.

e. Save the report as **rptMainShip**

f. Drag the OrderID field to the 1-inch horizontal mark in the Detail section, two rows of dots down.

g. Change the label to **Order Number**. Move the controls until the left edge of the label starts at the 0.25-inch horizontal mark, even with the label in the Header.

h. Drag the EmployeeID field to the 4.5-inch horizontal mark on the same line as the OrderID controls. Place the CarrierName field beneath the OrderID controls, leaving two rows of dots.

i. Drag the DeliveryMethod field to align beneath the CarrierName controls. Drag the NextDayDelivery field to align at the 3.5-inch horizontal mark on the same line as the DeliveryMethod controls.

 NOTE: The checkbox appears at the 3.5-inch horizontal mark; its label is to its right.

j. Change the controls in the Detail section to 12-point Times New Roman. Size them to fit, and deselect the controls.

k. Move the text boxes in the first column of controls to align at the 1.75-inch horizontal mark. Set the OrderID and EmployeeID text boxes to Align Left.

l. Move the controls in the first column until there is equal vertical space between each set of controls. Move and align the EmployeeID and NextDayDelivery controls appropriately.

m. Add a label at the .25-inch horizontal mark in the Page Footer to show your name in 10-point Arial.

n. Make sure all the data can be seen. Then save the report.

2. Use a text expression by following these steps:

a. Click the Text Box button [ab] and click at the 4-inch horizontal mark in the Page Header section.

b. Delete the label and open the property sheet for the unbound control. Open the Expression Builder.

c. Key **"As of "&** in the preview ("As of *space*" in quotes, ampersand).

d. Open the Common Expressions folder and paste Current Date after the ampersand. Click OK to close the Expression Builder.

e. Click the Format tab and use Medium Date. Close the property sheet.

f. Set the font for this control to 18-point bold italic. Size the control so you can see both the text and the date.

> *g.* Select both controls in the **Page Header** and open the property sheet. Set the **Height** to **.35** inch. Set the **Font** to Arial. Align these two controls at the top.
>
> *h.* Adjust the **Page Header** section to show one row of dots below the controls.
>
> *i.* Save and close the main report.

3. Create a subreport by following these steps:

> *a.* Create a new report in Design View for qrySubShip.
>
> *b.* Double-click the Field List title bar to select all the fields. Drag them to the 1-inch horizontal mark in the **Detail** section, two rows of dots down.
>
> *c.* Choose **F**ormat, **V**ertical Spacing, **I**ncrease. Increase the vertical spacing again.
>
> *d.* Drag the top of the **Detail** bar to meet the **Page Header** bar and close the **Header** section.
>
> *e.* Size the **Detail** section to show two rows of dots below the last control.
>
> *f.* Drag the right border of the design grid to the 2.5-inch horizontal mark.
>
> *g.* Save the report as **rptSubShip** and close the report.

4. Add a subreport to the main report by following these steps:

> *a.* Open rptMainShip in Design View.
>
> *b.* Double-click the **Detail** bar and make the section 4 inches high. Close the property sheet.
>
> *c.* Click the Subform/Subreport button .
>
> *d.* Position the pointer at the 1-inch horizontal mark about three rows of dots below the controls. Click to start the wizard.
>
> *e.* Choose **Use an e**xisting report or form. Choose rptSubShip. Click **N**ext.
>
> *f.* Verify that the listed link identifies OrderID as the common field. Click **N**ext.
>
> *g.* Click **F**inish to accept the default name for the subreport.
>
> *h.* Preview the report in **Fit** and **100%** sizes. Return to Design View and save the report.

Edit the subreport and its control. Add a calculated control.

1. Edit the subreport control by following these steps:

> *a.* With rptMainShip open in Design View, select the subreport label and press Delete.

> ✴ **TIP:** It is often easiest to select a subreport control by clicking its top edge.

 b. Select the subreport control and click the Properties button .

c. Set the Width to **3** inches and the Height to **2** inches. Set the Can Grow property to **Yes**.

 NOTE: The Can Grow property allows the height of the control to expand or contract to fit the data.

d. Set the Border Width to **1** point. Close the property sheet.

2. Add a calculated control by following these steps:

a. Click the subreport Report Selector.

b. Right-click anywhere in the subreport Detail section. Choose Report Header/Footer.

c. Scroll the sections in the subreport and add a text box in the Report Footer at the 1-inch horizontal mark.

d. Change the label to **Number of Animals**

e. Click the unbound control and open its property sheet. Open the Expression Builder for the Control Source row.

f. Open the Functions folder and then the Built-in Functions folder.

g. Click SQL Aggregate in the middle panel. Double-click Count in the right panel.

h. Click anywhere in <<expr>> to select it.

i. Click the rptSubShip folder in the left panel. Click <Field List> in the middle panel.

j. Double-click ProductID in the right panel. This expression counts how many products are listed on each order number.

k. Click OK and close the property sheet.

l. Preview the report. Check each page and verify that each OrderID matches the OrderNumber. Return to Design View. Save and close the report.

TIP: When creating or modifying a subreport, you can include the common field to check the accuracy of the link. When you are sure the report is working properly, you can delete the field.

3. Edit the subreport from the Reports window by following these steps:

a. Click the Reports button and open rptSubShip in Design View.

b. Press Ctrl + A to select all the controls. Change them to 10-point Times New Roman. Choose Format, Size, To Fit.

 c. Click anywhere to deselect the controls. Click on the horizontal ruler above the text boxes. Click the Properties button .

d. Set the Left property to **1.1** inches. Close the property sheet.

 e. Click the Align Right button .

f. Set the Left property for the labels to **.25** inches.

g. Edit the label in the Report Footer to **# of Animals**. Align it with the other labels.

h. Preview the report. Check to see that all information can be seen and that the count is at the end of the report. Return to Design View.

i. Delete the OrderID and its label. Move all other controls in the Detail section up to the first row of dots.

j. Two rows of dots under List Price, draw a short line. Click the Properties button 🖹.

k. Set the Width property to **1.5** inches and set the Left property to **.5** inch. The Height property should be **0** inches. Close the Property sheet.

l. Drag the Page Footer bar up, leaving one row of dots showing below the line.

m. Close the Report Header and Page Footer sections. Save and close the report.

n. Open rptMainShip. Preview all the pages in a Fit size. Return to Design View.

o. Double-click the Detail bar. Set the Force New Page property to After Section.

p. Choose File, Page Setup. Change the top and bottom margins to **.5** inch.

q. Print the shipment report for Order #20101.

r. Save and close the report.

EXERCISE 12-21

Create a subreport in the wizard. Edit the subreport.

1. Create a subreport in the wizard by following these steps:

a. Open qryStuffedAnimals in Design View and remove the Product field from the design grid.

b. Click the New Object button 📇 drop-down arrow and choose Report. Save the query.

c. Choose AutoReport: Columnar and click OK. Return to Design View.

d. Click the AutoFormat button 🖹 and choose Compact. Click OK.

e. Click the Subform/Subreport button 📇.

f. Position the pointer at the 3.5-inch horizontal mark on the second row of dots in the Detail section. Click to start the wizard.

g. Choose Use existing Tables and Queries and click Next.

h. Click the Tables/Queries drop-down arrow and choose tblStuffedAnimals.

i. Double-click ProductID, ListPrice, and QuantityOnHand. Click Next.

j. Choose Define my own to set the link.

k. Click the drop-down arrow for Form/report fields. Choose ProductID.

l. Click the drop-down arrow for Subform/subreport fields. Choose ProductID. Click Next.

m. Change the prefix in the name to **rpt** and click Finish.

n. Maximize the window and preview the report. Return to Design View.

2. Edit a subreport by following these steps:

a. Select the subreport label and press ⌨Delete.

NOTE: You need to size a subreport control so you can see its labels and text boxes.

b. Move the subreport closer to the main report controls, just below the horizontal line.

c. Select the subreport and drag the bottom middle handle to make the control taller, about 1.75 inch.

d. Select the ListPrice label and text box. Use the right-side sizing handle to make them about **1** inch wide.

e. Select and move the QuantityOnHand label and text box closer to the ListPrice controls. Make them both **1.2** inches wide.

f. Make the main report **6.5** inches wide. Make the subreport control **3.3** inches wide.

g. Preview the report and make changes so you can see all the data and not have blank pages.

h. Delete the date control. Add your name in a label in the Page Footer.

i. Right-align the page number control.

j. Print the third page of the report.

k. Save the report as **rptMainAnimals** and close the report.

l. Save and close qryStuffedAnimals.

m. Compact and close your database.

Lesson Applications

EXERCISE 12-22

Create relationships and queries for a main report and a subreport.

1. Open *[your initials]*CC-12 and refresh the linked tables to *[your initials]*CC-E-12.

2. Import another copy of tblPayroll. It is named **tblPayroll1**.

3. Open tblPayroll1 in Design View. Make the SocialSecurityNumber field the primary key.

4. Open the Relationships window and clear the layout. Maximize the window. Add tblPayroll1 and tblEmployees to the window.

5. Drag the SocialSecurityNumber field from tblEmployees to tblPayroll1. This is a One-to-One relationship because a social security number can appear only once in both tables.

6. Create the relationship. Close the Relationships window and save the layout.

7. Create a new query for tblEmployees in Design View.

8. Add these fields to the design grid: SocialSecurityNumber, FirstName, LastName, Address, City, State, and PostalCode.

9. Sort by SocialSecurityNumber in ascending order.

10. View the dynaset. Save the query as **qryMainPayroll**

11. In the Design window, choose Edit, Clear Grid.

12. Click the tblEmployees Field List and press Delete .

 13. Click the Show Table button and add tblPayroll1 to the query.

14. Add these fields to the design grid: SocialSecurityNumber, MonthlySalary, HourlyRate, FedTax, StateTax, FICA, and Savings.

15. Sort by SocialSecurityNumber in ascending order.

16. Choose File, Save As. Save this query as **qrySubPayroll**

17. View the dynaset and close the query.

EXERCISE 12-23

Create a main report. Use a text expression.

1. Create a new report in Design View for qryMainPayroll.

2. Add a label in the Page Header. Key **Confidential Payroll Information** and set it to 20-point bold Arial. Size the label.

REVIEW: When you size a label to fit, the section expands, too.

3. Change the font color to red. Set the Left property to **.25** inch.

 REVIEW: When a control is selected, you can press Alt + Enter to open its property sheet.

4. Size the section and nudge the label to show two rows of dots above and below it.

5. Add and align a label at the left edge of the Page Footer for your name.

6. Click a text box at the right edge of the Page Footer. Delete the label and open the Expression Builder for the unbound control.

7. In the preview, key **"Payroll Date "&** (there is a space after the word "Date").

8. Open the Common Expressions folder and paste Current Date. Click OK. Format the date as Medium Date and use Text Align, Right.

9. Preview the report and verify that you can see the entire expression and date.

10. Align the controls in the Page Footer at the top. Make the Page Footer tall enough for the labels with one row of dots below the controls.

11. Save the report as **rptMainPayroll**

12. Drag the SocialSecurityNumber field to the 2-inch horizontal mark in the Detail section, two rows of dots down.

13. Place FirstName two rows of dots below SocialSecurityNumber. Change the label to **Employee's Name**

14. Drag LastName to the 3-inch horizontal mark to the right of FirstName. Delete the label and align the text boxes.

15. Drag the Address field two rows below the name, at the 2-inch horizontal mark.

16. Click a text box two rows below Address. Delete the label.

17. Using the Expression Builder for the unbound control, combine the fields City, State, and PostalCode.

18. Name the new control **FullAddress** and key **@@@@@"-"@@@@** as a format. This will add a dash to the ZIP code.

19. Size the control to fit the address on one line.

 TIP: Select all the controls in a section by dragging down the vertical ruler edge in that section.

20. Set all the controls in the Detail section to 12-point Times New Roman and size them.

21. While the controls are selected, move them until the labels align at the .5-inch horizontal mark. Deselect the controls.

 22. Click the horizontal ruler above the text boxes. Deselect the main title. Click the Properties button and set the Left property at **2** inches.

23. In the drop-down arrow at the top of the Property Sheet, select LastName and set the left property to **3** inches.

24. Check several pages to verify that you can see all the data. Print page 3 and save your report.

EXERCISE 12-24

Draw a rectangle, change the page setup, and create a concatenated expression.

1. With rptMainPayroll open in Design View, draw a rectangle around the controls in the Detail section.

2. Change the rectangle to pale gray and send it to the back. Adjust the size of the rectangle or nudge the controls to get an even frame around the controls.

3. Apply a shadowed effect to the rectangle.

4. Change the Page Setup to use .75-inch left and right margins.

> **TIP:** Deselect the rectangle first and then select the controls inside the rectangle.

5. Delete the Employee Name label, the FirstName text box, and the LastName text box.

6. Place a text box where the name text boxes were located. Delete the label.

7. Create a new text box named **FullName** that will combine the employees' first and last names.

8. Copy the font from the text box Address to FullName. Double-click a sizing handle to size its height.

9. Delete the SS# and Address labels.

10. Move the text boxes to the 1.5-inch horizontal mark. Set their Fill/Back Color to transparent.

11. Adjust all labels and text boxes so all data can be seen.

12. Preview, save, print page 3, and close the report.

EXERCISE 12-25   *Challenge Yourself*

Use a query to add a subreport in the wizard.

1. With rptMainPayroll open in Design View, make the report **6.5** inches wide.

2. Start the Subreport Wizard aligned at the top, with the rectangle at about the 4.5-inch horizontal mark.

3. Use all the fields from qrySubPayroll. The common field is SocialSecurityNumber. Save as **rptSubPayroll**

4. Preview, save, and close the main report.

5. Open the subreport rptSubPayroll from the Reports window. Make the Detail section about 2 inches tall. Delete the SocialSecurityNumber label in the Report Header.

   NOTE: The SocialSecurityNumber field is necessary in the subreport for the link, but it does not need to be visible.

6. Move the SocialSecurityNumber text box to the lower right corner of the Detail section. Set the Visible property for SocialSecurityNumber to No.

   TIP: Move the text boxes out of the way so you can arrange the labels.

7. Move the labels from the Report Header to the left edge of the Detail section, arranging them in a single column format. Salary will be the first label, Hourly should be below Salary, Federal Income Tax should be below Hourly, and so on. Make all the labels 10-point Arial bold and set the text to Align Right.

8. Arrange the text boxes next to the appropriate labels, forming a second column. Make all the text boxes the same width. Format the money controls as Currency with two decimal places. Make all the text boxes 10-point Arial.

9. Move the SocialSecurityNumber text box below the Savings text box.

10. Make the subreport as narrow as possible, based on your controls. It should be between 2 and 2.5 inches wide.

11. Close all the Headers. Save and close the subreport.

12. Open rptMainPayroll. Make additional changes to the main or subreport so the data is easy to read and is fit to size. If the address controls in the main report are split, adjust the size and position of the subreport control.

13. Remove the border around the subreport.

14. Print page 3. Save and close the main report.

15. Compact and repair the database. Close the database.

On Your Own

In these exercises you work on your own, as you would in a real-life work environment. Use the skills you've learned to accomplish the task—and be creative.

EXERCISE 12-26
Review the design of the database you modified in Exercises 11-38. On separate sheets of paper, sketch three subreports that will enhance the design of your database. At least two of the reports must have a calculation in the main report. On each sheet of paper, write your name and "Exercise 12-26." Continue to the next exercise.

EXERCISE 12-27
On each subreport sketch, draw the relationship that will be required. Print the relationships in your database. For each report, identify the recordset (table or query) for the main report and the subreport. On the printout, write your name and "Exercise 12-27." Continue to the next exercise.

EXERCISE 12-28
Create a parameter query for one of the subreports. Create all main reports and subreports. Include your name and "Exercise 12-28" in the header of each report. If your tables do not have meaningful information, add data to make your reports more meaningful. Print each report. Submit the sketches and printouts from Exercise 12-26 through 12-28 to your instructor. Keep a copy of this database. It will be used in subsequent lessons.

Integrating Access with Other Data and Applications

OBJECTIVES

MOUS ACTIVITIES

In this lesson:
Ac2002e **6-1**
Ac2002e **6-2**
Ac2002e **7-1**
Ac2002e **7-2**
Ac2002e **7-3**
Ac2002e **7-5**
Ac2002e **8-2**

See Appendix E.

After completing this lesson, you will be able to:

1. **Use security tools.**
2. **Import and export text data.**
3. **Import and export XML data.**
4. **Use Data Access Pages.**
5. **Use PivotTables and PivotCharts.**
6. **Create a mail merge document.**

 Estimated Time: 2 hours

Data moves around the world in many forms. For example, the Internet is full of data moving from one location to another. In this lesson you learn how to share data by using Access.

When sharing information, the need for security is very important. So in this lesson you also learn how to set different levels of security for different needs.

Using Security Tools

Access has a set of security tools you can use to assign passwords and permissions. A *permission* is a property or attribute that determines whether you can use a file and what kind of use you can make of the file. To practice using these security tools, you first create a new database by using the Database Wizard.

> **TIP:** Typically, designing a database involves planning table structures, identifying fields, establishing relationships, designing forms and reports, and creating macros and modules.

EXERCISE 13-1 Create a Database by Using the Wizard

The Database Wizard provides sample databases with appropriate tables, queries, forms, and reports. It creates a Switchboard, too. A *Switchboard* is a master form that opens instead of the Database window. It allows you to navigate the objects in the database.

1. Click **Start** and choose **New Office Document**. Click the **Databases** tab. There are several sample databases available.

> **TIP:** You can create a new database from within Access by choosing General Templates in the New File task pane.

2. Click **Inventory Control** and click **OK**. The File New Database dialog box opens with a default filename.

3. Set your **Save in** location. Click **Create**.

4. The first dialog box explains what this database will track. Click **Next**.

5. The next dialog box lists the tables on the left and the fields for each table on the right. Click each table name on the left and review the field names. Access shows optional field names in italic. You can see an optional E-mail field name in the **Information about employees** table.

FIGURE 13-1
Reviewing table
names and fields

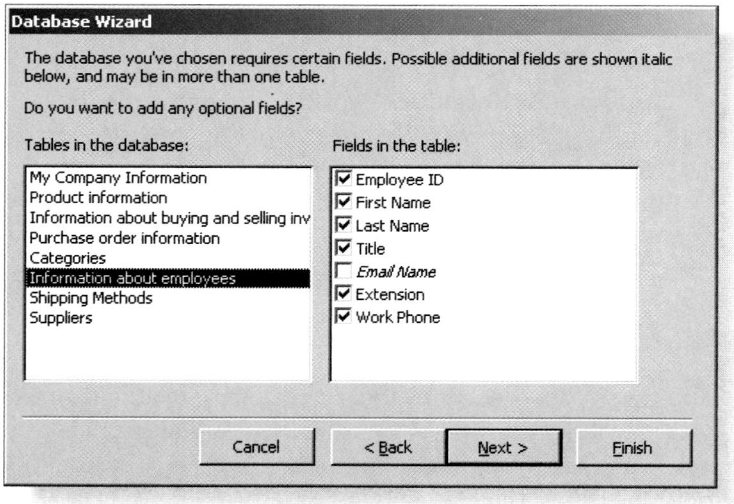

6. Click <u>N</u>ext. In the next dialog box, you select the AutoFormat to be used for forms. Choose Standard and click <u>N</u>ext.

7. Next you select the report AutoFormat. Choose Corporate and click <u>N</u>ext.

 NOTE: You can choose a picture to be used on all reports in the Database Wizard. The picture must be available in an accessible folder.

8. Title this database **Inventory Control** and click <u>F</u>inish. The title appears on the Switchboard. You see the database being built.

9. Before you can use the database, you need to enter company information. Click OK in the message box.

10. Key the following information:

Company Name:	**Carolina Critters**
Address:	**10900 South 88 Avenue**
City:	**Charlotte**
State:	**NC**
ZIP Code:	**28202-4567**
Country:	*Leave blank.*
Phone Number:	**704-555-1234**
Fax Number:	**704-555-4321**

11. Close the form. The database opens with a Switchboard form.

12. Click several buttons to open some of the forms. If a menu item has an ellipsis (…), it opens another Switchboard form.

 NOTE: The Database window is minimized in the corner.

13. If you are not at the Main Switchboard, click Return to Main Switchboard.

14. Close the Switchboard. Restore the Database window.

EXERCISE 13-2 Use the Database Splitter

In addition to its security tools, Access has a utility that will split a database into a back-end and a front-end database. A *back-end database* contains only tables (only data). A *front-end database* contains queries, forms, reports, and other objects that use the tables from the back-end database; it usually has no tables. Splitting a database in this way keeps the records (the data) in a single, centralized, protected file.

Splitting the database lets users customize their database with a unique front end. They can develop their own forms and reports without affecting other users. They link their unique front-end design to the data in the standardized back-end. If a user damages an object, only that user's front-end database is affected.

FIGURE 13-2
Front-end database
sharing
back-end data

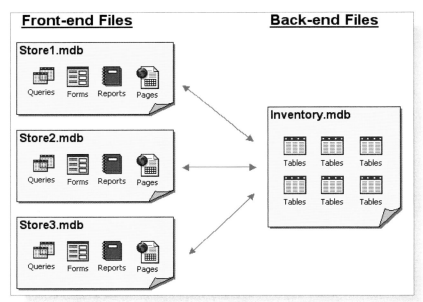

1. Choose Tools, Database Utilities, and Database Splitter. Read the information in the wizard
2. Click Split Database. The Create Back-end Database dialog box opens.
3. Set your usual Save in location.

 NOTE: The default name includes a "_be" suffix at the end of the name. This stands for "back-end."

FIGURE 13-3
Create Back-end
Database
dialog box

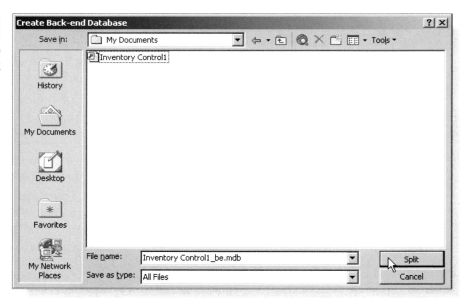

4. Click Split. The message box tells you that the database has been split.

5. Click OK. The front-end database, **InventoryControl1**, with the forms and reports, is open. The tables from the new back-end database, **InventoryControl1_be**, are linked.

 NOTE: Use the Linked Table Manager to update links when splitting a database.

6. Click the Forms button. Look at some of the forms.

7. Click the Reports button. Review some of the reports.

8. Compact and repair the database. Close the Switchboard and the Database window.

EXERCISE 13-3 Assign a Password

Password protection keeps anyone who doesn't know the password from using the database. You must key the password to open the file. To assign a password, you must open the database for exclusive use. This means no one else can open the database while you are using it. To change or remove the password, you also must open it exclusively.

Be cautious when creating and assigning passwords. If you forget the administrative password, you can lock yourself out of your own database.

 1. With no database open, click the Open button .

2. Click **InventoryControl1** to highlight it.

3. Click the Open drop-down arrow. Choose Open Exclusive. The Main Switchboard opens with the database.

FIGURE 13-4
Opening a
database for
exclusive use

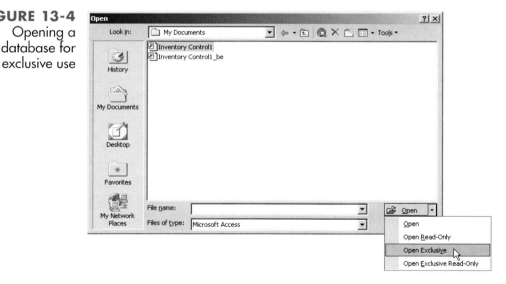

4. Choose <u>T</u>ools, Securi<u>t</u>y, and Set <u>D</u>atabase Password.
5. Key **123** in the Password box. Press [Tab].
6. Key **123** in the Verify box. Click OK.
7. Close the Database window in the lower left corner of the window.

 NOTE: When you close the database, the Main Switchboard closes with it.

8. Click the Open button and double-click **InventoryControl1**.
9. Key **123** in the Password Required dialog box. Click OK.
10. Choose <u>T</u>ools, Securi<u>t</u>y, and Unset <u>D</u>atabase Password. You see an error message because you did not open the database exclusively.

FIGURE 13-5
Error message when database is not opened for exclusive use

11. Click OK to remove the message box. Close the database.

 NOTE: Be sure to close the database, not just the Switchboard.

12. Click the Open button and select **InventoryControl1**.
13. Click the <u>O</u>pen drop-down arrow and choose Open Exclusi<u>v</u>e.
14. Key **123** in the Password Required dialog box. Click OK.
15. Choose <u>T</u>ools, Securi<u>t</u>y, and Unset <u>D</u>atabase Password. Key **123** and click OK.
16. Close the database. You can now open it without the password.

EXERCISE **13-4** **Create Users and Groups**

When you work in a networked environment, the network administrator usually identifies and sets up groups. A *group* is a collection or set of users who are allowed to work on certain files or computers. Each group is given rights, such as the ability to read or use the data, the ability to modify or edit data, or the ability to modify the basic design.

Rights to data usually follow personnel functions. Managers might have rights to modify data, while data entry clerks might only have rights to add new records or view existing records. Database designers have rights to modify forms and reports.

You can practice the steps for creating a group on your own computer. You will create individual users and assign them to a group. User account names, passwords, and group affiliations are stored in a workgroup information file that is read by Access.

Before proceeding with this exercise, obtain permission from your instructor or lab assistant. Make certain you have enough time to complete all steps from Exercise 13-4 through Exercise 13-6. It is important that at the end of this lesson you remove all groups and users from this workstation. The users and groups created in this exercise will exist not just for the current database but for all Access databases opened on your workstation.

1. Open **InventoryControl1**.
2. Choose Tools, Security, and User and Group Accounts. The User and Group Accounts dialog box opens.
3. Select the Groups tab and click New. The New User/Group dialog box opens.
4. In the Name box, key **Inventory Managers**
5. In the PersonalID box, key **InvMgrs**

FIGURE 13-6
New User/Group
dialog box

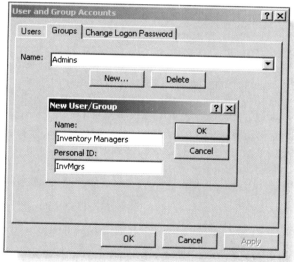

6. Click OK. You have created a group.
7. Click the Users tab. The Inventory Managers group is available.
8. Click New to create a new user.
9. In the Name box, key **Ivana Estrada**. In the Personal ID box, key **IEstrada**. Click OK.

10. In the Available Groups list, choose Inventory Managers.

11. Click Add>>. "Ivana Estrada" is added to this group.

New User
added to Group

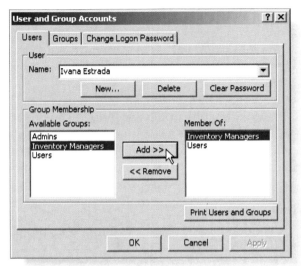

12. Click New to create a new user.

13. In the Name box, key **Warren Jackson**. In the Personal ID box, key **WJackson**. Click OK, and then click Add.

14. Click Print Users and Groups. In the Print Security dialog box, you can select what type of information to print. Click Cancel. If you clicked OK, you would get a generated report listing users and the groups to which they belong.

15. Click OK to close the User and Group Accounts dialog box.

EXERCISE 13-5 Set Ownerships and Permissions

After groups and users are identified, you can set permissions and change the owner. The *owner* is the individual or group who controls the object. Permissions can be set to read/write, read the design, modify the design, or administer the file or object. *Permissions* are attributes that specify what type of authorization a user has to use data or objects in a database.

Permissions granted directly to an individual user's account affect only that user. Permissions granted to a group account affect all users in the group. Removing a user from the group takes away the group's permissions from that user.

1. Choose Tools, Security, and User and Group Permissions.

2. Click the Change Owner tab. Each object is listed with the current owner.

3. In the Object Type list, click the drop-down arrow and choose Table. The tables are listed with their owners.

4. Click Inventory Transactions to highlight the table name.

5. In the List section, turn on Groups. This lists the names of the groups instead of the users.

6. For New Owner, click the drop-down arrow and choose InventoryManagers.

7. Click Change Owner. The new owner appears in the list.

FIGURE 13-8
Changing
ownership of object

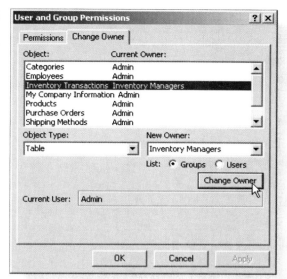

8. Click the Permissions tab. The User/Group Name box shows either the groups or individual users.

9. In the List section, choose Users. The individual user names appear.

10. Choose Ivana Estrada.

11. In the Object Type list, choose Table.

12. From the Object Name list, choose Employees.

13. In the Permissions group, select Update Data. Read Design and Read Data are automatically included. Ivana now has permission to read and modify data but cannot modify the design of the Employees table.

14. Click Apply. Click OK.

FIGURE 13-9
Changing
permissions for
Employees table

EXERCISE 13-6 Delete Users, Groups, and Permissions

Because you are working on a lab computer, you should delete the groups, users, and permissions you just created. In a normal office environment, you would not need to perform these steps.

1. Choose Tools, Security, and User and Group Accounts.

2. Click the User tab.

3. In the Name list, click the drop-down arrow and choose Ivana Estrada.

4. Click Delete and Yes in the warning dialog box.

5. Repeat these steps to delete Warren Jackson.

6. Click the Groups tab. In the drop-down Name list, chose Inventory Managers.

7. Click Delete and Yes. Click OK to close the User and Group Account dialog box.

8. Close the database.

EXERCISE **13-7** **Encrypt and Decrypt a Database**

Encryption compacts and scrambles database objects and data so the database cannot easily be deciphered. This safeguards the information as it travels across phone lines or the Internet. When you encrypt a database, you create a copy of the database. To encrypt a database, the original file must be closed and the new database must have a name different from the original file. When another person opens the encrypted database, Access decrypts each object as it is opened. This slows performance, but adds security.

1. Choose Tools, Security, and Encrypt/Decrypt Database.

2. Choose **Inventory Control1** as the database to be encrypted. Click OK.

3. Key **Encrypt** as the name of the encrypted database file. Click Save.

4. Open **Encrypt**. Access decrypts each object as it is opened.

5. Close the database.

Working with Text Files

You can import a plain text file into Access and use it like any table. A plain text file contains only data, without any type of formatting. It is usually delimited. *Delimited* means that the fields are separated by an identifiable character, such as a single space, a tab, or a hard return.

 NOTE: All word processors can convert a document into plain text.

EXERCISE **13-8** **Import a Text File**

Access cannot import a word processing file, such as a Word file, unless the document is converted to a plain text, delimited file. Plain text is often referred to as ASCII or ANSI text.

1. Open **InventoryControl1_be**.
2. Click the Tables button and right-click in the white space.
3. Choose Import. The Import dialog box opens.
4. Change the Files of type to Text Files.
5. Set the Look in location to find **NewEmployees**.
6. Click to select the file and click Import. The Import Wizard starts and correctly determines that the fields are delimited.

> **NOTE:** A fixed-width text file starts each field at the same character position. For example, the LastName always starts at Position 1, the FirstName always starts at Position 30, the Address always starts at Position 45, and so on. Mainframe computers often use this format.

7. Click Next. Common delimiters are listed across the top.
8. Choose Tab and turn on First Row Contains Field Names.

FIGURE 13-10
Selecting the delimiter and setting the first row

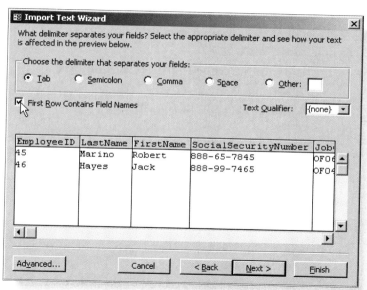

9. Click Next. You can choose where to import the data. Choose In a New Table. Click Next.
10. For each field, you can change the field name and data type, set an index, or skip the field.
11. Click in the SocialSecurityNumber field. Click the Indexed arrow and choose Yes (No Duplicates).
12. Scroll right to the Supervisor field. Click it and then select Do not import field (Skip).

FIGURE 13-11
Remove data you
do not want
imported

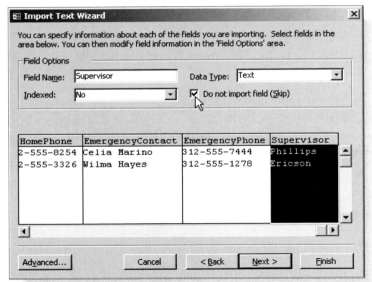

13. Click **Next**. Click **C**hoose my own primary key and click the field SocialSecurityNumber. Click **N**ext.

14. Edit the new table name to **tblNewEmployees**

15. Click **F**inish and then click OK.

16. Open tblNewEmployees in Datasheet View.

 NOTE: You usually need to clean up imported data by adding formats, input masks, proper sizes, and so on.

17. Look at the table in Design View. All text fields are 255 spaces wide, and there are no captions or input masks.

18. Close the table.

EXERCISE **13-9** **Export a Text File**

You can export a table or query as plain text for use in a word processor.

1. Right-click tblNewEmployees and choose **E**xport.

2. Set the Save as **t**ype to Text Files and set the Save **i**n folder. The text file will be named **tblNewEmployees** with a **.txt** filename extension.

3. Click E**x**port. The Export Text Wizard starts. Each field's data is enclosed in quotation marks. The quotation marks are a text qualifier.

4. Choose **D**elimited. You should export text with a delimiter so it can be easily edited in the word processor.

5. Click <u>N</u>ext. You can choose which delimiter to use.

6. Click Tab. Select Include Fields Names on First Row. This makes it easier to format the file in the word processor.

7. Click the Text Qualifier arrow and choose {none}. This removes the quotes for the text file.

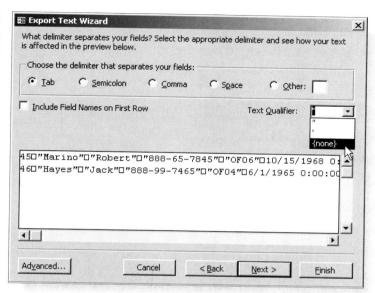

FIGURE 13-12
Setting the delimited and text qualifier options

8. Click <u>N</u>ext. Click in the filename and press the right arrow to see the filename.

9. Click <u>F</u>inish and then click OK.

10. Start Word and open the text file.

 NOTE: You need to set the Files of <u>t</u>ype in Word to find a text file. Word's standard file extension is **.doc**.

11. Close the document and Word.

Working with XML Files

XML (Extensible Markup Language) creates a text file that stores table names, field names, and data. It is designed for exchanging data between various programs across the Internet. Access can import an XML file, and it also can export to the format.

 NOTE: XML files work in conjunction with XLS (Extensible Stylesheet Language) and XSD (Extensible Scheme Standard) files.

EXERCISE 13-10 Import XML Data

Because an XML file stores table names and field names as well as data, Access creates a table to import XML data.

1. Right-click the white area of the database window and choose Import.

2. Set Files of type to XML Documents.

3. Select **NewProductData** and click Import. One table is found in the file called NewProducts listed in the Import XML dialog box.

FIGURE 13-13
List of table data
stored in the
XML file

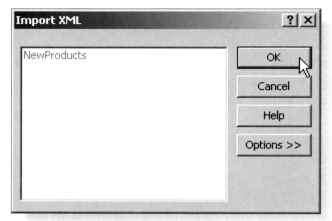

4. Click OK. The file is imported.

5. Click OK in the message box.

6. Open the NewProducts table. You can see that it's a regular Access table.

7. Close the table.

EXERCISE 13-11 Export a Table in XML Format

Just as data can be imported from an XML file, existing dynasets can be exported to an XML format. Data can be converted into viewable pages. When properly configured, a database stored online can be accessed through a browser.

1. Right-click the table tblNewEmployees and choose Export.

2. Set Save as type to XML Documents. Access will use the same filename, but with a different extension. (See Figure 13-14 on the next page.)

FIGURE 13-14
Save a table as an
XML file

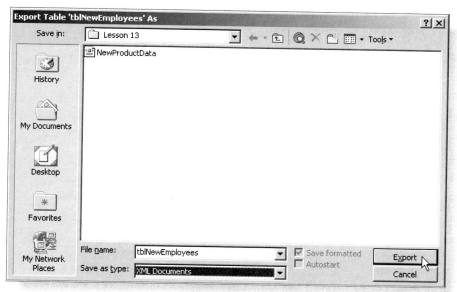

3. Click Export. The Export XML dialog box opens.

FIGURE 13-15
Determine if other
support files need to
be created

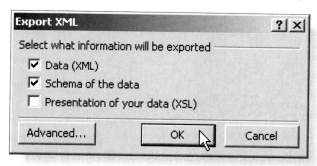

4. Select Data (XML) and Schema of the data. Click OK.

 NOTE: The Schema of the data includes the data types and sizes.

5. Close the database and exit Access.

 NOTE: You can work offline to open the XML file.

6. Start Internet Explorer. Choose File, and then choose Open.

7. Click Browse. Navigate to your folder and set the Files of type to All Files.

8. Open **tblNewEmployees**. If a program can interpret XML, the program can be used to read this text file and use the data. (See Figure 13-16 on the next page.)

FIGURE 13-16
XML code

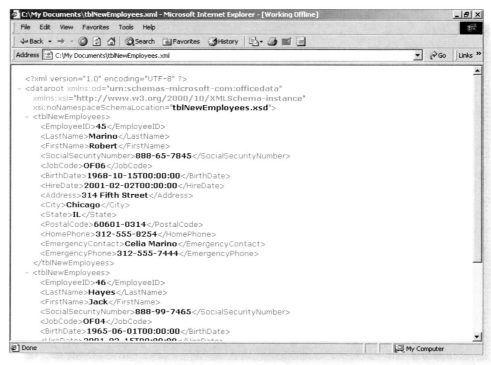

9. Close Internet Explorer.

Using Data Access Pages

A Data Access Page is an HTML file that is linked to a dynaset. You can use a Data Access Page to post information to a Web site. Users of your site can review, sort, add, and filter data. They cannot, however, change any existing data. This is helpful when publishing real-time sales data for salespeople who are out in the field.

NOTE: Data Access Pages are designed to be used with Internet Explorer 5.0 or higher, which must be installed on your computer for you to be able to create a page.

EXERCISE **13-12** **Create a Data Access Page**

A Data Access Page looks similar to a form because it displays information. However, unlike a form, a Data Access Page is an HTML file stored separate from the database. The object you see in the Pages window is actually a shortcut to the HTML file.

1. Create a copy of **CC-13** and name it *[your initials]*CC-13. Create a copy of **CC-E-13** and name it *[your initials]*CC-E-13.

2. Open *[your initials]*CC-13 and refresh the linked tables from *[your initials]*CC-E-13.

3. Click the Pages button. Double-click Create Data Access Page by using wizard.

4. Click the drop-down arrow for Tables/Queries and choose tblSalesOrders.

5. Click the Add All button >> . Click Next.

6. Do not use any grouping. Click Next.

7. Sort by OrderID in ascending order. Click Next.

8. Rename the title to pgeSalesOrders and choose the option Open the page. Click Finish. The page opens in Page View, similar to Form View.

FIGURE 13-17
Data Access Page in
Page View

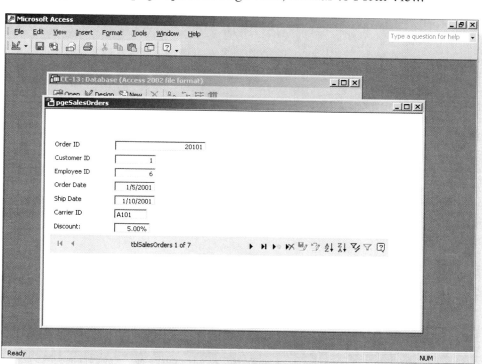

9. Maximize the window. View the page and switch to Design View.

EXERCISE 13-13 Modify a Data Access Page

The Data Access Page has objects or controls. You can move and size the objects and replace placeholders. *Placeholders* are words shown onscreen to mark the area where you enter a main title and body text. The title placeholder is the line that reads "Click here and type title text."

1. Click anywhere in the title placeholder line. Key **Sales Order Access Page**

2. If there is no body-text placeholder on your screen, click just above the table object. Key **This is the most recent list of orders received for Carolina Critters products.**

3. Press Shift + Enter. Key **This list is updated each day at 4 pm.**

4. Select the table object (as shown in Figure 13-18).

FIGURE 13-18
Data Access Page in
Design View

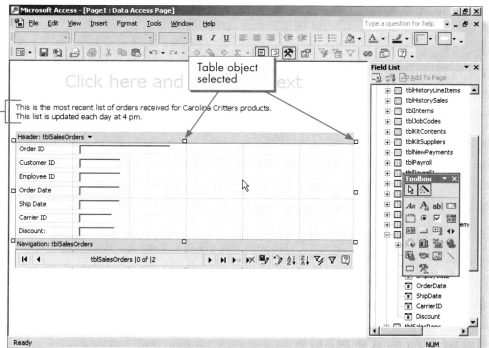

5. Click the Fill/Back Color arrow and choose a light color.

6. Click the View button . Save the page. Name it **pgeOrders**

7. Close the page. Compact the database and exit Access.

8. Start Internet Explorer. You must be online to use a Data Access Page.

9. Choose File, Open. Click the Browse button. Set the Look in box to the location where your files are stored.

10. Choose the HTM file **pgeOrders**. Click Open.

11. Click OK. The Data Access Page has a row of navigation buttons.

12. Click the New Record button . (See Figure 13-19 on the next page.)

FIGURE 13-19
Entering a
new record in a
Data Access Page

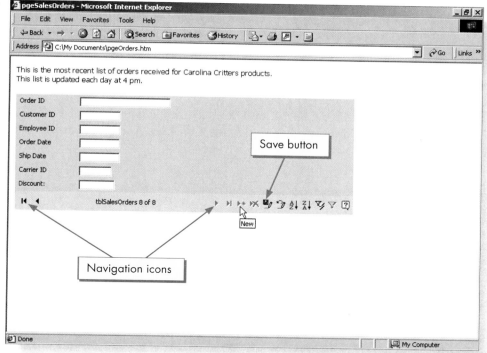

13. Key the following data in the Data Access Page. Press `Tab` to move from field to field.

Order ID:	**20120**
Customer ID:	**1**
Employee ID:	**29**
Order Date:	*Today's date using mm/dd/yy format*
Ship Date:	*Tomorrow's date using mm/dd/yy format*
Carrier ID:	**A101**
Discount:	**.05**

14. Click the Save button . Close Internet Explorer.

15. Start Access. Open *[your initials]*CC-13 and refresh linked tables from *[your initials]*CC-E-13.

> **NOTE:** Be sure to open the table, not the page.

16. Open tblSalesOrders and look for the record you added in the Data Access Page. Close the table.

Using PivotTables and PivotCharts

PivotTables and PivotCharts provide a way to view complex information in a summarized format. A PivotTable is a table with row and column headings that can be rotated or pivoted. A PivotTable summarizes data from a dynaset in a way that's easy to change.

PivotChart View shows a graphical analysis of a table's data. By specifying the layout and dragging items and fields, you can see different levels of detail similar to a PivotTable View.

EXERCISE 13-14 Create and Edit a PivotTable

A PivotTable View summarizes and analyzes data stored in a table or query. The information viewed through PivotTable View is the same information you see in Datasheet View. The only difference is the format in which it displays. By dragging fields and items, you can show different levels of detail.

1. Open tblStuffedAnimals. Click the View drop-down arrow and choose Pivot-Table View. A blank PivotTable opens with the PivotTable Field List.

FIGURE 13-20
Blank PivotTable

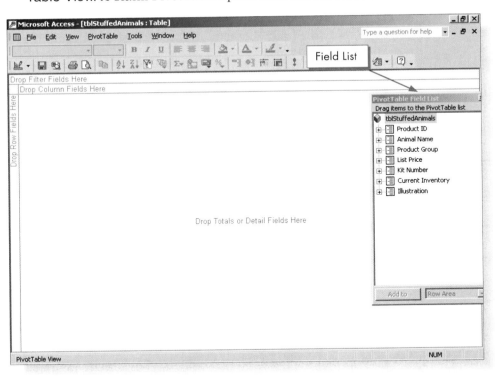

NOTE: If you do not see the PivotTable Field List, click the Field List button .

2. Click ProductGroup in the Field List. Drag the field to the Drop Row Fields Here column.

3. Release the mouse button when the blank column is outlined in blue. The ProductGroup field is entered as a row heading, and each field has an Expand button and a Collapse button .

4. Drag ProductID to the Drop Totals or Detail Fields Here section. Each Product ID for each group is listed.

FIGURE 13-21
Product ID by
Product Group

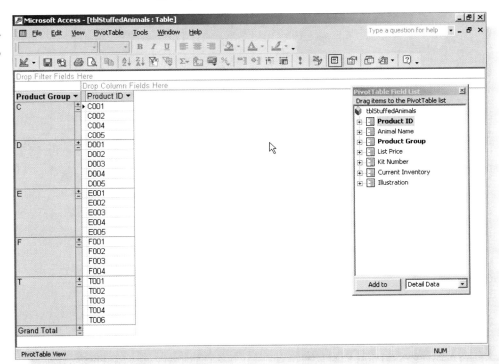

5. Click the Collapse button for each group. No IDs are shown.

6. Expand each group.

7. Right-click ProductID in the PivotTable.

8. Choose AutoCalc, Count. A count of the number of IDs is added to the field.

9. Right-click ProductID in the PivotTable again. Choose Hide Details. Now only the count is shown.

10. From the PivotTable Field List, drag Current Inventory on top of Count of Product ID. You will see a solid blue line to the right of the column.

11. Release the mouse button. The current inventory is summed or totaled for each group.

12. Click the Print Preview button. View the table in Fit and 100 percent sizes.

13. Close the preview.

EXERCISE Save a PivotTable as a Data Access Page

You can save a PivotTable as a Data Access Page to be posted on a Web site at a later time.

1. Choose File, and Save As. The Save As dialog box opens.

2. Click the drop-down arrow for As and choose Data Access Page. Click OK.

3. Set the File name to **pgeStuffedAnimalsTable** and set the Save in box. Click OK.

4. Save layout changes to the table. Compact and close the database.

 NOTE: You can work offline to open the Data Access Page.

5. Start Internet Explorer. Choose File and Open.

6. Click Browse. Navigate to your folder and set the Files of type to All Files.

7. Open pgeStuffedAnimalsTable. The Data Access Page displays in the same way as a regular Web page.

EXERCISE Create and Edit a PivotChart

Like a PivotTable, a PivotChart summarizes data stored in a recordset. The *chart* is a visual representation of the summarized data. You can rotate, or pivot, what is shown in the chart to see various summaries of the information.

NOTE: The terms chart and graph are often used interchangeably.

1. Open tblStuffedAnimals. This table already has a PivotTable.

2. Click the View drop-down arrow and choose PivotChart View. The information from the PivotTable is shown in a column PivotChart. The chart has two columns for each group, one for the Product ID count and one for the inventory. The count is very small in relation to the inventory, so you can barely see the column.

3. In the Chart Field List, right-click Count of Product ID. Choose Delete.

4. Close the Chart Field List.

5. Triple-click any column to select all columns. Click the Properties button 📇. Click the Border/Fill tab.

6. Click the Fill Color button 📥 and choose a different color.

7. Click the Type tab. Click the 3D Column chart type (second row, first column).

8. Click the General tab. Click the drop-down arrow for Select and choose Chart Workspace. Change the Wall Thickness to **0**

9. In the Add group, click the Add Title button 📧. A new section appears above the chart.

FIGURE 13-22
Adding a Title
to the chart

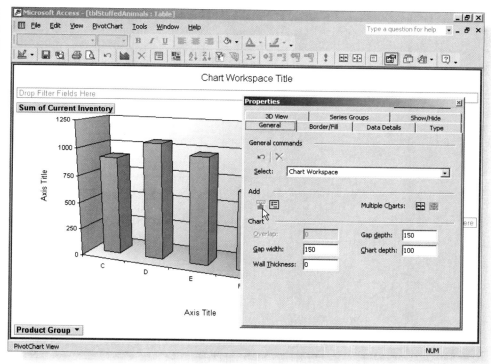

10. Click the drop-down arrow for Select and choose Title. Click the Format tab.

11. Change the Caption to **Carolina Critters Current Inventory**. Make the Title 14-point Arial, bold and italic.

12. Click the Axis Title to the left of the chart and change its Caption to **Units**

13. Click the Axis Title at the bottom of the chart and change its Caption to **Product Categories**

14. From the General tab, click the drop-down Select box and choose the Chart Workspace.

15. Click the Show/Hide tab. Click to deselect Field buttons/drop zones.

16. Close the Properties dialog box.

FIGURE 13-23
Finished PivotChart

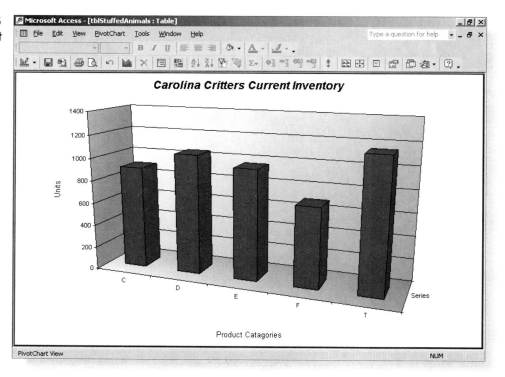

EXERCISE 13-17 Save a PivotChart as a Data Access Page

You can save a PivotChart as a Data Access Page to be posted on a Web site at a later time.

1. Choose File, Save As. The Save As dialog box opens.

2. Click the drop-down arrow for As and choose Data Access Page. Click OK.

3. Make the File name **pgeStuffedAnimalsChart** and set the Save in box. Click Save.

4. Save the layout changes and close the table. Compact and close the database.

5. Start Internet Explorer. Choose File and then Open.

6. Click Browse. Navigate to your folder and set the Files of type to All Files.

7. Open pgeStuffedAnimalsChart. The Data Access Page display in the same way as a regular Web page.

8. Close Internet Explorer.

Creating a Mail Merge Document

You can use your tables in Access to create a mail merge document in Word. A *mail merge document* is a form letter. The basic text is the same from letter to letter, but the names, addresses, and other specific information change for each person or company. In addition to the form letter, you use another file such as a database that has the names, addresses, and specific information for each individual.

EXERCISE 13-18 Create a Mail Merge Letter

1. Click tblCustomers to highlight it.

2. Click the drop-down arrow for the Office Links button . Choose **Merge It with MS Word**.

3. The first wizard asks if you have already created the Word file or if you need to create it now. Click **Create a new document and then link the data to it**. Click **OK**.

4. Word opens a blank document. Maximize the window.

5. The Mail Merge pane should be on the right side of the screen. If not, click **View** and then **Task Pane**.

> **NOTE:** The Mail Merge pane acts like a wizard by using steps.

6. In the task pane, from the **Select document type** group, choose **Letters**.

7. Click <u>Next: Starting document</u> to go to the next step.

8. Select **Use the current document**.

9. In the task pane, click <u>Next: Select recipients</u>. The middle area of the pane shows that you are using tblCustomers.

10. Choose <u>Next: Write your letter</u>.

11. Choose **Insert, Date and Time**. In the **Available formats** list, choose the third option (month spelled out, the date, and a four-digit year). Click to select **Update automatically**. Click **OK**.

12. Press [Enter] five times. As you write your letter, you can choose several standard parts of a letter in the task pane.

13. Choose Address block. The standard address block includes a person's name, the company name, and the postal address.

FIGURE 13-24
Insert Address Block

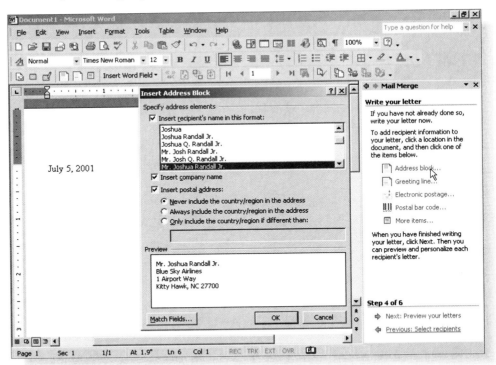

14. Click Match Fields. Word assumes certain field names for parts of the address block. You need to change them if they are not what are used in some fields to match data in your table.

15. Click the **First Name** drop-down arrow. Choose **ContactName**. This substitutes a field in the table.

 NOTE: You should use the First Name field because the Last Name field is inserted with a space in front of it.

16. Click the **Address 1** arrow and choose **BillingAddress**. The rest of the address matches.

17. Click **OK** and then click **OK** again to close the Insert Address Block dialog box. Word inserts a field <<Address Block>> that marks where the address information will be inserted.

18. Press [Enter] twice. Key **Dear** and press [Spacebar].

19. Click More items in the task pane. These are the fields from the table.

20. Double-click **ContactName**. Click **Close**. The field ContactName is inserted.

21. Key a colon after the field ContactName. Press [Enter] twice.

22. Key the following text to complete the letter.

FIGURE 13-25   Form letter

```
Thank you for your recent order. It will be shipped tomorrow.

Sincerely,



[Your first and last name]
```

23. In the task pane, click <u>Next: Preview your letter</u>. The first letter is displayed.

24. You can click the Prev Page `>>` or Next Page `<<` buttons near the top of the task pane to view other letters.

NOTE: Each recipient is a different record in the database table.

FIGURE 13-26
Completed
merge letter

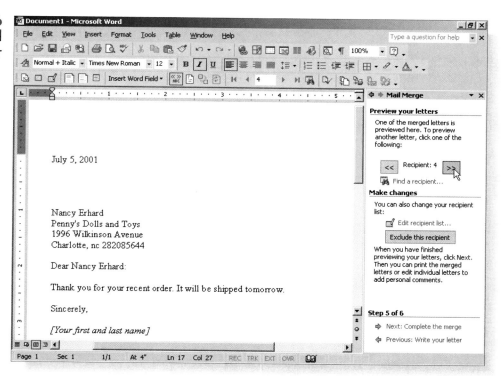

25. Click <u>Next: Complete the merge</u>. You can send the completed letters directly to the printer or edit them on the screen.

26. Click <u>Edit individual letters</u>. Choose <u>A</u>ll and click OK. A letter is created for each person in tblCustomers.

27. Exit Word without saving the documents.

28. Compact and close your database.

USING HELP

Access has many tools for securing data. Use Help to learn more about these features.

Use Help to learn more about security:

1. Press F1 to start Help.

 REVIEW: Turn off the Office Assistant if it starts.

2. Click the <u>C</u>ontents tab. Expand the topic Administering and Securing an Access File.

3. Expand Securing a Database.

4. Click Overview of Access security. Click <u>Show All</u>.

FIGURE 13-27
Microsoft Access
Help

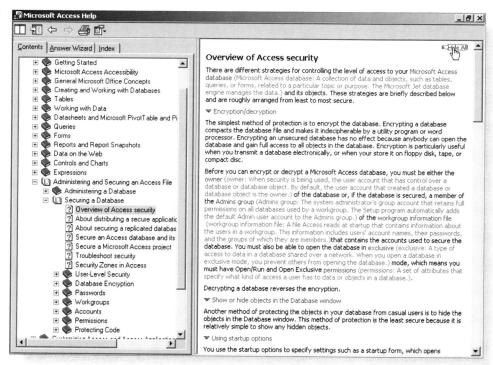

5. Read the Help window. Close Help.

LESSON 13 Summary

➤ Access security tools include the Database Splitter. It places the tables in a back-end database and the other objects in a front-end database.

➤ A database must be open exclusively before assigning a password to it.

➤ Giving different permissions to groups and users guards who can work with the objects in a database.

➤ You should encrypt a database before sending it across the Internet.

➤ Access can import and export plain text files. Many other programs can also read and create text files.

➤ XML files are text files that are easily exchanged across the Internet.

➤ Use a Data Access Page to view, delete, and add data to a database from the Web. Your users can then review and add data to the table from the Web. A Data Access Page is similar to a form.

➤ A PivotTable summarizes information from a table or query with movable fields. A PivotChart displays the data from a PivotTable with movable categories.

➤ You can create a mail merge document from a table or query by using the Office Links.

LESSON 13 Command Summary

FEATURE	BUTTON	MENU	KEYBOARD	SPEECH
Assign password		Tools, Security, Set Database Password		✓
Encrypt database		Tools, Security, Encrypt/Decrypt Database		
Export		File, Export		✓
Import		File, Get External Data, Import		✓
New Database	☐	File, New	Ctrl + N	✓
Office Links	▣			

continues

LESSON 13 Command Summary   *continued*

FEATURE	BUTTON	MENU	KEYBOARD	SPEECH
PivotChart		View, PivotChart View		
PivotTable		View, PivotTable View		
Set permissions		Tools, Security, User and Group Accounts		
Split database		Tools, Database Utilities, Database Splitter		✓

Concepts Review

TRUE/FALSE QUESTIONS

Each of the following statements is either true or false. Indicate your choice by circling **T** or **F**.

T F **1.** PivotCharts can show data that changes from record to record.

T F **2.** PivotTables can be printed in landscape format.

T F **3.** A new blank database has a default table named "Table1."

T F **4.** The Database Splitter creates an exact copy of a database.

T F **5.** Data that is imported into Access from other applications is stored in tables.

T F **6.** An XML file stores table names and field names as well as data.

T F **7.** Permissions granted to a group affect only new users added to the group.

T F **8.** A Data Access Page has Page View, Design View, and Datasheet View.

SHORT ANSWER QUESTIONS

Write the correct answer in the space provided.

1. Name two ways to make a table viewable on the Internet.

2. Name three common delimiters.

3. PivotCharts can be used by what two database objects to display data?

4. What database objects are included in a blank database?

5. Describe two ways to limit access to a database.

6. What is a mail merge document?

7. Describe the benefits of using a wizard to create a new database.

_____

8. What does encryption do?

_____

CRITICAL THINKING

Answer these questions on a separate page. There are no right or wrong answers. Support your answers with examples from your own experience, if possible.

1. Would you make your database accessible on your Web site? Why or why not?

2. Discuss the difference between, and the reasons for, a database password and encryption.

Skills Review

EXERCISE 13-19

Create a new database by using the wizard. Assign a password. Import a text file.

1. Create a new database by following these steps:

    a. Click the New button 🗋. Click General Templates on the New File pane. Click the **Databases** tab.

    b. Click **Service Call Management** and click **OK**.

    c. Verify the Save In location. Click **Create** to use the default filename.

    d. This database tracks customers, work orders, and related data. Click **Next**.

    e. Use all the suggested tables and fields. Click **Next**.

    f. Choose **Expedition** as the AutoFormat used for forms. Click **Next**.

    g. Choose **Corporate** for reports and click **Next**.

    h. Give the database the title **ServiceCalls**. This is the name used at the top of the Switchboard. Click **Next**.

    i. The wizard is complete. Make sure the option to start the database is checked. Click **Finish**.

    j. Click **OK** in the message box.

    k. Key the following information:

Company Name:	**Carolina Critters**
Address:	**10900 South 88 Avenue**
City:	**Charlotte**

State:	**NC**
ZIP Code:	**28202-4567**
Country:	*Leave blank.*
Sales Tax Rate:	**.0825**
Payment Terms:	**Net 15**
Invoice Description:	*Leave blank.*
Phone Number:	**704-555-1234**
Fax Number:	**704-555-4321**

l. Click the Close button to see the Switchboard form.

m. Explore the Switchboard choices to view the forms and reports. Close the database when you finish.

2. Assign a password to the database by following these steps:

   a. With no database open, click the Open button .

   b. Click **Service Call Management1** to highlight it.

   c. Open the database exclusively.

   d. Choose <u>T</u>ools, Securit<u>y</u>, and Set <u>D</u>atabase Password.

   e. Key **123** in the Password box and the Verify box.

   f. Close the Database window.

   g. Open the Service Call Management1 database and test the password.

   h. Close the database.

3. Import a text file by following these steps:

   a. Open your database *[your initials]*CC-13 and refresh the linked tables from *[your initials]*CC-E-13.

   b. Right-click in a blank white area of the Tables window and choose <u>I</u>mport.

   c. Click the Files of <u>t</u>ype drop-down arrow and choose Text Files. Set the Look <u>I</u>n location to find the text file **NewCustomers**.

   d. Select **NewCustomers** and click <u>I</u>mport.

   e. The wizard has determined that the fields are delimited. Click <u>N</u>ext.

   f. Click <u>C</u>omma to select it as the character used to separate the fields.

   g. Click the First <u>R</u>ow Contains Field Names check box. Click <u>N</u>ext.

   h. Choose In a Ne<u>w</u> Table. Click <u>N</u>ext.

   i. Click the CustomerID column. Click the Indexed drop-down arrow and choose Yes (No Duplicates).

   j. Click the CompanyName column. It is correctly identified as a Text data type.

 TIP: Access does not always choose the best data type when importing tables from other sources.

   k. Scroll and click the PostalCode column. Change the Data <u>T</u>ype to Text.

l. Scroll and click the PhoneNumber column. Change the Data Type to Text. Repeat these steps for the FaxNumber column.

m. Scroll and click the TaxStatus column. Change the Data Type to Yes/No.

 TIP: The Yes/No field initially shows the Visual Basic interpretation of yes or no (which is 0 or –1).

n. Scroll and click the TaxIDNumber column. Set the Data Type to Text. Click Next.

o. Click the option to Choose my own primary key. Choose CustomerID. Click Next.

p. Name the new table **tblNewCustomers**. Click Finish. Click OK in the message box.

q. Open tblNewCustomers in Design View. Switch to Design View.

r. Apply an appropriate input mask to each of these fields: PostalCode, PhoneNumber, and FaxNumber.

s. Change the Display Control on the Lookup tab for the TaxStatus field to Check Box.

t. Save the table and view the datasheet. Close the table.

EXERCISE 13-20

Export a table to XML. Create and edit a Data Access Page. Edit a Data Access Page.

1. Export a table to XML by following these steps:

a. Right-click tblJobCodes and choose Export.

b. Set the Save in folder to your usual location for saving work. Click the Save as type drop-down arrow. Choose XML Documents.

c. Click Export. Click OK.

d. Start Windows Explorer and find the file you just created. It has the same name as your table, but with an XML extension.

e. Exit Windows Explorer. Return to Access.

2. Create a Data Access Page by following these steps:

 NOTE: When you use Design View to create a Data Access Page, the same wizard helps you lay out the fields.

a. Click the Pages button. Double-click Create data access page by using wizard.

b. Click the Tables/Queries drop-down arrow and choose tblHistorySales.

c. Click the Add All button [>>]. Click Next.

d. Do not use any grouping. Click Next.

e. Sort by OrderID in ascending order. Click Next.

f. Name the page **pgeHistorySales** and choose the option <u>O</u>pen the page. Click <u>F</u>inish.

g. View the page and switch to Design View. Maximize the window.

 NOTE: If a Field List is displayed in Design View, close it.

3. Edit a Data Access Page by following these steps:

a. Click the title placeholder. Key **Sales History Access Page**

b. Click above the table object or click the body-text placeholder. Key **This is sales history for Carolina Critters products.**

c. Select the table object.

 d. Click the drop-down arrow for the Fill/Back Color button 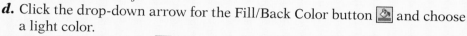 and choose a light color.

 e. Click the View button 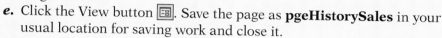. Save the page as **pgeHistorySales** in your usual location for saving work and close it.

 NOTE: Data Access Pages have an .htm extension.

f. Print the page in landscape and close the page.

EXERCISE 13-21

Build a summary query. Create and print a PivotChart.

1. Build a query for a report and its chart by following these steps:

a. Create a new query in Design View for tblHistoryLineItems.

b. Add ProductID and Quantity to the design grid.

c. Display the Total row and group by ProductID.

d. Use the Count function for Quantity.

e. Add criteria to show only the C product line.

f. Save the query as **qryCHistory*[your name]***

2. Create and print a PivotChart by following these steps:

a. Click the down arrow for the View button and choose Pi<u>v</u>otChart View. A blank PivotChart opens, showing the PivotChart Field List.

 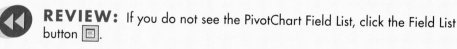 **REVIEW:** If you do not see the PivotChart Field List, click the Field List button.

b. Drag the ProductID field to the Drop Category Fields Here row.

c. Drag the CountofQuantity field to the Drop Data Fields Here area.

d. Open the property sheet for Category Axis Title. On the Format tab, change the Caption to *[your name]*.

e. Chick the Print Preview button . View the PivotChart in Fit and 100% sizes, with landscape orientation.

f. Print the PivotChart.

g. Close the query and save your changes.

EXERCISE 13-22

Create a mail merge document.

1. Create a mail merge document by following these steps:

a. Click tblEmployees to highlight it. Click the Office Links button arrow.

b. Choose Merge It with MS Word.

c. Click Create a new document and then link the data to it. Click OK.

d. Maximize the Word window.

e. Select the type of document as Letters. Click Next: Starting document.

f. Use the current document and click Next: Select recipients.

g. Click Next: Write your letter. Select more items.

h. Double-click FirstName, LastName, HomePhone, and JobCode. Close the dialog box.

i. Click between FirstName and Lastname; press [Space].

j. Click between Lastname and HomePhone; press [Enter].

k. Click between HomePhone and JobCode; press [Enter].

l. Click Next: Preview your letters.

m. Preview your letters. Click Next: Complete the merge.

NOTE: You can use merge features in Word to show all the records on one page.

n. Scroll through the pages in Word. Close the documents without saving, and exit Word.

o. Compact and close your database.

Lesson Applications

EXERCISE 13-23

Create a blank database. Assign a password. Import text files.

1. Start Access. In the opening dialog box, choose a blank Access database. Click OK.
2. Name the new database **Lesson13***[your initials]*.
3. Set a password for the database to 123. Close the database.
4. Open the **Lesson13***[your initials]* database you just created.
5. Import the text file **NewEmployees**. The first row has column headings. Use the SocialSecurityNumber as a primary key field, indexed with no duplicates. Name the new table **tblNewWorkers***[your initials]*.
6. Import the text file **Employees**. It is delimited with tab characters and has field names in the first row. Add to the table **tblNewWorkers***[your initials]*.
7. Choose Tools, Analyze, and Documenter. Click the Tables tab. Choose the table in the database.
8. Click Options. Include only the properties for the tables; Name, Data Type, and Size for the fields, and nothing for the indexes. Click OK.
9. Click OK in the Documenter dialog box to generate a report. Preview the report and print it.

 REVIEW: The Documenter generates a report that cannot be edited or saved.

10. Close the report and database.

EXERCISE 13-24

Create and edit a Data Access Page. Export data in XML format.

1. Open your database *[your initials]***CC-13** and refresh the linked tables from *[your initials]***CC-E-13**.
2. Use the wizard to create a Data Access Page for tblCarriers using all fields, no grouping or sorting.
3. View the page and switch to Design View.
4. Change the title placeholder to **Carolina Critters Carriers**
5. Change the fill color for the page object to a light color.

6. View and save the page as **pgeCarriers**

7. Print pgeCarriers. Close the page.

8. Save the data in tblCarriers as an XML file called **tblCarriers.xml**

9. View the file in your browser and print the first page.

EXERCISE 13-25

Modify a query. Create and print a PivotTable.

1. Copy qryDinoInv and rename the copy **qryOrderReorder[your name]**

2. Edit the query so it displays all stuffed animals.

3. Sort by ProductName and then ListPrice.

4. Change the reorder amount calculation from 20% to 25%.

5. Save the changes to the query.

6. Change to PivotTable View.

7. Display List Price and Animal Name fields in the Fields rows area. List Price should appear to the left of Animal Name.

8. Display Current Inventory and Reorder Amount fields to the Detail area. Current Inventory should appear to the left of Reorder Amount.

9. Print the PivotTable.

10. Close the query and save your changes.

EXERCISE 13-26 *Challenge Yourself*

Creating a Word merge document and a Data Access Page.

Write a letter in Word that informs all the Carolina Critters customers that they can now find information regarding company-wide sales on the Web site www.carolinacritters.com. Inform them that information will be updated on this page frequently. Also ask them to call their account manager if they have questions or would like to receive additional information e-mailed or mailed to them. Merge and print the last page of your merged document.

Generate a Data Access Page showing Carolina Critters' sales-promotion information. Include the name of the promotion, its description, and dates of the sale.

On Your Own

In these exercises you work on your own, as you would in a real-life work environment. Use the skills you've learned to accomplish the task—and be creative.

EXERCISE 13-27

Review the design of the database you modified in Exercise 12-28. Using the Documenter, print the structures for all your tables and queries. Include the properties, relationships, and permissions. Include the names, data types, and sizes for the fields. Include the names and field names for the indexes. On each printout, write your name and "Exercise 13-27a." Split your database. Verify your links. Print the structure of the split databases. On each printout, write your name and "Exercise 13-27b." Continue to the next exercise.

EXERCISE 13-28

Create two XML files and two Data Access Pages. Print the files and pages. On a sheet of paper, write one to three paragraphs describing when each would be more appropriate to use. Include your name and "Exercise 13-28" on each sheet. Continue to the next exercise.

EXERCISE 13-29

Create two PivotTables and two PivotCharts. Include your name and "Exercise 13-28" on each PivotTable and PivotChart. Print each PivotTable and PivotChart. Submit to your instructor printouts from Exercise 13-27 through 13-29. Keep a copy of each database. They will be used in subsequent lessons.

Unit 4 Applications

UNIT APPLICATION 4-1

Create a justified report with the Report Wizard. Build a calculated control. Use Access functions to show summaries in footers.

1. Copy the database CC-U4 and name it *[your initials]*CC-U4. Copy the database CC-E-U4 and name it *[your initials]*CC-E-U4. Update the linked tables to *[your initials]*CC-E-U4.

2. Edit qryStuffedAnimals. Add the ProductGroup, ListPrice, and QuantityOn-Hand fields to the query. Sort by the ProductGroup.

  TIP: In the Report Wizard, use the Add All button and then remove the QuantityOnHand field.

3. Use the Report Wizard with all fields except the QuantityOnHand field. Grouping is not necessary, but sort by ProductName in ascending order. Use a justified layout, portrait orientation, and the Casual style.

 NOTE: A justified report shows the fields side by side, left-to-right, and top-to-bottom. The text box and label are separate, with the labels above the text box.

4. Key **Stuffed Animals Retail Value** as the title.

 NOTE: This justified report is enclosed in a rectangle and all the controls have a hairline border.

5. Delete the ProductGroup text box and its label. Move the ListPrice text box and its label left to fill the space.

6. Copy and paste the ListPrice text box and its label. Move the copy to the right of the original ListPrice controls.

 TIP: Use a combination of nudging (using Ctrl and an arrow key) and mouse dragging to position the controls.

7. Change the label for the copy to **Retail Value**

8. Open the Expression Builder for the copied ListPrice text box. Build the following expression to show a retail value that reflects a 50% markup: **[ListPrice]*1.5**. Name this control **RetailValue**. Check that all currency controls shows two decimal places.

 TIP: To size a control in small increments, select it and press Shift and an arrow key to size the controls from any edge.

9. Center-align all labels, and then apply a light gray fill color.

10. Resize the Detail section, leaving one row of dots below the rectangle.

11. Group the records by ProductGroup with Group Header and Footer. Use Product Name to sort the records within the group.

12. Add the ProductGroup field to the Group Header, and format the label with a light gray fill and a thin black border.

13. Place a new text box in the group footer at the 2-inch horizontal mark. Build an expression to sum the quantity on hand. Change the label to **Group Quantity** and format it with light gray fill and a black border.

14. Place a new text box at the 5-inch horizontal mark in the Group Footer. Change the label to **Total Retail Value for Group**. Build an expression for the unbound control to compute the total retail value of the inventory: **Sum([ListPrice]*[QuantityOnHand]*1.5)**. Format the control as Currency, with two decimal places. Format and align the control to match the others. Right-align the text box with the Retail Value text box in the Detail section.

15. Open the Report Footer. Copy the Total Retail Value control in the Group Footer. Drag the copy to the Report Footer. Change the label to **Total Retail Value**

16. Force a page break before the ProductGroup header. Open the Page Header. Move the label from the Report Header to the Page Header and close the Report Header.

17. Format the main title in 18-point bold italic. Match the color and border to the rest of the report.

18. Delete the =Now() control in the Page Footer. Add a label in the same position, with your name.

19. Save the report and print page 5.

20. Edit the appropriate controls to determine what the retail values would be if the markup or margin were changed to 75%, instead of 50%. Print page 5.

21. Close the report without saving.

22. Find the report you just created and rename it **rptAnimalsValue**

UNIT APPLICATION 4-2

Build queries for a main report and its subreport. Create the main and subreports. Combine the reports.

1. Create a relationship between tblStuffedAnimals and tblKitContents without referential integrity.

2. Use the Simple Query Wizard to create a detail query with the following fields:

Table	Field
tblStuffedAnimals	KitNumber
	ProductID
	ProductName
	ListPrice
tblKitContent	SupplierID
	Cost

3. Save the query as **qryMainMarkup**

 REVIEW: You can enter a label for a calculated field in the Expression Builder by preceding it with a colon.

4. Add a calculated field to the query and title it **Markup**. The expression is **([ListPrice]–[Cost])/[Cost]** Change the format to percent with no decimal places.

 NOTE: You need to change the format in two steps. First, change the Format to Percent and view the query. Then set the decimal places.

5. Create another query in Design View by using tblKitContents and tblKitSuppliers.

6. Add KitNumber and SupplierID from tblKitContents. From tblKitSuppliers, add SupplierName, Address, City, State, PostalCode, and PhoneNumber.

7. Save the query as **qrySubMarkup**

8. Create a report in Design View for qryMainMarkup.

 REVIEW: Double-click the Field List title bar to select all the fields.

9. Drag all fields to the 1-inch horizontal mark in the Detail section. Change the font to 10-point Arial for all the controls. Show one row of dots between each pair of controls. Right-align the text boxes to better balance the text with the numbers.

10. Enter a label at the left margin in the Page Header that says **Stuffed Animals Suppliers**. Choose a font, size, and color.

11. Enter a label at the left margin in the Page Footer for your first and last name.

12. Use a text box at the right margin to place the long date in the Page Footer.

13. Save the report as **rptMainMarkup**. Close the report.

14. Create a report in Design View for qrySubMarkup.

15. Drag the following fields to the 1-inch horizontal mark in the Detail section: KitNumber, SupplierID, SupplierName, Address, and PhoneNumber.

16. Change the font to 10-point Arial. Position the controls to show one row of dots between each pair.

17. Arrange the controls so the phone number is below the supplier name and the address is below the phone number.

18. Create a new text box to align beneath the Address text box. Delete the label. Use the Expression Builder to create a concatenated text expression to show the city, state, and ZIP code on a single line.

19. Size the Detail section to show one row of grid dots below the last control. Close the Page Header and Footer sections.

20. Size the controls to see all the data, and make all controls the same font and size. Make the report **3.5** inches wide.

21. Save the report as **rptSubMarkup**

22. Open rptMainMarkup in Design View. Place a subform control to the right of the existing controls for rptSubMarkup. Define the link, using KitNumber. Use the default name.

23. Size the subreport control to closely fit the width of the subreport. Drag the right border of the main report to the 6.5-inch horizontal mark. Delete the subreport label.

24. Edit the subreport to make the KitNumber invisible. Size it to be very small, and move it to the top right edge of the design grid.

 NOTE: You might find it easier to edit the subreport in its own window rather than trying to edit from within the main report.

25. Move the other controls up until the top control is flush against the Detail bar. Keep one row of grid dots between controls. Adjust the height of the Detail section. Save the subreport.

26. Use no border for the subreport.

27. As a design element, add a horizontal line or an image to the report. Change the page margins or make other adjustments to fit four records per page.

28. Save the report and print page 2.

UNIT APPLICATION 4-3

Create a summary query and design a PivotChart.

1. Create a new query for tblCustomers and tblHistorySales. Show the OrderID and CompanyName fields. Group by CompanyName and Count by OrderID. Save the query as **qryNumOrders**

2. Switch to PivotChart View.

3. Set the bottom axis to be the field CompanyName.

4. Set the data for the chart to be the field CountOfOrderID.

5. Change the Caption of the Value Axis Title to **Number of Orders**

6. Change the axis title at the bottom of the chart to your name.

7. Add a main title and key **Number of Orders by Customer.** Set the font to 18-point Arial bold.

8. Select the Chart Workspace in the property sheet. On the Show/Hide tab, remove the check mark on Field buttons/drop zones.

9. Set print orientation to landscape and save.

10. Print the chart.

UNIT APPLICATION 4-4 *Using the Internet*

Find a table on the Web with data. Build a new database. Set a password for the database and import it into an Access table.

As we all know, the Internet is full of information. The trick is to be able to find and use it. Find a table on a Web page that lists information such as stock quotes, catalog items, college courses, or real estate listings. Look for a table that includes a row of headings at the top. Select and save the table. Access can recognize data found in HTML, XML, or HTM file formats.

 TIP: Not all tables in Web pages are well suited for this exercise.

Create a new database by using the wizard. Choose a name and set a password for your database.

Import the table you saved from the Web into your new database. View the data and check Design View. Apply input masks and other formatting that seems appropriate.

Create an appropriate report for your table and print it.

Using Advanced Features

LESSON 14

Building Forms with Subforms

OBJECTIVES

MOUS
ACTIVITIES
In this lesson:
Ac2002e **2-1**
Ac2002e **2-3**
Ac2002e **6-1**

See Appendix E.

After completing this lesson, you will be able to:

1. **Create a main form.**
2. **Format a main form.**
3. **Create a subform.**
4. **Add a subform to a main form.**
5. **Modify a subform control and a subform.**
6. **Add a command button to a form.**
7. **Create a form and a subform by using the wizard.**
8. **Create a grouped Data Access Page.**

 Estimated Time: 2 hours

Data from multiple tables is often required to answer business questions and present information in a meaningful way. Forms, like reports, enable you to work with more than one table at a time. You can base a form on a query, or use a link between two tables in the Form Wizard. In addition to using more than one table in a form, you can add enhancements that make a form easy and efficient to use.

You have learned that a Data Access Page is a Web document and provides access to tables. You can apply much of what you learn about designing forms to a Data Access Page.

562

Creating a Main Form

A *main form* is a form that contains one or more other forms. Forms that are placed in a main form are called *subforms*. Main forms and subforms generally use a One-to-Many relationship. The main form shows the "One" side; the subform shows the "Many" side.

Suppose you need to review sales orders onscreen. You need to know the customer's name as well as what and when the customer ordered. The Customers table includes names. The Sales Orders table includes basic information about the order, but not all the details. The Customers and Sales Orders tables are the basis for a main form. Other information is in a subform.

EXERCISE   14-1   View a Query and a Main Form

The form you work with in this exercise is a One-to-Many form. The top part of the form reflects the "One" side of the relationship. The entire form, which includes the subform, is the main form. You see one customer, with many items in the subform.

To scroll through the main form, place the insertion point anywhere except in the subform. When the insertion point is in the subform, you scroll through records in the subform.

1. Make a copy of **CC-14** and name it *[your initials]*CC-14. Make a copy of **CC-E-14** and name it *[your initials]*CC-E-14. Refresh your linked tables.

2. Open qrySalesReviewMain. The dynaset displays general information about each order.

3. Click the View button . Notice the join line. Close the query.

4. Open frmSalesReviewMain. The top part of the form shows the fields from qrySalesReviewMain. The subform shows information from tblSalesOrder-LineItems. Both parts of the form include the OrderID field. (See Figure 14-1 on the next page.)

    NOTE: The One-to-Many relationship is based on the Order ID field.

5. Click in the Order ID text box in the main form and click the Sort Ascending button . The Specific Record box for the main form shows that this is Record 1.

6. Click the Next Record button or press PgDn to go to the third record for Order ID 20103. The subform shows details about order 20103. The subform has its own Specific Record box. It shows the current record in the subform.

FIGURE 14-1
Sales Review
main form

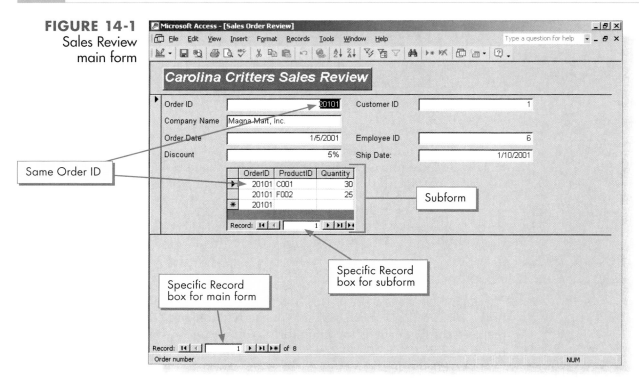

Same Order ID

7. Click the Next Record button ▶ in the subform. The Specific Record box in the subform shows "2," and the Specific Record box in the main form shows "3." Notice that the Order ID appears once in the main form but many times in the subform.

8. Click the Next Record ▶ and Previous Record ◀ buttons in both the main form and the subform until you are familiar with navigating in both parts of the form.

9. Close the form.

 EXERCISE 14-2 Create a Main Form

A main form is created in the same way that you create any other form. You can use wizards or Design View. You can base the form on a table or a query. You can format controls and add special features, such as command buttons.

NOTE: A main form and a subform can also be referred to as "a hierarchical form," "a master/detail form," or "a parent/child form."

1. Select qrySalesReviewMain and click the drop-down arrow for the New Object button . Choose **F**orm. Choose **Form Wizard** and click **OK**.

2. Add all **A**vailable Fields to the **S**elected Fields list. Click **N**ext and click **N**ext again.

3. Choose **C**olumnar for the layout. Click **N**ext.

4. Choose the **Standard** style. Click **N**ext.

5. Key **frmSalesOrdersMain** as the title. Choose the option **Open the form to view or enter information.**

6. Click **F**inish. Access creates and opens the form.

Formatting a Main Form

The main form is usually set to show a single form at a time. You can modify the position, size, and style of the controls and add a title in the **Form Header.** You have learned that you can use property sheets as well as toolbars to change most control properties. Like the controls, the form has its own property sheet.

EXERCISE **14-3** **Modify Form and Section Properties**

Through the form's properties dialog box, you can set the width of the form and the heights of each section.

1. Switch to Design View.

2. Double-click the Form Selector button.

3. Click the **Format** tab. Set the form **Width** to **4.125** inches.

4. Verify that the **Default View** is set to **Single Form**. (See Figure 14-2 on the next page.)

 TIP: Forms are in Single Form View by default.

5. Click the drop-down arrow for the Object box and choose **Detail.** The **Detail** section is shown in the property sheet. Set the **Height** of the section to **2.5** inches.

6. Click the **Form Header** bar. Set the **Height** to **.875** inch. Close the property sheet.

FIGURE 14-2
Main form in
Design View

Object box

Form Selector
button

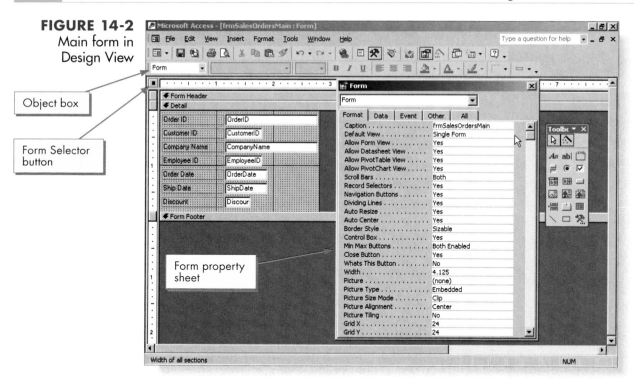

Form property
sheet

EXERCISE 14-4 Add and Format a Form Title

Each form should include a title. Proper titles help users identify the purpose
of each form.

1. Click the Label button and click at the left edge of the Form
   Header.
2. Key **Carolina Critters**. Press Ctrl + Enter and key **Sales Order Review** on
   the next line. Press Enter.
3. Change the font to 18-point bold italic Arial.
4. Double-click a sizing handle to size the label to fit.

5. Click the drop-down arrow for the Fill/Back Color button  and choose a
   dark color. Click the drop-down arrow for the Font/Fore Color button
   and choose white. Click the drop-down arrow for the Special Effect
   button and choose **Raised**.
6. Position the label to show two rows of dots above and below the label.
7. Save the form.

EXERCISE 14-5 Format Controls

Controls can be formatted as a group or individually.

1. Press [Ctrl]+[A] to select all controls.
2. Point at the center of the label in the **Form Header**, press [Shift], and click to deselect the control.

 TIP: It is easier to select all controls first and then deselect the one that should be excluded.

3. Set the font for the remaining controls to 10-point Arial.
4. While the controls are selected, choose F<u>o</u>rmat, <u>S</u>ize, and To <u>F</u>it.
5. Click anywhere to deselect the controls and view the form. Return to Design View.
6. Move and size the controls in the **Detail** section as shown in Figure 14-3. (Use the <u>A</u>lign command and the spacing tools on the F<u>o</u>rmat menu.

FIGURE 14-3
Modifying controls

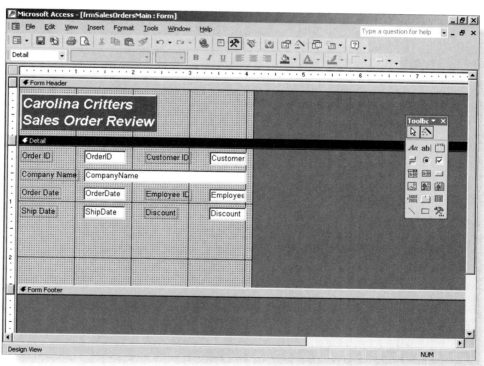

NOTE: The Make Equal command uses the vertical spacing between the first two selected controls as a guide and then spreads the controls to evenly fill the area between the top and bottom selected controls. The top and bottom controls do not move.

7. Save the form.

8. View your form to make sure you can see all the data.

EXERCISE **14-6** **Apply Conditional Formatting in Form View**

You can call attention to data on the screen by applying conditional formatting to a control. For example, you might highlight a product when its inventory level falls below the reorder level.

1. Switch to Form View and click the Discount text box.

2. Choose F̲ormat, Con̲ditional Formatting.

3. In the Condition 1 box, choose Field Value Is.

4. In the middle entry box, choose greater than.

5. In the third entry box, key **0**

6. Click the drop-down arrow for the Fill/Back Color button 🖌 and choose a bright color.

FIGURE 14-4
Setting conditional formatting

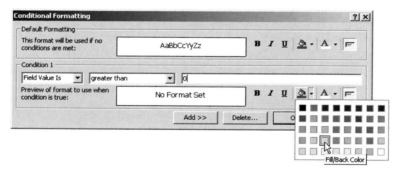

7. Click OK. Press PgDn to view the color changes for the field. Return to Design View.

8. Choose V̲iew, Ta̲b Order. Click the Auto Order button and then click OK. Test the order in Form View.

9. Save and close the form.

Creating a Subform

The Sales Review subform is a form in its own right, based on its own query. When you view the subform as a separate object in Form View, Access displays all the records. When you view the subform within the main form, however, only records that are related to the current record in the main form are displayed in the subform. As you work more with forms and subforms, the relationship between the two forms will become clearer.

EXERCISE 14-7 Change Views in a Subform

The subform is the bottom part of frmSalesReviewMain. It reflects the "Many" side of the relationship between the main form and the subform. It is based on a query that uses tblSalesOrderLineItems.

A main form is generally set for **Single Form** View so you see one form at a time. Many subforms are set to display records in Datasheet View.

1. Open qrySalesReviewSub. The dynaset displays specific information about each order.
2. Click the View button . The query uses all the fields from the table. Close the query.

   REVIEW: Queries process data more efficiently than tables and are better used as the basis for reports and forms.

3. Open frmSalesReviewSub. It includes the OrderID field, as does the main form.
4. Switch to Design View. Double-click the Form Selector button.
5. Click the **Format** tab and the **Default View** row. Select **Single Form**.

   REVIEW: Leave the property sheet open when you need to make additional changes.

6. Click the View button . This is a **Single Form** View showing one record per form, like the main form.
7. Return to Design View.
8. Switch to **Continuous Forms** View. View the form again. This form is designed in a tabular arrangement.

FIGURE 14-5
Changing the
Default View

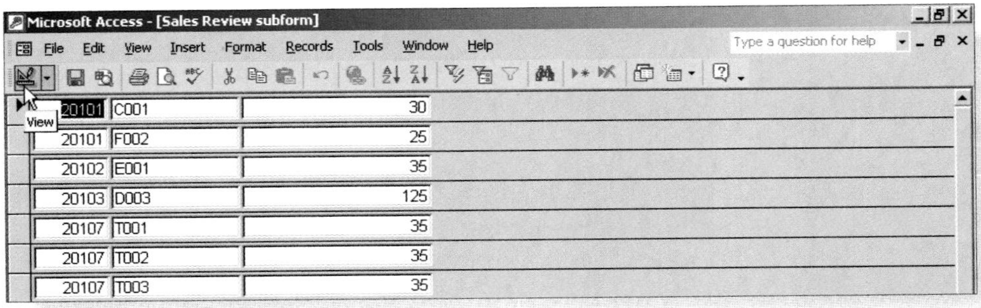

9. Return to Design View and set the Default View to Datasheet for this subform.

10. Close and save the form.

EXERCISE 14-8 Create a Tabular Form

You now create a subform on your own.

1. Click the Forms button and New. Choose Design View and qrySalesReview-Sub. Click OK.

2. Double-click the Field List title bar and drag the controls to the Detail section.

 REVIEW: Double-clicking the Field List title bar selects all the fields.

3. Select and delete the labels.

4. Drag the OrderID text box to the top left position in the Detail section.

5. Drag the ProductID text box to the right of the OrderID text box. Drag the Quantity text box to the right of the ProductID text box.

 REVIEW: Point at the edge of the vertical ruler to select all controls in a row.

6. Select and align these controls at the top.

7. Size the Detail section to show no grid dots below the controls.

FIGURE 14-6
Sales Orders
subform in
Design View

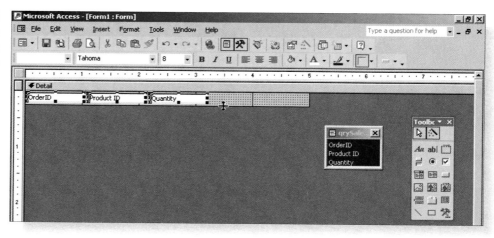

8. View the form. The Default View is Single Form.

9. Return to Design View and open the Form property sheet.

10. Set the **Default View** to **Continuous Forms** and close the property sheet.

11. View the form. Save it as **frmSalesOrdersSub** and close it.

Adding a Subform to a Main Form

You are now ready to add the subform to the main form. The subform is a database object just like any other form. It is also a control in the main form. For a form and subform to work as expected, there must be a common field between them.

EXERCISE **14-9** **Add a Subform to a Main Form**

When you use a wizard, Access looks for a common field to link. You could use the Subform/Subreport button in the toolbox to start the Subform/Subreport Wizard, or you could define and verify the link yourself.

REVIEW: The Control Wizards must be active to use the Subform/ Subreport button .

1. Open frmSalesOrdersMain in Design View. Maximize the window and close the Field List.

2. Scroll the window until you can see the empty part of the **Detail** section.

3. Click the Subform/Subreport button in the toolbox.

4. Position the pointer at the 1-inch mark horizontally, a couple of rows of grid dots below the lowest control. Click to start the wizard.

5. Click **Use an existing form** in the first dialog box, because the subform is already built.

6. Choose frmSalesOrdersSub. Click **Next**.

7. Click **Define my own** to verify and define the linking field.

8. In the **Form/report fields** group, click the drop-down arrow for the first row and choose OrderID.

9. In the **Subform/Subreport fields** group, click the drop-down arrow for the first row and select OrderID. (See Figure 14-7 on the next page.)

10. Click **Next** and use the default name for the subform. Click **Finish**.

11. Look at the completed form in Form View. Deselect the subform.

FIGURE 14-7
Defining the link
between a main
form and subform

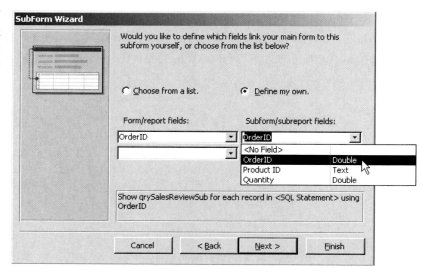

Modifying a Subform Control and a Subform

You place a subform in the main form as an object. It is a control and has many of the typical properties of other controls. You can format the subform control to set its size, border, and position. The subform has a label you can format or delete.

Although the subform is a control, it also is the subform itself. You can modify the usual form properties and controls directly from within the main form. You can also return to the Forms window and modify the subform just as you would any other form.

 NOTE: A subform can have its own subform with a One-to-Many relationship between the two.

EXERCISE **14-10** **Modify a Subform Control**

To select a subform control, point and click at its top or bottom edge. If you point near the scroll bars, you may scroll the subform in its window without selecting it. When the subform control is selected, its name appears in the Object box in the Formatting toolbar. You also see selection handles around the perimeter of the control.

1. While in Design View, choose frmSalesOrdersSub from the Object box.

FIGURE 14-8
Form and subform
in Design View

Object box

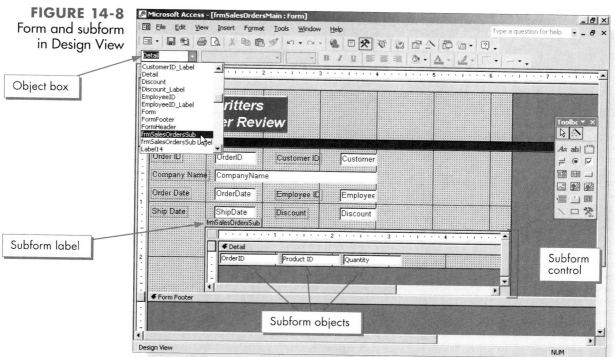

Subform label

Subform
control

Subform objects

2. Position the pointer to show an open hand and align the control's left edge at the .5-inch horizontal mark.

 3. Click the Properties button  to display the subform control's property sheet.

REVIEW: Check the title bar in the property sheet to verify which control is selected.

4. Set the Width to **3** inches and the Height to **2** inches. (See Figure 14-9 on the next page.)

5. Close the property sheet. Switch to Form View. The subform control is now not wide enough. Return to Design View.

NOTE: You might need to move the Form Footer bar to see the bottom selection handle on the subform.

6. Drag the right middle handle of the subform control to the 4-inch vertical mark. Drag the bottom middle handle to the 3-inch horizontal mark. View the form again.

FIGURE 14-9
Subform control
selected

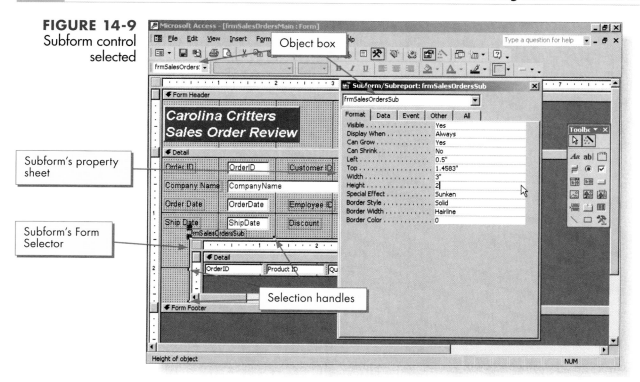

Subform's property
sheet

Subform's Form
Selector

Selection handles

7. Return to Design View. Select the subform label and delete it.

8. Size the Detail section of the main form so there is one row of grid dots below the subform control.

9. View the form. Return to Design View.

EXERCISE 14-11 Remove Navigation Icons and Scroll Bars

Modifying the subform control is one step in fine-tuning a form. For example, the subform on which you are working needs to be tall enough to show an order with five items (Order #20107). This requires modifying the subform control.

You also might discover that you need to make changes to the subform itself. Many subforms do not need to show navigation icons. You scroll to subforms through the main form. If you make the control tall enough, you also won't need scroll bars in the subform.

1. Double-click the subform's Form Selector to open the subform's property sheet.

 NOTE: The Data tab in the property sheet identifies the Record Source (where the form is getting data).

2. Click the Format tab and then click the Navigation Buttons row. Choose No.

3. Click the Scroll Bars row and choose Neither.

FIGURE 14-10
Subform
property sheet

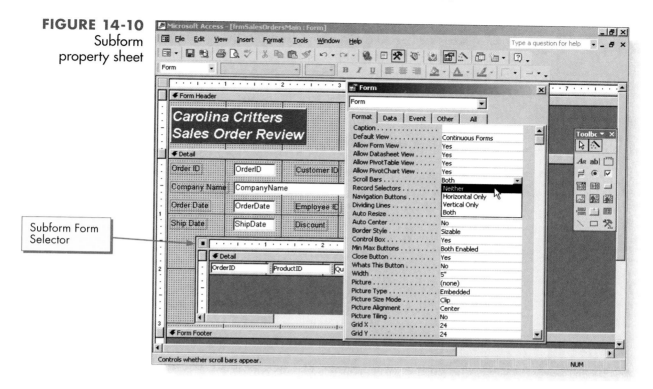

4. Close the property sheet and look at the subform in Form View. There are no navigation icons or scroll bars.

5. Return to Design View and open the subform's property sheet. Change the Default View to Datasheet. Close the property sheet.

 NOTE: There is a property sheet for the subform and the subform control.

 6. Click the Close button ⊠. The Save dialog box typically lists both open forms so you can save changes to both of them.

FIGURE 14-11
Saving changes to
all forms

7. Click Yes. Look at the main form in Form View. There are no navigation icons for the subform.

8. Return to Design View. Size the subform control to fit the data more closely. Save the form.

EXERCISE **14-12** Look at Subform Links

The main form is synchronized with the subform; therefore, the subform shows only records related to the current record in the main form. Access uses the **Link Master Fields** and **Link Child Fields** properties of the subform control to link the main form with the subform. Access enters these fields for you when you define the link by using the wizard.

If you create the link yourself, you enter the field names in the property dialog box of the subform. In the **Link Master Fields** row, you enter the name of the linking field from the main form. This is usually the primary key of the primary table in a One-to-Many relationship. In the **Link Child Fields** row, you enter the name of the linking field in the subform. The **Link Child Fields** row is a foreign key in the related table.

NOTE: Depending on how you create the form and subform and the relationship between the underlying tables or queries, Access determines the Link Child Fields and the Link Master Fields properties for you.

1. Open the property sheet for the subform frmSalesOrderSub.

2. Click the **Data** tab. Review the **Link Child Fields** row and the **Link Master Fields** rows. The OrderID fields are the linking fields between the two forms.

FIGURE 14-12
Linking fields
for the subform

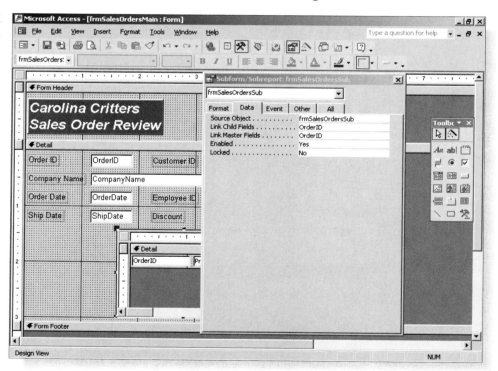

3. Close the property sheet and save.

4. Compact the database.

Adding a Command Button to a Form

A *command button* is a button you click to begin an action or a series of actions. You can create your own command buttons to run macros or Visual Basic procedures. (You will learn how to work with macros later in this text.)

EXERCISE 14-13 Add and Modify a Command Button

When the Control Wizards are on, you can click the Command Button button and click it to place a button on the form. When the wizard starts, you can select from six categories of commands or related actions. You can also specify the appearance of the button.

1. While in *[your initials]*CC-14, open frmSalesOrderMain in Design View.

2. Click the Command Button button in the toolbox. Click at the 5-inch horizontal mark, to the right of the subform control. The wizard starts.

3. In the first dialog box, choose Record Operations in the Categories list and Add New Record in the Actions list. This sets the category of command and the specific action.

FIGURE 14-13
Creating a
command button

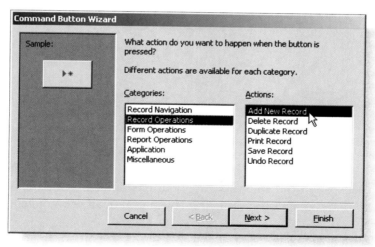

4. Click Next. Choose Text. A sample button with default text appears. (Rather than text, you could choose to display a picture in the command button.)

5. In the text box, key **Add New Order**

FIGURE 14-14
Choosing text for
the command button

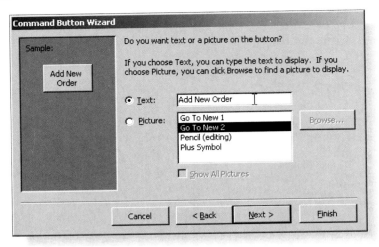

6. Click <u>N</u>ext. Name this control **cmdAddRecord** and click <u>F</u>inish.

 NOTE: The Leszynski naming convention also has prefixes for objects found in forms and reports. The prefix for a command button is "cmd."

7. Right-click the new command button and open its property sheet.
8. Click the **Format** tab. Set the **Width** to **1** inch. Close the property sheet.
9. Drag the command button into the Form header, aligned left at the 4-inch horizontal mark.
10. Save the form and switch to Form View.

 NOTE: Command buttons work in Form View when you click them, not in Design View.

EXERCISE 14-14   **Add a New Record by Using the Main Form**

You are now ready to add a new record by using the main form. As you add a new Order ID with its related line items, you are updating both underlying tables. Because of the One-to-Many relationship established between the tables in the underlying queries, some data is automatically completed, too.

1. Click the **Add New Order** button to open a blank form.
2. Click in the Order ID text box at the top and key **20121** as the order number. Press Tab.
3. Key **6** as the Customer ID and press Tab. Access fills in the Company Name. Press Tab.

4. Key today's date as the Order Date in mm/dd/yy format. Press ⌷Tab⌷. Key **7** as the Employee ID, a week from today as the Ship Date, and **.05** as the Discount.

5. Press ⌷Tab⌷ to move to the subform. The discount color appears because the discount is greater than zero, and the Order ID is filled in.

6. Press ⌷Tab⌷ and key **T005** as the first Product ID. Press ⌷Tab⌷ and key **35** as the quantity.

7. Enter a second line item. Key **F002** as the Product ID and **50** as the quantity.

8. Close the form.

9. Open tblSalesOrders. Look for Order ID 20121.

10. Expand the subdatasheet for this record. These are the related records from tblSalesOrderLineItems.

11. Collapse the subdatasheet. Close the table.

Creating a Form and Subform by Using the Form Wizard

If there is a One-to-Many relationship between tables, you can use the Form Wizard to create a main form with a subform. You choose both tables with the appropriate fields. The wizard lets you establish which is the main form and which is the subform.

EXERCISE **14-15** **Create a Form and Subform by Using the Form Wizard**

A simple way to create a main form with a subform is to use the Form Wizard to base the new form on a preexisting One-to-Many relationship.

1. Open the Relationships window. Verify that there is a One-to-Many relationship between tblHistorySales and tblHistoryLineItems. Close the window.

2. Click Forms. Double-click Create form by using wizard.

3. Choose tblHistorySales and all the fields.

4. Choose tblHistoryLineItems. Use ProductID and Quantity. Click Next.

5. When you use two tables, the wizard asks how you want to view the data. The table you choose becomes the basis for the main form. Choose tblHistorySales.

6. Click Form with subform(s).

FIGURE 14-15
Setting the
main form
in the wizard

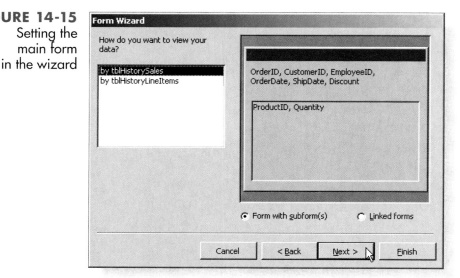

7. Click <u>N</u>ext. Choose a <u>D</u>atasheet layout for the subform. Click <u>N</u>ext.

8. Choose the Industrial style and click <u>N</u>ext.

9. Edit the name for the main form to **frmHistorySales**. Edit the subform name to **frmHistoryLineItems**. Choose the option to open the form, and click <u>F</u>inish.

10. View the form. In Design View, move the subform control down until there is the same amount of white space above it as the other controls.

11. Save the form.

EXERCISE 14-16 Add a Combo Box to a Main Form

A *combo box* is a control that shows a drop-down list. Using a combo box, you can choose a value from the drop-down list or you can enter a new value in the combo box.

To create the drop-down list, you can key the list of values or you can use another table as the basis for the list. In the form on which you are working, you can use a combo box to select the Order ID number in the main form. Then Access updates the subform to show the related line items.

1. Delete the OrderID control and label.

2. Click the Combo Box button 📑.

3. Click at the 1-inch horizontal mark where the OrderID control was located. The wizard starts.

4. Choose Find a <u>r</u>ecord on my form based on the value I selected in my combo box. (See Figure 14-16 on the next page.)

5. Click <u>N</u>ext. Double-click OrderID and click <u>N</u>ext.

FIGURE 14-16
Choosing how
a combo box
gets its values

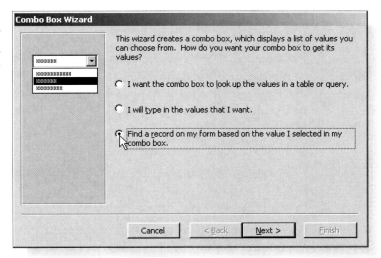

6. Adjust the width of the column to fit the data. Click Next.

7. Set the label to show **Order ID** and click Finish.

8. Size the label and combo box to match the others.

 TIP: Check the property sheet for the width of an existing control and then set the combo box to match.

9. Save and view the form.

10. Click the drop-down arrow in the combo box and choose an order number. The subform changes to match.

11. Return to Design View and open the property sheet for the combo box.

12. Click the Data tab and the Row Source row. Press Shift + F2 . Access builds SQL code for the combo box that chooses the OrderID field from the table.

 NOTE: SQL stands for "Structured Query Language." It is a widely used language for database queries.

FIGURE 14-17
SQL code for the
combo box

13. Click Cancel. Save and close the form.

Creating a Grouped Data Access Page

A Data Access Page has objects or controls similar to a form. You can apply your knowledge about designing and modifying forms to designing Data Access Pages. A Data Access Page uses a table or a query to display current data on a Web site, but it resembles a form layout. The controls are similar but limited.

EXERCISE	14-17	Create a Data Access Page in Design View

A Data Access Page is saved as an HTML document in the same folder as the database. It is not part of the database, however. Access creates a shortcut to the document and shows that shortcut in the Pages window.

Spacing in a Data Access Page is measured in pixels, not inches. A *pixel* is a unit of measurement for computer screens. A pixel is also known as a screen dot.

1. Create and save a query for tblCustomers, tblHistorySales, and tblHistoryLineItems.

 NOTE: If you do not see join lines, you must create them.

2. Add CompanyName to the design grid. From tblHistorySales, add OrderID and OrderDate. From tblHistoryLineItems, use ProductID and Quantity.

3. Save and close the query.

4. Click the **Pages** button and then click **New**. Choose Design View and your new query. Click **OK**.

5. Drag the CompanyName field from the Field List to the grid area. (See Figure 14-18 on the next page.)

 NOTE: The selection handles are hollow in Page Design. The move/size pointer is an open hand.

6. Select the Company Name label and delete it.

7. Select the text box control. Drag a corner handle to make it larger, and then open its property sheet.

FIGURE 14-18
New Data Access
Page in Design View

FIGURE 14-18
New Data Access
Page in Design View

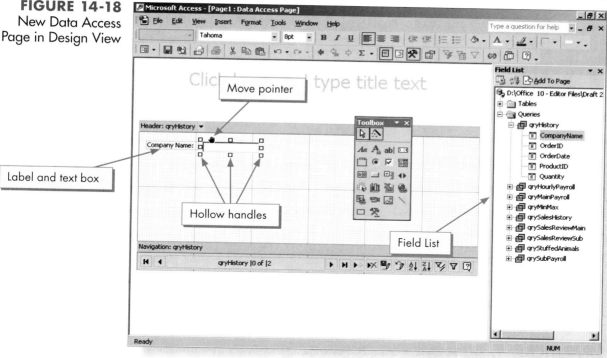

8. Click the Format tab. Set the Width to **350** for 350 pixels. Set the Height to **27**

FIGURE 14-19
Text box control
property sheet
in the
Data Access Page

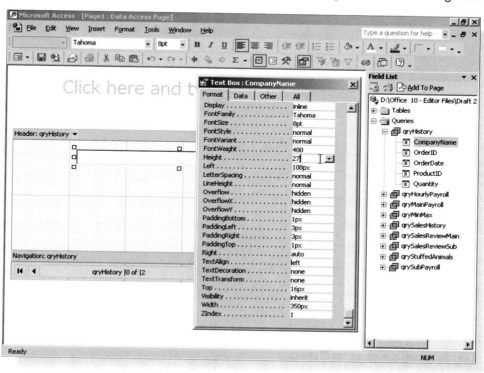

9. Close the property sheet. Set the font to 14-point bold italic Arial. Click the View button .

10. Click the Last Page navigation icon. There is a page for each order from the query, a total of 59 pages.

11. Return to Design View. Save the page as **pgeHistory**

EXERCISE **14-18** **Promote a Field to a Group Level**

If you use the Page Wizard, you can choose to use grouping in one of the dialog boxes. When you build a page in Design View, you promote fields from the main body section to the next highest group. Grouping uses levels similar to Word or PowerPoint outlining.

1. Click the text box. Click the Promote button . The text box is moved up one level to a Group Header. The Group Header shows the field name. There is an Expand button + to the left of the control.

FIGURE 14-20
Text box promoted to a group level

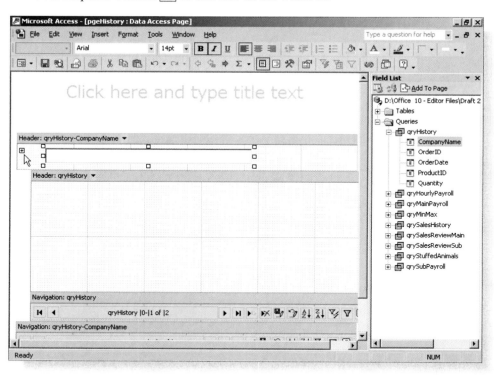

2. Switch to Page View. There are ten groups now, one for each company. The groups are collapsed.

3. Click the Expand button ⊞ for Children's Hospital. The group expands but there is nothing in it at this time.

FIGURE 14-21
Groups in the
Data Access Page

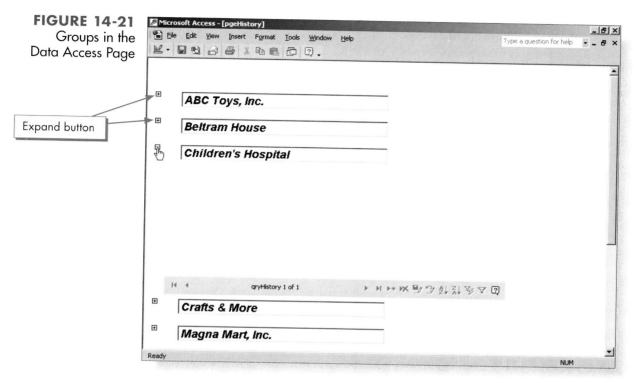

Expand button

4. Click the Collapse button ⊟. Return to Design View.
5. Click anywhere below the second **Header** bar, in the main body section. Click the OrderID field in the Field List. Click **Add To Page**, located at the top of the Field List. The control is added in the main body section.
6. Select the OrderID label and make it 12-point italic Arial. Resize it to fit.
7. Select the text box and make it 11-point bold Arial. Move the label away from the text box for better spacing.

TIP: It is easier to move the label away from the text box than to move the text box away from the label.

8. Select the text box and click the Promote button ⬅. Access promotes the OrderID field to a group beneath the CompanyName group.
9. Click the View button 🖽. Expand a company group and then an order group. There is nothing in the order group yet. Collapse all groups and return to Design View.
10. Save the page.

EXERCISE 14-19 Add Fields to the Body of the Page

The main body section of the Data Access Page is similar to the Detail section of a form or report. You add the fields that represent the data you want to see. If you accidentally place a control in the wrong section, drag it to the correct location.

1. Click in the main body section. Double-click OrderDate, ProductID, and Quantity. The fields are placed in the main section.

2. Close the Field List window.

3. Select the OrderDate label. Choose Edit, and Delete.

4. Open the property sheet for the OrderDate text box.

 TIP: You can use inches as the measurement unit by keying **in** immediately after the number, without a period.

5. Set the Left position to **1in**, the Top at **.083in**, the Height at **.26in**, and the Width at **1in**.

FIGURE 14-22
Text boxes in the main section of the Data Access Page

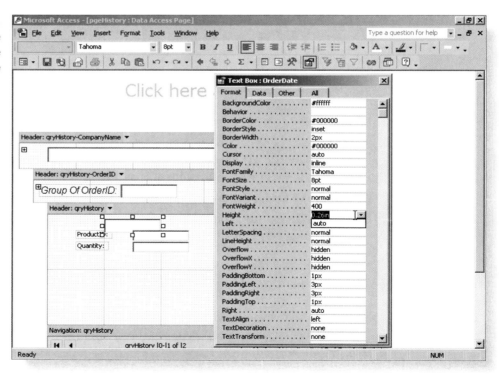

6. Close the property sheet. Select and delete the ProductID label. Drag the text box next to the OrderDate text box.

7. Select and delete the Quantity label. Drag the Quantity text box to the ProductID text box.

8. Make the text boxes the same height and align them.

9. Double-click the main body section and set the Height to **41px**

10. Click the title placeholder and key **Sales History by Customer**

11. Change the OrderID label to **Order ID** and save the page.

12. View the page. Expand Craft & More. Notice that the Order IDs are in ascending order. Expand one of the orders.

FIGURE 14-23
Expanded group in
Page View

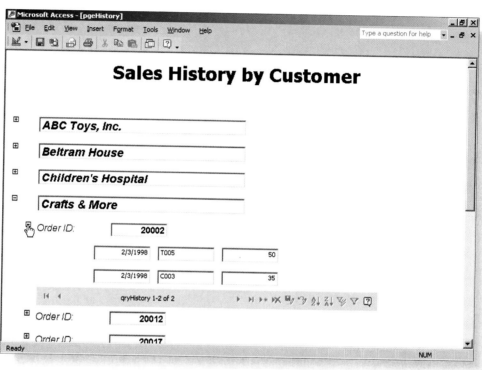

13. Return to Design View.

EXERCISE 14-20 Add Captions and AutoSum Function

Complete the form layout by changing the section captions and by adding an AutoSum function. Changing the captions makes the form more user-friendly. Adding AutoSum causes the form to count the total number of orders.

1. Click the Group Level Properties drop-down arrow for the CompanyName Header.

2. Choose Caption. A section for labels (caption) opens above the Group Header.

3. Click a new label in the section. Change the label to show **Company Names:** (include the colon).

4. Change the font to 14-point bold italic Arial.

5. View the page and then adjust the label if it needs it.

6. Click the Group Level Properties drop-down arrow for the Header qryHistorySales section (the main body).

7. Choose Caption. Add a new label.

8. Click the Properties button .

9. Click the Other tab. Change the InnerText to **Order Date**

NOTE: The label properties are named differently in a page.

10. Click the Format tab. Set the font to 10-point bold Arial.

11. Close the property sheet.

12. Position the label above the appropriate text box.

FIGURE 14-24
Adding a
Caption section

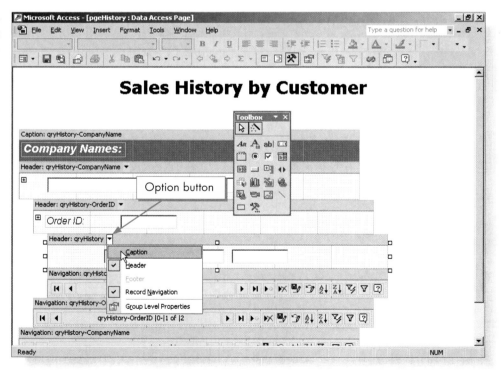

13. Add labels for ProductID and Quantity. Format appropriately.

14. Select the OrderID text box in the OrderID Group Header.

15. Click the drop-down arrow for the AutoSum button Σ.

16. Choose **Count**. A text box and label are added just above the control that counts the number of orders for each new company name.

17. Click to display a text insertion point and change the label to **Number of Orders:** (include the colon).

18. Drag the control to the right of the CompanyName control and resize it if it needs it.

19. Select the OrderDate text box in the main body section.

20. Click the drop-down arrow for the AutoSum button Σ and choose **Count**.

21. Change the label to **Number of Line Items:** (include the colon).

22. Drag the control to the right of the OrderID control in the OrderID Header, and resize it if it doesn't fit well.

FIGURE 14-25
New
calculated fields

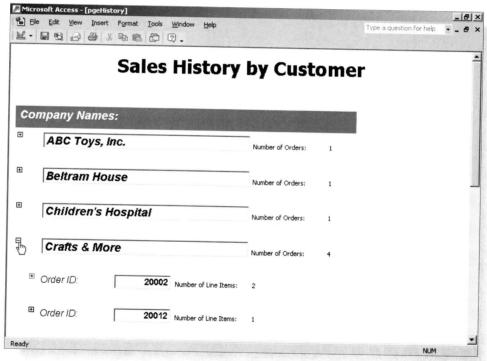

23. View the page and save it. Establish an Internet connection.

24. Choose **File**, **Web Page Preview**. The page opens in your browser.

25. Close the browser. Compact the database and exit Access.

USING HELP

In addition to the basic design ideas you applied to a Data Access Page, you can apply a "theme," similar to an AutoFormat for forms and reports. (If the Office Assistant starts, turn it off.)

Use the Answer Wizard to learn about Data Access Page themes:

1. Press F1 and click the Answer Wizard tab.

2. Key **what is a theme** and press Enter.

3. Click About themes in the list. Click Show All and read the Help window.

FIGURE 14-26
Microsoft Access
Help

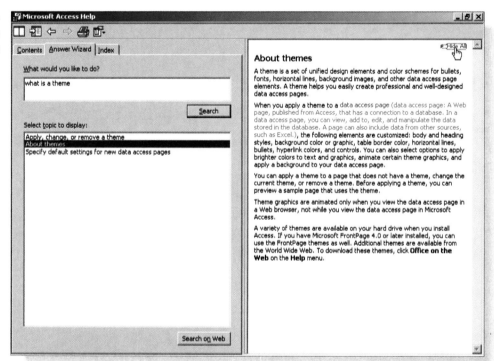

4. Click Apply, change, or remove a theme from the list. Click Show All and read the window.

5. Close Help.

LESSON Summary

➤ A main form is a container for a subform. Main forms and subforms are linked by a common field. The subform is a form on its own as well as a control in the main form.

➤ Main forms and subforms are formatted like typical forms. You can format a subform from within the main form.

➤ A subform is often set for **Datasheet View**, but the main form is set for **Single Form** View.

➤ A command button is a control that, when clicked, carries out a series of steps. Access provides several preset command buttons to carry out common tasks.

➤ A combo box is a control that shows a drop-down list.

➤ You can group a Data Access Page to show all records from a particular company or in a particular order in one section. Groups can be expanded or collapsed.

➤ Adding a calculated field to the **Caption** area summarizes the data in the group below it.

LESSON 14 Command Summary

FEATURE	BUTTON	MENU	KEYBOARD	SPEECH
Command Button	▭			
Combo Box	▤			
Expand group	+			
Collapse group	−			

Concepts Review

Each of the following statements is either true or false. Indicate your choice by circling T or F.

T F **1.** A main form is a container for other forms.

T F **2.** In a main form with a subform, the form on the "One" side of the One-to-Many relationship is the subform.

T F **3.** The Specific Record box in the main form tells you the current record of the main form and the subform.

T F **4.** A grouped Data Access Page displays the records in the same way as a grouped report.

T F **5.** A combo box shows two choices with option buttons.

T F **6.** The Link Child Fields property displays the linking field in the main form.

T F **7.** You can format the controls in a Data Access Page by using the same commands as for formatting controls in a form.

T F **8.** You can set a form to display one or several records at a time.

Write the correct answer in the space provided.

1. What button must be turned on to use the Subform/Subreport Wizard?

_____

2. What database object displays table or query data in a layout for Web viewing?

_____

3. What is the keystroke combination for entering a line break in a label?

_____

4. Name three views for records in a form.

_____

5. Which buttons do you click to see or hide the groups in a Data Access Page?

_____

6. What does a combo box do?

_____

7. How can you set a precise width, such as 1.35 inches, for a control?

_____

8. How do you open the Form property sheet?

_____

CRITICAL THINKING

Answer these questions on a separate page. There are no right or wrong answers. Support your answers with examples from your own experience, if possible.

1. What other main forms with subforms might be built for the tables in the Carolina Critters databases? Explain how the tables are related and which form would be the "One" form.

2. Discuss what types of command buttons you might find helpful on a form.

Skills Review

EXERCISE 14-21

Create and format a main form. Create a subform. Add a subform to a main form.

1. Create a main form by following these steps:

    a. Open *[your initials]*CC-14 and refresh the linked tables from *[your initials]*CC-E-14.

    b. Use the Form Wizard to create a new form for tblJobCodes. Add both fields to the <u>S</u>elected Fields list. Use a <u>C</u>olumnar layout and the Standard style. Name the form **frmJobCodesMain**. Make the form 6 inches wide. Make the Detail section 2 inches tall.

    c. Press Ctrl + A and change the font to 10-point Arial.

    d. Move the JobCode controls until the left edge of the label is at the 3-inch horizontal mark, two rows of grid dots down.

    e. Move the JobTitle controls up to align with the JobCode controls.

    f. Open the Form Header property sheet. Set the Height to **0.75** inch.

 **REVIEW:** Double-click the Form Header bar to open the property sheet.

    g. Key a label in the Form Header to show **Carolina Critters**. Press Ctrl + Enter and key **Job Codes** on the second line.

h. Change the font to 18-point bold Arial. Center-align the title.

i. Size the label box to be the same width as the form.

 NOTE: When you make a label the same width as the form and use the Center command, the text appears centered on the form.

j. Save and close the form.

2. Create a tabular subform by following these steps:

   a. Use the Form Wizard to create a form for tblEmployees.

   b. Use these fields: JobCode, EmployeeID, LastName, and FirstName, in that order. Use a Tabular layout and the Standard style. Name the form **frmJobCodesSub** and close the form.

3. Add a subform to a main form by following these steps:

   a. Open **frmJobCodesMain** in Design View and maximize the window.

   b. Verify that the Control Wizards button in the toolbox is turned on.

   c. Click the Subform/Subreport button 📇 and click at the 1-inch horizontal mark below the controls.

   d. Click the option Use an existing form and choose frmJobCodesSub. Click Next.

   e. The link is correctly identified. Click Next.

   f. Accept the default name for the subform control and click Finish.

   g. Save your form. View it and scroll through several forms.

EXERCISE 14-22

Modify the subform control. Add and format a command button.

1. Modify a subform control by following these steps:

   a. With frmJobCodesMain open in Design View, right-click the frmJob-CodesSub control and select Properties.

   REVIEW: Verify which property sheet is open in the title bar.

   b. Click the Format tab and change the Width to **4.75** inches. Change the Height to **2** inches. Close the property sheet.

   c. Delete the subform label.

   d. Double-click the subform's Form Selector and click the Format tab.

   e. In the Default View row, choose Datasheet. Close the property sheet.

   f. View the form and save the changes.

2. Modify a subform by following these steps:

   a. In the subform, make the JobCode text box and label smaller so they fit the data better. Move the other controls to the left and resize them as needed. Drag the right edge of the Subform to about the 4-inch mark.

TIP: Select all the controls and use F<u>o</u>rmat, Hori<u>z</u>ontal Spacing, and Make <u>E</u>qual to spread controls across the selected area.

    b. Open the subform property sheet and set the Default View to Continuous Forms.

    c. Switch to Form View. Use the navigation buttons to explore the main form and subform.

    d. Size all controls so no data is cut off. You can move labels if you need to.

3. Add a command button to a main form by following these steps:

    a. Size the Detail section of the main form to show space below the subform control.

    b. Click the Command Button button ⬛ and click below the subform control.

    c. Choose the Record Operations category and the Print Record action. Click <u>N</u>ext.

    d. Choose <u>P</u>icture to use the sample image. Click <u>N</u>ext.

    e. Name the control **cmdPrintRecord** and click <u>F</u>inish.

    f. Click the View button ⬛ to see and test the command button. The command button selects and prints the current form.

    g. Save the form.

4. Set the command button properties by following these steps:

    a. Return to Design View.

    b. Right-click the command button control and select <u>P</u>roperties.

    c. Click the Format tab and set the Left position at **2.5** inches. Set the Width at **1** inch. Close the property sheet.

    d. View, save all the changes, and close the main form.

EXERCISE 14-23

Create a subform with the wizard. Add a combo box control.

1. Create a subform in the wizard by following these steps:

    a. Open the Relationships window. Click the Show All Relationships button ⬛.

    b. Add tblCarriers to the layout. Set a One-to-Many relationship with tblSalesOrders. Close the window.

    c. Click Forms. Double-click Create form by using wizard.

    d. Choose tblCarriers and all the fields.

    e. Choose tblSalesOrders and all the fields. Click <u>N</u>ext.

NOTE: Because the CarrierID field is in both tables, the table identifier is included in the Selected Fields list.

    f. View the data by tblCarriers. Click the Form with <u>s</u>ubform(s) button. Click <u>N</u>ext.

g. Choose a <u>D</u>atasheet layout for the subform. Click <u>N</u>ext.

h. Choose the Industrial style and click <u>N</u>ext.

i. Edit the name for the main form to **frmCarriers&Sales**. Edit the sub-form name to **frmSales**. Choose the option to open the form, and click <u>F</u>inish.

j. In Design View, move the subform control down until there is the same amount of white space above it as in the other controls.

 REVIEW: You can nudge the subform control with Ctrl and any arrow key.

k. Save the form.

2. Add a combo box to a form by following these steps:

a. Delete the Carrier ID control and label.

b. Click the Combo Box button 📇.

c. Click at the 1-inch horizontal mark where the Carrier ID control was located.

d. Choose Find a <u>r</u>ecord on my form based on the value I selected in my combo box. Click <u>N</u>ext.

e. Double-click CarrierID and click <u>N</u>ext.

f. Adjust the width of the column to fit the data. Click <u>N</u>ext.

g. Set the label to show **Carrier ID**. Click <u>F</u>inish.

h. Size and position the label and combo box to match the others.

i. Save and view the form.

j. Make any necessary formatting changes to the subform and its label.

k. Print the form for Carrier A101 in landscape. Close the form.

EXERCISE 14-24

Create a grouped Data Access Page. Promote fields to a group level. Add fields to the main section. Add an AutoSum function.

1. Create a grouped Data Access Page by following these steps:

a. Create and save a query for tblCarriers, tblSalesOrders, and tblSalesOrderLineItems.

 REVIEW: If you do not see automatic join lines in the query, you must create the join.

b. Add CarrierName to the design grid. From tblSalesOrders, add OrderID and OrderDate. From tblSalesOrderLineItems, use ProductID and Quantity. Save as **qryCarrier**, and then close the query.

c. Click the Pages button. Click <u>N</u>ew. Choose Design View and the query qryCarrier.

d. Drag CarrierName from the Field List to the unbound section. Delete the label.

> *e.* Select the text box control and open its property sheet. Set the Width to **3in**. Set the Height to **.5in**. Close the property sheet.
>
> *f.* Set the font to 16-point bold italic Arial. View the page.
>
> *g.* Save the page as **pgeCarriers**
>
> *h.* Select the text box and click the Promote button .

2. Promote another field to a group level by following these steps:

> *a.* Click the main body section of the page. Click OrderID in the Field List. Click <u>A</u>dd to Page.
>
> *b.* Select the Order ID label and make it 12-point italic Arial.
>
> *c.* Select the text box and make it 11-point bold Arial. Move the label away from the text box.
>
> *d.* Select the text box and click the Promote button .
>
> *e.* View the page. Expand a carrier group and then an order group. Collapse all groups and return to Design View.
>
> *f.* Make any changes you feel are appropriate, and save the page.

3. Add fields to the main section by following these steps:

> *a.* Click to select the Header:qryCarrier section. Double-click OrderDate, ProductID, and Quantity. Close the Field List window.
>
> *b.* Open the Caption section for qryCarrier.
>
> *c.* Drag all three labels up into the Caption section.
>
> *d.* Open the property sheet for the OrderDate text box.
>
> *e.* Set the Height at **.25in**, the Left position at **1in**, the Top at **.25in**, and the Width at **1in**. Close the property sheet.
>
> *f.* Drag the ProductID text box next to the Order Date text box.
>
> *g.* Drag the Quantity text box next to the Product ID text box. Size the text boxes to match the first one. Move the labels so they are above their text boxes. Resize controls to show all data.
>
> *h.* Click the title placeholder and key **Sales by Carrier**
>
> *i.* Click the OrderID text box. Create a calculated field that will count the number of Orders.
>
> *j.* Drag the text box to the right of the CarrierName text box. Change the text of the label to **Number of Orders:** (include the colon).
>
> *k.* View the page. Expand a carrier company and its orders. Collapse each level after you view the data. Finish with the carrier All Air Ways and their Orders expanded.
>
> *l.* Print and save the page.

> **NOTE:** You can size a section in a Data Access Page by dragging a handle.

> *m.* Open the page in Internet Explorer. Expand and collapse again.
>
> *n.* Close the page and Internet Explorer.
>
> *o.* Compact the database and exit Access.

Lesson Applications

EXERCISE 14-25

Create and format a subform. Create and format a main form. Add the subform.

1. Open *[your initials]***CC-14** and refresh the linked tables from *[your initials]***CC-E-14**. Create a query in Design View for tblKitContents and tblStuffedAnimals. Show the KitNumber and SupplierID from tblKitContents and ProductName from tblStuffedAnimals. Sort by KitNumber. Save the query as **qryKitsSub**

2. Create a new form in Design View for the query. Drag all the fields to the Detail section.

3. Delete the labels. Position the text boxes in a single row in this order from left to right: KitNumber, ProductName, SupplierID. Start the row near the left edge of the form.

4. Set the form's Default View to Datasheet.

5. Switch to Form View. Select the SupplierID column. Then choose Format, Hide Columns.

6. Save the form as **frmKitsSub** and close it.

7. Create a columnar AutoForm for tblKitSuppliers. Apply the Blueprint AutoFormat.

8. Delete the SupplierNumber controls. Delete the City, State, and PostalCode controls. Delete all the remaining labels.

9. Select the text boxes and change the font to 10-point bold Arial.

10. Place the SupplierName text box at a Left position of **.25** inch and a Top position of **.125** inch. Make it **2.25** inches wide.

11. Place the Address text box two rows of grid dots below the SupplierName text box and make it the same size.

 REVIEW: Move controls out of the way when necessary.

12. Place the ContactName text box at a Left position of **3** inches and a Top position of **.125** inch. Make it **2** inches wide.

13. Draw a text box below the Address text box for a concatenated expression to show the city, state, and ZIP code. Make this control the same size as the Address text box. Delete its label and set the font to match.

14. Move the phone and fax fields below the ContactName text box. Make them the same width as the ContactName control.

15. Select all the controls and set the Height to **.25** inch.

16. View the form. Save the form as **frmKitsMain**

17. Open the property sheet for the SupplierID text box and set its Visible property to No. Move this control to the 5-inch horizontal mark, aligned right with the ContactName control.

18. Add a label in the Form Header and key **Supplier Kits**. Set the label font to 24-point bold italic Arial. Align the label on the left with the leftmost text box in the Detail section.

 REVIEW: Double-click a handle in a label to size it to the text.

19. Add frmKitsSub below the concatenated control. The link is the SupplierID field.

20. Determine how tall and wide the subform control should be. Size it and delete its label.

21. Size the Product Name column in Form View. Add a label with your name in the Form Header.

22. Print the first record only. Close and save all changes.

EXERCISE 14-26

Create a Data Access Page without groups.

1. Click the Pages button. Double-click Create Data Access Page by using wizard. Use tblJobCodes and all the fields.

2. Do not use any grouping. Sort by JobCode.

3. Edit the name to **pgeJobCodes** and open the page.

4. Select the main table object and apply a light fill color.

5. Click the title text placeholder and key **Job Codes**

6. Click just above the main section and key **These are current job codes and titles at Carolina Critters.**

7. Make any other appropriate design changes.

8. Add a label with your name to the Form Header. Save the page.

9. Print the record for the Vice President for Research and Development.

10. Open the page in Internet Explorer. Exit Explorer.

EXERCISE 14-27

Create a form and subform by using the wizard.

1. Create a One-to-Many relationship between tblJobCodes and tblEmployees.

2. Create a new form by using the wizard. Use both fields from tblJobCodes and the first and last name fields from tblEmployees.

3. View the data by tblJobCodes and make a form with a subform in datasheet layout.

4. Choose a style and name the main form with an **frm** prefix. Edit the subform name to use the prefix and remove the space.

5. View and save the form.

6. Use a combo box for the JobCode control.

7. Add a label with your name to the forms header.

8. Print the record for Administrative Support Specialist.

9. Save and view the form; then close it.

E X E R C I S E 14-28 *Challenge Yourself*

Add a command button to a form.

1. Add a command button in the Form Header of frmKitsMain to close the form.

2. Add another command button to print the current record.

3. Test the buttons.

On Your Own

In these exercises you work on your own, as you would in a real-life work environment. Use the skills you've learned to accomplish the task—and be creative.

EXERCISE 14-29

Review the designs of the databases you modified in Exercise 13-29. Create sketches of three new main forms with subforms. On each sketched form, write the name of the form, describe its purpose, and list the source dynaset(s). On at least one of the forms, add two or more command buttons. List the purpose of each button. On each sketch, write your name and "Exercise 14-29." Continue to the next exercise.

EXERCISE 14-30

Based on the sketches you created in Exercise 14-29, create three main forms with subforms. Select the style and layout most appropriate for each form. Arrange the controls appropriately. For all forms, include your name and "Exercise 14-30" in the footer and the title of the form in the header. Print a copy of each form. Continue to the next exercise.

EXERCISE 14-31

Sketch two Data Access pages. On each sketch, write the name of the page, describe its purpose, and list the source dynaset(s). Include your name and "Exercise 14-31" on each page. Create and print the pages. Submit sketches and printouts from Exercises 14-29 through 14-31 to your instructor. Keep copies of the databases. They will be used in subsequent lessons.

LESSON 15

Using Special Controls and Tools

After completing this lesson, you will be able to:

1. **Add and format an option group.**
2. **Change a control type.**
3. **Use list and combo boxes in a form.**
4. **Create a multipage form.**
5. **Use a hyperlink in a form.**
6. **Add a PivotChart to a form.**
7. **Create a Switchboard.**
8. **Replicate a database.**

 Estimated Time: 2 hours

As you work with forms, you will see how they can be more functional than tables for entering and editing data. In this lesson, you expand your knowledge of forms. You use option and toggle buttons for Yes/No fields. You create option groups for selecting from a list of choices. You also learn how to create multipage forms and Switchboards.

Adding and Formatting an Option Group

An *option group* is a control object consisting of a set of buttons or check boxes that represent choices for data entry. For example, the company's sales orders are shipped by one of three carriers. You could create an option group control with three option group buttons, one for each carrier. (An *option group button* indicates one of the choices in the option group.) When there are five or fewer choices, option groups are good to use.

FIGURE 15-1
An option group

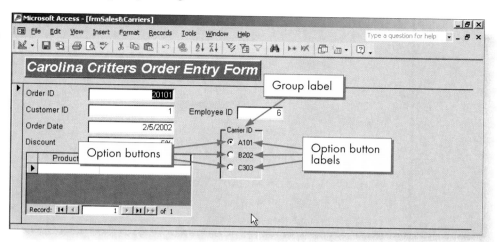

NOTE: In the above example, if you use one carrier most of the time, you could set that carrier as the default option.

EXERCISE **15-1** **Copy a Form**

When making advanced changes to forms, a good practice is to make a copy of the original form.

1. Make a copy of **CC-15** and name it *[your initials]***CC-15**. Make a copy of **CC-E-15** and name it *[your initials]***CC-E-15**. Refresh your linked tables. Click the Forms button.

2. Open frmSalesOrderEntryMain and maximize the window. This form is set for Data Entry, so you do not see existing records.

3. Switch to Design View and open the form's property sheet.

 REVIEW: Double-click or right-click the Form Selector to open the property sheet.

4. Click the Data tab. This form is based on tblSalesOrders. The Data Entry row shows **Yes**.

5. Click the Data Entry row and change its setting to **No** (See Figure 15-2 on the next page.)

FIGURE 15-2
Changing the
Data Entry property

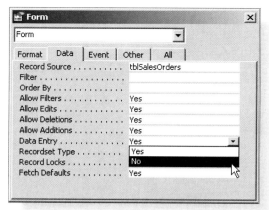

6. Click the Format tab. Change the Caption to **frmSales&Carriers**. Close the property sheet.

7. Choose File, Save As.

 NOTE: You can save a form as a report for printing.

8. The Save Form To text box shows the existing form name. Key **frmSales&Carriers.** Set the As type as **Form.** Click OK.

FIGURE 15-3
Save As dialog box

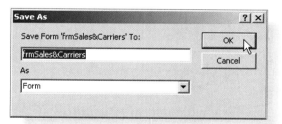

9. You now have two forms: the original frmSalesOrderEntryMain and a copy frmSales&Carriers.

EXERCISE 15-2 **Create an Option Group**

Option groups are linked to just one field. Each option group has an *option group frame* that borders the option group. *Option group labels* describe the content of the entire option group, while *option button labels* identify each button or check box. The buttons or check boxes represent what value will be stored in that field in the table.

1. Verify that the Control Wizards button ![icon] is turned on. In the toolbox, click the Option Group button ![icon].

2. Click at the 3.5-inch horizontal mark, two rows of dots below the Employee ID field. The Option Group Wizard starts.

 REVIEW: Don't worry about the exact positioning of the option group as you build it. You can move and resize controls after you create them.

3. In the first row of the Label Names column, key **A101**. In the second and third rows, key **B202** and **C303**

FIGURE 15-4
Entering labels for
the option buttons

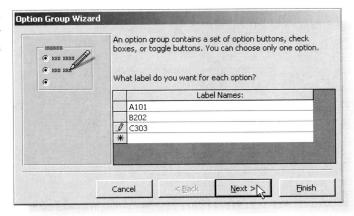

4. Click Next. Click the button for No, I don't want a default. Click Next.

5. In the next dialog box, the Wizard assigns each carrier a numeric value. These values, not the label names, are stored in tblSalesOrders, the underlying dataset for the form.

FIGURE 15-5
Each label is
assigned a value.

6. Click Next. Click the button for Store the value in this field. Click the dropdown arrow and choose CarrierID from the list. Click Next.

7. In the next dialog box, choose Option buttons for the type of control and Sunken for the style. Click Next.

8. Edit the default caption to **Carrier ID.** Click <u>F</u>inish.

9. Click the View button. Scroll through a few records. The current carrier is not shown for any of the existing records.

> **REVIEW:** This is a main form with a subform, so use the navigation buttons for the main form at the bottom of the window.

10. Return to Design View. Right-click any part of the option frame except the label. Choose <u>P</u>roperties. Check the title of the property sheet to be sure it's the option group.

11. Click the Other tab and name the control **grpCarriers**

FIGURE 15-6
Option group
property sheet

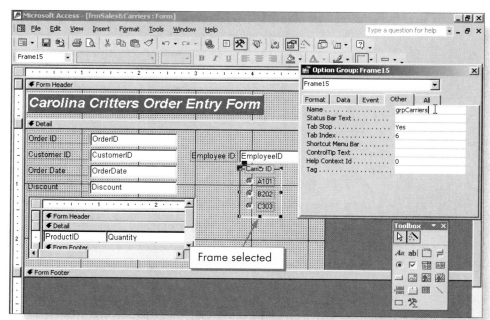

12. Press the down arrow. The object name updates. If you do not rename objects, they have names like "Frame15" that do not clearly identify them.

13. Close the property sheet. Close and save the form.

TABLE 15-1 **Prefixes for Control Objects**

PREFIX	OBJECT TYPE	EXAMPLE
cbo	Combo box	cboPaymentMethod
chk	Check box	chkCollate

continues

TABLE 15-1   Prefixes for Control Objects   *continued*

PREFIX	OBJECT TYPE	EXAMPLE
cmd	Command button	cmdPrint
grp	Option group	grpOrientation
img	Image	imgEmployee
lbl	Label	lblEmployeeID
lst	List box	lstDepartments
opt	Option button	optOrientation
txt	Text box	txtEmployeeID

EXERCISE 15-3 Use the Option Group

In an option group, each option has an option value. This value is a unique number assigned to the option. Currently the Carrier ID field used in the option group does not store numbers. That's why the value of Carrier ID is not displayed. You must change the current value in the Carrier ID field to numbers in order for the option group to match a button to the associated field.

1. Open tblSalesOrders. You will replace the current Carrier ID with the numbers assigned to these carriers.

2. Click the first record in the Carrier ID field. Click the Find button . Click the Replace tab.

3. Key **a101** in the Find What entry box. Key **1** in the Replace With entry box. Click Replace All and Yes to replace all occurrences.

> **REVIEW:** Find criteria is not case-sensitive.

4. For the next Replace, key **b202** in the Find What box and **2** in the Replace With box. Replace all occurrences.

5. Repeat these steps to replace **c303** with **3**.

6. Close the dialog box and the table.

7. Open frmSales&Carriers and scroll through several records to check the option group. The label for the button shows text, but the value is numeric in the table.

8. Before you add a new record, click in the Order ID field of any record and press Tab to check the tab order. Return to Design View.

REVIEW: The tab order should reach the option group before reaching the subform. If the tab order is not correct, change it now.

9. Choose View, Tab Order. Click Auto Order. Drag the Discount field before the grpCarriers field. Click OK.

TIP: You can place the dot in the option button by clicking or by pressing the Spacebar.

10. Add a new record with the following information:

Order ID	**20200**
Customer ID	**9**
Employee ID	**28**
Order Date	*Enter today's date in mm/dd/yy format.*
Discount	**.1**
Carrier ID	**A101**
Product ID	**C004**
Quantity	**25**

11. Close the form and save the design changes.

12. Open tblSalesOrders. Find the order you just entered and notice how the Carrier ID shows the value even though the option group displayed labels. Select and delete this record. Close the table.

TABLE 15-2   Standard Uses of Some Control Objects

OBJECT	USAGE
Check Box	• Used when all, some, or none of the choices can be selected. • Each check box is a Yes/No field. • Used stand-alone or in a group.
Option Button	• Used with a limited number of values. • Each button represents a unique value. • Frequently embedded in an option group.

continues

TABLE 15-2 Standard Uses of Some Control Objects   *continued*

OBJECT	USAGE
Option Group	• Often used to limit selection to only one choice. • Groups related objects sharing a common subject or purpose

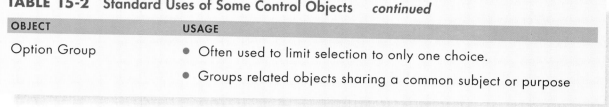

FIGURE 15-7
Example of
check boxes and
option buttons

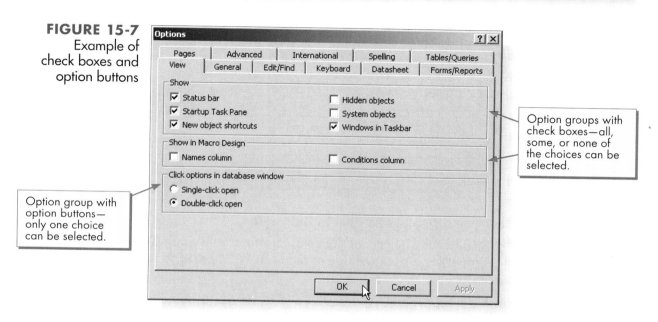

EXERCISE 15-4 Format the Option Group

An option group consists of several parts, each of which can be formatted separately.

- Option group frame

  The property sheet includes settings for the frame and the option group as a whole.

- Option group label

  This is the title for the frame, such as "Carrier ID."

- Option button

  Each button (or check box) has its own property sheet. The option value is on the **Data** tab.

- Option button labels

  Each option has its own label, such as A101, and its own property sheet.

FIGURE 15-8
Parts of an
option group

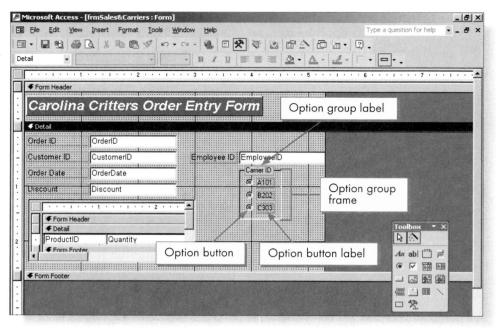

1. Open frmSales&Carriers in Design View.

2. Right-click any part of the option group frame except the label. Choose Properties. Check the title of the property sheet to be sure it's the option group.

3. Click the Format tab and the Special Effect row. Choose Shadowed. Close the property sheet and deselect the frame.

4. Select the frame's label. Change the font to 10-point Arial. Double-click a sizing handle.

5. Right-click one of the option buttons and open the property sheet. Click the Data tab and check its Option Value.

 NOTE: You could change the Name property of each option button by using the prefix "opt."

6. Click the label for the option button and check its caption. Close the property sheet.

7. Save and close the form.

Changing Control Types

Depending on the data type, you can change some controls to another type of control. A check box, for example, can be changed to an option button or a toggle button. They are all used for Yes/No fields. When you select a control and then choose Format, Change To, you see the other types of controls that are available.

EXERCISE **15-5** **Change a Check Box to an Option Button**

A check box is not a good choice for a control in a group. Check boxes normally are controlled by Yes/No fields and do not represent multiple values contained in a single field. Option buttons are more appropriate to use in a group.

1. Open frmNewCustomerEntry. It is set for Data Entry, so you do not see existing customers. The Tax Exempt field uses a check box control.
2. Choose File, Save As. Name the copied form **frmNewCustOption**
3. Open the form's property sheet and set the Data Entry property to **No**
4. Select the check box control, not its label.
5. Choose Format, Change To, and Option Button.
6. Switch to Form View and scroll through several records to find a customer who is tax-exempt.
7. Save and close your form.

EXERCISE **15-6** **Change a Check Box to a Toggle Button**

The default control for a Yes/No field is a check box. If you use any of the wizards to build a form or a report, a Yes/No field displays a check box. In addition to the option button, you can use a toggle button for a Yes/No field. The button appears to be depressed when it is selected, indicating "yes" or "true."

1. Open the Relationships window and delete the relationship between tblCarriers and tblSalesOrders.
2. Create an AutoForm for tblCarriers. Maximize the window and change to Design View.
3. Select the check box control.
4. Choose Format, Change To, and Toggle Button.
5. Delete the Next Day Delivery label.
6. Open the property sheet for the toggle button control and click the Format tab.
7. Make the button **1** inch wide and **.25** inch high.
8. Key the caption **Next Day Delivery?** (include the question mark). Close the property sheet.

 TIP: You can double-click a toggle button handle to size the button to fit the caption.

9. Size the button so you see the label.

10. Switch to Form View and scroll through the records.

FIGURE 15-9
Depressed toggle
button showing
"Yes/True"

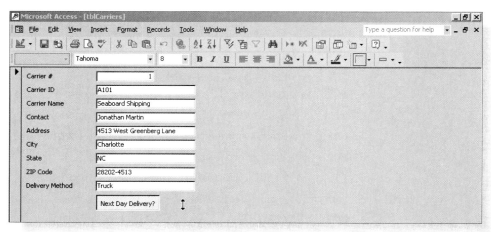

11. Close the form without saving it.

Using List and Combo Boxes

List and combo boxes allow you to choose an entry from a list rather than keying the entry. You used a combo box in an earlier lesson in main forms. A *list box* shows all the choices available; you cannot enter values not listed. A list box has a scroll bar if the height is small, but no drop-down arrow. A lookup field in a table is shown as a list box in an AutoForm.

A combo box shows a value list when you click a drop-down arrow. A *value list* is a list of displayed choices in a list or combo box. For a combo box you can also set whether or not to allow new items (items not already in the list) to be entered.

EXERCISE 15-7 **Create a Lookup Field for a List Box**

To use a lookup field in a table, the field cannot have any validation rules or other settings that interfere with the lookup.

1. Open tblSalesCampaigns in Design View.

2. Click the Supplier row in the top pane. Delete the validation rule for the Supplier field.

 REVIEW: You can click the Validation Rule row and press F2 to select all the text.

3. Click the Lookup tab in the Field Properties for the Supplier field.

4. Click the drop-down arrow for the Display Control and choose List Box.

5. Click the Row Source Type arrow and choose Value List. A value list is a list of choices that you key. Entries are separated by semicolons.

6. Click the Row Source row and key **AA-01;BB-02;CC-03;DD-04** (include the semicolons). You do not need to key a space after a semicolon.

FIGURE 15-10
Creating a value list
for a lookup field

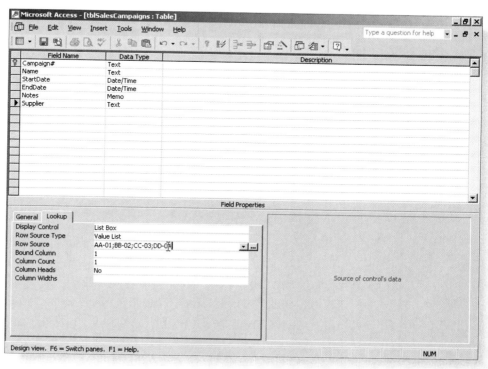

7. Save the table and return to Datasheet View. The Supplier field is now a lookup field.

8. Create an AutoForm using tblSalesCampaigns. Access shows the Supplier field in a list box.

9. Close the form without saving. Close the table.

EXERCISE **15-8** **Add a List-Box Control**

Rather than using the option group for the carriers in the form, you can use a list box or a combo box to list the choices.

1. Open frmSales&Carriers in Design View. Delete the option group control and its label.

2. Verify that the Control Wizards button ![icon] is turned on. Click the List Box button ![icon].

3. Click to place the list box where the option group was located. The List Box Wizard starts. The first dialog box asks how you want to get the data for the list.

4. Click the button for I want the list box to look up values in a table or query.

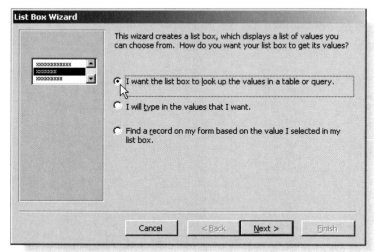

5. Click Next. Choose tblCarriers and click Next.

6. Double-click CarrierName to move it to the Selected Fields list. Click Next.

7. Adjust the column width in the next dialog box so you can see all the data. Click Next.

8. Click the button for Store that value in this field. The value is stored in the CarrierID field in tblSalesOrders. Select the CarrierID field and click Next.

9. Key **Carrier** for the label. Click Finish.

10. Open the control's property sheet and name it **lstCarriers**

11. Set the tab order for the form. Move Discount above Carrier. Move the labels closer to the controls.

12. Save the form and switch to Form View.

 REVIEW: Press any arrow key or click to select a choice in the list box.

13. Add a new record with the following information:

Order ID	**20200**
Customer ID	**9**
Employee ID	**28**

Order Date	*Key today's date in mm/dd/yy format.*
Discount	**.1**
Carrier ID	**Seaboard Shipping**
Product ID	**C004**
Quantity	**25**

14. Close the form.

 NOTE: Your form does not include the ShipDate, so information is missing from the table.

15. Open tblSalesOrders. Find the order you just entered and notice that the Carrier ID shows the primary key value (from tblCarriers) even though the list box shows the carrier names. Select and delete this record. The Cascade Delete option deletes the related record from tblSalesOrderLineItems.

16. Close the table.

EXERCISE **15-9** **Add a Combo Box Control**

A combo box can look up data, such as a list box, from another table or query.

1. Open frmSalesCampaigns in Design View.

2. Delete the Supplier control.

 3. Verify that the Control Wizards button ⬚ is on. Click the Combo Box button ⬚.

4. Click at a point two rows of dots below the Notes text box. The Combo Box Wizard starts.

5. Click the button for I want the combo box to look up values in a table or query. Click Next.

6. Choose **tblKitSuppliers** and click Next.

7. Double-click SupplierID and click Next.

8. Adjust the column width to show all the data. Click Next.

9. Click the button for Store that value in this field. Choose Supplier and click Next.

10. Key **Supplier** as the label. Click Finish.

11. Save the form and switch to Form View.

12. Scroll through the records and add the following new record. Click the drop-down arrow in the combo box to select the supplier.

Campaign #	**December 2002**
Name	**Critters for Christmas**

Start Date **11/25/02**

End Date **12/16/02**

Notes **This campaign will feature all animals at special prices and will introduce a new toy in the Cats & Dogs line.**

Supplier *Choose GG-07 from the list.*

 NOTE: Because all items in the list start with unique letters, you can key the first letter of the SupplierID to choose it.

13. Close the form.

14. Compact the database.

Creating Multipage Forms

A form lets you see one record at a time on the screen. Some forms, however, have so much information that the fields do not fit on one screen. You can create forms that require users to scroll up and down to see all the fields. You can also create forms with more than one page or tab. Users just click the page or tab to see the additional information.

 TIP: You could use a multipage form instead of a main form and subform.

FIGURE 15-12
Multipage form

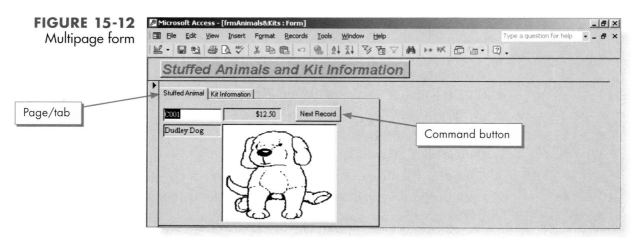

EXERCISE 15-10 View a Multipage Form

A multipage form uses tabs to indicate a page. You must select each tab to view the fields in the page indicated by that tab.

1. Open frmAnimal&Kits. This form is based on a query that uses the Stuffed Animals, Kit Contents, and Kit Suppliers tables.

2. If it is not open, click the **Stuffed Animals** tab. This page shows the fields from the Stuffed Animals table. There is also a command button on this page.

3. Click the **Kit Information** tab. This page shows information from the Kit Contents and Kit Suppliers tables.

4. Click the **Stuffed Animal** tab. Move to the fifth record. Click the **Kit Information** tab.

5. Close the form.

EXERCISE 15-11 Save a Query for a Multipage Form

Each page of a multipage form displays information from a dynaset. The dynaset may be the same for all pages or it may be different for some or all of the pages. Queries are the most common sources of dynasets in multipage forms.

1. Open qryHourlyPayroll in Design View. This query uses tblPayroll and shows only hourly workers.

2. Add tblEmployees and tblEmployeeDates to the Design grid. Notice the joins among these tables.

3. In the tblEmployees Field List, multiple-select LastName, FirstName, Job-Code, and HomePhone. When you have selected all four fields, drag them to the first column in the design grid.

 REVIEW: When you drag a field on top of an existing field in the query grid, Access moves the existing field(s) to the right.

4. Drag the BirthDate field to be the fifth column in the design grid.

5. View the dynaset. Choose File, Save As.

6. Enter **qryEmployeePayroll** as the new name. Close the query.

EXERCISE 15-12 Create and Print a Multipage Form

When creating a multipage form, it is best to start in Design View with a blank form, add pages, and then add the appropriate fields to each page. When you print a multipage form, each page prints on a separate piece of paper. If you want to print one record, first select the page and then print it.

1. Select qryEmployeePayroll. Click the New Object arrow and choose Form. Select **Design View**. Click **OK**.

2. Double-click the **Detail** bar to open its property sheet. Set the **Height** to **4** inches.

3. View the form's property sheet and set the **Width** to **7** inches. Close the property sheet.

4. Click the Tab Control button in the toolbox.

5. Draw a rectangular shape that starts at the .25-inch mark on both rulers and extends to the 3.75-inch mark on the vertical ruler and the 6.5-inch mark on the horizontal ruler. The Tab Control tool inserts a two-page object.

6. You can select the entire object or each page separately. Click each tab to select the page. Click the unused tab area across the top edge of the object to select the entire control. Check the Object Name box on the Formatting toolbar to verify the selection.

FIGURE 15-13
Tab control
in a form

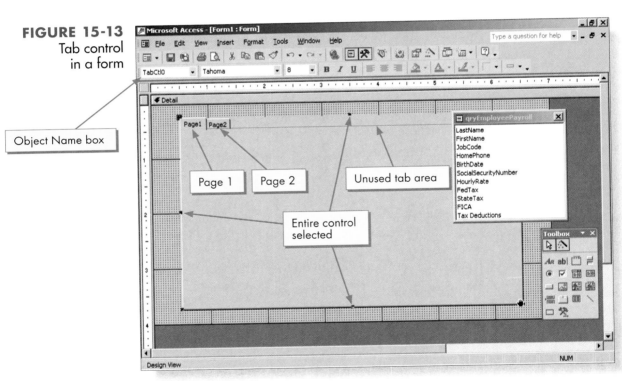

7. Double-click the "Page1" label to open the property sheet for the page. Change the **Caption** to **Employee Information**. Press the down arrow to apply the change. Leave the property sheet open.

TIP: There is a property sheet for the tab control and for each page.

8. Click the "Page2" tab and change the Caption to **Payroll Specifics**. Close the property sheet.

9. Click to select the Employee Information page.

10. Select these fields from the Field List and drag them to Page 1: LastName, FirstName, HomePhone, and BirthDate.

 NOTE: As you drag the fields, the page shows a black rectangle to mark where the fields will be placed.

11. Set the text boxes and labels to 12-point Arial. Make the labels bold. Arrange and size the controls as shown in Figure 15-14.

FIGURE 15-14
Page 1 controls

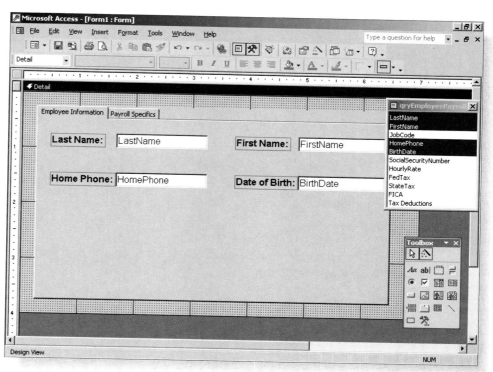

12. Click to select the Payroll Specifics page. Drag these fields to that page: JobCode, SocialSecurityNumber, HourlyRate, FedTax, StateTax, FICA, and Tax Deductions.

13. Arrange the controls as shown in Figure 15-15 on the next page. Format them to match the first page.

14. Save the form as **frmHourlyPayroll**

15. View the form in Form View and look at each page.

16. Click the Print Preview button . Set the page to print in landscape. Only the first page appears.

FIGURE 15-15
Page 2 controls

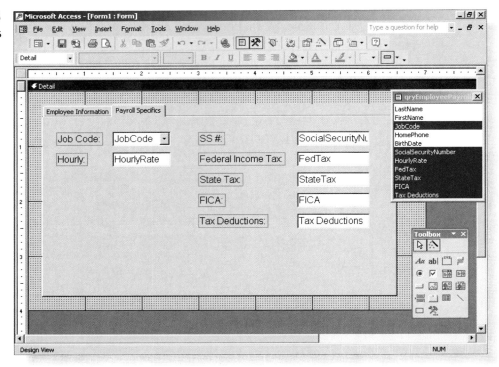

17. Select the second page of the same record and view it in Print Preview. Close the form.

Adding a Hyperlink

A *hyperlink* is a label with a link to a document, usually in another application or software program. When you click the hyperlink, the appropriate application starts and opens the document. When you click on a hyperlink in a form, table, or query, the associated document is displayed. You might, for example, keep employees' resumes online.

EXERCISE 15-13 Add a Hyperlink to a Form

In a table or form, you can create a hyperlink by using a Word document's filename. When you click the hyperlink object, Word starts and then opens the document. (You can also create hyperlinks that open other file types.)

1. Open frmStuffedAnimals in Design View.

2. Click the Insert Hyperlink button on the Form Design toolbar.

3. Key **Catalog** in the Text to display box.

4. Click Existing File or Web Page in the Link to: list. Click the Open button 📂.

5. Locate the file **StuffedAnimalsCatalog.doc**, select it, and click OK. Click OK again. The hyperlink appears on the form in a default location.

FIGURE 15-16
Insert Hyperlink
dialog box

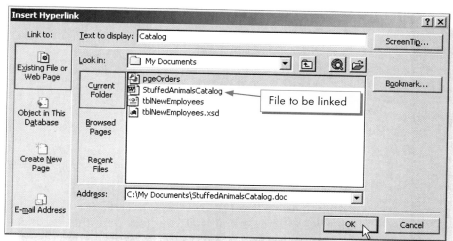

6. Drag the hyperlink below the ProductGroup controls.

NOTE: The hyperlink is a label.

7. Open the property sheet for the hyperlink control.

8. Change the Caption to **Display Catalog**

9. Change the Font Size to 12 points. Change Text Align to Center. (See Figure 15-17 on the next page.)

10. Resize the hyperlink label so all the text can be seen.

11. View the form. Point to the hyperlink; a tool tip displays the filename.

12. Test the hyperlink in Form View. Exit Word and return to Access.

13. Save and close the form.

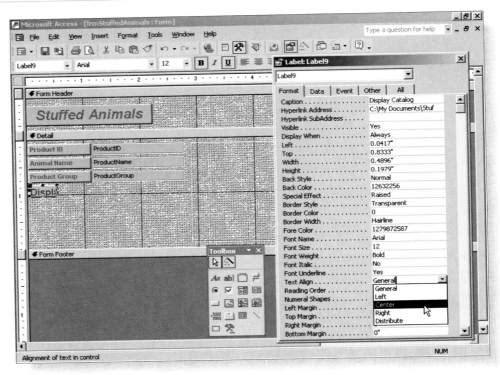

Adding a PivotChart to a Form

You can insert a PivotChart in a form (just as you can insert a chart in a report).
Of course, it is essential that you have data that lends itself to charting. Access
provides assistance in building a chart, but you must know how to analyze the
information.

EXERCISE **15-14** **Create a PivotChart**

To create a PivotChart, you must know which fields are appropriate for each drop
zone. A *drop zone* is the area in a PivotChart or PivotTable to which a field can be
assigned. The drop zone displays outlines and captions for associated fields. Each
PivotChart links with only a single underlying recordset.

1. Click the **Queries** button and the **New** button. The New Query dialog box
   opens. Choose **Design View** and click **OK**.
2. Add tblStuffedAnimals and tblKitContents to the design grid.
3. From tblStuffedAnimals, add ListPrice to the design grid. From tblKitContents, add KitNumber and Cost.

4. Save the query as **qryAnimal&KitsChart**

5. Click the drop-down arrow for the New Object button 🗗 and click <u>F</u>orm. Choose AutoForm: PivotChart and click OK. A blank PivotChart appears with a Chart Field List.

6. From the Chart Field List, click and drag KitNumber to the Drop Category Fields Here drop zone. Click and drag Cost to the Drop Data Fields Here drop zone. Click and drag ListPrice to the right of Cost.

FIGURE 15-18
Dragging a field to
a drop zone

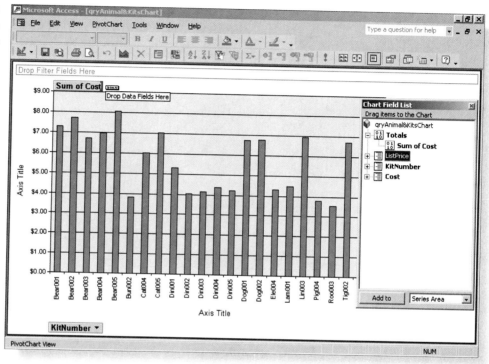

7. Close the Chart Field List.

8. Save the form as **frmAnimal&KitsChart** and close it.

9. Close the query.

EXERCISE 15-15 Place a PivotChart in a Form

A PivotChart summarizes information associated with a complete recordset. Because a PivotChart displays cumulative data, it is placed in the subform or subreport portion of a form or report.

1. In the Forms window, right-click **frmAnimals&Kits**. Choose Save <u>A</u>s from the shortcut menu.

2. Key **frmAddChart**. Set the As type as Form. Click OK.

3. Open frmAddChart in Design View.

4. Double-click the Form Selector and make the section **8** inches wide.

5. Click the Subform/Subreport button in the toolbox.

6. Position the pointer just to the right of the upper right corner of the tab control. Click to start the wizard.

FIGURE 15-19
Positioning the
Subform/Subreport

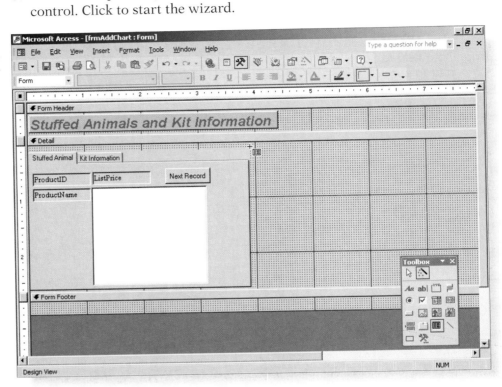

7. Click Use an existing form in the first dialog box. Choose frmAnimal&KitsChart. Click Next.

8. Click the button for Define my own. Choose KitNumber in both of the drop-down boxes. Click Next.

9. Use the default name and click Finish.

10. The subform is placed in the main form, but is the wrong size. Click the Properties button and change the Width to **4** inches and the Height to **3.5** inches.

> **NOTE:** The AutoForm formatted the subform just like a normal form. You see the PivotChart only in Form View.

11. Delete the subform label. Change to Form View. Click the Next Record button a few times.

NOTE: The chart shows the ListPrice and Cost for only one kit at one time.

12. Save and close both forms.

EXERCISE 15-16 Format a PivotChart

When you make changes to an existing PivotChart, you must open the chart in PivotChart View. You cannot make changes or edit the PivotChart while in Form View.

1. Open frmAnimal&KitsChart in PivotChart View.

 2. Click the Properties button 🖳. With **Chart Workspace** in the **Select** drop-down box, click the Add Title button 📊.

 3. Click the Add Legend button ☰.

4. Click the **Type** tab. Choose the **3D Column Clustered** chart.

FIGURE 15-20
Changing chart type

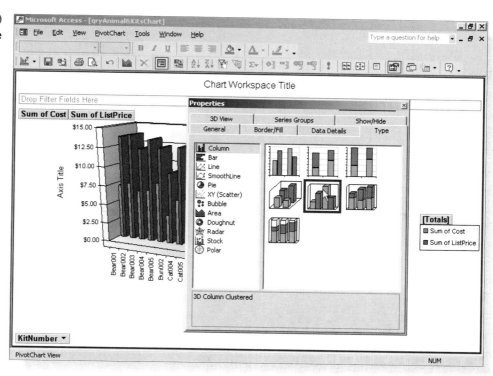

5. Click the **Border/Fill** tab. Change the **Fill Color** to a light color.

6. Click Chart Workspace Title at the top of the screen. Click the Format tab. Key **Cost vs. List Price** as the new caption. Set the font to 16-point Arial bold.

7. Click any open area away from the chart. The Select drop-down box shows Chart Workspace. Click the Show/Hide tab. Deselect the check box for Field buttons/drop zones.

8. Click Axis Title to the left of the chart. Click the Format tab and delete its caption.

9. Repeat the procedure in the previous step for the Axis Title at the bottom of the chart.

FIGURE 15-21
Completed
PivotChart

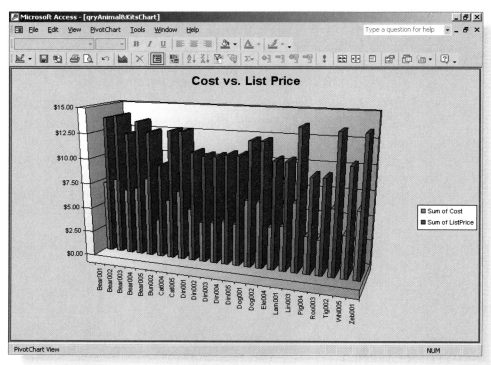

10. Save the form and close it.

11. Open frmAddChart. View the records and then close the form.

Creating a Switchboard

In previous lessons you were introduced to a Switchboard that was created by the Database Wizard. A Switchboard is a form that contains command buttons to switch to other forms or reports. It is a "master" form that functions as an application menu.

EXERCISE 15-17 Create a Main Switchboard

The default name given to a Main Switchboard is the database name. You can edit the control that displays the Switchboard title to change the title.

1. With the database open, choose Tools, Database Utilities, Switchboard Manager.

2. The message box alerts you that the database does not have a Switchboard. You can create one now. Click Yes.

3. The Switchboard Manager dialog box lists **Main Switchboard** as the default Switchboard form. Click Edit so you can add items to the page or form.

FIGURE 15-22
Switchboard Manager and Edit Switchboard Page dialog boxes

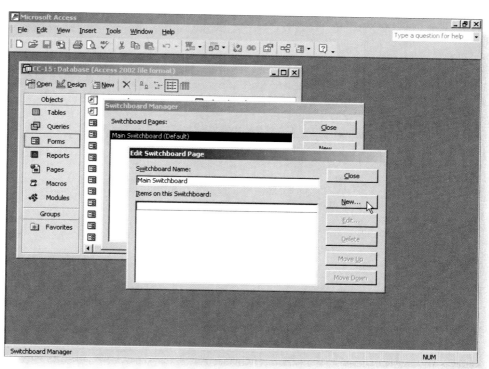

4. Click New in the Edit Switchboard Page dialog box to add the first item. The Edit Switchboard Item dialog box has three text entry boxes. In the Text box, key **Add/Edit Employee Information**

5. Click the drop-down arrow for the Command entry box. Choose Open Form in Edit Mode.

6. Click the drop-down arrow for the Form entry box and choose frmEmployeeInformation. (See Figure 15-23 on the next page.)

FIGURE 15-23
Edit Switchboard
Item dialog box

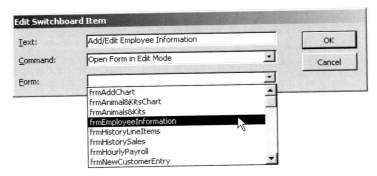

7. Click OK. Click <u>N</u>ew to add another item. The Edit Switchboard Item dialog box opens. In the <u>T</u>ext box, key **Preview Customer's Report**

8. Click the <u>C</u>ommand drop-down arrow. Choose Open Report.

9. Click the <u>R</u>eport drop-down arrow and choose rptCurrentCustomers. Click OK.

10. Click <u>C</u>lose. Click <u>C</u>lose again to generate the Switchboard. It is named Switchboard and is listed in the Forms window.

11. Double-click Switchboard to open it.

FIGURE 15-24
Completed
Switchboard

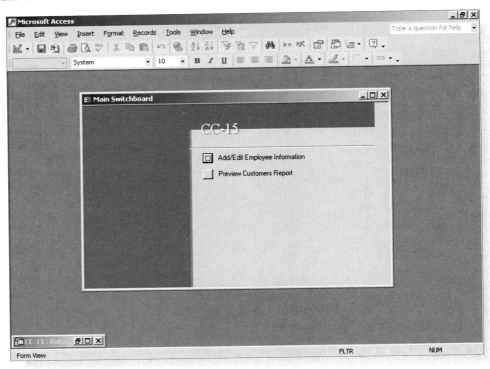

12. Test the buttons. Close the form or report to return to the Switchboard. Close the Switchboard.

13. Click the Tables button. Access has created a table named Switchboard Items. Open Switchboard Items. It is a list of the buttons and what they do. If you edit the Switchboard in Design View, it might not work as you expect because this table is not automatically updated to show changes.

14. Close the table.

EXERCISE 15-18 Set a Startup Option

You can set a particular form to open when you open the database. If you have a Switchboard form, it is usually the startup form. When you set start-up options, you can fine-tune what is shown in the opening window.

1. Choose Tools, Startup. The Startup dialog box lets you set a name and icon for the application, select menu bars, and choose what form or page is displayed at Startup.

2. Click in the Application Title entry box and key **Carolina Critters**

3. Click the Display Form/Page drop-down arrow and choose Switchboard.

4. Verify that Display Database Window and Display Status Bar are turned on.

FIGURE 15-25
Startup options

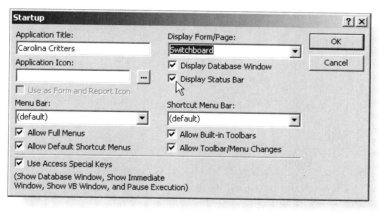

5. Click OK. Close the database. Open it again to see the Switchboard. The Database window is behind the Switchboard.

6. Close the Switchboard and the Database window.

7. Hold down [Shift] and open the database again. You can bypass the Switchboard by holding down [Shift] as you open the database.

 NOTE: Remove the startup Switchboard so it is easier to finish the lesson.

8. Choose Tools, Startup.

9. Click the Display Form/Page drop-down arrow and choose (none) at the top of the list. Click OK.

10. Compact and close the database.

Replicating a Database

A *replica* is a synchronized copy of a master database. Replicated databases are usually distributed to people working out in the field. Replication uses the Briefcase strategy that is available in Windows.

When you create a replica, the original database becomes the Design Master and is tagged as "replicable." A *Design Master* is a database to which system tables and system fields and replication properties have been added. It is the first member in a replica set. You change the design structure only in the Design Master.

You can replicate the master database for others to use on their computers. At some point, the replicas need to be synchronized with the Design Master. This process updates both databases so everyone has the same data.

EXERCISE 15-19 **Replicate a Database**

Replication is a sophisticated tool for mobile computing. Behind-the-scenes rules track and record changes, resolve conflicts, and register entries.

1. Make a copy of *[your initials]*CC-15 and name it **CentralDB**

2. Open the new database.

3. Choose Tools, Replication, Create Replica.

4. The database must be closed to be replicated. Click Yes.

5. A message box alerts you that you should make a backup. Click Yes.

6. You now need to set the location and name for the replica. The existing filename appears in the File name box. Key **Replica** and click OK.

7. The message box identifies the names of the master and its replica. The replica is the database that is taken out on a portable PC. Click OK.

8. A message box explains that the master is made. Click OK.

FIGURE 15-26
Message identifying
the Design Master
and the replica

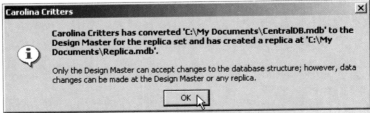

Carolina Critters

Carolina Critters has converted 'C:\My Documents\CentralDB.mdb' to the Design Master for the replica set and has created a replica at 'C:\My Documents\Replica.mdb'.

Only the Design Master can accept changes to the database structure; however, data changes can be made at the Design Master or any replica.

OK

9. The title bar includes Design Master with the database name. All the objects show a replication icon.

10. Close the master database and open **Replica**. Its title bar includes "Replica."

11. Close the database.

 NOTE: You can return to a plain copy of your database by deleting the master and replicas. Then rename the ".bak" files made by Access to include the ".mdb" extension.

USING HELP

In this lesson you have learned more about controls for a form.

Use Help to explore additional commands and properties about controls for forms:

1. Start Help and click the Contents tab.

2. Expand the Controls and Chart folder.

3. Click About types of controls in Access. Read the Help pane.

4. Expand the folder for List Boxes, Combo Boxes, and Drop-down List Boxes.

5. Click Properties of list boxes, combo boxes, drop-down list boxes and Lookup fields.

FIGURE 15-27
Microsoft Access Help

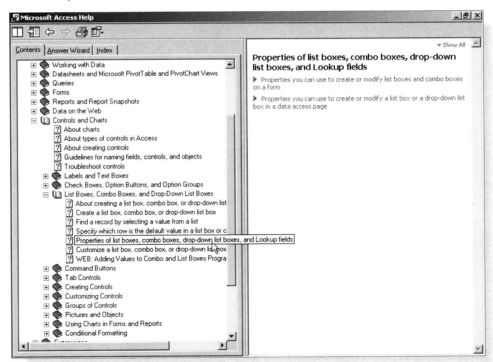

6. Read the Help window and then close it.

LESSON 15 Summary

➤ An option group includes buttons or check boxes for making choices in a form. It is best used for a field that has fewer than five possible choices.

➤ An option group includes a frame, a label, and the option buttons or check boxes. Each has its own properties.

➤ Most types of controls can be changed to another type.

➤ A list-box control lists the possible field values. It might show a scroll bar if the list is long.

➤ A combo box shows a single line with a drop-down arrow. You can choose from the list or set the control to allow entry of a new item as well.

➤ A multipage form places more than one page or form on the tab control. You can name each page and place controls where needed.

➤ A hyperlink is a label that includes a link to another document, either on the Web or on the computer. When you click the label, the other file opens.

➤ You can add PivotCharts to forms if there is data that is suitable for charting. You can show one PivotChart per dynaset.

➤ A Switchboard is a master form with links to other forms or reports. It is often set in the Startup dialog box to open when the database opens.

➤ A replica is a copy of the database that can be synchronized to the master database. This enables people to work on the files in different places at different times and compile all their work into the master database.

LESSON 15 Command Summary

FEATURE	BUTTON	MENU	KEYBOARD	SPEECH
Save As		File, Save As	F12	✓
Create Option Group	[xyz]	Format, Change to, Option Button		✓
Create Toggle Button	⇄	Format, Change to, Toggle Button		✓

continues

LESSON 15　Command Summary　　*continued*

FEATURE	BUTTON	MENU	KEYBOARD	SPEECH
Create List Box		Format, Change to, List Box		✓
Create Combo Box		Format, Change to, Combo Box		✓
Create Tab Control				✓
Insert Hyperlink		Insert, Hyperlink	Ctrl + K	✓
Insert Chart		Insert, Chart		

Concepts Review

Each of the following statements is either true or false. Indicate your choice by circling **T** or **F**.

T   F   *1.* A hyperlink field launches the related software when you click the button.

T   F   *2.* Each control object in an option group has a value, set to a number.

T   F   *3.* A Switchboard can be set to open in place of the Database window.

T   F   *4.* You can use a check box control for a number or logical data type.

T   F   *5.* A combo box occupies less space than a list box.

T   F   *6.* When you set the Data Entry property to Yes, you don't see existing records in Form View.

T   F   *7.* To see information from two different tables, you just link both tables to a form.

T   F   *8.* You can create the illusion of pages in a form by using the Subform Wizard.

Write the correct answer in the space provided.

1. How can you set a Switchboard as the opening screen for a database?

_____

2. What is the main benefit of using a combo box in a form for data entry?

_____

3. What types of controls might you use for Yes/No fields?

_____

4. What control do you use to create multiple pages in a form?

_____

5. What form property permits you to see only a blank record?

_____

6. In Design View, how do you select the entire form?

_____

7. What control do you place in a form to show a PivotChart?

_____

8. For what type of data can you use an option group?

_____

CRITICAL THINKING

Answer these questions on a separate page. There are no right or wrong answers. Support your answers with examples from your own experience, if possible.

1. Develop ideas for a hyperlink. What kind of information might be linked?

2. You can set a form to allow someone only to view data, or you can set it to allow data entry. Why might you use this property?

Skills Review

EXERCISE 15-20

Add, format, and use an option group. Change a control type.

1. Add an option group to a form by following these steps:

    a. Open *[your initials]*CC-15 and refresh the links to tables in *[your initials]*CC-E-15.

    b. Open tblSalesReps. Click the first record in the Region field. Click the Find button . Click the Replace tab.

    c. Key **east** in the Find What entry box. Key **1** in the Replace With entry box. Click Replace All to replace all occurrences.

    d. For the next replacement, key **north** in the Find What entry box and **2** in the Replace With entry box. Replace all occurrences.

    e. Repeat these steps to replace **south** with **3** and **west** with **4**

    f. Close the dialog box and the table.

    g. Create an AutoForm for tblSalesReps. Switch to Design View.

    h. Click the AutoFormat button and choose Expedition. Click OK.

    i. Delete the Region controls and make the form **5** inches wide.

    j. Save the form as **frmSalesReps**

    k. Verify that the Control Wizards are turned on. Click the Option Group button .

l. Position the pointer at the 3.**5**-inch mark, aligned with the SocialSecurityNumber controls, and click.

m. In the first row of the Label Names column, key **East**. Press Tab. On the next three rows, key **North**, **South**, and **West**. Click Next.

n. Click the button for N<u>o</u>, I don't want a default. Click Next. Note the number values. Click Next.

o. Click the button for Store the <u>v</u>alue in this field. Choose Region as the field and click Next.

p. Choose Toggle buttons for the type of control. Choose Raised for the style. Click Next.

q. Change the caption to **Region**. Click Finish. View the form.

2. Format and use an option group by following these steps:

a. With tblSalesReps open in Design View, double-click the option group frame to open its property sheet.

 REVIEW: Name a control on the Other tab.

b. Set the Special Effect to Etched. Name the control **grpRegion**. Close the property sheet and deselect the option group.

c. Check the tab order for the form.

d. View the form and scroll through the records.

3. Change a control type by following these steps:

a. In frmSalesReps, click the Salary text box and choose F<u>o</u>rmat, C<u>h</u>ange To, <u>C</u>ombo Box.

 NOTE: The wizard adds the necessary SQL code for a combo box. When you change the control type, the code needs to be changed too.

b. View the form and click the drop-down arrow. The combo box does not have a Row Source.

c. Open the property sheet for the Salary combo box control.

d. Change the Name property to **cboSalary**

e. Click the Data tab, the Row Source row, and the Build button ⬚.

f. Add tblSalesReps to the query design grid. Add Salary to the grid. Close the query and click Yes to update the Row Source.

 TIP: You are building a SQL query. Press Shift + F2 in the property sheet to see the code.

g. Close the property sheet and view the form. Test the drop-down list.

h. Close and save the form.

EXERCISE 15-21

Add a combo box control. Use a combo box.

1. Add a combo box by following these steps:
   a. Right-click frmEmployeeInformation and choose Save As. Key **frmEmployees** and click OK. Open frmEmployees in Design View.
   b. Open the form's property sheet and change the Caption to **New Employees**. Close the property sheet.
   c. Delete the Job Code controls.
   d. Verify that the Control Wizards are turned on. Click the Combo Box button .
   e. Position the pointer where the Job Code text box was located. Draw a control that is about .25 inch tall and 1 inch wide.
   f. Choose I want the combo box to look up values in a table or query. Click Next.
   g. Choose tblJobCodes to provide the values. Click Next.
   h. Double-click JobCode. Click Next. Adjust the column width to show all the data. Click Next.
   i. Choose Store that value in this field and use JobCode. Click Next.
   j. Edit the label to **Job Code**. Size, position, and format the combo box and its label to match the rest of the form.
   k. Set the tab order. Save and view the form.

2. Use a combo box by following these steps:
   a. Add the following new record:

Last Name	**Morris**
First Name	**Sharon**
Employee ID	**34**
Address	**1167 Highland Street**
Photograph	*Skip*
City	**Charlotte**
State	**NC**
Postal Code	**28205-1167**
SS#	**888-46-8976**
Home Phone	**(704)-555-1689**
Job Code	*Select MF04 from the list.*
Contact Name	*Key [your first and last name].*
Emergency Phone	**(704)-555-1269**

   b. Print the new record.

   NOTE: Adjust the form/page width if it is too wide to print.

   c. Delete the record you just added and close the form.

EXERCISE 15-22

Create a multipage form. Add and format controls.

1. Create a multipage form by following these steps:
   a. Create a new query in Design View for tblEmployees and tblEmployeeDates.
   b. From tblEmployees, add EmployeeID, LastName, FirstName, Address, City, State, PostalCode, and HomePhone to the grid.
   c. From tblEmployeeDates, add SocialSecurityNumber, BirthDate, and HireDate to the grid.
   d. Save the query as **qryPersonalInfo**. Check the dynaset and close the query.
   e. Create a new form in Design View for qryPersonalInfo.

    **REVIEW:** Double-click the Detail bar to open its property sheet. Double-click the Form Selector button to open the form's property sheet.

   f. Make the Detail section **4** inches tall. Make the form **6.5** inches wide.
   g. Click the Tab Control button .
   h. Draw a rectangular shape that starts at the .25-inch mark on both rulers and extends to the 3.75-inch mark on the vertical ruler and the 6.25-inch mark on the horizontal ruler.

    **REVIEW:** Leave the property sheet open and click the control to be formatted.

   i. Double-click the "Page1" tab and change the caption to **Address Information**. Change the "Page2" caption to **Confidential**
   j. Save the form as **frmPersonalInfo**

2. Add and format controls on a multipage form by following these steps:
   a. With frmPersonalInfo open, click to select the Address Information page.
   b. Drag the EmployeeID field from the Field List to the 1.5-inch mark about .25 inch down on the first page.
   c. Draw a text box control below these controls to align with the EmployeeID text box. Change the label to **Employee's Name**
   d. Click the Build button 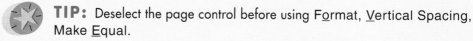 for the Control Source of the unbound control.
   e. Build a concatenated expression to show the first and last name:
      [FirstName]&" "&[LastName]
   f. Make all the labels 10-point bold Arial. Make all the text boxes 10-point Arial. Size, position, and align the controls to see all the data.
   g. Drag the Address field to align beneath the Employee's Name control. Copy the formats.

   TIP: Deselect the page control before using Format, Vertical Spacing, Make Equal.

   h. Draw a text box control below the Address controls. Change the label to **City and State**. Build a concatenated expression to show the city, state, and Postal code. Size, position, align, and format the controls. Make the vertical spacing equal.

  i. Add the HomePhone field so its right edge is at the 6-inch mark, and format it to match the page. Align this field with EmployeeID at the top.

  j. Click to select the Confidential page. Drag the following fields to the page: SocialSecurityNumber, BirthDate, and HireDate.

  k. Format the controls to match the first page.

  l. Resize all controls so all information can be seen.

  m. View and save your form; then close it.

EXERCISE 15-23

Add a PivotChart to a form. Format a PivotChart. Add a hyperlink. Create a Switchboard. Set a Startup option.

1. Create a PivotChart by following these steps:

  a. Create an AutoForm using tblSalesOrderLineItems. Switch to PivotChart View.

  b. Drag and drop Product ID from the Chart Field List to the Drop Category Fields Here drop zone.

  c. Drag and drop Quantity to the Drop Data Fields Here drop zone.

  d. Save the form as **frmSalesChart** and close.

2. Add a PivotChart to a form by following these steps:

  a. Open frmSalesReviewMain in Design View. Make the Detail section **4** inches tall.

  b. Click the Subform/Subreport button 🖽 in the toolbox. Click at the upper right corner of the other subform control.

  c. Select the form frmSalesChart. Click Next.

  d. Use OrderID to link the controls. Click Finish.

  e. Click the Properties button 🗟 and set the subform to a width of **4** inches and a height of **2.5** inches.

  f. Click the Form Selector for the subform. Click the Format tab. Set the Default View to PivotChart. Close the property sheet.

  g. Delete the PivotCharts label.

  h. Preview the form to see if the chart needs to be sized. Resize the other subform to match the PivotChart height.

  i. Add your name in a label in the Form Header.

  j. Save and close the form.

3. Format a PivotChart by following these steps:

  a. Open frmSalesChart in PivotChart View.

  b. Click the Properties button 🗟. Click the Axis Title to the left of the chart. Click the Format tab and change the Caption to **Quantity**

  c. Click the Axis Title below the chart and change its Caption to **Sales**

  d. Click an unused (white) part of the chart. Click the Show/Hide tab and deselect the Field buttons/drop zones check box.

e. Close the form and return to frmSalesReviewMain.

f. Save and close the form.

4. Add a hyperlink by following these steps:

a. With frmSalesReviewMain open, click the Insert Hyperlink button 🌐.

b. Key **Catalog** in the Text to display box.

c. Click Existing File or Web Page in the Link to: list. Click the Open button 📂.

d. Locate and select **StuffedAnimalsCatalog.doc** and click OK to close the Insert Hyperlink dialog box.

e. Drag the hyperlink below the Discount label.

f. Open the property sheet for the hyperlink control. Change the Caption to **Display Catalog**. Change the Font Size to **10** and align the first column of labels.

g. Double-click a sizing handle to size the hyperlink label.

h. Test the hyperlink in Form View. Exit Word and return to the form.

i. Print the record for Order ID 20107 in landscape orientation.

j. Save and close the form.

5. Create a Switchboard by following these steps:

a. Delete the Switchboard form. Delete the Switchboard Items table.

b. Choose Tools, Database Utilities, Switchboard Manager. Click Yes to create a Switchboard.

c. Main Switchboard is the default Switchboard form. Click Edit.

d. Click New. In the Text box, key **Add/Edit Products**

e. As the Command, choose Open Form in Edit Mode.

f. As the Form, choose frmAnimals&Kits. Click OK.

g. Click New to add another item. In the Text box, key **Preview Stuffed Animals Report.**

h. For the Command, choose Open Report. For the report, choose rptStuffedAnimals. Click OK.

i. Click Close. Click Close again to generate the Switchboard.

j. Double-click Switchboard in the Forms window.

k. Test the buttons. Close any forms or reports to return to the Switchboard. Close the Switchboard.

6. Set a startup option by following these steps:

a. Choose Tools, Startup.

b. Click the Display Form/Page drop-down arrow and choose Switchboard.

c. Verify that Display Database Window and Display Status Bar are turned on. Click OK.

d. Close the database and reopen it.

e. Close the Switchboard and the database window.

f. Hold down Shift and open the database again to bypass the Switchboard.

g. Choose Tools, Startup. Click the Display Form/Page drop-down arrow and choose (none) at the top of the list. Click OK.

h. Close and compact the database.

Lesson Applications

EXERCISE 15-24

Create a form with an option group.

1. Open *[your initials]*CC-15 and refresh the links to tables in *[your initials]*CC-E-15. Create a new form named **frmNewCustomers** that is based on frmNewCustomerEntry.

 NOTE: You can use File, Save As, or Copy and Paste to create a copy of the form.

2. Change the caption of the new form to **New Customers**. Set the Data Entry property so you can edit existing records.

3. Delete the Tax Exempt? check box. Create an option group in its place.

4. Set the label names to **Yes** on the first line and **No** on the second line. Use **No** as the default option.

5. Replace the option values with **–1** for Yes, **0** for No. These are standard Access and Visual Basic values for Yes and No.

6. Store the value in the TaxStatus field. Use the most appropriate control and Etched as the style. Enter **Tax Exempt?** as the caption. View the form and make changes as necessary.

7. Add your name in the Form Header.

8. Save your changes and add the following records:

Customer ID:	**20**
Company Name:	**The Helping Hand**
Billing Address:	**273-16 Mount Fillmore Road**
City:	**Greensboro**
State:	**NC**
Postal Code:	**27406-6557**
Phone Number:	**(910) 555-3892**
Fax Number:	**(910) 555-2113**
Contact Name:	**Larry Mills**
Tax Exempt:	**Yes**

 TIP: Use Ctrl + ⌐ to duplicate the field from the previous record.

Customer ID:	**21**
Company Name:	**Samantha's Playpen**

Billing Address:	**1169 Overlook Court**
City:	**Greensboro**
State:	**NC**
Postal Code:	**27406-1169**
Phone Number:	**(910) 555-5234**
Fax Number:	**(910) 555-1278**
Contact Name:	**Samantha Wilson**
Tax Exempt:	**No**

9. Print the record for Customer ID 12.

10. Close the form and open tblCustomers. Notice that the Yes/No values show a check mark and no check mark because you entered the actual Access value for Yes/No fields. Close the table.

EXERCISE 15-25

Create a multipage form. Format and arrange controls. Add a subform to a page.

1. Create a new form in Design View for tblCustomers. Make the form **6.5** inches wide and **4** inches tall.

2. Draw a Tab Control object that is about the same width as the form and **3.5** inches tall.

3. Change the "Page1" caption to **Customer Information**. Change the "Page2" caption to **Sales History.**

4. On the Customer Information page, add these controls: CustomerID, CompanyName, ContactName, BillingAddress, PhoneNumber, and FaxNumber.

5. Change all the controls to 10-point Arial and size them to fit.

 TIP: Controls on a form look best when they are aligned and are the same size.

6. Arrange the CustomerID and ContactName controls as the first row on page 1, with the CustomerID label about .25 inch from the left edge of the page. Position the ContactName label at the 3.5-inch mark.

7. Arrange the labels and text boxes so there appears to be the same amount of space between the label and the text box for both controls.

8. Arrange the CompanyName and BillingAddress controls to start at the 1-inch vertical mark with the BillingAddress below the CompanyName.

9. Create a concatenated expression for the city, state, and Postal code. Position the control below the BillingAddress controls. Do not use a label.

10. Make the vertical spacing equal for the address controls. Size them appropriately.

11. Position the PhoneNumber and FaxNumber controls to align left with the ContactName control but below the concatenated expression.

12. Save the form as **frmCustSalesInfo**

13. Add a subform control to the Sales History page. Use existing Tables and Queries with tblHistorySales. Add these fields: CustomerID, OrderID, OrderDate, and ShipDate. Verify the linking field as CustomerID. Name the subform **frmCustSalesHist**

14. Open the subform's property sheet and set the Default View to Continuous forms.

 NOTE: Open the subform in Design View and apply an AutoFormat to match its design to the first page.

15. Make the CustomerID text box invisible and delete the label. Then move the text box out of the way.

16. Modify the subform so the text boxes are on one line, with a label above each text box in the Form Header.

17. Delete the subform label. Size and position the subform.

18. Add your name in a label in the lower left corner of the Detail section, outside the tab/page.

19. Drag the bottom of the tab/page to cover your name. A control behind the tab appears on all pages.

 TIP: You can't copy and paste the label from one page to the other.

20. Resave the form, and print both pages for the first record.

EXERCISE 15-26

Create a Switchboard by using the Switchboard Manager.

1. Delete the Switchboard Items table and the Switchboard form.

2. Create a Switchboard named Main Switchboard that has buttons to view the frmAnimalsAndKits and frmSalesReviewMain forms.

3. Add buttons to enter a new customer into frmNewCustomerEntry.

4. Add a button to exit the application.

5. Print the Switchboard.

6. Delete the Switchboard Items table and the Switchboard form.

EXERCISE 15-27 *Challenge Yourself*

Create a form with a PivotChart.

Replace the subform in frmHistorySales with a 3-D bar chart that changes from record to record. Place the chart below the other controls. Format the chart as you prefer, but remove the drop zones. Add a label with your name in the **Form Header** and print one record.

On Your Own

In these exercises you work on your own, as you would in a real-life work environment. Use the skills you've learned to accomplish the task—and be creative.

EXERCISE 15-28

Review the designs of the databases you modified in Exercise 14-31. Select three existing forms to modify by adding a variety of special controls. Print the forms and sketch your changes. You may modify your table structures to better accommodate your designs. List the purpose of each change. On each printout, write your name and "Exercise 15-28." Continue to the next exercise.

EXERCISE 15-29

Based on the sketches you created in Exercise 15-28, make the modifications to your forms. Sketch a new form that includes a chart. Create the form. For all forms, include your name and "Exercise 15-29" in the footer. Include the title of the form in the header. Print a copy of each form. Continue to the next exercise.

EXERCISE 15-30

Print a list of all the reports and forms in your databases. Sketch a multipage Switchboard that will allow a user to run each form and report. Organize the Switchboard selections logically by function of the object being selected. Include your name and "Exercise 15-30" on each page. Create and print the Switchboard. Submit sketches and printouts from Exercises 15-28 through 15-30 to your instructor. Keep copies of the databases. They will be used in subsequent lessons.

Working with Macros and Modules

OBJECTIVES

After completing this lesson, you will be able to:

1. **Run a macro.**
2. **View and edit a macro.**
3. **Create a macro.**
4. **Name and group macros.**
5. **Use conditions in a macro.**
6. **Create a module and a Visual Basic routine.**
7. **Create a form module routine.**
8. **Optimize a database.**

MOUS
ACTIVITIES
In this lesson:
Ac2002e **7-4**
Ac2002e **8-1**
Ac2002e **8-3**

See Appendix E.

 Estimated Time: 2 hours

You might have an idea what a macro does from your work with other software programs. A *macro* is a program (typically a small program) that carries out the steps for a routine activity. If every Friday you run a particular query and print its related report, you could write a macro to do it automatically for you. In this lesson, you create, name, and run simple macros and use conditions in macros. A *condition* is a logical expression that can be true or false.

A module is similar to a macro. A *module* is a collection of Visual Basic for Applications declarations and procedures that are stored together as a unit. *Visual Basic for Applications (VBA)* is an object-oriented programming language used to enhance Office applications.

Both macros and modules are ideal for automating repetitive or complex tasks. For example, you might write a module to add interest charges to outstanding balances for all customers who are past due 30 days.

The main difference between a macro and a module is the level of complexity. Macros are generally simple procedures with a limited number of steps. Most modules are involved procedures used to build user interfaces. A module contains VBA code and follows the same syntax rules as any Visual Basic program.

Because both macros and modules are multi-stepped activities, it is important that you properly plan the sequence of these activities. A good programmer plans, develops, and writes a macro or a module, using the same systematic approach as in writing a program. Proper planning helps avoid costly and time-consuming corrections or modifications to the code.

Running a Macro

In earlier lessons you used a command button when you added the control to a form. When you use the Command Button wizard, Access develops a Visual Basic module and assigns it to the appropriate event for the command button. An *event* is an action such as clicking a button, pressing a key, or opening a form. Many controls list events in the property sheet. You can assign a macro or a Visual Basic module to an event. When you perform the event, the macro or module executes.

EXERCISE **16-1** **Run a Macro from a Command Button**

1. Make a copy of **CC-16** and name it *[your initials]***CC-16**. Make a copy of **CC-E-16** and name it *[your initials]***CC-E-16**. Update the linked tables. Click the Forms button.

2. Open frmEmployeeInformation and maximize the window. This form has a command button that runs a macro.

3. Click the Preview Salary Report button. Click OK in the message box. Close the preview window.

4. Switch to Design View. Open the property sheet for the command button.

5. Click the Event tab and find the On Click event. When you click the command button, mcrPreviewSalaryRpt runs. (See Figure 16-1 on the next page.)

 NOTE: On Click events trigger instructions when you click a command button in Form View. The event does not trigger the instructions in Design View.

6. Close the property sheet and the form.

FIGURE 16-1
Property sheet for a
command button

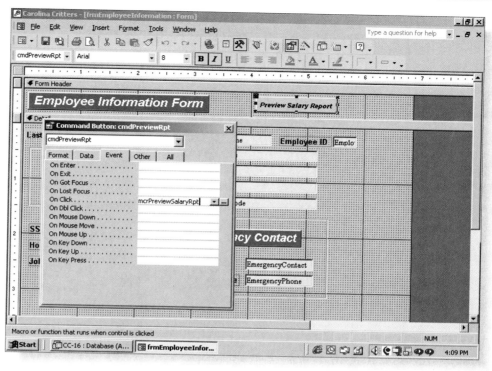

EXERCISE **16-2** Run a Macro from the Macros Window

Macros are often assigned to a command button. By viewing the property sheet of
the command button, you can view the name of the associated macro.

1. Click the **Macros** button.

2. Double-click mcrPreviewSalaryRpt. The macro runs. Click **OK** and close the
Preview window. You return to the Macros window.

3. Choose <u>T</u>ools, <u>M</u>acro, Run <u>M</u>acro. The Run Macro dialog box has a drop-
down list for all the macros in the database.

FIGURE 16-2
Run Macro
dialog box

4. Choose mcrPreviewSalaryRpt and click **OK**. Click **OK** in the message box
and close the Preview window.

Viewing and Editing a Macro

The Macro Design window has two panes. The top pane shows **Actions**, which are selected from a list. The lower pane shows **Action Arguments**. An *argument* is the object, element, expression, or condition for the action to be carried out.

 TIP: Arguments for a macro are similar to arguments for functions such as Sum() or Count().

FIGURE 16-3
Macro window

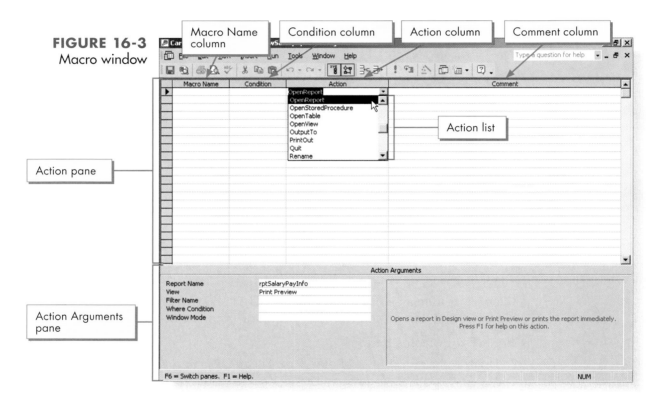

Macro Name column · Condition column · Action column · Comment column · Action list · Action pane · Action Arguments pane

Report Name	rptSalaryPayInfo
View	Print Preview
Filter Name	
Where Condition	
Window Mode	

Opens a report in Design view or Print Preview or prints the report immediately. Press F1 for help on this action.

F6 = Switch panes. F1 = Help.

EXERCISE 16-3 View and Edit a Macro in Design View

In Design View, you can show the **Macro Name** and **Condition** columns. There is also a **Comment** column for optional descriptions of what each action does in the macro.

1. Click once to select mcrPreviewSalaryRpt.

2. Click **Design**. The first action in this macro is OpenReport. The five arguments for this action are Report Name, View, Filter Name, Where Condition, and Window Mode.

3. Click the Report Name row in the Action Arguments pane. The report that is opened is rptSalaryPayInfo.

4. Click each row in the Action Arguments pane and read the information in the Help area.

FIGURE 16-4
PreviewSalaryRpt
macro

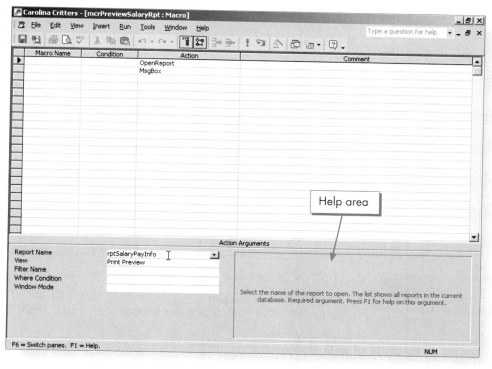

5. Click the second action in the upper pane, MsgBox. It has four arguments. Click each argument line and read the Help area.

6. Click the Message row in the Action Arguments pane and press ⟨Shift⟩ + ⟨F2⟩ to open the Zoom window.

7. Key **-Thank You** at the end of the message (include the hyphen). Click OK to close the Zoom window. (See Figure 16-5 on the next page.)

8. Click the Title row in the Action Arguments pane. Key **Preview Report**. This appears as the title in the Message dialog box's title bar.

 9. Click the Save button to save your changes.

 10. You can run the macro from this window to test the new message. Click the Run button . Read the message and note the title for the dialog box. Click OK in the Message box and close the preview.

FIGURE 16-5
Editing the
Message argument

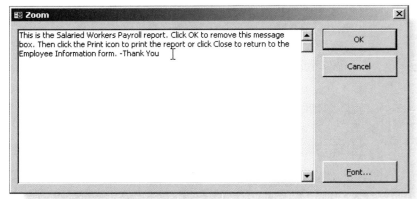

EXERCISE 16-4 Add an Action and Comments to a Macro

An action argument is similar to the arguments needed to complete a built-in function in Access or Excel. A few Access actions do not have arguments.

1. In the Macro Design window, click the MsgBox **Action** row in the top pane.

2. Click the Insert Rows button ⧉ to insert a blank row.
3. Display the list of actions and key **m** to scroll to actions that start with the letter "M." The first action is "Maximize." Press [Enter].

   REVIEW: You can press [F4] to display a drop-down list instead of clicking the arrow.

4. Key this comment: **This action will maximize the report preview window.** There are no arguments for this action.
5. Click the fourth **Action** row and display the list of actions.
6. Set the **Action** to **Close**. This action has three arguments.
7. Enter this comment for the **Close** action: **This action closes the preview window.**
8. Click the **Object Type** row in the **Action Arguments** pane. Display the drop-down list and choose **Report**.
9. Click the **Object Name** row and choose rptSalaryPayInfo. (See Figure 16-6 on the next page.)
10. Save the macro and click the Run button 🔘 to test the macro.
11. Click **OK** in the Message box. The preview closes as part of the macro.
12. Close the Macro Design window.

FIGURE 16-6
Adding the Close
action and comment

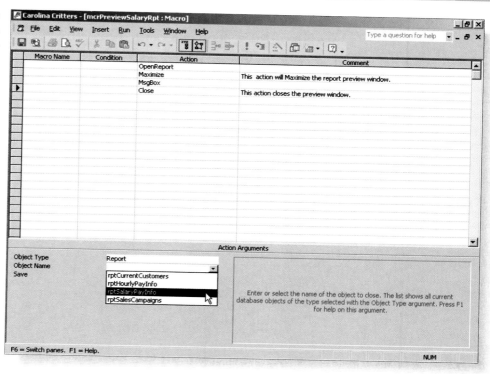

Creating a Macro

Macros are database objects like tables, forms, and reports. Macros must be written in the Design window. You can access the Design window from one of the Build buttons or from the Database window. Unlike macros you might have recorded in Word or Excel, Access macros are not recorded.

To create a macro, you must open the Macro Design window, select the actions, and complete the arguments. You also can add a command button to a form and then build a macro for its **On Click** execution.

NOTE: You can build the macro first and then add the button to the form.

EXERCISE 16-5 Assign a Macro to an Event

The report rptHourlyPayInfo is similar to the report that is opened by the existing command button. You will add another button to the same form to open this report.

1. Open frmEmployeeInformation in Design View.

2. Draw a command button to the right of the existing button, about the same size as the existing button. Because the Control Wizards are on by default, the Command Button Wizard starts. Click Cancel.

3. Open the new control's property sheet. Click the All tab. Change the Caption to **Preview Hourly Report**

4. Change the Name property to **cmdHourly**

5. Click the Event tab and the On Click row.

6. Click the Build button . The Choose Builder dialog box opens. You can start the Expression Builder, the Macro Builder, or the Code Builder.

FIGURE 16-7
Choose Builder
dialog box

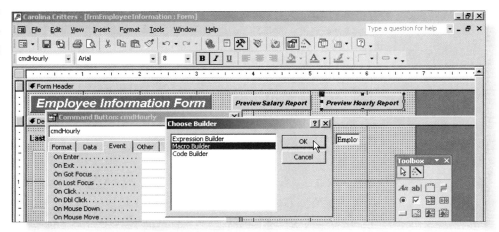

> **NOTE:** The Code Builder opens a Module window for Visual Basic procedures an'd functions.

7. Click Macro Builder and click OK.

8. Name the macro **mcrPreviewHourlyRpt**. The Macro Design window opens.

EXERCISE 16-6 Add Actions and Arguments to the Macro

This macro uses the same commands as the mcrPreviewSalaryRpt macro.

1. Click the first Action cell and display the list of actions.

2. Key **openr** to move to OpenReport. Press Enter.

3. Key the following for the comment (including the period): **This action opens the Hourly Payroll Report.**

4. Move to the Report Name of the Action Arguments pane.

5. Click the drop-down arrow or press F4 to display the report names. Choose rptHourlyPayInfo.

6. Press Tab to move to the View argument. This sets how Access opens the report. Display the list and choose Print Preview.

7. Move to the Filter Name row. You can apply queries or filters to the report. There are no filters for this report.

FIGURE 16-8
OpenReport action

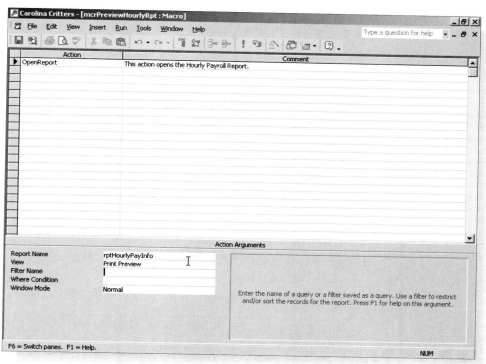

8. Click the second Action cell in the top pane. Key **max** to move to the Maximize action. Press Enter.

9. Key **This action maximizes the preview window.** (Key the period.) This action does not have any arguments.

10. Click the third action cell and key **ms** and press Enter. Key this comment (including the period): **This action displays a message box.**

11. Move to the Message argument in the Action Arguments pane.

12. In the Message row, press Shift + F2 to open the Zoom window. Key this message:

    This is the Hourly Pay Report for this week. Click OK to close this message box. Then click Print to print the report or close the report.

13. Click OK. Press Tab to move to the Beep argument. If you have a sound card and speakers for your machine, set this to Yes.

14. Move to the Type row. There are four types of message boxes: Critical, Warning!, Information, and Warning? The Type argument controls what symbols you see in the message box.

TABLE 16-1 Message Box Icons

ICON	MACRO NAME	VB NAME	DESCRIPTION
❌	Critical	vbCritical	Display Critical Message Icon
⚠️	Warning!	vbExclamation	Display Warning Message icon
ⓘ	Information	vbInformation	Display Information Message icon
?	Warning?	vbQuestion	Display Warning Query icon

15. Choose Information as the Type.

16. Move to the Title argument. Key **Preview Hourly Report**

17. Click the fourth Action cell and select the Close action.

18. Key this comment (including the period): **This action closes the preview window.**

19. Click the Object Type row in the Action Arguments pane. Key **r** and press Tab to select "Report."

20. Click in the Object Name row and choose rptHourlyPayInfo.

FIGURE 16-9
Completed macro

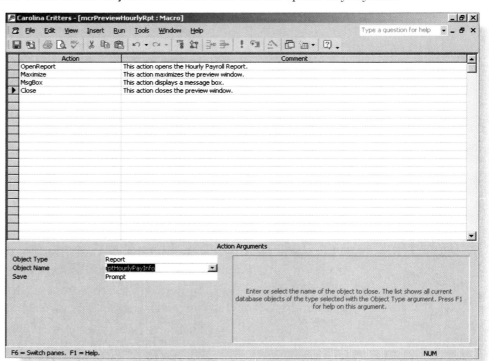

21. Save the macro. Close the Macro Design window. You are back in the Form Design window and the macro has been assigned to the **On Click** event.

FIGURE 16-10
Macro assigned to
On Click event

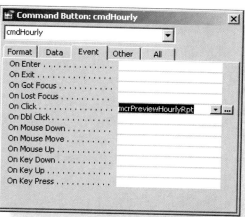

22. Close the property sheet, save the form, and switch to Form View.

23. Click the new command button to test it. Click **OK** to close the message box.

EXERCISE **16-7** **Edit a Macro**

The new macro closes the preview without giving you a chance to print the report. Therefore, you should not include the **Close** command in this macro. Because you are still in the form, you can edit the macro from the property sheet for the control.

1. Switch to Design View and open the property sheet for the **Preview Hourly Report** button.

2. Click the **Event** tab and the **On Click** row.

3. Click the Build button . The Macro Design window opens, not the Choose Builder dialog box, because you have already listed a macro name here.

NOTE: The row selector is the same in the Macro window as it is in the Datasheet.

4. Click the row selector for the **Close** action.

FIGURE 16-11
Selecting the
Close action

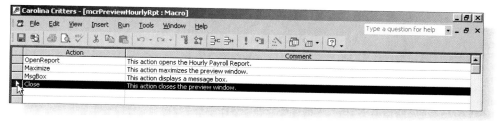

5. Delete the action. Save and close the macro window. Close the property sheet and return to Form View.

6. Save the form and test the button.

7. Close the Print Preview and the form.

Naming and Grouping Macros

You can place more than one macro in a macro object. When you do this, however, you must name each individual macro. This means you need to display the Macro Name column. When you see macros in a list, the macro object name appears, followed by a period and then the name of the macro.

 NOTE: If you run a macro by the object name without the individual macro identifier, only the first macro in the group executes.

EXERCISE **16-8** **Use and View a Grouped Macro**

When macros are grouped, each macro has a name and an action. The action for the individual macro executes when that specific macro is run.

1. Open frmAnimalsByGroup. A cluster of command buttons enables you to choose which category group to show. Each command button executes a macro that applies a filter to the form.

FIGURE 16-12
Cluster
command buttons

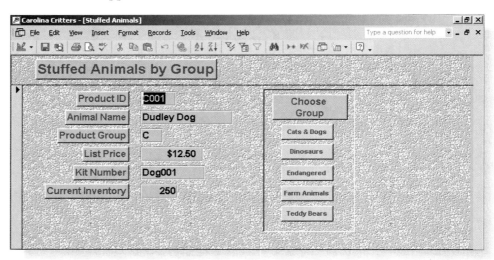

2. Click the Cats & Dogs button. Only the records that belong to the C product group are shown.

3. Switch to Datasheet View to better see the filtered records. Return to Form View.

  REVIEW: To change to Datasheet View in a form, click the drop-down arrow for the View button .

4. Click the Remove Filter button 🔽.
5. Click the **Dinosaurs** button and switch to Datasheet View.
6. Return to Form View and remove the filter.
7. Test the **Endangered** and **Farm Animals** buttons. The **Teddy Bears** button is not complete. Close the form without saving changes.
8. Click the **Macros** button and open mcrAnimalGroups in Design View.
9. Each macro has a name and an action. The **ApplyFilter** action applies the filter entered as the **Where Condition** argument.

FIGURE 16-13
Grouped Macro in
Design View

Macro names

Filter

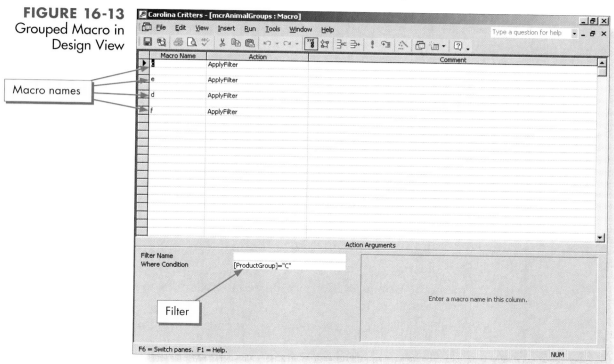

EXERCISE **16-9** **Add a Macro to a Grouped Macro**

You can now write a macro to show the Teddy Bear category. Then you will assign the macro to the appropriate button on the form.

1. Click the second blank row after the "f" macro.
2. Key **t** as the Macro Name and press Tab .
3. Choose the ApplyFilter action.
4. Click the Where Condition argument row in the lower pane.
5. Key **[productgroup]="t"** to set a criteria that the product group field must show a "T."

FIGURE 16-14
Adding an
individual macro
to a group

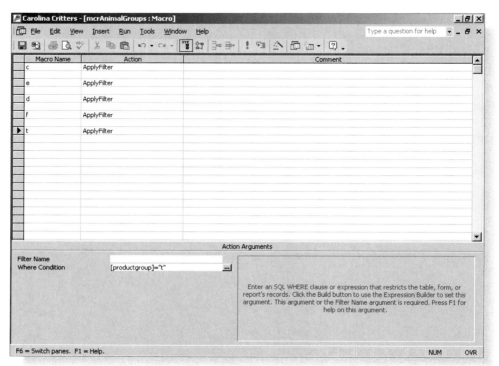

6. Save the macro and close the window.
7. Open frmAnimalsByGroup. You need to assign the macro to the command button in the form.
8. Switch to Design View and open the property sheet for the Teddy Bears command button.
9. Click the Event tab and the On Click row.
10. Click the drop-down arrow to list the existing macros. Choose mcrAnimalGroups.t. (See Figure 16-15 on the next page.)
11. Close the property sheet.
12. Save the form, switch to Form View, and test the Teddy Bears button.
13. Remove the filter and close the form.

FIGURE 16-15
Click the arrow to
list existing macros

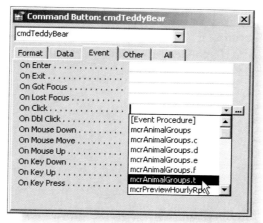

Using Conditions in a Macro

If you add a condition to a macro, you can control whether the macro carries out the commands and what commands it actually runs. Here's an example: The Customers table includes a field for the tax status of a customer. If a person is tax exempt, you need to enter a special Tax ID. This means you need to see the tax ID number field only if the tax status field is checked for "Yes."

You can write a macro to show the Tax ID field when the tax status is exempt and to hide the field when the customer is not exempt. Showing and hiding a control uses the SetValue macro action. The SetValue action has an Item argument in which you name the control and property to be changed. Its Expression argument is where you set the value for how the control should be changed.

EXERCISE 16-10 **Add a Text Box Control and Set Properties**

Because macros can be attached to events in forms and reports, you can use this condition in a form, not in the table. You first need to edit a form to add the TaxID control and make it invisible.

1. Open frmNewCustomerEntry. This form is set for Data Entry, so you do not see the existing records. There is no control for the Tax ID number. Switch to Design View.

2. Drag the TaxID field from the Field List to the 3-inch mark at the right of the Tax Exempt control. The new control shows the TaxID field and label.

3. Size, align, and format the control to match the others.

4. Open the property sheet. Change the name to **txtTaxID**.

5. Click the Format tab. Set the Visible property to No. You start with the control hidden and display it if the Tax Exempt check box is checked. Close the property sheet and view the form.

6. Save and close the form.

EXERCISE 16-11 Write a Macro with Conditions and the SetValue Action

After you add the hidden field to the form, you create a macro to display the field based on the value of another field. You will use a condition.

1. Create a new macro.

2. Click the Conditions button ⊞ to display the Condition column.

3. Although you can key a condition, you can also use the Expression Builder. Click the Build button ⬚.

4. Double-click the Forms folder in the left panel. Double-click All Forms. Click once to open frmNewCustomerEntry.

5. In the middle panel, click <Field List>. Double-click TaxStatus in the right panel.

6. The condition appears in the preview window. Key **=yes** to complete the condition.

FIGURE 16-16
Building an expression

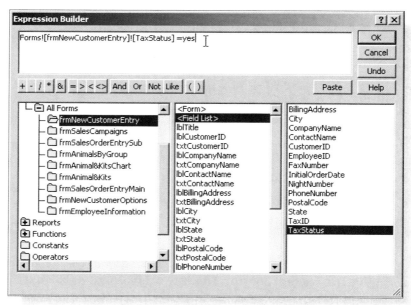

7. Click OK. Press [Tab] to move to the Action column. Choose SetValue. Move to the Item row in the Action Arguments panel.

8. The Item argument requires that you name the object/control property that will be set. You will be setting the Tax ID control and its Visible property if the TaxStatus field is "Yes." Click the Build button [...].

9. Double-click the Forms folder in the left panel. Double-click All Forms. Click frmNewCustomerEntry.

10. In the middle panel, scroll and click once to select txtTaxID. The properties for the control appear in the right panel.

 TIP: Control properties are preceded by a period in an expression.

11. Scroll to find and double-click the Visible property in the right panel. The complete identification for the control appears in the preview area.

FIGURE 16-17
Item argument in the
Expression Builder

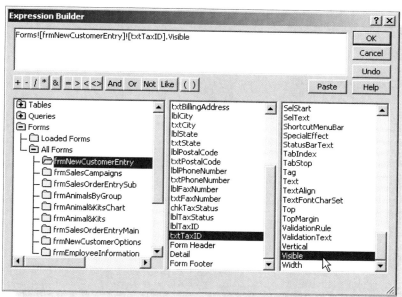

12. Click OK. Click the Expression row in the Action Argument panel. Key **true**

13. Click the first Condition cell and press [Shift] + [F2].

14. Press [Ctrl] + [C] to copy and click Cancel.

15. Click the second Condition cell for the macro and press [Ctrl] + [V] to paste the condition.

16. Edit the condition to show **no** instead of "yes."

17. Click the Action column and choose SetValue. The Item argument is the same as the first SetValue action, so you can copy it.

18. Click the first SetValue action and click its Item argument. Press ⟦F2⟧ to select the field. Press ⟦Ctrl⟧ + ⟦C⟧.

19. Paste the Item argument for the second SetValue action. Set the Expression for the second SetValue action as **false**

FIGURE 16-18
Completed macro

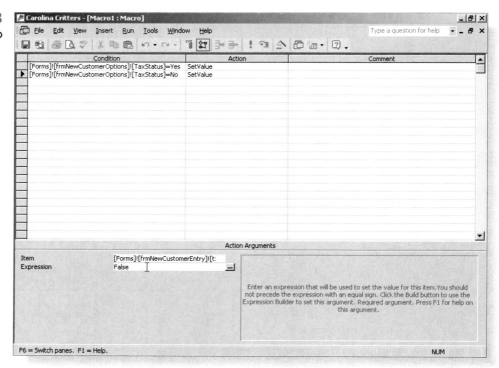

20. Save the macro as **mcrTaxExempt** and close the macro.

EXERCISE **16-12** **Assign a Macro to the After Update Event**

Some fields in a table might not be applicable to all records. For example, it might be important to list the name of a spouse for a married employee, but obviously not for a single employee. You can assign a macro to display or hide a field based on the value of another field.

In this example, you will display or hide the tax identification number of a customer, based on their tax-exempt status. If the customer is tax-exempt, the field for the tax identification number will display.

1. Open frmNewCustomerEntry in Design View. Open the property sheet for the checkbox named chkTaxStatus.

2. Click the Event tab. Click the After Update row and its drop-down arrow.

3. Choose mcrTaxExempt from the macro list.

FIGURE 16-19
Assigning the
TaxExempt macro
to an event

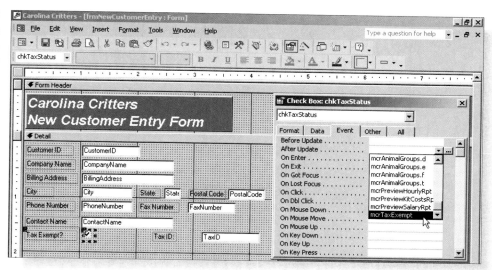

4. Close the property sheet. Save the form and return to Form View.

5. Enter the following record:

Customer ID	**15**
Company Name	**Dreams Made Home**
Billing Address	**8788 Marple Lane**
City	**Chicago**
State	**IL**
ZIP	**60621-8788**
Phone Number	**(773) 555-8788**
Fax Number	**(773) 555-8789**
Contact Name	**Anthony McLean**
Tax Exempt?	**Yes**
Tax ID	**13-4567**

6. Move to the next record. Notice that the Tax ID control remains visible.

7. Close the form. Compact the database.

Creating a Module and a Visual Basic Routine

Automating database applications with VBA modules is preferable to creating numerous embedded macros. Modules are faster to run, more flexible to design, and can recover from errors. Most database professionals prefer writing modules when automating applications.

Understanding the basic concepts of VBA is important. However, to truly use the power of VBA in a database application, you need to become familiar with VBA's syntax, coding techniques, and control structures.

EXERCISE 16-13 Explore Visual Basic Editor

The Visual Basic Editor defaults to display three docked panes. On the left are the **Project** and **Properties** panes. On the right is the **Code** pane. Listed in the **Project** pane are the modules associated with the current database.

There are two major types of modules—standard modules and class modules. *Standard modules* are global and may be assigned to numerous objects. *Class modules* are modules that are attached to individual objects such as a form or a report. Only standard modules are seen as objects in the module portion of the Database window. Both types of modules can be viewed in the Visual Basic Editor.

When you double-click an object in the **Project** pane, the associated code is displayed in the **Code** pane. Code is broken into procedures. A *procedure* is a series of commands and properties that performs a specific task. When a module has multiple procedures, horizontal lines separate each procedure. A procedure can be either a subroutine or a function.

1. While in *[your initials]*CC-16, update the links to **CC-E-16**. Click the Forms button.

2. Choose <u>T</u>ools, <u>M</u>acro, <u>V</u>isual Basic Editor. The VB Editor opens.

NOTE: If you do not see the Project and Properties panes on the left, turn them on from the View menu.

3. If the database is not already expanded, click the Expand button ⊞ for the database in the **Project** pane. The **Microsoft Access Class Objects** folder is shown.

4. Click the Expand button ⊞ for the **Microsoft Access Class Object** folder. Forms with VB code are listed.

5. Double-click frmAnimal&Kits. The forms module opens in the **Code** pane. Access created its own VB code when you created the form. (See Figure 16-20 on the next page.)

6. Click the View Microsoft Access button 🔑 to return to Access. The VB Editor is still open.

FIGURE 16-20
Visual Basic Editor

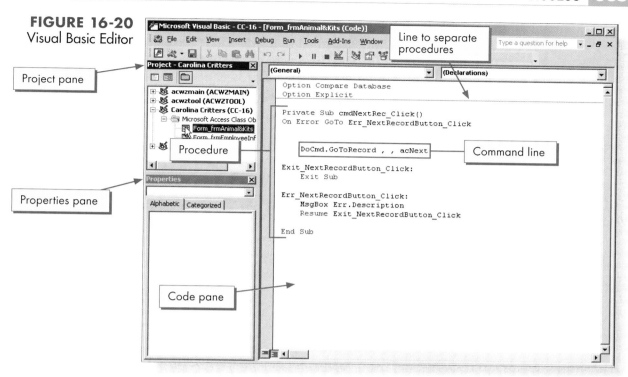

EXERCISE **16-14** Create a Module and Visual Basic Routine

Creating a Visual Basic routine often requires you to use special characters and system functions. The special characters and system functions you will use in this lesson are listed in Table 16-2.

TABLE 16-2   Common Visual Basic Symbols and Functions

SPECIAL CHARACTER/SYSTEM FUNCTION	DESCRIPTION
&	Used to concatenate two strings
_ (underscore)	Used to join one line to another
Chr(13)	Function that inserts a hard return
Date	Function that returns current date
Time	Function that returns current time

1. Click the Modules button and click <u>N</u>ew. Access switches back to the Visual Basic Editor. In the Project pane, a subfolder called Modules is added to the project Carolina Critter. This folder contains all stand-alone modules. The new module within the Modules folder is named "Module1" by default.

2. In the Property window, click the Name row and replace "Module1" with **basMessages**. Click in the Code pane to see the change.

 NOTE: The Leszynski naming convention uses "bas" as the prefix for modules.

FIGURE 16-21
Renaming a module

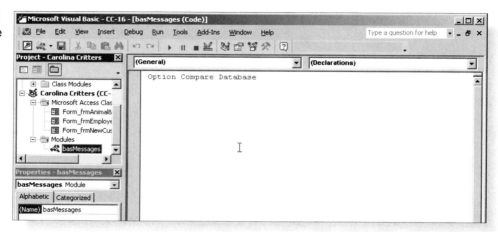

3. Click <u>I</u>nsert, <u>P</u>rocedure. This opens the Add Procedure dialog box.

4. Key **ShowDateTime** in the Name box. Click OK. The VB Editor adds the first and last line of the new procedure for you.

5. Press Tab . Key **msgbox** followed by a space. Key the following parameters.

 TIP: By keying the comma (,) you end one parameter and start the next one.

Prompt:

First line of text	**"Today's Date is:** Spacebar **"**
Concatenate	*Press* Spacebar **&**
Date function	**date**
Concatenate	*Press* Spacebar **&**
Carriage Return	**chr(13)**
Concatenate	*Press* Spacebar **&**
Join to next line	*Press* Spacebar _
New line in the editor	*Press* Enter *then* Tab

Second line of text	**"The Time is:** Spacebar **"**
Concatenate	*Press* Spacebar **&**
Time function	**time,**
Button style:	**vbInformation,**
Title:	**"Current Date and Time"**

6. Press ⬇ to see the completed message box statement.

 NOTE: The VB Editor will capitalize the first letter of keyword.

FIGURE 16-22
Completed Msgbox
statement

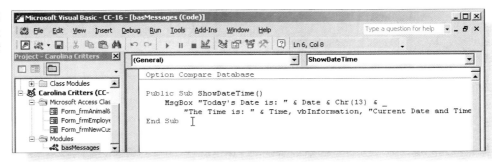

7. Click the Save button 🖫. Click **OK** to keep the name.

8. Click the Run button ▶ to test your message box. Click **OK**.

FIGURE 16-23
Current Date and
Time dialog box

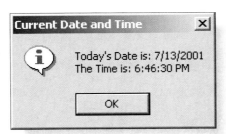

9. Click the Access button 🔑 to return to Access.

EXERCISE **16-15** **Assign a Procedure to the On-Click Event**

As you know, a procedure (or "routine") is a series of commands and properties that performs a task. When you write a procedure, you should first think it through in logical steps. In this exercise, you create a procedure to print the current record when a button is clicked. This is similar to the macro you wrote.

NOTE: The terms "procedure" and "routine" are used interchangeably by database professionals.

1. Click the Forms button. Open frmNewCustomerOptions in Design View.

2. Turn off the Control Wizards. Add a Command Button under the "Tax Exempt?" label.

3. Change the Name of the new button to **cmdDateTime** and its Caption to **Show Date and Time**

4. Click the Event tab. In the On Click row, click the Build button [...].

5. Choose Code Builder from the Choose Builder dialog box. The VB Editor opens and a new procedure has been added.

6. Press [Tab]. Key **basmessages.** (Include the period.) After you type the period, the name of the procedure in the Module basMessages appears.

7. Key **s** and then press [Tab] to complete the statement.

FIGURE 16-24
Call the procedure
ShowDateTime

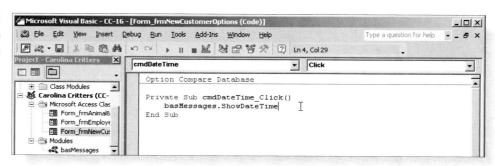

8. Save the procedure and return to Access. Test the Show Date and Time button.

9. Save and close the form.

Creating a Form Module Routine

All forms and reports possess class modules. A class module can be opened only when the form or report is open. Form and report modules often contain event procedures that run in response to an event in the object. An *event procedure* is a procedure automatically executed in response to an event initiated by the user or program code or triggered by the system. You can use event procedures to control the behavior of your form or report.

EXERCISE **16-16** Create a Command Button that Uses VBA Code

Before creating a Visual Basic procedure, you should first think through the steps and then determine the event. In this case, the event you create is to print the current record when a button is clicked. Finally, you need to assign the activity to an object that will be attached to a button. All this is done through the Command Wizard.

1. Open frmEmployeeInformation in Design View. Make sure the Control Wizards button [image] is on.

2. Add a new Command button [image] below the Job Code label.

3. In the Command Button Wizard, choose **Record Operations** in the Categories. Choose **Print Record** in Actions. Click **Next**.

4. Choose **Picture** and use the default printer image. Click **Next**.

5. Key **cmdPrint** as the name. Click **Finish**. The button is added to the form.

6. Open the property sheet for the button. Click the **Event** tab. The **On Click** event has an [Event Procedure] assigned to it.

7. Click in the **On Click** event. Click the Build button [...]. The VB Editor shows the module you just created. Access wrote this code for you.

FIGURE 16-25
cmdPrint_Click
procedure

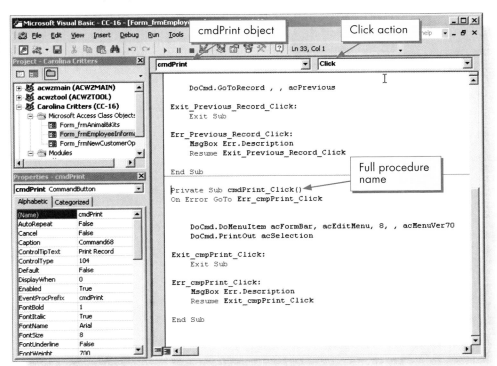

TIP: When using the Command Wizard, Access inserts error-trapping code automatically.

8. Click the View Microsoft Access button [image] to return to Access.

9. Close the property sheet and return to Form View. If you test the button, you will see that the procedure selects and prints one record.

10. Save and close the form.

EXERCISE 16-17 **Create a Procedure to Change the Appearance of a Form**

In this exercise you create a procedure that hides a PivotChart on a form. Although the PivotChart is not visible, it is still a control in the form.

1. Open frmAnimal&Kits in Design View. Click the drop-down arrow for the **Object** box. Note that all controls have been named by using the Leszynski naming convention.

2. Click the Control Wizards button [image] to turn it off.

3. Click the Command Button button [image] and click below the Tab control.

4. Open the property sheet for the command button. On the **Format** tab, change the **Caption** to **Chart OFF**. Press [↓] to see your changes.

5. Click the **Other** tab and change the **Name** to **cmdChartOff**

6. Click the **Event** tab and click in the **On Click** event. Click the Build button [...]. In the Choose Builder dialog box, choose **Code Builder**. Click **OK.** Notice that the name of the procedure is the name of the button, followed by the event.

7. Press [Tab]. Key **me**. This stands for the forms in which this procedure is located.

8. Key a period. A list box appears with all the object and actions that are part of the form. Key **frm**. The list box scrolls down to find "frm" in the list. The subform is at the top of the list and is highlighted.

FIGURE 16-26
List box with properties and actions

[image: Microsoft Visual Basic screenshot - Form_frmAnimal&Kits (Code) window showing code editor with cmdChartOff selected and Click event, with code:
Option Compare Database
Option Explicit

Private Sub cmdChartOff_Click()
    me.frm
End Sub
and a drop-down list box showing frmAnimal_KitsChart, FrozenColumns, GoToPage, GridX, GridY, HasModule, HelpContextId]

NOTE: VBA does not allow the "&" symbol, so it is replaced by an underscore "_".

9. Press Tab. Key a period. A list box appears with all the properties and actions that are part of the subform. Key **v**. The list box scrolls down to find "v" in the list. When "Visible" is highlighted, press Tab.

10. Key **=**. A box with two choices appears: "True" and "False." Key **f** and press Tab to complete the statement. Press ↑.

FIGURE 16-27
Completed
procedure

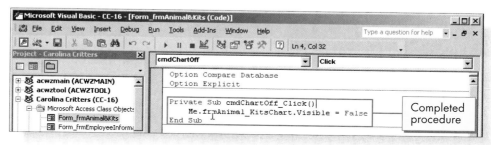

11. Click the Save button 🖫 and then click the Access Button 🖉. The form reappears.

12. The property sheet now shows the [Event Procedure] in the **On Click** event.

13. Switch to Form View and test the **Chart OFF** button.

14. Close the form and open it again. The chart has returned.

EXERCISE 16-18 **Add a Control Structure to a Procedure**

In this exercise you add a logical expression to the module. The procedure checks whether the PivotChart is visible. If it is not, a message appears on the screen when the command button is pressed.

1. Switch to Design View. Double-click cmdChartOff to open its property sheet. On the **Event** tab, click the Build button ⋯ for the **On Click** event. You return to the VB Editor and the procedure cmdChartOff_Click.

2. Press Tab. Press Enter and then ↑.

3. Key the following:

    if *Press* Spacebar

    me.frm *Press* Tab

    .v *Press* Tab

    =t *Press* Tab *and then* Spacebar

    then *Press* ↓ *to see the changes.*

FIGURE 16-28
First line of the
If-Then statement

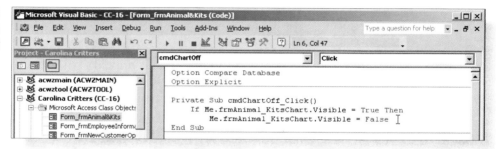

Press Enter and then Backspace.

else Press Enter and then Tab

msgbox "ERROR - Chart is unavailable", vbc Press Tab

Press Enter and then Backspace

endif Press ↑ to see the completed procedure

TIP: The use of tabs makes the code easier to read.

FIGURE 16-29
Finished If-Then
statement

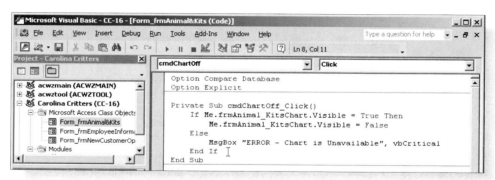

4. Press the Save button 🖫. Return to the form and switch to Form View.

5. Test the **Chart OFF** button. Click it a second time. Click **OK** to close the error message.

6. Close the form.

Optimizing Databases

A database containing VBA code can be saved as an *MDE file,* a compacted Access database containing compiled VBA code that cannot be edited. Converting a database to an MDE file compiles all modules, removes all editable source code, and compacts the destination database. The MDE database is smaller than the MDB database because the code has been removed. Memory usage is optimized and performance improves. The Visual Basic code continues to function as before. Forms and reports continue to function normally.

What is different is that users are not able to modify or create forms, reports, and modules. Users are not able to view or edit the VBA code. They are not able to add, delete, or change references to object libraries. They also are not allowed to import or export forms, reports, or modules. However, they can import tables, queries, Data Access Pages, and macros from or export to non-MDE databases.

EXERCISE 16-19 Compact a Database on Closing

As you delete data or objects, the database becomes fragmented and begins to use space on the disk inefficiently. Periodically you should compact your database to ensure optimal performance. When compacting a database, Access copies the file, rearranges its contents to reclaim unused space, deletes the original file, and renames the new file to the original database name. Because Access actually creates a copy of the original database, you should always have at least equal the amount of free space on your storage media as the original size of the database.

1. Click Tools, Options. Click the General tab.
2. Select the check box for Compact on Close. Click OK.
3. Close the database. Notice that the database is compacting automatically.

EXERCISE 16-20 Create an MDE File

MDE files cannot be modified. If you ever lose the original Access database file, including the modules with the Visual Basic code you have written, you will not be able to make changes to the procedures you have created. Therefore, it is very important that you always safeguard the original file and its source code.

1. Open *[your initials]*CC-16.
2. Click Tools, Database Utilities, Make MDE File.
3. Name the file **CCritters** and click Save. Close the database.
4. Compare the size of the files *[your initials]*CC-16 and **CCritters**. Is there a difference?
5. Open **CCritters**. Click Tools, Macro, Visual Basic Editor.
6. Expand the folders in the Project window until you find Form_frmAnimal&Kits. Double-click it. All the code is locked.

FIGURE 16-30
The project is locked

7. Click OK. Close both the VB Editor and the database.

USING HELP

Macros and Visual Basic modules can automate much of your work. Use Help to learn more about these features. Turn off the Office Assistant if it starts.

Use Help to explore application development.

1. While in any database object window, press F1.

2. Click the Contents tab.

3. Expand the Programming in Access topic. Expand the Basic Programming Concepts topic. Click the topic Should I use a macro or Visual Basic?

4. Read both When should I use a Macro? and When should I use Visual Basic?

FIGURE 16-31
Microsoft Access
Help

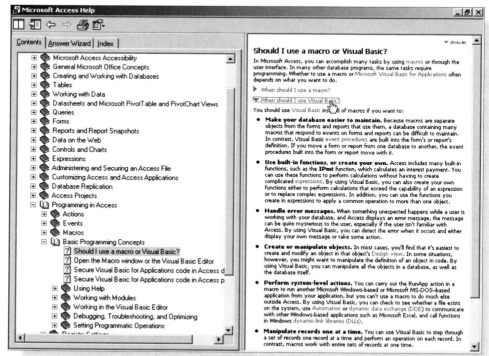

5. Expand the Macros topic. Click the topic Convert macros to Visual Basic. Read how to convert macros into standard and Class VB modules.

6. Explore other macros or Visual Basic topics of interest to you. Close Help when you have finished.

LESSON Summary

➤ Macros and Visual Basic modules are event-driven, sequenced activities containing customizable arguments, conditions, actions, and comments.

➤ Events that execute macros and Visual Basic modules include clicking a button, pressing a key, and opening a form or a report.

➤ After creating a standard module, you may assign it to a single object or numerous objects. A class module, such as a form or report module, is the property of the object in which it originated.

➤ Creating an MDE file should be the last step in the development of a database that you plan to distribute.

LESSON 16 Command Summary

FEATURE	BUTTON	MENU	KEYBOARD	SPEECH
Run Macro	!	Tools, Macro, Run Macro		✓
Show Macro Names	xyz	View, Macro Names		✓
Show Conditions		View, Conditions		✓
Launch VBA		Tools, Macro, Visual Basic Editor	Alt +F11	✓
Run Procedure	▶	Run, Run Sub/UserForm	F5	✓
New Procedure		Insert, Procedure		✓
Return to Access		View, Microsoft Access	Alt +F11	✓

Concepts Review

Each of the following statements is either true or false. Indicate your choice by circling T or F.

T F **1.** A command button runs a macro if the macro is assigned to an event in the button's property sheet.

T F **2.** Modules run faster than macros.

T F **3.** All macro actions have at least one argument.

T F **4.** You can test a macro by running it from the Macro Design window.

T F **5.** The Type argument for the MsgBox action sets the title for the message box.

T F **6.** You can insert, but not delete, **Action** rows in a macro.

T F **7.** Standard modules can only be used by one form or report.

T F **8.** Modules can be written to trap errors.

Write the correct answer in the space provided.

1. What action or command displays a dialog box on the screen?

_____

2. What two columns appear in the Macro Design window as a default?

_____

3. What two columns can you turn on and off in the Macro Design window?

_____

4. In the Database window, what type of module is listed?

_____

5. What property hides or shows the control?

_____

6. What are the two arguments for the SetValue action?

_____

7. List the Visual Basic names of the four icons that can be displayed in a message box?

_____

8. What does Chr(13) represent in a Visual Basic module?

_____

CRITICAL THINKING

Answer these questions on a separate page. There are no right or wrong answers. Support your answers with examples from your own experience, if possible.

1. Discuss the similarities and differences between using a macro and a Visual Basic module.

2. Open the property sheet for a command button in one of your forms and look at the Help screen for several events. Develop ideas for macros or modules that might be appropriate for three new events.

Skills Review

EXERCISE 16-21

Create a macro. Assign a macro to a command button. Add an action to a macro.

1. Open the file *[your initials]***CC-16**. With your database open and with refreshed links, create a macro by following these steps:

   a. Click the Macros button and New.
   b. Click the first Action cell and display the list of actions.
   c. Key **openr** to move to the OpenReport action and press Enter.
   d. Key **This action opens the Sales Campaign report.** (Include the period.)
   e. Move to the Report Name argument in the Action Arguments pane.
   f. Display the report names and choose rptSalesCampaigns.
   g. Move to the View argument and choose Print Preview.
   h. Click the second Action cell and key **max**. Press Enter.
   i. Key **This action maximizes the preview window.** (Include the period.)
   j. Save and name the macro **mcrPreviewSalesCampaigns**. Close the Macro window.

2. Assign a macro to a command button by following these steps:

   a. Open frmSalesCampaigns in Design View.
   b. Draw a command button below the label in the Form Header. If the Command Button wizard starts, click Cancel.
   c. Open the property sheet and set the Caption to **Preview Report**

    d. Name the button **cmdPreviewReport**

    e. Click the Event tab and the On Click row. Choose mcrPreviewSalesCampaigns from the drop-down list.

    f. Close the property sheet and save the form.

    g. Switch to Form View and test the button.

3. Add an action to a macro by following these steps:

    a. Open the property sheet for the command button.

    b. Click the Event tab and the On Click row. Click the Build button .

    c. Click the third Action cell and choose the **msgbox** action.

    d. Key this comment: **This action displays a message box.** (Include the period.)

    e. Move to the Message argument and open the Zoom window. Key this message:

      This is the current Sales Campaigns report. Click OK to close this message box. Then click the Print button to print the report or click Close to close the preview.

    f. In the Type argument row, choose Information.

    g. In the Title argument row, key **Preview Report**

    h. Save the macro and close the window.

    i. Close the property sheet and save the form.

    j. Switch to Form View and test the button. Close the form.

EXERCISE 16-22

Add labels to a form. Use conditions and SetValue. Add a command button to a form.

1. Add hidden objects to a form by following these steps:

    a. Open frmNewCustomerEntry. Add a label aligned with the CustomerID control at the right edge of the Detail section. Key **Out of State Customer** and press ⌷Enter⌷.

    b. Open the property sheet for the label. Click the Format tab and set the Visible property to No. Name the control **lblOutOfState**. Close the property sheet.

    c. Format and size the label to use 10-point bold italic Arial.

    d. Save and close the form.

2. Create a macro by following these steps:

    a. Click the Macros button and <u>N</u>ew. Display the Macro Name column by clicking the Macro Names button .

    b. Save the macro as **mcrLocation**

3. Use conditions and the SetValue action by following these steps:

    a. Click the Conditions button ⌷📋⌷.

b. Click the Build button for the first **Condition** cell.

c. Double-click the **Forms** folder in the left panel. Double-click **All Forms**. Click frmNewCustomerEntry.

d. Click <Field List> in the middle panel. Double-click **State** in the right panel. Key **="nc"** to complete the condition. Click **OK**.

e. Press Tab to move to the **Action** column. Choose SetValue. Move to the **Item** row in the **Argument** pane. Click the Build button.

f. Double-click the **Forms** folder and then **All Forms**. Click frmNewCustomerEntry.

g. In the middle panel, select lblOutOfState. Double-click **Visible** in the right panel. Click **OK**.

h. Click the **Expression** row in the **Argument** pane. Key **false**

i. Click the **Condition** cell and press Shift + F2. Press Ctrl + C to copy and then click **Cancel**. Click the second **Condition** cell and press Ctrl + V to paste the condition.

j. Edit the condition to show **<>"nc"** instead of =nc.

REVIEW: The operator **<>** means "is not equal to."

k. Click the **Action** column and choose SetValue. Move to the **Item** row in the Argument pane. Click the Build button.

l. Double-click the **Forms** folder and **All Forms**. Click frmNewCustomerEntry. In the middle panel, select lblOutofState. Double-click **Visible** in the right panel. Click **OK**. Key **true** for the **Expression** argument.

m. Save and close the macro.

4. Assign macros to an event by following these steps:

a. Open frmNewCustomerEntry in Design View.

b. Open the property sheet for txtState. Click the **Event** tab and the **After Update** row.

c. Choose mcrLocation from the list of macros.

d. Close the property sheet and save the form. Switch to Form View.

e. Add the following record:

Customer ID	16
Company Name	**Crystal Carousel**
Billing Address	**413 West Lee Street**
City	**New York**
State	**NY**
ZIP	**10022-0431**
Phone Number	**(202) 555-7788**
Fax Number	**(202) 555-1234**

Contact Name   **Robert Schmitt**

Tax Exempt?   **No**

   f. Close the form.

EXERCISE 16-23
Add a Visual Basic routine to a module.

   1. Add a new routine to a standard module by following these steps:

      a. Click the Modules button. Click basMessages. Click Design.

      b. Click Insert, Procedure. Name the new procedure **LegalNotice**. Click OK.

      c. Press Tab and key **msgbox**

      d. Key the following:

Press Spacebar "CONFIDENTIALITY STATEMENT"

Press Spacebar & *Press* Spacebar chr(13) *Press* Spacebar & *Press* Spacebar

chr(13) *Press* Spacebar & *Press* Spacebar _ *Press* Enter

"This database contains information that is confidential. *Press* Spacebar "

Press Spacebar & *Press* Spacebar _ *Press* Enter

"Dissemination, distribution, copying, or use of this information *Press* Spacebar "

Press Spacebar & *Press* Spacebar _ *Press* Enter

"by anyone other than current employees of Carolina Critters *Press* Spacebar "

Press Spacebar & *Press* Spacebar _ *Press* Enter

"is prohibited."

,vbc *Press* Tab

, "Legal Notice" *Press* ↓

      e. Save the procedure and click the Access button 🔑.

   2. Assign a procedure to an event by following these steps:

      a. Open frmEmployeeInformation in Design View.

      b. Open the property sheet for the form.

      c. On the Event tab, click in the On Open row.

      d. Click the Build button ... and choose Code Builder. Click OK.

      e. Press Tab and key **basmessages.leg**. Press Tab.

      f. Save and click the Access button 🔑.

      g. Switch to Form View. Click OK to the Legal Notice dialog box.

      h. Close the form and then reopen it. Click OK.

      i. Close the form.

EXERCISE 16-24

Add a command button. Create a procedure to make a chart visible.

1. Add a command button to a form by following these steps:

   a. Open frmAnimal&Kits in Design View. Verify that the Control Wizards button  is off.

   b. Click the Command Button button  and click to the side of the Chart OFF button.

   c. Change the new button's Caption property to **Chart ON**

   d. Change the new button's Name property to **cmdChartOn**

2. Create a procedure by following these steps:

   a. In the Event tab, click the Build button 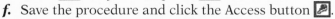 for the On Click event.

   b. Choose Code Builder and click OK.

   c. In the VB Editor, press Tab. Key **me.frm**

   d. Press Tab. Key **.v**

   e. Press Tab. Key **=t** and press Tab.

   f. Save the procedure and click the Access button .

   g. Test both command buttons.

   h. Compact and close the database.

Lesson Applications

EXERCISE 16-25

Create a grouped macro. Assign macros to events.

1. Create a columnar AutoForm for tblKitContents. Make the form wider and the Detail section taller. Add a command button to the right of the controls in the upper right corner of the Detail section and then cancel the wizard. Copy and paste the command button so you have seven buttons. Change the Caption for each button to show one of the Supplier ID numbers (AA-01, BB-02, and so on). Save the form as frmKitContents and close it.

 TIP: To set the captions, open the property sheet and leave it open. Just click each control in succession.

2. Create a grouped macro named mcrKits. Name the first macro **a** and have it apply a filter that shows only the kits from Supplier AA-01.

 TIP: Write the first macro, assign it the appropriate button in the form, and test it before writing the other macros.

3. Add six more macros with appropriate names. Apply a filter to show one of the other suppliers. You can copy, paste, and edit the Where Condition. Save and close the macro.

4. Assign the appropriate macro to the related event for each of the command buttons. Save the form.

5. Test the buttons. Notice that there are no kits from Supplier DD-04 or FF-06.

6. Use the Documenter to print only the actions and arguments for this macro.

7. Print one record of the form.

EXERCISE 16-26

Add a Visual Basic routine to a module. Add a button to run it.

1. Add a new procedure to the basMessages module.
2. Name it **CompanyInfo**
3. Have the procedure display a message box with the following text:

FIGURE 16-32

Carolina Critters, Inc., was formed in 1946 by Hector Fuentes upon his
return from serving in the U.S. Navy in World War II. Hector's son, Carlos,
took over the company in 1962 and ran it until 1997 when his daughter Lisa
assumed the presidency. Originally producing only stuffed teddy bears and
a dog modeled on Franklin Delano Roosevelt's dog, the company has branched
out over the years. It now has 5 product lines and 25 products, producing
over $25 million in annual sales.

4. The icon should be the exclamation mark.
5. The title should be **Company Information**
6. Add a button, named cmdCompanyInfo, to frmEmployeeInformation that, if clicked, will run the procedure CompanyInfo.
7. Use the Documenter to print only the code for basMessages.

EXERCISE 16-27

Add a command button and procedure that will turn a chart on and off.

1. In frmAnimal&Kits you created a button that controlled the visibility of the chart. Replace that button with a single button.
2. Create a procedure named ChartOnOff for when the button is clicked:
   - If the subform is not visible then
   - Set visible to true.
   - Change the command buttons **Caption** to "Chart OFF."
   - Else (the subform is visible)
   - Set visible to false.
   - Change the command buttons **Caption** to "Chart ON."

 TIP: There will be no need for an error message.

3. Use the Documenter to print only the code for frmAnimals&Kits.

EXERCISE 16-28 *Challenge Yourself*

Create a routine in a form module. Assign it to an event.

For frmEmployeeInformation, add a command button in the **Detail** section that toggles the form between being used only for adding a new employee record to being used only to view all employee records.

If Data Entry for the form is equal to true then
- Set Data Entry property to False.
- Change the command button **Caption** to "Add Employees."
- Change the form title to "Employee Information Form."

Else (the form is viewing all employee records)
- Set Data Entry property to True.
- Change the command button **Caption** to "View Employees."
- Change the form title to "Add New Employee."

Use the Documenter to print only the code for frmEmployeeInformation.

On Your Own

In these exercises you work on your own, as you would in a real-life work environment. Use the skills you've learned to accomplish the task—and be creative.

EXERCISE 16-29
Review the designs of the databases you modified in Exercise 15-30. Sketch a combination of three macros or Visual Basic modules that will enhance your design. You can modify your table structures to better accommodate your designs. For each sketch, write the name of the macro or module, describe its purpose, list the source dynaset(s), and list all object(s) with which the macro or module will be associated. Below each macro, write one to two paragraphs explaining why using a macro is more appropriate than using a module. Below each module, write one to two paragraphs explaining why using a module is more appropriate than using a macro. On each printout, write your name and "Exercise 16-29." Continue to the next exercise.

EXERCISE 16-30
Based on the sketches you created in Exercise 16-29, create the macros and modules. Associate each macro or module to the appropriate objects. Test each macro or module and all associated object(s). Print documentation for each macro or module. On each printout, write your name and "Exercise 16-30." Continue to the next exercise.

EXERCISE 16-31
Document your databases by providing printouts of the databases' structures and printouts of all your objects. Organize the printouts in an organized and logical manner. Include a cover page with your name, class information, and current date. Immediately behind the cover page, write at least three pages describing the most significant or important skills you learned and how you might approach designing a similar database differently in the future. Submit sketches and printouts from Exercises 16-29 through 16-31 to your instructor.

Unit 5 Applications

UNIT APPLICATION 5-1

Create a new database. Add tables to the database. Establish relationships.

1. Start Access and create a blank database named **[YourInitials]SchoolDB**. This database will track students, courses, and instructors for a school similar to yours.

2. Create a new table named **tblStudents**. Use the following fields: LastName, FirstName, MI, SS#, Address, City, State, ZIP, Phone. Determine the data type, size, captions, input masks, primary key, and formats.

3. Create a new table named **tblCourses**. Use these fields: CoursePrefix, CourseNo, Title. In this table you will list course codes and titles. Assume that courses are listed in the format "COM101 Communications I" with "COM" as the course prefix, "101" as the course number, and "Communications I" as the course title. Establish a numbering pattern so you know how wide to make the fields. Determine the data type, size, captions, input masks, and formats. Use CoursePrefix and CourseNo as a two-field primary key.

  TIP: To set a two-field primary key, select both row selectors before clicking the Primary Key button .

4. Create a new table named **tblInstructors**. Use these fields: LastName, FirstName, InsCode. Decide how you will set an instructor code. Determine the data type, size, captions, input masks, and formats.

5. Create a new table named **tblSchedule**. Use these fields: CoursePrefix, CourseNo, Section, Day(s), StartTime, EndTime, Room, InsCode. Two of these fields must use the same data type and size as fields in tblCourses. One must match a field in tblInstructors. Determine the data type, size, captions, input masks, and formats. The primary key is a three-field combination: CoursePrefix, CourseNo, and Section.

6. Create a new table named **tblEnrollment**. Use these fields: CoursePrefix, CourseNo, Section, SS#. Three fields must match the information in tblSchedule. The SS# field must match tblStudents. Do not assign a primary key.

7. Show all tables in the Relationships window and establish the appropriate relationships without referential integrity. The relationship between tblCourses and tblSchedule uses two fields. Select both and drag. Then set the fields in the Edit Relationships dialog box. There is a three-field relationship between tblEnrollment and tblSchedule.

8. Print the relationships in landscape orientation.

UNIT APPLICATION 5-2

Add records to tables. Print tables.

1. Add ten students to tblStudents, using data that is relevant to your location and school. Key a period after the middle initial. Notice the automatic subdatasheet assigned to the table based on the relationships.

   REVIEW: You can remove a subdatasheet in Design View. Right-click in the upper pane and choose Properties.

2. Add five instructors to tblInstructors. The table also has an automatic subdatasheet.

   REVIEW: To determine which table is used for the subdatasheet, choose Insert, Subdatasheet.

3. Add information about seven courses offered at your school to tblCourses. No subdatasheet is automatically assigned.

4. Add at least two sections of each course listed in tblCourses to tblSchedule. To enter times, check the **Format** property in Table Design. Use existing instructor codes.

5. Add records in tblEnrollment that show at least four students registered in each class listed in tblSchedule. As you complete each CoursePrefix group, make sure no student has registered for two sections of the same course.

   REVIEW: Copy the immediately preceding field by pressing Ctrl + ' .

6. Open tblStudents and expand a few subdatasheets.

7. Print all tables in landscape orientation.

UNIT APPLICATION 5-3

Create a main form with a subform. Create a multiple-page form. Write a macro. Add a command button to a form. Assign a macro to an event. Create a Switchboard.

1. Create an AutoForm for tblStudents. Delete the subform control. Make the form 6.5 inches wide and reposition the controls to better use the form grid. Add a **Form Header** with a label that says **Student Schedule.** Save the form.

   NOTE: The subform is automatically created because of the existing relationship between the tables.

2. Create a query for tblCourses, tblEnrollment, and tblSchedule. Include the CoursePrefix, CourseNo, and the Title from tblCourses and the SS# from tblEnrollment. Do not include any fields from the other tables. Create a new form in Design View for this query. Drag all the fields to the design grid and delete the labels. Arrange the text boxes in a single row at the top edge of the Detail section in this order (left to right): CoursePrefix, CourseNo, Title, SS#. Make the SS# field invisible and set the form to Continuous Forms View. Add this form as a subform to the main Student Schedule form and format it appropriately. Print one record of this form.

 NOTE: You need to show tblSchedule in the query as a junction table to establish a link between tblEnrollment and tblCourses.

3. Create a multiple-page form for tblInstructors. Name the first page **Instructor Info.** Show the instructor's first and last name and code on this page. Name the second page **Current Schedule**

 REVIEW: You can widen the fields in the subform in Form View.

4. Insert a subform on the second page, using tblSchedule. Show all the fields except Room and InsCode. Determine what field links the subform to tblInstructors on page1. Format the subform.

5. Create a tabular AutoReport for tblSchedule. Make it landscape and format it with a professional design.

6. Write a macro that opens this report in Print Preview. Include an appropriate message box.

7. Create a columnar AutoForm for tblCourses. Add a command button and assign the macro to the relevant event.

8. Create a Switchboard for your database. Include buttons to view the forms and reports.

9. Set the Switchboard to display when you open the database. (Use the Move Up and Move Down arrows in the Edit Switchboard Page dialog box to rearrange your items.)

UNIT APPLICATION 5-4   *Using the Web*

Create two Data Access pages.

1. Create a new Data Access Page that shows the course and section by instructor. Concatenate the fields CoursePrefix and CourseNo to create a Course field. Concatenate the first name and last name fields to create an Instructor field. Format the page to look appealing. Expand one group and print the page.

TIP: You will need to create new queries that contain the fields and concatenated fields needed to build these Data Access Pages.

2. Create a new Data Access Page that shows the Section, Meeting Days, Start Times, End Times, Room, and Instructor grouped by Course. Concatenate the fields CoursePrefix, CourseNo, and Title to create a Course field. Concatenate the first name and last name fields to create an Instructor field. Format the page to look appealing. Expand one group and print the page.

Portfolio Builder

List of Files/Tables Produced in the Portfolio Builder

Files/Tables Produced (Possible Capstone Project)

Filename	Description
*[Your initials]***Printouts**	Your printout list. A list of printouts to include in your representational portfolio.
*[Your initials]***Prospects**	List of prospective employers for use in targeting your database objects and printouts.
Up to 10 printouts	Printouts listed in your printout list (your representational portfolio).

Additional Documents Discussed (Actual Job Search)

Résumé	
*[Your initials]***AppInfo**	Information for use in filling out employment applications.
Cover letter	
Thank you letter	
Contact log	

Portfolio Builder

OBJECTIVES

After completing this lesson, you will be able to:

1. Create and adapt Access databases for a portfolio.
2. Identify prospective employers.
3. Target your portfolio to a specific employer.
4. Feature your Access skills in your résumé.
5. Fill out an employment application.
6. Prepare and present yourself at an interview.
7. Follow up an interview.

Finding a job is difficult—especially if the economy is bad or companies are downsizing. The number of applicants often exceeds the availability of jobs. It is important for you to distinguish yourself from other people interested in the same job. You need to show a prospective employer what you can do.

This Portfolio Builder helps you build a "representational portfolio"—a collection of your best work that you can show as evidence of your Access skills. The databases and printouts in your portfolio will be geared to specific employers and could actually accompany a résumé and cover letter, or they could be brought with you to a job interview. Some instructors might use this representational portfolio as a capstone project for the course.

Objectives 4 through 7 of this Portfolio Builder lead you though an actual job-search process, including identifying and contacting prospective employers, filling out employment applications, presenting yourself, and following up after interviews.

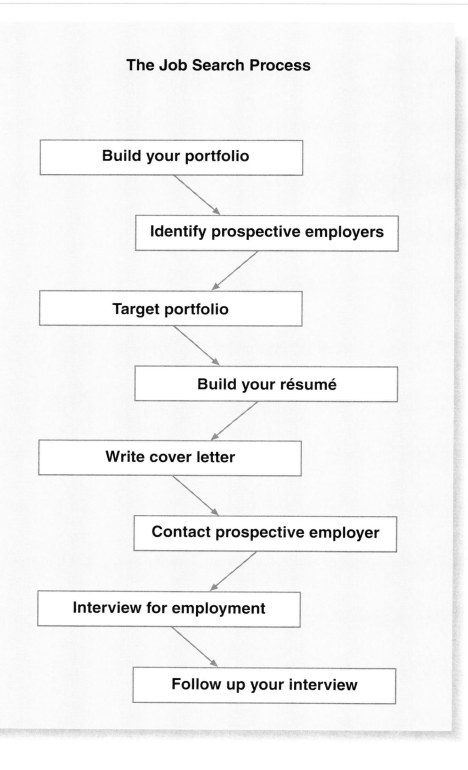

The Portfolio Builder will be helpful to you if you're planning to search for immediate employment. However, Objectives 1 through 3 are also a useful final project, because it requires you to demonstrate skills you have gained over the entire course. Even if you're not looking for a job, it will help prepare you for an eventual job search.

Building Your Portfolio

While your résumé describes your experience and your skills, your portfolio actually demonstrates your skills by representing the best work you can do. It also should be work with which a prospective employer can identify—that is, tables, reports, and forms that the employer will understand.

The first step in building your portfolio is to decide what types of printouts belong in it. Use the following checklist as a starting point for creating a list of possible printouts for your portfolio.

TABLE P-1   Possible Printouts for Portfolio

WORKSHEET	COMMENTS
Customers Report	Indicates that you know your target company's market. Customers may be entirely artificial, but should be realistic. To identify your target company's customers, research the company on line or at your local library. Read their annual report (if they are a publicly-owned company). Additional printouts: portion of a customer table, customer entry form, mailing labels.
Products Report	Indicates that you know your target company's products and services. To obtain information about your target company's products, research the company's product line either on line or in print. Additional printouts: portion of a products table, product entry form. In some cases it may be appropriate to scan a company's catalog and include images in the report.
Sales Report	Indicates that you are aware of your target company's sales history. This type of information is available on line, in the company's annual reports, or in press releases carried by the local paper. If such information is not available, discuss possible strategies for estimating sales realistically (so as not to underestimate a company's sales, and in so doing, to hurt your chances for employment). Additional printouts: portion of monthly sales table, sales entry form.

NOTE: The printouts produced in the course of the Lesson and Unit Applications may also be used in your portfolio. You can personalize them (using the suggestions above) so that the Carolina Critters database contains data that might be more appropriate for your target company. (Obviously, any changes to the Carolina Critters database should be made on a copy of the original database.)

EXERCISE **P-1** Develop a List of Printouts for the Portfolio

1. Develop a list of up to 10 printouts for inclusion in your portfolio. Use Table P-1 as a checklist, but also consider printouts that you may have prepared in the Access course. If you have work experience, list actual printouts that you have created. Use the following headings for your list (see Figure P-2):

   Number   **Type of Printout**   **Description**

2. Save the list as *[your initials]***Printouts** and print it.

3. Finalize your list by reviewing it with someone who is familiar with your job-search area. Adjust the list as needed. Save and print it.

FIGURE P-2   Sample printout list for student seeking a database-entry position with a high-technology manufacturing company

No.	Type of Printout	Description
1	Customer Report	Customers, sorted alphabetically.
2	Customer Report	Customers, grouped by state, with a calculation showing the number of customers from a state (or region).
3	Customer Report	Filtered list, showing only customers from a particular region.
4	Product Report	Products, grouped by product line. (If possible, add images.)
5	Product Report	Products, sorted by product ID (add a ProductID field if the company's products do not have a product ID number).
6	Sales Invoice	Shows customer information and product information.
7	Sales Report	Sales by product, sorted by product line.
8	Sales Report	Sales by group, sorted in ascending order over a period.

continues

FIGURE P-2 Sample printout list for student seeking a database-entry position with a high-technology manufacturing company   *continued*

No.	Type of Printout	Description
9	Sales Report	Sales by product, for products over a specific sales goal.
10	Inventory Report	Products in inventory, filtered to show products for which inventory is low.

EXERCISE P-2 Build Your Portfolio

It isn't necessary to begin a database from scratch. In fact, it may not even be a good idea. You may be able to modify an existing database (perhaps even the Carolina Critters database used in the course or the sample NorthWind database provided by Microsoft).

TABLE P-2 Possible Exercises for a Representational Portfolio

LESSON/UNIT	EXERCISES/APPLICATIONS*
Lesson 1	1-26
Lesson 2	2-27
Lesson 3	3-29
Unit 1	U1-2, U1-3
Lesson 4	4-22
Lesson 5	5-21
Lesson 6	6-28, 6-29
Lesson 7	7-30, 7-31
Unit 2	U2-2, U2-3
Lesson 8	8-27, 8-28, 8-29
Lesson 9	9-25, 9-26, 9-27

continues

TABLE P-2   Possible Exercises for a Representational Portfolio   *continued*

LESSON/UNIT	EXERCISES/APPLICATIONS*
Lesson 10	10-22, 10-23
Unit 3	U3-2, U3-3,
Lesson 11	11-33, 11-34, 11-35
Lesson 12	12-23, 12-24, 12-25
Lesson 13	13-24, 13-25, 13-36
Unit 4	U4-2, U4-3
Lesson 14	14-26, 14-27, 14-28
Lesson 15	15-25,15-26, 15-27
Lesson 16	16-26, 16-27, 16-28
Unit 5	U5-2, U5-3, U5-4

*The "On Your Own" exercises are especially suitable as a representational portfolio. Note, however, that they build from the first lesson to the last.

1. Create each of the printouts on your list.

2. Adjust every printout to give it as professional an appearance as possible. Focus on formatting. Demonstrate the skills you learned in this course.

3. Consult the appropriate style reference for your profession to check that your formatting is acceptable.

4. Spell-check your report labels and, if appropriate, the data itself.

5. Ask someone familiar with your future profession to review your printouts (and, possibly, your database). Then modify them appropriately.

Identifying Prospective Employers

Your next step is to identify prospective employers, starting with the companies in your area (and the people within those companies) that might be hiring people with your skills.

Always try to identify the manager in each company or organization who heads up the division, department, or group in which you hope to work. Avoid applying through a Human Resources staff member, if at all possible. In the Human Resources Department, it's easy to become just another applicant who receives no special attention.

Help-Wanted Ads

Help-wanted ads can be a useful way to research the hiring trends of a local company. Help-wanted ads are, however, less useful as a source of real employment opportunities. They should never be used as the primary focus of your job search. In fact, some experts believe that only 10 percent of all available jobs are listed in the newspaper.

Use back issues of your local newspapers to find out whether a company has been hiring recently, what kinds of jobs have recently been advertised, and who was listed as a contact person in the ad.

Networking

Talk to people who are in a position to provide information about job leads and the hiring process at particular companies. They can be friends, relatives, acquaintances—anyone who can put you in touch with a job contact. Try to identify the people within a company who have the power to hire you. Get the correct spelling of each person's name and their official correct job title, department, company, and, if possible, telephone number.

Company Research

An easy way to begin your company research is with the Yellow Pages. Use it to locate businesses in the field in which you're interested. (You might need to use the "Business-to-Business" section for some types of businesses.)

The business section of your local library contains reference books that can give you even more information about local companies. Some of the best sources are:

- *Standard & Poor's Register of Corporations*, Directors, and Executives. McGraw-Hill. (Volume 2 lists companies by location.)
- *The National Directory of Addresses and Phone Numbers*. Gale Research, Inc.
- *Million Dollar Directory*. Dun & Bradstreet.
- *Job Seeker's Guide to Private and Public Companies*. Gale Research, Inc.
- *Peterson's Job Opportunities. Business*. Peterson's Guides, Inc.
- *Peterson's Job Opportunities. Engineering and Computer Science*. Peterson's Guides, Inc.

Some of these sources are also available in easy-to-use software versions with which you can search for particular companies based on specific criteria. Your local librarian can often provide help in locating information about specific companies, as well.

Using the Internet

Many sources of company and career information are available on the Internet. Many companies operate their own Web site or home page, and some even list their job openings there. If a prospective employer is a large company, search the Internet based on the company's name. Often, promotional materials from the company will indicate its Internet or Web site address. (Promotional materials from local companies are often available in your local public or school library.)

Many Web search engines (such as Google.com, Lycos.com, Excite.com, or Go.com) offer career-oriented services. Search for such general keywords as "career," "employment," or "job." A targeted search using more specific keywords might produce results more immediately useful to your job search.

You can also use your Internet browser to search for locations with appropriate keywords. For example, one recent search showed 600,000 matches for the keyword "career." Obviously, the more targeted your search of the Internet, the more useful it might be.

Specialized employment search engines on the Internet might prove useful. Because these services list jobs from across the nation (and around the world), they might be less useful for a local job search. A list of places to look for jobs on the Internet follows (remember that Internet options change rapidly, so this list might need to be updated and new options might be available):

- HotJobs
  One of the most widely used Web-based job-search sites
  www.hotjobs.com

- The Monster Board
  Another well-established Internet job-search service
  www.monster.com

- CareerBuilder (formerly CareerPath)
  One-stop "mega job search" of 75 Internet job-posting sites
  www.careerbuilder.com

- Headhunter (formerly CareerMosaic)
  www.headhunter.net

- JobOptions (formerly E-Span)
  www.joboptions.com

EXERCISE   P-3   Identify Prospective Employers

1. Identify at least five prospective employers. They may be located anywhere but should represent the type of company for which you could imagine working.

2. For each prospective employer, obtain the name of a job contact. (This person would typically be a manager of the department, division, or group in which you would like to work.)

3. Key the list of prospective employers in a database or a worksheet. Include the contact's name, department, company name, address, city, state, ZIP code, telephone number, and FAX number. Save the list as *[your initials]***Prospects** and then print it. You'll use this list throughout the remainder of this Portfolio Builder.

Targeting Your Portfolio

So far you've created a portfolio of printouts that reflect something about you. Now it's time to target a specific company and tailor your portfolio to that company.

EXERCISE | **P-4** | **Target Your Portfolio to an Employer**

The job contact at your targeted company is likely to respond more favorably to your portfolio if you take the time to tailor it to the company. Doing so shows that you made an effort to learn about your prospective employer. It might also provide more conversational opportunities in a job interview.

1. From your list of five prospective employers, choose one as your target. Review the information you've gathered about the company. If you feel you don't have enough information, collect additional material. Ultimately, you should be very familiar with the company—and the position—you've targeted.

2. Review Table P-3.

TABLE P-3   Targeting Your Portfolio

☑	TARGETING SUGGESTIONS
☐	Use the targeted company's name in reports and other printouts. Use the company's address where appropriate.
☐	Modify the contents of your database so it applies specifically to the targeted company.
☐	You may decide not to change some of the more specialized database objects created for your class (other than to make any corrections your instructor might have recommended). Sometimes it's a good idea to let the targeted company know that the printout was submitted as a class assignment, especially if it relates to your chosen field.

3. Based on the checklist shown in Table P-3, modify your database objects to increase their appeal to the targeted company.

4. Spell-check your database and save it.

5. Create the printouts for your portfolio. Use standard printer paper.

NOTE: If you are building your portfolio as a capstone project for your course, it is not necessary to go beyond this point. You can turn in your representational portfolio. The following information is presented for students who might be constructing a representational portfolio for use in an actual job search.

Creating a Résumé

To present yourself properly to a potential employer, you'll need more than just a portfolio. You'll also need a résumé describing your education and work experiences and a cover letter that introduces you, expresses your interest in the position, and summarizes your credentials. (Many good books are available about developing résumés. You could also consult the Portfolio Builder in *Word 2002: A Professional Approach* by Deborah Hinkle.)

Your Access skills should be a prominent feature of your résumé and cover letter. For example, if you interned at a company where you were required to use a monthly accounts-payable report, you might include the following line in your résumé:

- "Created monthly accounts-payable Access report."

Or, if you are a whiz at using Access's graphics features, you might write:

- "Created weekly national sales report in Access, showing state-by-state distribution as a pie chart."

It is usually considered acceptable to include any printouts produced for a previous employer in your portfolio, provided that they honestly represent examples of your work and provided that you change any proprietary or confidential information contained in the printouts. It's best to indicate clearly on such printouts that the data has been altered. This demonstrates your integrity.

Filling Out an Employment Application

Some companies require that every applicant, at every level, fill out an employment application. Other companies don't even use one. Generally, however, companies do use some form of an employment application. Whether you need to fill out such a form will depend on the company's internal personnel policies.

Often applicants are asked to fill out an employment application when they arrive at the company for an interview. To minimize stress in an already stressful situation, prepare for the employment application beforehand by creating a reference sheet that contains any information that might be included in the application and isn't found on your résumé. (Of course, you should refer to your résumé in filling out your employment application. Make sure to bring an extra copy for reference.)

Tips for Employment Applications

- Be as specific as possible when describing the position you are seeking.
- Be careful when listing a required salary. A salary that is too high might eliminate you for some acceptable jobs, and a figure that is too low might weaken your negotiating position. Sometimes it is better to leave this line blank.
- Be prepared to list dates (month and year) for the schools you have attended. Some applications might also ask for your grade-point average and your class rank.
- Be prepared to list the following information for your previous employers: address, telephone number, name and title of supervisor, start date and end date (month and year), and a description of your duties.
- If some questions are not applicable to the job you are seeking, it is usually acceptable to write "Not Applicable" next to the question.

EXERCISE **P-5** **Create a Reference Sheet for an Employment Application**

1. Review the "Tips for Employment Applications." Note any information that isn't covered by your résumé.
2. Key all information that you will need to fill out an employment application. Use any format that makes sense to you.
3. Save the file as *[your initials]*AppInfo and then print it.

Preparing for Employment Interviews

After you have contacted a potential employer and scheduled an appointment to meet, you'll need to prepare yourself to make a good impression in person. No matter how good your résumé or credentials are, only the interview can, ultimately, land you the job.

The more interviews you go on, the better your interviewing skills will be.

 NOTE: If possible, avoid scheduling an interview on a Monday, which is often the most hectic day in a business environment.

Preparing Yourself

- Confirm your appointment the day before, and make sure you arrive at the interview on time.

- Become as familiar with the company as possible. Read articles about the company, if they are available, or talk to people who are or have been employed by the company. It's always flattering to a prospective employer when an applicant appears knowledgeable about the company in an interview.

- Approach the interview with a clear mental picture of your capabilities and your job objective. Review your résumé immediately before meeting the prospective employer. Think positively.

Presenting Yourself

- Come to the interview equipped with copies of your résumé, your references, and any recommendation letters you have gathered. Have your portfolio on hand, as well as a notepad and a pen.

- Look your best. Your attire and grooming are critical to making a good impression. Dress neatly and professionally, in a manner that is appropriate to the company you are visiting. If necessary, get help in selecting an interview outfit from someone who is familiar with your prospective company's style of dress.

- Be yourself. Act as relaxed as you possibly can, sit in a comfortable position, and focus on the interviewer.

- Ask questions. Learn what you can about the job, the company, to whom (or to how many people) you'd report, and so on. If no job is available or the job opening is not appropriate for you, ask for recommendations about other people you might contact in the company.

- At the end of the interview, if you want the job, express your interest in it and be ready to explain why the company should hire you.

Frequently Asked Interview Questions

The following questions are frequently asked in interviews. You might want to rehearse your answers before the interview. Never offer negative or unnecessary information to an interview question.

- Can you tell me about yourself?
- Why should I hire you?
- What are your major strengths? Weaknesses?
- What are your short-term goals? Long-term goals?

- Why do you want to leave your present job (if employed)?
- Why did you leave your previous job?
- What do you enjoy most (or least) about your current (or previous) job?
- Why do you want to work here?
- What salary do you expect to receive?

Following Up the Interview

To be successful in the interview process, you should take two important follow-up steps:

- Send a thank you letter.
- Keep track of your contacts.

Thank You Letters

Always send a thank you letter within 24 hours after you've interviewed with someone. It creates a positive impression, shows that you have good follow-up skills and appropriate social skills, and reminds the person of your meeting.

The letter should be short and friendly, thanking the person for his or her time and for any information he or she might have provided. You might want to mention something that reminds the person of who you are, in case many people have interviewed for the position.

Even if you know that the interview will not lead to a specific job offer, a thank you letter demonstrates your professionalism.

FIGURE P-3   Sample thank you letter #1

Dear Ms. Jones:

Thank you for the opportunity to interview for the sales position. I enjoyed meeting you and appreciate the information you shared with me.

I am very interested in the position and believe I could quickly become a productive member of your sales team.

Thanks again for the interview, and I look forward to hearing from you.

Sincerely,

FIGURE P-4   Sample thank you letter #2

Dear Ms. Jones:

Thank you for the interview and the information you gave me yesterday. I really appreciate your recommendation that I meet with John Doe in the Marketing Department.

I have scheduled an interview with Mr. Doe and look forward to meeting him. If this contact eventually leads to a job offer, I will be most grateful.

Thanks again for your time and help.

Sincerely,

Keeping Track of Contacts

Be organized in your job search. Create a contact log to keep track of everyone who has received your résumé.

FIGURE P-5
Sample format for
contact log

Date Sent	Contact Name	Company	Telephone	Comments

In addition, develop a system for organizing your contacts so you can follow up with telephone calls as appropriate. You can use your contacts log for this, as well.

Appendices

APPENDIX A

Windows Tutorial

If you're unfamiliar with Windows, review this Windows Tutorial carefully. You'll learn how to use a mouse; how to start Windows; how to use the taskbar, menus, and dialog boxes; and other important aspects of Windows.

If you're familiar with Windows but need help navigating Windows files and folders, refer to Appendix B: "File Management." There you'll find information on how Windows stores information and how to use Windows Explorer.

NOTE: All examples from this Tutorial refer specifically to Windows 2000. If you are using any other version of Windows, your screen might differ slightly from the images shown in this Tutorial. However, because most basic features are common to all versions of Windows, this Tutorial should be helpful to you no matter what version of Windows you use.

Using the Mouse

Although you can use the keyboard with Windows, you'll probably find yourself using the mouse most of the time. A *mouse* is a pointing device that is typically attached to your computer. You roll the mouse on any flat surface, or on a *mouse pad*, typically a smooth pad on which the mouse rests. The mouse is used to move a pointer on the computer screen. A *pointer* is typically a small arrow that you move on the computer screen to accomplish specific tasks.

As you roll the mouse (typically on a mouse pad), the pointer on the computer screen moves in the direction you move the mouse. Thus, when you roll the mouse to the left, the pointer on the screen moves to the left. When you roll the mouse to the right, the pointer on the screen moves to the right. By using the mouse you can position the pointer on objects on the computer screen.

TIP: When moving the mouse on the mouse pad, if you reach the edge of the pad, just pick up the mouse and place it in the center of the pad. This won't change the position of the pointer on the screen.

A mouse typically has two buttons at the front (the edge of the mouse where the cord attaches)—one on the left and one on the right. (A mouse might also have a center button or a wheel, but these are not typical; therefore, a center button or wheel isn't discussed in this Tutorial.)

To choose an item on the computer screen by using the mouse, roll the mouse until the pointer on the screen is over the desired item. Then press and release the left mouse button once. Pressing and releasing the mouse button is referred to as a *click*. Doing this twice is referred to as a *double-click*. Whenever you're told to "click" or "double-click" an item on the computer screen, use the left mouse button.

The right mouse button is used less frequently. Pressing and quickly releasing the right mouse button is referred to as a *right-click*.

You can use the mouse to *drag* an object to another location on-screen. To do this you position the pointer on the object you want to drag, hold down the left mouse button, and roll the mouse until the pointer is at the position where you want to drop the object. Then release the mouse button and the object is dropped at the specified location. (You can see why this type of mouse action is also referred to as *drag-and-drop*.)

You can also select an object by using the mouse. To do this you position the pointer on one side of the object, hold down the left mouse button, and roll the mouse until the pointer reaches the other side of the object. Then release the mouse button. The selected object is highlighted in some way. In Windows, you often need to select an object before you can perform some action on it. For example, you often need to select an object before you can copy it.

As you progress in this Tutorial you will become familiar with the terms in Table A-1 describing the actions you can take with a mouse.

TABLE A-1   Mouse Terms

TERM	DESCRIPTION
Point	Roll the mouse until the tip of the pointer is touching the desired item on the computer screen.
Click	Quickly press and release the left mouse button.
Double-click	Quickly press and release the left mouse button twice.
Drag (or drag-and-drop)	Point to an object on-screen, hold down the left mouse button, and roll the mouse until the pointer is in position. Then release the mouse button.
Right-click	Quickly press and release the right mouse button.
Select	Hold down the left mouse button; roll the mouse so the pointer moves from one side of an object to another. Then release the mouse button.

As you perform actions on-screen using the mouse, the on-screen pointer changes its appearance, depending on where it's located and what operation you are performing. Table A-2 shows the most common types of pointers.

TABLE A-2   Frequently Used Mouse Pointers

POINTER	DESCRIPTION
⬉ Pointer	Used to point to objects.
I I-Beam	Used in keying, inserting, and selecting text.

continues

TABLE A-2   Frequently Used Mouse Pointers   *continued*

POINTER	DESCRIPTION
↗ 2-Headed Arrow	Used to change the size of objects or windows.
↔ 4-Headed Arrow	Used to move objects.
⧗ Hourglass	Indicates the computer is processing a command. While the hourglass is displayed, it is best to wait rather than try to continue working.
☝ Hand	Used in Window's Help system to display additional information.

Starting Windows

All computers are not set up the same way. In most cases, however, when you turn on your computer, Windows loads automatically and the Windows desktop appears. The *desktop* is the area that first appears on the computer screen after you start Windows. The desktop is your on-screen work area. All the elements you need to start working with Windows appear on the desktop.

1. Turn on the computer. Windows begins loading, and a Windows log-on screen displays.

NOTE: On some computers, the log-on screen does not appear automatically. You might have to press the following keys, all at once, and then quickly release them: Ctrl , Alt and Delete . If your computer is on a network, your instructor might need to provide you with special start-up instructions.

2. You now need to log on to Windows, using your user name and password. To start this process, move the pointer to the U̲ser name box. The pointer turns into an I-beam. If someone else's name appears in the U̲ser name box, use Delete or Backspace to delete the name before keying yours. Key your user name. If you make a mistake, press Backspace to delete your mistakes and then key correctly.

NOTE: If you don't know your Windows user name and password, ask your instructor for help. If your computer is attached to a network, you also might be prompted to log on to the network before you log on to Windows.

3. When you finish keying your user name, move the pointer to the P̲assword box and key your password.

4. When your user name and password are correctly keyed, click OK. The Windows desktop appears.

The Windows Desktop

The left side of the Windows desktop contains *icons*, small pictures that represent programs, files, or folders. If you double-click an icon, the program, file, or folder represented by that icon opens. (Appendix B: "File Management" contains a complete discussion of files and folders.)

FIGURE A-1
Windows desktop

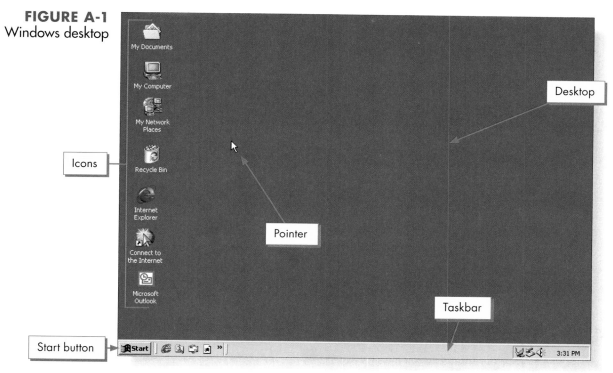

NOTE: Depending on how your computer is set up, your icons might be different from those shown in Figure A-1.

Two important icons are found on virtually all Windows desktops:

- My Computer
  When you double-click this icon, a new window opens showing icons representing the disk drives available on your computer (and on your network, if you are on one). Use My Computer when you want to view the contents of a hard disk or a floppy disk.

- Recycle Bin
  When you double-click this icon, a new window opens listing files you have deleted. Until you empty the Recycle bin, these files can be undeleted and used.

Another important component of the desktop is the *taskbar.* This bar usually appears at the bottom of the desktop. Buttons on the taskbar show which programs and windows are currently open.

Using the Start Menu

The taskbar contains the Start button , which is the most important button in Windows. Clicking the Start button causes the Start menu to appear. This menu provides a list of commands and shortcuts to files. From the Start menu you can perform many Windows tasks. Table A-3 describes the components of the Start menu.

FIGURE A-2
Start menu

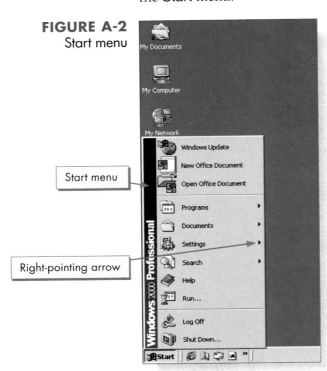

Start menu

Right-pointing arrow

Some items on the Start menu also show a right-pointing arrow. This means additional choices are available on a secondary menu, called a *submenu*. When you point to a menu item with a right-pointing arrow, the submenu appears.

1. Click the Start button on the Windows taskbar.

2. The Start menu appears.

NOTE: The Start menu can be customized. It might not show the Log Off command. It might show the Favorites command, which displays a list of favorite Internet addresses. It might also show the commands with individual letters underlined. You can use the underlined letters as an alternate method of executing a command. Instead of clicking the command, you key the letter that is underlined.

TABLE A-3   Start Menu

COMMAND	USE
Windows Update	Connects to the Microsoft Web site for Windows updates.
New Office Document	Starts a new Microsoft Office document of any type.
Open Office Document	Opens an existing Microsoft Office document.
Programs	Displays a submenu listing the programs on your computer. Clicking a program instructs Windows to start the program.
Documents	Displays a submenu listing recently opened documents.
Settings	Displays a submenu listing system components for which you can change settings.

continues

TABLE A-3	Start Menu *continued*
COMMAND	**USE**
Search	Displays a submenu listing commands that enable you to locate a file, folder, Internet address, or people.
Help	Starts the Windows Help function. Windows Help instructs you how to perform tasks in Windows.
Run	Allows you to type a command to start a program.
Log Off	Closes all programs, disconnects your computer from the network and Internet, and prepares your computer for someone else to use.
Shut Down	Shuts down, restarts, or places your computer in a stand-by mode.

Using the Programs Command

Most programs on your computer can be started from the **Programs** command on the **Start** menu. This is the easiest way to open a program.

The **Programs** menu normally uses the *Personalized Menus* feature in Windows. This feature keeps the menus relatively uncluttered by hiding items that have not been used recently. You expand the menu to its full size, showing all its options, by clicking the down arrow at the bottom of the menu.

1. With the Start menu open on your screen, point to **Programs**. (Or, you can click **Programs**.) The Programs submenu appears, listing the programs installed on your computer. Every computer has a different list of programs.

2. Point to the down arrow at the bottom of the **Programs** submenu (or click it). The Programs menu is expanded to its full size.

FIGURE A-3
Programs submenu

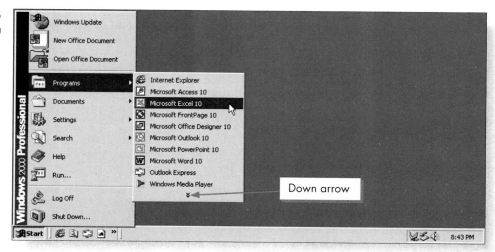

3. Point to the program you want to open and click. (For the purposes of this Tutorial, you can open Excel, a spreadsheet program in Microsoft Office.) In a few seconds, the program you selected loads and its first screen appears. Notice that a button for the program appears on the taskbar.

Using the Taskbar

Using the taskbar, you can switch between open programs and between open documents within a program. Windows displays a button on the taskbar for each program and document that is currently open.

The window in which you are working is called the *active* window. The title bar for the active window is highlighted, and its taskbar button is also highlighted.

1. The program window you opened in the previous procedure should still be open. To open a second program, click the Start button 🏁Start, choose **Programs** from the **Start** menu, and then choose an option from the **Programs** submenu. (For the purpose of this Tutorial, you can open Word, a word-processing program in Microsoft Office.) Notice how the second program covers the first. The window containing the second program is now active. Its title bar is highlighted, as is its button on the taskbar.

2. Click the button on the taskbar for the first program you opened. The first program (Excel) appears again.

3. Click the button on the taskbar for the second program (Word) to switch back to it.

4. Start a new blank document in Word by clicking the New Blank Document button 🗋 on the Word toolbar. (Toolbars are usually located near the top of the screen. See Figure A-4 on the next page.) Notice that each open document has its own taskbar button so you can easily switch between documents.

5. Click the button on the taskbar for the first program you opened (Excel). Now practice using the taskbar to switch between program windows and between document windows until you feel comfortable.

6. Move the pointer to the top edge of the taskbar until it changes from a pointer to a two-headed arrow ↕. Using the two-headed arrow, you can move the taskbar or change its size.

7. With the pointer displayed as a two-headed arrow, hold down the left mouse button and move the arrow up until the task bar moves up, changing position with the status bar at the bottom of the program window. (See Figure A-4 for the location of the status bar.)

8. Move the pointer to the top edge of the taskbar once again until the two-headed arrow displays. Hold down the left mouse button and move the arrow down to the bottom of the screen. The taskbar is restored to its original position.

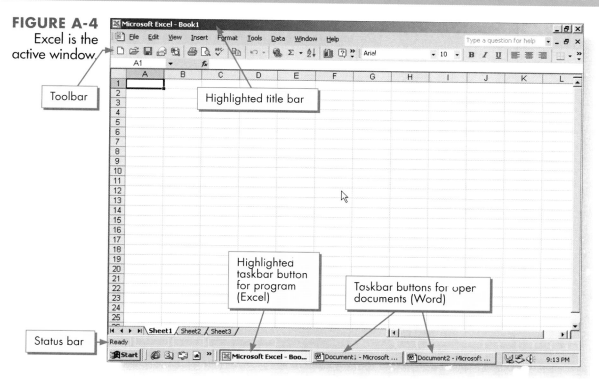

FIGURE A-4
Excel is the active window

Toolbar

Highlighted title bar

Highlighted taskbar button for program (Excel)

Taskbar buttons for oper documents (Word)

Status bar

NOTE: You might sometimes see the taskbar displayed along the sides or the top of the desktop. You can change the position of the taskbar on the desktop by dragging it. You do this by placing the pointer over the taskbar, holding down the left mouse button, moving the pointer to the new location, and then releasing the mouse button.

Using Menus

Most Windows applications use a similar menu structure. You use the mouse to open a menu containing various menu options (these are often called commands). You can open a menu by clicking the name of a menu from the *menu bar,* a row of menu names just below the title bar. Then you can click a menu option from the menu to execute that menu option.

Alternatively, you can use the keyboard to open menus and choose menu options. To open a menu, you press Alt and the underlined letter of the menu name at the same time. For example, to open the File menu, you hold down Alt and press F. You can use the keyboard again to choose a menu option. For example, with the File menu open, you use Alt + S (the underlined character from the Save command) to choose the Save command. Using a combination of Alt and a key underlined in the command you want to choose is a type of *keyboard shortcut.*

1. Make the Excel window the active window (if it is not already) by clicking its button on the taskbar.

2. Click <u>E</u>dit on the menu bar. The Edit menu appears.

Three dots following a menu option indicate that a dialog box is displayed when that menu option is chosen. (The next section of this Tutorial discusses dialog boxes.) Some commands also show toolbar buttons or keyboard shortcuts next to the command name. These are alternative ways to execute the command.

Notice that each of the menu names has an underlined character.

FIGURE A-5
Edit menu
from Excel

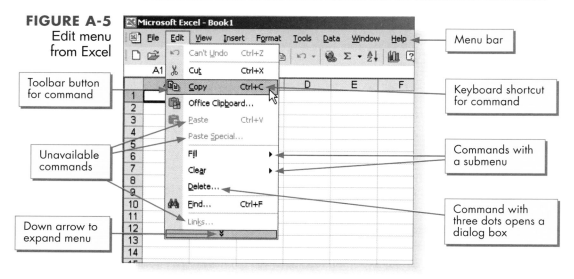

3. Click <u>E</u>dit on the menu bar again. The menu closes.

4. Press [Alt] + [E], the keyboard shortcut for the Edit menu. The Edit menu appears again.

5. Click <u>E</u>dit on the menu bar again to close the Edit menu.

6. Press [Alt] + [V], the keyboard shortcut for the View menu. The View menu appears.

FIGURE A-6
View menu
expanded from
Excel

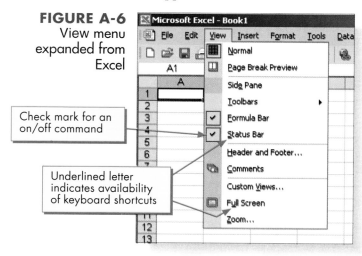

7. Click the down arrow at the bottom of the menu to display the entire View menu. Some commands have check marks next to them. This means the command can be turned on or off.

Notice also that all the commands in the menu have an underlined letter, indicating that they, too, have keyboard shortcuts.

8. Click <u>V</u>iew to close the View menu.

Using Dialog Boxes

Windows applications make frequent use of dialog boxes. A *dialog box* is a window that requests input from you related to a command you have chosen. All Windows applications use a common dialog box structure.

1. Make the Word program the active window.

2. Choose <u>F</u>ile on the menu bar. The File menu appears.

3. Click the down arrow at the bottom of the menu to display the entire **File** menu. The three dots following the <u>P</u>rint command indicate that when you choose <u>P</u>rint, a dialog box will be displayed.

4. Choose <u>P</u>rint. The Print dialog box appears. It contains some of the most common types of dialog box options.

FIGURE A-7
Print dialog box in Word

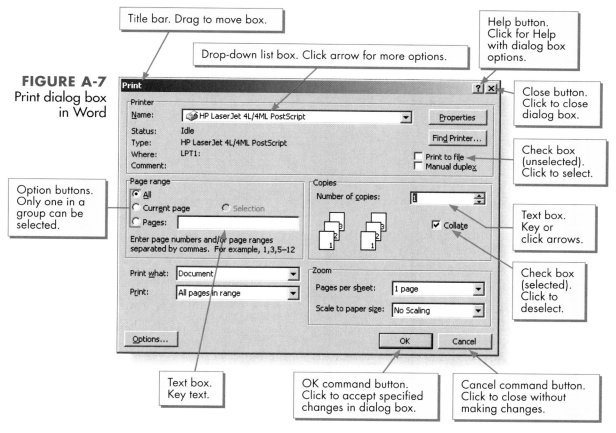

NOTE: The underlined letters indicate the options that have keyboard short-cuts. For example, to choose <u>A</u>ll as the print range, you would key [Alt] + [A].

5. Click **Cancel**, which is located in the lower right corner of the dialog box. The Print dialog box closes without making any changes.

6. Make Excel the active window.

7. Click Format on the menu bar. The Format menu appears.

8. Choose Cells. The Format Cells dialog box displays.

The tabs under the title bar are the most significant feature of this type of dialog box. (See Figure A-8.)

9. Click the Font tab, if it is not already displayed.

To use the scroll bar in the Font, Font style, or Size list boxes, you can click the vertical scroll arrows to scroll through the options. You can also drag the scroll box up or down to scroll through the options.

FIGURE A-8
Format Cells
dialog box,
Font tab, in Excel

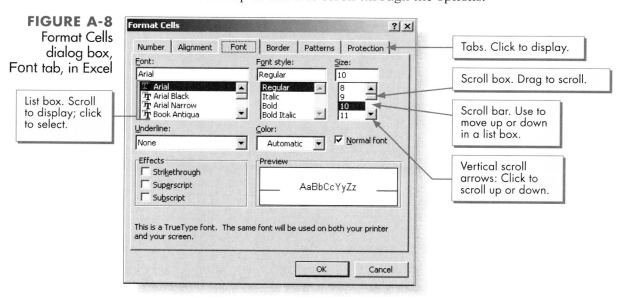

10. Click Cancel in the lower right corner of the dialog box to close it without making any changes.

Changing the Size of a Window

You can change the sizes of your windows by using either the mouse or the sizing buttons. *Sizing buttons* are the small buttons on the right side of the title bar that allow you to resize, minimize, or maximize the window. (See Figure A-9.) This can be especially useful when you'd like to display several open windows on your desktop and see them simultaneously.

There are three sizing buttons that can appear on the title bar of every window: the Minimize button , the Maximize button , and the Restore Down button . Table A-4 (on the next page) describes each of these buttons.

1. Make Excel the active window, if it is not already. Click the Maximize button on the Excel title bar if the Excel window does not fill the entire desktop.

2. Click the Restore Down button on the Excel title bar. The Excel window reduces in size, and the Word window appears behind it. Notice that the highlighted title bar of the Excel window indicates it is the active window.

TABLE A-4	Sizing Buttons
BUTTON	**USE**
▬ Minimize	Reduces the window to a button on the taskbar
☐ Maximize	Enlarges the window to fill the entire desktop (appears only when a window is reduced)
⧉ Restore Down	Returns the window to its previous size and desktop position (appears only when a window is maximized)

3. Move the pointer to the border of the Excel window. The pointer changes to a two-headed arrow ↔.

TIP: Sometimes the borders of a window can move off the computer screen. If you're having trouble with one border of a window, try another border or drag the entire window onto the screen by using the title bar.

4. With the two-headed arrow displayed, drag the border to make the window smaller.

5. Click the title bar of one of the Word windows behind the Excel window. The Word window becomes the active window. The Excel window is still open, but it is now behind the Word window.

6. Click the Maximize button ☐ if the Word window does not fill the entire desktop.

7. Click the Minimize button ▬ on the title bar of the Word window. The Excel window becomes the active window. The second Word window appears behind the Excel window.

8. Click the Close button ☒ on the title bar of the second Word window. The Excel window is still the active window. Notice there are only two program buttons on the taskbar now.

9. Make the Word window the active window by clicking the Word button on the taskbar.

10. Click the Restore Down button ⧉ on the Word window. The Word window reduces in size. The Excel window might be partially visible behind the Word window. You can drag the two reduced windows so parts of both can be seen simultaneously.

11. Drag the title bar of the Word window until you can see more of the Excel window. Use both title bars to reposition the windows.

Some program windows, such as those for Excel and Word, contain two sets of sizing buttons. The upper set (on the title bar) controls the program window. The lower set controls the sizing of the document within the program window. See Figure A-9 (on the next page) for the location of the lower set in Word and Excel.

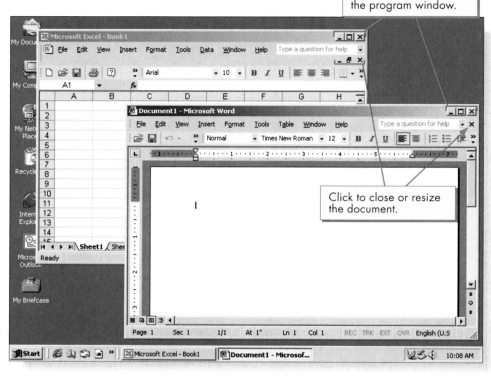

FIGURE A-9
Displaying two
program windows
simultaneously

> **12.** Click the Close button ⊠ on the title bars of each of the two program windows to close them. You have a clean desktop again.

Using the Documents Command

Windows lets you open an existing document by using the Documents command on the Start menu. This command allows you to open one of the last 15 documents previously opened on your computer.

1. Click the Start button 🏁Start on the taskbar to display the Start menu.

2. Choose Documents. The Documents submenu appears, showing you the last 15 documents that were opened.

3. Click a document. The program in which the document was created opens and the document displays. For example, if the document you chose is a Word document, Word opens and the document appears in a Word program window.

4. Click the program window's Close button ⊠ (remember, it is the Close button on the title bar). The program window closes and the desktop is clear once again.

Using the Settings Command

The Settings command on the Start menu lets you change the way Windows looks and works. Because your computer in school is used by other students, you should be very careful when changing settings. Others might expect Windows to look and work the standard way. Having Windows look or work in a nonstandard way could easily confuse them.

FIGURE A-10
Settings submenu

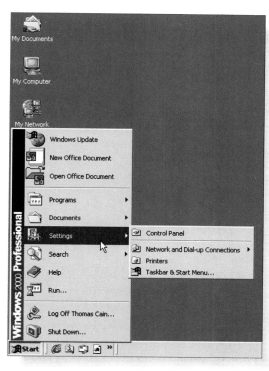

NOTE: Talk to your instructor before changing any settings on your computer.

1. Click the Start button 🏁Start on the taskbar.

2. Choose Settings. The Settings submenu displays.

3. Click anywhere on the desktop to close the Settings submenu without making any changes.

TABLE A-5	Settings Options
OPTION	**USE**
Control Panel	Displays the Control Panel window, which lets you change screen colors, add or remove programs, change the date and time, and change other settings for your hardware and software.
Network and Dial-up Connections	Displays a submenu that lets you make connections with other computers or a private network.
Printers	Displays the Printers window, which lets you add and remove printers, as well as modify your printer settings.
Taskbar & Start Menu	Displays the Taskbar and Start Menu Properties dialog box, which you use to customize the taskbar and add and remove programs on the Start menu.

Using the Search Command

If you don't know where a file or folder is located, you can use the Search command on the Start menu to help you find and open it.

1. Click the Start button on the taskbar.

2. Choose Search. The Search submenu appears.

3. Choose For Files or Folders. The Search Results dialog box appears.

FIGURE A-11
Search Results
dialog box

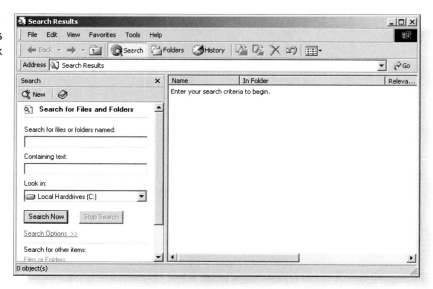

4. In the Search for files or folders named text box, key the name of the file or folder you want to find. Remember, you can use Backspace or Delete to delete any keying errors you make.

TIP: To search files for specific text, use the Containing text text box. To search for files by date, size, type, or other attributes, click Search Options.

5. Click the down arrow next to the Look in text box to specify where you want Windows to search. The default location is the C drive.

6. Click Search Now to start the search. Any matches for the file are shown on the right side of the dialog box.

7. Double-click on any found item to open the program and view the file or folder Windows has located.

8. When you are finished with your search, close all open windows and clear your desktop.

Using the Run Command

Windows allows you to start a program by using the Run command and keying the program name. This command is often employed to run a "setup" or "install" program that installs a new program on your computer.

1. Click the Start button ![Start] on the taskbar.

2. Choose Run. The Run dialog box appears.

FIGURE A-12
Run dialog box

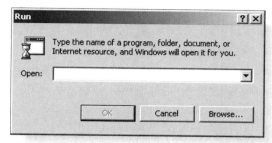

3. If you know the name of a program you want to run, key the name in the Open text box. Often you will need to click Browse to open a drop-down list of the disk drives, folders, and files available to you.

4. Click Cancel to close the Run dialog box.

Displaying a Shortcut Menu

When the mouse pointer is on an object or an area of the Windows desktop and you right-click, a shortcut menu appears. A *shortcut menu* typically contains commands that are useful in working with the object or area of the desktop to which you are currently pointing.

FIGURE A-13
Shortcut menu for the desktop

1. Position the mouse pointer on a blank area of the desktop and right-click. A shortcut menu appears with commands that relate to the desktop, including arranging icons and displaying properties.

2. Click outside the shortcut menu to close it.

3. Right-click the time in the bottom right corner of the taskbar. A shortcut menu appears with a command that relates to adjusting the time.

4. Click Adjust Date/Time. The Date/Time Properties dialog box appears. You can use this dialog box to adjust your computer's date and time.

5. Click Cancel.

6. Click outside the shortcut menu to close it.

7. Right-click an icon to display its shortcut menu, and then close the menu.

Exiting Windows

You should always exit any open applications and Windows before turning off the computer. This is the best way to be sure your work is saved. Windows also performs other "housekeeping" routines that ensure everything is ready for you when you next turn on your computer. Failure to shut down properly will often force Windows to perform time-consuming system checks the next time it is loaded.

To exit Windows, use the **Shut Down** command on the **Start** menu. This command has several shut-down options:

- **Log off.** Logs off the current Windows user and makes Windows available for another user to log on.
- **Restart.** Restarts the computer without shutting off the power. This is sometimes necessary when you add new software.
- **Shut down.** Closes all open programs and makes it safe to turn off the computer. Some computers will turn off the power automatically.
- **Stand by.** Places the computer in stand-by mode, which generally turns off the screen display and puts the computer in "hibernation." (This option is not available on all computers.)

1. Click the Start button ⊞Start on the taskbar.

2. Choose **Shut Down** from the **Start** menu. The Shut Down Windows dialog box appears.

FIGURE A-14
Shut Down
Windows
dialog box

3. Click the down arrow next to the text box and select **Shut Down** if it is not already selected.

4. Click **OK**. Windows prompts you to save changes in any open documents. It then prepares the computer to be shut down. Windows will tell you when it is safe to turn off your computer.

5. When Windows tells you it is safe to turn off your computer, turn off your computer and your monitor.

APPENDIX B

File Management

Most of your tasks in Windows 2000 will involve working with information stored on your computer. This Appendix briefly explains how information is stored in Windows 2000.

It also introduces you to one of the most useful programs for managing information in Windows—the Windows Explorer. This program shows you how information is organized on your computer and provides you with the tools to manage it.

Files and Folders

The basic unit of storage in Windows is a *file*. The documents you create and use, as well as the programs you use, are all files. These files are stored in *folders*, which can contain other folders as well as files.

Filenames in Windows may be up to 255 characters, including spaces. A filename also has a three-letter extension, which identifies the type of file. For example, the extension "doc" identifies a file as a Word document. The extension is separated from the filename by a period (often called a "dot"), as in "Birthday.doc."

NOTE: By default, file extensions are not displayed. To display them in Windows Explorer, open the Tools menu, choose Folder Options, diplay the View tab, and then clear the Hide file extensions for known file types check box.

Opening Windows Explorer

One of the most useful tools in Windows 2000 for managing folders and files on your computer is *Windows Explorer*. This program displays folders and files in a hierarchical structure, similar to a family tree. It allows you to browse through all your computer's drives and folders in a single window. You can also use it to see the contents of other computers on your network.

To open Windows Explorer:

1. Click the Start button ⊞Start on the taskbar.
2. Choose Programs.
3. From the Programs submenu, choose **Accessories**.
4. From the **Accessories** submenu, choose **Windows Explorer**. (If **Windows Explorer** does not appear on the **Accessories** menu, click the down arrow at the bottom of the menu to display the entire **Accessories** menu.). (See Figure B-1 on the next page.)

FIGURE B-1
Starting Windows
Explorer

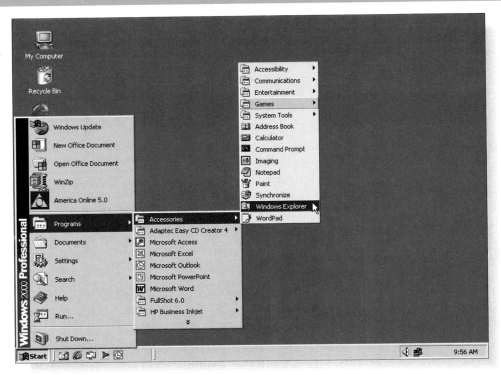

Windows Explorer appears. The window is divided into two panes: The left pane shows the network (if any) and the hierarchy of computers, drives, and folders. The right pane shows the contents of the item you click on the left pane. Various icons are used to represent folders, computers, drives, and networks. Notice the Plus symbols ⊞ and Minus symbols ⊟. These are used to navigate among the drives and folders on your computer.

FIGURE B-2
Windows Explorer

Computer icon

Click minus symbol
to hide lower-level
folders.

Disk drive icon

Selected folder

Folder icons

Click plus symbol
to show lower-
level folders.

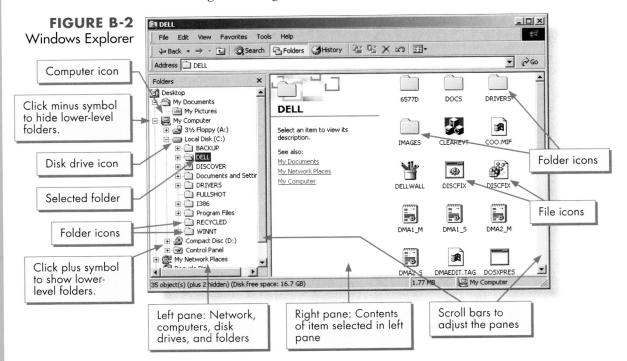

Folder icons

File icons

Left pane: Network,
computers, disk
drives, and folders

Right pane: Contents
of item selected in left
pane

Scroll bars to
adjust the panes

NOTE: The right pane of your Windows Explorer window might look different than the one shown in Figure B-2. Windows Explorer enables you to control the way in which files and folders are displayed in the right pane. The icons might be sized differently, or the contents of the folder might be arranged in a column format, showing details such as file type, date, and size.

Navigating Using Windows Explorer

Practice navigating through your computer's files and folders using the Windows Explorer:

1. Click the Plus symbol ⊞ next to a folder or disk drive icon. The lower-level branches under that folder or drive display.

TIP: Any folder displaying a Plus symbol ⊞ contains one or more folders within that folder.

2. Click the Plus symbol ⊞ next to other folder icons.

Notice that as you display the branches of the hierarchy, the symbol next to the folder icon changes to a Minus symbol ⊟.

3. Click a Minus symbol ⊟ next to a folder icon. The hierarchy under the folder collapses and the lower-level branches under it are hidden.

4. Click a folder icon. The contents of the folder display.

Folders selected in the left pane are displayed in the right pane.

5. Use the scroll bars on the right sides of the two panes if the contents of either pane extend beyond the viewing area.

Copying Files and Folders

You can use Windows Explorer to manage files and folders on you computer. Common management tasks include copying files or folders, moving files or folders to new locations, renaming files or folders, deleting unneeded files or folder, and creating new file folders.

To copy a file or folder from one location to another:

1. In the left pane, click the folder icon containing the file you wish to copy. The files within that folder appear in the right pane.

 NOTE: You might have to click several folders in the hierarchy to finally display the folder containing the file you wish to copy.

2. Locate the file in the right pane and right-click it. A shortcut menu appears.

TIP: You can select multiple files to copy. When files are adjacent to one another, select the first file, press and hold Shift, and click the last file. All files between the first and last files will be selected for copying. To select nonadjacent files, select the first file, press and hold Ctrl, select the remaining files, and then click.

3. Select <u>C</u>opy from the shortcut menu.

4. In the left pane, locate the folder to which you will copy the file. Right-click the folder icon. A shortcut menu appears.

 TIP: Use the Plus symbols ⊞ and the scroll bar to adjust the viewing area if the folder isn't displayed.

5. Choose Paste from the shortcut menu. The file is copied to the new folder. The file is now located in both the original location and the new location.

Copying Files on to Floppy Disks

To transport a file from your school to your home, you will typically need to copy the file onto a floppy disk. To copy a file from your computer to a floppy disk:

1. Insert a floppy disk in your floppy disk drive (typically this is Drive A).

2. In the left pane, click the folder icon containing the file you wish to copy. The files within that folder appear in the right pane.

 NOTE: You might have to click several folders in the hierarchy to finally display the folder containing the file you wish to copy.

3. Locate the file in the right pane and right-click it. A shortcut menu appears.

 TIP: You can select multiple files to copy to a floppy disk. When files are adjacent to one another, select the first file, press and hold Shift, and click the last file. All files between the first and last files will be selected for copying. To select nonadjacent files, select the first file, press and hold Ctrl, select the remaining files, and then click.

4. Choose Send <u>T</u>o from the shortcut menu.

5. Choose 3½ Floppy (A) from the submenu. The file is copied to the disk.

Moving Files and Folders

You can also move file or folders from one location to another. This process is very similar to copying a file to another location. However, rather than choosing <u>C</u>opy from the shortcut menu when you right-click the file, you choose the Cut command.

To move a file or folder from one location to another:

1. In the left pane, click the folder icon containing the file you wish to move. The files within that folder appear in the right pane.

 NOTE: You might have to click several folders in the hierarchy to finally display the folder containing the file you wish to move.

2. Locate the file in the right pane and right-click it. A shortcut menu appears.

 TIP: You can select multiple files to copy. When files are adjacent to one another, select the first file, press and hold (Shift), and click the last file. All files between the first and last files will be selected for copying. To select nonadjacent files, select the first file, press and hold (Ctrl), select the remaining files, and then click.

3. Select Cut from the shortcut menu.

4. In the left pane, locate the folder to which you will move the file. Right-click the folder icon. A shortcut menu appears.

 TIP: Use the Plus symbols ⊞ and the scroll bar to adjust the viewing area if the folder isn't displayed.

5. Choose Paste from the shortcut menu. The file is moved to the new folder. The file is located in only the new location. It has been moved from the original location.

Files can also be moved using the drag-and-drop method:

1. In the left pane, click the folder icon containing the file you wish to move. The files within that folder appear in the right pane.

 NOTE: You might have to click several folders in the hierarchy to finally display the folder containing the file you wish to move.

2. Locate the file in the right pane and select it.

3. Hold down the left mouse button and drag the file to the left pane. Position the pointer over the desired folder. The folder icon is highlighted.

 TIP: If the folder contains lower-level branches and your target location is within a lower level, the lower level will automatically display after a few moments. You can move the pointer near the top or bottom edge of the pane to scroll if the desired folder doesn't appear on-screen.

4. Release the mouse button when the desired folder is highlighted. The file is moved from the original location into the highlighted folder.

 NOTE: You can only move a file from one location to another on the same disk when using the drag-and-drop method. If the target location is a different disk, a copy is made. You can also use the drag-and-drop method to copy a file by pressing (Ctrl) and holding down the left mouse button when selecting the file to copy.

Deleting Files and Folders

When you delete a file or folder, it is placed in the Recycle Bin. To delete a file or folder:

1. Locate the file or folder. A folder can be located in the left or right pane. A file will always be in the right pane.
2. Right-click the file or folder.
3. Choose <u>D</u>elete from the shortcut menu.

> **TIP:** If you mistakenly delete a file or folder (and you haven't emptied the Recycle Bin), you can restore it by clicking the Recycle Bin to open it, right-clicking the item you want to restore, and choosing Restore from the shortcut menu.

Renaming Files and Folders

A common file management task is renaming files and folder. Often companies develop a unique naming structure for their files.

1. Locate the file or folder and right-click it. A shortcut menu appears.
2. Choose Rena<u>m</u>e from the shortcut menu.
3. Key the new name. Delete the old filename.
4. Press Enter to complete the process.

Creating New Folders

Creating folders is a necessary part of file management. They are like folders in a file cabinet. Some people like to use many folders, with a few items in each one. Others use fewer folders with many files in each. You will develop your own system, but try to be consistent in your folder structure. Consistency makes it easier to locate files easily.

To create a new folder:

1. Select (highlight) the disk or folder in the left pane where you want to locate the new folder.
2. Choose <u>F</u>ile from the menu bar.
3. Choose <u>N</u>ew from the File menu.
4. Choose <u>F</u>older from the submenu. The folder is created in the folder or disk you selected. You can now rename the folder.

APPENDIX C

Speech Recognition

The *speech recognition* feature in Microsoft Office enables you to dictate text into any Office program. You also can use your voice to select menu commands, toolbar buttons, dialog box selections, and task pane items. The speech recognition feature is not intended for completely hands-free operation. It is best used in combination with the mouse or keyboard.

To use speech recognition, your computer must be equipped with the following:

- A high-quality close-talk (headset) microphone with gain adjustment. (You use gain adjustment to make your input louder for use by the system.)
- A 400 megahertz or faster computer.
- 128 MB or more of memory.
- Windows 98 or later or Windows NT 4.0 or later.
- Microsoft Internet Explorer 5 or later.

Installing the Speech Recognition Feature

The speech recognition feature is installed in Word (typically by performing a custom installation). To install the speech recognition in Word:

1. Start Word.
2. Choose **Tools** from the menu, and then choose **Speech**. (You might need to click the down arrow at the bottom of the **Tools** menu to display the entire menu.) You'll be asked if you wish to install the feature.
3. Click **Yes**. After the feature is installed, it is available in the **Tools** menu in all Office programs.

 NOTE: Installation requires the Office XP CD-ROM.

Speech Training

You increase speech recognition accuracy by training the computer to recognize how you speak. You are offered training when the speech recognition feature is first installed. You also can train the computer at any time after installation.

Speech training helps the computer learn to recognize how you speak. You train the computer by reading text out loud. Microsoft Office listens to your voice and creates a speech recognition user profile. A *user profile* is information created and stored by the speech recognition training program that the computer uses in recognizing your unique voice. After you've created the profile and have completed the initial training, you can improve the computer's accuracy by completing additional voice training sessions. There are eight different voice training sessions. The more training sessions you complete, the more accurate the computer will be in recognizing your voice.

Microsoft Office lets you create multiple speech recognition user profiles. This is particularly useful when more than one individual uses the speech recognition feature on a single computer.

To create your user profile and begin speech recognition training, complete the following steps:

1. Press the Start button .

2. On the Start menu, choose Settings, and then choose Control Panel. The Control Panel appears.

3. Double-click the Speech icon . The Speech Properties dialog box appears. One or more Recognition Profiles might already be listed. You now will create your own profile.

FIGURE C-1
Speech Properties
dialog box

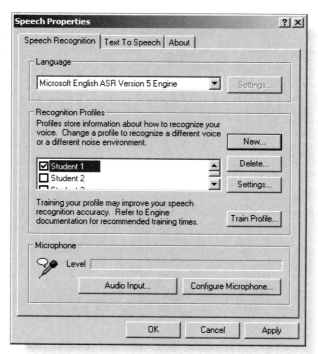

NOTE: You can also access the Speech Properties dialog box by clicking the Tools button on the Language toolbar and then choosing Options from the menu.

4. Click New. The Profile Wizard dialog box appears.

5. In the Profile text box, key *[your name]* and then click Finish. The Speech Properties dialog box reappears. Your profile is added to the list of available profiles.

6. Make sure your profile is the currently selected profile shown under Recognition Profiles. This means your profile is the profile the computer will use when speech recognition is activated in any Microsoft Office program.

 NOTE: To begin voice training, you could have clicked Next instead of Finish in the Profile Wizard dialog box. However, Office requires users with new profiles to complete voice training the first time they activate speech recognition, even if they have already completed training in the Profile Wizard dialog box. You will be prompted to begin voice training the first time you use the speech recognition feature in any Office program.

7. Click OK to close the Speech Properties dialog box, and then close the Control Panel.

8. Click the Start button 🔲Start on the Windows taskbar. Choose Programs on the Start menu, and then choose Microsoft Word. (You can open any Office program in which you want to use speech recognition; in this exercise, you will use Word.) When Word opens, the Language bar is displayed automatically.

TIP: If the speech recognition feature has been installed and the Language bar does not appear in the Office programs, its display has been turned off. To redisplay the Language bar, click the Start button 🔲Start on the Windows taskbar, choose Settings from the Start menu, and then choose Control Panel. On the Control Panel, double-click the Text Services icon 🖳, and then click Language Bar. Select Show the Language bar on the desktop.

9. Click the Microphone button 🎤 Microphone on the Language toolbar to activate speech recognition training. The Welcome to Office Speech Recognition dialog box appears.

NOTE: If the Welcome to Office Speech Recognition dialog box does not appear when you click the Microphone button 🎤 Microphone, you need to make sure Office considers you the current user and is using your profile. Click the Tools button 🖉Tools on the Language toolbar, choose Current User, and then select your profile. Now when you click the Microphone button 🎤 Microphone, you will activate the speech recognition training.

10. Click Next to begin the Office Speech Recognition training. There are two parts to the training: microphone training and voice training. The Microphone Wizard dialog box appears first. This wizard helps you adjust your microphone for the best results in speech recognition.

FIGURE C-2
Microphone Wizard

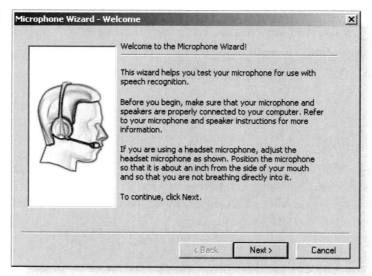

11. Click **Next** and complete the Microphone Wizard. When you click **Finish** at the last Microphone Wizard screen, the Voice Training dialog box for the Microsoft Speech Recognition Training Wizard appears. This wizard trains the computer to recognize your voice.

FIGURE C-3
Voice Training

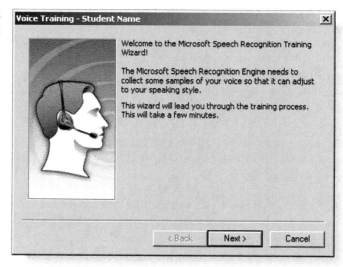

12. Click **Next** to begin the voice training. You'll first be asked some questions about your gender and age, and then you'll read some text out loud.

13. When you complete the voice training, click **Finish**. A short video follows that demonstrates the use of the speech recognition feature. To improve the computer's accuracy in recognizing your speech, it is recommended that you conduct additional training sessions.

NOTE: The video that follows the voice training requires the Flash Player plug-in to run. This is a free program by Macromedia that is used to play movies. If this program is not already installed on your computer, your browser might automatically connect you to the Macromedia Web site. You'll be prompted to begin downloading the plug-in. The video appears only once, after you complete your first speech recognition voice training session.

14. To conduct additional training sessions, click the Tools button [Tools] on the Language bar, and then choose <u>Training</u>. The Voice Training dialog box appears. Notice that there are eight different sessions. Each contains different material for you to read aloud. You can perform sessions more than once. After you have used speech recognition, you might wish to do more training.

FIGURE C-4
Voice Training,
additional sessions

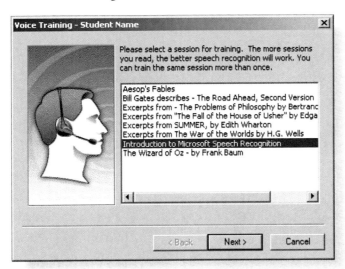

15. Click Cancel to close the Voice Training dialog box, and close Word.

Beginning Speech Recognition: Dictation Mode

After the speech recognition feature is installed and you have completed your initial training, you can use it in any Microsoft Office program. There are two modes of speech recognition:

- *Dictation mode* lets you dictate text into any Office program. For example, you can use the Dictation mode to dictate a Word document or an Outlook e-mail message.
- The *Voice Command mode* lets you select menu commands, toolbar buttons, dialog box options, and task pane items by using your voice.

Speech recognition commands are activated by using the buttons on the Language toolbar. The Language toolbar is displayed automatically in all Office programs if the speech recognition feature has been installed. Table C-1 describes each of the buttons on the Language toolbar.

TABLE C-1   Language Toolbar

BUTTON	PURPOSE
Correction	Presents correction options for selected text. (Not present in applications where there is no text entry.)
Microphone	Turns the microphone on and off.
Dictation	Turns on the Dictation mode so the words you speak are turned into text.
Voice Command	Turns on the Voice Command mode so you can select menu, toolbar, dialog box, and task pane items using your voice.
Tools	Displays a drop-down menu for various options, including selecting the current user profile and performing additional voice training.

To begin using the speech recognition feature, perform the following steps:

1. Start Word. (You can open any Office program in which you want to use speech recognition; in this exercise, you will use Word.) When Word opens, the Language bar is displayed automatically.

2. If the microphone is not already turned off, click the Microphone button ✐ Microphone on the Language toolbar to turn it off.

3. Click the Tools button 🗐Tools on the Language toolbar, and then choose <u>C</u>urrent User. Select your profile if it is not already selected.

 NOTE: Make sure the computer is using your voice profile before you begin using speech recognition.

4. Position your microphone.

5. Click the Microphone button ✐ Microphone. The microphone is activated, and the Language toolbar expands.

6. Click the Dictation button 🗐Dictation on the Language toolbar or say "*Dictation.*" You are now in the Dictation mode.

7. Say "*I am now using Microsoft Office speech recognition.*" As you speak, the computer displays a blue bar for text it is processing. The words appear when processing is completed.

FIGURE C-5
Speech recognition
processing spoken
text in Dictation
mode

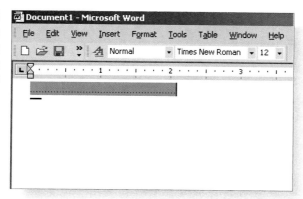

8. Say *"Period."* The computer places a period at the end of the sentence and adds a space for the next sentence.

Correcting Mistakes

Mistakes can be corrected in several ways:

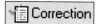

- You can place the insertion point on the incorrect word and click the Correction button ⌐Correction on the Language toolbar. You'll be shown a list of correction alternatives.
- You can select the incorrect word or phrase and dictate the correct text.
- You can key over errors by using the mouse or keyboard. In Dictation mode, you can select the text, say *"Spelling mode,"* pause slightly, and then spell the correction.

The computer recognizes many common punctuation and keyboard symbols. For example, "semicolon," "question mark," and "open parenthesis" all generate the appropriate characters in Dictation mode.

1. Say *"As I speak, comma, the words I speak appear on the screen. Period."* The computer places a comma after the first phrase and a period at the end of the sentence, and the first letter in the sentence is capitalized.

2. If the computer has made any mistakes in the text you dictated in the previous step, try using some of the techniques just described to correct them.

Using Voice Command Mode

In Voice Command mode, you can activate menus, toolbar buttons, dialog box and task pane items, and certain keystrokes. Table C-2 provides some other useful voice commands.

TABLE C-2   Useful Voice Commands

COMMAND	RESULT
Say "spelling mode"	In Dictation mode, lets you spell a word.
Say "new line"	In Dictation mode, inserts a line break and places the insertion point at the beginning of the new line.
Say "force num"	In Dictation mode, lets you dictate all numbers as digits.
Say "new paragraph"	In Dictation mode, inserts a new paragraph and places the insertion point at the beginning of the new paragraph.
Say "expand"	In Voice Command mode, displays an entire menu when all commands on a menu are not visible.
Say "escape"	In Voice Command mode, cancels a menu.

1. Say "*Voice Command.*" The computer is now in Voice Command mode.

 NOTE: You can switch between Dictation mode and Voice Command mode by saying "*Dictation*" or "*Voice Command.*"

2. Say "*Return.*" The computer places a Return (Enter) after the sentence. The insertion point is now on the next line.

3. Say "*Backspace.*" The computer backspaces to the end of the sentence.

4. Use the mouse to select "speech recognition" in the first sentence.

5. Say "*Italic.*" The selected text is italicized. In Voice Command mode, you can activate toolbar buttons.

6. Move the insertion point to the end of the second sentence.

7. Say "*Return.*" The computer places a Return after the sentence.

8. Say "*Return.*" The computer moves the insertion point down another line.

9. Click the Dictation button [🖉 Dictation] or say "*Dictation.*" The computer switches back to Dictation mode.

10. Say "*Speech recognition is a powerful tool. Period.*"

FIGURE C-6
Text dictated into a
Word document

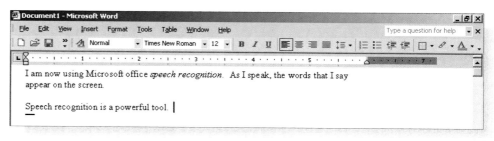

11. Click the Voice Command button [🖈 Voice Command] or say "*Voice Command.*"

12. Say *"File."* The File menu displays. You can activate menu commands in Voice Command mode.

13. Say *"Print."* The Print command on the File menu is selected, and the Print dialog box displays.

14. Say *"OK."* The document prints. You can make dialog box selections by using your voice in the Voice Command mode.

15. Click the Microphone button Microphone or say *"Microphone"* to turn off the microphone. It is good practice to turn off the microphone when it's not in use.

16. Close Word without saving the document.

NOTE: If you find the computer making a significant number of mistakes, make sure your microphone is adjusted correctly. You can also improve the computer's accuracy by completing more training sessions.

APPENDIX D
Proofreaders' Marks

PROOFREADERS' MARK		DRAFT	FINAL COPY
¶	Start a new paragraph	ridiculous! If that is so	ridiculous!
			If that is so
⌒	Delete space	to gether	together
#	Insert space	It may be	It may not be
⟳	Move as shown	it is (not) true	it is true
∩	Transpose	beleivable	believable
		(is it) so	it is so
◯	Spell out	(2) years ago	two years ago
		16 Elm (St.)	16 Elm Street
∧	Insert a word	How much *is* it?	How much is it?
—ρ OR —	Delete a word	it may ~~not~~ be true	it may be true
∧ OR ⁄	Insert a letter	temper*a*ture	temperature
↑ OR ⌐	Delete a letter and close up	commit*t*ment to bun*y*	commitment to buy
—ρ OR —	Change a word	*but* ~~and~~ if you ~~won't~~ *can't*	but if you can't
(Stet)	Stet (don't delete)	I was ~~very~~ glad (Stet)	I was very glad
/	Make letter lowercase	Federal Government	federal government
≡	Capitalize	Janet L. greyston	Janet L. Greyston
∨	Raise above the line	in her new book*	in her new book*
∧	Drop below the line	H2SO4	H_2SO_4

PROOFREADERS' MARK	DRAFT	FINAL COPY
⊙ Insert a period	Mr⊙Henry Grenada	Mr. Henry Grenada
∧ Insert a comma	a large∧old house	a large, old house
∨ Insert an apostrophe	my children∨s car	my children's car
∨ Insert quotation marks	he wants a ∨loan∨	he wants a "loan"
= OR ⹀ Insert a hyphen	a first⹀rate job	a first-rate job
	ask the co⹀owner	ask the co-owner
⌐M Insert an em-dash	Here it is∧cash!	Here it is—cash!
⌐N Insert an en-dash	Pages 1⌐N5	Pages 1–5
___ Insert underscore	an issue of <u>Time</u>	an issue of <u>Time</u>
(ital)___ Set in italic	(ital) The New York Times	*The New York Times*
(bf)〰 Set in boldface	(bf) the <u>Enter</u> key	the **Enter** key
(rom) Set in roman	(rom) the *most* likely	the most likely
{ } Insert parentheses	left today{May 3}	left today (May 3)
⌐ Move to the right	$38,367,000⌐	$38,367,000
⌐ Move to the left	⌐Anyone can win!	Anyone can win!
ss [Single-space	ss [I have heard / he is leaving	I have heard / he is leaving
ds [Double-space	ds [When will you / have a decision?	When will you / have a decision?
(+ 1 line) Insert 1 line space	<u>Percent of Change</u> / 16.25 (+ 1 line)	<u>Percent of Change</u> / 16.25
(– 1 line) Delete (remove) 1 line space	Northeastern / (– 1 line) / regional sales	Northeastern / regional sales

APPENDIX E

MOUS Certification

TABLE E-1

Access 2002: Core MOUS Activities Related to Lessons

CODE	ACTIVITY	LESSON
Ac2002 1	**Creating and Using Databases**	**Lessons**
Ac2002 1-1	Create Access databases	1, 4
Ac2002 1-2	Open database objects in multiple views	1, 2
Ac2002 1-3	Move among records	1, 2
Ac2002 1-4	Format datasheets	1
Ac2002 2	**Creating and Modifying Tables**	
Ac2002 2-1	Create and modify tables	1, 2, 3, 4, 5
Ac2002 2-2	Add a pre-defined input mask to a field	5
Ac2002 2-3	Create Lookup fields	5
Ac2002 2-4	Modify field properties	4, 5
Ac2002 3	**Creating and Modifying Queries**	
Ac2002 3-1	Create and modify Select queries	1, 2, 3, 6
Ac2002 3-2	Add calculated fields to Select queries	6
Ac2002 4	**Creating and Modifying Forms**	
Ac2002 4-1	Create and display forms	2, 6
Ac2002 4-2	Modify form properties	6
Ac2002 5	**Viewing and Organizing Information**	
Ac2002 5-1	Enter, edit, and delete records	2, 4
Ac2002 5-2	Create queries	3
Ac2002 5-3	Sort records	3
Ac2002 5-4	Filter records	3
Ac2002 6	**Defining Relationships**	
Ac2002 6-1	Create one-to-many relationships	5
Ac2002 6-2	Enforce referential integrity	5
Ac2002 7	**Producing Reports**	
Ac2002 7-1	Create and format reports	7
Ac2002 7-2	Add calculated controls to reports	7
Ac2002 7-3	Preview and print reports	7

continues

TABLE E-1

Access 2002: Core MOUS Activities Related to Lessons   *continued*

CODE	ACTIVITY	LESSON
Ac2002 8	**Integrating with Other Applications**	**Lessons**
Ac2002 8-1	Import data to Access	4
Ac2002 8-2	Export data from Access	6, 7
Ac2002 8-3	Create a simple data access page	6

TABLE E-2

Access 2002: Lessons Related to Core MOUS Activities

LESSON	CODES*
1 Getting Started with a Database	1-1, 1-2, 1-3, 1-4, 2-1, 3-1
2 Adding and Editing Data	1-2, 1-3, 2-1, 3-1, 4-1, 4-2, 5-1
3 Finding and Sorting Records	2-1, 3-1, 5-2, 5-3, 5-4
4 Creating Databases and Tables	1-1, 2-1, 2-4, 5-1, 8-1
5 Managing Data Integrity	2-1, 2-2, 2-3, 2-4, 6-1, 6-2
6 Adding Forms to a Database	3-1, 3-2, 4-1, 4-2, 8-2, 8-3
7 Adding Reports to a Database	7-1, 7-2, 7-3, 8-2

*MOUS Activity codes are abbreviated in this table.

TABLE E-3

**Access 2002: Expert MOUS Activities Related to Lessons

CODE	ACTIVITY	LESSON
Ac2002e1	**Creating and Modifying Tables**	**Lessons**
Ac2002e 1-1	Use data validation	11
Ac2002e 1-2	Link tables	8, 9
Ac2002e 1-3	Create lookup fields and modify Lookup field properties	9
Ac2002e 1-4	Create and modify input masks	11
Ac2002e 2	**Creating and Modifying Forms**	
Ac2002e 2-1	Create a form in Design View	11, 14, 15
Ac2002e 2-2	Create a switchboard and set startup options	15
Ac2002e 2-3	Add subform controls to Access forms	14
Ac2002e 3	**Refining Queries**	
Ac2002e 3-1	Specify multiple query criteria	8, 9
Ac2002e 3-2	Create and apply advanced filters	8, 10
Ac2002e 3-3	Create and run parameter queries	10
Ac2002e 3-4	Create and run action queries	10
Ac2002e 3-5	Use aggregate functions in queries	10 *continues*

**Since the original printing of this book, Microsoft has revised its certification standards and eliminated Expert objectives.

TABLE E-3

Access 2002: Expert MOUS Activities Related to Lessons *continued*

CODE	ACTIVITY	LESSON
Ac2002e 4	**Producing Reports**	**Lessons**
Ac2002e 4-1	Create and modify reports	8, 11, 12
Ac2002e 4-2	Add subreport controls to Access reports	12
Ac2002e 4-3	Sort and group data in reports	11, 12
Ac2002e 5	**Defining Relationships**	
Ac2002e 5-1	Establish one-to-many relationships	9, 12
Ac2002e 5-2	Establish many-to-many relationships	9
Ac2002e 6	**Operating Access on the Web**	
Ac2002e 6-1	Create and modify a data access page	13, 14
Ac2002e 6-2	Save PivotTables and PivotCharts views to data access pages	13
Ac2002e 7	**Using Access Tools**	
Ac2002e 7-1	Import XML documents into Access	13
Ac2002e 7-2	Export Access data to XML documents	13
Ac2002e 7-3	Encrypt and decrypt databases	13
Ac2002e 7-4	Compact and repair databases	16
Ac2002e 7-5	Assign database security	13
Ac2002e 7-6	Replicate a database	15
Ac2002e 8	**Creating Database Applications**	
Ac2002e 8-1	Create Access modules	16
Ac2002e 8-2	Use the Database Splitter	13
Ac2002e 8-3	Create an MDE file	16

TABLE E-4

Access 2002: Lessons Related to Expert MOUS Activities

LESSON	CODES*
8 Designing Queries	1-2, 3-1, 3-2, 4-1
9 Using Joins and Relationships	1-2, 1-3, 3-2, 5-1, 5-2
10 Designing Advanced Queries	3-2, 3-3, 3-4, 3-5
11 Building Tables, Forms, and Reports	1-1, 1-4, 2-1, 4-1, 4-3
12 Working with Subreports	4-1, 4-2, 4-3, 5-1
13 Integrating Access with Other Data and Applications	6-1, 6-2, 7-1, 7-2, 7-3, 7-5, 8-2
14 Building Forms with Subforms	2-1, 2-3, 6-1
15 Using Special Form Controls	2-1, 2-2, 7-6
16 Working With Macros and Modules	7-4, 8-1, 8-3

*MOUS Activity codes are abbreviated in this table.

For more information about the Microsoft Office User Specialist (MOUS) program, go to www.mous.net.

APPENDIX F

Designing A Database

The most important, but often overlooked, task in learning database software is designing a database. *Designing a database* does not mean that you add a table, a query, or a report to a database. It means you visualize and identify the basic parts of a database and think carefully about how these parts should work together. You determine what information you need to track, how you break down that information into tables and fields, and how the tables are related.

Good database design comes with years of practice, experience, and troubleshooting. Your work with the Carolina Critters database used in this textbook is an introduction to a well-designed database. The Access Database Wizard can also be helpful in designing a database. You can choose tables and fields that are similar to the ones you plan to use in your own database. The Wizard creates a relational database to help you see how to build a database that will accomplish your goals.

Use the following questions and guidelines to help you design your database (whether you do it from scratch or use the Database Wizard):

1. What do you want the database to do?

- How do you plan to use the database?
- What information do you need from the database?
- Will you be keeping track of products, people, vehicles, events, equipment, etc.? Will you be keeping track of several such items?
- Will you enter phone orders directly on screen?
- Will you print reports for all the data?
- Will the data need to be grouped and counted in various ways?
- Do you need to print a report on a regular basis (for example, a weekly shipment report)? If so, sketch it on paper.
- Do you have paper forms used to record information? If so, build them into a reference file you can use when you design forms and reports.
- Will other people use the database? If so, ask them for their input.

2. What tables will you need?

- Do you need to collect information about employees? You usually need name and address information, a social security number, tax information, possibly family information, etc.
- Do you need to maintain an equipment inventory? If so, do you need the serial number, date of purchase, vendor, department, etc.?

Sketch on paper the tables you need. List the fields in each table. Check the tables against these table design rules.

- *Include information about only one subject in each table.*
  The entity could be a person, product, order, service, or transaction. You need to keep information about one subject separate from another subject. For example, you would keep student addresses in a different table from student courses and grades. If data are in separate tables, you can delete a student's courses without having to delete the student.

- *Do not duplicate information within a table.* If you were to show a student's addresses with their courses, you would need to repeat the address for each course the student takes. When the addresses are in a separate table, you only need to show the address once.

- *Do not duplicate data between tables.* The addresses should only be in the Student table. If an address changes, you edit it in one table. Not only is this faster and more efficient, but you also reduce the likelihood of errors and duplicates. With the proper links, you enter the information only once.

3. What fields do you need?

A field is an *individual fact*. This may seem easy to identify, but you need to think about how you will use data. For example a student table might include the following data for each student: student name, social security number, street address, city, state, and phone number. You might think that each of these would be a field. However, you may need to consider whether you should show the name as one field or two (first and last). Another consideration might be whether the phone number should be one field or two (area code and number).

Your next step is to layout the basic structure or design of each table, indicating field names, data types and sizes, and other properties. Follow these rules for identifying fields in your tables:

- Make sure each field is directly related to the subject.

- Do not include calculated fields (such as the number of courses taken, grade point average, or tuition due.)

- Store information in the smallest logical part (for example, use "City" and "State" rather than "Location").

- Identify fields that are common to a set of two tables. This allows you to establish relationships between tables. A Student table,

for example, would typically have a Social Security Number field. The Courses table would have the same field as a way to identify the student without needing to show the student's name.

4. What is the primary key for each table?

The *primary key* is the unique field(s) for each record. Although a table does not need to have a primary key, having one allows you to establish more useful relationships. For example, if you want to connect a student with all the courses he or she has taken, a primary key is necessary in the Student table. A primary key can be a single field or a set of fields in a table.

5. How are tables related?

You need to identify the links or connections between tables in the database. This allows you to show related information in forms and reports. A *relationship* is based on a common field between two tables. This means both tables have the same field. Sometimes, however, you need to use a *junction table* to link two tables that otherwise would not be related. The junction table includes a field from each of the related tables.

6. Have you tested your design?

Your final step is to create a *test database*. Enter sample data and establish relationships between tables. Build sample queries. Design sample reports and forms. It is easier to refine the design now than after you enter actual data.

Access's Table Analyzer can help you evaluate the design. This wizard reviews the design of each table and makes recommendations for better database design. Another wizard, Performance Analyzer, can help you analyze the performance of your database.

Glossary

Action query   Query type that changes the data in a table. (10)

Aggregate function   Sum, average, count, minimum, maximum, and other calculations for a specific group. (10)

AND condition   Used when two or more parameters must be true. (3)

Append query   Action query that adds records from one table to another. (10)

Argument   Object, element, expression, or condition that a user can change to customize a macro or module. (16)

AutoCorrect   Feature that corrects spelling and capitalization errors as you type. (2)

AutoForm   Form layout that includes all fields in a specified arrangement. (6)

AutoFormat   Predefined style template for forms and reports. (6)

AutoReport   Default report that includes a style and all fields for the query or table; can be either columnar or tabular. (7)

Background image   Image that displays behind data in a form or report. (11)

Bound control   Control that is linked to a field in a recordset. (6)

Bound object frame   Control in a form or report that displays OLE data. (7)

Calculated control   Control that uses an expression or formula as its data source. (6)

Calculated field   Unbound field that uses an expression or formula as its data source. The definition and properties of a calculated field are stored in the query object. (8)

Caption   The field property that controls the column selector in Datasheet View. (4)

Chart   Visual representation of numerical data. (13)

Class modules   Modules that are attached to individual objects, such as a form or a report. (16)

Clip mode   Image property that shows image at its original width and height. (11)

Column selector   Thin bar at the top of each column in a query in Design View. (8)

Combo box   Control that shows a drop-down list. (14)

Command button   Button that, when clicked, begins an action or a series of actions. (14)

Common expression   Control with built-in commands to display dates, times, and page numbers. (7)

Concatenated expression   Expression that joins fields so they appear as one field. (12)

Condition   Logical expression that can be true or false. (16)

Conditional formatting   Formatting that displays under certain conditions. (7)

Control   Object that displays information, performs an action, or enhances appearance in a form, report, or Data Access Page. (2) A control can be bound, unbound, or calculated. (6)

Criteria   Requirements or specifications data must meet. (1) Text strings or expressions used to find matching records. (3)

Crosstab query   Query that displays sums, averages, or other calculations for data arranged in spreadsheet style. (10)

Data Access Page   Object that acts like a form but whose controls are Internet compatible. A direct link is established between the Data Access Page and the source recordset. (6)

Data type   Type of information in a field (such as alphabetic, numeric, or OLE object). Set in Design View. (4)

Database integrity Stability and soundness of the data. (3)

Database properties Dialog box that provides descriptive information about the database, such as filenames, most recent editing date, author, size of database, and others. (1)

Database software Collection of data that tracks information for a business or individual. (1)

Database template A wizard that creates a functional database structure based on user selections. (4)

Database, back-end Databases that only contain data in tables. (13)

Database, front-end Databases that contain support objects but no data. (13)

Datasheet View Way of looking at a table that displays the records in rows and columns, similar to a spreadsheet. (1)

Default value Field property that sets the same value for all new records. (5)

Default View Form property that determines how many forms appear onscreen at once. (2)

Delete query Action query that removes records from a table. (10)

Delimited Fields separated by a unique character. (13)

Design grid Pane in the Query Design window in which you specify fields and criteria for a query. (8)

Design Master Database to which system tables, system fields, and replication properties have been added. The first member in a replica set. (15)

Design View Screen used for determining, formatting, and editing the structure or layout of a table, a form, a query, or a report. (1)

Detail section Form or report part that shows data for one record. (6)

Drop zone Area in a PivotChart or Pivot-Table to which a field can be assigned. (15)

Dynaset Results of a query. If data is edited or changed in the dynaset, the source table's data will be changed also. (1) Recordset created by a query allowing dynamic changes to the data in the source table. (3)

Encryption Compacting and scrambling a database and its objects for transmission across data lines. (13)

Event Action such as clicking a button, pressing a key, or opening a form. (16)

Event procedures Procedure automatically executed in response to an event initiated by the user or the program code or triggered by the system. (16)

Expression Any legal combination of text, numbers, or symbols that represents a value. (6)

Expression Builder Dialog box that enables you to build a formula or calculation by selecting field names, constants, functions, or other elements. (6)

Field Individual piece of information in a record, represented by a column in a table. (1)

Field description Optional clarification of purpose of a field in a table. Set in Design View. (4)

Field name A description of the information in a field (a column). (4)

Field properties Formats, settings, and other attributes set in Design View for a table. (4)

Filter Used to create a subset of records that match criteria. (3)

Flat Database Database that contains all data in a single table. (1)

Focus The active control in an object. (11)

Foreground image Image that appears exactly where it is placed on a report or form. (11)

Foreign key   Non-primary key that is common to a related table. (9)

Foreign key field   Field that refers to the primary key field in the related table. (5)

Form   Database object that displays information from the table or query in an attractive, easy-to-read screen format. Forms can be used to edit and add records. (1)

Form Footer   Section that appears once at the bottom of a form. (6)

Form Header   Section that appears once at the top of a form. (6)

Form View   Screen layout for a record that is designed to be easy to read and to improve the speed and accuracy of data entry. (2)

Format   Field property that determines how data is displayed. (5)

Format Painter   Tool that copies the font, size, color, and alignment from one control to another. (7)

Group   Section of a report that organizes or categorizes the records by a particular field. (7) Collection of users given specific authorization to data or objects. (13)

Group Footer   Section of a report that prints once at the bottom of each group. (7)

Group Header   Section of a report that prints once at the top of each group. (7)

History table   Table designed to keep track of past sales or other activities. (10)

HTML   Hypertext Markup Language, a standard formatting language for Web documents. (6)

Hyperlink   Label that links to a document or application. When you click the hyperlink, the document or application opens. (15)

IIF expression   Expression that checks a condition that you specify and then shows one or the other of your choices. (12)

Image frame   Control structure that allows the placement of an image on a report or form. (11)

Indeterminate relationship   Relationship that occurs when Access does not have enough information to determine the relationship between the two tables. (5)

Index   Record sort order that is identified in the table design. (9)

Inner join   Link that shows all fields for all records that have matching values. (9)

Input mask   Field property that displays a pattern for entering data. (5)

Join   Link made in a query between common fields in multiple tables. (9)

Join line   Graphical representation of a relationship between two tables. Each end of the join line connects to a related field in a table. (5)

Junction table   Table linking two other tables that do not have a common field. Used for Many-to-Many relationships. (9)

Label   Control that shows text such as a title. (2)

Layout   Design of a table, report, or form. (1)

Left outer join   Join that shows all the records from the right table and only the records from the table on the left where the joined fields are the same. (9)

Leszynski Naming Conventions   Object-naming standard widely recognized and used by database designers. Object names are preceded with standardized prefixes signifying their object type. (LNC) (1)

Like operator   Operator used in wildcard criteria in a query. (8)

List box   Control object that displays all available choices in a column. (15)

Literal characters   Characters that are displayed exactly. (11)

Literal text   Characters, words, or phrases that appear in a control, enclosed in quotes in the expression. (12)

Lookup field   Field property that displays input choices from another table, enabling you to enter data by choosing from a list. (5)

Macro   Database object used to run routine tasks with a series of commands. (1) Program (typically a small program) that carries out the steps for a routine activity. (16)

Mail merge document   Form letter. Basic text is the same from letter to letter, but names, addresses, and other specific information change for each person or company the letter is sent to. (13)

Main form   Form that contains one or more related forms. (14)

Main report   Report that is a container or holder for other reports. (12)

Main Switchboard   A form that helps a user navigate around a database. (4)

Make-table query   Action query that creates a new table from an existing one. (10)

Many-to-Many relationship   Relationship between tables in which a junction table links two tables that do not share a common field. (9)

MDE file   Compacted Microsoft Access database containing compiled VBA code that cannot be edited. (16)

Module   Collection of Visual Basic for Applications (VBA) declarations and procedures that are stored together as a unit. (1), (16)

Normalization   Process of separating data into tables without redundant fields. (10)

NULL   Reserved Access word that means "empty" or "blank." (8)

Null value   Value that is nothing. Blank field that does not contain either numbers or spaces. (3)

Object   Element or part of a database. Main objects include tables, queries, forms, reports, pages, macros, and modules. (1)

OLE object   Object linking and embedding for a data type created in another program. Examples include picture, sound, and movie files. (2)

One-To-Many relationship   Relationship that occurs when the common field is a primary key in the first table and not a primary key in the second table. (5) Relationship between tables in which a value occurs once in the primary table and many times in the related table. (9)

One-to-One relationship   Relationship between tables in which the primary key in the main or primary table matches the primary key value in one record in the related table. A One-to-One type of relationship is unusual. (5), (9)

Option button label   Label of the embedded object in an option group. (15)

Option group   Control object consisting of a set of buttons or check boxes that represent choices for data entry. (15)

Option group button   Button in an option group. (15)

Option group frame   Component of the option group that borders the embedded objects. (15)

Option group label   Component of the option group that describes the content of the group. (15)

Option value   Numeric value assigned to each choice in an option-group control. (15)

OR condition   Used when only one of two or more parameters must be true. (3)

Owner   Individual or group who has authorization to an object. (13)

Page   Database object used to post a table or query as a Web page. (1)

Page Footer   Section that prints at the bottom of each printed page. (6)

Page Header   Section that prints at the top of each printed page. (6)

Parameter   Determining factor or characteristic. (10)

Parameter query   Query that prompts for selection criteria each time it is run. (10)

Permission   Attribute that specifies the authorization a user has for data or objects. (13)

Pivot Chart View   Screen with data displayed in a chart form. (1)

Pivot Table View   Screen with data displayed in a table format with columns and rows. (1)

PivotTable   Interactive table that can quickly summarize large amounts of data. (10)

Pixel   Unit of measurement for computer screens. Also known as a screen dot. (14)

Placeholder   Words shown onscreen to mark text entry areas. (13)

Primary Key   Field whose data is different for each record. Used to identify record. (3)

Procedure   Series of commands and properties that performs a specific task. (16)

Property sheet   Dialog box that lists format, data, and other settings for an object. (2), (6)

QBE grid   Query by Example grid; another name for the design grid. Pane in the Query Design window in which you specify fields and criteria for a query. (8)

Query   Database object that extracts information from the table or other queries. (1)

Record   One entity (person, place, thing, or event) in a table holding related data, shown as a row. (1)

Record selector   Icon that marks the current or active record. It changes shape depending on the status of the record. (1)

Recordset   Collection of data from a table or query. (2)

Referential integrity   Database rules for checking and validating data entry; keeps track of changes in related tables. (5)

Relational database management system   Database software that uses relationships between data to eliminate duplication of data. (1)

Relational operators   Operators that make comparisons between two values. (8)

Relationship   Link or connection between two tables sharing a common field. (5) Permanent link or join made at the table level. Relationships can be created in any query, form, or report. (9)

Replica   Synchronized copy of a master database. (15)

Report   Database object that displays information from a table or query in a printable page format. (1)

Report Footer   Section of a report that prints once at the bottom (last page) of the report. (7)

Report Header   Section of a report that prints once at the top (first page) of the report. (7)

Report Page Footer   Section of a report that prints at the bottom of every page. (7)

Report Page Header   Section of a report that prints at the top of every page. (7)

Right outer join   Join that shows all the records from the left table and only the records from the table on the right where the joined fields are the same. (9)

ScreenTip   Name or function of an object. It appears when you rest the mouse pointer on the object. (1)

Select query   Query that locates data from one or more tables and displays the results in a datasheet. (8)

Selection handles   Small black rectangles around an active object in a form or report. (6)

Selection marquee   The dotted line indicating that an object is selected. The settings for the selection marquee can be adjusted, requiring objects to be selected by clicking and dragging over the entire object or only over a portion of an object. (7)

Sizing handle   Any selection handle on a control except the top left one. Sizing handles are used to adjust the width or height of the control. (6)

Standard modules   Global modules that may be assigned to numerous objects. (16)

Stretch mode   Image property that shows image sized to fit the control. (11)

Subdatasheet   A related table nested within a primary table. The subdatasheet shows records from the related table while user is in the primary table. (5)

Subform   Form that is placed in a main form. (14)

Subreport   Report that is inserted into another report. (12)

Summary query   Query that shows totals, averages, counts, minimums, or maximums for grouped records. (10)

Switchboard   A master form that opens instead of the Database window. It allows you to navigate the objects in the database. (13)

Tab order   Form setting that determines insertion point movement through a form. (6)

Table   Database object that stores related data in records with fields. (1)

Text box   Object that shows data from a field in a form, report, or data access page. (2)

Text expression   Expression that is entered as text in a text box control, not entered in a label. (12)

Unbound control   Control that is not linked to a recordset; includes titles, lines or images. (6)

Unbound object frame   Control for placing an OLE object that might need to be edited within the original software used to create the OLE object. (11)

Update query   Action query that edits the data in a field for many records with one command. (10)

Validation rule   Rule or requirement for data entry. (11)

Validation text   Onscreen message displayed when a validation rule is violated. (11)

Value list   List of displayed choices in a list or combo box. (15)

VBA   Visual Basic for Applications. Object-oriented programming language used to enhance office applications. (16)

Wildcards   Search characters (* # ?) used to represent one or more alphabetical or numerical positions. (3)

Zoom dialog box   A text-editing window for lengthy text. (4)

Zoom mode   Image property that shows image proportionally fit to the control. (11)

Index

Photo Credits